Thomas Walter Perry

Notes on the judgment of the Judicial Committee of the Privy Council

In the appeal Hebbert v. Purchas, delivered February 23, 1871

Thomas Walter Perry

Notes on the judgment of the Judicial Committee of the Privy Council
In the appeal Hebbert v. Purchas, delivered February 23, 1871

ISBN/EAN: 9783337735609

Printed in Europe, USA, Canada, Australia, Japan

Cover: Foto ©ninafisch / pixelio.de

More available books at **www.hansebooks.com**

NOTES

ON

THE JUDGMENT OF

THE

Judicial Committee of the Privy Council

IN THE APPEAL

HEBBERT *v.* PURCHAS,

Delivered February 23, 1871.

BY THE

REV. THOMAS WALTER PERRY,

(Member of the Royal Commission on Ritual, 1867-1870.)
VICAR OF ST. MARY THE VIRGIN, ARDLEIGH, ESSEX.

LONDON:
J. MASTERS & Co., 78, NEW BOND STREET.

TO

ALEXANDER JAMES BERESFORD BERESFORD-HOPE, ESQ., D.C.L., &c.,

M.P. for the University of Cambridge.

My dear Mr. Beresford-Hope,

Your great interest, shewn for so many years, in all questions touching the Law and Practice of Ceremonial and Ritual in the Church of England, would alone have been a sufficient reason for my asking permission to Dedicate to you this Volume relating to that subject. I might also have mentioned, as another plea, the pleasant recollections of our co-operation during the 108 Meetings of the Royal Commission on Ritual, from June 17, 1867 to June 28, 1870.

The real ground, however, of my application was—that at your instance I undertook, in 1871, to prepare some Notes on the Judgment of the Judicial Committee of the Privy Council, in the Case of Hebbert v. Purchas, when a re-hearing of it was about to be applied for, on the ground that, owing to circumstances, the Argument had been *ex parte ;* and, consequently, the Court lacked the advantage of that fuller information which discussion by opposing Counsel would, no doubt, have elicited for the guidance of their Lordships.

There was, as you know, a strong and wide-spread conviction, that this Judgment of the Final Court of Appeal in Causes Ecclesiastical, affecting seriously, as it did, the future of the Church of England, could not be regarded practically as merely a Decision against one of her Clergy, *personal* though it was in Legal strictness.

Hence the Petition to Her Majesty in Council that the Cause might be re-heard: the particulars of this Application and the Reasons for the Prayer not being granted, will be found at pp. 444-48 of this Publication.

But, although the immediate object of the Notes had thus passed away when they were in part prepared, it seemed worth while, perhaps, to finish them; consequently they have expanded into the present Volume which, up to p. 217, was printed off before April 1872; and soon afterwards most of the succeeding pages relating to the Vestment question were composed. The work was then unavoidably laid aside owing to my most unexpected appointment to this Benefice, in October 1872, by the Lord Chancellor (Lord Hatherly) whose kindness I am glad here gratefully to acknowledge.

Since that time Duties in this Parish have only permitted these Notes to be resumed at intervals, and thus the completion of them has been delayed until now. During their progress your own Book, "Worship in the "Church of England" (1874), appeared; and also some other important Publications have been issued in reference to the Points adjudicated upon in the Purchas Suit. I delayed, however, to read them until this Work was finished; for this reason alone—that if the independent investigations should agree in their general Conclusions, the Inquiries and their Results might, probably, be regarded as somewhat reliable.

For the very kind readiness with which you responded to my request, and so enabled me thus to address you, I beg leave now to return my best thanks. It need scarcely be said that your acceptance of this Dedication in no way implies your concurrence with any opinions or arguments which I have advanced in the course of this Volume: indeed I must add that you have not yet seen it.

The last sheets were being revised when the Hearing of the Appeal, Ridsdale *v.* Clifton and Others, was commenced before the Judicial Committee, on January 23rd. Let us trust that the able Arguments, addressed to an unusually strong Court, (See p. 449), on behalf of the Appellant, by Sir James Stephen and Mr. Arthur Charles, may lead their Lordships to the conviction (at which the Court, in the Purchas Case, might have arrived under the like favourable circumstances) viz., that the Vestments, the Wafer-bread, and the Eastward Position of the Celebrant—three of the Points decided adversely in the Appeal Hebbert *v.* Purchas, but now included in Mr. Ridsdale's Appeal—are all LAWFUL according to the Rubrics of the present Book of Common Prayer.

Believe me, my dear Mr. BERESFORD-HOPE,

Yours very sincerely,

THOS. W. PERRY.

THE VICARAGE,
   ARDLEIGH, COLCHESTER.
     March 9, 1877.

CORRIGENDA.

Page 27, Note, line 2, *for* "Burleigh Papers, vol. 8, No. 16" *read* "Lansd. 8, f. 16. *in dorso*, '14 Nov. 1564 Varieties in the Services y⁶ Churche of precisians.'"

„ 67, line 21, *for* "II" *read* "III."

„ 69, line 21, *for* "1557" *read* "1577."

„ 150, Note, line 22, *for* "Salisbury" *read* "Sarum."

„ 154, Note, line 12, *for* "when approved" *read* "when they were approved."

16, *for* "consequently only" *read* "consequently from this, or from some other cause, only."

„ 165, line 7 from Note, *for* "never made" *read* "never yet made."

„ 211, Note §, line 2, *for* "p. 67" *read* "p. 627."

„ 232, line 6 from bottom, *for* "institutam" *read* "instituta."

„ 241, Note *, line 3 from bottom, *for* "p. 318-88" *read* "p. 318. 8vo."

„ 322, last line, *for* "touching Faires Markets" *read* "touching Faires and Marketts."

„ 335, line 7, *for* "seem to have raised" *read* "seem to have then raised."

„ 379, line 12, *for* "That Ridley must" *read* "That Ridley, or whoever was Celebrant, must."

„ 389, line 9, *for* "pp. 379-81" *read* "370-81."

NOTES
ON THE JUDGMENT OF
THE JUDICIAL COMMITTEE OF THE PRIVY COUNCIL,
HEBBERT *v.* PURCHAS.

※ To ensure accuracy the text of the Judgment, which is here given in full, is reprinted from the Official copy: the insertions between square brackets are corrections of the quotations.

"*Judgment of the Lords of the Judicial Committee of the Privy Council on the Appeal of Hebbert, heretofore Elphinstone* v. *Purchas, from the Arches Court of Canterbury; delivered* 23rd *February,* 1871.

Present:

LORD CHANCELLOR [Hatherly, W. Page Wood].
ARCHBISHOP OF YORK [Dr. Thomson].
BISHOP OF LONDON [Dr. Jackson].
LORD CHELMSFORD [F. Thesiger].

" IN this case, which comes to us from the Arches Court of Canterbury, the learned Judge of that Court has directed a monition to issue to the Rev. John Purchas as to several matters and things complained of by the Promoter, and has condemned him in costs; and the Defendant has not appealed. But as to certain charges contained in the 16th, 17th, 20th, 25th, 36th, and 38th Articles of Charge, the learned Judge has refused or omitted to direct a monition to issue against the Defendant, and to condemn him in the costs of these Articles; and against the decision upon these Articles the Promoter has appealed.

"The substitution of Henry Hebbert as Promoter, for the purpose of this Appeal, for Charles James Elphinstone, the Promoter in the Court below, since deceased, has been allowed by a former judgment of this Committee.

"The Rev. John Purchas, the Respondent, has not appeared, and the Committee has not had the assistance of the argument of counsel on his behalf.

"The charges which are the subject of this Appeal are that the Respondent has offended against the Statute Law and the Constitutions and Canons Ecclesiastical, by administering wine mixed with water, instead of wine, to the communicants, as pleaded in the 16th Article; and by standing with his back to the people, between the people and the Holy Table, whilst reading the Prayer of Consecration in the Holy Communion, as pleaded in the 17th Article; and by the use of wafer bread instead of bread such as is usual to be eaten, in the administration of the Holy Communion, as pleaded in the 20th Article; and by causing holy water, or water previously blessed or consecrated, to be poured into divers receptacles for the same in the said church, in order that the same might be used by persons in the congregation, or by causing or permitting the same to be used by others, as pleaded in the 25th Article; and by himself wearing and sanctioning and authorizing the wearing by other officiating ministers, whilst officiating in the Communion Service, and in the administration of the Holy Communion in the said church, a vestment called a chasuble, as pleaded in the 36th Article; and by himself wearing, and causing or suffering to be worn by other officiating clergy, when officiating in the Communion Service in the said church, certain other vestments called dalmatics, tunics or tunicles, and albs, and by himself wearing, carrying, or causing or suffering other officiating clergy in the same church to wear or bear in their hand, a certain cap called a biretta, during Divine Service, as pleaded in the 38th Article. (Case pp. 9, 10.)

"We find it convenient to adopt the order followed by the learned Dean of the Arches, and to examine first, the charge of wearing and causing to be worn, a chasuble, tunics, or tunicles and albs, in the celebration of the Holy Communion."

I. Their Lordships, after these preliminary remarks, proceed as follows :—

"It is necessary to review shortly the history of the Rubric, usually known as the 'Ornaments-Rubric,' which governs this question.

"The first Prayer Book of King Edward VI, 1549, contains the following Rubric at the beginning of the Communion office :—

"'Upon the day and at the time appointed for the ministration of the Holy Communion, the priest that shall execute the holy ministry shall put upon him the vesture appointed for that ministration, that is to say, a white albe, plain, with a vestment or cope, and where there be many priests or deacons, then [*for* then *read* there] so many shall be ready to help the priest in the ministration as shall be requisite, and shall have upon them likewise the vestures appointed for their ministry, that is to say, albes with tunicles.' "

II. They next observe that :—

"In the second Prayer Book of Edward VI (1552) this was altered, and it was ordered that the minister 'shall use neither albe, vestment, nor cope, but being archbishop or bishop he shall have and wear a rochet, and being a priest or deacon he shall have and wear a surplice only.' "

It is worth while to notice here that, notwithstanding the language of this Rubric, regard was had to the feelings and wishes of the people where they were attached to the old practices; for the Royal Commissioners, who were appointed to take Inventories of the Church goods after the Second Prayer Book came into use, had a "discretion" to leave in the Churches other things besides those which they were *expressly ordered* to reserve for Divine Service. The Judicial Committee in Liddell *v.* Westerton themselves refer to this, they say " the Com-

"missioners are enjoined to leave 'in every Church or Chapel "'of common resort, one, two, or more chalices or cups, according "'to the multitude of people in every such Church or Chapel, "'and also such other ornaments as by their discretion shall "'seem requisite for the Divine Service in every such place for "'the time.'" (*Moore's Report*, p. 157.)

It is quite plain from numerous Inventories of the period, that in many cases they did leave "for use in the Church" Ornaments which it was clearly illegal and highly penal to use if the Rubric had been construed strictly by the Authorities at that time. (See English Church Union case, Dec. 1866, pp. 47—59, reprinted in First Ritual Report, pp. 149—151.)

It may be mentioned here that the Judicial Committee in Liddell *v.* Westerton, were not indifferent to the *feelings* of the parties interested, for they observe that—

"The evidence as to the wishes of the parishioners upon this subject appears to their Lordships to show (what, in such a case, might perhaps be expected) that with respect to these Ornaments there are many persons of great respectability, who, from conscientious motives, are strongly attached to them; many of equal respectability, who, from motives equally conscientious, feel an invincible repugnance to them; and some, it may be hoped not a few, who, whatever opinion they may form of their intrinsic value, consider them as of no importance whatever in comparison with Christian charity and concord, and who, whether they approve, or whether they disapprove, of them, would infinitely rather sacrifice their individual feelings and opinions than secure their triumph at the expense of disturbing and distracting the Church of which they are members." (*Moore*, p. 151.)

III. The Judicial Committee then proceed to say that:—

"The Prayer Book of Elizabeth (A.D. 1559) provided that 'the minister at the time of the communion, and at all other times of [*for* of *read* in] his ministration, shall use such ornaments in the church as were in use by authority of Parliament in the second year of the reign of King Edward [the *sic*] VI, according to the Act of Parliament set in the beginning of this book.'"

Upon this Rubric their Lordships comment thus:—

"This Committee has already decided (Liddell *v.* Westerton), that the words 'by authority of Parliament in the second year of the reign of King Edward VI,' refer to the first Prayer Book of King Edward VI."

The Judicial Committee treat this Decision as having settled the meaning of this one part of the Rubric: yet the same Court also "decided," in equally explicit terms, the meaning of the rest of the Rubric; for, comparing the language of the Rubric of 1662 with the Rubric of 1604 and with the Rubric and Act of Elizabeth, they said that " they all obviously mean the same " thing, that the same dresses and the same utensils, or articles, " which were used under the first Prayer Book of Edward the " Sixth may still be used." (*Moore*, p. 159.) The Court, in the case of Hebbert *v.* Purchas, appear to have considered themselves bound *by one part* of the interpretation of the Ornaments Rubric, given in Liddell *v.* Westerton and adopted in Martin *v.* Mackonochie; if, as it would seem, they held these decisions to have stereotyped the *construction* of that part, how were they free to re-consider *the rest* of a construction which had also been given and adopted under the same conditions and on the same occasions? Had their Lordships referred, indeed, to objections which notoriously have been made to the meaning assigned to "Second Year" in Liddell *v.* Westerton, and said that they were satisfied with that meaning, the position would have been consistent with their discussing the remaining interpretation of the Rubric: as it is their course is unintelligible and seems entirely arbitrary.

Under these circumstances it may be useful to point out some difficulties which lie in the way of accepting unreservedly the interpretation of "Second Year" as laid down by the Judicial Committee in Liddell *v.* Westerton, and which would at least deserve consideration should the construction of the entire Rubric be discussed at any future time before this or some other Court competent to decide the question. That Court, after noticing the argument "at the Bar," thus comments upon it:—

"There seems no reason to doubt that the Act in question received the Royal Assent in the Second year of Edward the Sixth. It concerned a matter of great urgency which had been long under consideration, and was the first Act of the Session; it passed through one House of Parliament on January the 15th, 1549, N.S., and the other on the 21st of the same month; and the Second Year of the Reign of Edward the Sixth did not expire till Jan. 28th. In the Act of the 5th and 6th Edward the Sixth, cap. 1, sec. 5, it is expressly referred to as the Act made in the second year of the King's Majesty's reign.

"Upon this point, therefore, no difficulty can arise. It is very true that the new Prayer Book could not come into use until after the expiration of that year, because time must be allowed for printing and distributing the Books; but its use, and the Injunctions contained in it, were established by authority of Parliament in the second year of Edward the Sixth, and this is the plain meaning of the Rubric." (*Moore*, p. 160.)

Now, with the utmost deference to the opinion of the Court on this matter, it is not in the least disrespectful to point out that there are very strong reasons for questioning its conclusions; nor is it improbable that a fuller knowledge of the facts might have varied their Lordships' view. And, first, it must be said that there is really *much* reason, instead of "no reason to doubt "that the Act in question received the Royal Assent in the "Second Year of Edward the Sixth." For :—

(1) The date of the Royal Assent is no where given, apparently. It is not mentioned in the *Journals of the Lords*, nor in the *Statutes of the Realm*, nor in the *Parliament Roll;* indeed it appears doubtful whether it was the practice to record the date in any Instrument used for giving the Royal Assent: the Commissions of the period are said to have been destroyed some years since, as being useless; but probably they would not have determined the point.

(2) The custom of the time was to give the Royal Assent at *the end* of the Session to all the Acts of the Session; and it appears from the Journals of the Commons, Nov. 21, 1554, that a question arose whether the Session would be terminated by the Royal Assent being given to a single Bill.* The point was, indeed, ruled in the negative: but in 1670-71 it appears to have been considered necessary to prevent the doubt; for in a case

---

* "The Bill for Cardinal *Poole*, sent up to the Lords by Mr. Treasurer, Mr. S. *Petre*, &c.

"Mr. Treasurer declared, that the King and Queen will be To morrow Afternoon in the Parliament-house, to give their Assent to that Bill.

"Upon a question asked in the House, if, upon the Royal Assent, the Parliament may proceed without any Prorogation;

"It is agreed by Voices, that it may."

of emergency* which led to the enactment of the 22 & 23 Car. II., cap. 1, the 7th Section is in these words—" Provided " alwayes and it is hereby declared and enacted That His " Majesties Royal Assent to this Bill shall not determine this " Session of Parliament."

(3) The Journals of the House of Lords mention that the King was present ("Presens Rex") on March 14th, 1548-9, and prorogued the Parliament until the 4th November following; therefore nothing can be more likely than that this Act, together with all the Acts of the 2nd Session, received the Royal Assent on that day. They are *sixty* in number and are styled "Acts passed in the Second Session of Parliament, " holden and begun at *West.* the 24th Day of *November*, Anno " Regni Regis *Edwardi* Sexti Secundo; and continued until " the 14th Day of *March*, Anno Regni dicti Regis *Edwardi* " Sexti Tertio."

(4) The original Act is endorsed "2 and 3 Edward VI;" and in the margin of the "Long Calendar of the Acts" it is marked, with the rest, " a° 2° et 3° Edw. VI. 1."

But, further, their Lordships mention that the Act is " ex- " pressly referred to" in the 5 and 6 Edw. VI, cap. 1, s. 5, as being "made in the Second Year" of that King. No doubt the Act was "made" in that year, in the sense of having passed both Houses of Parliament before January 28th, but the question is—whether it was *in force* in that year in virtue of the Royal Assent having been given before the Second Year expired—and certainly no evidence has hitherto been produced to prove this: while, as to the reference itself, it has been pointed out that "this " is no conclusive evidence," owing to the language of other contemporary Statutes: "for we find," says Mr. Pinnock, "the Act, " 2 and 3 Edw. VI, c. 10, cited in 5 and 6 Edw. VI, c. 3, s. 4, " as having been passed in the *third year* of Edw. VI; while two " *later* Statutes are cited as having been passed in the *second* year: " the Act 2 and 3 Edw. VI, c. 20, is represented in 1 Eliz., c. " 4, s. 13, as having been passed in the *second year* of Edward " VI; and 2 and 3 Edw. VI, c. 21, is stated in 5 and 6 Edw. VI,

---

* It was "An Act to prevent malitious maiming and wounding" made in consequnence of an attempt to injure Sir John Coventry when attending Parliament: it was necessary for the ends of Justice that it should take effect at once.

"c. 12, s. 1, as having also been passed in the *second* year of "Edward VI." (*The Law of the Rubric*, p. 97. Camb. 1866.)

Next, there seems no ground for saying that the Act "concerned a matter of great urgency." The New Prayer Book was not *required* by the Act to be used before "the Feast of "Pentecost," *i.e.* June 9, 1549, therefore there was abundance of time and no need of the Royal Assent until the Session ended on March 14, 1548-9.

If it be thought that the printing of the Book could not safely be proceeded with until the Royal Assent had been given, the answer seems to be that the printing did proceed, for a copy exists one part of which is dated "the viii" and another "the xvi. daye of Marche in the third yeare," (*Cardwell, Two Liturgies*, p. xl.) and printing was not very rapid in those days.

There is another ground for doubting this alleged "urgency" and consequently for thinking that the Royal Assent was not given before Jan. 28th, and therefore not in the *Second* Year of Edw. VI. The 8th Section of the Act provides that "where "the said Books shall be attained and gotten before the said Feast "of Pentecost," the New Service was to be used "within three "weeks" after the Books were procured. Now if the Royal Assent was not given until the 14th March this order would pretty certainly prevent the Book being used illegally before that date, seeing that no part of the Book appears to have been ready before the 8th March. Whereas if the Royal Assent had been given as early as the Judicial Committee suppose, and if the matter was so urgent as they think, it would have been natural to order its use at once: unless indeed it was supposed it might need three weeks' study, notwithstanding that, in the Preface, the Book was so especially commended for its simplicity.

It may be replied that to mention a *year* and not a *document* would have left the Clergy in 1559 without any definite guide as to what Ornaments they were to use:* yet precisely the

---

* This was Dr. Lushington's difficulty: he said, "I find that I am referred to a guide, the existence of which I cannot with certainty discover" (*Moore*, p. 35): he added that "As to the Ornaments of Ministers, there was enough in the First Prayer Book of Edward the Sixth to satisfy the meaning of the direction" (*Ibid*): whereas with respect to "Ornaments of the Church" he had previously said, "I know of none deserving notice on this occasion" as being "prescribed by that Book of Common Prayer" (*Ibid*, p. 31). The Judicial Committee, also construing "second year" as *First Book* and limiting "Ornaments" to "the

same difficulty (if it was a difficulty) must have beset them at the beginning of Mary's Reign when she referred them to "the "last year of Henry 8th": the interval, however, was very short in each case; only 7 years for the Marian and but 11 years for the Elizabethan Clergy: the latter were, of course, most of them the same men who had alike used the Sarum Missal and the Prayer Book of 1549, and therefore they were perfectly acquainted with the customary Ornaments at each period although only *some* of them were prescribed *nominatim* in either of those Service Books. Indeed it is quite easy for us at this distance of time to ascertain from Documents of the period, which are perfectly accessible, what were the Ornaments of the Church of England and her Ministers in the Second year of King Edward 6th, whichever we regard as the true meaning of that expression.

It must, then, I think, be admitted that the definition of "Second year," given in Liddell *v.* Westerton, is open to question; and that, consequently, the meaning of this part of the Rubric is still an arguable point: *practically*, however, it was not of much consequence, originally, because the Court did not regard the Rubric as being *exclusive*. For, although they said "that the word 'Ornaments' applies, and in this Rubric "is confined to those articles the use of which in the Services "and Ministrations of the Church is *prescribed* by the Prayer "Book of Edward the Sixth" (*Moore*, p. 156), they did not say that *nothing was to be included* among this class of Ornaments but those things expressly named in that Book. On the contrary, their Lordships took a larger and more liberal view: they repeated their definition of "Ornaments" in somewhat varied

several Articles used in the performance of the Services and Rites of the Church," said that "no difficulty will be found in discovering, amongst the articles of which the use is there enjoined, ornaments of the Church as well as ornaments of the Ministers." (*Ibid*, pp. 156,-7.) But the fact is that that Book does not prescribe some of those notoriously and necessarily in use of both kinds, *e.g.*, the Stole for the Minister; the Linen Cloth for the Altar: these it would have been *illegal* to use from 1549 to 1552 if *only* what the Book prescribed was *lawful:* but the Court, aware of this difficulty, also employed the larger expression, "used under the First Prayer Book of Edward the Sixth." (*Ibid*, p. 159.) I must adhere to this distinction in the terms used by the Court, notwithstanding that Canon Robertson calls it "frivolous" and cites Mr. B. Shaw in proof of the terms being employed interchangeably "in legal language." (*How shall we conform to the Liturgy?* p. 294; Ed. 1869.)

and less exclusive language, saying of the Elizabethan Rubric—
"Here the term 'Ornaments' is used as covering both the
"Vestments of the Minister and the several Articles used in
"the Services; it is confined to *such* things as, in the perform-
"ance of the Services, the Minister was to use" (*Ibid*, p. 159):
they did not say that *the Ornaments themselves* are *confined* to
those *mentioned* in the Book; and then, as though to leave no
doubt that they did not mean to lay down a rule which should
limit the List of "Ornaments" to those *in terms prescribed* by
the Prayer Book, they further say "they are not prepared to
"hold that the use of all articles *not expressly mentioned* in the
"Rubric, although quite consistent with, and even subsidiary
"to the Service, is forbidden. Organs are not mentioned, yet
"because they are auxiliary to the singing, they are allowed.
"Pews, cushions to kneel upon, pulpit cloths, hassocks, seats
"by the Communion-table, are in constant use, yet they are
"not mentioned in the Rubric." (*Ibid*, p. 187)—some of
these, *e.g.* "Cloths" and "Organs," being in the "list" of
Ornamenta which the Court referred to (*Ibid*, p. 157) as being
given by Lyndewood, or recognized "in modern times." But
this liberal definition has been greatly *restricted* by the Judgment in Martin *v.* Mackonochie, the Court having then decided
that "Lighted Candles" used during the celebration of the
Holy Communion "are clearly not 'Ornaments' within the
"words of the Rubric," because, besides not being *prescribed*
by the Rubric, "they are not subsidiary to the Service";
although it is impossible to hold that "pulpit cloths" *e.g.* are
subsidiary if the lights are not. It has therefore become
necessary to draw attention to *the great probability*, to say the
least, that "Second year" is capable of another and larger
meaning than that assigned to it in Liddell *v.* Westerton.

IV. Their Lordships continue their argument thus :—

"The Act of Parliament set in the beginning of Elizabeth's book is Queen Elizabeth's Act of Uniformity, and the 25th Clause of that Act contains a proviso, 'that such ornaments of the Church and [of *sic*] the ministers thereof shall be retained and be in use, as was in this Church of England by authority of Parliament in the second year of the reign of King Edward VI, until other order shall be therein taken by the authority of the Queen's Majesty, with the advice of the [*for* the *read* her] Commissioners as [*dele* as] appointed and authorized under the Great Seal of England for causes Ecclesiastical, or of the Metropolitan of this Realm.'

"The Prayer Book, therefore, refers to the Act, and the Act clearly contemplated further directions to be given by the Queen, with the advice of Commissioners or of the Metropolitan. It was not, apparently, thought desirable to effect an immediate outward change of ceremonies, although the adoption of the second Prayer Book of Edward VI, in lieu of the first, had effected a great change in the very substance of the Communion Service, with which the theory of the peculiar vestments (the albe and chasuble) was closely connected."

The Court, in this passage, appears to assume that this Law as to the "Ornaments of the Church and of the Ministers" was only designed to serve a temporary and passing purpose, and was intended to be superseded as soon as possible. It is important to remark that this view does not seem consistent with the aspect of this period of English Church History which presented itself to the minds of the Judicial Committee fourteen years ago; and therefore those who are acquainted with that History are at least free to prefer the following account given by the Court in Liddell *v.* Westerton:—

"After the overthrow of Protestantism by Queen Mary, and its restoration on the accession of Queen Elizabeth, a great controversy arose between the more violent and the more moderate Reformers as to the Church Service which should be re-established, whether it should be according to the First, or according to the Second Prayer Book of Edward the Sixth. The Queen was in favour of the First, but she was obliged to give way, and a compromise was made, by which the Services were to be in conformity with the Second Prayer Book, with certain alterations; but the Ornaments of the Church, whether those worn or those otherwise used by the Minister, were to be according to the First Prayer Book." (*Moore*, p. 158.)

The Judicial Committee in Hebbert *v.* Purchas assume that the power given to Queen Elizabeth to take "other order" as to the "Ornaments" was governed by the consideration that "it was not, apparently, thought desirable to effect an imme- "diate outward change of ceremonies." Their Lordships' language might imply that they have not carefully attended to the words of the Statute, for they treat "Ornaments" and "Ceremonies" as though they were interchangeable terms; whereas the 25th section of 1 Eliz., cap. 2 enabled the Queen to take "other order" as to "Ornaments," and the 26th section enabled her to "publish such further ceremonies" as might be requisite if "any contempt or irreverence" were "used in the "ceremonies" provided in the Prayer Book. If "Ornaments" were "Ceremonies" this distinction was useless. But, not to dwell now upon this point, the question arises whether this provision of the Statute cannot be satisfactorily accounted for on an entirely different ground. It must be remembered that a power to regulate such matters, which had been possessed by the Crown, was taken away by the 1 Edw. VI, cap. 12, s. 4, which repealed the Statutes (31 Hen. viii., c. 8, and 34 and 35 Hen. viii., c. 23) rendering Royal Proclamations valid as Acts. Henry VIIIth and Edward VIth had both used this power in issuing Injunctions which limited the general Law as to Ornaments and Ceremonies: in proof of this it is sufficient to refer to the Letter sent by the Council on May 13, 1548, to the Licensed Preachers bidding them not to "stir and provoke the "people to any alteration or innovation:" its words are "What "is abolished, taken away, reformed and commanded, it is easy to "see by the Acts of Parliament, the Injunctions, Proclamations, "and Homilies." (*Cardwell, Doc. Ann.*, I., p. 65.)

Queen Mary, in abolishing what was done in the Reign of Edward VI, had adopted "the last year of Henry VIII" as the standard for "Divine Service and Administration of Sacra- "ments." (1 *Mary*, 2, *cap.* 2.) Queen Elizabeth chose "the "Second Year of the Reign of King Edward VI" as the Reformed Standard for "Ornaments." The Court, in Liddell *v.* Westerton, said, indeed, that these Ornaments "were to "be according to the first Prayer Book": if this only means, as their Lordships elsewhere say, what was "used under" that Book, and is not *restricted*, as in Martin *v.* Mackonochie, to what "is prescribed by that Prayer Book," there need be no difficulty in accepting the definition; for the Injunctions of 1547 embodied the latest changes which were made by Authority, and " the Order of Communion," of March 8, 1548, expressly forbade " the varying of any other rite or ceremony in the Mass " (until other order shall be provided) "—no " other order" being provided until the first Prayer Book was published in March, 1549. To have taken the mere directions of this Book of 1549 as the *sole* rule of Ornaments in 1559, would have been to choose a Standard which was either too high or too low: *too high*, because it provided some Ornaments* for which there was no use in the Book of 1552, which had been taken as the Book of Service; *too low*, because it did not order several Ornaments† which were alike deemed indispensable in 1549 and in 1559.

Accordingly, the Elizabethan Prayer Book must either have specified *nominatim* every Ornament which was to be used, (a thing which no preceding Service Book had ever done); or it must have selected (as it did) what was deemed a suitable period as the *general* Standard for Ornaments, reserving (as it also did) a regulating power which could be legally exercised. Edward's limiting Injunctions of 1547 were not restored by the 1 Eliz., cap. 1, 1558-9, reviving certain Statutes which Mary had repealed; therefore it was necessary for Elizabeth to issue some Directions to shew what, if any, of the accustomed Ornaments in Queen Mary's reign were not to be employed, in order to make the new rule correspond with the usage of Edward's Second Year: this was first done by the Injunctions

---

* The Book of 1549 prescribed or implied the following which were not needed by the Book of 1559.
(1) The White Vesture or Chrism for the Child in Baptism, offered at the Woman's Purification. (prescribed.)
(2) The Vessel for the anointing oil in Baptism, (implied.)
(3) The Vessel for the oil to anoint the Sick (implied).

† The Book of 1549 did not prescribe any of the following :—
(1) Vestment for the Minister at Litany, Matrimony, Commination.
(2) Covering for the Altar at any time.
(3) Linen Cloth for the Altar at Celebration.
(4) Stole for the Priest though, notoriously, it was in use.
(5) Credence Table for the Elements, which were only to be put upon the Altar after the Offertory.

of 1559, which were mainly a re-production of Edward's Injunctions of 1547, with some additions and omissions. Thus the 23rd of Elizabeth prohibited the very same Ornaments which had been abolished by the 28th of Edward,* and thus so far applied the standard of the Act to regulate the existing custom. The Injunctions, both of Edward and Elizabeth regulated many other matters besides Ornaments.

This view is clearly supported by a passage in the Letter of Archbishop Parker to Sir W. Cecil, on January 8, 1570-1 (touching Wafer-bread) in which the Archbishop quotes the 26th Section of the Act, giving power to provide " further " Ceremonies or Rites"; he says, "but for which Law her " Highness would not have agreed to divers orders of the Book. " And by virtue of which Law she published further order in her " Injunctions both for the Communion-bread, and for the placing " of the Tables within the quire. They that like not the " Injunctions force much the Statute in the book. I tell them " that they do evil to make odious comparison betwixt Statute " and Injunction, and yet I say and hold, that the Injunction " hath authority by proviso of the Statute." (*Parker Correspondence*, p. 375.) This mention of "the Tables" shews that the Injunctions were an exercise of the powers given in the 25th Section relative to "Ornaments," no less than to the 26th Section; for "the placing of the Tables" could not be regarded as one of the "Ceremonies or Rites" contemplated in the latter Section.

Their Lordships, in Hebbert *v.* Purchas, having assumed that the Elizabethan Act of Uniformity contemplated an "outward "change of Ceremonies," endeavour to support their theory by saying that "the adoption of the second Prayer Book of " Edward VI, in lieu of the first, had effected a great change in " the very substance of the Communion Service, with which the " theory of the peculiar Vestments (the Albe and Chasuble) was

---

* The 28th Injunction of Edw. 6th orders "That they shall take away, utterly extinct and destroy all shrines, coverings of shrines, all tables, candlesticks, trindles or rolls of wax, pictures, paintings, and all other monuments of feigned miracles, pilgrimages, idolatry and superstition : so that there remain no memory of the same in walls, glass windows, or elsewhere within their churches or houses. . . ." (*Cardwell, Doc. Ann.*, I., p. 17.)

"closely connected." I have already shown that the idea of an incompatibility between the Ornaments of the First Book and the Service of the Second Book, such as is here implied, was not favoured by the Judicial Committee in Liddell v. Westerton; but the notion of the Second Prayer Book having "effected "a great change* in the very substance of the Communion "Service" is wholly opposed to the opinion of a contemporary prelate, who at least ought to have been cognizant of the change if it was made. Bishop Latimer being asked by *Weston*, in the "Disputation at Oxford," 1554, "which Communion [Book] "the first or the last" he was referring to, replied, "I find no "great diversity in them; they are one Supper of the Lord, but "I like the last very well." To this Weston rejoined, "Then "the first was naught, belike"; and Latimer answered, "I do not

* A similar mistake was made by the Judicial Committee in Liddell v. Westerton. Their Lordships said that by the Second Prayer Book "material alterations were introduced in the Prayer of Consecration": yet this was only "a correction" (?) of a most strange blunder which appeared in the Report as confirmed by the Queen. The present writer privately pointed out the error in the proper quarter, and the following note was appended to the words above quoted in Mr. Moore's Report, p. 179:—"The reporter has been requested to add the following note:—A correction has here been introduced of an erroneous passage, which in the judgment as delivered, stood thus: 'that the prayer for the Consecration of the Elements was omitted, though in the present Prayer Book it is restored.' T. P. L." (The initials are those of the Member of the Committee who read the Judgment.) But upon this error, in part at least, the Stone Altar at St. Barnabas was condemned. There was no opportunity of asking for a re-consideration of this part of the Judgment on account of this error; for, owing to peculiar circumstances, the Report had been confirmed by the Queen in Council before the reading of it was finished in the Council Chamber at Whitehall. It is somewhat surprising that the *Episcopal* Members of the Committee appear to have overlooked, in both cases, the mistakes here mentioned. The note I have quoted from Mr. Moore's Report does not appear in the reprint given in the "Ecclesiastical Judgments of the Privy Council," edited under the direction of the Bishop of London, by Messrs. Brodrick and Fremantle, 1865.

The Members of the Committee in Liddell v. Westerton were the following:
 The Right Hon. the Lord Chancellor (Lord Cranworth.)
 The Right Hon. Lord Wensleydale.
 The Right Hon. T. Pemberton Leigh.
 The Right Hon. Sir John Patteson, Knt.
 The Right Hon. Sir William H. Maule, Knt.

Her Majesty also summoned "to attend and advise at the hearing," (*Moore* p. 133):—
 The Most Rev. and Right Hon. the Lord Archbishop of Canterbury [Dr. Sumner.]
 The Right Rev. and Right Hon. The Lord Bishop of London [Dr. Tait.]

"well remember where they differ." (*Latimer's Remains, Parker Society, p.* 483.)

If it be objected, that this was but the opinion of one Bishop (though as a contemporary he was surely not less able to judge of the changes of the Book than are Bishops or Lawyers 300 years later) the language of the Statute 5 and 6 Edward VI., cap. 1, which authorised the Book cannot be disregarded. That Act said that the Prayer Book of 1549 was " a very godly order, agreeable to the Word of God and the " Primitive Church, very comfortable to all good people desiring " to live in Christian conversation, and most profitable to the " estate of this Realm." Yet if " the very substance of the " Communion Service" was affected by a Law which thus highly praised it, the alleged " great change " must have been either for the better or for the worse; but what could be *better* than the " order" so commended? or what more blameworthy than to compel, under penalties, the people to come to Church for something worse?

The Court asserts that " the theory of the peculiar Vest- " ments (the Albe and Chasuble) was closely connected" with this " very substance of the Communion Service," which was subjected to this assumed "great change." But it was the same Service, with no *material* alteration for which the Statute of Elizabeth provided these supposed unsuitable Vestments; and, moreover, this Service satisfied the Roman party in England for the first ten years of Elizabeth's reign. Indeed there seems good reason to believe that it would have received Papal sanction if only the Queen had chosen to acknowledge the Pope's Supremacy.

Their Lordships have not stated what part of the Service they include under the term " very substance": most probably they refer to the Prayer of Consecration; but, then, one of these "peculiar Vestments"—the Albe—might be worn when there was no Consecration, and only the first part of the Service (which was merely transposed in the Book of 1552) was used; for a Rubric directed that " Upon Wednesdays and Fridays, " . . . though there be none to communicate with the Priest, yet " these days (after the Litany ended) the Priest shall put upon "him a plain Albe or Surplice, with a Cope, and say all things "at the Altar (appointed to be said at the celebration of the "Lord's Supper) until after the Offertory. . . . ." The next Rubric extends this direction by saying, "And the same order "shall be used all other days, whensoever the people be custom-"ably assembled to pray in the Church, and none disposed to "communicate with the Priest." Whatever then is "the "theory" of these Vestments to which the Court alludes (for "the theory" is not stated, though presumably the sacrificial "theory" is meant), it fails to condemn the "Albe" as un-suitable for the Book of 1552, even if the supposed "great "change" could be admitted to have been made; and if it were not, as it is, the case that in both Books the Service is alike called "our sacrifice of praise and thanksgiving."

V. The Court thus continues its argument upon this point:—

"The Rubric and the proviso together seem to restore for the present the Ornaments of the minister which the second Prayer Book of King Edward had taken away. But Sandys, afterwards Archbishop of York, who assisted at the Revision of the Prayer Book, gives to Archbishop Parker a different suggestion:—'Our gloss upon this text,' he says, 'is, that we shall not be forced to use them (the Ornaments), but that others in the meantime shall not convey them away, but that they shall [*for* shall *read* may] remain for the Queen.' (Burnet's Reformation, vol. ii., Records, p. 332.) The Injunctions of Elizabeth appeared in the same year, 1559, and one of them orders that 'the churchwardens of every parish shall deliver unto the [*for* the *read* our] visitors the inventories of Vestments, Copes, and other Ornaments, Plate, Books, and specially of Grails, Couchers, Legends, Processionals, Hymnals, Manuals, Portasses, and such like appertaining to the Church.' (Cardwell, Doc. Annals, I., 228.) Commissioners began to carry out these Injunctions in the same year. One of their Returns is in the Record Office (Calendar of State Papers, Domestic, 1547-1580, p. 148), which shows that they chiefly occupied themselves in taking inventories of Church Ornaments and of the Service Books in use."

In making this conjecture the Court is referring to those Ornaments of the Book of 1549 which were dispensed with in the Book of 1552. But if the entire statement of Sandys is examined, the "different suggestion" which their Lordships find in it must be rejected or materially qualified. The words before "Our gloss," &c., are these—"The Parliament "draweth towards an end; the last Book of Service is gone "through with a Proviso to retain the Ornaments which were "used in the First and Second Years of Edward VI., until it "please the Queen to take other order for them." (*Parker Correspondence*, p. 56. Ed. Parker Society.)

It is as well to mention here that Strype remarks upon Sandys' statement, "But this must be looked upon as the "conjecture of a private man." (*Annals*, vol. i., p. 84.)

However, if it be assumed that Sandys' "gloss" was warranted by his knowledge of the circumstances, as one of the Reviewers of the Book, it by no means substantiates the inference which the Judicial Committee appear to have drawn from it, viz., that the Ornaments were only meant to be safely kept. Sandys disliked the Ornaments, and so he evidently hoped that regard would be paid to himself and to others who felt with him, and that they would "not be *forced* to use them." But he also knew that no objection to the Ornaments existed among a much larger party, and there is nothing in his words to indicate that he thought or wished that *they* were to be *prohibited* from using them.

Moreover the statement of Sandys suggests a further reason for his "gloss": he says that the Ornaments which it was intended "to retain" were those "used in the first and second "years of King Edward": a return to that period may well have disturbed him, especially as Guest, one of his co-revisers, had said *No* to Secretary Cecil's question, "Whether, in the cele-"bration of the Communion, Priests should not use a Cope, "besides a Surplice?" the "Surplice only" having been ordered by the Book of 1552, which was then about to be revived: it is easy therefore to understand his words—"that they may "remain for the Queen"—as the expression of his hope or belief that a more restricted and definite Standard would be the one actually *imposed* by Authority. Indeed it seems not unlikely that his complaint helped to procure some change; for it was "the second year" of Edward VI. which the Statute ultimately adopted, probably because the Injunctions of 1547 and other subsequent Orders had considerably limited the Ornaments of "the first year."

The citation by the Court of Sandys' statement, which supports what has been already said (pp. 5—10) as to the meaning of "second year," induces me to quote the following remarks which I made upon the passage previous to the Judgment in Liddell *v.* Westerton:—

"But, notwithstanding Strype's comment on Sandys' account, his statement is, I think, a most important contemporary elucidation of the meaning of these much debated words, 'The Second Year of the Reign of King *Edward* the Sixth,' which lie at the root of the whole controversy. Here is a man whom Strype himself tells us was 'diligently employed' in preparing the New Prayer Book; who (though, like Guest, he was plainly opposed to the Ornaments) must have been well aware of Cecil's question as to resuming those taken away by Edward's *Second* Book, and of the intentions of his co-revisers; who, if the Parliament was really rejecting the decisions of the reviewers, would be likely to know and to watch carefully its proceedings, and would hardly hazard a 'conjecture' on the subject; yet he, writing 'hastily' to Parker upon the state of his own finances and other matters,—could not avoid mentioning, as it seems, a subject which evidently annoyed him. And what does he say was the Standard for Ornaments, which *The Parliament* was taking?—*the* 'FIRST *and second years of King Edward.*' It is quite true that, as the Statute and the Rubric prove, 'the SECOND Year' was ultimately selected to regulate the Ornaments; in all probability because the majority of the Reviewers, or the Parliament, or both, felt that, while there were *important* distinctions between the Ornaments of the *First* Year and those of the *Second* (as I have already shewn), the standard of Ornaments had, after the latter date, been reduced much lower than was consistent with the Ritual, which they themselves wished to settle in the Church of England. Yet, in all this, there is no allusion whatever to Edward's First *Book*—an allusion most natural, if that *Book*, and not the Second *Year*, had been in the minds of these various witnesses, more especially, as the Secretary Cecil's questions had drawn the especial attention of the Reviewers to Edward's two Books, and had referred to the later Book as taking away 'Ceremonies' (not *Ornaments*), the propriety of restoring which they were to consider." (*Lawful Church Ornaments*, pp. 128, 129. London, 1857.)

Their Lordships, after quoting Sandys, say that "The in-"junctions of Elizabeth appeared in the same year, 1559." But it is most important to notice that these Injunctions, though prohibiting some things which were used in Edward's first year (see *e.g.* No. 23*) made no change whatever as to the Vestments; nor was any alteration authorized for the next two years: it was not until about March 1561, (*Strype, Annals*, vol. 1, p. 213) that the "Interpretations and further considerations" of the Injunctions directed "That there be used only but one "apparel; as the Cope in the Ministration of the Lord's Supper, "and the Surplice in all other Ministrations." It is plain, therefore, that *during the first two years* after the Elizabethan Prayer Book came into use, Albe, Chasuble, and Tunicle, were perfectly lawful, though doubtless Sandys and those who sympathized with him were not "forced to use them."

Nor, indeed, did the "Interpretations" affect the *legal* character of the Ornaments; for, according to Strype, "they "were drawn up in writing by the Archbishop and Bishops, for "the further regulation of the Clergy" (*Annals*, vol. 1, p. 213) or, as he elsewhere says, "by the diligent Archbishop in his own "name, and in the name of the rest of the Bishops." (*Parker*, p. 92.) Strype gives no hint, nor does there seem any reason for supposing, that they had any Authorization from the Queen, at least under the provisions of the Statute of Uniformity, which enabled her to take "other" or "further order" touching the requirements of the Prayer Book. It is a reasonable inference, therefore, that in places where the fuller Vestments had been *retained* there was no *legal* hindrance to their *use*, if the Clergy and People chose to continue them, whatever dispensing or controlling power the Bishops might have been capable of lawfully exercising in cases where their employment was refused by the Clergy or opposed by the People.

Considering the reactionary feeling which Mary's reign had produced, and the Genevan opinions which so many of the returned exiles had embraced, it is not surprising that great opposition was made to the Ornaments which the Elizabethan

---

* Which is the same as No. 28 of Edward 6th. (*See above, p.* 14.)

Statute authorized; and therefore nothing is more likely than that the Cope was enjoined as a relaxation of the Rubrical requirement which might be accepted by all parties as a reasonable compromise. Guest, who had at first objected to it, might well be content to accept a rule which released him from the greater obligation of the Rubric; while those who wished to retain the fuller Vestments were no doubt content to acquiesce in a Garment which certainly was magnificent enough to distinguish the Eucharistic Service from other Offices. How little the compromise availed is but too plain from the subsequent history.

Having referred to the issue of the Elizabethan Injunctions, their Lordships quote the 47th, which ordered the "Church-"wardens" to "deliver" to the "visitors the Inventories of" the Church Ornaments; and, from one of the Returns, they conclude that the Commissioners "chiefly occupied themselves "in taking inventories of Church Ornaments, and of the Service "books in use." Such an employment (if, indeed, it was their chief occupation) affords, at least, the presumption that their business was not to *remove*, much less to *destroy*, the Ornaments; and the *verification* or the *making* of Inventories, coupled with the language of the Statute, indicated a present continuance of those in use at the period named. Judging however from Strype's account the Commissioners in London either were not very careful to adhere to their instructions, or they did not (perhaps could not) restrain the ignorant zeal of the people which this 47th Injunction was probably designed to curb. Strype states that:—

"On the 18th of July the Visitors sat at the Bishop of London's palace. In this visitation they took care to have all the utensils and instruments of superstition and idolatry demolished and destroyed out of the churches where God's pure service was to be set up; such as the roods, that is, the images of Christ upon the cross, with Mary and John standing by; also images of other saints, tutelaries of the churches, to whom they were dedicated; popish books, altars, and the like. . . . . ." Then, after giving some instances, he adds:—"So that from Bartholomew-tide, and so forward, within a month's time, or less, were destroyed all the roods, church images, church goods, with copes, crosses, censers, altar-cloths, rood-cloths, books, banner-staves, wainscoat, with much other such-like gear, in and about London." (*Strype's Grindal*, pp. 25, 26.)

This account shows plainly enough that the authors or abettors of this wanton destruction were by no means discriminating; "Copes," which two years later were expressly prescribed for use, no less than "crosses" and "altar-cloths," shared the fate of whatever were regarded as "instruments of super-"stition and idolatry."

Some of the results of this raid on the old Ornaments are expressly stated in the following very important mandatory Letter from the Queen which, as its language shows, was a direct exercise of the power given in the 26th Section of her Act of Uniformity: the Document is addressed *"To the most Reverend father in God, our right trusty and "right well-beloved Matthew, Archbishop of Canterbury; the "Right Reverend father in God, our right trusty and well-beloved "Edmund, Bishop of London; and to the rest of our Commissioners "for causes Ecclesiastical."* It is dated from "Westminster the "two and twentieth of January, the third year of our reign," *i.e.* Jany. 22, 1560-1, and recites at the commencement that "by "act of Parliament, holden in the first year of our reign," the Queen had authority " to take further order in any rite or cere-"mony appointed in the Book of Common Prayer " in concert with the Ecclesiastical Commissioners or the Metropolitan: it goes on to mention the need which Her Majesty understood there was of supplying "other Chapters or parcels of Scripture" tending more to the "edification" of the " lay people " than some "lessons and other things appointed to be read," and then it continues thus:—

"and that furthermore in sundry churches and chapels where divine service, as prayer, preaching, and ministration of the sacraments be used, there is such negligence and lack of convenient reverence used towards the comely keeping and order of the said churches, and specially of the upper part, called the Chancels, that it breedeth no small offence and slander to see and consider, on the one part the curiosity and costs bestowed by all sorts of men upon their private houses, and on the other part the unclean or negligent order and spare keeping of the house of prayer, by permitting open decays and ruins of coverings, walls and windows, and by appointing unmeet and unseemly tables with foul cloths for the communion of the Sacraments, and generally leaving the place of prayers desolate of all cleanliness and of meet ornaments for such a place, whereby it might be known a place provided for divine service."

After this preamble the Queen directs the Commissioners " to "cause some new calendars" of lessons "to be imprinted," giving order about the condition of the Churches as follows :—

"And further also to consider, as becometh, the foresaid great disorders in the decays of churches, and in the unseemly keeping and order of the chancels, and such like, and according to your discretions to determine upon some good and speedy means of reformation, and, amongst other things, to order that the tables of the Commandments may be comely set or hung up in the east end of the chancel, to be not only read for edification, but also to give some comely ornament and demonstration that the same is a place of religion and prayer; and diligently to provide, that whatsoever ye shall devise, either in this or any other like point, to the reformation of this disorder, that the order and reformation be of one sort and fashion, and that the things prescribed may accord in one form as nigh as ye may; specially that in all collegiate and cathedral churches, where cost may be more probably allowed, one manner to be used; and in all parish-churches also, either the same, or at the least the like, and one manner throughout our realm."

The Letter concludes with Her Majesty's authorization for carrying out their reforms when agreed upon, which runs thus :—

"And for the publication of that which you shall order, we will and require you, the Archbishop of Canterbury, to see the same put in execution throughout your province, and that you, with the rest of our Commissioners before mentioned, prescribe the same to the Archbishop now nominated of York, to be in like manner set forth in that province, and that the alteration of anything hereby ensuing be quietly done, without shew of any innovation in the Church. And these our Letters shall be your sufficient warrant in this behalf." (*Parker Correspondence*, pp. 132—4, and *Cardwell, Doc. Ann.*, I., p. 294.)

That these Orders of the Queen were at once acted upon, as regards at least the Province of Canterbury, appears by a Letter in Latin, from Parker to Grindal, dated the 15th February 1560-1, the contents of which are thus conveniently summarized in the margin :—

"The Queen has addressed to the Archbishop her letter of the 22nd January last past, commanding that the Ecclesiastical Commissioners should make certain alterations or reformations. The Archbishop thereupon commands the Bishop of London with all speed to publish the orders for reformation of the Kalendar, and setting up tables of Commandments, whereof a printed copy is annexed, to the Suffragan Bishops of the province of Canterbury, charging them to see that the same be inviolably observed." (*Parker Correspondence*, p. 135.)

It is of much consequence to notice particularly the concluding directions of the Queen's Letter to the Ecclesiastical Commissioners, touching the *general uniformity* of the reformations which they were to prescribe; for they distinctly contradict the theory so often put forward, and apparently held by the Judicial Committee itself as regards Vestments, namely that Parish Churches were not intended* to have Ornaments of the same character as those used in Cathedral and Collegiate Churches: the Letter plainly makes "cost" the ground of any distinction which might be allowed; and this would seem to be a true, as it is a natural, explanation of all subsequent Documents, such as the Advertisements and Canons, which do not *prescribe* so high a standard of Ornaments for Parochial as they do for Cathedral Churches: the Church Goods so recklessly destroyed could not easily have been replaced in most Parishes for lack of necessary funds, even if there had been none of the opposition to their use which existed in so many places.

The "Interpretations and further Considerations" of the Injunctions of 1559 already mentioned (p. 20) appear to have been published by the Bishops about the time of the Queen's Letter, whether before or after does not seem certain, though according to Strype it was towards the close of 1560, and in that case may have been after the 22nd January. There is a passage

* Seventy-two years later, the same principle as that enunciated in Queen Elizabeth's Letter was recognized in "An Order of Council for placing the Communion Table in St. Gregory's Church," near St. Paul's Cathedral, dated "Whitehall, November 3, 1633," which states that " . . . His Majesty having heard . . . [the] proceedings in this cause . . . was also pleased to observe, that if those few Parishioners [but five in number who complained] might have their wills, the difference thereby from the aforesaid Cathedral mother Church, by which all other Churches depending thereon ought to be guided, would be the more notorious . . . (*Rushworth, Coll.* ii., fol. 207, cited by *Cardwell, Doc. Ann.*, II., p. 238). Also, Canon vii. of 1640 (which is still in force) orders, in reference to the place of the Altar, "we judge it fit and convenient, that all Churches and Chappels do conform themselves in this particular to the example of the Cathedral or Mother Churches, saving always the general liberty left to the Bishop by Law, during the time of Administration of the Holy Communion." And thirty years later still, Abp. Sheldon, in his "Circular Letter to Cathedrals," June 4, 1670, says—"Our Cathedrals are the standard and rule to all Parochial Churches of the solemnity and decent manner of reading the Liturgy, and administering the Holy Sacraments." (*Cardwell, Doc. Ann.*, II., p. 331.) Unfortunately, owing to the negligence of past times, as these passages shew, so far from this being the case, the intended order has been reversed, and Parish Churches have in many instances become models which might advantageously be followed in Cathedrals.

in a Letter from Archbishop Parker and the Bishops of London and Ely to the Queen, believed to be about 1560 though its exact date is unknown,* which seems very likely to refer to these "Interpretations," especially as Strype says they were "framed, as it seems to me, by the pen of Cox, Bishop of Ely, "and revised by the Archbishop." (*Annals*, I., p. 216.) The words are these:—

". . . . according to our duty of vigilancy over your loving people, we have of late in our consultations devised certain orders for uniform and quiet ministration in religion. We trust your gracious zeal towards Christ's religion will not improve† our doings, though such opportunity of time hath not offered itself as yet to be suitors to your princely authority to have a public set synod to the full determination of such causes." (*Parker Correspondence*, p. 130.)

If my conjecture about this passage be correct, it confirms the remark already made (p. 20) as to the "Interpretations" not being any *limitation*, in the sense of *repeal*, of the prescription in the Elizabethan Rubric as to the Vestments: but merely an Episcopal manifesto, permitted by the Queen, to declare how much of the Statutable requirement the Bishops deemed it necessary to enforce, namely the *Surplice* and the *Cope*, in all Churches alike whether Cathedral and Collegiate or Parochial.

VI. The Court, passing over entirely the "Interpretations" of the Injunctions, thus continues the History of the period:—

"In the year 1564 appeared the advertisements of Elizabeth. They make order for the vesture of the minister in these words:—'In the [*dele* the] ministration of the Holy Communion now in [*for* now in, *read* in the] Cathedral and Collegiate churches, the principal minister shall use a cope, with gospeler and epistoler agreeably; and at all other prayers to be said at the said [*dele* said] Communion Table to use no copes but surplices.'

"'That every minister saying any public prayers or

---

* The Editor of the *Parker Correspondence* says, "It is very difficult to determine the exact date of this letter. Some considerations would lead to the conclusion that it was written a little later than 1560, but it has been usually ascribed to that year, and the reasons to the contrary are not sufficiently demonstrative to warrant an interference with the old ascription."

† Editor's Note—" To improve in the sense of *improbare*, to disapprove."

ministering [of *sic*] the Sacraments or other rites of the Church, shall wear a comely surplice with sleeves, to be provided at the charge [s *sic*] of the parish.' (Cardwell, Doc. An., I, 326.)"

The way in which the issue of the Advertisements is here introduced is likely to convey a very erroneous impression of their origin; and, indeed, it is incorrect to say that they "appeared" in 1564, for, as will be seen later, although prepared in March 1564-5 they were not issued until above a year afterwards. Probably most readers of the Judgment would infer from the passage—that they were simply the result of a determination on the part of Authority further to reduce the Standard of Ornaments. But the Queen's Letter of January 25, 1564-5, to Archbishop Parker, suggests that the disregard of even that lower compulsory Standard which the "Interpreta-"tions" of the Injunctions had set up, only about four years before, rendered it necessary to take some step to stay the downward progress of a growing indifference or opposition to all external order and propriety in the conduct of Divine Service. Her Majesty complained that, owing to "lack of "regard" on the part of "the Primate and others, the Bishops" of the Province of Canterbury, there was "an open and mani-"fest disorder and offence to the godly wise and obedient "persons, by diversity of opinions and specially in the external, "decent, and lawful rites and ceremonies to be used in the "churches:" and she declared her determination "to have all "such diversities......against the laws, good usages, and ordi-"nances of our Realm, to be reformed and repressed and brought "to one manner of uniformity through our whole realm and "dominions......" (*Parker Correspondence*, p. 223.)

In consequence of the Queen's Letter the Archbishop desired his Suffragans to send him information "at the farthest" by the end of February, as to the actual state of things; and Strype has furnished a paper found in Secretary Cecil's MSS., dated Feb. 14, 1564, which appears to be a summary of the Episcopal Returns: it is called "Varieties in the Service and Adminis-"tration used," and among those mentioned this, touching the "Administration of the Communion," occurs, "Some with

"Surplice and Cap* [? Cope]; some with Surplice alone; "others with none." (*Strype's Parker*, p. 152.)

The Archbishop followed up this by framing, in conjunction with some of the Bishops, regulations to correct the evil which these Returns disclosed: these he sent to Cecil, with a letter, on March 3, 1564-5 (*Parker Correspondence*, p. 233), hoping, apparently, to get some sanction for them, and especially asking for a letter from the Queen to the Bishop of London (Grindal) "to execute Laws and Injunctions." A year, however, elapsed, during which the Archbishop wrote several Letters to the Secretary, urging the need of the Queen's help if he was to effect any improvement in the matters of which Her Majesty had complained: they are dated March 8, 1564-5; March 24, 1564-5; April 7, 1565; March 12, 1565-6; and March 28, 1566: in this last letter he says:—

"I pray your honour to peruse this draft of Letters, and the Book of Advertisements with your pen, which I mean to send to my Lord of London. This form is but newly printed, and yet stayed till I hear your advice. I am now fully bent to prosecute this order, and to delay no longer, and I have weeded out of these articles all such of doctrine, &c., which peradventure stayed the Book from the Queen's Majesty's approbation, and have put in but things advouchable, and, as I take them, *against no law of the realm*. And where the Queen's Highness will needs have me *assay with mine own authority what I can do for order, I trust I shall not be stayed hereafter*, saving that I would pray your honour to have your advice to do that more prudently in this common cause which must needs be done." (*Parker Correspondence*, p. 271.)

The words which I have here put in italics require especial notice: the Archbishop says that the Advertisements which he then sent were "against no law of the realm": but this could not be true if, as some contend, they were *prohibitory* of what the Statute of Elizabeth required; and it may be inferred from Parker's expression, that they were not *intended* to *repeal* the

---

* Strype prints this "Cap," but *Cope* is certainly the more likely reading, and on examining the MS. (*Burleigh Papers*, vol. 8, No. 16, British Museum) I cannot doubt that *Cope* is the word: it is written thus—Cōpe—the o, which is quite distinct, *appearing* to have a line over it, like a mark of contraction for *pp*, though it may only be part of the head of the *C*: the word *Cap* occurs later three times, under the head of "Apparel;" in two cases it is clearly written "Cappe," and in the third "Capp."

Rubric even if they received the Queen's assent. Neither could the Advertisements operate as any *prohibition* of that general use of the Cope which the Bishops in their " Interpretations " of the Injunctions deemed sufficient, unless they contained words to that effect, which indeed they do not.

That the Archbishop did not expect to obtain the Royal sanction to the Advertisements seems plain from his saying, " And where the Queen's Highness will needs have me *assay* " *with mine own authority what I can do for order, I trust I shall* " *not be stayed hereafter ;* " and his language is very different from, and much less hopeful than, what he had used a year before, in his Letter of March 8th, when he said, " If the Queen's " Majesty will not authorise them, the most part be like to lie " in the dust for execution of our parties, *laws be so much* " *against our private doings* [the italics are mine]. ' The " Queene's Majestie, with consent, &c.' I trust shall be obeyed," (*Parker Correspondence*, p. 234,)—the reference being, apparently, to the *original* Preface of the Advertisements, viz., " The Queen's Majesty . . . . hathe by the assent of the " Metropolitane, and withe certeine other her Commissioners " in causes ecclesiasticall, decreed certein rules and orders to " be used as hereafter followith."   (*Strype, Parker*, App., No. 28, vol. iii., p. 84.)

There is an important passage in a Letter from Archbishop Grindal to Zanchy at Heidelberg, which seems decisively to prove two things about the Advertisements: *First*, that they were not designed to be and were not the " other order " of the Statute ; *Next*, that they were designed to and did prescribe a positive rule as to Vestures. Zanchy, it appears, had been persuaded to write to Queen Elizabeth in favour of the non-conforming party in England, and had sent his Letter to Grindal to present it to Her Majesty: the Archbishop replied in a Letter which, though undated, appears to have been written about the end of 1571 or the beginning of 1572 ; in it he tells Zanchy why he and others whom he had consulted thought "it " were better not to present" his Letter, and then he goes on to explain what was " the state of the case " in England as to Religion and Ecclesiastical Discipline; he says :—

"When first her highness Elizabeth, under most happy auspices, began her reign, the popish doctrine and worship being cast off, she restored all things to that standard of the administration of the word of God, and the Sacraments, and the whole of religion, which had been drawn up and established during the reign of Edward VI. of happy, but also of most lamented memory. To this all the States of the Kingdom with full consent gave their voices in the great council of the nation, which in our vernacular language we call the Parliament. The authority of this Council is so great, that the laws made therein cannot by any means be dissolved, except by the sanction of the same. Whereas, then, in this form of religion of which I have spoken, drawn up by King Edward, there were many commands respecting the habits properly adapted to ministers of the Church, and also concerning other things which some good men wish to be abolished or amended, it was forbidden by the authority of the law that any one should meddle with this matter. Yet the law itself allowed the Queen's majesty, with the advice of some of the bishops, to alter some things. Nothing however of the law is either altered or diminished; nor, as far as I know, is there a bishop, who does not himself obey the prescribed rules, and also lead or persuade the rest to do the same. Wherefore there is no reason why you should give yourself the trouble to persuade what they themselves have some time ago willingly yielded to you, viz., either that they should remain in their several posts, or that the Queen should deal more gently with those who decline conformity. Almost all the other ministers of the Church also, learned and unlearned, seem not unwillingly to give in to the same opinion with the bishops. [A part of the letter is here wanting.] As for *doctrine*, hitherto we retain it unshaken and unadulterated in our churches. And therefore, since all our controversy has flowed from *discipline*, these are the usual grounds of complaint. Ministers are required to wear commonly a long gown, a square cap, and a kind of tippet over the neck hanging from either shoulder, and falling down almost to the heels. In public prayers and every sacred administration, besides this ordinary dress, the Ecclesiastical discipline requires the ministers to wear a linen garment, called, by a new appellation, a *Surplice*. And since the priests of corrupt religion are distinguished from those who administer the light of the Gospel by these things, as it were by certain tokens, some allege that it is not lawful for them by such compliances either to approve the hypocrisy of idolaters, or to pollute their own ministry. The more moderate, though they will by no means allow themselves to be compelled to obey the prescribed rites, yet neither are willing to censure others as sinful for yielding obedience, nor esteem the use of these things as impious. But some there are who so defend that peculiar mode of dress, that without it they eagerly contend that all sacred offices are all but profaned, and both the ministry deprived of a great ornament, and the people of instruction; but the greater part, as I have said, of the Ecclesiastical order seem to persist in this opinion, that however they think that these things may be abolished, (and many certainly desire it,) yet, whereas they conceive that there is more sin in deserting their posts than in taking the garments, they think it better, as the smallest of evils, to obey the commands than to give up their places. And in so great a variety of sentiment, each man is confident that he holds his own opinions well supported by solid arguments. But I let arguments pass; for I resolved to relate naked facts." (*Remains of Archbishop Grindal.* Parker Society, pp. 338—340.)

Although this passage is long it seemed best not to abridge it lest an imperfect or one-sided view should be given of Grindal's statement: but the point to be especially noticed is—that Grindal, who was himself, be it observed, one of the framers of the Advertisements, writing five or six years after they were issued and referring plainly to the Elizabethan Act of Uniformity and its two Provisos giving power to make alterations, distinctly says, " Nothing however of the Law is either altered or dimin- "ished;" clearly, therefore, the Advertisements had not *repealed* the Rubric. But he adds that the Bishops " obey the prescribed "rules, and also lead or persuade the rest to do the same:" now as this could not refer to the Rubric which certainly was not then enforced or obeyed, Grindal must have intended some other " prescribed rules " as being alone *obligatory*, although as he says the " law" was not " either altered or diminished"; this in fact is entirely consistent with Sandys' view as to the Ornaments of Edward's Second year, viz. " that we shall not be "forced to use them, but that others in the meantime shall not "convey them away, but that they may remain for the Queen"— remain, no doubt, for the Queen, with " the advice" named in the Act, to decide the extent to which they should be *required* in the Public Services.

These "prescribed rules," then, were not the *unaltered* " Law," *i.e.*, the Rubric, but resulted from " the Ecclesiastical "discipline" of which Grindal speaks a few lines farther on in his Letter where he mentions the particular Garments it " re- "quires the minister to wear." That " discipline" manifested itself in three especial ways at three different periods: they were these:—

First, in 1559, the Elizabethan "Injunctions" which, in no way referring to the Rubric and therefore neither enforcing it nor dispensing with any part of it, declared in No. xxx. that "Her Majesty . . . willeth and commandeth, that all archbishops and bishops, and all other that be called or admitted to preaching or ministry of the sacraments, or that be admitted into vocation ecclesiastical, or into any society of learning in either of the universities, or elsewhere, shall use and wear such seemly habits, garments, and such square caps, as were most commonly and orderly received in the latter year of the reign of King Edward the Sixth. . . . ." (*Cardwell, Doc. Ann.*, I., p. 225.)

Secondly, in 1561, the "Interpretations and further Considerations" of the Injunctions, drawn up by the Archbishops and Bishops, which gave a direction "Concerning the Book of Service" in ordering "That there be used only but one apparel; as the Cope in the ministration of the Lord's Supper, and the Surplice in all other ministrations. . . ." (*Ibid*, p. 238.)

Thirdly, in 1566, the "Advertisements" which, in the "Articles for administration of prayer and sacraments," did not require so much as the "Interpretations" had prescribed for *Parish* Churches; only directing "That every minister sayinge any publique prayers, or ministringe of the sacramentes or other rites of the churche, shall weare a comely surples with sleeves . . . ." (*Ibid*, p. 326); and also giving precise "Articles for outwarde apparell of persons ecclesiasticall," one of which mentions the Gown and Cap named by Grindal; for it orders "That all inferiour ecclesiastical persons shall weare longe gownes of the fashion aforesayde, and cappes as before is prescribed," viz., in the previous *Items* which, moreover, refer to what is "appointed by the Injunctions." (*Ibid*, p. 329.)

These successive changes in "the Ecclesiastical Discipline" resulted finally in the *positive rules* of the Advertisements; they were obviously, however, not *prohibitions,* but only *dispensations* of the previous directions of 1559 and 1561; and they left untouched, as Grindal says, the Statute Law; its more comprehensive prescription of Ornaments remaining in abeyance.

The Court states that "Commissioners began to carry out" the "Injunctions" of 1559, "in the same year," and refers to "one of their Returns" catalogued in the "Calendar of State Papers, Domestic, 1547-1580, p. 148," as showing "that they chiefly occupied themselves in taking inventories of "Church Ornaments and of the Service Books in use." The Document here mentioned is thus described in the Calendar:—

"Vol. X. 1559. A book of the Visitation of the Province of York, comprehending the Dioceses of York, Durham, Carlisle, and Chester, taken before Dr. Edwyn Sandes, and Dr. Henry Harvye, and others, the Queen's Commissioners for the visitation of that province. *Also containing,*

"Certificate of recognizances taken before Drs. Sandes and Harvye, Commissioners General, for offences detected in the visitation of the province of York."

This Document has been carefully examined, but its contents do not bear out the description given in the Judgment. The heading says it was "visitacio regia actualiter exercita," and the Book begins with a copy of the Commission, corresponding to that given by Cardwell (*Doc. Ann.*, I., p. 249, Ed. 1844), dated June 24, 1559; but no direction is given about *Inventories* among the Instructions* given to the Commissioners to visit the Ecclesiastical State and Persons; nor is there any Inventory among the Returns in the Volume, or anything to indicate that the Commissioners were engaged in taking Inventories: in fact the contents of the Book shew that this was not "chiefly" their occupation. The Commissioners were authorized to punish those who obstinately refused to subscribe the Religious Forms; to examine into such subjects as the proper administration of Wills, and the vacancies in Churches; to consider matters relating to Benefices; to inquire about persons imprisoned on account of Religion, and cases of deprivation; and to appoint pious and prudent persons to investigate all matters relating to the Visitation.

The Volume has an account called "Detectiones et comperta," which includes presentments touching persons and things; others relate to immoralities, to clerical absentees, to recognizances taken in the Provinces touching punishments decreed for offences discovered during the Visitation and for the appearance of the offenders before the Commissioners when commanded. If anything was done relative to the Inventories of Church

---

* They are "Ad visitandum igitur tam in capite, quam in membris Ecclesias cathedrales, civitates, et diœceses Eboracen. Cestrens. Dunelmen. et Carliolen. [Ebor. Dunelmēn. Carliolen̄. et Cestr̄.] necnon quascunque alias collegiatas, parochiales, et præbendales ecclesias, et [ac] loca alia ecclesiastica quæcunque, tam exempta, quam non exempta, in et per easdem civitates et diœceses visibiliter [ubilibet] constitutas, clerumque et populum earundem in eisdem degentes [em] sive residentes [em]; deque statu ecclesiarum et locorum hujusmodi, necnon vita, moribus, et conversatione, ac etiam qualitatibus personarum in ecclesiis et locis prædictis degentium sive commorantium [ministrantium], modis omnibus, quibus id melius aut efficacius poteritis, inquirendum et investigandum. . . . ." (*Cardwell, Doc. Ann.*, I., p. 251.) The readings in square brackets are from the MS. State Paper in the Record Office.

Goods, it must have been under the general direction "to do "all and singular other things which may to you seem fit and "necessary concerning such visitation and reformation of matters," for there is no special mention of them. At page 8, however, which records the first sitting of the Commissioners (Aug. 22nd), it is stated that the Parishioners and others concerned came before them in the Church of St. Mary, Nottingham, and there *exhibited* their Bills of Detection "together with Inventories of "Goods of their Churches:" but this seems to be the only reference by name to "Inventories," nor is there any indication that they were to be taken subsequently: in one case (p. 94) the Clergy appearing are monished to produce their Letters of Orders, Institutions, Dispensations, and "other their muniments;" this perhaps was always done. At pp. 219 to 321 is a return of Presentments of defects in the fabric, insufficient means of performing Service, etc.; and here occur many references to there being no Communion book, and some to books of Service burnt in Queen Mary's time: but the greater part of the entries relate to Church Discipline, denial of the Supremacy, acts of immorality and other scandals.* It must be presumed, therefore, either that the Judicial Committee has been misinformed as to the character of this Document, or that a wrong reference is given in the Judgment; yet no other paper answering to their Lordships' description is to be found in the Catalogue.

Some time after writing this last passage I noticed, what seems to be, the probable source of their Lordships' error in Mr. Raine's pamphlet to which they refer elsewhere in the Judgment, and from which they appear to have substantially quoted the paragraph discussed at pp. 17 to 25; referring to the Ornaments Rubric of 1559, he says:—

"She [the Queen] had the Romanists as well as the Protestants to consider, and she did therefore what her brother did, and probably with the same intention. She obliged the Reformers, apparently against their wishes, to put the rubric, as it stands, in her book. But there was a thorough understanding between the Protestant party and their royal mistress. Sandes, afterwards Archbishop of York, who was one of the revisers, gave the following explanation of his view of the rubric

---

* Strype (*Ann.*, I., 165) examined this Return; his short account of it agrees, so far as it goes, with the above.

in a letter to Archbishop Parker :—'Our gloss upon this text is, that we shall not be forced to use them (*i.e.* the Ornaments), but that others in the meantime shall not convey them away, but that they shall remain for the Queen.'* This is crooked policy, but the event proved that this was the intention. The truth of this remark is pretty plain from what soon followed, for the Queen took the things herself. Like Edward VI, she looked upon the vestments, etc., as the property of the Crown. In her Injunctions, published in 1559, it is ordered '*that the churchwardens of every parish shall deliver unto our visitors the inventories of vestments, copes and other ornaments, plate, books, and specially of grayles, couchers, legends, processionals, hymnals, portuesses, and such like appertaining to the Church.*'† On the 24th of June, the royal council for the North, then established at York, had power to visit the cathedrals, collegiate churches, etc., throughout the Northern Province, with plenary authority to punish and deprive.‡ On the 25th of July another body of commissioners was appointed for the same district,§ consisting, I believe, of Dr. Sandes, Dr. Harvey, and others, and they continued working until December, when the Queen recalled them, allowing them, however, to complete all matters which had already been begun.‖ The book of their proceedings is preserved in the Public Record Office.¶ They seem to have occupied themselves for the most part in making inventories and in taking particular notice of the service books that were in use. This was a preparatory step. But the vestments began gradually to disappear." (*Vestments*, etc., by James Raine, M.A., 1866, pp. 8, 9.)

Mr. Raine mentions in a Note that the MS. was examined for him by Mr. Lawley: the account which I have given of it is derived from the inspection of three competent persons with two of whom I have myself examined the Book. The Judicial Committee have evidently received an impression of its contents substantially different from its real character. So, then, it appears that their Lordships were misled by Mr. Raine, who himself was misguided by Mr. Lawley.

I must observe, further, that this passage and other parts of the Pamphlet (as will be seen later) convey, however unintentionally,

" * Burnet's History of the Reformation, ii., Records, p. 332.

" † Wilkins, iv., p. 187. Cardwell's Doc. Annals, i., 228. Sparrow, 79.

" ‡ Wilkins, iv., 193-4. Cardwell, *ut supra*, i., 249, etc.

" § Quoted by Mr. Blunt. Preface to Annotated Prayer Book, xxxiv. There is in a MS. at York a set of injunctions given by them to the Chapter of Durham, on Sept. 25, 1st Eliz."

" ‖ Cal. of State of Papers, Domestic, 1547-80, 145.

" ¶ Ibid, p. 148. I have to thank Mr. Lawley for his kindness in examining this MS. for me."

an erroneous impression as to the object and effect of some of the Documents to which Mr. Raine refers: thus he states that "the "Queen took the things herself. Like Edward she looked upon "the Vestments, etc., as the property of the Crown." If, as it would seem, the reference immediately following to the Order of the Injunctions to deliver to the Queen's Visitors the Inventories of the Ornaments, is supposed to imply this claim, I venture to dispute the inference. The object of the inquiry (I do not refer to the *Special Commissions*) was to secure the safe custody of the Goods of the Churches, and to prevent their misappropriation or unauthorized removal. There seems no proof that Elizabeth either wished to follow or did imitate Edward's example in taking them herself: nor do either the proceedings or the instructions of the Commissioners to whom Mr. Raine refers, countenance any notion that they were aiding such a project.

VII. The Court goes on to say :—

> "These Advertisements were very actively enforced within a few years of their publication. An Inventory of the Ornaments of 150 parishes in the Diocese of Lincoln, A.D., 1565-1566, has been published by Mr. Edward Peacock; and it shows that the Chasubles or Vestments and the Albs, were systematically defaced, destroyed, or put to other uses, and a precise account was rendered of the mode of their destruction. Proceedings took place under Commissions in Lancashire in 1565 and 1570; in Carlisle in 1573 and following years, when 'vestments seem to have disappeared altogether.' (Rev. J. Raine, 'Vestments,' London, 1866.) There is no reason to doubt that all through the country, commissions were issued to enforce the observance of the advertisements within a few years after they were drawn up."

No doubt there was an endeavour to enforce the Advertisements, but in what direction? Their Lordships' language implies that it was against what may be termed the "Ritualists" of that day; yet there is not a single word in the Document which countenances such an opinion. It was the *Anti-Ritual* party upon whom they had to be "enforced," those who would hardly or not at all tolerate so much as the *Surplice:* to them, most certainly, it would have been no grievance had it been the *object* of the Advertisements to destroy the Vestments; on the contrary, they would then have the rather welcomed them; whereas the effect of the attempt to carry them out is thus stated by Cardwell (*Documentary Annals,* I., 321):—

"These advertisements and the proceedings consequent thereon occasioned the first open separation of the Nonconformists from the Church of England, the professed ground of separation being the necessity of wearing the same apparel that was used by the Romanists; but the real point at issue being, and soon afterwards showing itself to be, the right principle of Church government. In February, 1566, Humphrey and Sampson proposed the following questions to Bullinger: 'Whether any Ecclesiastical Constitutions may be tolerated, which though from their nature they are free from anything impious, do not nevertheless tend to edification? Whether anything of a ceremonial nature may be prescribed to the Church by the Sovereign, without the assent and free concurrence of Churchmen? Whether good pastors of unblemished life and doctrine may rightfully be removed from the Ministry on account of their non-compliance with such ceremonies?' These and other questions were answered by Bullinger and Gualter in a way calculated to allay the growing discontent, but without satisfying the two impatient theologians who had proposed them. (*Zurich Letters,* pp. 154, 354.)"

In support of their view as to the result of the enforcement of these Advertisements, their Lordships refer to Mr. Peacock's interesting publication of the Lincoln Inventories of 1565-6, and they remark that "it shews that the Chasubles or Vestments, "and the Albs, were systematically defaced, destroyed, or put to "other uses." In the Argument for the Appellant this Book was much quoted by Dr. Stephens, who, not unfairly, presented that *primâ facie* aspect of it which supported his own contention: the Court had not the advantage of hearing the criticisms of an opposing Counsel, and perhaps could scarcely be expected to investigate its extensive and minute details in order to ascertain the precise bearing and value of the Documents. Yet an examination of these Records not only fails to sustain the Court's supposed effect of the Advertisements, but, further, proves a great deal too much for their Lordships' purpose. In the following Table I have given a correct analysis (I think) of such parts of the 153 Inventories as bear upon the subject here discussed.

Name of Ornaments destroyed.	Number of Inventories.	Date at which they are named as destroyed, &c.									
		1552	1559	1560	1561	1562	1563	1564	1565	Tot to 1566	No Date	1566
Censers.	75		6	6	2		4		19	37	1	37
Cruets.	76		10	8	1	4	3	1	14	41	1	34
Copes.	44		3	3	1	1	1	1	14	24	1	19
Vestments.	136	1	9	6	3	5	5	5	36	70	1	65
Albes.	128		8	5	2	2	3	2	36	58	1	69
Tunicles.	8			1	1		1		3	6		2
Crosses.	124		7	8	3	5	5	1	34	63	1	60
Candlesticks.	86		5	7	2	4	6	1	22	47	1	38
Fanons.	31		2	2	1	2	1	1	2	11	1	19
Amices.	45	1	6	3	1	3		.	6	20	1	24
Stoles.	54	1	5	3	1	4	2	1	10	27	1	26
Corporasses.	29		3	2			1	2	5	13		16
Linen Cloths.	16		2	2	1			1	2	8		8
Towels.	12		1	1	1	1			4	8		4
Pillows.	5			1				1	1	3		2

Now in considering the supposed bearing of these Inventories upon the Advertisements it is essential to keep in mind the date of Archbishop Parker's letter just quoted (See p. 27) viz., 28th March, 1566, in which he told Cecil that he was "fully "bent to prosecute this order," *i.e.* the Advertisements: on the same day the Archbishop drafted a Letter (*D. A.*, p. 334) to the Bishop of London desiring him to transmit them to the other Suffragans of the Province. It is obvious therefore that none of the Ornaments which were destroyed or sold before March 26th, when the year 1566 began, could have been affected by an Order not issued from Lambeth until three days after: yet, as will be seen by the Table, *fully half* of them were made away with between 1559 and the end of 1565. This, however, is to take the view *most favourable* to the presumed witness of these Inventories: but they do not prove so much: their dates range from March 4, 1565-6 to May 26, 1566: of the whole number, 39 are *prior* to the Archbishop's letter of 28th March; 97 are between March 29 and April 30; and 15 date from May 1st to 26th. Time of course must be allowed for the Bishop of London sending the Advertisements to his brethren, and for the Commissions to be issued (if indeed there were any): it is highly probable that this would occupy most of the time between March 28 and April 30; so that, even supposing the Archbishop to have actually sent his Letter to the Bishop of London on the day of its date (a very unlikely thing, since he had written the same day to Cecil "to peruse this draft of letters," viz., that to the Bishop of London, and had also said "the Book of "Advertisements . . . is . . . yet stayed till I may hear your "advice") few, if any, of the 97 Inventories just mentioned could have been made *in consequence* of the Advertisements; so that only the 15 Inventories of May are at all likely to have sprung from this imagined source. Even these, however, it appears must be excluded, since it seems that a month elapsed before the Archbishop received an answer to his application; for, writing to Cecil on April 28th, he mentions that the Queen had told the Archbishop of York "to declare her pleasure "determinately to have the Order go forward." (See p. 63.) The Advertisements were not issued by Grindal to the Dean and Chapter of St. Paul's until May 21st, 1566 (See p. 64), and therefore it is most unlikely that they had found their way into Lincolnshire by the 26th of the same month (which is the latest date of any of the Inventories): consequently there can be no reason whatever to suppose that they bore any relation at all to the Inventories.

Moreover the Inventories themselves (including those of May) shew that the Ornaments were not put away *in consequence* of the Advertisements: they mention them as being mostly *already* got rid of, and state what remains.

Further, the Inventories prove too much as regards the purpose for which the Judicial Committee cite them; for if the Advertisements were the taking of the "other order" provided for by the Act of 1559, it follows that from that date till 1566 the Ornaments in question did not "remain for the Queen," as

Sandys supposed they would, but were *illegally* removed; for, as I have shewn (See p. 20), the Royal Injunctions did not touch them; and the Interpretations of the Injunctions, which only *required* the Cope, was an Order emanating from the Bishops alone.

Yet this is not all; *Copes* were destroyed, as well as Chasubles and Albes, during the same period; the Table shews 24 instances, and of these 18 were effected after 1561—the date at which the "Interpretations" positively ordered them in all Churches. Besides this there are 19 instances in the Inventories of 1566; of these, two things must be said: either they were destroyed before the date of the Advertisements (as I have already said the Inventories indicate) and thus their destruction was in defiance of the Episcopal Orders to use them; or, not being *required* by the Advertisements in *Parish* Churches, they were gladly turned out by those who were indifferent to them or who accounted them no less "superstitious" than the Chasubles which the "Interpretations" had *dispensed* with, but had not *forbidden*.

But, in truth, the re-action of those days was accompanied by a wanton destruction of "popish ornaments" which was neither discriminating nor consistent, as these Inventories shew, and could not well be more opposed to the principle subsequently enunciated in the 30th Canon of 1603—that "the abuse of a "thing doth not take away the lawful use thereof." Crosses* were as obnoxious as Chasubles and Albes: Stoles shared the fate of Amices: linen Altar Cloths and Altar Cushions (Pillows), were reckoned among the "monuments of superstition:" in fact it was only necessary that an Ornament should have been used in the Mass to ensure its demolition: even a Chalice was accounted " prophane " and must be converted into " a Communion Cup": while, as to consistency, the Cope remained where it was not

---

* But that they were *legal* and were destroyed without *lawful* Authority is plain from Bishop Jewel's Letter to Peter Martyr, Feb. 4, 1559-60, in which he says—"...... matters are come to that pass, that either the Crosses of silver and tin, which we have everywhere broken in pieces, must be restored, or our bishoprics be relinquished." (*Zurich Letters*, 1st Series, No. xxix., p. 67.) Such an alternative the Queen could not have presented to men who had destroyed the Crosses under the sanction of the Law. The Letter shews that Parker and Cox at this time defended the use of the Crucifix against Grindal and Jewel.

considered a "monument of superstition" (*e.g.* Lundonthorp, p. 115), but was cast out with the "tromperie of popish "peltrie" (*e.g.* Kelbie, p. 109) when it found no favour among the more advanced Protestants.

By what Authority the Goods mentioned in these Lincolnshire Inventories were destroyed there seems no evidence at present to shew: the Judicial Committee appear to think that it was done under one of the "Commissions" which "were issued to "enforce the observance of the Advertisements:" Mr. Peacock informs me that he was unsuccessful in his endeavours to discover any Commission, and that he believes other Antiquaries have alike failed: my own inquiries have been also in vain. It is certainly desirable to know what were the precise Instructions of the Commissioners, for those Gentlemen were often not very particular in their proceedings: though, indeed, considering the contents of the Advertisements there is not the least reason to suppose that the orders to enforce them gave any directions at all as to the disposal of the Church Ornaments. In all probability the Commissioners to whom these Inventories were exhibited were acting under one of the general Commissions for executing the Statutes 1 Eliz. c. 1 and 2, touching the Ecclesiastical Jurisdiction of the Crown, and the Uniformity of Divine Service: but as this latter Act retained the Ornaments, it is wholly unreasonable to suppose that a Royal Commission should have *authorized* (although it may have *connived* at) their destruction at a time when the Law unquestionably had not been *altered* although it was not *enforced.*

In making the preceding remarks upon the Lincolnshire Inventories I have assumed that the Court was warranted in connecting, to some extent, the Proceedings to which they relate with the Advertisements: but the fact is that they had nothing whatever to do with each other. There is not the slightest reason for supposing that the Commissioners to whom the Inventories were exhibited were discharging any duty imposed upon them by the Advertisements, or indeed that they knew anything about those Orders.

VIII. In support, however, of their Lordships' view the Judgment goes on to remark that:—

" The Visitation Articles of the Archbishops and Bishops about this time show that the operation of the advertisements had been rapid and complete. Archbishop Grindal, in 1571, inquires, ' whether all vestments, albs, tunicles, stoles, phanons, pixes, paxes, hand-bells, sacring-bells, censers, crismatories, crosses, candlesticks, holy water stocks, images, and such other reliques and monuments of superstition and idolatrie be utterly defaced, broken and destroyed.' (2nd Report, Ritual Commission, p. 408a.) Archbishop Parker in 1575 asks, ' in the time of celebration of Divine service, whether they wear surplices.' (2 Ritual Commission, p. 416a.) Aylmer, Bishop of London, uses the same form of question as Archbishop Grindal (Ibid, p. 418b.) Sandys, Archbishop of York, inquired in 1578, ' whether your parson, vicar or curate, at all times in saying the Common Prayer upon Sundays and holydays, and in administering of the Sacrament [s *sic*] doth use and retain [*for* retain *read* weare] the surplice yea or nay' [*for* nay *read* no]. (Ibid, p. 422a.)"

Yet it might well be thought that the more natural inference from Grindal's inquiry would have been that the Advertisements had *not* been so "rapid and complete" in their "operation" as that Prelate desired, else he need not have asked at all about the condemned Ornaments. Indeed such inquiries continued much later; their Lordships refer to those of Aylmer, Bishop of London in 1577; and to this may be added Sandys, Archbishop of York in 1578 (2nd *Rit. Report*, p. 423, No. 32). After this time such questions seem (so far as these Articles shew) to have ceased for the next twenty-three years, but in 1601, Bancroft, Bishop of London, asks thus:—

" Whether there be any in your parish who are noted, knowne, or suspected to conceale or keepe hidden in their houses any masse bookes, portesses, breviaries, or other bookes of poperie and superstition or any challices, copes, vestments, albs, or other ornaments of superstition, uncancelled or undefaced, which it is to be conjectured they do keep for a day, as they cal it." (2nd *Rit. Report*, p. 438.)

The same enquiry is made by Babington, Bishop of Worcester, 1607; Abbot, Archbishop of Canterbury, 1611; King,

Bishop of Lincoln, 1612; Howson, Bishop of Oxford, 1619; and Articles for Peculiars of Canterbury, 1637 (*Ibid*, pp. 457, 459, 463, 477, 575): the cause of these questions would seem to have been the dread of "Popish recusants" and of their supposed designs to restore " their religion " which culminated in the two Statutes made against them—2 James I., c. iv., 1604, and 3 James I., c. iv., 1605—the latter of which required the *Churchwardens* to make presentments in order to assist in " discovering and repressing them."

However, whether the destruction of the Ornaments was slow and sure, or the reverse, enough has, I think, already been said here to prove that the Advertisements were not the *cause* of their disappearance.

The Judicial Committee quote the Visitation Inquiries of three Bishops in order to shew, apparently, that after the issue of the Advertisements the *Surplice* alone was permitted in *Parish* Churches: yet such a conclusion could only be reliable if the Advertisements or the Questions of the Bishops had been of a *negative* or *prohibitory* character: but this is not the case with either of them. It must be borne in mind, too, that the unwillingness or refusal to wear the Surplice itself not only necessitated the distinct mention of it, but also furnished an obvious reason for not asking about any other Vesture than that which the Bishops themselves had considered it necessary to *insist* upon. Further, if the *Cope* was forbidden by the "Advertisements" it is surprising that Grindal, Aylmer and Sandys did not name it in their detailed enumeration of Ornaments about whose destruction they so minutely enquired from 1571 to 1578: it was indeed asked for, as I have mentioned, in the Inquiries touching concealed "ornaments of superstition;" but, as even the Canons of 1604 ordered it for Cathedrals, it cannot be reasonably supposed that the question referred to that particular Vesture itself; therefore it would seem to have been only aimed at any Copes which were thought to be "reliques "and monuments of superstition" from having been "heretofore "used at Masse," and which it was "conjectured they do keep for "a day, as they cal it," *i.e.* in the hope of reviving them with a restored Roman Worship under the Papal Supremacy.

The first example given by the Court is from Archbishop Parker in 1575, who asks, "in the time of Celebration of Divine "Service, whether they wear surplisses." But Parker asked the very same question in 1563—"3. Item. Whether your Prestes, "Curates, or Ministers do use in the time of the celebracion of "Divine Service to weare a surplesse, prescribed by the Queenes "Majesties Injunctions, and the boke of Common Praier." (2nd *Report of Ritual Commission*, p. 403.) The *Surplice*, it should be noticed, is not "prescribed" in the "Injunctions" themselves, but in their "Interpretations" of 1561 which also *prescribe* "the *Cope* in the ministration of the Lord's Supper:" if, then, not to inquire for an Ornament meant that it was not to be used, it follows that in 1563 no less than in 1575 the Cope was *prohibited* by silence though it was actually *required* by the Bishops' "Interpretations" of the Injunctions at that very time in force.

It might be thought a *suppressio veri* not to notice the fact (which, however, is not mentioned by the Judicial Committee) that Grindal in his Visitation Articles of 1571 enquires—"7. "Whether your person, vicar, curate, or minister doe weare any "Cope in your Parish Church or Chappell."* It may be that he only referred to Copes which had been used in Mary's reign, for he adds "or minister the Holy Communion in any Chalice here- "tofore used at Masse:" but if he designed to give a *prohibitory* character to the Advertisements and so to *discourage* the use of *any* Copes in the Northern Province, it is noticeable that in his 4th *Injunction* of the same year (2nd Rit. Report, p. 411) he did not *forbid* that Ornament, though, except in this particular, it corresponds with his Article 7 : neither did he order its destruction in *Injunction* 7 (*Ibid*, p. 414) which wholly agrees with his Article 6 (*Ibid*, p. 408.) These considerations seem to prove that he knew the *Cope* to be *lawful* in *Parish* Churches, under

---

* The same inquiry occurs in his "Articles" for "the Metropolitcall visitation" of "the Province of Canterburie," 1576 (*Remains, Parker Society*, p. 159). The Editor says, "These Articles of Inquiry are taken from a printed copy in the Cambridge University Library. They are not noticed by Strype, nor are they given by Wilkins or Cardwell. The Archbishop's sequestration, which took place in this year, seems to have interrupted the progress of this metropolitical visitation."

the Advertisements whether he *liked* it or not;* and its legality is the more presumeable from the fact that in not one of the long Series of Articles and Injunctions from 1563 to 1728, printed in the 2nd Report of the Ritual Commission does any Bishop or Archdeacon follow Grindal's example by asking whether the Cope was worn in Parish Churches.

* Subsequently to this being written I observed, and have since considered, Mr. Raine's remarks upon this Injunction: he says (p. 14)—" The word cope is not mentioned in the above order; perhaps it is here included under the word 'Vestmentes'; perhaps it is accidentally omitted. If there is an omission, it is an accidental one, as is shewn by the following proceedings of the Archbishop's Commissioners upon some of the comperts in the Visitation. There are only three relating to vestments from the whole province.

"1571. Office against George Sutton par. Hornsey, the two churchwardens, and Stephen Vavasour, the parish clerk.

"Sutton says, '*he did hang up the* ij *copes in the revestrie of Hornesey churche. The said Vavasour saieth he did se the said* ij *copes sence at the desyre of the said Sutton who hanged the same in the revestrie, having in his companye the said Vavasour, who denieth the same. And for so much as the said Sutton confessed the having of the said copes, and coulde not discharge himselfe of the same, he was ordered to gyve* x s *to the churche of Hornesey before Law-Sunday next, of condicion that if at any tyme hereafter the copes be founde he shall have the* x s *agayn.*'

"1571. Office against Thomas Cooke, clerk of the Holy Trinity church, Hull.

"' *He hath* ij *copes, but what he haith done with them it is not knowne. He says that he boughte* ij *copes of one Grimston, and the same are defaced. And so, the matter is referred to Mr. dean of Hull, and he to make certificate after in letters whether the said copes were lawfullie solde or no from the churche.*'

"1571. Office against Leonard Lewtie, of the parish of Spofforth.

"' *He haith had the custodie of divers churche gere serving for Latten servyce, as vestimentes, tunycles, crosses, with others, so muche as did fill one di. quarter sack; and there is come to the handes of one of the churchwardens sence the visitacion one crosse and* iij *vestmentes which are now defaced; and the rest yt is not knowen where it is.*' He appears and denies the truth. Afterwards he says that the things were given to Mr. Haworth and others, the Queen Majesty's Commissioners, at Leeds, and defaced. These Commissioners must have been acting under the Advertisements."

In the last of these instances the *Cope* is not mentioned, and I do not see that the other two sorve the purpose for which Mr. Raine cites them. They show, as was to be expected, that persons who had the custody of Church goods were obliged to give an account of them; but so far from proving that Copes were illegal and might therefore be destroyed, they appear to indicate the reverse; for in one case a fine was to be remitted if the missing "Copes be founde," and in the other a certificate was to be produced "whether the said Copes were lawfullie solde or no from the Churche." Probably, as the Advertisements did not *order* the Cope in *Parish* Churches, a Parish might lawfully sell it and apply the proceeds to some Church purpose; but this is no evidence that it was a duty to make away with it as a forbidden Vestment. It seems to me that Mr. Raine was under an entirely wrong impression in saying "these Commissioners must have been acting under the Advertisements": very likely they may have had to see that the Advertisements were observed; but those Orders had nothing in common with the proceedings quoted.

IX. The conclusion to which the Court comes from its preceding review is thus stated :—

"Upon the whole, there is abundant evidence that within a few years after the advertisements were issued, the vestments used in the Mass entirely disappeared."

No doubt this statement is substantially correct; yet it materially affected the Decision of the Court to assign the *fact* to its true *cause:* I have already shewn that the Advertisements were not that cause; unless *indirectly*, and then only to a very small extent: they did but sanction any desires to abolish the Vestments by rendering the use of some of them still less obligatory under the Rubric than it was after the Bishops had issued the "Interpretations" of the Injunctions.

There is sufficient proof that the destruction of the Vestments began very soon after the passing of the Elizabethan Act of Uniformity, notwithstanding its provision that they should "be retained and be in use :" that this proceeding was then illegal, even if Sandys' "gloss" upon the proviso (See p. 18) be accepted, cannot be doubted ; for there is no proof that they were destroyed by any Authority contemplated by the Statute. On the contrary, a proceeding of the Ecclesiastical Commissioners in 1561, *subsequently* as it would seem to the "Inter-"pretations" of the Injunctions (See p. 24) which required at least the Cope in all Churches, is very strong evidence that no *lawful* order had been given for their destruction. Strype, writing under this date, says :—

"The Archbishop of Canterbury, with Thomas, Archbishop of York, the Bishops of London and Ely, and some others of the Ecclesiastical Commission, were now sitting at Lambeth, upon the regulating and ordering of the matters of the Church. And on the 12th day of April, (being their second session,) certain Articles were agreed upon by them, with the assent of their brother Bishops to the same : namely,"

Among these Articles is the following :—

"*Item*, That all old service books, grails, antiphoners, and others, be defaced and abolished by orders in visitations." (*Life of Parker*, ii., 97.)

This order was perfectly legal, being consistent with the Act of Uniformity which forbad the public use of any other Book of Service than the one provided by the Statute: if it had been also legal to deface and abolish the Vestments, it is unaccountable that the order of the Commissioners should not have included them as well: perhaps it will be said that, as Strype relates, the Vestments had been destroyed previously, soon after the Prayer Book and the Injunctions were issued in 1559 (See p. 21), and therefore there was no need to give any orders about them; but he relates the same of the Books: the fact being that the destruction of both was only *partial*, as is shewn by contemporaneous and later Documents, *e.g.*, the Lincolnshire Inventories. Therefore it can hardly be doubted that, the *Vestments* being retained* by the Statute which *abolished* the *Books*, the Commissioners, whatever may have been their wishes, would not have imperilled their own Authority by issuing Orders which they could not *legally* justify.

That the destruction of the Vestments was in part justified or excused as though warranted by the Instructions given to the Royal Commissioners for the Visitation of the Dioceses seems plain, although indeed no mention whatever is made of such Ornaments either in the Injunctions or in the Articles with which they were furnished in 1559. No doubt it was the words "all other monuments of . . . . superstition" in the 2nd of these Articles and the corresponding 23rd Injunction† of which advantage was unfairly taken both then and later: the Article is in these words:—

* It was only 15 months before this that *Thomas Sampson*, writing to *Peter Martyr* (Jan. 6, 1559-60), says—"What can I hope, when three of our lately appointed Bishops are to officiate at the table of the Lord, one as priest, another as a deacon, and a third as subdeacon, before the image of the crucifix, or at least not far from it, with candles, and habited in the golden vestments of the Papacy; and are thus to celebrate the Lord's Supper without any sermon?" (*Zurich Letters*, 1st Series, No. xxvii., p. 63.) The Queen's known regard for the Law, often referred to by the Bishops, makes it certain that she would not have retained these things in her Chapel if they had been unlawful.

† The 23rd Injunction is as follows:—
"XXIII. Also, That they shall take away, utterly extinct, and destroy all shrines, coverings of shrines, all tables, candlesticks, trindals, and rolls of wax, pictures, paintings, and all other monuments of feigned miracles, pilgrimages, idolatry, and superstition, so that there remain no memory of the same in walls, glass-windows, or elsewhere within their churches and houses: preserving nevertheless, or repairing both the walls and glass-windows; and they shall exhort all their parishioners to do the like within their several houses." (*Cardwell, Doc. Ann.*, 1., p. 221.)

"2. Item, whether in their churches and chapels all images, shrines, all tables, candlesticks, trindals, and rolls of wax, pictures, paintings, and all other monuments of feigned and false miracles, pilgrimages, idolatry, and superstition be removed, abolished, and destroyed." (*Cardwell, Doc. Ann.*, I., p. 242. Ed. 1844.)

Collier, referring to the matter, says:—

"They proceeded upon the plan of the Injunctions; and had, over and above, a book of Articles printed for that purpose.

"By these directions all carved images [*i.e.* those images, as the Article shews, which had been abused to superstitious purposes—*conf.* Liddell *v.* Westerton, *Moore*, p. 169], paintings of counterfeit miracles, and other superstitious remains, were removed out of churches and defaced. They inquired likewise into the preaching, morals, and management of the clergy. In London the Commissioners were Sir Richard Sackville, Dr. Huick, Mr. Horne (afterwards Bishop of Winchester), and one Salvage. These gentlemen, calling such persons of every parish before them as they thought fit, gave them an oath to present upon the Articles delivered. And here some people's ignorant zeal carried them too far: for not only images were destroyed, but copes, altar-carpets, prayer-books, other church furniture, and even crucifixes, were burnt together. There is an odd, bantering, letter, written from *London* into the country, upon this occasion, the words are these—
'(29th Aug. 1559). Since the day before our *Bartholomew* fair, we have had such bonfires, as passes all the blazes that were made for the winning of St. *Quintins:* For all our church patrons, *Maries, Johns, Roodes*, and all the rabblement of the pope's ornaments, were sent to *Terra Sancta* in this fiery sacrifice.' (Biblioth. Robt. Harley Armig.)

"To worship images, is pushing regard much too far: 'tis without doubt a criminal excess, unpractised and condemned by the primitive church: but then on the other hand, to treat them coarsely and burn them, looks like an affront to those they represent, and is altogether unbecoming Christians. To burn the figure of the cross, and especially that of our Saviour, is, to speak softly, a horrid profanation: and, if we may reason from such indignities done to men, must be superlatively wicked. The *Reader*, therefore, is to suppose, that all this disorder was without commission, and nothing but mob-execution: for 'tis evident the practice of the Queen and Court was quite different, and therefore would give no countenance to such singular extremes." (*Collier, E. H.*, II., fol. p. 434; *or* 8°, vol. vi., p. 250.)

The evidence given at p. 21 points to this and to another cause for the disappearance of *Vestments* which is well expressed by the Judicial Committee (in Liddell *v.* Westerton) when considering the subject of *Crosses*: their Lordships said:—

"That many of the English Bishops objected both to Crosses and Crucifixes, and either ordered or sanctioned their removal from Churches within their Dioceses, and that in many others they were defaced or destroyed by the violence of the people, can admit of no doubt; and that this violence extended also to monuments in Churches, appears by a Proclamation issued by Queen Elizabeth against defacers of monuments in the year 1560; for it speaks of these proceedings as ' to the slander of such as either gave or had charge in times past only to deface monuments of idolatry and false feigned images in Churches and Abbeys.' (1 Card., Doc. Ann., No. liv., pp. 289, 290, Ed. 1844); expressions which tend strongly to confirm the meaning their Lordships have already attributed to the Injunctions and Acts of Parliament of Edward the Sixth." (*Moore*, p. 174.)

This "meaning," to which their Lordships refer, may most fitly be reproduced here; the passage is all the more applicable to the case of *Vestments* because they most certainly had not been "excluded" in 1560 (the date given in the last passage) "from use in the Services." The passage runs thus:—

"But although their Lordships are of opinion that the law did not require the removal from Churches of Crosses, merely as such, both Books of Common Prayer had excluded them from use in the Services. They were no longer to be employed; and nothing is more probable, therefore, than that if they could be turned to any profit, they would be made the subject, either of sale or robbery, and that in the popular disturbances which accompanied the great change in the religion of the nation, and in many cases anticipated and outran the acts of the government, crosses would share the fate of images; so that between the fanaticism of the populace, and the cupidity of the courtiers, the ornaments of the Churches, in every sense of that term, would be subject to spoliation and destruction. We find, indeed, by the Injunction of the Council of the 30th April, 1548, already referred to (ante, p. 156) that even at this early period such proceedings were going on, for that Letter expressly forbids the sale or alienation of the chalices, silver crosses, bells, or other ornaments, which it declares were not given for that purpose to be alienated by parishes at their pleasure, but rather to be used to the intent they were first given, or to some other necessary and convenient service of the Church.

"Under these circumstances, it cannot be matter of surprise if comparatively few crosses remained either standing in the Churches or preserved in the repositories of its ornaments." (*Moore*, p. 171.)

This non-existence of Crosses did not, however, lead the Judicial Committee in 1859 to declare them illegal when "standing in Churches," though they are not named in the Canons of 1603 or in the Prayer Book of 1662; on the contrary when, in 1860, Mr. Beal alleged that their Lordships' Monition had not been complied with because "the metal cross "which was standing . . . on or attached to the super altar, on "the stone altar . . . was then placed on the sill of the great "eastern window of the Church," the complaint was dismissed, the Court observing that "the Cross has been placed in another "part of the Church or Chapel, not in any sense upon the Table "which has been substituted for the stone Table . . ." (*Moore's P. C. Reports*, 14, p. 1.) Neither did the like non-existence of Vestments influence the Court when interpreting the Ornaments Rubric in 1857; nor has the almost total disappearance of Copes and their entire disuse in Cathedrals for above 100 years* induced the Judicial Committee, in the Case now under discussion, to disregard the order of the 24th Canon of 1603 to use them at the Celebration of the Holy Communion.

X. The opposition to the Surplice is next referred to by their Lordships, they say :—

> "It is true that for some years after the appearance of the Advertisements, great reluctance was exhibited by the Puritan party to the use of the surplice, and, in the struggle against the use, they sometimes asserted that, if the surplice were insisted upon,

---

* In Durham Cathedral the Copes were first disused in 1759, when Bishop Warburton was Prebendary, owing, it is said, to the edge of the Cope interfering with his wig. Mr. Raine (p. 19) has this Note about them: "The following extract from an unpublished diary is of value—'1759: at the latter end of July or beginning of August the old copes (those raggs of Popery) which had been used in the communion service at the abbey ever since the time of the Reformation were ordered by the d. and ch. to be totally disused and laid aside. Dr. Warburton, one of the prebendary's and bp. of Gloucester, was very zealous to have them laid aside, and so was Dr. Cowper, the dean.'" Five Copes now remain there: 1. Purple Velvet, richly embroidered, and with a crucifix on the back; 2. Purple Silk, embroidered in Gold, with Saints on the Hood; 3. Crimson Velvet, embroidered in Gold with Saints on the Orphrey; 4. Cloth of Gold and Blue Velvet, woven 'together in a pattern; 5. Crimson Satin, embroidered in Gold, David with the Head of Goliath on the Hood: this Cope was given by King Charles I.

The Copes at Westminster Abbey were ordered by the Parliament in 1643 to be destroyed. (*Neale's West.* I. 164: *Stanley's Memorials of West.*, p. 93): yet, as Copes were worn at the Coronation of Charles II., new ones would seem to have been provided: possibly not all the old ones perished, for Abp. Juxon is said to have worn "a rich antient Cope" (*Ogilby, Coron. of Charles II.*, 177): but, although Copes have been worn at the subsequent Coronations and at Royal and other great Funerals, there does not appear to be any evidence of their being used (though this would not prove that they were not employed) in the ordinary Communion Service at the Abbey since the Restoration; at all events, it seems pretty certain that they have been disused there for at least the last century, which is all that I am concerned to shew here.

then, by virtue of the Rubric and Act of Parliament, the other vestments mentioned in the first Prayer Book of Edward VI should also be used.

The expression, "some years," falls much short of the period during which this "reluctance"—it should rather be said *opposition*—to its use was exhibited: such at all events is the legitimate inference to be drawn from the long series of Visitation Articles, dating from 1563 to 1728, published in the 2nd Report of the Ritual Commissioners, 1868: in these 82 Documents the general questions, "Have you a Surplice?" or "Doth "your Minister wear a Surplice?" indicate a very common laxity about it, or they would have been needless; but the more stringent enquiries in 16 instances, coming down to 1679 —that is, 113 years after the Advertisements—prove the long and continuous resistance or indifference: "always use and "wear," "continual wearing," "never omit wearing," "con-"stantly wear," are terms which prove that the Ecclesiastical Authorities had extreme difficulty in enforcing the Surplice upon many of their Clergy.

XI. Having noticed this "great reluctance" to wear the Surplice, the Judicial Committee remark that:—

> "In a somewhat rare tract, printed in the reign of James I, 1605, and addressed to the Bishop of Worcester, defending 'the not exact use of the authorized Book of Common Prayer,' the writer (p. 34) argues that no such order was made by the Queen as was directed by the Act of Parliament, yet even he admits that the Metropolitan, 'on the Queen's mandative letters that some order might be taken, had conference and communication, and at the last, by assent and consent of the Ecclesiastical Commissioners, did think such orders as were specified in the Advertisements meet and convenient to be used and followed' (p. 36); but he asserts that they were of no value, since 'the Queen's assent was not yielded.'"

This Tract, which is a remarkable one, has an introductory "Epistle," addressed "To the Right Honorable Lords, the "Lords of his Majesties most honorable privie Counsell" (a noticeable point considering that the present Judgment proceeds from a Committee of that body) : the Writers complain :—

"That a third or fourth part of three or four hundred painfull, discreet, learned, grave and godly ministers, within lesse then sixe monethes, should be suspended, deprived, or deposed some from their offices, and some from their benefices; . . . only for omission of the least of the commaundements and traditions of men," *viz.*, "the wearing of a whit Surplice, and the feyned making of an ayrie crosse in Baptisme." And they ask the Council "to bee petitioners unto his Majestie, that by his Regale and Supreame power, there might bee an healing of the former errour, and uncharitableness of the Diocesans and other Ordinaries."

It appears to me that this Tract has a more important bearing upon the Advertisements than the Judicial Committee seem to allow, and therefore it may be useful to produce its arguments somewhat more fully than their Lordships have done.

Referring (p. 1) to the Canons of 1603-4 the Writers contend, that by "the Statute 25, H. 8, cap. 19," these Canons were not " made by the whole Clergie of the Realme," inasmuch as the Clergy of the Northern Province were not parties to them (as indeed they were not at that time); therefore they urge "that they "ought not to have bene promulged and executed at all, especi-"ally within the Province of Yorke." Further, while saying that they were "ready, upon better reasons, to alter" their "opinion," (an opportunity for which occurred the next year, 1606, when the Convocation of York assented to the Canons) they said " that the Synod never intended, that the peyne of deprivation " should follow . . . . for the not use of any Ornaments . . . "enjoyned by those Canons," seeing that " there is not so much " as meċion once made " in them of such a penalty.

Next they argue (p. 32) that by the Elizabethan Act of Uniformity, then in force, the Legal Ornaments were those of the First Prayer Book ; they also maintain that the Provincial Constitutions were still in force, though, ingeniously enough, they meet an argument supposed to be drawn from them in favour of the Surplice, by saying that "the provinciall" does not apply to "a Minister of the Gospel," since they only provide for "the "masse." They also allege that the penalties of the Statute do not apply to the non-use of the prescribed *Ornaments*, because the Proviso respecting them comes after the Penal Clauses of the Act: if the Statute will bear this construction (which certainly seems natural and grammatical) it may help to explain Sandys' "gloss" upon the Rubric that "we shall not be *forced* " to use them." Then, after comparing the Elizabethan Statute and Rubric with the Rubrics of the Book of 1549, they conclude that *the Surplice alone* was not required by Law, and so they endeavour to excuse themselves for not wearing it at all.

Having given this outline of the argument it may be useful to give one portion of it in full, though somewhat long, especially as the Tract (of which I possess a copy) is not very accessible:—

"*Considerations against the deprivation of a Minister, for the not vse of a Surplice in divine service.*"

"In the whole body of the statute, there is not one syllable or letter, frō the which any semblance of reason can be deduced, that any Minister of the church, for refusing to vse, or for the not vsing of any ornament appointed by the statute, or by the book to bee in vse, should be punished with the peyne of deprivatiō. For what soever punishment a Minister, for the breach of the Statute, may sustayne, by the king's justices, the same is only to be imposed for such offences, as are specified before the last provisoe of the statute. Ornamentes therefore of the church provided to be reteyned, and to be in vse, being not cōteyned in those premises, or things mencioned before the second provisoe, concerning the Archbishops and Bishops authoritie, and for refusing whereof, a Minister, by the premises is punishable, it followeth (there being no punishmēt for refusing the vse of ornaments in the last provisoe) that the not use of ornaments, is not punishable before the king's justices. And if there be no punishment appointed to be inflicted before the king's justices for the refusing to vse any ornament, thē much lesse is there any punishment to be inflicted for the refusall of the vse of a Surplice. For the Surplice is so farre from being commanded to be worne, as an ornament, in every service of the church, as the same is not so much as once particularly mencioned, either in the parish booke, or in the statute.

"Nay by the generall wordes, both of the statute and the booke, the Surplice is wholly secluded from being appointed to be an ornament of it selfe, in some part of the service of the Church. For if with the same in some part of the Service there be not a Cope provided to bee worne, the Surplice may not be worne. For the better manifestation whereof, it is necessary that we set downe the wordes of the Statute, of the parish booke, and of the booke of the second of K. Edw. the sixth: vnto which booke of king Edward, for the use of ornaments, the Ministers be referred, both by the parish booke & statute of 1 Eliza. c. 2. the words of which statute are these:

"*Provided alwayes and be it enacted, That such ornamentes of the Church, and of the Ministers shall be retayned and be in use as was in the church of England, by authoritie of Parliament, in the second yeare of the raigne of King Edward the 6. vntill other order shalbe therein taken by authoritie of the Queenes Majestie, with the advise of her Commissioners, appointed and authorised under the great seale of England, for causes Ecclesiasticall, or of the Metropolitane of this Realme.*

"Thus farre the statute: the wordes of the parish booke follow:

"*It is to be noted, that the Minister at the time of the Communion and other times in his ministration shall use such ornamentes in the Church, as were in use by authoritie of Parliament, in the second yeare of King Edw. the sixth, according to the act of Parliamēt, in that case enacted and provided.* The words of which booke of the second of King Edward, are these:

"*Vpon the day and at the time appointed, for the ministration of the holy Communion, the Priest that shall execute the holy ministerie, shall put upon him the vesture appointed for that ministration, that is to say,* A white Albe playne, with a vestiment or cope:

"Afterward it is said thus: *Upon Wensdayes and Fridayes the English Letany shal be said or song, &c. And though there be none to communicate with the Priest, yet those dayes (after the Letany ended) the Priest shall put upon him a playne Albe, or Surplice, with a Cope, and say all things at the Altar, &c.*

"From all which places it is plaine, First, that no Minister, at any time upon Wensdayes and Fridayes, after the Letany ended, was bound simplie to weare a surplice at the Altare, for it was in his choyse, to put upon him a playne Albe or Surplice, with a Cope.

"Secondly, that no Priest upon the day and at the time appointed for the Ministration of the holy communion, might put vpon him a Surplice, but only a white Albe playne, with a vestiment or cope.

Thirdly, that no Minister upon Wensdayes and Fridayes, when hee read the Letany, did weare, or was bound to weare an Albe, or Surplice and Cope. For it had been in vayne and a thing ridiculouse for the booke to have willed the Minister, after the Letany ended, to put vpon him those ornaments, if in the time of reading the Letany, hee had had them vpon his backe.

"Fourthly, that no minister at or in any of the times and services aforesaid, is bound to put upō him a Surplice, vnless therewithall he weare a Cope. For the use of ornamentes ought to be according to the act of Parliament. And therefore where no Cope, there by the act no Surplice: where no Altar to goe vnto after the Letany ended, there no Surplice to be put on after the Letany: where a Communion with a white Albe plaine, and a vestiment or Cope, there a Cōmunion without a Surplice.

"There is yet one other speciall observation before touched, though for an other purpose, worthy to be reiterated in this place against the vse of the Surplice at the Communion, reading the Letany, and saying prayers at the Altar. And that is this: Namely for that as well tho

Statute 1 *Eliza.* as the parish booke hath revived and commaunded the vse of those ornamentes, according to the Act of Parliament, 2 *Edw.* 6. which were repealed and forbidden by the booke of the 5 and 6 of *King Edward the sixth.*

"*It is to be noted,* saith the booke of 5 and 6 of *King Edw.* 6. *That the Minister, at the time of the communion, and all other times, in his ministration, shall use neither Albe, vestiment nor Cope, but being an Archbishop or Bishop, he shall have and weare a Rochet, and being a Priest or Deacon, he shall have and weare a Surplice only.*

"And here it is to be noted (sayeth the parish booke) that the Minister at the time of the communion, and at all other tymes, in his ministration, shall vse such ornamentes in the church as were in vse by Authoritie of Parliament in the 2. yeare of the reigne of *King Edw. the* 6. according to the Act of Parliament in that case made and provided, which were as the Booke of *K. Edw.* saith, an Albe with a vestiment or Cope, at the communion, and an Albe or Surplice with a Cope, upon Wensdayes and Fridayes, after the Letany ended." (Pages 32—34.)

After these "Considerations" and some other remarks the Writers proceed to argue against the enforcement of the Advertisements, on the ground of their lack of adequate Authority. As the statement was made within forty years of the issue of those Orders there can be no reasonable doubt that it was founded upon a sufficient knowledge of the facts, and that it is therefore the reliable contemporary testimony of competent witnesses. It runs thus :—

"For our partes we acknowledge, that the Queenes Highnes had authoritie by the statute with the advise of her Commissioners, &c. or Metropolitane, to take other order for ornamentes. But wee never yet vnderstood, that any other order was taken accordingly: and especiallie in any such sorte, as that the Archbishops, Bishops & other Ordinaries might warrant their sentences of deprivation to be lawfull against the Ministers, which refuse to vse the Surplice. By the Advertisements wherevpon (as it seemeth) they did principally rely, and by authoritie whereof they did chiefly proceed, it is apparent that neither the letter, nor intendement of the statute (for the alteration of ornamentes) was observed: And that therefore the commaundement of wearing a Surplice in steed of a white Albe playne, by the advertissementes, was not duely made.

"For though by her Highnes letters it doth appeare, that she was desirous, as the preface to the advertisemēts importeth, to have advise from the Metropolitane & Cōmissioners, that she might take order; nevertheless that her Highnes, by her authority, with their advise, did take order & alter the ornamēts : this (I say) doth no where appeare, no not by the advertisements them selves. Howsoever then the Metropolitane vpon the Queenes mandative letters, that some orders might be taken, had conference and communication, and at the last, by assent, and consent of the ecclesiasticall commissioners did think such orders as were specified in the advertisements, meete and convenient to be vsed and followed ; nevertheless, all this proveth not that these orders were taken by her Maiesties Authoritie. For the Metropolitane and Commissioners, might thinke, agree and subscribe, that the advertisementes were meete and convenient, and yet might these advertisements be never of any valew, as wherevnto her Highnes authoritie was never yeelded." (Pages 35, 36.)

XII. Adverting to the concluding passage, here quoted from this Tract, their Lordships observe that :—

"This last proposition can hardly be maintained; for if the Queen's mandative letter preceded the compilation of the Advertisements, and if, as it appears abundantly, they were afterwards enforced as by her authority, her assent must be presumed. It appears probable that the Queen hesitated before the Advertisements were thus enforced, as to which see a remarkable letter from the Archbishop to Cecil, on the 28th March, 1566, cited by Mr. Perry in his book on ' Lawful Church Ornaments (p. 209), from the Parker Correspondence, on which Mr. Perry remarks 'it would seem that the Archbishop's application had at length some success, for immediately afterwards he sent his letter to the Bishop of London for conformity,' and in the letter to the Bishop he requests him 'to transmit the Book of Advertisements to the other Suffragans of the Province.'"

Upon this it must be remarked first of all, that it is not said that the Queen issued a Mandative Letter for " the compila-"tion of the Advertisements"; all that is stated is that, in consequence of "the Queen's Mandative Letters that some "order might be taken," the Metropolitan and other Bishops took counsel, which resulted finally in the Advertisements. The " Letters " referred to are plainly the Document already noticed (See p. 26) which the Queen sent to Archbishop Parker on January 25th, 1564-5 (*Parker Correspondence*, No. clxx., p. 223), and which the Archbishop, writing to Grindal, Bishop of London, on January 30th, speaks of as " her letters." (*Ibid*, No. clxxi., p. 227.) But there is nothing whatever in the

Queen's Letter to indicate that she was acting upon the 25th or 26th Sections of her Act of Uniformity. Her Majesty's complaint was—that owing to want of proper care on the part of the Bishops great disorders had arisen with reference to the "lawful rites and ceremonies to be used in the churches" (See p. 26); therefore the Queen said:—

"We do by these our present letters require, enjoin, and straitly charge you, being the Metropolitan, according to the power and authority which you have under us over the Province of Canterbury, (as the like we will order for the Province of York,) to confer with the Bishops your brethren, namely, such as be in commission for causes Ecclesiastical, and also all other head officers and persons having jurisdiction Ecclesiastical, as well in both our Universities as in any other places, collegiate, cathedral, or whatsoever the same be, exempt or not exempt, either by calling to you from thence whom you shall think meet, to have assistance or conference, or by message, process, or letters, as you shall see most convenient, and cause to be truly understand [sic] what varieties, novelties and diversities there are in our clergy or amongst our people within every of the said jurisdictions, either in doctrine or in ceremonies and rites of the Church, or in the manners, usages, and behaviour of the clergy themselves, by what name soever any of them be called. And thereupon, as the several cases shall appear to require reformation, so to proceed by order, injunction, or censure, according to the order and appointment of such laws and ordinances as are provided by Act of Parliament, and the true meaning thereof, so as uniformity of order may be kept in every church, and without variety and contention." (*Ibid*, p. 225.)

Now if these Directions are compared with the two clauses * of the Statute it cannot be maintained, I think, that they are a taking of "other order" as to "Ornaments" or a publishing of "further ceremonies or rites;" besides this, the persons named are more than those specified in the Act: their duty also was different, they were to ascertain what varieties of practice

---

* "XXV. Provided always, and be it enacted, that such Ornaments of the Church and of the Ministers thereof, shall be retained and be in use, as was in the Church of England by authority of Parliament, in the second year of the reign of King Edward the Sixth, until other order shall be therein taken by the authority of the Queen's Majesty, with the advice of Her Commissioners appointed and authorised under the Great Seal of England for causes Ecclesiastical, or of the Metropolitan of this realm."

"XXVI. And also, that if there shall happen any contempt or irreverence to be used in the ceremonies or rites of the Church, by the mis-using of the orders appointed in this book, the Queen's Majesty may, by the like advice of the said Commissioners or Metropolitan, ordain and publish such further ceremonies or rites, as may be most for the advancement of God's glory, the edifying of His Church, and the due reverence of Christ's holy mysteries and sacraments."

In the *Statutes of the Realm* and in *The Statutes Revised* (1870) these are printed as one Section and numbered XIII.; usually they are printed as above.

existed; and they were to deal with "the several cases," which should "appear to require reformation," by "order, injunction, "or censure, according to the laws then in force." All this is very different from a proceeding under the Statute to alter its requirements, and shews, as it seems to me, that the Queen did not in the least contemplate any such change when she issued these Letters. The "Preface" to the Advertisements themselves, while referring to the Queen's Letters, does not in the least imply that they were *alterations* of the Law, but speaks of them as being "orders and rules . . . . thoughte meete and "convenient to be used and followed," (*Cardwell, Doc. Ann.*, p. 323): nor, indeed, does it state anything as to their possessing Royal Authority.

The question, therefore, arises—whether this Letter from the Queen was not a proceeding under the 1st Elizabeth, c. 1, which was "An Act to restore to the Crown the ancient Jurisdiction "over the Estate Ecclesiastical and Spiritual," and so was an exercise of the *Visitorial* Authority of the Crown. The direction to "proceed by order, injunction, or censure, according to "the order and appointment of such laws and ordinances as are "provided by Act of Parliament," entirely agrees with the language of "The Queen's warrant for the court of High Com- "mission in Causes Ecclesiastical" (July 19, 1559) where reference is made to this Act and to the Act of Uniformity as the foundations of the "power and authority" which the Commissioners were to wield. The 4th Paragraph directs them

"to inquire, hear, and determine all and singular enormities, disturbances and misbehaviour, done and committed, or hereafter to be done and committed, in any church or chapel, or against any divine service, or the minister or ministers of the same, contrary to the law and statutes of this realm." (*Cardwell, Doc. Ann.*, I., 258.)

And the 5th Paragraph orders them

". . . . from time to time, and at all times during our pleasure, to visit, reform, redress, order, correct and amend, in all places within this our realm of England, all such errors, heresies, crimes, abuses, offences, contempts and enormities, spiritual and ecclesiastical wheresoever, which by any spiritual or ecclesiastical power, authority, or jurisdiction, can or may lawfully be reformed, ordered, redressed, corrected, restrained, or amended, to the pleasure of Almighty God, the increase of virtue, and the conservation of the peace and unity of this our realm, and according to the authority and power limited, given and appointed by any laws or statutes of this realm." (*Ibid.*)

This view of the authority upon which the Queen acted in writing to Archbishop Parker is fully confirmed by comparing with it the language of her Letter of Jany. 22, 1560-1 to the Ecclesiastical Commissioners (See p. 22) and also of King James's Letter to the same body in 1603-4 (See p. 86): in both those cases, where the Provisions of the Act of 1559 to take "other" or "further" Order concerning the Ornaments and Ceremonies were to be acted upon, those Provisos are distinctly recited: in this case, where the object was to enforce conformity, no such reference is made, but only Her Majesty's general power to reform abuses is stated.

Their Lordships say that "it appears abundantly" that the Advertisements "were afterwards enforced as by her authority:" but they do not give any instances; and certainly this is not the conclusion to be drawn from the following Documents which refer to them :—

1. The Archbishop's Letter to the Bishop of London, March 28, 1566, charges the latter "to see Her Majesties Lawes and Injunctions ducly observed within" his "Diocese and allso theis *our convenient orders described in theis bookes*, at thies present sent unto your Lordship." (*Cardwell, Doc. Ann.,* i., 336. *Parker Corresp.*, p. 273.)

2. A Letter of George Withers and John Barthelot to Henry Bullinger and Rodolph Gualter, August, 1567, mentions "*the Advertisements of the Bishops,*" and, again, it says—"For all that we have above treated of is manifest from *the Advertisements of the Bishops*, from certain Royal Injunctions, from the formularies of Baptism, both of adults and infants." (*Zurich Letters*, 2nd Series, pp. 149 and 151.)

3. A Letter of George Withers to the Prince Elector Palatine, probably 1567, says—"In what way the Sacraments are disfigured by human inventions, will easily appear from the public form of prayer, the Royal injunctions, and *the admonitions*, or (as they call them) *the Advertisements of the Bishops*." (*Ibid.*, pp. 162-3.)

4. Archbishop Parker, in his Visitation Articles, 1569, asks "whether the holy sacramentes be likewise ministred reverently in such manner, as by the Lawes of this Realme, and by the Quene's Majesties Injunctions, and by *thadvertisements set forthe by publike authority* is appointed and prescribed." (*Card., Ibid*, 355.)

"IV. Item. Whether your curates or ministers do publiquely in theire open churches reade in manner appoynted the Quene's Majestic's

Injunctions and Homelies; *the aduertisementes lately sette forthe by publique authoritie."* (*Ibid*, 356.)

5. The Injunctions of Cox, Bishop of Ely, *cir.* 1570-74, require the "surplesse, prescribed by the Queene's Majesties Injunctions and the Booke of Common Prayer," and also the "priestlyke apparell, to be worne accordyng to *the precept set foorth in the booke called the* Aduertisementes." (2nd *Rit. Report*, p. 406.)

6. In Archbishop Whitgift's Articles, 1584, there is this direction :— "IV. That all preachers, and others in Ecclesiastical orders, do at all times wear, and use such kynde of apparel, as is prescribed unto them *by the Book of Advertisements*, and Her Majesty's Injunctions 'anno primo.'" (*Doc. Ann.*, i., 468.)

The words which I have printed in *Italics* in these examples plainly assign to the Advertisements a very different rank from that which is accorded to the Formularies, Injunctions, Laws, and Homilies.

It would be uncandid, however, not to notice the following cases in which the Advertisements are referred to the Queen under the same terms which are applied to other Orders :—

1. Archbishop Parker's Articles for Winchester, 1575, inquire— "50. Item, whether they [Archdeacons] haue uprightly and unfeynedly both obserued in their own persons, and towardes all other put in due execution the Ecclesiasticall Lawes of this realme the Queene's Majesties Injunctions and other her Highness commaundements, orders, decrees, and aduertisementes set forth for the publike administration of God's holy word and sacramentes." (2nd *Rit. Report*, p. 418.)

2. The 7th Canon of 1640 mentions "the Injunctions and Advertisements of Queen Elizabeth of blessed memory."

Yet it must be also noticed that the 24th Canon of 1603-4 only styles them "Advertisements published anno. 7 Eliz.," and it may therefore fairly be argued that in the two instances just quoted the mention of the Queen's name was only intended to indicate (like the Canon of 1603-4) the *period* at which they were made. But, be this as it may, more weight is due to the *discriminating* terms in which the Injunctions and Advertisements are spoken of in the former instances ; and the evidence ought to be very strong, and wholly in one direction, to warrant the conclusion of the Judicial Committee—that the Queen's "assent "must be presumed."

Their Lordships do indeed say that "It appears probable "that the Queen hesitated before the Advertisements were thus "enforced:" in proof of it they refer to Archbishop Parker's letter of March 28, 1566 (See p. 27), and they do me the honour of citing a remark of mine upon it, made in a former publication (*Lawful Church Ornaments*, p. 210), viz., " It " would seem that the Archbishop's application had, at length, " some success." In saying this, however, I certainly had no intention of implying that the " success," whatever it was, gave an Authority to the Advertisements equivalent to their being the " other order " of the Elizabethan Statute; the remarks and references at pp. 204 and 212, and the Lists of Ornaments "disused" though "legally usable" given at pp. 306 and 310 of the same Volume, shew this. The following quotations prove, as it seems to me, not only that the Queen, "hesitated," but that she would not consent to give her own *sanction* to the Advertisements, and at length did no more than allow or direct them to be issued, on the Authority of the Metropolitans, fortified, to whatever extent it was so, by the concurrence of others in the Ecclesiastical Commission.

1. ARCHBISHOP PARKER to SIR WILLIAM CECIL, 3rd March, 1564-5. "Sir, I send your honour a Book of Articles, partly of old agreed on amongst us, and partly of late these three or four days considered, which be either in papers fasted on, as ye see, or new written by secretary hand. Because it is the first view, not fully digested, I thought good to send it to your honour to peruse, to know your judgment, and so to return it, that it may be fair written and presented. The devisers were only the Bishops of London, Winchester, Ely, Lincoln, [viz., Grindal, Horne, Cox, and Bullingham] and myself.*

* Strype (*Life of Parker*, p. 158) says that "These Articles were printed with a Preface this year 1564, by Reginald Wolf, according to Bishop Sparrow's Collections, and entitled *Advertisements*, though by a writing on the back side of the fair copy that was sent to the Secretary, when they were first framed, it seems they were not presently published, nor authorized. For these are the words written upon them by the Secretary's own hand. *Mar.* 1564. *Ordinances accorded by the Archbishop of Canterbury, &c., in his Province. These were not authorized nor published.*"
There is a copy in the British Museum (cat. 3106, *d.* 13, 1—34) the Title-page of which is as follows :—" Advertisements partly for due order in the publick Administration of the Holy Sacraments, and partly for the apparel of all persons Ecclesiastical, by virtue of the Queens Majesties letters commanding the same; the 25 day of *January* in the seventh year of the reign of our Sovereign Lady Elizabeth, by the grace of God, of *England, France* and *Ireland*, Queen, defender of the Faith &c. : Londini, *Cum privilegio ad imprimendum solum. Anno. Dom.* 1564, *Anno 7. Eliz. R.*" The Colophon is " Imprinted at London by *Reginald Wolf.*" The contents agree with the copy in *Sparrow* and in *Cardwell:* but, in part at least, the date might mislead : " Anno 7. Eliz. R." is not indeed inconsistent with the dates of the Letters above given; for the " Book" had been sent in rough draft to Cecil on March 3, 1564-5, that after his "judgment" it

" . . . . I must earnestly pray your honour to obtain a private letter from the Queen's Majesty to my lord of London, to execute laws and injunctions; which he saith, if he be so charged, he will out of hand see reformation in all London; and ye know there is the most disorder, and then is the matter almost won thorough the Realm. I pray you earnestly, expeditely to procure these letters, for he is now in a good mood to execute the laws, and it will work much more good than ye would think, &c. This third of March." (*Parker Correspondence*, p. 233.)

2. ARCHBISHOP PARKER to SIR WILLIAM CECIL, 8th March, 1564-5. "Sir, I send your honour our Book, which is subscribed to by the Bishops conferrers, which I keep by myself. I trust your honour will present it upon opportunity which ye can take in removing offences that might grow by mine imprudent talk. If the Queen's Majesty will not authorize them, the most part be like to lie in the dust for execution of our parties, laws be so much against our private doings. 'The Queen's Majesty, with consent, &c.' I trust shall be obeyed.

" . . . . If this ball shall be tossed unto us, and then have no authority by the Queen's Majesty's hand, we will set still. I marvel that not six words were spoken from the Queen's Majesty to my Lord of London, for Uniformity of his London, as himself told me; if the remedy is not by letter, I will no more strive against the stream, fume or chide who will." (*Ibid*, p. 234.)

3. ARCHBISHOP PARKER to SIR WILLIAM CECIL, 24th March, 1564-5. "Sir, I would ye had not have stirred *istam camarinam*, or else to have set on it to some order at the beginning. This delaying works daily more inconvenience, *et obfirmatiores fiunt*. . . . . If my Lord of Leicester and your honour would consult with my Lord Keeper how to deal in

might "be fair written and presented" to the Queen: it was returned to Cecil, apparently in MS., on March 8, 1564-5, that he might get the Queen's sanction to it: if it was *printed* between this date and Nov. 18th it would have been in the 7th year of Her Majesty's reign, for Elizabeth came to the throne on Nov. 17, 1558. But, to agree with the date 1564, it must have been printed between March 8th and 26th, 1564 O.S. Yet, judging from Parker's complaints of delay on the Queen's part in his Letters of March 24, 1564-5, and April 7, 1565, it seems unlikely that he should have already *printed* the Advertisements. Moreover, in his Letter to Cecil of March 28, 1566, he says, "this form is but newly printed, and yet stayed till I hear your advice." It would seem that 'shortly before this Cecil had advised some alteration of another copy which Parker sent him on March 12, 1565-6; for the substitution of "sequestration" for "deprivation" in "the fourth chapter, littera K," which Parker speaks of in that Letter, seems to have been abandoned by omitting the Article entirely (See p. 62 and Note). If, therefore, this were one of the original printed copies, I could only conclude that, whether the Book was or was not entirely printed between March 12th and March 28th, 1566, the *original* date of the Advertisements was preserved, and this certainly was 7th Elizabeth 1564. But there are grounds (partly typographical) for thinking that this copy is extracted from the first Edition of Sparrow's Collections of 1661: in that case the date is at once accounted for and so has no bearing upon the earliest Edition of the Advertisements: there is every reason to think that the first printed copies were *undated*. In the British Museum (CAT. *C.* 25, *c.* 6; T. 775. 10, 1013. 8; and 3505. *c*) are four undated copies: whether these are originals or not, I do not know.

this cause to do good and to pacify the Queen's Majesty, I think ye shall spend a piece of your afternoon well." (*Ibid*, p. 236.)

4. ARCHBISHOP PARKER to SIR WILLIAM CECIL, 7th April, 1565. " Sir, The talk, as I am informed, is much increased, and unrestful they be, and I alone they say am in fault. For as for the Queen's Majesty's part, in my expostulation with many of them I signify their disobedience, wherein, because they see the danger, they cease to impute it to Her Majesty, for they say, but for my calling on, she is indifferent. Again, most of them dare not name your honour in this tragedy, for many must have your help in their suits, etc. My Lord of London is their own, say they, and is but brought in against his will. I only am the stirrer and the incenser. And my Lord of Durham will be against us all: and will give over his Bishopric rather than it shall take place in his Diocese. . . . . If this matter shall be overturned with all these great hopes, etc., I am at point to be used and abused." (*Ibid*, p. 237.)

After this last Letter nearly a year elapsed before anything more appears to have been done touching the Advertisements; for the next letter seems to be :—

5. ARCHBISHOP PARKER to SIR WILLIAM CECIL, 12th March, 1565-6. " Sir, I am much astonished, and in great perplexity to think what event this cause will have in the proceeding to an end. . . . . I have written to the Queen's Majesty, as you see [referring apparently to an enclosed Letter.] I pray your honour use your opportunity. And where once this last year certain of us consulted and agreed upon some particularities in Apparell (where the Queen's Majesty's Letters were very general), and for that by Statute we be inhibited to set out any constitutions without Licence obtained of the Prince, I sent them to your Honour to be presented; they could not be allowed then, I cannot tell of what meaning; which I now send again, humbly praying that if not all yet so many as be thought good, may be returned with some Authority, at the least way for particular Apparel: or else we shall not be able to do so much as the Queen's Majesty expecteth for, of us to be done."

In a P.S. the Archbishop says—" Sir, in our book of articles, the fourth chapter, littera K, we made the pain sequestration, and not deprivation. For that much depriving with new fruiting [the allusion is to *first fruits*] will be taken *in malam partem*." (*Ibid*, p. 262.)

It is to be remarked that in the copy of the Book given by Cardwell as issued (*Doc. Ann.*, p. 329) no mention is made of either of these penalties, or indeed of any punishment for non-compliance. The Article relating to them is given by Strype in his copy of the original draft of these " Ordinances," as they were called when first sent to Cecil for his approval: it authorized the Bishops to " convente " before them all who should be complained of; to reform them, if necessary, by suspension;

and in case of contumacy " to aggravate the peine with seques-
" tration of the fruites of his lyving." (*Life of Parker, Appendix*,
No. xxviii., vol. iii., p. 92, Ed. 1821.) The omission of this
" Item " was one of the changes* which the Advertisements
underwent before they were ultimately published.

Three Letters, Nos. 205, 206, and 207 (pp. 267-9) follow,
which shew that the Archbishop endeavoured to bring the
London Ministers to conformity; these are succeeded by—

6. ARCHBISHOP PARKER to SIR WILLIAM CECIL, 28th March, 1566:
it has been already quoted and commented upon at p. 27. (*Ib.* p. 271.)

7. ARCHBISHOP PARKER to BISHOP GRINDAL, 28th March, 1566.
This is, no doubt, the "draft of letters" which Parker sent to Cecil
with his own Letter (No. 6) for his perusal before he forwarded it to the
Bishop of London: in it the Archbishop reminds the Bishop of London
that " the Queen's most excellent Majesty, now a year past and more,
addressed her Highness' letters" requiring " obedience " to the Laws:
he then goes on to state the steps which had been taken in consequence, and to "require and charge" him "to see her Majesty's Laws
and Injunctions duly observed within " his Diocese " and also these
our convenient orders described in these books at this present sent unto
your Lordship. And furthermore, to transmit the same books with "
his " letters (according as hath been heretofore used) unto all others
of our brethren within this Province, to cause the same to be performed in their several jurisdictions and charges." (*Ibid*, p. 273.)

8. ARCHBISHOP PARKER to SIR WILLIAM CECIL, 4th April, 1566.
". . . . And so, at length, my Lord of London and I dismissed them
all [viz.: Crowley and some other Non-conformists] with our Advertisements, in their obedience." (*Ibid*, p. 277.)

9. ARCHBISHOP PARKER to SIR WILLIAM CECIL, 28th April, 1566.
" Sir, The Queen's Majesty willed my Lord of York to declare her
pleasure determinately to have the order to go forward. I trust her
Highness hath devised how it may be performed. I utterly despair
therein as of myself, and therefore must sit still, as I have now done,
always waiting either her toleration, or else further aid. Mr. Secretary,
can it be thought, that I alone, having sun and moon against me, can
compass this difficulty? If you of her Majesty's council provide no
otherwise for this matter than as it appeareth openly, what the sequel
will be *horresco vel reminiscendo cogitare*. In King Edward's days
the whole body of the council travailed in Hooper's attempt. My
predecessor, Dr. Cranmer, labouring in vain with Bishop Farrar, the
council took it in hand; and shall I hope to do that the Queen's
Majesty will have done?" (*Ibid*, p. 280.)

* Also in the following Article the concluding words which I have printed in
Italics were omitted:—"Item, That the Bisshoppe do call home once in the yere
any Prebendaries in his churche, or benyficed in the diocos, which studiethe at
the Universities: to knowe howe he profitteth in learnynge, and that he be not
suffered to be a servinge or waytinge man dissolutelye: *or ells to sequester the
fruits of his lyvinge*." (*Ib.*, p. 89. Conf. *Cardwell, Doc. Ann.*, I., 328.)

The subsequent " Correspondence " of Parker does not contain any further allusion to his difficulties with regard to the " Advertisements ;" so that, unless there is any other evidence to be produced upon the subject, this last letter of the Archbishop appears to shew plainly the final result of his endeavours to obtain from Elizabeth the kind of sanction which he deemed necessary to ensure success in enforcing these Orders.

It appears that, shortly after this Letter, the Archbishop must have given directions to the Bishop of London to issue the Advertisements ; probably sending to him for that purpose the Letter of March 28th which he had submitted for Cecil's perusal (See above, No. 7). For on May 21st the Bishop sent them to the Dean and Chapter of St. Paul's, as appears by the following Letter (*State Papers, Domestic*—Elizabeth, vol. xxxix., No. 76) :—

"After my hartie Comendacyons. these are to require and to give you in especyall charge that with all convenyent speed you call before you all and singuler the mynisters and Ecclesiastical persons within your deanry of Poules and office, and to prescribe and enioyn everie of them upon payne of deprivacon to prepare forthwith and to weare such habit and apparell as is ordeyned by the Queenes maiesties authoritie expressed in the treaty entituled The Advertisements &c which I send heerein enclosed unto you, and in like to inioyne everie of them, under the said payne of deprivacon as well to observe the order of ministracon in the church with Surples, and in such forme as is sett forth in the saide treatie as alsoe to require the subscription of every of them to the said Advertisements, And yf you shall perceive any of them to be disobedient, which shall refuse to comform themselves heerein, that then without any delay you certifie me the names of all such before Trynitie Sundaie next ensuinge, to the intent I maie procced to the reformacon and deprivacon of everie of them as apperteyneth in this case with a certificate allsoe of the names of such as promiseth conformytie. And thus I bidd you farwell from my howse in London this 21st of Maie, 1566.
"Yors in Christ,
EDM. LONDON.

"Indorssed—To the right worshipful the Deane and Chapter of Powles yeve thise."

One expression in this Letter may seem at first sight to favour the notion that the Queen had at last sanctioned the Advertisements with that "*Authority*" which, on the 28th March, Parker complained she would not accord ; and which his Letter of April 28th proves to have not then been given (See No. 9, p. 63) : but a little consideration of the words shows that this is not their probable meaning, at all events that they are clearly capable of another interpretation. The Bishop orders that "the ministers and ecclesiastical persons" are "to wear such " habit and apparel as is ordained by the Queen's Majesty's autho- " rity, expressed in the treaty entitled The Advertisements &c.": this evidently relates to that part of the Advertisements headed "Articles for outwarde apparell of persons ecclesiasticall," in which the *Injunctions* are referred to; in the 30th of these this " apparell" was " ordained by the Queen's Majesty's authority," and the particulars of this apparel were also "expressed" in "the "Advertisements" themselves. This is really all that Grindal asserts, and it certainly does not amount to claiming the Queen's Authority for "the treaty entitled The Advertisements &c."; but only for the *details* of that " outward apparel " which the Queen had prescribed in her Injunctions, only *in general terms*, as " such seemly habits, garments, and such square caps, as were " most commonly and orderly received in the latter year of the " reign of King Edward the Sixth." (*Cardwell, Doc. Ann.*, I., 226.) If Grindal had intended to claim direct Royal sanction for the Advertisements themselves, surely he would have said " ordained by the Queen's Majesty's authority in the Adver- " tisements."

But, further, the *Surplice* is not referred to in this part of the Letter but is mentioned separately and in other terms: Grindal could not refer to the *Injunctions* with respect to this, for they did not mention it ; and so he requires the Clergy " to " observe the order of ministration in the church with Surplice, " and in such form as is set forth in the said Treaty": this is not equivalent to saying " ordained by the Queen's Majesty's " authority, expressed in the Treaty entitled The Advertise- " ments &c." The case of the Surplice, therefore, stood thus— the Queen now, as previously, required conformity; the Bishops five years before had endeavoured to secure it in their own " Interpretations " of the Injunctions by ordering only the Cope and Surplice in all Churches: this attempt had failed, and so they relaxed their own rule, and limited their requirement

K

in Parish Churches to the Surplice. Grindal's Letter to Zanchy five years later (See p. 29) confirms this view; shewing, as it does, that the original Law was not "either altered or "diminished," although "prescribed rules" had been issued by competent Authority.

This view of Grindal's Letter to the Dean and Chapter of St. Paul's, touching the Advertisements, is supported by Parker's own Letter when sending them to his Peculiars: the Letter is of the same date as that prepared by Parker for the Bishop of London and submitted to Cecil, viz., March 28, 1566: Strype writes as if both Letters were sent, with the Advertisements, at the time they were written; the probability is that they were delayed until Cecil had expressed his opinion upon the Letter to Grindal: and so Grindal's Letter to the Dean of St. Paul's on May 21st, most likely points to about the time Parker sent to his Peculiars. Moreover, there is nothing to indicate in the least that Cecil objected to the Letter to Grindal, and therefore it must be assumed that both Letters were sent in their original form. Strype's account of the Archbishop's Letter to his Peculiars is as follows:—

"The same 28th of March, the Archbishop sent these books of orders to the several Deans of his own peculiar jurisdiction, with his letter to this purport to the rest, as he wrote to the Dean of Bocking; 'That he had heard, that divers Parsons, Vicars, and Curates, within his peculiar jurisdiction of the deanery of Bocking, had not conformed themselves to the Queen's Injunctions, that he sent him a book of certain orders, agreed upon by him and his brethren of the province of Canterbury, and hitherto not published: willing him to call before him, and to publish to them the said orders prescribed in that Book, to move, persuade, and command them, as they would answer at their peril, duly to observe her Majesty's laws in the administration of public prayers and sacraments, and in their extern apparel, and all the orders sent to them therewith. And upon obstinate disobedience to suspend them from public ministration, and also sequester all the fruits of their livings so long time as they shall remain in disobedience. And to signify to him the names of all, to the intent that he might take further order with them: and to signify to them, that if they continue so three months they are to be deprived.'

"A like letter was writ to Mr. Denne, Commissary of Canterbury; to the Bishop of Chichester, Commissary of the peculiar jurisdiction of South Malling, Pagham, and Terring; and to Mr. Dr. Weston, Dean of the Arches, Shoram, and Croydon, with several of the Books above mentioned inclosed therein." [Margin—"Archbishop Park. Regist."] (*Strype's Parker*, I., p. 431.)

The only reliable conclusion to be drawn from the history which these Letters reveal must, surely, be this—That the Queen demanded the suppression of the nonconformity of which she so seriously complained; that the Archbishop with others prepared the Advertisements in order to carry out Her requirements; that, after a year's delay, they were allowed by Her Majesty, who also insisted upon having " the Order to go forward;" but that she could not be induced, whether from the objections of Her Council or for whatever reason, to have these Regulations issued in her Name; and that consequently the Metropolitans and their Suffragans were reluctantly compelled to do the best they could with them on the strength of their Episcopal Authority aided, probably, by the terrors of the High Commission Court.

That this was the real state of the case is also shewn by the negative evidence of Documents which, in requiring conformity, base the demand upon the Act of Uniformity, or the Injunctions of 1559, or upon both; but do not even mention the Advertisements, as the following instances shew :—

1. Archbishop Parker's Visitation Articles for Cathedral and Collegiate Churches, 1567, inquire—"II. Item, Whether your Divine Service be used, and your Sacraments ministred in manner and forme prescribed by the Quenes Majesties Injunctions, and none other way ? . . . . Whether in al points according to the Statutes of your Church, not being repugnant to any of the Quenes Majestys Laws or Injunctions?" (*Cardwell, Doc. Ann.*, I., p. 339, ed. 1844.)

2. Archbishop Parker's Visitation Articles for his Diocese, 1569, ask—" III. Item, Whether youre prestes, curates, or ministers do use in the time of the celebration of Divine Service to weare a surples, prescribed by the quene's majestie's injunctions and the boke of common prayer. And whether they do celebrate the same divine service in the chauncell or in the churche, and do use all rites and orders prescribed in the boke of common prayer, etc., and none other." (*Ibid,* p. 356.)

3. Queen Elizabeth's Letter to the Archbishop for uniformity in Church Matters, 20th August, 1571, states—" that none shall be suffered to decline either on the left or on the right hand from the direct line limited by authority of our said laws and injunctions." (*Ibid,* p. 368, and *Parker Correspondence,* p. 386.)

4. Archbishop Parker in his Letter to Lord Burghley, 9th May, 1573, points out the probable consequences "if the Queen's Majesty's Injunctions, if her chapel, if her authority be so neglected, if our book of service be so abominable . . . ." (*Parker Corresp.*, p. 426.)

5. A Proclamation of Queen Elizabeth, June 11, 1573, which orders all—"to kepe the order of common prayer, diuine seruices, and administration of the Sacramentes, accordyng as in the sayde booke of diuine service they be set foorth." (*State Papers, Domestic, Elizabeth*, vol. 91, No. 47.*)

6. Queen Elizabeth's Proclamation against the despisers or breakers of the orders prescribed in the book of common prayer, 20th October, 1573, requires the Archbishops and others—"to have a vigilant eye and care to the observation of the orders and rites in the said book prescribed." (*Cardwell, Doc. Ann.*, I., p. 386.)

* It may be useful to append here the whole (printed) Document: Strype has given it (*Life of Parker*, bk. iv., 421.)

"By the Queene.

"The Queene's Maiestie consydering that notwithstanding that by great and mature deliberation of the wysest of this Realme, a godly & good order of publique prayer and administration of the Sacramentes hath been set foorth and allowed by Parliament, and commonly through the whole Realme, in al the tyme of her Maiesties raigne receiued and vsed: yet some persons of theyr natures unquietly disposed, desyrous to change, and therefore redy to fynde fault with al well established orders, do not only refrayne from comming to the Church, where the diuine seruice and common prayer is orderly vsed, but also do vse of theyr own deuises, other rites and ceremonies then are by the lawes of the Realme receiued and vsed: and besydes that, some of them haue rashly set foorth, and by stealth imprinted certayne bookes vnder the title of an admonition to the Parliament, and one other also in defence of the sayde admonition, the whiche bookes do tend to no other ende, but to make diuision and dissention in the opinions of men, and to breede talkes and disputes agaynst common order. Her highnesse therefore, both to represse suche insolent and inordinate contemptes of suche as refuse to come to common prayer and diuine seruice, according to the order established by Parliament, to the euil and pernitious example of others, and to kepe her subiectes in one uniforme, godly, and quiet order within her Realme, to auoyde all controuersies, scismes, and dissentions that may aryse: doth strayghtly charge and commaunde al her Maiesties faythful and true subiectes, them selues to kepe, and to cause others suche as be under them, to kepe the order of common prayer, diuine seruices, and administration of the Sacramentes, accordyng as in the sayde booke of diuine seruice they be set foorth, and none other contrary or repugnant, upon payne of her hyghnesse indignation, and of other paynes in the sayd act comprysed.

"And as concerning the said bookes, called, The admonition to the Parliament, and al other bookes made for the defence of the sayde admonition, or agreeable therewith, the whiche bookes do cheefely tende to the deprauyng and fyndyng fault with the sayde book of common prayer, and administration of the Sacramentes, and of the orders receiued here in this Churche and common wealth of Englande: Her highnesse strayghtly chargeth and commaundeth al and euery Prynter, Stationer, Booke bynder, Marchaunt, and al other men of what qualitie or condition be or they be, who hath in theyr custodie any of the sayd bookes, to bring in the same to the Byshop of the diocesse, or to one of her hyghnesse priuie Counsel, within twentie dayes after that he shal haue notice of this Proclamation, and not to kepe any of them without licence or allowance of the sayde Byshop, upon payne of imprysonment, and her highnesse further displeasure.

"Geuen at our Manour of Greenwiche, the, xi. day of June. 1573. the fyfteenth yere of our raigne."   "God saue the Queen."

"¶Imprinted at London in Powles churchyarde, *by Richarde Jugge, Printer to the Queenes Maiestie.*

"Cum priuilegio Regiæ Maiestatis."

7. A Letter from the Council about uniformity and a parochial visitation, 7th Nov., 1573, directs the Bishops and Archdeacons—"to take a more vigilant eye to this uniformity, and to the keeping of the orders [in the book of common prayer allowed by parliament] and by her majesty's injunctions . . . ." (*Ibid*, p. 387.)

8. Archbishop Parker writing to Sandys Bishop of London, 24th Nov., 1573, speaks of "the Queen's Majesty being very careful and desirous, that one uniform order in the celebration of divine service and ministration of the sacraments should be used and observed in all places of this her Highness' realm and dominions, according to the Book of Common Prayer set forth by public authority and her Majesty's Injunctions, without alteration or innovation . . . ." (*Parker Correspondence*, p. 451.)

9. Archbishop Grindal in his Articles for Cathedral and Collegiate Churches in his Province of Canterbury, 1576, inquires—"VI. Item, Whether your divine service be used, and the sacraments ministred in manner and forme prescribed in the quenes majesties injunctions, and none otherwaies." (*Cardwell, Doc. Ann.*, I., p. 419, ed. 1844.)

10. Bishop Barnes, in his "Monicions and Injunctions . . . to the Clergie and Churchwardens" in his "Sinode" held at Durham "on Tewsdaie the first daie of October 1557", orders thus:—"7. ITEM, that no rites or ceremonies be used at the ministracion of the Sacramentes and celebracion of Divine service other then ar expressed, set downe, and prescribed, in the Booke of Common Prayer and Administracion of Sacramentes, or any ther prescribed be omitted or neglected, or left unused ; and that the Parsons, Vicars, and Curates at ministracion of Sacramentes were cleane and comelie surplesses, and that they abrode do were grave, clerkely, and decent apparell, as gownes" &c. (*Eccl. Proceedings of Bp. Barnes.* Surtees Society, 1850, p. 17.)

Two modern Writers, well informed on the subject, take the view which has been here given of the Advertisements:—

Dr. A. J. Stephens, commenting upon the words of the Elizabethan Act, "until other order," says—"Which *other* order (at least in the method prescribed by this Act) was never made; and therefore, legally, the Ornaments of Ministers in performing Divine Service are the same now as they were in the second of Edward VI." (*Eccl. Stat.*, i., p. 370, note ; 1845.

The Rev. T. Lathbury remarks—"A loud outcry was raised by the Puritans against the Advertisements, as though some new rites had been imposed, whereas they were only intended to enforce such as were already in use, because some of the Clergy were lax in their practice. They were allowed by the Queen to be published, but not under her Majesty's authority ; consequently they never possessed the same force as the Injunctions." (*Hist. of the Book of Common Prayer*, p. 72, note ; 1848.)

There is, indeed, a passage in a Letter from Archbishop Parker to Lord Burleigh, Nov. 15, 1573, which might seem at first to support the opinion that the Advertisements were issued agreeably to the Proviso of the Elizabethan Act of Uniformity; it runs thus—

"In London our fonts must go down, and the brazen eagles, which were ornaments in the Chancel and made for Lectures, must be molten to make pots and basins for new fonts. I do but marvel what some men mean, to gratify these puritans railing against themselves, with such alteration where order hath been taken publicly this seven years by Commissioners, according to the Statute, that fonts should not be removed." (*Parker Correspondence*, p. 450.)

The "order" here referred to is, no doubt, the direction of the Advertisements "That the fonte be not removed, nor that "the Curate do baptize in parishe churches in any basons" (*Cardwell, Doc. Ann.*, I., p. 326): and the words "this seven "years" seem clearly to point to the date of their issue, viz., about April or May, 1566, as appears from the Letters of Parker to Cecil and of Grindal to the Dean and Chapter of St. Paul's, (quoted at pp. 63 and 64.) The expression "taken publicly this "seven years by Commissioners, according to the Statute" would have given a colour to the view of the Judicial Committee had they quoted it; for it is stated at the end of the Advertisements that they were "agreed upon, and subscribed by" the six Bishops who signed them—"Commissioners in causes ecclesi-"asticall, with others;" and that they were in all probability taken under *a* Statute, viz., the 1st Elizabeth, c. 1, I have already argued at p. 57.

If indeed it could be proved that the proceedings were under the 25th Section of the 1st Elizabeth, c. 2, it would also be true that the Commissioners acted "according to the Statute" so far as that in preparing the Advertisements and presenting them to the Queen for approval they were tendering "advice" to her Majesty: but it certainly could not be truly said that "order "hath been taken publickly . . . according to" *that* "Statute" unless the Queen had either authorized the Commissioners to publish what, in their discretion, they should order; or had subsequently given her formal sanction to what they proposed: for the Act requires the "order" to be "taken by the authority of "the Queen's Majesty with the advice of her Commissioners." This was done on two other occasions; first, when the alteration of the Lessons and the restoration of the Chancels were ordered in 1561, the Queen said that "for the publication "of that which you shall order, . . . these our Letters shall be "your sufficient warrant." (See p. 23). Next, when King James, having approved the revision of 1604, authorized the Archbishop of Canterbury (as being Metropolitan and also head of the Ecclesiastical Commission) to order the new Prayer Book to be provided and used in the two Provinces. (See p. 86.)

The difference, which Strype points out, between the *original* and the *published* copy of these Advertisements, as regards the Title and Preface, materially strengthens the argument against their having received the Queen's Authority according to the Statute: with reference to the *Title* of them he says:—

"The matter, I suppose, was this: When these Articles (by Leicester's means no question) were refused to be confirmed by the Queen's Council, the Archbishop however thought it advisable to print them under his and the rest of the Commissioners' hands, to signify at least what their judgment and will was; and to let their authority go as far as it would. Which was probable to take some effect with the greater part of the Clergy; especially considering their canonical obedience they had sworn to their Diocesans. But because the Book wanted the Queen's Authority, they thought fit not to term the contents thereof *Articles* or *Ordinances*, by which names they at first went, but by a modester denomination, viz., *Advertisements*." (*Life of Parker*, I., 314, 8vo., or *fol.* II. 158.)

The Title of the *original*, as printed by Strype, is "Ordin-"nances accorded by the Archbishop of Canterbury, etc., in his "Province" (*Ib.*, iii., 84, 8vo.): the *published* copy which Cardwell gives is headed "Advertisements partly for the due order "in the publique administration of common prayers, and usinge "the holy sacraments, and partly for the apparell of all persons "ecclesiasticall, by vertue of the Queene's Majestie's Letters, "commanding the same, the 25th day of January in the seventh "year of our soveraigne Lady Elizabeth, by the grace of God "of Englande, Fraunce, and Ireland, queene, defender of the "faith, etc." (*D. A.*, I., 321; and *Sparrow's Coll.*, p. 123.)

With regard to the *Preface*, Strype says that—

"This was the reason that there is some difference in the Preface thereof, as we have it printed in Bishop Sparrow's Collections, from that which is in the MS. copy sent unto the Secretary. That Preface is all the same, but only whereas in the MS. it ran thus—'The Queen's Majesty . . . hath, by the assent of the Metropolitan, and with certain other her Commissioners in causes ecclesiastical, decreed certain rules and orders to be used, as hereafter followeth.'" (*Life of Parker*, i., 314, 8vo., *see also the Document*, No. xxviii., vol. iii.)

In the published copy, as he remarks, it runs thus:—

"'The Queen's Majesty . . . hath by her Letters directed unto the Archbishop of Canterbury, and Metropolitan, required, enjoined, and strictly charged, that with assistance and conference had with other Bishops, namely, such as be in commission for causes ecclesiastical, some orders might be taken, whereby all differences and varieties among them of the Clergy and the people, as breeding nothing but contention, offence, and breach of common charity, and be against the laws, good usages, and ordinances of the realm, might be reformed and repressed, and brought to one manner of uniformity throughout the whole realm: that the people may thereby quietly honour and serve Almighty God, in truth, concord, unity, peace, and quietness, as by her Majesty's said Letters more at large doth appear. Whereupon by diligence, conference, and communication in the same, and at last by assent of the persons beforesaid, those orders and rules ensuing have been thought meet and convenient to be used and followed.' There be also some other small alterations, as the word *constitutions* in the MS. is changed into *temporal orders* in the Collections: and *positive laws in discipline*, is changed into *rules in some part of discipline*. I have also diligently compared the printed book with the aforesaid MS. copy, and find them different in many places, and sundry things are left out which are in the copy: the Archbishop thinking fit in that manner to publish them, because of their want of the stamp of authority to oblige persons to the observance of them." (*Life of Parker*, I., 314, 8vo., and *Cardwell, Doc. Ann.*, I., 321.)

It will be observed that in this latter Preface there is no mention, as in the former, of the Queen having "decreed" the "orders:" they are made to claim no other authority than that of the Commissioners.

Strype, in his "Annals of the Reformation," thus remarks upon the Authority which the Advertisements possessed:—

"All this book was signed and subscribed by the composers, the aforesaid metropolitan and bishops: whereof four were commissioners ecclesiastical. They designed this book should have been enforced upon the clergy, by getting the queen's ratification, and as a book of *decrees* proceeding from her, by their advice and assent. But the queen declining to sign it, (however she had, in her foresaid letter to the archbishop [viz. Jan. 25, 1564-5], commanded him, with others of the commission ecclesiastical, to proceed by orders and injunctions, and in her name to enjoin them,) this labour of theirs lost much of its power and efficacy. But she was persuaded not to add her own immediate authority to the book by some great persons at court;

because, upon their suggestion, she said, the archbishop's authority and the commissioners alone were sufficient. And so instead of calling them *articles* or *ordinances*, they only named them *advertisements*. They are set down in bishop Sparrow's Collection.

"These orders, (called now *advertisements*,) by the metropolitan and some ecclesiastical commissioners drawn up, if the queen had established them, would have had the strength of the law, by a proviso in the act for the *Uniformity of the Common Prayer and Service*: viz. 'That if there should appear any contempt or irreverence to be used in the ceremonies or rites of the church, by misusing of the order appointed in that book, the queen might, by advice of her commissioners ecclesiastical, or the metropolitan, ordain and publish such further ceremonies and rites, as might be most for the advancement of God's glory, the edifying of his church, and the due reverence of Christ's holy mysteries and sacraments.' By virtue of this clause,* I suppose it was, the metropolitan framed these orders, in expectation of the queen's interposing her authority to ordain them; which, without it, proved afterwards but weak and languid." (*Ann.* I., 462 : or 8vo. Oxford, I., pt. 2, p. 130.)

I cannot better conclude these observations upon the Advertisements than by quoting the following confirmatory statement from an old and scarce Volume of Tracts which the Judicial Committee have themselves cited as evidence that the Alb and Chasuble had, "within ten years after the date of the Adver-"tisements," "ceased to exist." The Book is called "A parte "of a Register" and was published about 1590: the Treatise now quoted is called "The copie of a Letter written by a "Gentleman in the Countrey, unto a Londoner, touching an "answere to the Archb. articles" it was written in 1583, for the author speaks of a "visitation holden this present yeare 1583" (p. 157); so that the evidence which the passage furnishes is only 17 years after the publication of the Advertisements: the writer, objecting to

"The thirde article [of the Archbishop—Whitgift] . . . . that all Preachers, and all other in Ecclesiasticall orders, doe at all times weare, etc."

Thus comments upon it :—

" . . . . he [the Archbishop] might have put in execution this article without further supplication, for this *articuli ex confesso* (as they saye) is alreadie established by the Advertisements which were never yet revoked, yea rather as I say, which were yet never duelie published, as being advertisementes, onelie in name ordinaunces, and not in deede. For though her Maiesties name and commaundement by her

---

* Compare remarks at pp. 57, 58 and 70; and "very general" No. 5, p. 62.

highness Letters, be used by the publishers of the saide advertisementes for the confirmation of them, yet nevertheles because the booke it selfe commeth foorth without her Maiesties' priviledge, and hath bin printed not by her Maiesties printer, nor any in his name, Therefore the same caryeth as yet no such credit and authoritie with it, as whereunto *propter falsitatem expressam,* or *veritatem tacitam in impetracione,* her Maiesties subjects are necessarilie bounde to subscribe, especiallie having either Iniunctions under her Maiesties owne name, and authorized by her Maiesties priviledge, contrarie to the same, as in the article, concerning not preaching without licences shall appeare." (p. 162.)

The evidence, then, appears to me to establish conclusively that, whether the proceedings of the Queen, which led to the preparation of the Advertisements, were taken under the 1st Elizabeth, c. 1, as is most probable; or whether under the 25th section of her Act of Uniformity, of which there is no proof; in neither case can the Advertisements claim any higher Authority than that of the Ecclesiastical Commissioners themselves, or be regarded as any legal repeal of the Ornaments Rubric.

XIII. Their Lordships thus sum up their previous remarks as to the supposed effect of the Advertisements upon the Vestments:—

> "But, as has been said, the contemporaneous evidence as to the abolition of all vestments obnoxious to the Puritan party (other than the surplice, hood, and tippett, and the square cap) is abundant."

The Lincolnshire Inventories (upon which the Court itself relies) will, however, be found to qualify this statement, as the following extracts from Mr. Peacock's book show:—

"BASINGHĀ," p. 41. "18. March 1565[6]."—". . . haue a cope in the churche the wch wee are admitted [by the injunc*] tions to kepe for o' mi'ster."

"BELTON," p. 47. "12. April 1566."—"Itm one cope—remayninth (*sic*)."

"BICHEFELD," p. 48. "21. March 1565[6]."—"Itm one cope—remaynīg in o' said pishe church."

"BILLINGBOROWE," p. 49. "14. March 1565[6]."—"Itm one cope—remayneth in or pishe churche wt a surplesse and 5 towelles wch we occupie about the coion† but all the tromperie and popishe Ornamentes is sold and defaced so that ther remaynethe no supersticious monumente wt in o' pish churche of Billingborowe."

* Mr. Peacock has a blank, the letters being missing in the MS.; I have given the probable reading.

† *i.e.* communion.

"LITTLE BITHAM," p. 52. "21. March 1565[6]."—"Itm one Cope—remaynīge in o' pishe church."

"BLYTON," p. 52. "20. April 1566."—Ornamtes of the priest—a cope wch remaynith, an alb whearof is made a surples, and a vestm' of the wch is made a coveringe for o' pulpit by the said churchwardens the said yeare," viz., "A° quinto Elizabth," *i.e.*, 1562.

"MARKET DEEPINGE," p. 68. "18. March 1565[6]."—"Itm fyve table clothes xv towelles a fonte clothe a surples a rocket or ij for the clark and a silver coppe—Remainith in o' pishe church a° dni 1565 Wm Harvie and W^m affen churchwardens so that no popish peltrie remaineth in o' said pishe church."

"EDNA9," p. 75. "18th day of Marche 1565[6]."—"Itm an old cope of blew velvet wth two surplishes remayninge at this tyme."

"EPWORTH," p. 77. "21. April 1566."—"Itm one cope and a chalice—remaynith."

"FFULLETBIE," p. 81. "24. April 1566."—"Itm one cope and a sacringe bell remaynith."

"HOLLYWELL," p. 106. "21. March 1565[6]."—"Itm one cope and one surplese remayninge in o' churche at this pnte."

"LENTON ALS LEVINGTON," p. 114. "22. March 1565[6]."—"Itm a cope wth all thother thinges according to thininctions* remaineth in o' said pish church A° dni 1565 Symon Scarson and John Barlemaman churchwardens."

"LUNDONTHORP," p. 115. "11. April 1566."—"Itm one cope—remaynīge in or said pishe so that wee haue no monument of supersticon now remaynige."

"MINTINGE," p. 117. "30. April 1566."—"Itm one cope—yet remaininge."

"MARKET REASON," p. 124. "24. April 1566."—"Itm one cope remaynith."

"RISKINGTON," p. 130. "26. April 1566."—"Itm one cope—Remaynith.
"Itm all other popish peltrie as candlesticks sensors chrismatories and suche like—weare restored to Tho Graue of Ashbie thexequut' of Sr Robt Graue A° p' mo Elizabeth of whom we borowid the same in Quene Maries tyme."

"SIBSAIE," p. 137. "2. May 1566."—"Itm ij copes—thet ar a covar ffor our polpet and the other Remayng in or churche."

"SOMERBIE," p. 141. "21. April 1566."—"Itm a cope and a chalice—remaynith in o' said pishe church."

"SWATON," p. 148. "18. March 1565[6]."—"Itm one cope—remayninge wt in or churche at this p'nte."

"SWYNESTED," p. 149. "18. March 1565[6]."—"ltm old cope—remayning in o' churche at this pn'te."

"TEDFORTH," p. 151. "24. April 1566."—"ffyrste one cope wch wee have."

* *i.e.*, the *Injunctions* of 1559 together with their *Interpretations* of 1561.
† *i.e.*, probably "the one."

"Totill," p. 154. "25. April 1566."—"Itm one cope—remayneth."
"Vffington," p. 154. "18. March 1565[6.]"—"Itm one cope—remayninge in oŕ churche at this pn'te tyme vndefaced."
"Welbie," p. 159. "10. April 1566."—"Itm one cope—remaynith."
"Winthorpe," p. 165. "30. April 1566."—"Itm a cope yet remaninge."
"North W'tham," p. 167. "18. March 1565[6.]"—"Itm one cope remayninge in oŕ churche at this pn'te."

It is plain from these instances that in 1566 the Cope was considered legal in *Parish* Churches, and was not regarded, in the Parishes here named, as being either "popish" or "superstitious," although its lawfulness did not screen it from such a character in other places. It was retained for use most likely under the order of the *Interpretations of the Injunctions*, as is shewn by the case of Lenton and (probably) by that of Basingham. If, as the Judicial Committee assume (See p. 35), these Inventories were the *result* of the Advertisements, which in their *original* form were submitted by Parker to Cecil a year before (See p. 60), then it is obvious that the Advertisements allowed the Cope in *Parish* Churches. On the other hand, if the Advertisements, which were not *issued* until after the date of the latest of these Inventories (See p. 64), were not within the *official* (or even *actual*) cognizance of the Visitors—and there is no ground for thinking that they were—then it is equally plain that the Inventories were in no way affected by the Advertisements.

XIV. The Court, having endeavoured, unsuccessfully as I humbly think, to prove that the Advertisements were issued and received as if they possessed the Authority contemplated by the 25th and 26th Sections of the Act of Uniformity of 1559, thus continues its observations:—

> "In a scarce book, called 'A Part of a Register,' in which is a considerable number of documents collected by those who objected to Church Ritual, the complaint is uniformly against copes and surplices. Thus, in a letter by A. G., 1570, page 13, he complains of 'crossing, coping, and surplessing.' A Report of the Examination of Smith, Nixon, and others before the Lord Mayor, the Bishop of London, and other Commissioners, 1567, page 28, describes

> Hawkins, one of the accused, as saying, 'Surplesses and copes be superstitious and idolatrous.' Ireland, another of them (page 32) says to the Bishop, ' But you go like one of the Mass priests still;' to which the Bishop replies,—' *You see me wear a cope or a surpless at Paul's. I had rather minister without these things, but for order's sake and for obedience to the Prince.*'"

It is desirable to mention, with regard to this passage, that *Parish* Churches must be referred to in the quotation from page 13, though from the last passage it might be thought perhaps that only Cathedrals were here complained of; the words are:—

> "they can not thinke the worde of God to be safely inough preached, and honorably inough handled without cappe, Cope, or surplesse: but that the Sacramentes, the Marrying, the Burying, the Churching of women, and other church seruice, as they call it, muste needes be declared with Crossing, with Coping, with Surplessing, with kneeling, with prety wafer kakes, and other knackes of Poperie."

This language is much too general unless Parochial Churches were included by the writer as being *liable* to use or as *using*,* in 1570, things which were *positively ordered* by the Injunctions

---

* Two other passages in the same volume ("A Part of a Register") support this view. At p. 401 of *"Notable reasons against the use of Popish Ceremonies"* this *"Question"* is asked—" The Brethren doe demaund, whether the Ministerie bee for certaine ceremonies that are of the dregges of Poperie (namelie the Cope, the surplesse, the crosse in Baptism, and other like) laid vppon them vnder pretence of Church pollicie onlie, and not with any opinion of worship or religion to be forsaken or no?" And at p. 406, in *" The Judgment of certaine brethren concerning the matters premised,"* occurs the following :—" 13. For as much as the holy Font, & the signe of the crosse, are as it were knit vnto Baptisme, for as much as the cope and surples in the common prayers and ministration of the Sacraments, the ring likewise in the publique celebration of Matrimonie, for as much I say, as these and other, which haue been worships and sacraments of Papists, are nowe required for the ministring of our diuine seruice reuerently and diuinely, these may thereupon by no meanes be more accounted among things indifferent, then may censers, tapers, holie bread, or holy water, neither doe they any better agree with the light of the Gospell, then light with darknesse, or the Temple of God with Idols." The writer of these passages must have considered that the Advertisements were not a *repeal* of the Statute or of the Injunctions with their Interpretations, otherwise he could not have spoken of the Cope being "laid uppon" and "nowe required" in the same way as he speaks of the Surplice, the Cross in Baptism, and the Ring in Marriage: evidently, he considered that the Advertisements were only a *minimum* demand of the *maximum* legal requirements. Moreover he could not have been merely referring to what the Advertisements ordered in *Cathedral* Churches; for that was not a matter which touched the Clergy at large; whereas the writer is obviously speaking of a grievance felt by some of those whose *Parochial* Ministrations commonly exposed them to what they deemed obnoxious requirements.

and their Interpretations, and were not *excluded*, as I have already shown, by what the Advertisements prescribed. That there was a great division of opinion as to the *propriety* of using them is plain from what occurred in Convocation only two years before the Advertisements were prepared; for, in the Synod which began January 13, 1562-3, a Paper was presented in which, among other things, it was proposed :—

"That the use of Vestments, Copes and Surplices, be from henceforth taken away." (*Strype, Ann.*, I., 315; and *Card., Syn.*, II., 498.)

Besides this a Paper signed by 33 Members of the Lower House was also brought forward in which it was proposed :—

"That the Copes and Surplices may be laid aside, and that the habit of the desk and the pulpit may be the same." (*Collier, E. H.*, II., 486; conf. *Strype, Ann.*, I., 316.)

This proposal appears to have been afterwards discussed in the following modified form :—

"That it be sufficient for the Minister, in time of saying of Divine Service, and ministring of the Sacraments, to use a Surplice: and that no Minister say Service, or minister the Sacraments, but in a comely garment or habit. (*Card., Conf.*, p. 118; conf. *Collier, E. H.*, II., 486, and *Strype, Ann.*, I., p. 337.)

Upon a division the proposal, even in this form, was lost, after being "warmly contested," by 59 to 58 (including Proxies); so that, as Collier says :—

" . . . . notwithstanding the struggle, the protesting party carried it. And thus the ceremonies and religious decorations continued in their former condition. However, it is plain, by the contest, the Frankfort and Geneva Precisians had no small interest. Many of the English exiles were willing to reform away the Ornaments and solemnity of Divine Worship, and thought Calvin's platform a much better regulation than that of the Primitive Church; but, God be thanked, the majority of our Reformers had a different sense of these matters, and had more learning and judgment, more steadiness and resolution, than to be overruled with noise and novelty." (*E. H.*, II., 486.)

These proceedings are clear evidence of four things: *First*, That the full Vestments, as sanctioned by the Statute of 1559, were considered in 1563 to be still in *legal* use; *Secondly*, That the Cope at least was extensively in *actual* use; *Thirdly*, That the opinions of the Clergy, so far as represented in the Lower House of Convocation, were nearly equally divided for and against *continuing* the use of the Cope; *Fourthly*, That a large minority wished to have the Surplice "laid aside" by Authority.

But, further, there is nothing to indicate that within the next two years the two parties had undergone any relative change; it is, therefore, most unreasonable to suppose that the Bishops who framed or sanctioned the Advertisements in 1564-5 intended to do *more* than the majority (bare though it was) of the Lower House of Convocation in 1562-3 refused to sanction : the latter would not allow that it was "sufficient" to use the Surplice for *all* Ministrations; it is wholly improbable, therefore, that the former could have designed, as the Judicial Committee hold, to *forbid* by the Advertisements every Eucharistic Vestment—even the Cope—in *Parish* Churches. The Bishops may, indeed, have thought that, as the opponents of the Surplice bore a large proportion to the supporters of the Cope, it would be a convenient compromise to *require* no more than the Surplice in all *Parish* Churches; yet the antagonism of the parties, and especially any Episcopal opposition such *e.g.* as that of the Bishop of Durham (See No. 4, p. 61), may have influenced the Queen in withholding her sanction from the Advertisements.

The quotations from this volume, " A Part of a Register," are thus continued :—

> " In another of these documents, called 'A View of Antichrist, His Laws and Ceremonies,' there is a careful enumeration of ornaments complained of as Popish, not mentioning alb nor chasuble; but (page 63) there is mention of 'the cap, the tippet, the surplice for small churches, the cope for great churches, furred hoods in summer for the great doctors, silken hoods in their quiers upon a surplesse, and the grey amise with the catte's tails.' This mention of the amise is the only notice in the many tracts collected in the Register of any specific vestment other than the surplice and cope being worn. But in the same book is contained 'A Letter by Master Robert Johnson to Master Edwin Sandys (1573), in which, at page 104, he says, 'You must yield some reason why the tippet is commanded and the stole forbidden; why the vestment is put away and the cope retained; why

the alb is laid aside and the surplice is used; or why the chalice is forbidden in the Bishop of Canterbury's Articles or the grey amice by the Canon more than the rest, why [*for* why *read* what] have they offended, &c.' Edward Dering (1593), in another tract in the same book, speaks of the grey amice having been specially forbidden in the 'Book of the Discipline of the Church of England.' He goes on to say that other vestments, equally superstitious, are used; and in a passage immediately before this he asks, 'how he can subscribe to the ceremonies in Cathedral Churches, where they have the Priest, Dean, and Sub-dean in copes and vestments, all as before;' but that he is alluding in this to the cope and surplice is plain both from the before-cited statement of the Bishop of London to Hawkins, and from the question in Johnson's tract 'Why the vestment is put away and the cope retained, the alb laid aside and the surplice in use;' and the enumeration of Popish ornaments in 'The View of Antichrist.'"

It would seem that the Court had no very clear idea what "the amise" resembled, else it could hardly have said "This "mention of the amise is the only notice in the many tracts "collected in the Register of any specific vestment other than "the Surplice and Cope being worn"; for the statement is contradicted by the context itself where the *tippet* and *hood* are mentioned, the *tippet* being also named at pp. 54 and 59 of the "Register": yet the Tippet or the Hood is as much a *Vestment* as is the Amice.

Further, this "View," to which the Court refers, includes more "Grosse poyntes of poperie, evident to all men" than their Lordships have selected from it; among them are—

"20. The popishe apparell of the Archbishoppe and Bishop, the blacke Chimere, or sleaueles coate put vpon the fine white rotchet.

"21. The great wyde sleeued gowne commaunded to the Ministers, and the charge to weare those sleeues vppon the armes, be the weather neuer so whote."

"35. The Organes playing away halfe of the psalmes."

So that, even granting the statement to imply the entire absence of Vestures other than the Surplice and Cope, it is a striking contemporaneous proof of the utterly unreasonable, though perfectly consistent, character of the opposition; and it is impossible to believe (as indeed the passage quoted at p. 77 from the "Register," p. 406, shews) that the *writer*, and those who held with him, would have had any greater objection to the Alb and Chasuble. Indeed Johnson's argument, next referred to, is most reasonable and logical; nor could anything well be more condemnatory of the course pursued by those who judge of the fitness of Ornaments by the fact of their use or disuse in times when irreverence, disorder, decay, and ruin were the prevailing features of the vast proportion of the Services and Churches of the Kingdom.*

It is worth while to notice here that the "Book of the "Discipline of the Church of England," referred to by Dering,

---

* The Returns to the Royal Commissioners (see *e.g.* p. 33) and to the Bishops abundantly prove this. The proceedings *e.g.* at the Visitations of Bishop Barnes of Durham, 1577 to 1586, (*Surtees Society*, vol. 22, p. 113 ff,) shew plainly the gross neglect in the Churches at that period, (yet there is no instance of Vestments being destroyed; perhaps it may be said, because there were none; and yet they were found elsewhere in the North about the same period—See p. 44); also they exhibit fines for talking in Church, absence from Church, repelling from Communion, punishments for immoralities, absence from benefice; the following are some instances as to the state of the Churches :—

"1578-9. 8 Mar. STOCKTON. The office of the Judge against Ralph Wright, churchwarden. They lack the Communion Boke. Excommunicated. Absolved." (p. 116,)

"1579. 28 March. SCHAM. The office of the Judge against Henry Lyddel and George Parkins, churchwardens. 'They doo not demaund the fyne of 12*d.* upon those that doothe absent themselves from devine service. They have not a decent pulpitt. Ther churche's dore ys broken, so that swyne or other beastes maye come in to the churche. They want the Appologie.' Suspended." (p. 118.)

"1579. 28 Mar. TRINDON. The office of the Judge against the Churchwardens. 'They lacked divers bokes in their church and my Lord's Injunctions.' Certified and are dismissed." (p. 118.)

"1579. 11 May. ELWICKE. The office of the Judge against Robert Woode and Richard Morland, churchwardens. 'Ther churche garthe lyethe downe so as boithe sheipe and swine commithe in.' Monished to repair." (p. 119.)

"1579. 3 Oct. WITTON GILBERT. The office of the Judge against the churchwardens. 'Theire churche is in decay in sclats, lyme and glass wynders, they cannot say service in fowle wether.'" (p. 124.)

"1579. 16 Oct. SIMONDBURNE. They lack a Bible, a Communion Book, and a silver cup." (p. 125.)

"[1579. October.] OVINGHAM. Their church is in great decay in the body, and glasse windowes and sclates, that service cannot be said in wete wether." (p. 126.)

"[1580. Aug.] NORTON. 'Their Bible is not sufficient, being old and torne, lackinge fowre or five leaves together in sundrye places of St. Paul's Epistles.' Supplied and dismissed." (p. 127.)

M

is, no doubt, the Canons of 1571 (to which Johnson also refers), one of which orders that :—

"No Deane, nor Archdeacon, nor Residentarie, nor Master, nor Warden, nor head of any college, or cathedrall churche, neither President, nor Rector, nor any of y^t order, by what name soeuer they be called, shall hereafter weare the Graye Amice, or any other garment which hath bene defiled with the like superstition. But euery one of them in their churches shal weare onely that linnen garment, which is as yet retained by the Queene's commandment, and also hys schollers hoode, according to euerye mans calling, and degree in schole."

These Canons did not, however, receive the Queen's assent, and therefore the prohibition had no *legal* force: I have not met with any account of the reasons for her refusal: if the words " shall weare onely that linnen garment" were intended to forbid the Cope, this may have been a cause why, as Strype says, " The Archbishop laboured to get the Queen's allowance " to it, but had it not." (*Parker*, iv., p. 322.)

Upon the quotations (at pp. 79-80) the Court observes :—

" Now all the Tracts above cited are dated within ten years after the date of the Advertisements, and the complaints so bitterly made as to the cope and surplice would certainly have been extended to the alb and chasuble had they not then ceased to exist."

There is no need to question the general truth of this statement, yet its bearing upon the *lawfulness* of the Alb and Chasuble *now* is really unimportant : no one contends, I suppose, that these Vestments continued long or to any extent in use ; but that cannot be a *sufficient* reason for not reviving them ; if it were, it must at the same time condemn other Ornaments which have in the last thirty years been largely restored in the Churches throughout the country.

Their Lordships further say that :—

" In the correspondence with foreign Reformers, called the 'Zurich Letters,' the controversy is treated as having become confined to the cope and surplice."

But then this very limitation proves how useless it was to endeavour to allay opposition by abandoning the Alb and

Chasuble, since the Surplice and Cope were quite as obnoxious to the objectors. The following quotation from Whitgift's Defence (in 1574) of his Answer to "The Admonition to the "Parliament, by T.C.," *i.e.* Thomas Cartwright will serve as an illustration :—

Cartwright, in the "Admonition," had said, "We marvel that they could espy in the last Synod [1571], that a grey Amice, which is but a garment of dignity, should be a garment (as they say) defiled with superstition, and yet that Copes, Caps, Surplices, Tippets, and such like baggage, the preaching signs of Popish priesthood, the Pope's creatures, kept in the same form to this end, to bring dignity and reverence to the Ministers and Sacraments, should be retained still, and not abolished." (*Whitgift's Works, Parker Society*, II., p. 50.)

T. C., replying to Whitgift's "Answer," observed that while the "Admonition" had not "misliked of the taking away of the grey amice," yet "to take away the amice out of the Church, and leave the Surplice, &c., is to heal a scratch, and leave a wound unhealed." (*Ibid.* p. 51.)

Whitgift rejoined that—" The grey Amice was justly taken away, because the use of it is not established by any Law of this Realm, as the use of other Vestures be; and in mine opinion the Bishops deserved commendation in so doing; for thereby they declared that they will not suffer any Rites or Ornaments to be used in this Church, but such only as are by public Authority established." (*Ibid*, p. 52.)

Now, however, after 300 years, the controversy has changed its ground and exhibits itself in a resistance to the renewed use of Ornaments, which at that time were *imposed* by Authority, no less than to others which the same Authority deemed it undesirable to insist upon, although in strictness they were required by Law. The opposition to the Surplice so long (and at times so fiercely) maintained during the last 30 years is an example of this, the more so since it exceeded that which has been made to the later revival of the Eucharistic Vestments.

XV. The Court, passing on to the time of James 1st, thus continues the reasoning of its Judgment :—

"At the Hampton Court Conference the Puritans objected to the surplice, as 'a kind of garment which the priests of Isis used to wear.' (Cardwell Conferences, p. 200.) There was evidently no other vestment in use to which they could object. The revised Prayer Book, issued soon after, retained the ornaments-Rubric in the same form as in the Prayer Book of Queen Elizabeth. The Canons of 1603-4 enacted by both Convocations, and ratified by the King's consent, sanctioned the use of this Prayer Book. But whilst thus implicitly sanctioning the ornaments-Rubric, the Canons also provide specially for the vesture of the minister. Canon 24 directs the use of 'a decent cope' for the principal minister in the Holy Communion in Cathedrals and Collegiate Churches 'according to the Advertisements published Anno 7 Elizabeth;' and Canon 58 directs that 'every minister saying the public prayers or ministering the Sacraments or other rites of the church shall use [*for* use *read* wear] a decent and comely surplice with sleeves, to be provided at the charge of the parish.'"

The inference which their Lordships here draw from this objection of the Puritans to the Surplice is by no means a necessary one; on the contrary, the comparison they used prevented them from naming the Vestments unless they could have alleged that those garments were also worn by "the priests of "Isis." This new ground of opposition to the much-hated Surplice may well have surprised the King and led him to say, "Surely . . . untill of late, I did not think that it had been "borrowed from the heathen, because it is commonly tearmed a "ragge of popery, in scorn." (*Cardwell, Conf.*, p. 200.) If this new anti-heathen line had attained the object which their anti-popery raid failed to secure, they knew perfectly well that there would be no need to continue the attack on other Vestures: yet their objection to the Cope (no less than to Albe and Chasuble) was not diminished, and certainly that Garment was in *legal* "use," even on the showing of those who hold that the Advertisements repealed the Rubric; that it was also in *actual* "use," to some extent, cannot, I believe, be disproved.

The Judicial Committee mention that "the Ornaments- "Rubric" of 1604 was "in the same form as in the Prayer Book "of Queen Elizabeth:" this fact seems to me an important additional proof that the Advertisements were not the "other "order" of the Elizabethan Statute; for, if they had been, it follows that the Elizabethan Rubric, being thus repealed, was actually revived in all its original force by the Prayer Book of

James 1st. But the Crown could have had no Authority to do this if the "other order" had been taken by the Advertisements, unless indeed it can be shewn that, nevertheless, that one proceeding did not *exhaust* the Proviso of the Statute; and, besides, nothing could well be more unlikely than that the Rubric of 1559 should have been retained in the old form when it was only necessary to restore the Rubric of 1552 with a slight change, to shew that the Advertisements had retained the *Cope* which that Rubric had set aside in the same terms with the Albe and Vestment.

Their Lordships remark that "the Canons of 1603-4 . . . . " sanctioned the use of" the " Prayer Book" of the same year: if "sanctioned" only means *recognised* it, the statement is perfectly true, for the 80th Canon orders that "The Church-" wardens or quest-men of every Church and Chapel shall, at " the charge of the parish, provide the Book of Common Prayer, "lately explained in some few points by his Majesty's authority, " according to the laws and his Highness's prerogative in that "behalf." But the Court, further on, also asserted that the Book "rested upon the Canons of 1603-4:" the former term must, therefore, be construed by the latter; or, at least, they must be taken together; and either way they imply that the Authority to use the Book was derived from the Canons. Yet the Canon itself states that the Book had been prepared " according to the Laws :" indeed if this had not been the case the Convocation could not *legally* have ordered it to be provided instead of the Book of 1559 then lawfully in use; and it is strange that the Court appears to have overlooked those " Laws," and so has mis-stated the Authority which put the Book in use.

Now the fact is that the Prayer Book of 1604 was professedly prepared under the Powers of the 25th and 26th Sections of the Elizabethan Act of Uniformity, and was afterwards issued by Authority of the King's Proclamation: Dr. Cardwell gives a summary of the proceedings in his " History of Conferences" (p. 143, Ed. 1841): here it will be more convenient to quote from the Documents which relate to the subject. The Hampton Court Conference ended on January 18th, 1603-4; some few alterations in the Book of 1559 were there agreed upon; what was subsequently done in reference to them and to the Book generally is stated in King James's Letter to the Archbishop of Canterbury, the Bishops of London and Chichester, " and to "the rest of our Commissioners for Causes Ecclesiasticall." The Letter begins by referring to the Authority "united and " annexed to the imperiall crowne " for " the Visitation of the "Ecclesiastical state and persons," and then it thus proceeds to quote, in a condensed form, the two Sections of the 1st Elizabeth, c. 2:—

" And whereas also by Act of Parliament it is provided and enacted, that whenever we shall cause to take further order for or concerning any ornament, righte, or ceremony appointed or prescribed in the booke commonly called 'The Book of Common Prayer, Administration of the Sacraments, and other rites and ceremonies of the Church of England,' and our pleasure knowne therein, either to our Commissioners, authorized under our great seal of England, for causes Ecclesiasticall, or to the Metropolitane of this our realm of England, that then further order should be therein taken accordingly." (*Cardwell, Conf.*, p. 217.)

The Letter goes on to state that the King " understanding "that there were in the said booke certeyne thinges which might "require some declaration and enlargement by way of explana- "tion," and having required the Bishops and others above mentioned " to take some care and payns therein," had " received "from" them " the said particular thinges" which are then fully set out in detail. (*Ibid*, pp. 218-24.) These the King says, " Wee by virtue of the said statutes, and by our supreme " authoritie and prerogative royall, doe fully approve, allowe " and ratify," and he goes on to direct the Archbishop to " command our printer, Robert Barker, newly to print the said " Communion Book " as thus altered, concluding in these words:—

" And that you take such order, not only in your own province, but likewise in our name with the Archbishop of Yorke for his province, that every parish may provide for themselves the saide booke so prynted and explained, to be onely used by the minister of every such parish in the celebration of divine service and admynistration of the sacramentes. And duely by him to be observed according to the lawe in all the other parts, with the rites and ceremonies therein contained and prescribed for him to observe." (*Ibid*, p. 224.)

The Book thus prepared was issued under "A Proclamation "for the Authorising and Uniformity of the Book of Common "Prayer, to be used throughout the Realme," dated March 5, 1603-4; the Document recites the Hampton Court Conference; the Commission " to the Archbishop of Canterbury and others, "according to the form, which the Laws of this Realm in like " case prescribe to be used"; and the direction for the Book, with its alterations ("explanations," as they are termed) " to be "newly-printed." It then expresses the King's confidence that " all our subjects, both ministers and others, will receive the "same with such reverence as appertaineth, and conform them-"selves thereunto" adding, " yet have we thought it necessary to "make known by proclamation, our authorising of the same "; and then it continues thus:—

"Wherefore we require all Archbishops, Bishops, and all other public Ministers, as well Ecclesiastical as civil, to do their duties in causing the same to be obeyed, and in punishing the offenders according to the laws of the realm heretofore established for the authorising of the said Book of Common Prayer. And we think it also necessary, that the said Archbishops and Bishops do each of them in his province and diocese take order, that every parish do procure to themselves, within such time, as they shall think good to limit, one of the said Books so explained." (*Ibid.* p. 227.)

These Documents prove incontestably that the Prayer Book of 1604 did not rest upon the Canons for its Authority: indeed it was impossible it could be so, for the Canons did not exist when the Book was thus issued. The Convocations of the two Provinces did not meet until March 20th, 1603-4: no business of importance was transacted in the York Convocation; and nothing was done in reference to the Canons in the first three Sessions of the Canterbury Convocation:—

". . . . but on the 13th of April the Bishop of London," says Mr. Lathbury, "exhibited the Royal Licence, authorising them, according to the powers vested in the Crown by the Act of Submission, to make Canons and Constitutions. The License bears the date of April 12, 1604.* . . . . . the consideration of the Canons was the commencement of the regular Synodical business. The Canons, which were subsequently passed, were submitted to the Convocation by the Bishop of London on the 2nd of May." (*Hist. of Convocation*, Ed. 1853, p. 202.)

* The King's Ratification also mentions a second License, viz., the 25th June.

The same Writer states, on the authority of the "Tanner "MSS. 282," that in the "27th Session, July 9th, 1604," the "King's writt to prorogue the Convocation to the 8th of "February, 1604 [*i.e.*, 1604-5]," was issued; and that "after "this the Canons of 1603-4 were printed and published." (*Ibid.* Note n., p. 215.)

The Judicial Committee state that "The Canons of 1603-4 "enacted by both Convocations, and ratified by the King's con- "sent, sanctioned the use of this Prayer Book." The preceding remarks have shewn that these Canons could not have "sanc- "tioned" the Book except in the sense of recognising it as a book already authorised under the provisions of the Elizabethan Act of Uniformity: if, however, their Lordships' view were correct it involves the singular consequence, which would have been very inconvenient at the time, that in the Province of York the Book was not obligatory for about eighteen months after it had been in force in the Province of Canterbury; for the Northern Convocation did not accept the Canons until 1605-6: according to Mr. Lathbury, that—

"Convocation assembled on the 6th of November [1605]. Their business was interrupted by the death of the Archbishop; but the King, by a new writ, dated January 22nd, addressed to the guardian of the Spiritualities, commanded them to proceed. In the vacancy of the See, the Bishop of Bristol, as Dean of York, acted as President (*Wake's State of the Church*, 507). They addressed his Majesty for a royal commission to treat, conclude, and do such things in Convocation as should be for the general good of the province. This request was made in consequence of the Canons already published, and, by the King's confirmation, ordered to be executed in the province of York.* The Canons were not disliked by the Bishops and Clergy in this province, but they were anxious to maintain their own privileges; for, as they had not concurred in enacting the Canons, it was not reasonable to expect them to submit until they had actually sanctioned them in their own Convocation. The Convocation of Canterbury could not bind the Province of York. They wished, by passing the Canons in due form, to submit to his Majesty, and at the same time to vindicate their own privileges. (*Wake's State*, 507; *Wilkins*, iv. 426-428.)

"The Licence was therefore granted, according to their request. It

* The Ratification says "We do . . . command . . . by these our Letters patents, the same to be diligently observed, executed, and equally kept by all our loving subjects in this our kingdom, both within the Provinces of Canterbury and York."

was in the usual form; and after it had been communicated to the Convocation, the Canons of the preceding year, agreed upon in the Province of Canterbury, were read, agreed to, and adopted as their own." (*Hist. of Convocation*, p. 229.)

The Court, repeating the error just pointed out, says, " But " whilst thus implicitly sanctioning the Ornaments Rubric, the " Canons also provide specially for the vesture of the Minister." The obvious question which arises from this remark is—did the Canons, then, mean to forbid every Vesture which they did not prescribe? If they did, the proceeding must have been very strangely contradictory if not, indeed, unconstitutional: it was nothing less than the King and the Convocation of Canterbury repealing *pro tanto* the Rubric which His Majesty and the Ecclesiastical Commission had issued under the express Provision of a Statute only four months before—a repeal, moreover, which was wholly unnecessary if the Advertisements had been issued conformably to the Act, for then they must still have been of Statutory obligation. Perhaps it will be replied that as the Rubric in the Book of 1604 retained the words of the Elizabethan Rubric—" according to the Acte of Parliament "set in the beginning of this booke"—there was clearly an intention to limit the Rubric; and that a proof of such intention is afforded by the 24th Canon which requires the Cope in Cathedral and Collegiate Churches *only* " upon principal feast-days," whereas the Advertisements required it *always* "in ministra- " tion of the Holy Communion" in those Churches: but, even if this be the meaning of the Canon, which I doubt (See xxi.), the answer plainly is, as the Dean of the Arches pointed out, that Convocation was not the body empowered to act by the Statute of Elizabeth. There is no difficulty in understanding the proceedings of Convocation if it be admitted that the 24th and 58th Canons were only designed to rule how much of the general requirements of the Rubric was to be *enforced* by the Ordinaries; and there was no inconsistency in this at a time when neither the Crown, nor the Parliament, nor the Bishops, wished to compel more: but upon any other theory their course is unintelligible.

The Court, after thus referring to the Prayer Book and Canons of 1603-4, states that :—

> "Their Lordships think it needless to adduce authorities to show that there was no attempt to revive or use the chasuble, alb, and tunicle, between the years 1604 and 1662."

But the question suggests itself—what inference is intended to be drawn from this remark? If it be meant—that no such attempt ought to be made now—it may fairly be replied, that a sufficient warrant for it is to be found in what was done during that period as to the Cope which certainly had fallen into pretty general disuse. Collier, speaking of Archbishop Bancroft in 1605, says that under his government "the use of Copes was "revived, the Surplice generally worn, and all things in a manner "recovered to the first settlement under Elizabeth." (*Eccl.Hist.*, ii., 687.) Archbishop Laud's Visitation Articles, 1635, shew that in the Cathedrals of Worcester, Gloucester, Winchester, and Chichester, there were no Copes, but that the Authorities were to procure them. (*E. C. Union Case*, p. 64. 1st *Rit. Report*, p. 152.) The Petition of 15,000 persons, "many of his "Majesty's subjects in and about the City of London, and "several Counties of the Kingdom," to the House of Commons, Dec. 11, 1640, complained of the "encreased" use of "the cope "and surplice." The "Ordinance" of the Parliament, 1643, decreed that "'no copes, surplices, superstitious vestments, "'roods, or holy water-fonts' (as they called them) 'were to be "'used.'" (*Collier*, *E. H.*, ii., p. 830.) *

---

* Mr. Robertson (*How shall we conform to the Liturgy?* p. 297, 3rd Ed., 1869) speaking of "the use of the Cope" under the Canons of 1604, "until the great Rebellion," says—" on the one hand the use of the cope was much neglected in cathedrals, while on the other hand it is possible that one or two clergymen may, under the primacy of Laud, have attempted to introduce it into parish churches." But it seems to me that the *Petition* and *Ordinance* above mentioned imply a much more extensive use in *Parish* Churches than Mr. Robertson allows; the same is, I think, to be gathered from the mention of *Parish* Churches in the following Documents when read together :—

1. "April 24, 1643. Sir Rob. Harley, Mr. Gurdon, Mr. Rous, Sir Gilb. Gerard, Mr. Bond, Mr. White, Mr. Moore, Mr. Corbett, Mr. Browne. This Committee is to receive information, from time to time, of any monuments of Superstition or Idolatry in the Abbey Church at Westminster, or the windows thereof, or in any other Church or Chapel, in or about London. And they have power to demolish the same, where any such superstitious or idolatrous monuments are informed to be : And all Churchwardens, and other officers, are hereby required

XVI. The Rubric itself is next referred to by the Court in these words:—

"The Ornaments-Rubric of 1662, is as follows:—
'And here it [*dele* it] is to be noted that such ornaments of the church and of the minister [s *sic*] thereof at all times of their ministration, shall be retained and be in use as were in this Church of England by the authority of Parliament in the second year of the reign of King Edward VI.' The form of this Rubric is different from that of the preceding Prayer Book, and follows, for the most part, the wording of the proviso of the Act of Queen Elizabeth."

In order to see clearly at one view the variations, to which their Lordships refer, in these Rubrics and the Elizabethan Statute, it will be convenient to put them in parallel columns.

to be aiding and assisting in the execution of this order: and are to meet at two o'clock this afternoon in the Exchequer Chamber." (*Journals of the House of Commons*, iii., 57.) See also Aug. 28, 1643. (*Ibid.*, p. 220.)

2. "May 31, 1643. *Ordered.* That the Committee for putting down and abolishing all monuments of superstition and idolatry, do take into their custody the Copes in the Cathedrals of Westminster, Paul's, and those at Lambeth: and give order that they be burnt, and converted to the relief of the poor in Ireland." (*Ib.*, p. 110.)

3. "Oct. 3, 1643. *Ordered.* That the Committee for removing of scandalous and superstitious monuments do take away all Copes and Surplices out of all Cathedral, Collegiate, and Parish Churches and Chapels, and apply them to the relief and succour of the wounded and maimed soldiers; and enjoin the Deans, Prebends, Parsons, Vicars, and Rectors of all Cathedral, Collegiate, and Parish Churches and Chapels; all Masters, Ushers, Scholars, Singingmen, and Choristers of all Cathedral, Collegiate, and Parish Churches and Chapels, Schools, and Colleges, not to wear any Surplice in any of the places aforesaid, upon any occasion, during any time of Divine Service or Sermons." (*Ib.*, p. 262.) It must be presumed that there was a large number of them, or they could not have afforded *much* "relief." See also Feb. 5 and March 9, 1643-4. (*Ib.*, iii., pp. 389 and 422.)

4. "May 9, 1644. Cap. 38. That no Copes, Surplisses, superstitious vestments, roods or roodlons or holy-water fonts shall be or be any more used in any church or chappell within this realm ..... and that all Copes, Surplisses, superstitious Vestments, Roods and Fonts aforesaid be likewise utterly defaced; whereunto all persons within this kingdom, whom it may concern, are hereby required at their peril, to yield due obedience." (*Scobell's Collection of Acts*, 1658, p. 70.) See also *Journals of the House of Commons*, iii., 486.

Allhallows, Barking, appears to have escaped these *Ordinances*, for in the Churchwardens' Account occurs the following entry:—"6 Oct. 1654, was sold to Mr. Quintaine an old silke Cope siluer guilt, by order of the Vestry, for £2 0s. 0d."

In Walcott's History of Christchurch, Hants, (2nd *Ed.*, p.81) it is mentioned that the "Book of Benefactors," now in the Parish Chest, records the gift of "a rich cope" in 1617 by Jo. Marsten the Vicar. This may fairly be regarded as a "contemporaneous exposition" of the meaning of the Canons of 1603-4.

Prayer Book, 1559.	Stat. 1 Eliz. c. 2, § 25, 1558-9.	Prayer Book, 1603-4.	Prayer Book, 1662.
"And here is to be noted, that the Minister at the time of the cōmunion, and at all other tymes in hys ministracion, shall use suche ornamentes in the church, as wer in use by aucthoritie of parliamēt in the second yeer of the reygne of king Edward the vi. according to the acte of parliament set in the beginning of thys booke."	"Provided alwayes & be it enacted, that suche ornamēts of the Churche, and of the ministers therof, shalbe reteined and be in use as was in this Churche of England, by aucthority of Parliament, in the second yeer of the raygne of Kyng Edward the vi. until other order shalbe therin takē by thaucthority of the Quene's Maiestie, with the aduise of her	"And here is to be noted, that the Minister at the time of the Communion, and at all other times in his ministration, shall vse such ornaments in the Church, as were in vse by authority of Parliament in the second yeere of the reigne of Edward the Sixt, according to the Acte of Parliament set in the begining of this booke."	"And here is to be noted, that such Ornaments of the Church and of the Ministers thereof at all times of their Ministration, shall be retained and be in use, as were in this Church of England, by the Authority of Parliament, in the second year of the Reign of King Edward the Sixth."

Cōmissioners appointed and auctorized under the great Seale of England, for causes ecclesiastical, or of the Metropolitan of this Realme."

The Judicial Committee says—that the Rubric of 1662 "follows, for the most part, the wording of the Proviso of the "Act of Elizabeth." The change was really due to Bishop Cosin; for in a Prayer Book of 1619 (now in the Cosin Library at Durham, D. iii.) prepared, as it seems, by Cosin for the Revision of 1661, the Rubric is thus altered in his own handwriting:—

THe Morning and Euening prayer shalbe vsed in the accustomed place of the Church, Chappell, or Chauncell, except it shall be otherwise determined by the Ordinarie of the place : And the Chancels shall remaine as they haue done in times past.
And here is to be noted, that ~~the Minister at the time of the Communi-~~ *all*
~~omitt~~ ~~on, and at other times in his Ministration, shall vse such ornaments~~
~~in the Church, as were in vse by authoritie of Parliament, in the se-~~
~~cond yeere of the Reigne of Edward the sixt, according to the Acte~~
~~of Parliament set in the beginning of this Booke.~~ =tayned & be in vse as were in this Church
place at ye end herof on   of England by the Authority of Parliament
the other side a fleuron.   in the Second yeere of ye Reigne of K. Edw. vi.
                             that is to say   A Surplice &c.

¶ An order for Morning Prayer dayly
                             ~~and Euening~~
                             these are ye words of ye Act itselfe. v. Supr.
place here a fayre Compartment.
throughout the yeere.

{to the right of the struck-out block:}
~~be divided from ye body of the church, &~~
~~& adds this Title here~~
~~order for~~
~~An Of Ornaments~~
~~to be~~ ^used in ye Church
nall ∴ Such ornaments
of the Church, & of the
ministers therof at all times
of their ministration shalbe re-

N.B. The words underlined are so marked either by Cosin or Sancroft.

N.B. The words "these are" &c. are in Sancroft's hand.

Cosin designed, then, to substitute the words of the Statute for the words of the Book: apparently Sancroft, who was Cosin's Chaplain, so understood him; and if Sancroft wrote these words in his capacity of Secretary to the Committee of Bishops, it would imply that they concurred in Cosin's proposal. But, however this may have been, Cosin having proposed to use the language of the Act, it follows that whatever he understood the Act to mean, that he must have intended the Rubric to mean; and, as his form was adopted by the Revisers in 1662, it is most reasonable to believe that they adopted it in his sense.* What that sense was is plain enough from his well-known three Series of Notes;† for there is no reason to suppose

---

* Cosin had wished to have the Vestments specified, for in his "Particulars to be considered, explained, and corrected, in the Book of Common Prayer," (which seem to have been used at the Revision of 1661, as most of them were adopted,) he says—"And in the same rubric, 'The Minister is appointed to use such ornaments in the church, and at all times in his ministrations, as were in use in the second year of King Edward the Sixth, according to the Act of Parliament.' But what those ornaments of the Church and of the ministers were, is not here specified, and they are so unknown to many, that by most they are neglected. Wherefore it were requisite that those ornaments used in the second year of King Edward, should be particularly named and set forth, that there might be no difference about them." (*Works, Ang. Cath. Lib.*, v., p. 507.) At the end of his revised form of the Ornaments Rubric, in the Durham Book (See p. 92), he began to write a List of the Ornaments, but only wrote thus—"that is to say— A Surplice, &c.": the words were afterwards erased by a line drawn through them, but whether by Cosin himself or by the Committee of Bishops appears uncertain. Probably it was thought that to specify the Ornaments might cause the Rubric itself to be rejected. If it be suggested that Cosin having written "Surplice" implies that he did not contemplate naming the other Vestments of the Book of 1549; it is obvious to reply that, while "&c" would certainly have admitted any details, the words need not have been erased on account of any risk in merely specifying what was prescribed in the Book of 1552, which was referred to with satisfaction by "the Ministers" at the Savoy Conference.

† FIRST SERIES. .*cir*. 1619 to 1638. "[*As were in use.*] And then were in use, not a surplice and hood, as we now use, but a plain white alb, with a vestment or cope over it; and therefore, according to this rubric, are we all still bound to wear albs and vestments, as have been so long time worn in the Church of God, howsoever it is neglected. For the disuse of these ornaments, we may thank them that came from Geneva, and in the beginning of Queen Elizabeth's reign, being set in places of government, suffered every negligent priest to do what him listed, so he would but profess a difference and opposition in all things (though never so lawful otherwise) against the Church of Rome, and the ceremonies therein used. If any man shall answer, that now the 58th Canon hath appointed it otherwise, and that these things are alterable by the direction of the Church wherein we live; I answer, that such matters are to be altered by the same authority wherewith they were established, and that if that authority be the convocation of the Clergy, as I think it is (only that), that the 14th canon commands us to observe all the ceremonies prescribed in this book. I would fain know how we should observe both canons. (But the act of parliament, I see, refers to the canon, and until such time as other order shall be

that he had changed his opinion at the last Review of the Prayer Book.

XVII. The Court, adverting to the Judgment of Sir R. Phillimore, goes on to say :—

taken.)" (*Ang. Cath. Lib.* v. p. 42.)' For remarks upon these last words "But the act" &c., see *infra*, xxiv.

SECOND SERIES. *cir.* 1638 to 1656. "*At the time of the Communion.*] And at the celebration of the holy Communion it was ordained, by the rules and orders of the first liturgy set forth by the Church of England, and confirmed by authority of parliament, in the second year of the reign of King Edward the VIth: 'That the priest who shall then execute the holy ministry, shall put upon him the vesture appointed for that ministration; that is to say, a white alb plain, with a vestment or cope': and, 'that other priests and deacons, who shall help him in that ministration, shall have upon them likewise the vestments appointed for their ministry; that is to say, albs with tunicles': but 'if he be a bishop, who either celebrateth the holy Communion, or executeth any other public ministration, that then he shall have upon him, besides his rochet, a surplice or alb, and a cope or vestment; and also his pastoral staff in his hand, or else borne or holden by his chaplain.'

"*And at all other times of his ministration.*] That is, (as is set forth in the first liturgy of King Edward before mentioned,) 'in the saying or singing of matins and evensong, baptizing and burying, the minister in parish churches, and chapels annexed, shall use a surplice. And in all cathedral churches and colleges, the deans, archdeacons, provosts, masters, prebendaries, and fellows, being graduates, may use in the quire, besides their surplices, such hoods as pertain to their several degrees which they shall have taken in any university within this realm; and when they do preach, it is seemly also that they should wear their hoods belonging to their degrees.'

"The word 'all' here had been divers years omitted in the editions of this book [See the Rubric, p. 92], contrary to the true copy of it, set forth in the first year of Queen Elizabeth, (which was done either by the negligence of the printer or upon design,) until King Charles the First, in the first year of his reign, commanded it to be restored, and sent me to his printing-house to see it done; ever since which time it has so continued.

"*In the Church.*] For 'in all other places,' as it was declared by the same authority in the second year of King Edward the Sixth, 'Every minister shall be at liberty to use any surplice or no.'

"*As were in use, &c.*] Among other ornaments of the church that were then in use, the setting of two lights upon the communion-table or altar was one, appointed by the King's Injunctions, (set forth about that time, and mentioned or ratified by the Act of Parliament here named,) whereby all other wax-lights and tapers, which in former times of superstition men were wont to place before their shrines and images of saints, being taken away and utterly abolished, it was required, that two lights only should be placed upon the altar, to signify the joy and splendour we receive from the light of Christ's blessed Gospel. Bene B. *Lutherus in formula missæ sive Communionis, quam Wittenburgensi Ecclesiæ anno superioris seculi vicesimo tertio præscripsit, Nec candelas (inquit) nec thurificationem prohibemus, sed nec exigimus; esto hoc liberum.*

"*By authority of Parliament.* Which confirmed both the first liturgy and the Injunctions of King Edward the Sixth.

"*In the second year of the reign of King Edward the Sixth.*] For it is here to be noted, that in his time there were two several liturgies, and two several acts of parliament made to confirm them. One in the second year, and another in the fifth year of his reign. In which fifth year, (upon the disuse which some

"The learned Judge, in the Court below, assumes (Appendix, p. 74) that the Puritan party at the Savoy Conference, objected to *this* Rubric: whereas it was the Rubric of James that they were discussing. Upon that, the Puritans observed that, 'Inasmuch

men made of the former ornaments, or upon the displeasure that other men took against them both at home and abroad,) it was appointed by the second liturgy, and enacted by parliamentary authority, 'That the minister, at the time of the Communion, and at all other times in his ministration, should use neither alb, vestment, nor cope; but being an archbishop or bishop, should have and wear a rochet; and being a priest or deacon, should have and wear a surplice only.' And yet this latter book, and act of parliament thereunto annexed, did not condemn either the ornaments, or anything beside that was appointed in the former book, but acknowledged it all to have been 'a very godly order, agreeable to the Word of God and the primitive Church.' Whereupon, by authority of parliament, in the first year of Queen Elizabeth, albeit it was thought most meet to follow and continue the order of divine service in Psalms, lessons, hymns, and prayers, (a few of them only varied,) which was set forth in the fifth year of King Edward; yet for the ornaments of the Church, and of the ministers thereof, the order appointed in the second year of his reign was retained, and the same are we bound still to observe. Which is a note wherewith those men are not so well acquainted as they should be, who inveigh against our present ornaments in the Church, and think them to be innovations introduced lately by an arbitrary power, against law; whereas, indeed, they are appointed by the law itself. And this Judge Yelverton acknowledged and confessed to me, (when I had declared the matter to him, as here I set it forth,) in his circuit at Durham, not long before his death, having been of another mind before." (*Ibid*, pp. 230-233.)

This matter came before Judge Yelverton in 1629, when Cosin was Prebendary of Durham, upon the complaint of Peter Smart; Yelverton "died January 24, 1630 [*i.e.* 1629-30] at his house in Aldersgate Street." (*Fuss's Judges of England*, vi., 395. Conf. *Dodd's Ch. Hist.*, iii., 81; *Chalmers' Biog. Dict.*; and *Wood's Ath. Ox.*, ed. Bliss, ii., 477.) These Notes were written in a Prayer Book of 1638, and, therefore, it is plain that Cosin held this view of the Rubric at least as late as 1638. But the Editor shews (p. xviii) that these Notes range from 1638 to 1656; it may be, therefore, that this Note is of the latter date; indeed there is reason for thinking that it is still later. Mr. Ornsby, who has long been engaged in editing Cosin's Remains for the Surtees Society and who is familiar with Cosin's handwriting, has kindly examined the MS. of this Note: he informs me that having compared it with some Notes in the Prayer Book of 1619 which Cosin prepared for the Revision of 1661, and with a MS. Account of the Revenues of the See of Durham—a Volume written in the Bishop's own hand, bearing the date of 1662—the similarity between these several specimens confirms him in the conviction he had expressed to me—that the Note in question is of the date of 1660 or 1661 and consequently represents the Bishop's views at the time of the Revision.

"*According to the act of parliament set forth in the beginning of this book.*] § *penult.*, in these words: 'Provided always, and be it enacted, that such ornaments of the Church, (whereunto the adorning and decent furniture of the communion table relate,) 'and of the ministers thereof,' (as the alb or surplice, vestment or cope, with the rochet and the pastoral staff before mentioned,) 'shall be retained and be in use, as was in this Church of England, by authority of Parliament, in the second' (not the fifth) 'year of the reign of King Edward the Sixth; until other order shall be therein taken, by the authority of the queen's majesty, with the advice of her commissioners appointed and authorized

[*read* Forasmuch] as this Rubric seemeth to bring back the cope, alb, [&c. *sic*] and other vestments forbidden by the Common Prayer Book, 5 & 6 Edward VI, and so for [*for* for *read* our] reasons alleged against ceremonies under our eighteenth general exception, we deem [*for* deem *read* desire] it may be wholly left out.' The Rubric had been in force for nearly 60 years, and they do not allege that the vestments had been brought back; nor would a total omission of the Rubric have been a protection against them. The Bishops in their answer show that they understand the surplice to under the great seal of England, for causes ecclesiastical, or of the metropolitan of this realm.' Which other order, so qualified as is here appointed to be, was never yet made." (*Ibid.*, p. 233.)

THIRD SERIES. Prob. most before 1640. "*Such ornaments, &c.*] Without which (as common reason and experience teaches us,) the Majesty of Him that owneth it, and the work of His service there, will prove to be of a very common and low esteem. The particulars of these ornaments (both of the Church and of the Ministers thereof, as in the end of the Act of Uniformity,) are referred not to the fifth of Edw. VI., as the service itself is in the beginning of that Act, for in that fifth year were all ornaments taken away, (but a surplice only,) both from bishops and priests, and all other ministers, and nothing was left for the church, but a font, a table, and a linen cloth upon it, (at the time of the Communion only,) but to the second year of that king, when his Service-book and Injunctions were in force by authority of parliament. And in these books many other ornaments are appointed; as, two lights to be set upon the altar or communion-table, a cope or vestment for the priest and for the bishop, besides their albs, surplices, and rochets, the bishop's crozier-staff, to be holden by him at his ministration and ordinations; and those ornaments of the church, which by former laws, not then abrogated, were in use, by virtue of the statute 25 Henry VIII., and for them the provincial constitutions are to be consulted, such as have not been repealed, standing then in the second year of King Edw. VI., and being still in force by virtue of this rubric and act of parliament.

"That which is to be said for these vestures and ornaments, in solemnizing the service of God, is, that they were appointed for inward reverence to that work, which they make outwardly solemn. All the actions of esteem in the world are so set forth, and the world hath had trial enough, that those who have made it a part of their religion to fasten scorn upon such circumstances, have made no less to deface and disgrace the substance of God's public service.

"*Such ornaments as were in use in the second year of King Edward VI.*] In that year, by the authority of parliament, was this order set forth, in the end of the Service-book then appointed. At Morning and Evening Prayer, the administration of baptism, the burial of the dead, &c., in parish-churches, the minister shall put upon him a surplice; in cathedral and collegiate churches, and in colleges, the archdeacons, deans, presidents and masters, may use the ornaments also belonging to their degrees and dignities. But in all other places it shall be free for them whether they will use any surplice or not. The bishop administering the Lord's Supper, and celebrating the Sacraments, shall wear a rochet or alb, with a cope or vestment; and he shall have also his pastoral staff. And before the Communion, upon the day appointed for the celebration of the Lord's Supper, the priest having on him an alb, with a vestment or cope, shall stand at the altar; and where there be many priests and deacons, so many of

be in question, and not the vestments. (Cardwell Conferences, 314, 345, 351.) But the learned Judge through this oversight has overlooked the most important part of the proceedings."

The Dean of the Arches was much too well read in the History of the Prayer Book to make any such false assumption as the Court here imputes to him: he did indeed assume that the Rubric which the Puritans objected to was essentially the same as the Rubric of 1662; and their Lordships knew that, upon the supposed controlling authority of a Superior Court, he

them as be needful shall help the chief minister, having albs or tunicles upon them.
"These ornaments and vestures of the ministers were so displeasing to Calvin and Bucer, that the one in his letters to the Protector, and the other in his censure of the liturgy, sent to Archbishop Cranmer, urged very vehemently to have them taken away, not thinking it tolerable, that we should have anything common with the papists, but shew forth our Christian liberty, in the simplicity of the Gospel.
"Hereupon, when a parliament was called, in the fifth year of King Edward, they altered the former book, and made another order, for vestments, copes, and albs not to be worn at all; allowing an archbishop, and a bishop, a rochet only, and a priest or deacon to wear nothing but a surplice.
"But by the Act of Uniformity the parliament thought fit, not to continue this last order, but to restore the first again; which since that time was never altered by any other law, and therefore it is still in force at this day.
"And both bishops, priests and deacons, that knowingly and wilfully break this order, are as hardly censured in the preface to this book concerning ceremonies, as ever Calvin or Bucer censured the ceremonies themselves. Among other ornaments of the Church also then in use, in the second year of Edw. VI. there were two lights appointed by his injunctions (which the parliament had authorized him to make, and whereof otherwhiles they made mention, as acknowledging them to be binding,) to be set upon the high-altar, as a significant ceremony of the light which Christ's Gospel brought into the world; and this at the same time, when all other lights and tapers superstitiously set before images, were by the same Injunctions, with many other absurd ceremonies and superfluities, taken away. These lights were (by virtue of this present rubric, referring to what was in use in the Second of Edw. VI.) afterwards continued in all the queen's chapels, during her whole reign; and so they are in the king's, and in many cathedral churches, besides the chapels of divers noblemen, bishops, and colleges to this day.
"It was well-known, that the Lord-treasurer Burleigh (who was no friend to superstition or popery) used them constantly in his chapel, with other ornaments of fronts, palls and books, upon his altar. The like did Bishop Andrewes, who was a man who knew well what he did, and as free from popish superstition as any in the kingdom besides. In the latter end of King Edward's time they used them in Scotland itself, as appears by Calvin's Epistle to Knox, and his fellow-reformers there, *anno* 1554, *Ep.* 206, where he takes exception against them, for following the custom of England.
"To this head we refer the organ, the font, the altar, the communion-table, and the pulpit, with the coverings and ornaments of them all; together with the paten, chalice, and corporas, which were all in use in the second of Edw. VI. by the authority of the acts of parliament then made." (*Ibid.*, pp. 438 to 441.)

o

was not at liberty to take any other view, since their own Court had laid it down in express terms that the three Rubrics and the Section of the Act, above quoted, "all obviously mean the "same thing, that the same dresses and the same utensils, or "articles, which were used under the First Prayer Book of "Edward the Sixth may still be used." (*Moore,* p. 159.)

Their Lordships, citing the objection at the Savoy Conference, remark that "the Rubric had been in force for nearly 60 years, and "they [the Puritans] do not allege that the vestments had been "brought back"; but, *first* among the Vestures which they held it to restore, was "the cope," which they and others had all along vehemently protested against : they knew that, not for 60 years only but for 100 years it had maintained a *legal* position quite as obnoxious to them as the Chasuble, and an *actual* position still more obnoxious because the Chasuble had probably fallen into general disuse—a position which it would not easily, if at all, have maintained had the Rubric been abolished which was the basis of Injunctions, Interpretations, and Advertisements.* In the opinion of the Court, moreover "a total omission of the "Rubric" would not "have been a protection against them" : if this means, as it seems to imply—that *any* Vestures might have been introduced where no Rubric specified anything— then, happily, a principle is restored which was most strangely rejected in Martin *v.* Mackonochie when their Lordships held that "a Rubric which is silent as to" a thing "by necessary "implication abolishes what it does not retain." No doubt the Bishops "understood the Surplice to be in question," but they could not have supposed it was *that alone,* when the Cope had been specified, whatever they might have thought about "the "[other] Vestments"; so that really, if there was any "over- "sight" in the Court of Arches, the Judicial Committee has itself "overlooked" a point which materially affected "the "proceedings" of the Conference as to the Ornaments Rubric.

* The Committee of the House of Lords, in 1640-41, when complaining of the "Innovations" of the period, speaks thus of the Authority of the Injunctions and Advertisements—"10. By pretending for their innovations, the Injunctions and Advertisements of Queen Elizabeth, which are not in force, but by way of commentary and imposition . . . . ." (*Cardwell,* Conf. p. 273.)

XVIII. Having thus noticed the Puritans' objection to the Rubric, as it stood in the Prayer Book of 1604, the Court proceeds as follows :—

> "The Bishops determined that the Rubric 'should continue as it is.' But after this they did, in fact, re-cast it entirely. It must not be assumed that alterations made under such circumstances were made without thought, and are of no importance. The Rubric had directed the minister to 'use at the time of the Communion, and at all other times of [*for* of *read* in] his ministrations [*dele* s],' the ornaments in question. The statute of Elizabeth did not direct such use nor refer to any special times of ministration, but it ordered simply the retaining of the ornaments till further order made by the Queen. The Bishops threw aside the form of the old Rubric and adopted that of the Statute of Elizabeth, but added the words 'at all times of their ministration' without the words which had in all former Rubrics distinguished the Holy Communion from other ministrations; a mode of expression more suitable to a state of things wherein the vestments for all ministrations had become the same. The change also brought in the word 'retained,' which, it has been argued, would not include things already obsolete. Whatever be the force of these two arguments, the fact is clear that the Puritans objected to a Rubric differing from this; and that after their objections, the Rubric was re-cast, and brought into its present form."

Their Lordships' intimation—that the Bishops *changed their minds* after the Savoy Conference (for this is the natural meaning of the beginning of this passage) seems to me a view of the History which has not before been taken: it may be a true one, though the known evidence would appear to refute it. However, the Court in speaking of the Rubric of 1604 as "re-cast," and as "differing" from the Rubric of 1662, admits that the former Rubric did *legally* continue the Vestments "forbidden," as the Puritans said, by the Book of 1552. Thus their Lordships really abandon their theory of the repealing* force of the Advertisements and of the Canons of 1604. Of course to "re-cast" a thing does not *necessarily* alter its original character: but the Court not only says that "alterations" were made; it further negatives any assumption that they were "of no importance." The draft Rubric of Bishop Cosin, already mentioned (at p. 92), coupled with what the Court states the Bishops to have "determined" at the Savoy Conference, does not favour the notion that any alteration of consequence was intended to be made; however, the following piece of contemporary evidence appears to me decisive on the point.

The changes at the Revision of 1661 were written in a folio edition of the Prayer Book of 1604, dated 1636: this Book† contains a comparative List of "Alterations," the "old" and "new" portions being placed in parallel columns: no notice whatever of this Rubric occurs in it, though other Rubrics are mentioned: at the end of the List this "Note" is written:—

"These are all yᵉ materiall alterations, yᵉ rest are onely verball, or yᵉ changing of some Rubrick's for yᵉ better performing of yᵉ Service, or yᵉ new moulding some of yᵉ Collects."

Now if the "re-cast" Ornaments Rubric had been included in this comparative Table it must have been one of these "materiall alterations," and so the Table would have been a reasonable proof that the view of the Judicial Committee was correct: but, not being inserted, it is no less conclusive the other way. Or, again, if the Rubric of 1604 had been legally changed by the Canons, this *Note* would have supported their Lordships' opinion—that the varied language of the 1662 Rubric was only co-extensive with the requirements of those Canons: on the other hand, the Rubric of 1604 not having

---

* The form of the Rubric in the Scotch Prayer Book of 1637 shews that it was not then regarded as *legally* altered by the Advertisements or Canons:— "And here is to be noted, that the Presbyter or Minister at the time of the Communion, and at other times in his Ministration, shall use such Ornaments in the Church, as are prescribed, or shall be by his Majestie, or his successors, according to the Act of Parliament provided in that behalf."

† The Volume (together with the MS. copy of it signed by the Convocations of the two Provinces and the original Act of 1662 to which the MS. was the Schedule) is now deposited in the Victoria Tower at Westminster: it was Photozincographed, by direction of the Lords of the Treasury, at the instance of the Ritual Commission and is published by Mr. Pickering.

been legally limited by the Canons (as I have shewn that the Court practically admits), the Rubric of 1662 is a *material alteration* (according to the Judicial Committee) and then the MS. *Note* in the Book of 1636 is not true. Yet it will be allowed, surely, that the Writer of the Note would have been more likely to know in 1662 the real meaning of the Rubric, than the Judicial Committee in 1871.

Their Lordships moreover say, that the Elizabethan Act " ordered simply the retaining of the Ornaments till further " order made by the Queen " : the substitution here of *further* for "other," as it is in the 25th Section, is a not unimportant error: but it is strange that the Court should not only have fallen into the greater mistake of omitting to notice the words " and be in use," but also of stating that " the Statute did not " direct such use [as the Rubric of King James had directed] " nor refer to any special times of ministration." The obvious meaning of this statement is—that the Statute and the Rubric *do not agree* : a *new* view, at all events, I think ; and one which certainly would have alike surprised the Elizabethan and the Jacobean Authorities, for it need hardly be said that the Rubrics of 1559 and 1604 are identical. By what ingenuity, then, can any real distinction as to *use* be shewn in the Act and the Rubric ? The Act says " such Ornaments of the Church and " of the Ministers thereof, shall . . . . be in use as was in this " Church ": the Rubric says " the Minister at the time of the " Communion, and at all other times in his Ministration, shall use " such Ornaments in the Church, as were in use :" both refer to the same Ornaments—the *general* order must include the " special " order ; " was in " must mean " were in use ;" shall " be in use " necessarily refers to occasions when they could be used, and they could only be used, with any consistency, at the times *i.e.* at the Services mentioned in the Rubric, for the Book of 1549 (which the Court holds to be the " Authority of Parlia- " ment in the Second year" of Edward VIth) expressly "pro- " vides," as the same Court said in 1857 (*Moore*, p. 157), "the " vestments differing in the different Services."

Again, the Court remarks that the Bishops, in abandoning the old Rubric for the direction of the Statute, "added the "words 'at all times of their ministration'" without the distinguishing words of the Rubric; and their Lordships consider this to be "a mode of expression more suitable to a state of "things wherein the Vestments for all Ministrations had become "the same." But they had not "become the same" in Cathedral and Collegiate Churches, and it is absurd to suppose that the Rubric did not include them; if it be replied that—the 24th Canon provided for *them*, it must be rejoined that—the 58th also provided for other Churches; and then the question naturally arises, Why did not the Rubric of 1662 follow the example of the Rubrics of 1559 and 1604 (which referred to the Act) and use some such expression as "shall be in use "according to the Canons of 1604"? There is moreover this fatal objection to the opinion of the Court, as to the intent and meaning of the newly added words—that it flatly contradicts the later words of the Rubric, viz., "as were in [*i.e.* according "to the Elizabethan Act and Rubric *were in use in*] this Church "of England by the Authority of Parliament, in the second year "of the reign of King Edward the Sixth" *i.e.* as their Lordships decide, the First Prayer Book; for that Book does not order the Surplice for the Celebration of the Holy Communion, but distinctly prescribes the Albe and Vestment, *i.e.* Chasuble; the Surplice or Albe with a Cope being ordered for use when no Consecration is intended.

Once more, the Judicial Committee say that "the change also "brought in the word 'retained,' which, it has been argued, would "not include things already obsolete": but they were quite as "obsolete" in 1604, yet the Rubric ordered their "use" and in doing so referred to the Act which, like the present Rubric, said they "shall be retained."

Their Lordships seem doubtful of the reasoning to which they refer, for they say "whatever be the force of these two "arguments, the fact is clear that . . . . the Rubric was re-"cast, and brought into its present form:" but it was both necessary and convenient to "re-cast" it; *necessary*, because the reference to the Statute could not be retained, as it stood, for the Ecclesiastical Commission had been abolished; *convenient*, because the Rubric alone might easily have been held to refer only to the Ornaments of the Ministers, whereas the Act expressly mentioned also the Ornaments of the Church.

XIX. This next passage in the Judgment has been already in part disposed of by the preceding remarks (See p. 99) upon the alleged *difference* of the Rubrics of 1604 and 1662: the Court says:—

> "With regard to the suggestion attributed to the House of Lords, 'whether the Rubric should not be mended where all vestments in time of Divine service are now commanded which were used by [*for* by *read* 2] Edward VI." ('Cardwell Conferences, p. 274,) the learned Judge has overlooked the fact that this applies to the earlier Rubric; and the suggestion did not emanate from the House of Lords, nor was it ever adopted by that body. And the learned Judge omits to observe that the Rubric of James, which was objected to, was amended after the suggestion."

The seeming readiness, here and elsewhere in the Judgment (See p. 95), to impugn the accuracy or care of the Dean of the Arches is, to say the least, unfortunate in a Review of his Judgment which (apart from other errors) has not a few mistakes in mere quotations, as is shewn by the corrections which I have put in square brackets here and in several other places. But the contradiction of Sir Robert Phillimore's remark—that the suggestion to alter the Rubric was made by "the House of "Lords"—is really unworthy of the Court; for what is the exact fact? It is thus stated by Cardwell:—

"On the 1st of March, 1641 [i.e. 1640—1], the House of Lords appointed a committee consisting of ten Earls, ten Bishops, and ten lay-Barons, to 'take into consideration all innovations in the Church respecting religion.' On the 10th of the same month, they were empowered to associate with them as many learned Divines as they pleased, and Archbishop Usher, and Drs. Prideaux, Warde, Twisse, and Hacket, are particularly mentioned as selected for the purpose." (*Conferences*, p. 238, Edit. 1841. *Conf. Collier*, E. H., p. 799, who dates the appointment a few days later.)

The "suggestion" itself is then given by Cardwell (p. 274) under the heading "Proceedings of the Committee appointed "by the House of Lords." To say, as the Judicial Committee does, that "it did not emanate from the House of Lords," is surely not more strictly accurate than the words of the Court below; for proposals made by a Committee of Peers appointed by the House of Lords may not improperly be said to "emanate" from that House. However, "the suggestion," whether made by the Lords' Committee, or laid before them by others, as may have been the case, clearly proves this—that 37 years after the Canons of 1604, which are assumed by the Court to have prohibited certain Ornaments of the Minister, all the Vestments "which were used 2 Edward VI" were regarded as then "com-"manded" by the Rubric of 1604 which, on that account, they thought should "be mended." The observation of the Judicial Committee, that the suggestion was never "adopted by" the House of Lords, if of any importance here, is an argument against the Court's statement—"that the Rubric of James, " which was objected to, was amended after the suggestion."

XX. In order to sustain this theory of an *amended* Rubric their Lordships go on to state that:—

> "From the passing of the Act of Uniformity there is abundant evidence to show that the vestments in question were not used at all. Their Lordships may refer to the various Visitation Articles published in the Second Report of the Ritual Commission and elsewhere, as showing that the surplice alone was to be used, and that deviations from that rule were on the side of defect, and not in the direction of returning to the vestments of the Mass. Some of these Articles were published by Bishop Cosin and others who took part in the revision of the Prayer Book. In the 6th Article Bishop Cosin inquires 'have you a large and decent surplice (one or more) for the minister to wear at all times of his publick ministration in the church?' (2 Ritual Commission, 601, *a*.) This repetition of the words 'at all times of his ministration,' the exact words of the Rubric, is very significant as a contemporaneous exposition of it by one of its framers."

It was needless for their Lordships to remove an *imaginary* obstacle to their argument, for, so far as I am aware, no one has advocated the lawfulness of "the Vestments in question" on the ground that they *were used* after 1662; although it may not be necessary absolutely to accept the assertion* that "there is abundant evidence to show that the Vestments

---

* The following Correspondence is an instance of the use of the ALB 100 years ago, and, therefore, *refutes* their Lordships'. assertion: indeed it is an obvious fallacy to suppose that the "evidence" to which they refer could sustain the inference which they draw from it, for it would be equivalent to saying—that nothing was used which was not mentioned in Visitation Articles; which is absurd. It is very likely that if the Ritual Commission had instituted the Inquiries which were proposed to. it (See 4th Report, pp. 65, 68, 69 and 139) other evidence would have been obtained similar to the following:—

The Guardian (Supplement) July 5, 1871. "The Rev. W. Frank Shaw sends us this 'vestment' note:—'The following extract from the churchwarden's accounts of this parish (Bledlow, Bucks) for the year 1771-2 may interest some of your readers, as showing the use of the alb in a country parish so recently as towards the close of the last century.

"'Paid him (*i.e.* the clerk) for washing the tablecloth, napkins, the surplice and *the alb* . . . . 0 7s. 0d.'

"The entries are made in a very clear and distinct hand, leaving no room for misinterpretation."

In *The Guardian (Supplement)*, July 26, 1871, the statement was thus questioned:—

"'W. M.' suggests that 'the alb mentioned in the Bledlow book (Table-Talk, 5th July) in 1771 is the white dress long worn by the clerk in parish churches, being a surplice without sleeves, or rochette. If further search were made in the book there would probably be found an entry:—'Linen for an alb for the clerk, so many shillings,' or more probably 'for altering the old surplice into an alb for the clerk, so many pence.'"

To which Mr. Shaw replied in *The Guardian*, August 2, 1871. "Sir—In reference to 'W. M.'s' suggestion in this week's 'Table Talk,' that 'the alb mentioned in the Bledlow book in 1771 is the white dress long worn by the clerk in parish churches, being a surplice without sleeves, or rochette,' I would merely remark that not only are there no such entries as he imagines would be found concerning the making of an *alb* for the clerk or the turning of an old surplice into an alb for him, but that constant mention is made of the alb from 1771 to 1783 (when the book from which I quote concludes), and in no single instance is any hint given of its being for the use of the clerk : whilst in an inventory of books, utensils, and ornaments of the Church 'exhibited at the parochial visitation of the Rev. and Worshipful Mr. Archdeacon Heslop, holden here the 19 of May, 1783,' a clear distinction is drawn between the alb for the Priest and the surplice without sleeves for the clerk in the following entry, which is the only one relating to vestments in the Inventory of Articles, 'many of which had been long in use, and others were provided against the Visitation.'

"'An alb, a short surplice for funerels [*sic*] and another for the clark without sleaves [*sic*], 0 15 0.'

"I must apologise for the length of this note, but merely wished to show *you* that I was right in my original assertion that some hundred years ago the alb was one of the vestments used by the Priest (John Davey, D.D.) in this parish.

"W. FRANK SHAW.

"Bledlow Vicarage, Tring, Bucks: July 28, 1871."

This evidence is the more valuable as showing that the *use* of the ALB was recognized by Ecclesiastical Authority as lawful in 1783.

"in question were not used at all": the only contention, I believe, has been that, though disused, they were and are *legally usable* by the Rubric; and this was the opinion of the same Court in 1857. But the citation of the Visitation Articles in the 2nd Ritual Report to prove "that "the surplice alone was to be used" is, I humbly submit, a summoning of witnesses who, to say the least, must be embarrassing to the Court when they are cross-examined: one inference which the Court derives from their testimony is— "that deviations from that rule were on the side of defect"; yet this "defect" itself furnishes the reason for the explicit and stringent direction to use the surplice, though indeed there is not a single word in any of these Inquiries, so far as I know, which even implies that this Vestment "alone" might be used. The great difficulty of that time was to overcome the indifference or opposition of large numbers of the Clergy to wear *any* prescribed Vesture whatever; as the following instances show:—

1662. Cosin (Bishop of Durham), III, 4.—" Doth he alwaies . . . . constantly wear the surplice. . . . . And doth he never omit it?" (2 *Rit. Report*, p. 601.)
1662. Pory (Archdeacon of Middlesex), 12.—" . . . . doth the Parson . . . . use the same [surplice] as oft as he officiates . . . . in the Congregation?" (*Ib.*, p. 625.)
1662. Quarles (Archdeacon of Nottingham), III.—" . . . . doth he at every time . . . wear the surplice . . . ?" (*Ib.*, p. 630.)
1670. Hammond (Archdeacon of Huntingdon), II., 4.—" Doth he . . . . constantly wear the surplice . . . ?" (*Ib.*, p. 637.)
1674. Pearson (Bishop of Chester), II., 5.—" . . . . doth he make use of the surplice . . . ?" (*Ib.*, p. 642.)
1679. Barlow (Bishop of Lincoln), II., 4.—" . . . . doth he make use of the surplice . . . ?" (*Ib.*, p. 645.)
1679. Gunning (Bishop of Ely), 18.—" Doth your minister always . . . . constantly wear the surplice . . . ?" (*Ib.*, p. 649.)

Moreover, this laxity or repugnance was but the continuation of the same obstacles to Rubrical conformity which had increasingly manifested themselves for nearly a century before the Rubric of 1662, and which unquestionably had not been weakened during the Commonwealth: the annexed extracts illustrate this :—

1569. Parker (Archbishop of Canterbury), III.—"Whether youre prestes, curates, or ministers do use in the time of the celebration of divine service to weare a surples, prescribed by the Quene's Majestie's Injunctions [*i.e.*, the *Interpretations* of them—See p. 20.] and the boke of Common Prayer." (*Cardwell, D. A.* I., p. 356.)

1570-74 *cir.* Cox (Bishop of Ely).—". . . . whether any licensed to serue any Cure, do not weare at the celebration of the diuine seruice and sacramentes a comely surplesse, and obscrueth all other rightes and orders prescribed in the booke of Common prayer, and the Quecnes maiesties Iniunctions, and in the booke of Aduertisements." (2nd *Rit. Report*, p. 407.)

1578. Sandys (Archbishop of York), 3.—"Whether your Person, Vicar, or Curate, at all tymes in saying the Common Prayer upon sundayes and holydays, and in administering of the Sacraments, doth use and weare the surples, yea or no? or doe suffer any other to saye the common prayer, or minister either of the Sacraments in your Church, not wearing the same?" (*Ib.*, p. 422.)

1599. King (Archdeacon of Nottingham), 9.—". . . . whether doth your minister in time of divine service and at the ministration of the Sacramentes alwaies use and weare the Surplesse . . . . ?" (*Ib.*, p. 435.)

1601. Bancroft (Bishop of London), 4.—"Whether doth your Parson, vicar, or curate read publike praier and administer the Sacraments ordinarily himself . . . . and generally whether doth he . . . . eyther upon Sundaies holidaies wednesdaies and fridaies weare a surplice." (*Ib.*, p. 436.)

1603. Thornborough (Bishop of Bristol), 10.—"Whether at any time and during the whole celebration of divine service and ministration of the Sacraments, in everic your churches, your Parson, Vicar, or Curate doth weare a surplice, according to the Lawes and statutes of this Realme of England in that behalf provided, and howe often default hath beene heerin, and by whom." (*Ib.*, p. 440.)

⁎⁎* It is important to notice that "the Lawes and Statutes of the Realme" are here cited as the authority for the Inquiry: the Bishop's question in No. 19, whether the Elizabethan Injunctions are read quarterly, shews that his Articles are earlier than the Canons of 1603-4; for, *e.g.*, Archbishop Bancroft in 1605 (*Ib.*, p. 450) and Bishop Babington in 1607 (*Ib.*, p. 453) ask whether the Canons of 1603-4 are read in Church.

1604. Chaderton (Bishop of Lincoln), 14.—". . . whether your minister at all times upon Sundaies and holidaies doe weare in time of divine service and administration of the Sacraments, the surplesse, yea or no, or doe suffer any other to saie the common praier, or minister either of the Sacraments in your Church not wearing the same." (*Ib.*, p. 447.)

1607. Babington (Bishop of Worcester), 3.—". . . . whether doth your minister duly observe . . . . the saide booke of Common Prayer, ... wearing the surplesse as by the booke of Common Prayer by law now established is injoyned?" (*Ib.*, p. 453.)

1608. [Jegon ?] (Archdeacon of Norfolk), 15.—" If you minister saying publicque prayers or ministring the Sacraments weare not a comely surplice. . . . ?" (*Ib.*, p. 458.)

1615. Sharpe (Archdeacon of Berks), 8.—". . . . whether doth your minister in time of divine service and at the ministration of the Sacraments alwaies use and weare the Surplisse?" (*Ib.*, p. 469.)

1619. Overall (Bishop of Norwich). *Tit.* iv., 3.—" Whether doth your Minister alwaies, and at everie time both morning and evening, reading Divine Service, and administering the Sacraments, and other Rites of the Church, weare the Surplice according to the Canons, and doth he never omit wearing of the same at such times." (*Ib.* p. 482.)

1620. Harsnett (Bishop of Norwich). *Tit.* ii., 8.—" Whether doth your Minister alwaies and at every time, both morning and evening, reading Divine Service, and administring the Sacraments, weare the Surplice, and doth he never omit the wearing of the same, at such times or at any of them." (*Ib.*, p. 485.)

1625. Andrews (Bishop of Winchester). 8.—" Whether doth he in the time of Divine Service, weare a Surplice, both morning and evening; and never omit the same in ministering the Sacraments, and other Rites of the Church." (*Ib.* p. 494.)

1627. Cosin (Archdeacon of the East Riding in York). II. 14.— " Doth he in the time of public and Divine Service, as well morning and evening, and at all other times of his ministration, when any Sacrament be administered, or any other rite or ceremony of the Church solemnized, use and wear the Surplice, without any excuse or pretence whatsoever? And doth he never omit the same?" (*Works, Ang. Cath. Lib.*, ii., p. 9.)*

II., 40.—"If any such lecturer be in your parish, doth he twice at the least in every year read morning and evening prayer in the lower pulpit, the Litany in the midst of the Church, the latter Service at the communion-table, all distinctly and reverently two several Sundays, publicly, in his Surplice?" (*Ibid*, p. 14.)

II., 41.—" Doth he twice a year at least, administer the Sacraments of Baptism and the Lord's Supper, in such order, words, rites, and ceremonies only as are prescribed in the church-book, and no otherwise, still wearing the Surplice?" (*Ibid*, p. 15.)

The following are from Cosin's Articles of the same date printed "from the original MS., in Cosin's hand-writing," in a volume of Bishop Cosin's Correspondence, &c., published in 1869, by the Surtees Society.†

---

* The Editor, in the Preface to this Volume, says—that these Articles "are transcribed from the original manuscript preserved in the Bishop's library at Durham. Although dated in 1627, the draft was framed in 1626. It would appear to have been intended for the Press: but if printed, no copy has reached the Editor's notice."

† The Rev. George Ornsby, who Edited this volume, says, p. 106—"The manuscript from which these Articles are printed is a rough draft, with many

Cap. IV., 27.—" Doth he not only sometimes weare, or usually weare, but always weare, and never omit the wearing of a Surplice, when he readeth Divine Service, either Morning or Evening, or when he administereth the Sacraments, and performeth any other part of his priestly or ministeriall function in the Church?" (*Correspondence, Surtees Society*, I., p. 113.)

Cap. VII., 8.— " Doth he use the whole forme of prayers appointed for the celebration of this Holy Mysterie, and none other, or otherwise than the Book hath ordered the same? Doth he at any time (or the Minister assisting him) administer the same without a Surplice faire and cleane upon him?" (*Ibid*, p. 118.)

Cap. VIII., 4.—" . . . Hath he his Surplice upon him when he doth at any time solemnize a marriage?" (*Ibid*, p. 119.)

Cap. X., 1.—" Whether doth your Minister burie the dead according to the full forme, manner, and rites, prescribed in the Book, meeting the corps at the Church-stile, and in his Surplice?" (*Ibid*, p. 119.)

Cap. XI., 1.—" Doth your Minister duly observe the order and forme prescribed in churching of women after child-birth? Is the same done publikely and reverently in the Church, the woman coming in that decent and grave attire which hath bin accustomed, and the Minister attending in his Surplice?" (*Ibid*, p. 120.)

Cap. XII., 1.—" . . . And in performance herof [the Commination Service] doth he weare his Surplice, as at this and at all other times of executing his office in the Church he is bound and commanded to doe?" (*Ibid*, p. 121.)

1628. Neile (Bishop of Winchester). 18.—" Whether doth your Minister alwaies in saying the publike prayers and administring the Sacraments weare a decent Surplice with sleeves. . . . " (*2nd Rit. Report*, p. 504.)

1629. Potter (Bishop of Carlisle). 8.—" Whether doth your Minister usually weare the Surplesse whilst he is saying the publike prayers, and ministring the Sacraments . . . ." (*Ib.*, p. 506.)

1629. Eland (Archdeacon of Bedford). 15.—" Whether doth your Minister alwaies in saying the publike prayers, and administering the Sacraments, weare a decent Surplesse with sleeves. . . . " (*Ib.*, p. 510.)

1632. White (Archdeacon of Norfolk). 15.—" Doth your Minister alwaies in sayinge the publike prayers and administring the Sacraments weare a decent surplice with sleeves . . . . ?" (*Ib.*, p. 531.)

1633. Lindsell (Bishop of Peterborough). 8.—" Whether doth the Minister, reading Divine Service, and administring the Sacra-

---

interlineations and alterations. It is on loose sheets, and the second part, if it ever existed, is lost. Whether Cosin ever propounded his Visitation Articles, as regarded the Clergy, in the form here given, or whether he eventually decided upon giving them in the more condensed shape in which they appear as printed in his Works, (*Ang. Cath. Lib.*) vol. ii., p. 1, it is of course impossible to say. Their minuteness and particularity render them, at all events, well worthy of preservation."

ments, and other rites of the Church, alwayes weare the Surplice; and doth he never at such times omit the wearing of the same? . . . ." (*Ib.*, p. 539.)

1636. Wren (Bishop of Norwich). 8.—" . . . and doth he, in performing all and every of these [the offices in the Prayer Book], weare the Surplice duly, and never omit the wearing of the same. . . . .?" (*Ib.*, p. 559.)

1636. Pearson (Archdeacon of Suffolk). *Tit.* v., 2.—" Whether doth your Minister alwaies, *viz.*, every Sunday and Holy-day, both Morning and Evening reading Divine Service, and administring the Sacraments, and other Rites of the Church, weare the Surplesse, according to the Canons, and doth hee never omit the wearing therof at the times aforesaid? If at any time he have omitted, specifie the times." (*Ib.* p. 570.)

1638. Montague (Bishop of Norwich). *Tit.* v., 16.—" Doth your Minister officiate Divine Service in one place, upon set times, in the habit and apparel of his order, with a Surplice, an Hood, a Gown, a Tippet; not in a Cloak, or sleevelesse Jacquet, or horseman's coat? for such I have known." (*Ib.* p. 582.)

1639. Pearson (Archdeacon of Suffolk). v., 5.—" . . . doth he in performing all and every of them [the Services], weare the Surplice duely, and never omit the wearing of the same. . . . .?" (*Lawful Church Ornaments*, p. 394.)

1640. Juxon (Bishop of London). 12.—" . . . . doth the Parson, Vicar, or Curate, use the same [Surplice], as oft as he officiates God's publike Service administreth the Sacraments, or dischargeth any publike duty in the Congregation." (*2nd Rit. Report*, p. 589.)

N.B.—Juxon's Articles are those provided and ordered by Can. 9. 1640.

1640. Bostock (Archdeacon of Suffolk). v., 5.—" . . . doth he [your Minister] in performing all and every of these [Offices of the Prayer Book], weare the Surplice duely, and never omit the wearing of the same . . . . ?" (*Ib.* p. 597.)

Now, looking at the language of all these Articles from 1569 to 1640, and comparing them with those of 1662 to 1679, it seems to me perfectly plain that they alike present the same history, namely,—(1) That the Statute and Rubric of 1559 made a general Law for the Ornaments of the Church and of the Ministers (the Court itself says that they " together seem " to restore for the present the Ornaments of the Minister which " the Second Prayer Book of King Edward had taken away ") (2) That this Law was retained in the Prayer Book of 1604 and continued until the Revision of 1661 (even on the showing of the Judicial Committee who say that " the Rubric [of James] " had been in force for nearly 60 years ") when the Puritans at the Savoy Conference asked that it might "be wholly left "out"; (3) That the same Law was re-enacted in 1662 (at all events in the common opinion* of standard Writers and Authorities subsequent to that date); But (4) That in this

---

* 1708.—BENNET, THOMAS. "[As for the Second Rubric] 'tis notorious that by those Ornaments of the Church, and of the ministers thereof, at all times of their Ministration, which were in this Church by the Authority of Parliament, in the second year of King Edward the Sixth, we are to understand such as were prescrib'd by the first Common Prayer Book of that Prince." (*Paraphrase on the Book of Common Prayer*, p. 2; 2nd Ed., 1709. Cited by Stephens, Book of Common Prayer, Eccl. Hist. Society, 1849, vol. i., p. 351.) But the statement, as quoted by Dr. Stephens, is somewhat qualified by the context, for Bennet, referring to the Rubrics of 1549 and 1559, says "From hence it seems to follow, that the present Rubric, and that of Queen Elizabeth, which are in effect the same, do restore those ornaments, which were abolished by King Edward the Second's Book [he means the Second Book of King Edward], and which indeed have been disus'd ever since that time." And then he goes on to say that Elizabeth took "other order" in the "Advertisements" which he cites together with the Canons of 1571 and 1604; after which he adds "From hence 'tis plain, that the Parish Priests (and I take no notice of the case of others) are obliged to no other ornaments, but surplices and hoods. For these [the Advertisements and Canons] are authentic Limitations of the Rubric, which seems to require *all* such ornaments as were in Use in the second year of King Edward's reign. Besides, since from the beginning of Queen Elizabeth's Reign down to our own times, the Disuse of 'em has most notoriously been allow'd; therefore, tho' it were not strictly reconcilable with the Letter of the Rubric, yet we cannot be suppos'd to lie under any obligation to restore the use of them. And indeed, if that Practice which our Governors do openly and constantly permit and approve, be not admitted for a good Interpretation of Laws, whether Ecclesiastical or Civil: I fear, it will be impossible to clear our hands of many other Repugnancies, of different kinds, besides this now under debate." (Pages 2 to 7, Ed. 1708 and 1709.) The sum of Bennet's argument is —that the Rubric remains in its fulness, but that the strictness of its requirements are authoritatively dispensed with. This is not, however, the view of the Judicial Committee.

1710.—NICHOLLS, WILLIAM.—" Primo Elizabethæ [c. 2, Sect.] xxv.

"*Ornaments.*] This Clause as to Ornaments seems to be restrain'd to the Person of Queen *Elizabeth*, and she making no Alteration in them, they remained at her Death the same as they were in the 2nd of *Edw.* 6. See the Rubric immediately preceding the Morning Service in the Common Prayer Book, confirm'd by 14, C. 2, c. 4, where the Ornaments appointed for that Service, are enjoyned as they were in the 2nd of *Edw.* 6. (*Que.* If the ancient Ornaments and no other, ought not to be used at this Day ?)

"*Rule for the Ornaments of Churches and Ministers.*

"*Ornaments of the Church, and the Ministers thereof.*] It being here said, *That the Ornaments of the Church, and the Ministers thereof, at all Times of their Ministration, shall be retained, and be in use, as were in this Church, by the Authority of Parliament, in the Second year of King Edward VI;* but no Ornaments particularly mention'd; it is necessary to enquire, What they are ? If we have Recourse to that Act, we shall find it there enacted, '*That all and singular Ministers, in any Cathedral or Parish-Church, &c., shall, after the Feast of Pentecost next coming, be bounden to say the Mattens, Evening-Song, &c., and the Administration of the Sacraments, and all the Common and Open Prayer,* in such Order and Form, *as is mentioned in the said Book* (viz. First Book of Edward VI) *and not other, or otherwise.* So that by this Act, we are sent to enquire into

case (as in other Rubrics* whose meaning is unquestioned and unquestionable) the Authorities of the Church, with the active or passive sanction of the State, were compelled by the course of events to dispense† with the larger requirements of the

the Rubricks of King *Edward's* first Common-Prayer-Book, for the Habits in which Ministers are to Officiate. And among them we find these Rules. That *in the Saying or Singing of Mattens and Evening Song,' &c.*
"*And whensoever the Bishop shall celebrate the H. Communion in the Church,*" *&c.* " But in the Rubrick of King *Edward's* Second Common-Prayer-Book, confirmed likewise by Act of Parliament, the *Cope and Pastoral Staff* are omitted; and therefore were not used by the Bishops, either since the Restoration, or all along Q. *Elizabeth's* Time, that I can find: Tho' in Queen *Elizabeth's* Act of Uniformity, there is likewise Reference made to the Act of the 2 of K. Edw. VI. *Provided always, and be it enacted, That such Ornaments of the Church, and of the Ministers thereof, shall be retained,*" *&c.* " To which this Clause is further added; *Until further Order shall be therein taken,*" *&c.* "Which last Clause, whether it be a Qualification personally Empowering this Queen, and dying with her; or declarative only of the Regal Power, antecedently inherent in her, and derivable upon her Successors; has afforded Matter of much Dispute." (*Commentary on the Book of Common Prayer*, 1st Ed., 1710, and 2nd Ed., 1712.)

1710.—WHEATLY, CHARLES. "By the Ornaments of the Church and of the Ministers thereof mentioned in the Second part of this Rubric it is plain from the Rubric itself we are to understand such as were prescribed by the first Common Prayer Book of Edward the Sixth. As for the Ornaments of the Church viz. the Communion Cloth &c. prescribed by that Book [not *nominatim*] I shall say nothing of them here as having an occasion to treat of them hereafter. As for the Ministerial Ornaments Surplices are prescribed for all Ministers whatsoever and Graduates are therewith to use such hoods as pertain to their several degrees, and Bishops besides these are to have Rochets Copes Pastoral Staves. But most of these things are now discontinued and none of them in general use but the Surplice and therefore I shall only offer a few words in vindication of that." (*A rational illustration of the Book of Common Prayer*, 1st Ed., 1710, p. 32.)

1720.—IBID. "SECT. IV. *Of the Ministerial Ornaments.* The second part of this rubric is concerning the *ornaments of the Church, and the ministers thereof, at all times of their ministrations:* and to know what they are, we must have recourse to the Act of Parliament here mentioned, viz. *in the second year of the reign of King Edward the Sixth;* which enacts, That *all and singular Ministers, in any Cathedral or Parish-church, &c. shall, after the feast of Pentecost next coming, be bounden to say the Mattens, Evening Song, &c. and the administration of the Sacraments, and all the common and open Prayer, in such order and form as is mentioned in the said book,* (viz. first book of Edward VI.,) *and not other or otherwise.* So that by this Act we are again referred to the first Common Prayer-book of King Edward VI. for the habits in which ministers are to officiate; where there are two rubrics relating to them, one prescribing what habits shall be worn *in all public ministrations* whatsoever, the other relating only to the habits that are to be used *at the Communion.* The first is in the last leaf of the book, and runs thus:

---

* *e.g.* The order to use the Athanasian Creed; the Notice and Observance of Holy-days; the Weekly Communion in Cathedrals; public Catechising in Church; and the Commination Service.

† Compare the remarks of Bishop Mant in his Notes on the Rubric (See p. 116.)

Statute; and could only with extreme difficulty, by means of Regulations, none of which had the force of the Acts of Uniformity, secure a partial compliance with the Rubric, and even failed to do that in numerous cases.

"*In the saying or singing of Mattens; or Even-song, Baptizing and Burying, the Minister in Parish-churches and Chapels annexed to the same shall use a Surplice. And in all Cathedral Churches and Colleges, Archdeacons, Deans, Provosts, Masters, Prebendaries, and Fellows, being Graduates, may use in the Choir, besides their Surplices, such Hoods as pertain to their several degrees which they have holden in any University within this Realm, but in all other places every Minister shall be at liberty to use any Surplice or no. It is also seemly that Graduates, when they do preach, should use such Hoods as pertaineth to their several Degrees.*

"*And whenever the Bishop shall celebrate the holy Communion in the Church, or execute any other public ministration; he shall have upon him, besides his Rochette, a Surplice, or Alb, and a Cope, or Vestment, and also his Pastoral Staff in his hand, or else borne or holden by his Chaplain.*

"The other rubric that relates to the habits that are to be worn by the minister *at the Communion,* is at the beginning of that office, and runs thus :

"*Upon the day, and at the time appointed for the ministration of the holy Communion, the Priest that shall execute the holy ministry, shall put upon him the Vesture appointed for that ministration, that is to say, a white Alb plain, with a Vestment or Cope. And where there be many Priests or Deacons, there so many shall be ready to help the Priest in the ministration, as shall be requisite. And shall have upon them likewise the Vestures appointed for the ministry, that is to say, Albes with Tunicles.*

"These are the ministerial ornaments enjoined by our present rubric. But because the Surplice is of the most general use, and what is most frequently objected against; I shall therefore speak more largely of that, and only give a short account of the rest."

Wheatly next proceeds to give an account of the different Vestments and of the Pastoral Staff, and then he continues thus :—

"These are the ministerial ornaments and habits enjoined by our present rubric, in conformity to the first practice of our church immediately after the Reformation; though at that time they were so very offensive to Calvin and Bucer, that the one in his letters to the Protector, and the other in his censure of the English Liturgy, which he sent to Archbishop Cranmer, urged very vehemently to have them abolished; not thinking it tolerable to have anything in common with the Papists, but esteeming everything idolatrous that was derived from them.

"However, they made shift to accomplish the end they aimed at, in procuring a farther reform of our Liturgy : for in the review that was made of it in the fifth of Edward VI. amongst other ceremonies and usages, these rubrics were left out, and the following one put in their place, viz.

"*And here it is to be noted, that the minister, at the time of the Communion, and at all other times in his ministration, shall use neither Alb, Vestment, or Cope; but being Archbishop or Bishop, he shall have and wear a Rochette; and being a Priest or Deacon, he shall have and wear a Surplice only.*

"But in the next review under Queen Elizabeth, the old rubrics were again brought into authority, and so have continued ever since; being established by the Act of Uniformity that passed soon after the Restoration."

"VIII. I must observe still farther, that among other ornaments of the church then in use, there were *two lights* enjoined by the injunctions of King Edward VI. (which injunctions were also ratified by the Act of Parliament here mentioned) to be set upon the altar, as a significant ceremony to represent the light which Christ's Gospel brought into the world. And this too was ordered

If, indeed, dispensations with positive Laws were unknown or unrecognised, a theory of their being resorted to in the case of the Ornaments Rubric might fairly be rejected; but, passing over any other examples, it is enough to say that many of the

by the very same injunction, which prohibited all other lights and tapers, that used to be superstitiously set before images or shrines, &c. And these lights, used time out of mind in the Church, are still continued in most, if not all, cathedral and collegiate churches and chapels, so often as divine service is performed by candle-light; and ought also, by this rubric, to be used in all parish churches and chapels at the same times.

" IX. To this section we might also refer the Pulpit-Cloth, Cushions, Coverings for the Altar, &c. And all other ornaments used in the Church, and prescribed by the first book of King Edward VI." (*A rational illustration of the Book of Common Prayer*, pp. 99—107; Oxford, 1810; containing " the Author's last corrections." The passages are the same in the fol. Ed. 1720.)

1713.—GIBSON, EDMUND (Bishop). "Until other order] Which *other* order (at least in the method prescribed by this Act [1 Eliz. c. 2, s. 25]) was never yet made; and therefore, *legally*, the ornaments of Ministers in performing Divine Service, are the same now as they were in 2 E. 6." (*Codex.* I., 363, Ed. 1713, or p. 297, Ed. 1761.)

1735.—SHARP, THOMAS (Archdeacon). ". . . . such ornaments of the church," &c. (*The Rubric in the Book of Common Prayer*, &c., p. 65. Oxford, 1834.) "There was one sentence . . . . authentic limitations of this rubrick." (*Ibid.* Cited *verbatim* by Bishop Mant. See p. 115.)

" It is true some disputes have been made concerning this power given her, whether it was only during her life, (as her powers in some other statutes of the same year are expressly limited,) or derivable upon her successors, and annexed to the crown. But this makes little difference in our present question. Her injunctions [which the *Advertisements* were not] have the sanction of that Parliament which granted her the said power, and the sanction too of the Act of Uniformity after the Restoration, which by this rubric now under consideration refers, according to the explanation now given of it, to her injunctions. [Yet see remarks on Bp. Mant (2), (3), and (4), p. 117.] But if, by the Act of Uniformity in the first year of her reign, there is a reservation of the said power to the crown, and it is derivable upon her successors, then it will follow further, that although such injunctions had not been set forth by her, yet we should have been secured in the present allowed usages concerning habits and ornaments: because it is a rule, that, wherever a discretionary power is left with our governors, a constant practice permitted, and for that reason supposed to be approved by them, is equivalent, by interpretation, to their command: of which more hereafter." (*Ibid*, p. 66.)

1746.—IBID. " And upon the fifty-eighth canon, which enjoins 'ministers reading divine service, and administering the sacraments, to wear surplices, and graduates therewithal hoods,' I need say the less, because it is superseded by the Rubric before the Common Prayer, in 1661, which is statute-law, and determines, that 'all the ornaments of the ministers, at all times of their ministration, shall be the same as they were by authority of Parliament in the second year of King Edward VI.' So that the injunction concerning the habits and ornaments of ministers, which is at the end of King Edward VI.'s first Service Book, with its explanation in the Act of Uniformity by queen Elizabeth, is the legal or statutable rule of our church-habits at this day: and is so far from being explained by this canon, that it rather serves to explain the canon itself: as I shall shew in an instance or two." He then mentions the surplice " in all other places " than " parish churches " and the " hood with the surplice

Canons of 1604, which are *Statutably* binding on the Clergy, have for a long period of years been entirely dispensed with by the Bishops, and, wisely, are not enforced, though Clergymen could of course act upon them if they wished. The 28th

'in parish churches'"; and, after some remarks upon these, concludes thus, "The whole truth of the matter is, that both the use of hoods, and disuse of copes and tunicles, are now so notoriously and universally allowed of by the ordinaries, that although neither of them could in strictness," &c. (*Ibid*, pp. 203—6. The remainder is cited by Bp. Mant. See p. 116.)

1763.—BURN, RICHARD, Dr. "1. By the 1 Eliz. c. 2, s. 25, 'Such ornaments of the church, and of the ministers thereof, shall be retained and be used, as was in the Church of England by authority of Parliament in the second year of the reign of King Edward VI., until other order shall be therein taken by the authority of the Queen's majesty, with the advice of her commissioners appointed and authorized under the great seal of England for causes ecclesiastical, or of the metropolitan of this realm.'

"*Other order.*]—Pursuant to this clause, the Queen in the third year of her reign, granted a commission to the Archbishop, Bishop of London, Dr. Bill, and Dr. Haddon, to reform the disorders of chancels, and to add to the ornaments of them, by ordering the Commandments to be placed at the east end. (*Gibs.* 201.)

"And by the rubric before the Common Prayer, 'Such ornaments of the Church, and of the ministers thereof, at all times of their ministration, shall be retained and be in use as were in this Church of England by authority of Parliament in the second year of the reign of King Edward VI.'" (*Eccl. Law*, vol. i., p. 367 *e*; 9th Ed., 1842.)

"By can. 58, 'Every minister saying the public prayers, or ministering the sacraments, or other rites of the church, shall wear a decent and comely surplice with sleeves,' &c.

"But this Canon (which is somewhat observable) is in part destroyed by the statute law, and by the rubric before the present common prayer.

"For by the 1 Eliz. c. 2, s. 25, it is provided, 'that such ornaments of the church, and of the ministers thereof, shall be retained and used,' &c. 'until other order shall be therein taken' &c. Which other order as to this matter was never taken.

"And by the rubric before the Common Prayer of the 13 & 14 Car. 2, 'It is to be noted, that such ornaments' &c.

"Therefore it is necessary to recur in this matter to the Common Prayer Book established by act of parliament in the second year of King Edward the Sixth: in which there is this rubric: 'In the saying or singing of *matens* and *evensonge baptizing* and *burying*, the minister in paryshe churches and chapels annexed to the same shall use a *surples*' &c.

"So that in marrying, churching of women, and other offices not here specified, and even in the administration of the holy communion, it seemeth that a surplice is not necessary. And the reason why it is not enioined for the holy communion in particular, is, because other vestments are appointed for that ministration, which are as followeth." He then quotes the Rubric from the Communion Office of 1549 " Upon the day," &c. (*Ibid*, iii. 437—8.)

1820.—MANT, RICHARD (Bishop). "*Such Ornaments of the Church, and of the Ministers thereof,* &c.] Without which, as common reason and experience teacheth us, the majesty of him that owneth it, and the work of his service there, will prove to be of a very common and low esteem. *Bp. Cosins.* [sic.]

"There was one sentence at the end of this rubrick, left out at the Restoration, which would have explained it more fully. The words were these, 'according

Canon which orders Copes in Cathedrals is a most pertinent instance; and hardly less so is the 74th, where "Decency in "Apparel" is "enjoined to Ministers," for unquestionably the Garments, which the Canon requires the Clergy to "usually

to the Act of Parliament set in the beginning of the book.' And these words will lead us to the proper limitation of this rubrick. For, if we look into the first Act of Uniformity by Queen Elizabeth, we shall find the words of this rubrick taken verbatim from that Act, and to be only a part of a clause whereby the Queen expressly reserved to herself a power of 'ordering both the ornaments of the church and of the ministers thereof' otherwise hereafter: which power she did afterwards actually make use of, though not perhaps just in the method prescribed in that Act, yet so effectually, that our habits 'at the times of our ministration' stand regulated by her injunctions to this day." (*Quoted verbatim from Archdeacon Sharp*, p. 65.)

"Now putting these things together, that the rubrick hath an immediate reference to the Act: and that the Act is made with an express reservation to the Queen's future appointments; and that the Queen, pursuant to this power given her, did, in the year 1564, publish her 'Advertisements,' as they are called, 'concerning the Habit of Ministers to be worn by them in time of divine service': it will appear that her injunctions thus set forth are authentic limitations of this rubrick." (*Ibid.*)

"The rubrick then, thus limited by the Queen's 'Advertisements' in 1564; and limited to the like sense by her Canons in the year 1571; as likewise by the 58th Canon of the year 1603, in the reign of her successor, King James the First; obliges the ministers of the Church, at the times of their parish ministration, to the use of no other ornaments but surplices, and hoods agreeable to their degrees." (*Ibid*, p. 204, *referring to Bennet*.)

"Since however some ritualists are of opinion, that this rubrick does not admit of the foregoing limitation, but is to be understood as still prescribing the use of all the ancient ministerial habits injoined by the First Book of King Edward the Sixth; it may be convenient to remark, that from the beginning of Queen Elizabeth's reign down to our times, the disuse of some of those ornaments has been, and is now, so notoriously and universally allowed of by the ordinaries; that, although it could not in strictness be reconciled with the letter of the rubrick, yet we are not bound, at this time, to make any alteration in our practice. For, whatever our governours in the Church do openly and constantly permit, and consequently by a fair construction approve of, whether it will be admitted as a good interpretation of Ecclesiastical laws or not, yet there is no doubt it is a sufficient dispensation for the continuance of the usage, till further order be taken therein; and more especially in all doubtful or disputable cases, the resolution of which is left to the ordinary. *Archdeacon Sharp, Dr. Bennet.*"* (*Ibid.*, p. 206, from "in strictness.")

Then follow two passages from *Cosin* and *Wheatly*, as to Altar-lights, Pulpit and Altar-clothes, &c. (*Common Prayer*, p. lxxi, 4th Ed., 1830.) See pp. 97 and 114.

There are some points in these remarks of Bishop Mant which require notice: thus (1) he says that "the words" of the Rubric of 1662 are "taken verbatim from" the Act of 1559. But the words "at all times of their ministration," in the Rubric, are not in the Act: no doubt the writer thought that, being in the Rubric of 1559 (though in a varied form, viz. "at the time of the communion, and at all other times in his ministration"), they were *practically* in the Act because the Rubric referred to it. In that case (if he were writing now) he

---

* Upon which Dr. Stephens remarks—"The irresistible answer to Bishop Mant's argument is this, that neither the 'Governors in the Church' nor 'usage' can supersede the positive enactments of the Statute Law." (*Notes on the Bk. of Com. Prayer*, I., 367.)

"wear" "hoping that in time newfangleness of apparel in some "factious persons will die of itself," have been but little seen during the last 100 years.

It is to be regretted that the Court, in speaking of "devia-

must have coincided with the Judicial Committee of 1857 who decided that all the Rubrics and the Act "obviously mean the same thing," and he must have dissented from the Judicial Committee of 1871 who said that the words "at all times of their ministration" are an *alteration* of the Rubric.

(2) Bishop Mant seems to have overlooked the fact that the words "according to the Act of Parliament" &c. could not have been retained "at the Restoration," at least in that form, because the Ecclesiastical Commission had ceased to exist.

(3) If in saying "that the Rubric hath an immediate reference to the Act" he means the Rubric of 1662, he is clearly in error; and therefore his inference, as to the Advertisements being now (if he means now) "authentic limitations" of it, is unsound. Also if he calls them "injunctions" in a *technical* sense, it is a misnomer.

(4) It cannot be true to say that the Rubric of 1559 was "limited to the like sense [of "the Queen's 'Advertisements' in 1564"] by her Canons in the year 1571," because those Canons never received the Royal Assent; probably, in part, as I have argued at p. 82, because of the attempt in one of them to *limit* the vestments to "onely that linnen garment [*i.e.* probably the surplice], which is as yet retained by the Queene's commandment." If these words were intended to refer to the Advertisments, the apparent claim of *Royal* authority for them may have been a further ground of opposition by the Queen, considering the course she had taken respecting them.

(5) The Bishop, in the last paragraph, recognizes the contrary opinion which rejects the legal "limitation" theory; and he is content with what he regards as "a sufficient dispensation" by Authority from the "strictness" of "the letter of the Rubric." This view is most reasonable and is, in fact, commonly held by those who have felt themselves at liberty under the Rubric to revive the use of the Vestments which it prescribes.

1832.—PALMER, WILLIAM. "The Rubric of the English ritual, which immediately precedes the office for morning prayer, contains the following words relative to the ornaments of the church and ministers: 'And here it is to be noted'" &c. "This refers to the Act of Uniformity, passed in that year, authorizing 'the Book of Common Prayer,' &c. And that book contains the following directions relative to the subject; which, for the sake of clearness, I shall compare with the version of Alese, who translated the English ritual into Latin immediately after it was published in 1549." Then follow the various Rubrics of the First Prayer-book relative to the Vestments. (*Origines Liturgicæ*, II., p. 396, 4th Ed., 1845.)

1843.—JEBB, JOHN, Dr., (*The Choral Service*, &c.,) has a chapter on "the Ornaments of the Church, and of the ministers thereof," in which, after mentioning other things, "The Vestment and Cope," he says:—

"The Cope, or the Vestment, specially prescribed to be used by the Clergy administering the Holy Communion, by the regulation referred to in the Rubric, and expressly ordered to be used in the Cathedral Churches by the twenty-fourth Canon, has now fallen into almost total disuse, being retained only at Westminster Abbey, at coronations, when all the Prebendaries are vested in Copes, as well as the Prelates who then officiate. The ancient Copes, used till some time in the last century, still exist at Durham; and at Westminster, as tradition informs us, they were used till about the same time. We have sufficient evidence from documents, that not only in Cathedrals, but also in the University Colleges, &c., they were in common use till at least the Great Rebellion.

"The Vestment and Cope were ignorantly objected to by many after the

"tions" from (what they deem) the "rule" of "the Surplice "alone," should have said that they were "not in the direction "of returning to the Vestments of the Mass": their Lordships must have known that the expression was calculated to arouse or deepen opposition to Vestures which were expressly provided for use in the first *Reformed* Communion Office.

The Court attaches great importance to Bishop Cosin's use of the words "at all times of his ministration," in his 6th Visitation Article of 1662, and says that "this repetition of"

Reformation, as Popish Ornaments. It is sufficiently well known that these as well as the other ecclesiastical garments retained, or enjoined by our Church, were common also to the Eastern Church, and were as ancient as any ritual record now extant; that they are Catholic and Anglican, and therefore ought to be retained.

"I must honestly acknowledge, that I can find no argument to justify the disuse of these ancient vestments, so expressly enjoined by authorities to which all Clergymen profess obedience, except that rule of charity, which, as Bishop Beveridge expressed it, is above rubrics; that loving regard for the edification of the people, to which every rite and ceremony should tend. . . ." (p. 216.)

1844.—PHILPOTTS, HENRY (Bishop of Exeter), after citing the Rubrics of 1549 and 1552, the changes under Mary, Elizabeth, and Charles II., says:—"From this statement it will be seen, that the surplice may be objected to with some reason [in the Communion Service]; but then it must be because the law requires 'the albe, and the vestment, or the cope,'

"Why have these been disused? Because the parishioners—that is, the churchwardens, who represent the parishioners—have neglected their duty to provide them; for such is the duty of the parishioners by the plain and express canon law of England. (Gibson, 200.) True, it would be a very costly duty, and for that reason, most probably, churchwardens have neglected it, and archdeacons have connived at the neglect. I have no wish that it should be otherwise. But, be this as it may, if the Churchwardens of Helston shall perform this duty, at the charge of the parish, providing an albe, a vestment, and a cope, as they might in strictness be required to do, (Gibson, 201,) I shall enjoin the minister, be he who he may, to use them. But until these ornaments are provided by the parishioners, it is the duty of the minister to use the garment actually provided by them for him, which is the surplice. . . . ." (*Judgment, re* Walter Blunt, Oct. 23, 1844. Cited, Stephen's *Eccl. Stat.*, II., 2049 and Bk. of Com. Prayer, I., 377; also *Hierurgia Anglicana*, 1848, p. 388.)

1845.—STEPHENS, A. J., Dr. "Which *other* order (at least in the method prescribed by this Act [1 Eliz. c. 2, s. 25],) was never made; and therefore, legally, the Ornaments of Ministers in performing Divine Service are the same now as they were in the 2nd of Edward VI." (*Eccl. Stat.*, I., 370.)

1849.—*Ibid.* After noticing the Rubrics of 1549, 1552, and 1559, he says: "And this Rubric of 1559, slightly altered, was a second time authorized at the last review.

"Copes were worn at Durham and Westminster till the middle of the last century, and copes are worn now by the bishops at the coronations; indeed all directions contained in the first Book of Edward VI., as to the ornaments of the church and of the ministers thereof at all times of their ministration, are by Stat. 14, Car. II., c. 4, the Statute Law of the Anglican Church." (*Notes Legal and Historical on the Book of Common Prayer*, 1849, I. 367.)

"the exact words of the Rubric, is very significant as a "contemporaneous exposition" of the Rubric "by one of its "framers." As their Lordships wish to be *precise*, it may be observed that it is not *accurate* to call them "exact "words," for Cosin says "*publick* ministration." And it will be seen that *in almost every instance* above quoted, from 1569 to 1640, *substantially* though not *verbally* the same inquiry appears as that which Cosin made in 1662: there can be no *real* difference between Cosin's expression "at all times of his ministration," and that, e.g., of Archbishop Sandys (1578) "at all tymes in saying the Common

---

1845.—CRIPPS, H. W. After naming the Ornaments prescribed in the Provincial Constitutions he says—" It will be obvious, however, that the things here enumerated were not applicable to the reformed religion; an alteration consequently took place, and the goods and ornaments of the Church were settled by authority of Parliament in the year 1548, the second year of the reign of Edward VI." He then quotes *Burn*, including the passage, (see p. 115,) "And by the rubric," etc. (*The Law relating to the Church and Clergy*, 1st Ed., p. 416; and 3rd Ed., 1857, p. 434.)

"As to the habit to be worn by the officiating minister, there seems to be some slight, or it may be only an apparent, variance between the canon and the statute law. The Canon law directs, that every minister," &c. Then follows Can. 58. (See p. 127.)

"But in the rubric of the Common Prayer Book, established by act of parliament in the second year of Edward the Sixth, it is directed, that in saying or singing of matins and evensong, baptizing and burying, the minister in parish churches, and chapels annexed to the same, shall use a surplice," &c. (See p. 113.) This is the present statute law upon this subject. For by the 1 Eliz. c. 2, and also by the Rubric before the Common Prayer, which, as we have before seen, is a part of the statute law, it is directed that such ornaments of the church, and of the ministers thereof, shall be retained and used as were in the Church of England, by authority of parliament, in the second year of Edward the Sixth.

"Where the statute law is opposed to the canon law, the latter would seem to be null; and as the statute law has not mentioned the solemnization of marriage, or the churching of women, as occasions on which the surplice is to be worn, it was probably at that time considered optional; and although custom has now strongly sanctioned its use upon such occasions, it must be doubtful whether it could be legally enforced. The administration of the Holy Communion is omitted in this part of the rubrical directions from the occasions on which the surplice is to be used; but it is directed in another part of that same Prayer Book, that the vesture worn on such occasions shall be a plain white alb, with a vestment or cope. This alb differs very little from the surplice, being close-sleeved; and indeed in the same place, where directions are given for the habit of the bishop in officiating at the ministration of the communion, it is said that he shall have upon him, among other things, his surplice or alb. And a difficulty might consequently here arise, if custom should in any case be so far disregarded, as that a minister should take upon himself to adopt an alb instead of a surplice in the administering the Sacrament; for the alb is in fact the only habit which the strict letter of the law sanctions on such occasions. . . . . ." (*Ibid*, pp. 640—1; or pp. 705—6, 5th Ed., 1869.)

"Prayer upon Sundays and Holy-days, and in administering the "Sacraments," or that of Archdeacon King (1599) "in time of "divine service and at the Ministration of the Sacraments." Before 1662 the Rubric mentioned separately "the Commu- "nion" and "all other times in his Ministration"; consequently the Visitation Articles would probably adopt a like separate phraseology; Cosin, in fact, as Archdeacon in 1627, uses the words "at all other times of his ministration" (See p. 108): in 1662 both are combined in the words "all times of their Ministration," and so Cosin *might* naturally quote the new Rubric. But it is quite plain that he held the words of the old Rubric to mean exactly the same thing, for he says (see Note * p. 93) "And in "the same Rubric [of 1604] the Minister is appointed to use such "ornaments in the church, *and at all times in his ministrations.*" If, therefore, the inquiry for a Surplice *only*, in Visitation Articles prior to 1662 does not prove that Albe and Chasuble were then *illegal* (and the Court admits that they were not, See pp. 84 and 96), the like inquiry since that date cannot *of itself* condemn those Vestments, especially as *primâ facie* at least, the old Rubric was re-imposed in 1662.

There is, however, a further difficulty in accepting the conclusion which the Court draws from Cosin's 6th Visitation Article: the Court, in speaking of his "repetition of the "words 'at all times of his ministration,'" assumes what has to be proved, namely—that Cosin *did* quote the Rubric. But, judging from the internal evidence of the Articles themselves, they appear to have been drafted before the Prayer Book of 1662 was in use; for they make no reference to it: Cosin merely asks "have you two books of Common Prayer set forth "by public authority," (*Tit.* I., 5, 2nd *Rit. Report*, p. 601); whereas Bishop Henchman, in the same year, inquires for "the Book of Common Praier newly established and set "forth," (II., 1, *Ibid.*, p. 610), and Bishop Reynolds asks for "the Book of Common Prayer now established" (IV., *Ibid.*, p. 619). But further, Cosin asks for "the books or forms of Divine "Service for the Fifth of November, the Thirtieth of January "and of the Twenty-ninth of May": now if his Inquiries were *subsequent* to the Book of 1662 he *need* not have asked for these Services *separately*, for they were to be printed with the Book, according to the direction at the end of the MS. Book annexed to the Act of Uniformity (4th *Rit. Report*, p. 40*). Henchman and Reynolds, who did ask for the new Book, make no such inquiry: the former only asks whether the *days* are "observed and kept holy, according to the Order set forth "in that behalf?" (2nd *Rit. Report*, p. 612), and the latter enquires whether "doth he [the Minister] observe" them. (*Ib.*, p. 620.)†

Some time after writing this last paragraph I inquired of the Rev. George Ornsby, (the Editor of *The Surtees Society's* Volume of Bishop Cosin's Correspondence) whether he was aware of any information as to the true date of Cosin's Articles or of the Visitation at which they were used; for although they are dated " In the second year of his Consecration, *Anno* "*Dom.* 1662," the *first* year ended December 2, 1661; and,

* "The Forms of Prayer for ye v. of November, ye xxx of Januarie, and for ye xxix of May, are to be printed at ye End of this Book."

† It is right, however, to state that HACKET, Bishop of Lichfield, 1662, inquires "V. Have you in your Church the Common-Prayer Book of the largest Volume, set forth by Authority, with the books of Divine Service for the fifth of November, the thirtieth of January, and the nine and twentieth of May?" (*Ib.*, 608.) That he is referring to the Book of 1662 is plain from another inquiry—"III. Hath he read the Book of Common-Prayer, as it is injoyned by the late Act of Uniformity, for public Prayer, Administration of the Sacraments &c. on some Sunday before the four and twentieth of August last past?" (*Ib.*, 609.) The expression " with the Books " may mean that they formed part of the New Prayer-Book, according to the direction.

Also IRONSIDE, Bishop of Worcester, 1662, asks "1. . . . . Have you the Book of Common-Prayer, approved and commanded by the late Act of Parliament?" and he further inquires "6. Have you in your Church the Book of Divine Service, to be used upon the fifth of November, the Thirtieth of January, and the Nine and Twentieth of May?" (*Ib.*, 614.)

But GRIFFITH, Bishop of St. Asaph, 1662, asks "*First.* Have you the Common praier book?" (*Ib.*, 606); also "6. *Item*, Whether is the Fifth of November kept holy, and thanksgiving made to God, according to the Order set forth in that behalf." (*Ib.*, 608.) He does not ask about the two other days, nor about the Book of Service for the three days.

LAYFIELD, Archdeacon of Essex, 1662, inquires "3. Whether have you provided the Book of Common Prayer lately commanded by his Majesty's Authority onely to be used?" (*Ib.*, 622), and does not ask for the other Books.

PORY, Archdeacon of Middlesex, 1662, asks "13. Have you . . . . the Book of Common Prayer . . . . also . . . . A book of prayer for the 5 of November, and for the 30th of January, and the 29th of May?" (*Ib.*, 625.)

QUARLES, Archdeacon of Northampton, 1662, inquires "IV. Whether you have . . . . the Book of Common Prayer?" (*Ib.*, 630); and he asks "XXX. Are the fifth of November, the thyrtieth of January, and the twenty-ninth of May observed according as is ordained in that behalf?" (*Ib.*, 631); but he does not ask for the Books of Service for those days.

by Sect. xxxii. of the new Act of Uniformity, the new Prayer Book did not come into use until August 24, 1662. In reply to my questions Mr. Ornsby kindly furnished me with some Extracts from the *Mickleton MSS.* and other Documents which will appear in a *Second* Volume he is preparing for the same Society; they render it certain that these Visitation Articles were *prepared* in the latter part of 1661; at latest, apparently before February 25, 1661-2, the day on which the King sent the Revised Prayer Book to the House of Lords: for in a Letter from *R. Neile* (an attorney who was with Cosin in London and appears to have been acting as his Secretary and man of business) to *Miles Stapylton* (Bishop Cosin's Secretary, who was then in Durham), dated "London, March 4, 1661," *i.e.*, 1661-62 Old Style, he says, "I am now writing my "Lorde's Booke of Articles of Visitation for the presse, which "are very strict I assure you." (*Mickleton MSS.*) The date of this Letter is consistent with the imprint of the Articles, "*London:* "Printed by *T. Garthwait*, 1662." For as they were only being prepared "for the Presse" on the 4th March they are not likely to have been printed before the 26th; and this would be 1662. That the Visitation was also held before the new Prayer Book was in use is shewn by the two following extracts.

The *First* is from a Letter of DAVENPORT (*Chaplain to Bishop Cosin*) to SANCROFT (*Tanner*, MSS., xlviii., 12): he writes thus :—

"Auckland, Jun. 16th, 1662.—Sir, Yours of the 10th I received the 13th instant..... My Lord desires at all times to know particularly what progress you make in the Common Prayer, [this, no doubt, refers to the Printing of the Book, after the Bill for Uniformity had received the Royal Assent on May 19th, 1662.]....We are all well, and about 3 weeks hence are to goe into Northumberland to visitt the diocess, and at our return I guess the Assizes will be at hand.

"Your affectionate servant

"G[EORGE] D[AVENPORT]."

"For Dr. William Sandcroft,
&c., &c., &c.

The *Second* Letter (*Ibid.*, 19) is from *the same* to *the same:* the writer says :—

"Auckland, July 15th, 1662.—Sir, I have received two from you, one of July the 5th, at Newcastle, the other of the 8th, at Duresm, at our return on Friday last.....On Thursday we go to Durham, the Visitation being the day following for the Diocess, and on Saturday for the Church.......

"Your most affectionate servant
"For Dr. William Sandcroft, &c., &c., &c.
G. D."

It must be allowed, I think, that this evidence disposes of any argument based upon the supposition that Cosin's Articles of 1662 were *subsequent* to the enactment of the Rubric and so were "a contemporaneous exposition of it by one of its "framers." Perhaps it will be said that as Cosin had signed the MS. of the Revised Prayer Book on 20th December, 1661, he knew what the Rubric was to be, and framed his Article accordingly: but it is too much to suppose that the Judicial Committee would assume that the Bishop might have issued Visitation Articles based upon a Prayer Book which had to pass the ordeal of Parliament before it would become Statutably binding upon his Clergy, and so alter (if it did alter) the Rubric of 1604 which was then in force. Yet if Cosin had done so absurd a thing it would have been useless, for he could not have *legally* inquired until after St. Bartholomew's Day whether the Rubric (*altered* as the Judicial Committee alleges) was obeyed; not even in the case of any Incumbent who, by Section III. of the Statute, had, before that Feast, "publicly, and solemnly read the Morning and Evening Prayer ".... according to the" new "Book of Common Prayer....: "and after such reading thereof" had "openly and publicly, "before the Congregation" declared "his unfeigned assent and "consent to the use of all things in the said book contained and "prescribed," as in the form required by Section IV. However, the Letters just cited prove that Cosin's Visitation was held in the middle of July and shew, probably, that the printing of the New Prayer Book had not then been completed.

Their Lordships appear to hold that if an Ornament was not inquired for in these Articles, it was intended that it should not be used, though it might not be inconsistent with another Ornament which the Articles named. But the argument is self-destructive, for it would prove that, in all Churches, the Cassock and the Black Scarf or Stole, no less than the Cope in Parish Churches, were prohibited; unless it be contended that general and continuous usage would suffice, though indeed it would be very difficult to establish this in their favour. There is, however, another *prescribed* Ornament which is adverse to this argument: the Prayer Book of 1662 orders "a fair linen cloth" for covering the remains of the Sacrament: no such order occurs in the Books of 1552, 1559, and 1604; and it is notorious that the "Corporas," which was used for that purpose, disappeared in the general destruction of other Ornaments—hence, no doubt, the need of ordering it. Yet of all the 29 Sets of Visitation Articles after 1662, published in the 2nd Ritual Report (besides 11 others collated with them (*Ib.*, p. 615) only two inquire for this Ornament—viz., Bishop Gunning, 1679, who asks, " when all "have communicated, doth he cover what remaineth of the Conse- "crated Elements with a fair Linen Cloth?" (No. 9, p. 648,) also, "have you . . . a fair Linen Cloth for covering the Consecrated Elements?" (No. 5, p. 651); and Bishop Fleetwood, 1710, who says, " Have you . . . a fair Linnen Cloth to cover the "Consecrated Bread and Wine?" (No. 8, p. 673.) If the Judicial Committee are right in the inference they make from the *silence* of these Visitation Articles, then this *newly prescribed* Ornament was only lawful in the Dioceses of the two Bishops who asked whether it was used.

XXI. The following portion of the next passage in the Judgment does not call for any remark :—

> "These, then, are the leading historical facts with which we have to deal in the difficult task of construing the Rubric of Ornaments. The vestment or cope, alb, and tunicle were ordered by the first Prayer Book of Edward VI. They were abolished by the Prayer Book of 1552, and the surplice was substituted. They were provisionally restored by the Statute of Elizabeth, and by her Prayer Book of 1559."

These words, however, must not be passed over :—

> "But the Injunctions and the Advertisements of Elizabeth established a new order within a few

years from the passing of the Statute, under which chasuble, albe, and tunicle disappeared."

The Injunctions, as I have already shewn (See p. 20), did not make the slightest change in the Rubrical requirements as to these Vestments: the Episcopal "Interpretations" of them, as has also been pointed out there and at p. 25, limited the *required* "apparel" to "the Cope in the Ministration of the Lord's "Supper, and the Surplice in all other Ministrations": no doubt this so far "established a new order" that the Chasuble and Tunicle were *not needed:* but it did not touch the Albe, for no direction was given as to the garment to be worn under the Cope in the Communion Service, and therefore the Celebrant and his assistants (if any) were free to use with it Albe or Surplice, just as they could by the directions of the Prayer Book of 1549. The Advertisements also did not say what was to be worn with the Cope in Cathedrals, therefore they too did not interfere with the Albe there: though, in Parish Churches, by ordering the Surplice for Sacraments (as well as other Services) they implicitly made the Albe needless, though they did not *prohibit* the Cope. But of neither the Injunctions and their Interpretations, nor of the Advertisements, can it be correctly said that " under" them " chasuble, albe, and tunicle disappeared "; for, as the History already quoted (See pp. 21, 39, 45—8) shows, they were not the *causes* of their destruction.

Further, this next remark is contradicted by the Documents to which it refers:—

"The canons of 1603-4, adopting anew the reference to the Rubric of Edward VI, sanctioned in express terms all that the advertisements had done in the matter of the vestments, and ordered the surplice only to be used in parish churches."

What their Lordships mean by speaking of the Canons "adopting anew the reference to the Rubric of Edward VI" I am unable to make out; there is no such "reference." It is not true to say that the Canons sanctioned "all" the Advertisements ordered touching Vestments, as will be seen by placing them in parallel columns:—

CATHEDRALS &c.

Advertisements. | *Canons.*

"Item, In ministration of the holy communion in the cathedrall and collegiate churches, the principall minister shall use a cope with gospeller and epistoler agreably;*

and at all other prayers to be sayde at the Communion Table, to use no copes but surplesses."

"Item, That the deane and prebendaries weare a surplesse with a silk hoode in the quyer; and when they preache in the cathedrall or collegiate churche, to weare theire hoode." (*Cardwell, Doc. Ann.*, i., 326; Ed. 1844.)

XXIV. "In all Cathedral and Collegiate Churches, the holy Communion shall be administered upon principal Feast-days, sometimes by the Bishop, if he be present, and sometimes by the Dean, and at sometimes by a Canon, or Prebendary, the principal Minister using a decent Cope, and being assisted with the Gospeller and Epistler agreably, according to the Advertisements published *Ann.* 7 *Elizabethæ*: the said Communion to be Administered at such times, and with such limitation as is specified in the Book of Common Prayer. Provided, that no such limitation by any construction shall be allowed of, but that all Deans, Wardens, Masters, or Heads of Cathedral and Collegiate Churches, Prebendaries, Canons, Vicars, Petty-Canons, Singing men, and all others of the Foundation, shall receive the Communion four times yearly at the least."

XXV. "In the time of Divine Service and Prayers in all Cathedral and Collegiate Churches, when there is no Communion, it shall be sufficient to wear Surplices: Saving that all Deans, Masters and Heads of Collegiate Churches, Canons and Prebendaries, being Graduates, shall daily at the times both of Prayer and Preaching, wear with their Surplices such Hoods as are agreeable to their degrees."

* It has been questioned whether the word "agreably" means that the Gospeller and Epistoler were to wear Copes or Tunicles: the original form of this Article of the Advertisements appears to decide that Copes were at first intended, though the subsequent alteration of the language *may* imply that a choice was left, especially in cases where Tunicles remained. The first wording was as follows—"*Item*, In the mynistracion of the Communyon in cathedrall and collegiate churches, the Executor, with Pistoler and Gospeller, mynster the

PARISH CHURCHES, &c.

Advertisements.

"Item, That every minister, sayinge any publique prayers, or ministringe of the Sacramentes, or other rites of the churche, shall weare a comely surples with sleeves, to bee provided at the charges of the parishe . . . . "
(*Ibid.*)

Canons.

LVIII. "Every Minister saying the Publick Prayers, or ministring the Sacraments, or other Rites of the Church, shall wear a decent and comely Surplice with sleeves, to be provided at the charge of the Parish. And if any Question arise touching the Matter, Decency, or Comeliness thereof, the same shall be decided by the discretion of the Ordinary. Furthermore, such Ministers as are graduates, shall wear upon their Surplices at such times, such hoods as by the Orders of the Universities are agreeable to their Degrees, which no Minister shall wear (being no graduate) under pain of Suspension. Notwithstanding it shall be lawful for such Ministers as are not graduates, to wear upon their Surplices, instead of Hoods, some decent Tippet of Black, so it be not Silk." (*Ed.* Lond. 1724.)

Now a comparison of these two Documents shews that, in their APPARENTLY *literal* reading (and this is what the Court professes to regard) there is *a marked difference* in their respective orders touching Cathedral and Collegiate Churches; for, whereas the Advertisements prescribe the Cope at *all** Celebrations of the Holy Communion, the Canon *seems* to require it only " upon "principal Feast-days." The Canon relating to it is indeed quite patient of another and more probable rendering which so far would support the contention of the Judicial Committee that it " sanc- " tioned . . . all that the Advertisements had done in the matter " of the vestments," though not " in express terms " as their

same in coopes; and at all other praiers to be said at the communyon table, to have no coopes but surplesses." (*Strype, Parker,* App., Bk. ii., 49; or 8vo. Oxf., 1821, vol. iii., 87.)

* No distinction of days is made in that "Item" which orders the Cope; and that none was intended is plain from the "Item" immediately preceding it which directs—"That in cathedrall churches and colledges the holye com-

Lordships say: but then this support must be at the cost of the Court's consistency; for, later in the Judgment, their Lordships rule that by the 24th and 25th Canons " the Cope is to " be worn in ministering the Holy Communion on high feast-" days in Cathedrals, and Collegiate Churches, and the Surplice " in all other ministrations "—words which seem, and certainly are understood, to mean that it is to be used *only* on those days: moreover the rendering I propose is adverse to the Court's ruling both in this case and in that of Martin *v.* Mackonochie, viz.: that silence is prohibition. It may most fairly and reasonably be contended that the object of the Canon in mentioning " prin-" cipal Feast-days " was to make the Celebration specially obligatory on those days, and also to secure that the Celebrant should be either the Bishop or one of the principal members of the Cathedral: the duty, probably, being too commonly left to the Minor Canons.* That it could not be intended to *limit* the *Celebration* to " principal Feast-days " is plain from the reference of the Canon to "such limitation as is specified in the Book of " Common Prayer " of 1604, where the Rubric says " And in "all Cathedrall and Collegiate Churches, where there be many " Priests and Deacons, they shall all receive the Communion with "the Minister every Sunday at the least, except they have a " reasonable cause to the contrarie." According to the Canon, then, the Celebration *should* be *weekly;* it *might* be only *five times a year, i.e.* on the probable supposition that " principal " Feast-days " means those Days for which " Proper Prefaces " were appointed. Unless, therefore, it was designed to have a more ornate Service on these Feasts, the Cope was available at

munion be ministred upon the firste or seconde Sundaye of everye monethe at the leaste. So that both deane, prebendaries, priests, and clerkes do receave and all other of discretion of the fundation do receave foure tymes in the yeare at the leaste." (*D. A.*, I., 326.)

* This was certainly the case a century later, for Archbishop Sheldon, referring to " the Deans, Canons, Prebendaries, and other Dignitaries," in his " Circular Letter to Cathedrals," says : " But with some trouble I must needs tell you, I have from many places heard, that the duties of reading the Church Service, and administering the Holy Communion, have been too much neglected by those dignified persons ; and as if it were an office below them, left for the most part to be performed by their vicars, or petty canons, to the offence of some of our friends, the advantage of sectaries, and their own just reproach." (*Cardwell, Doc. Ann.*, ii., p. 331.)

all other Celebrations; for it cannot be supposed that the framers of the Canon, professing, as the Court points out that they did (See p. 84), to follow the Advertisements, would consider any *principle* to be invaded by the use of that Vestment at *all* Celebrations in the Churches where its use was prescribed.

Again, it is important to consider the language of the *Title* of the Canon—" *Copes to be worn in Cathedral Churches by* "*those that administer the Communion*" *:* the words are as comprehensive as can be; and unless it were possible to prove that the Canon was intended to forbid Celebrations on any days but "principal feast-days" or to prohibit any one, except those whom it names, to Celebrate at any time, it seems to me impossible to deny that Copes are to be used *whenever* the Holy Communion is administered. The *Title* of the 25th Canon necessarily leads to the same conclusion; for when it says "*Surplices and Hoods to be worn in Cathedral Churches when* "*there is no Communion,*" the inference is, surely, unavoidable— that "when," that is, *whenever there is* a Communion, something *different*, or at least something *additional* must be worn.

Further, the Advertisements direct "at all other prayers to be " sayde at the communion table, *to use no copes but surplesses:*" whether this refers to the Ante-Communion Service only, or includes the Marriage Service, the language is more *exclusive* than that of the Canon which merely says "In the time of "Divine Service and Prayers in all Cathedral and Collegiate "Churches, when there is no Communion, *it shall be sufficient* to "wear Surplices:" the Canon makes no distinction of *place*, as the Advertisements do, it follows therefore that for the Ante-Communion Service (which would be said at the Altar) and for other Offices (which would not be said at the Altar) the Cope *may* be used with the Surplice in these Churches.*

* I venture to think that these considerations dispose of Canon Robertson's conclusion in the following passages which I did not see until after the above was written:—" Under Archbishop Bancroft, we are told, ' the use of copes was revived, and the surplice generally worn.' (Collier ii., 6 and 7.) It is, of course, to be understood that the copes were worn according to the limitations of the late canons; these having been chiefly drawn up by Bancroft himself while bishop of London. He appears, indeed, to have gone a step further, in prescribing for his own cathedral, 1608, that the epistle and gospel be read in copes *every* Sunday and holy-day. [The *Order* is ' That the Epistle and Gospel be every Sunday and holy day read, according to the book of Common Prayer, in some convenient place near the communion table, and in copes.'] (Wilkins, iv. 426;

Once more, as regards "parish Churches" their Lordships make the Advertisements and the Canons *prohibitory* by introducing the word "only," although there is nothing whatever in the language of either which can even imply that they "ordered the "surplice *only* to be used in Parish Churches:" if, however, silence is *exclusive* then the Surplice may not be worn in Cathedrals and Collegiate Churches at Services for which the Cope is ordered; yet who ever heard of the Cope being worn without an Albe or a Surplice under it? "shall use a Cope" and "shall wear a Surplice" must mean the same thing, viz.: that the particular Vesture mentioned is *obligatory:* the expressions cannot, by any ordinary construction, mean that no other Vesture may be used with it, unless indeed the context varies the import of the words. Perhaps it will be said that such a variation does occur in the 58th Canon which orders the Hood*

but although he inquires about habits at Wells cathedral in 1605, there is no mention of the cope in his articles on that occasion. (Ib. 415.)" It appears to me, as I have argued above, that there are no "limitations" in these Canons as to the use of the Cope in Cathedrals for the Communion Service: at all events Bishop Bancroft must have known the meaning of Canons which he had himself framed, and therefore the usage which he prescribed "for his own Cathedral" cannot reasonably be supposed to have been at variance with them. Bancroft's silence upon the point, in his "Articles" (*i.e.* INQUIRIES) for Wells in 1605, is not inconsistent with his "ORDERS" for *his own* Cathedral in 1608.

* *Archdeacon Sharp* says "... I take it, the clause in this Canon, which enjoins graduates to wear the hoods of their respective degrees in parish Churches, is not strictly binding; forasmuch as the present rubric, which is of later date, and decisive of all questions about the habits in ministration, refers us to a rule [viz., the "Certain Notes" at the end of the Prayer Book of 1549] by which the said practice is not required." And in a Note, (after referring to the various interpretations of the Rubric given by Cosin, Grey, Bennet, Wheatly, and "the author of the Rubric examined, Lond. 1737") he says, "Now under this variety of sentiments about the sense and extent of this Rubric, when it is said 'to be decisive' about the habits, no more is meant than that it is *the rule*, however understood, by which our habits ought to be now regulated; (a point in which all parties agree;) and that no canon should take place in enjoining anything contrary to it or inconsistent with it. But there is no way in which the rubric can be so explained, as to include the use of graduates' hoods in parish churches, or of black tippets to non-graduates, during the ministration of divine service. The former being restrained to be used only in cathedral and collegiate churches and chapels, or by graduates in the pulpit, both in King Edward's first Service-Book, and in the Queen's Advertisements, 1564, and in the canons of 1571. And in none of these is the use of the tippet once mentioned." (*The Rubric in the Book of Common Prayer*, &c., p. 205. See also Note, *supra*, p. 114.) I am not here concerned to enquire whether the Rubric *does* refer exclusively to what is prescribed in the Prayer Book of 1549, as the Judicial Committee held in Liddell *v.* Westerton; but, if so, Archdeacon Sharp's argument is fatal to that of the Judicial Committee in Hebbert *v.* Purchas, as to the obligation to wear Hoods under the 58th Canon.

to be worn over the Surplice, and therefore that as it could not be intended to wear the Cope over the Hood it was meant that it should not be worn at all. No doubt the Hood was not designed to be hidden, for it was to be worn as an Ornament: but the same order to wear it over the Surplice in Cathedral and Collegiate Churches is given in the 25th Canon ; yet, unless " it "shall be sufficient " is a positive order not to wear aught but what is prescribed, it is clear, as I have already said, that the Cope might be worn consistently with the direction of the Canon, in which case the Hood would of course not be worn ; and the same reasoning applies to the Surplice and Hood in Parish Churches—the Cope, which is the greater Ornament, superseding the lesser *i.e.*, the Hood. It cannot be pretended that, in the abstract, there is any such incongruity as that a Cope is right in a Cathedral or Collegiate Church but wrong in a Parish Church; not to say that some Collegiate Churches are now Parochial Churches: the difference in the Canonical requirement in the two cases is sufficiently accounted for by the consideration that in the latter the Surplice was "to be " provided at the charge of the Parish," and therefore nothing more than is *necessary* is *commanded.*

The 82nd Canon is in point here, it orders the Lord's Table to be " covered, in time of divine service, with a carpet of silk " or other decent stuff . . . and [it does not say *and also*] with "a fair linen cloth at the time of the ministration"—the Rubric, moreover, only ordering the latter : if it were possible to maintain the dictum of the Judicial Committee (in Martin *v.* Mackonochie) that " a Rubric which is silent as to an Orna- "ment," which was "previously in use," also "by necessary "implication abolishes what it does not retain," it would be reasonable to say that the ordinary Altar covering must not be put on as well as the Linen Cloth, and that a Cope must not be worn with a Surplice, because neither the one nor the other is ordered. But there being neither inconsistency nor impropriety in using a Cope with a Surplice, the dictum of the same Court (in Liddell *v.* Westerton) applies, viz., that their Lordships were "not prepared to hold that the use of all "articles not expressly mentioned in the Rubric [or Canon], "although quite consistent with, and even subsidiary to the "Service, is forbidden." (*Moore*, p. 18). Nor is their Lordships' reasoning with regard to Altar Cloths wholly inapplicable to the question—whether Copes are prohibited in Parish Churches by the order of the Canon that a Surplice is to be worn? Their Lordships said :—

"Next, as to the embroidered cloths, it is said that the Canon orders a covering of silk, or of some other proper material, but that it does not mention, and therefore, by implication, excludes more than one covering. Their Lordships are unable to adopt this construction. An order that a Table shall always be covered with a cloth surely does not imply that it shall always be covered with the same cloth, or with a cloth of the same colour or texture. The object of this Canon seems to be to secure a cloth of a sufficiently handsome description, not to guard against too much splendour." (*Ibid*, p. 188.)

The last of what their Lordships term "the leading historical "facts," which relate to the Rubric, is thus mentioned :—

> "The revisers of our present Prayer Book in 1662, under another form of words, repeated the reference to the second year of Edward VI, and they did so advisedly, after attention had been called to the possibility of a return to the vestments."

There is certainly nothing *fictitious* about this statement, although it has been shewn, I think, that the same cannot be said of all the Court's "facts"—moreover, it is a *fact*, the natural inference from which might have seemed to be that it was an *easy*, not a "difficult task," as their Lordships say, to construe the Rubric : its literal and grammatical meaning was plain enough to the same Court in 1857, no less than to others who have interpreted it before and after that date. It is true, indeed, that the term "second year" has by some been referred to 1548, and by others to the Prayer Book of 1549 ; but none have doubted that, among the Ornaments in use at the period intended to be indicated, at least those *prescribed* in the Prayer Book of 1549 were *included;* although, as has been noticed, the Advertisements of 1565 and the Canons of 1604 have been held to be *continuous lawful dispensations* from the strictness of the Rubric. The Revisers of 1661 were well aware what the reference implied and what (as the Court admits) the opponents of Vestments understood it to imply: therefore it must be presumed that in making it "advisedly" they must have meant what they said, viz., that the *Second Year* of King Edward VIth was to be taken as the legal standard for the Ornaments of the Church and of the Minister; for if their purpose was to *prohibit* the Eucharistic Vestments of that year, the words they employed were certainly, to say the least, "dangerous deceits."

XXII. In the following passage (which reads much like a further adaptation from Mr. Raine*) the Court returns again to the question of the Advertisements:—

* "Now great exception has been taken to the value of these Advertisements, because it has not been shewn that they received the Royal assent. They were, I believe, enjoined by Royal proclamation, and I shall show soon that they were enforced by the Royal officers. But, putting this aside, supposing that they did not possess the Royal authority, the Queen seems generally to have held that the power of the Bishops was sufficient to carry such orders out, inasmuch as it was derived from her; and it is certain that several Bishops *did* act upon these Advertisements. At all events they are quoted by the Canons of 1603, and the orders which they contain relative to dress are then perpetuated in a manner to which no one can make any exception. The canons supersede them, but the mere fact of their being quoted and referred to therein, shews that they were of weight and authority." (*Vestments*, p. 10.)

Mr. Raine here expresses his *belief* that the Advertisements were "enjoined by Royal proclamation"; it is unfortunate that he has not given some reason for it, because, so far as I know, there is no ground whatever for supposing this to have occurred: on the contrary, the abolition, by 1 Edw. vi. c. 12, s. 4, of the Statute which made Proclamations valid as Acts, (See p. 12) is adverse to the notion. The Injunctions of 1559 were not, apparently, issued by Proclamation; why then should recourse have been had to it for the Advertisements? If, however, like the Prayer Book of 1604 (See p. 87) they had been issued by Proclamation under the 1st Eliz. c. 1 & 2, it is wholly improbable that the proceeding should not be equally well known.

So, too, it seems to me that Mr. Raine has failed to "shew" that the Advertisements "were enforced by the Royal officers": his references, at p. 12, to various Royal Commissions do not, I humbly think, at all support his theory. (See pp. 138-42.)

Further, in a Note to the sentence "it is certain that several Bishops *did* act upon these Advertisements," he says—"Archbishop Parker acted on them in his Metropolitical Visitation of the diocese of Gloucester (Strype's Parker, iii. 317) and of Hereford. See a letter from C. J. R. in the 'Guardian.' Other Prelates acted upon them in their spirit and intention without naming them." The only account I can find of the Gloucester Visitation, in Strype's Parker, is in Bk. ii. 160, or Vol. I., p. 319 of 8vo. Ed. Oxford, 1821. It is as follows:—

"But to return to the Advertisements. At length, it seems, the Archbishop's patience and persistence prevailed, and these ecclesiastical rules (now called Advertisements) recovered their first names of Articles and Ordinances: as may appear by the metropolitical visitation of the Church of Gloucester, anno 1576, by Lau. Humfrey, Herbert Westphaling, Doctors in Divinity, and some other Civilians, by the Archbishop's deputation; when among the Injunctions (eight

"The authority of the Advertisements has been questioned on the ground that it has never been shown that they received the assent of the Queen. Supposing, for the sake of argument, that the

in number) given to that Church, one was this, 'Not to oppose the Queen's Injunctions, nor the Ordinations nor Articles made by some of the Queen's Commissioners, (which are there said to be, Matthew, Archbishop of Canterbury; Edmund, Bishop of London; Richard, Bishop of Ely; Edward, Bishop of Rochester; Robert, Bishop of Winton; and Nic. Bishop of Lincoln;) January the 25th, in the 7th year of the Queen's reign.' To which that Archbishop (next successor to our Archbishop) subscribed his name. Where we may observe, that these Ordinances of the Queen's Commissioners are joined with her own Injunctions to be observed. Of such force they were now become."

If this is the passage to which Mr. Raine intended to refer, it is plain that the Visitation was held when *Grindal* was Archbishop of Canterbury, for Parker died May 17, 1575 : indeed the latter part of the passage shows that Strype was referring to Grindal, for he says "To which that Archbishop (next successor to our Archbishop) subscribed his name." However, if the Injunction had been signed by *Parker* it would not have supported the notion that the Advertisements had "received the Royal Assent," for a clear distinction is drawn between "the Queen's Injunctions" and "the Ordinations" or "Articles made by some of the Queen's Commissioners": nor does Strype imply anything to the contrary in saying—"Where we may observe, that these Ordinances of the Queen's Commissioners are joined with her own Injunctions to be observed. Of such force they were now become." Indeed, as I have shown at p. 58, this *joint enforcement* but *separate authority* was exhibited by Parker and others.

With regard to "Hereford," I do not find in *Strype's Parker* any account of Parker holding a Visitation there; and I presume, therefore, that the Letter of "C. J. R." is Mr. Raine's reference for it. That Letter (See *The Guardian*, March 21, 1866) is as follows :—

"Sir—I do not think that any of your correspondents upon the subject of Ritualism have noticed some (apparently) *authorized* proceedings which took place nine years later than the Advertisements of 1564. I quote the following from Duncomb's *History of Hereford*, vol. i., p. 486 :—

"'Whilst he (*i.e.*, Herbert Westfaling, D.D., afterwards Bishop of Hereford) was Canon of Christ Church, he was appointed by Queen Elizabeth a joint Commissioner with John Kennall, another Canon, Laurence Humphrey, President of Magdalen, and William Cole, President of C.C.C., for causing all 'monuments of superstition to be defaced at Christ Church ;' and they issued an order, accordingly, for the destruction of all 'copes, vestments, albs, missals, books, crosses, and other such idolatrous and superstitious monuments.' This order (*Collect. Curiosa*; Oxford, 8vo., 1781) was dated 'from Magdalen College in Oxford, May 5, 1573.'

"As at this date the Puritans had received a severe check, and were certainly regarded by the Queen with anything rather than favour, it is somewhat surprising that such an order as the above should have been issued at all.—C.J.R."

Upon this Letter I remark (1) That this was not a Visitation of the Diocese of Hereford, but of Christ Church, Oxford ; (2) That it was not a Metropolitical Visitation of the Archbishop, but the proceeding of a Royal Commission ; (3) That there is nothing to suggest that the Commissioners were charged to enforce the Advertisements; (4) That if this was their plea, then, as the Advertisements prescribed Copes in Cathedrals, this order to destroy them, *as such*, could not have been "*authorized ;*" (5) That their destruction, together with the other Ornaments, may have been decreed upon the false principle then so commonly acted upon, viz., that whatever had been used in "the Mass" was "idolatrous and superstitious." See remarks at pp. 21—22, 39—42, and 46.

Advertisements did not receive the official assent of the Queen, but were acted upon under a number of Royal Commissions, and with the approval of the Metropolitan, their Lordships think this was a 'taking other order' within the meaning of the Statute. There is no doubt that the Advertisements were carried into effect as legally binding, and were enforced by Royal Commissions. There is no doubt that they were accepted in some cases by reluctant people, as of legal obligation; and their authority is expressly recognized by the 24th canon of 1603-4."

Here their Lordships appear to admit that no evidence has been produced as yet to prove that the Queen *authorized* the Advertisements, and so they proceed to argue their legality from the way in which they state them to have been employed. But, as Lord Chelmsford in effect remarked at the hearing, the prescribed proceeding was a *Statutable* one, and therefore must be strictly followed. All the known evidence leads to a conclusion which is nearly demonstrative—that the "other order" of the Elizabethan Act of Uniformity was not taken as the Statute required; indeed the presumption is, as I think has been shewn at p. 57, that the Advertisements were a proceeding under a different Statute, and so could not be in any sense the supposed "other order."

In face of the strong presumption (seemingly recognized by the Court) against the alleged authority for the Advertisements, it is difficult to understand how their Lordships could allow themselves, especially in a criminal suit, to seek to establish them upon a ground not recognized in the Statute; yet this is what they do, for they say "supposing . . . . that the Adver-"tisements . . . . were acted upon under a number of Royal "Commissions, and with the approval of the Metropolitan, their "Lordships think this was a 'taking other order' within the "meaning of the Statute." Yet how could this be? The Statute legalized certain things "until other order" should be taken about them: that order was to be taken in a particular way, viz., by the Queen acting with the advice either of (1) the Ecclesiastical Commissioners, or (2) the Archbishop of

Canterbury. The Court considers it would equally satisfy the Statute if a *Royal Commission* (which, be it remembered, need not and, as it would appear, ordinarily did not, consist of the *Ecclesiastical Commissioners*) executed orders which the Metropolitan approved. I must take leave to doubt whether Courts in general would deem this a compliance with the Proviso of the Statute. Nor, indeed, would it mend the matter if the Royal Commission were the Ecclesiastical Commission; for although the latter was a standing body acting under the authority of the Crown, its power as regards the 25th Section of the Act of Uniformity was to give " advice" to the Queen in exercising the " authority" which that Section gave to her. No doubt it was part of their duty, under the Queen's Warrant which constituted the Commission (See *Cardwell, Doc. Ann.*, i., p. 257) to procure obedience to the Act of Uniformity and to punish disobedience to it: but, obviously, they could not enforce any " other order" than the Statute prescribed, until it had become a branch of the Statute by being strictly developed under the power of that Statute.

But, further, the Advertisements themselves do not correspond with the kind of "other order" which the 25th Section of the Act contemplated; that Section limited the *Order* to Ornaments of the Church and of the Ministers, used in the Services, whereas the *Advertisements* dealt with many other subjects; and even if it be allowed that they were designed also to carry out the 26th Section which provided in the same manner for publication of " further ceremonies and rites," the Orders in question far outrun that category.

The Advertisements consist of (1) " Articles for doctrine and preachinge," (2) "Articles for administration of prayer and "sacraments," (3) "Articles for certayne orders in ecclesiasticall " policy," (4) " Articles for outward apparell of persons ecclesi- " asticall," (5) "Protestations to be made, promised, and sub- " scribed by them that shall hereafter bee admitted to any office, " roome, or cure in any churche, or other place ecclesiasticall."

Of these five divisions Nos. 1, 3, and 5 have nothing to do with Ornaments, Ceremonies, or Rites: No. 4 relates only to the ordinary dress of the Clergy when not officiating: No. 2, which contains but 14 out of the whole 38 Articles, is the only division at all answering to the subjects mentioned in the two Provisos of the Act; and, of the 14 Articles, just 5 deal with the Ornaments mentioned in the 25th Section.

Can it, then, be seriously contended that these Advertisements were an "Order" prepared under the Elizabethan Act of Uniformity? Is it in the least likely that the Law Officers of the Crown would have advised Queen Elizabeth to sanction such a composite Document as this, upon the plea that it was a legal compliance with the 25th Section of the Act of Uniformity, which authorized Her Majesty to take "other" "order" concerning the Ornaments which that Section prescribed?

The Judicial Committee having, however, suggested the theory that "Royal Commissions" carrying out the Advertisements might bring them "within the meaning of the Statute," proceed to say:—" There is no doubt that the Advertisements "were carried into effect as legally binding, and were enforced by "Royal Commissions." If by the expression "legally binding," their Lordships mean that they were a Statutable requirement according to the 25th and 26th Sections of the Elizabethan Act of Uniformity, I humbly think there is the greatest doubt of it to be drawn from all the known evidence. If the Court only refers to the fact of their being a body of positive Directions, compiled from existing Laws by the Ecclesiastical Commissioners who subscribed them, and designed to secure a certain degree of actual compliance with those Laws, no doubt they were "*legally* binding," at all events in so far as all Ecclesiastical Laws were of legal obligation on the Clergy or Laity, for the Advertisements touch both. Yet all this is very different from the view which the Judicial Committee appears to take of the Advertisements—viz., that they were a collection of Orders designed to *prohibit* and *banish*, at least in the matter of Vestments, whatever they did not expressly command to be used or done.

The Court is equally positive that the Advertisements "were "enforced by Royal Commissions": if "there is no doubt" of this, how does it happen that the Court produced no proof of

T

it? It is quite plain that Archbishop Parker had not the slightest expectation of any such assistance, for in his Letter to Cecil, of April 28th, 1566—the time when the Queen had decided "to have the order go forward"—he evidently was hopeless of his power to execute it; his language is, "I trust "her Highness hath devised how it may be performed. I utterly "despair therein as of myself, and therefore must sit still, as I "have now done, alway awaiting either toleration, or else further "aid." (See p. 63.) Now it cannot be competent even to the Final Court of Appeal in Ecclesiastical Causes to invent Ecclesiastical History, although it practically makes Ecclesiastical Laws; yet their Lordships, in this case, have either done so or have again borrowed a view of it from Mr. Raine, who thus writes :—

"During the first few years of Elizabeth's reign a vast destruction of Ecclesiastical goods seems to have taken place throughout England. Of course things were kept back and hid, and sometimes, perhaps, used after they were declared to be illegal. The officers of the Crown and the Bishops must have been continually occupied in hunting after them. The chief agents, however, in this work of destruction were Commissioners appointed by the Queen, who, having their legal warrant in the Act of Uniformity, and being directed in accordance with it by the Advertisements, did their work most thoroughly and expeditiously, independently of the Bishops, who followed in the same track. The account of their proceedings in Lincolnshire is in print. They over-ran the North, and I find them acting in all the Northern dioceses. All this labour soon removed the Vestments, and showed that the task of carrying out the Advertisements was not deputed to the Bishops only; and even if the Advertisements were not alluded to by name that would be a matter of little moment, if only what they *specially* ordered was carried out by Church and Queen. The consequence of this zeal was obvious. From a year or two after the issuing of the Advertisements to the present time I cannot trace the use of Vestments in any parish church in the North of England. The instances which I shall mention in which they were discovered are merely cases in which the goods had been concealed." (*Vestments*, p. 12.)

It seems to me that an examination of this statement made by Mr. Raine will be the best mode of replying to the assertion of the Judicial Committee as to the Royal Commissioners. I venture, then, with all respect, to state in opposition to Mr. Raine :—

1. That the Royal Commissioners had no " legal
"warrant in the Act of Uniformity" to destroy " Ecclesias-
"tical goods," though they had a defined authority in the
Injunctions, which, however, did not include the Vestments.

2. That the Advertisements gave no direction whatever as
to such destruction.

3. That, whatever the Royal Commissioners or the
Bishops did, in reference to the destruction of Vestments,
no evidence has been produced to prove that it was done in
consequence of the Advertisements.

4. That all the 153 Lincolnshire Inventories, except 15, are
of an earlier date than April 28th, 1566, the time at which the
Queen allowed the Advertisements to be issued; and that,
unless the Commission acted upon the Advertisements within
ten days afterwards, only 7 of these 15, dating from May 13 to
May 26, could possibly have been presented to them, though
even that is wholly improbable.

5. That supposing (what has to be proved) that the Royal
Commissioners received any directions for or had any " task "
whatever in "carrying out the Advertisements," the removing
of Vestments does not seem to have been part of their duty or
labour; for that work appears to have been done before.

6. That it cannot " be a matter of little moment " whether a
Royal Commission did what it was not authorized to do.

7. That the Advertisements were *conservative* not *destructive*,
and "what they *specially* ordered" was *the use* of certain
things.

8. That unless Vestments were in use in the Churches
referred to, when the Advertisements were issued, their non-use
afterwards cannot fairly be attributed to the Advertisements.

Mr. Raine, in his Note to p. 12, mentions that several
Royal Commissions were acting between 1565 and 1639, but
he does not quote anything from their proceedings to prove
that, as he says, they were occupied in destroying Vestments
or in enforcing the Advertisements. The duties assigned to
those Commissioners were, in truth, of a wholly different kind,
and may be fairly gathered from a description of a Commission
in 1570, given in the Ecclesiastical Proceedings of Bishop

Barnes of Durham, to which Mr. Raine refers: in fact all the Royal Commissions for Ecclesiastical purposes, of the period now under discussion, were of the type furnished by the following example :—

"The Injunctions and other Ecclesiastical proceedings of Richard Barnes, Bishop of Durham, from 1575 to 1587." (*Surtees Society, vol.* 22. 1850.)

In his "Monicions and Iniunctions . . . to the Clergie and Churchwardens" in his "Sinode" held at Durham "on Tewesdaie the first daie of October 1577" in No. 3 (p. 14) he orders that if persons who are debarred from Holy Communion on account of immoralities, cannot be reclaimed, they are to be presented "to the Ordinary or to the Quenes Highnes Commissioners for causes Ecclesiastical within this said diocos of Duresmne."

A summary of the Commission is then given, it commences thus :—

"The Contentes of the Quenes Commission for Causes Ecclesiasticall, within the Province of Yorke, bearing date the xxvjth of July, anno Elizabethæ xijo (1570), directed to lix. persons, or thre at leaste, durante beneplacito. Dr. Swift's Book, p. 60 [Swift was Chancellor to the Bishop.]

"'To execute two Actes of Parliament made anno 1° Eliz., th' one intituled An Acte ffor Uniformitie of Common Praier and Service of the Church, etc., th' other entituled An Acte restoringe to the Crowne the aunccient jurisdiction, &c.'"

The rest of Dr. Swift's summary of the Commission shews that the Commissioners duties were :—

1. To inquire into heretical opinions, seditious books, attacks upon the Crown, and the laws and government of the realme—by Jury and witnesses and other means.

2. "To hear and determine all and singuler enormities, disturbances, assaultes, affraies and misbehaviours, done or committed in any churche or churchycarde or chappell, or against any devine service, or the ministers of the same, in or aboute the doing of devine service, contrary to the lawes and statutes of this realme, or shall obstinately absent themselves from the churche."

"To enquire of all such errours, heresies, schismes, abuses, offences, contemptes, enormities, spirituall or ecclesiasticall, whatsoever, which by any spirituall power and jurisdiction can or may be lawfully reformed."

"To enquire and search out all persons, being in the ministry, or having ecclesiasticall livinges, lurking or hiding themselves in secret places within the limits, etc."

To deal with cases of immorality.
To devise means of detecting offenders and to punish.
To imprison obstinate and disobedient persons.
To take recognizances of offenders or those suspected.
To appoint Registrars of proceedings.
To appoint Receivers of fines &c.

After the Commission has expired to certifie to the Exchequer the names of Receivers of fines &c.

Justices of the peace and others are to aid the Commission.

" These Letters patentes are a sufficient warrant against the Queene and all other persons for doing the premises."

As an illustration of the way in which the later Commissions followed an earlier form, I give the following description of one issued five years before the Advertisements appeared :—

" 1561 [May 5] 10. Minute of a Commission to the Archbishop of York, Earl of Rutland, Bishops of Durham and Carlisle, and 12 others, to take oaths of all manner of spiritual persons and ministers within the Province of York. Also of a Commission to the same, with the Bishop of Chester and 20 others, to inquire of all offences committed against the Act for Uniformity of Common Prayer, and the Act for restoring to the Crown the ancient jurisdiction over the State Ecclesiastical, &c. within the same Province; also of all heretical opinions, seditious books, conspiracies, slanderous words, &c. against the Queen or State; and of misbehaviour in Church or Chapel, or against the Minister. Also to punish such as absent themselves from Church; amend errors and heresies; punish masterless men and vagabonds; determine complaints of Matrimony, and of them wrongfully deprived of their Livings for religion; hear complaints of all Ecclesiastical crimes; take recognizances of offenders, committing the obstinate to ward; Thos. Clerk and Edm. Eyre to be registrars. Power given to name a receiver of fines, out of which expences are to be paid, and on the expiration of the Commission the fines to be certified into the Exchequer. [1 *page. Entered on the Patent Roll*, 3 *Eliz.*, pt. 10. *The first of these Commissions is printed by Rymer*, Vol. ix., p. 611, *and bears date 5 May* 1561.]" (*Calendar of State Papers, Domestic— Addenda*, Elizabeth, Vol. xi., p. 510.)

A further example of the *erroneous impression* which (as I said at p. 35) Mr. Raine's Pamphlet is likely sometimes to give, occurs in another Note to the passage on which I am commenting : speaking of these Royal Commissioners he says " They " over-ran the North, and I find them acting in all the Northern " dioceses. All this labour soon removed the Vestments, and " shewed that the task of carrying out the Advertisements was " not deputed to the Bishops only "; the Note to the word " dioceses " refers to seven different instances of Commissions. I have just shewn (pp. 138-41) that two of these, viz., the Commission mentioned by Bishop Barnes and the Lincolnshire Commissions, have no bearing upon the point. The third instance given is that of two Commissions " acting in Lancashire " in 1565 and 1570, mentioned at pp. 177 and 243 of the *Chetham Society's* Volume of "Lancashire Chantries": but these, again, are not in the least *ad rem*. Neither are three other cases, viz. Durham 1577, York 1626 to 1639 (*Surtees Society*), and York 1570 (*Eccl. Pro. of Bp. Barnes*). The seventh case, viz. "a book "of the Proceedings of the Commissioners for the Diocese of "Carlisle between 1573 and 1576," I have not seen ; but if its contents are of the same character as those contained in the Volumes already mentioned, I can only say (though Mr. Raine remarks "Vestments seem to have disappeared altogether ")— that any one will be completely misled who expects to find proofs of the conclusions which he arrived at and which the Judicial Committee seem to have accepted as a basis for part of their argument from the Advertisements.

The Court says, "There is no doubt that" the Advertisements "were accepted in some cases by reluctant people, as of "legal obligation:" but who were they? Not, I apprehend, the "Ritualists" of that day, but the "Anti-Ritualists" who abhorred the Surplice which the Advertisements enjoined no less than the Cope which was only ordered in Cathedral or Collegiate Churches, or the Chasuble which they did not require at all. If the case be otherwise the Court should have cleared up the point by giving an illustration of its statement: it is at least unsatisfactory that upon a disputed and somewhat obscure point of English Church History their Lordships should make positive assertions unsupported by evidence—a course which was not pursued in the analogous case of Liddell and Westerton. "Their authority is expressly recognized by the 24th Canon of 1603-4," says the Court: no doubt, as I have before said, they had *authority*, but the Canon does not say so, much less does it state what was the nature of that authority; it only speaks of them in the barest and most indefinite terms as " the "Advertisements published *Ann. 7 Elizabethæ.*" The language of their Lordships appears to imply that the Canon recognizes them as an authoritative order *altering* the Rubric of 1559, otherwise there seems no object in the reference: that they possessed no such "authority" has been, I hope convincingly, shown.

XXIII. To meet the objection arising from the want of proof that the Advertisements received the Queen's assent, the Court remarks that:—

> "In the case of Macdougall v. Purrier (4 Bligh's Reports, 433) the House of Lords presumed the enrolment in Chancery of a Decree of Commissioners appointed by an Act of Henry VIII for settling the tithes in London, although no such enrolment could be found, on the principle that where instruments have been long acted on and acquiesced in by parties interested in opposing their effect, all formalities shall be presumed to have been observed. No special form of consulting the Metropolitan is prescribed to the Queen."

But this case does not seem to be at all to the purpose unless it can be shewn that objections were raised on the part of Authorities to the Enrolment of this Decree: if the Advertisements had not encountered opposition from the Queen it might have been reasonably supposed that the Queen assented to them although the evidence was missing: as, however, their entire history is altogether adverse to the supposition that they obtained that degree of sanction which Archbishop Parker felt they needed in order to enforce them effectually and thus secure their object, it is not unreasonable to suppose that the House of Lords would come to an opposite conclusion in this instance, and would hold that the presumption was against the formality having been observed.

There is no reason, however, to think that any Document or Instrument is missing in this case: the original (but rejected) draft of the Advertisements with their Preface claiming the Queen's formal sanction has been preserved (See pp. 71-2): the altered Document was published at the time; copies of it remain, and their accuracy has not, I believe, been questioned; it bears the signatures of those who composed it or agreed to it; but its preamble does not contain certain words which were in the draft submitted for the Queen's approval (See p. 28), and which had they been retained would have given the desired sanction. What is the natural inference to be drawn from this fact, especially when considered in connexion with Parker's repeatedly recorded disappointment? Surely it must be that the Queen ultimately refused to comply with the formality so urgently requested.

As to the intimation that the Advertisements, like the Decree referred to, were "long acted on and acquiesced in by parties "interested in opposing their effect," it is needless, after what has already been remarked (See pp. 35 and 50), to say more than that no one was interested in opposing them except those who opposed the Act of Uniformity and almost all Ecclesiastical Discipline arising out of it. But that some of them did object to the Advertisements on the ground here in question is plain from two instances already given (See pp. 54 and 73).*

* The "Letter written [Nov. 6, 1583] by a Gentleman living in the Countrey, unto a Londoner, touching an answere to the Arch. articles" (quoted at p. 73), shews that the party adverse to "the Habits" not only continued their resistance to the Advertisements (which, indeed, they held not to possess the Queen's formal sanction), but were also opposed to the Queen's sanction being given to these new Articles of Whitgift and other Bishops; one of them being a further enforcement of that Article of the Advertisements which related to the Habits. There is a Paper in the Record Office (Domestic—Elizabeth, 1583, Vol. 163, No. 31) which contains (with some additions) the twelve Articles dated 1584 as printed by Cardwell (*Doc. Ann.*, i., 466, *Ed.* 1844: see also *Strype's* Whitgift, iii., 115; and *Wilkins*, iv.): as this Document has never, I believe, been printed, it is worth while to give it here entire; it is as follows:—

STATE PAPERS (DOMESTIC), ELIZABETH, 1583—Vol. 163, No. 31.

"Howe this may bee executed so farre fourth as concerneth Ordinaries, I have declared in a schedule wch I have sent to yor Lo

"[1] That it may please yor Ma^{ty} to geve strayte order that the lawes late made against the Recusantes may bee putt in more due execution: considering the benefite that hath growen unto the churche thereby, where they have bene so executed and the encouragem^t wch they and others do receave by remisse executing thereof.

"[2] That no bookes be printed beeing not before perused and allowed under the hande of the Archebishopp of Canterbury or Bishopp of London for the tyme being And that Printers bee restrayned from setting fourth other editions or Translations of the Byble or Newe Testament then that wch is *allowed*: Nor to add annotations to the same till they be seen and perused by the Archebishopp of Canterbury and Synode of Bishoppes And that like order bee taken for such treatises as in any way touche the state of the Realme or the Churche

"* Allowed: viz: by the sayd Archebishopp or Bishopp of London

"This article onely forbiddeth the resorting of Straungers to private houses to the

"[3] That all preaching reading catechizing and other suche like exercises in private places and families whereuntoo others doo resorte being not

The Court remarks that " No special form of consulting " the Metropolitan is prescribed to the Queen " : the object of this remark is not apparent, and the point does not touch the

entent to heare those exercises Because it withdraweth them from their ordinary Pastor & Parish sheweth a myslike in them of the public ministery & service & geveth suspicion of schisme In consideration whereof suche private exercises have bene restrayned by Provinceall & Generall Counciles (as the Councile of Laödicea & the sixth generall Councile) : and by Christian Emperors as namely Constantyne the great and Justinian : Neither is it suffered (as I thinke) at this day in any Reformed Churche in Christendom where the Gospell is by publike authority established Besides that it smelleth of Donatisme & Anabaptisme

of the same familie bee utterly inhibited Seing the same was never permitted as lawfull under any Christian magistrate but is a manifest signe of Schisme and a cause of contention in the churche

" This is most necessary & according to the doctrine of those that are most præcise whiche have sett it downe for a principle that Idem debet esse minister verbi & sacramentorū. Besides the Counselles letters directed to all Bishoppes in January anno 1579 commaunding that they should suffer none to preache but suche as ministred the Sacramentes also

" [4] That none be permitted to preache reade or cathechize in the Churche or ellswhere unlesse he doo fouer tymes in the yere at the least say service and minister the Sacramentes according to the Booke of Common Prayre

" The last wordes viz Cloak with sleeves &c may be leafte out yf it bee thought good But the article is warranted both by the Advertisementes sett out by Her Maties authoritie & also by the Q's Injunctions anno primo Elizab

" [5] That all preachers and others in Ecclesiasticall orders doo at all tymes weare and use suche kynde of apparrell as is præscribed unto them by the Booke of Advertisementes [That is Cloke with sleeves Square capp gowne tippett &c]
N.B.—In the 1584 copy, given by Cardwell, the following is substituted for the words I have put within square brackets—" and her majesty's injunctions ' anno primo.' " (See p. 59.)

" [6] That none be permitted to interprete the Scriptures or preache unlesse he bee a priest or deacon at the least admitted thereunto according to the lawes of this Realme

question of the Queen's assent to the Metropolitan's proposal as to the Advertisements: yet it is to be observed that in two known instances where the Metropolitan was consulted under

"[7] THAT none be permitted to preache reade catechize ministre the Sacraments or to execute any other ecclesiasticall function by what authoritie so ever he bee admitted thereunto unlesse he first consent and subscribe to theis Articles following before the Ordinary of the Dioceise wherein he preacheth readeth catechizeth or ministreth the Sacram^{ts} &c

"1 THAT her Ma^{ty} under God hath and ought to have the Soveraignetie and rule over all maner persons borne within Her Realmes Dominions and Contrees of what estate either Ecclesiasticall or Temporall so over they bee And that none other forren power Prelate State or Potentate hath or ought to have any Jurisdiction power superioritie prœeminence or authoritie Ecclesiasticall or Spirituall within Her Ma^{ts} sayd Realmes Dominions or Contrees

"THEIS bookes are warranted by acte of Parliament & every one in the ministerie is or ought to be ordered accordinge to the tenor thereof

"2 THAT the Booke of Common Prayer and of ordering Bishoppes Priestes and Deacons conteyneth in it nothing contrarie to the worde of God and that the same may lawfully be used and that he himself will use the forme in the sayd Booke prescribed in publike prayer and administration of the Sacram^{ts} and none other

"THIS book of Articles by Act of Parliament must be Publikely readd by every beneficed person in the Churche whereof hee hath cure who must also then geve his unfayned consent thereunto & subscrybe to the same before the Ordinary upon payne of losse of his benefice

"3 THAT he alloweth the booke of Articles of Religion agreed upon by the Archebishoppes and Bishoppes of bothe Provinces and the whole Clergie in the Convocation holden at London in the yere of our Lorde God 1562 and sett fourth by her Ma^{ts} authoritie And that he thinketh all the Articles therein conteyned to be agreeable to the worde of God

"[8] THAT from hencefourth none bee admitted to any orders ecclesiasticall unlesse he doo then presently shew to the Bishopp a true presentation of himself to a benefice then voyde within the Diœcese or Jurisdiction of the sayd Bishopp Or unlesse hee shewe unto the sayd Bishopp a true Certificat where presently he may be placed to serve some cure within the same Diœcese or Jurisdiction Or unlesse hee be placed in some Cathedrall or Collegiat Church or College in Cambridge or Oxford Or unlesse the sayd Bishopp shall then fourthwith place him in some vacant benefice or cure

the 25th and 26th Sections of the Elizabethan Act of Uniformity, the "form" is recorded (See pp. 22 and 86); and as this form was not used in the Queen's letter of January 25,

"[9] AND that no Bishopp henceforth admitt any into orders but such as shall bee of his own diœcese unlesse he bee of one of the Universitees or bringe his letters dimissaries from the Bishopp of the Diœcese and bee of age full xxiiij^{ty} yeres and a graduate of the Universitee Or at the least able in the Latin tounge to yelde an accompt of his Fayth according to the Articles of Religion agreed upon in Convocation and that in suche sorte as that he can note the sentences of Scripture whereupon the trueth of the sayd Articles is grounded and bring a sufficient Testimoniall with him of his honest lyfe and conversation either under the seale of some College in the Universitees where he hath remayned or from some Justice of the Peace with other honest men of that parish where he hath made his abode for three yeres before And that the Bishopp wch shall admytt any into orders being not in this maner qualified bee by the Archebishopp with the assistance of some one other Bishopp suspended from admitting any into orders for the space of two yeres

"[10] AND that no Bishopp institute any into a Benefice but suche as bee of the habilitee before described And if the Arches by Double Quarrell or otherwise proceede against the sayd Bishopp for refusall of suche as be not of that habilitee That the Archebishopp of Canterbury either by his owne authoritee or by meanes procured from yor Ma^{ty} may stay suche processe that the endeavo^{rs} of the Bishopp may take place

"VARIETEE of translations specially in publike service doth give great offence & ministreth occasion of quarrell to the Adversary

"[11] THAT one kynde of the Translation of the Bible bee onely used in Publike Service as well in Churche as Chappell And that to bee the same wch is nowe authorized by Consent of the Bishoppes

"[12] THAT no dispensations be graunted unto persons absent to take the benefice of great Residence specially in Cathedrall Churches of the old foundation: the same being the onely or principall cause why suche Churches are not furnished with learned and grave men to the great hurte and slander thereof

"[13] THAT from henceforth there bee no Commutation of Pennaunce, but in rare respectes and upon great consideration, and when it shall appoere to the Bishopp himself that that shall bee the best way for the wynninge and reforming of the offendo^r And that the penaltie bee employed either to the relieffe of the poore of that parish or to other godly uses and the same well

1564-5 which led to the Advertisements (See pp. 26 and 55—58) the presumption is that Her Majesty was not then acting upon those Provisos.

wittnessed and made manifest to the Congregation And yet if the fault be notorious that the Offendor make some satisfaction either in his owne person with declaration of his repentañce openly in the Churche or ells that the ministre of the Churche openly in the pulpitt synifie to the people his submission and declaration of his repentañce done before the Ordynarie and also in token of his repentañce what portion of money he hath geven to be employed to the uses above named

"[14] As psons of honest worshippfull and honorable calling may necessarily & reasonably have occasions sometymes to solemnize mariage by license for the banes asking or for once or twyse without any great harme so for avoidinge generally of Inconveniences noted in this behalf it is thought expedient that no dispensations bee graunted for mariage without banes but under sufficient and large bondes wth theis conditions followinge First that there shall not afterwardes appeere any lawfull lett or impediment by reason of any præcontract consanguinitee affinitee or any other lawfull meanes what soever Secondly that there be not at that present tyme of graunting suche dispensation any suite playnte quarrell or demaunde moved or depending before any Judge Ecclesiasticall or Temporall for and concerning any suche lawfull impediment betwene suche the parties Thirdly that they proceed not to the solemnization of the mariage without consent of Parentes or Governors And lastly that the mariage be openly solemnized in the churche (The Copie of wch bond is to be sett downe and geven in charge for every Bishopp in his Diocese to followe) Provided that whosoever offend against this order bee suspended ab executione officii for one half yere

"[15] THAT when Excommunication doth proceed upon some cause or contempt of some originall matter specified in a Statute made in the fyfte yere of yor Matts reigne entituled An Acte for the due execution of the writt De Excommunicato Capiendo That then the saide Writt may goe fourth upon the Significavit from the Ordinary without any charge of the sayd Ordinarie the same to be deducted out of the fynes and amercements growing thereby to yor Maty wch will both encourage Ordinaries so to proceed against obstinat persons and also encrease yor Matts commoditie by reason of the great number that shall be certified

These remarks were written before I had an opportunity of examining the Report of the Case: the facts therein stated entirely confirm those remarks and further prove that there is no real

"[16] THAT Sheriffes at the taking of their Oathes may have an earnest and speciall charge geven them in yor Ma^{ts} name aswell for the straite emprisoning of suche as are committed by vertue of the sayd writtes as also for the carefull execution of the whole Statute De Excommunicato Capiendo so farre fourth as it concerneth them

[Indorsed]

"Octob. 1583. Articles presented to hir Mat^r by ye Archb of Cant^{eb} [John Whitgift] and ye Bish of Sar [John Piers] in the names of thēselves and ye B B of Lōdon [John Aylmer] Rochist^r [John Young] Lȳcoln [Thomas Cowper] Peterb [Edmund Scambler] Glocest^r [John Bullingham] At St James."

The Dean of the Arches, in his Judgment *re* Purchas, referring to this Document which was quoted by Dr. Stephens (who has kindly allowed me the use of his certified copy) thus comments upon it:—
"It is said, however, that though it has been hitherto supposed that these Advertisements were issued without the observance of the conditions prescribed in the Statute, and therefore illegally, recent discoveries in the State Paper Office have brought to light documents which establish that these conditions were complied with, and that the Advertisements had therefore statutable Authority. I am unable to draw so large an inference from the Manuscript Document, copied from the State Paper Office, which has been submitted to me. It does not seem to me to do more than contain a recital in an informal Document, 'that the Advertisements were sett out by Her Majesties authoritee,' which would not carry the matter further, I think, than the reference to them in the 24th Canon, 'according to the Advertisements published Anno 7 Eliz.' or, as the Latin version has it, 'juxta admonitiones in septimo Elizabethæ promulgatos.' It is impossible to conceive that the authority which published these Canons was not perfectly aware both of the fact and law relating to these Advertisements, and the manner in which they are referred to would rather lead to the inference that they were not at that time considered to have *per se* a statutable authority." (4th *Rit. Report*, p. 242.)

If the Letter from which I have quoted at p. 73 had been brought to Sir Robert Phillimore's notice it must have strongly confirmed his view of the Document to which his Judicial attention was called; for the writer, commenting upon the 5th of these Articles, only seventeen years after the publication of the Advertisements, says that the latter "were never yet duelie published." There is no reason indeed to suppose that the "Gentleman living in the Countrey" had seen this same State Paper with its Marginal Notes, but it is plain that the Articles themselves had come under his notice, for he begins his "Letter" by saying "You wished greatly (belouered in the Lorde) that one louing the trueth, and not placed in the ministerie, would yeelde some sounde reasons, why the articles lately crepte abroade frō the Archb. of *Canturburie*, and Bi. of *London*, might by her Maiesties authoritie be rejected as matters friuolous and vnworthie her Roiall assente, that so execution pretended against diuers godlie Pastours and Preachers, if it were possible, might graciouslie be stayed." (*A parte of a Register*, p. 132.) In the course of the Letter he says (p. 162) of the above "article" [5] that "unles the Archb. suspecte that in time to come her Maiestie vpon the lamentable complaints of her people, may not onelie be mercifullie

analogy between the *Advertisements* and this *Decree of the Commissioners*. A legal friend who, *independently*, examined the Report also considers that it is not in the least *ad rem*.

inclined to tender their peace and prosperitie: but also may rightlie be moued in jelousie against himselfe for so seuerely exacting these things at the subiectes handes; vnlesse (I saye) the Archb. suspecting these thinges, minde to haue her Maiestie the principall authour and protectour of all his harde intreaties yet to come, he might haue put in execution this article without further supplication," &c. (See p. 73.) The writer, who opposes all the sixteen Articles, mentions *four* which are in this MS. but which do not appear among the *twelve* in the printed versions; viz.—No. 2, Against the printing and publication of Books, and also Editions of the Bible without authority; No. 12, Against certain Dispensations for non-residence, especially in Cathedrals; No. 15, Touching Writs "*de Excommunicato Capiendo*"; and No. 16, As to Sheriffs being obliged to imprison those committed under No. 15.

STRYPE, in his account of these Articles (Whitgift, iii., 115—119; or 8vo., vol. i., 228—237. 1822), does not refer to this MS. State Paper, and so it may be doubted whether he ever saw it; indeed it raises a question as to the accuracy of his statement. For, writing under the date of 1583, he says "in the month of September, divers good articles were drawn up and agreed upon by himself and the rest of the Bishops of his province, and signed by them. Which the Queen also allowed of, and gave her royal assent unto, to give them the greater authority." Then he gives the Articles, twelve in number, from "Regist. Whitgift, fol. 97"; they are signed by "Jo. [Whitgift] Cant., Jo. [Aylmer] London, Jo. [Piers] Salisbury, Ed. [Scambler] Petriburgh, Tho. [Cowper] Lincoln, Edm. [Scambler] Norwich, Jo. [Young] Roffen, Tho. [? John Wotton] Exon, Marmad. [Middeton] Menoven." They are the same, with a few unimportant verbal differences, as those given by WILKINS and CARDWELL, who both cite them as from "Reg. I., Whitgift, fol. 97, a."; but they both alike date them 1584, whereas STRYPE dates them 1583. No date is attached to these Articles in the Register at Lambeth, but, as they follow a series of Documents in the Register, ranging from December 1583 to June 1584, the date might seem to be 1584; unless indeed the Documents are not inserted in chronological order. There are no *Signatures*, however, in this Register to these Articles; and thus the question arises—from what source did Strype obtain these signatures? He must have seen either the original or some copy of it.

STRYPE continues thus:—"The Archbishop and the Bishop of London soon after, upon a review of these articles, and the addition of three more (viz., against the printing and publishing of books and pamphlets without licence from the Archbishop or Bishop; against granting dispensations to persons absent; and for writs to go forth *de excommunicato capiendo*, upon the *Significavit*), set them forth (having got the Queen's allowance thereunto) for all persons concerned to take notice of, at their own perils, being resolved to put them in force." (See *supra*, Nos. 2, 12, 15, and 16.) STRYPE does not give any authority for this statement, and I cannot find anything in Whitgift's Register to warrant it; no such additional Articles are there recorded.

STRYPE goes on to say:—"And in the next month (*viz.* October) the Archbishop issued out his letters to the Bishops and Ordinaries of his province, for their diligent putting in execution the above specified articles: the copy of his letter is extant to the Bishop of London, dated from Lambhith, wherein these articles are recommended to his care. And certain directions about the first Article, were subjoined to the same Letter. The Bishops were enjoined in the same Lettor, to certify him about certain Particulars for his better knowledge, and understanding of the present state of the Church and the Clergy thereof. The Archbishop's letter is as follows." STRYPE then professes to quote it from "Regist. Whitgift": but the original varies considerably from Strype's copy:

The case was this: The impropriate Rector (Macdougall) of St. Helen's, Bishopsgate, filed (in 1830) a Bill in Chancery against Purrier for non-payment of Tithes under a settlement made by the 37th Hen. VIII., c. 12: the Report says:—

the portions which I have printed within Square Brackets are those which occur in the Lambeth Register. The Letter, which is on fol. 90, runs thus :—
" After our [my] hearty commendations unto your Lordship. Where, of late by [the] advice, as well of your Lordship as of certain others of my brethen, the Bishops of my province, I have set down certain articles for good orders to be observed in the Church of England, the true copy whereof I have sent unto you herewith [herewith unto your Lordship], whereunto it hath pleased her Majesty, of her princely clemency, to yield her most gracious assent [consent] and allowance; to the intent the said articles may take the better effect throughout [my Province] your diocese of London, I have thought good to will [pray] and require you [your Lordship], that with such [convenient speede as you maye, you transmitte a true copie of the said articles togithir with the tenoure of this my Letters to every one of my brethren the Bishopps of my Province, willinge and requiringe them and every of them with such care and diligence as appertayneth to cause the same Articles effectually to be put in execution in every of their severall Dioceses and Jurisdictions] care and diligence as appertaineth, you cause the same articles effectually to be put in execution throughout the same diocese of London. And because I am desirous to know the state of the Clergy of my Province, that I may be the better furnished to govern the same, I have thought good to pray your Lordship to send unto me a catalogue of the names of all the ecclesiastical persons within your diocese, with signification of their benefices and promotions, degrees of school, and of the conformity of every of them to the laws and orders any ways established by her Majesty, and to require my brethren to do the like in their several dioceses: and to certify your Lordship as well thereof, as also how these Articles are put in due execution. That I thereupon may receive certificate of all from your Lordship. And so I commend you to the grace of God. From my house at Lambhith, this 19th of October, 1583."

STRYPE then mentions a similar Letter (which occurs on fol. 89-90 of the Register), dated Oct. 29th, sent "to Dr. Griffith Lloyd, for Oxford, who had the care of that see now vacant," and having further remarked that " these articles gave the discontented party (that called themselves *the maintainers of the discipline of God*) great offence," proceeds to quote parts of the Letter before mentioned "from a Gentleman in the Country," &c., in proof of the " offence" to which he refers.

Now the questions which arise upon a comparison of Strype's account with the State Paper are these—1. Was the State Paper of October, 1583, either the *original* or an *amended* draft of the 12 Articles which Strype prints ? 2. Did the Archbishop send to the Bishop of London, on Oct. 19, 1583, the 12 or the 16 Articles (15 if, as it seems, 15 and 16 were regarded as *one*) ? 3. If the 16 (or 15) Articles were " put in execution " by the Bishop of London in consequence of the Archbishop's Letter, and provoked the Letter of Nov. 6th from " a Gentleman in the Country "; were Articles 2, 12, 15, and 16 afterwards withdrawn and the 12 Articles ultimately published in 1584—the date given by Wilkins from Whitgift's Register ?

Without some further evidence I do not see that a clear answer can be given to these questions: but, whether 1583 or 1584 is the true date of the 12 Articles, it would seem that Strype has mistaken the procedure with regard to them. One thing, however, is plain ; viz., that in the State Paper presented for the Queen's sanction, the 5th Article does not correspond with the 4th of the 12 printed Articles. The marginal Note (See p. 145) says that the words "That is Cloke with sleeves square capp gowne tippett &c " of the 5th Article " may be

"It appeared that at various times, from the date of the Act to the time of filing the Bill, decrees and orders had been made in all the Courts of Westminster Hall, and in the House of Lords, upon the supposition or presumption that a decree according to the Act had been

leafte out yf it bee thought good;" and they do not appear in Whitgift's Register at Lambeth or in the printed copies: they may indeed have been substituted in the State Paper for the words "and her Majesty's Injunctions, *anno primo*" which occur in the Register, these latter words being finally restored: but if this was not the case the alteration seems to indicate that the State Paper is really the *original*, and so furnishes a presumption that the four (three) Articles which are not among the 12 were not allowed by the Queen, though Strype represents them as having been *added* to the 12 prepared "in the month of September" and which, as he says, "the Queen also allowed of, and gave her royal assent unto."

It is also to be observed that the 12 Articles are signed by three Bishops whose names are not attached to the 16 Articles of the State Paper; and it seems unlikely that the Queen would have sanctioned the additional stringent Articles upon the application of a smaller number of the Bishops.

There is another point in the State Paper which also appears to shew that it was the *original* of the Articles which the Queen sanctioned: the First Article, for enforcing "the Lawes late made against the Recusantes," which agrees with Strype's copy from Whitgift's Register, has the following marginal note— "Howe this may bee executed so farre fourth as concerneth Ordinaries, I have declared in a schedule wch I have sent to yor Lo." This schedule appears to have consisted of the Four Articles which are found at fol. 91 of the Register and are marked in the margin "A direction to the Ordinaries for their better proceeding in the execution of the First Article touching Recusantes:" Strype has printed these (III. 118 or Vol. I. 234, 8vo. "First, That every Minister in his own cure" &c.) and says that the Archbishop sent them with his Letter of Oct. 19, 1583. The fact that these four Articles are recorded in the Whitgift Register, though the three additional ones to which Strype refers (and which are in the State Paper) are not in the Register, tends to shew that the latter were not ultimately allowed, and that the Twelve Articles in the Register are the "true copy" to which the Archbishop refers in his Letter.

It may be useful to give here the following order of documents in this part of Whitgift's Register:—

(1) Fol. 90 (*dorso*).—Margin, "His Grace's Letters with the Articles for good orders in Churche."
(2) „ The Letter of Oct. 19, 1583 to the Bishop of London to issue the Articles to the Suffragans. (See p. 151. Also Cardwell, D. A., i., 459.)
(3) Fol. 91.—The Four Articles as to the mode of enforcing Art. I touching Recusants, given by Strype, Bk. III., 118, or Vol. I., 234, 8vo. —"First, That every Minister in his own cure," &c. See also Cardwell, D. A., i., 460.
(4) „ A Letter on a different subject.
(5) „ The Archbishop's Letter to the Bishop of London, Dec. 12, 1583, —"After my very hearty commendations to your good Lordship. I have herein sent" &c. Printed by Strype, Bk. iii., 120, or Vol. i., p. 239, 8vo. Also Cardwell, D. A. i. 462.
(6) „ Then Ten Articles given by Strype, Bk. iii., 119-20, or Vol. i., 238, 8vo.—"I. A general examination" &c. Also Cardwell, D. A., i., 463.
(7) Fol. 91 (*dorso*), & 92 to 97.—Various Documents of the Dates December 1583; January, February, March 1583-4; April, May, June 1584.
(8) Fol. 97.—"Articles touching preachers and other orders for the Church," as

made and enrolled; but no proof of such enrolment was produced in the cause; and the Defendants to the Suit proved that the Records had been searched, and that no such enrolment was to be found.

in Strype, Bk. iii., 115-17, or Vol. i., 229-32. See also Cardwell, D. A., i., 466-71.
There are no other Articles under the date of 1584 or 1585.

In addition to Sir R. Phillimore's remark upon the Note to the 5th Article of the State Paper I must observe (1) That the Article itself only uses the expression "the Book of Advertisements"; (2) That the expression in the Note, "sett out by Her Mat^{ies} authoritie," is quite consistent with the *Preface* to the Advertisements and with *Parker's* Letter of April 28, 1566 (See p. 63), in which he says—"The Queen's Majesty willed my Lord of York to declare her pleasure determinately to have the order go forward"; (3) That the Note itself distinguishes between the *Advertisements* and the *Injunctions* by calling the latter what they really were—" the Q's"; and that the printed Article of 1583 or 1584 (No. 4) makes precisely the same distinction. (See p. 59.) It is plain, then, I think, that this State Paper is *adverse* to the claim of *Statutable* Authority for the Advertisements which it was produced to uphold. Compare Cardwell's Note on these Articles (D.A., i. pp. 466—467.)

When the preceding remarks had been some time in type (and after a fruitless search for further evidence at Lambeth, in the London Registry, in the Foxe and other MSS. at the British Museum, and also among contemporary Documents in the Record Office) my attention was directed to the Petyt MSS., in the Library of the Inner Temple, which Mr. Martin (the Librarian) kindly allowed me to examine. In No. 538, Vol. 52, there is a *copy* of the *Twelve* Articles, with the Signatures; but there is nothing to indicate from what Document the copy was made : it agrees, however, with that given by Strype (See p. 150) : it is entitled (fol. 5, *dorso*) "Articles agreed upon by the Bishops exhibited to her Mat^{ie} Anno Domini. 1583. September." Immediately after the Signatures the following occurs (fol. 7) :—" Articles sent from the Lords of the Counsell ult^o Nouembris 1583.

"It was also further ordered that the Archbishop of Canterburie should be spoken withall upon the pointes followinge—viz."

These "pointes" are the *Ten* Articles given by Strype (*Whitgift*, iii., 119-20; or Vol. i., 238, 8vo.), beginning thus :—" I. A general examination," etc. : they are, moreover, entered in the Lambeth Register. (See No. (6), p. 152.)

Now, as Strype frequently quotes the Petyt MSS. it is not unlikely that he took the Signatures to the *Twelve* Articles from that source (though he refers to the *Whitgift Register* for the Articles themselves and also for the *Ten* Articles just mentioned) : the probability is increased by Strype's remark (p. 238) "that on the last day of November, it was ordered by the Council, that the Archbishop should be spoken withal upon these several points following "—*i.e.*, the *Ten* Articles. But, then, this apparent reference to the Petyt MS. (or its original) increases the doubt as to the accuracy of Strype's own statement—that after the *Twelve* Articles were "allowed" by the Queen, "three more" had also her "allowance" and that "in the next month (viz. October) the Archbishop issued out his Letters .... putting in execution the above specified articles" (See p. 150)—though whether he means the *twelve* or the *fifteen* is not clear. It appears very unlikely that if the Twelve Articles (which were "exhibited" to the Queen in September) were afterwards supplemented by the *Three* which Strype mentions (and which appear among the *Fifteen* presented to the Queen, in the State Paper of Oct. 1583), the Council should have returned only the *Twelve* in November, although (as Strype says) the *Three* were also sanctioned by the Queen. The improbability is increased by the fact that, although the *Twelve* and the *Ten* Articles do appear in the Lambeth Register, the *Three* are

"Upon these pleadings and evidence an issue was directed in the Court below [the Rolls], to try whether the Decree mentioned in and authorized to be made by the Statute was duly enrolled according to the provision in the Statute.

not given in that important Record of authorized Ecclesiastical Proceedings. The preservation of the Document of Oct. 1583 in the Record Office may, perhaps, imply that it was not sanctioned and therefore not returned to the Archbishop. Some light might have been thrown on the subject by the contemporary Records of the Privy Council, but, unfortunately, the *Council Register* is missing from 26th June 1582 to 19th February 1586.

The only conclusion which, as it seems to me, can be drawn from the whole case in its present form is this:—That (1) in September 1583 the *Twelve* Articles agreed upon by the Bishops were presented for the Queen's sanction; that (2) in October an altered draft was sent, containing the *Three* additional Articles; that (3) Whitgift prepared his Letter of October 19th to be issued with the Articles when approved by the Queen; that (4) meanwhile the proceedings of the Bishops had transpired and all the *Fifteen* Articles were attacked, as is shown by the Letter of November 6 (See pp. 73 and 149); that (5) consequently only the *Twelve* Articles were allowed and "sent from the Lords of the Counsell ultm° Nouembris 1583"; and that (6), then, Whitgift sent them to the Bishops (through the Dean of the Province) accompanied by his already prepared Letter to the Bishop of London.

There is another Publication, *cir.* 1583 or 4, which speaks of the Advertisements in almost the same language as the "Letter" uses; the Writer says—"Touching the first protestation to be made, promised, and subscribed, by them that shall hereafter be admitted to any office, room, or cure in any church, or other place ecclesiastical, contained in these words, in the book of Advertisements. *In primis*, I shall not preach, or publicly interpret, but only read that which is appointed by public authority, without special licence of the Bishop, under his seal,—though her Majesty's excellent name be used by the publishers of the said Advertisements for confirmation of them, and that they affirm her Majesty to have commanded them thereunto, by her highness' letters: yet because the book itself cometh forth without her Majesty's privilege, and is not printed by her Majesty's printer, nor any in his name, therefore it carrieth no such credit and authority with it, as whereunto her Majesty's subjects are necessarily bound to subscribe, having other laws, and other Injunctions under her name, and authorized by her Majesty's privilege, contrary to the same. For her Majesty by her Injunctions, commandeth every Minister to preach within his own cure, without licence." (*An abstract of certain Acts of Parliament: of certain of her Majesty's Injunctions: of certain Canons, Constitutions, and Synodals provincial, established and in force, for the peaceable government of the Church, within her Majesty's Dominions and Countries, for the most part heretofore unknown and unpractised;* p. 47, 4to.)

But it must be stated that a reply was made to this "Abstract" in which the writer says—"The objection, which to this purpose against the author might be brought out of the Advertisements, he handleth as Alexander did Gordian's knot, which because he could not handsomely untie, he heweth it in sunder with his sword. And so doth he, by denying the authority of them, because they are not with privilege, nor printed by the Queen's printer, although they were commanded by her Majesty's express letters. And is any man to surmise, that those reverend and wise Fathers, who subscribed unto the said book of Advertisements, would or durst publish them in her Majesty's name, and as by her Highness' authority and letters, dated such a certain day, if it were not so: or that they would enterprize to forbid or restrain that which the law had so expressly charged and commanded?" (*An Answer to the two first and principal*

" This order was reversed upon appeal ; and it was declared, that if to give effect to the Statute it was necessary that the Decree should be enrolled, it ought to be presumed that the Decree had been duly enrolled." (Pages 433—34.)

Treatises of a certain factious libel, put forth lately, without name of author or printer, and without approbation of authority, under the title of an Abstract, &c. Published by Authority. Page 74, 4to., 1584.)

STRYPE (Ann., vol. iii., fol. 1737, p. 233) says that this "Answer" was written by some civilian, Dr. Cosin perhaps, or Dr. Bancroft : if it was Cosin, then it is certain that he could not have been defending their *authority* as being the "other order" of Elizabeth's Act of Uniformity, because (See p. 96.) he considered that that order had never been taken. But, indeed, it is immaterial who was the Author; for the point then in dispute was not that which was under consideration in Hebbert *v.* Purchas—viz., whether the Advertisements were made conformably to the 1 Eliz., c. 2. The writer of this "Abstract" and the writer of the "Letter" *may* both have been wrong in their inferences from the Advertisements not having been "printed by the Queen's printer"; nay, more, the Advertisements may even have possessed a *Statutable* authority under 1 Eliz., c. 1, as I have argued at p. 57 : but this is wholly consistent with their not being the "other order" which if duly made would have varied the Ornaments legalized by the Act and Rubric of 1559 : a *positive direction* given under the authority of one Statute (A) to use certain things which are required by another and concurrent Statute (B), cannot (without negative words) be a *prohibition* of other things also ordered by Statute B.

The assertion of the writer of the "Abstract"—that the book of Advertisements, coming forth as it did, "carrieth no such credit and authority with it, as whereunto her Majesty's subjects are necessarily bound to subscribe, having other laws, and other Injunctions under her name"—is a very pertinent comment upon Parker's fears as to their fate if the Queen would not give that *kind* of authority to them which he unsuccessfully sought. (See his Letter to Cecil, March 8, 1564-5 ; *supra*, p. 61.)

The same conclusion follows from a scarce publication at least seven years later than the "Letter" (of 1583) bearing the following title :—"A Petition directed to Her most excellent Majesty, wherein is delivered a mean how to compound the civil dissensions in the Church of England : a proof that they who write for Reformation do not offend against the Stat. of 23 Eliz., c. [2], and therefore, till matters be compounded, deserve more favour," &c. This Petition has no date or printer's name, but as it mentions (p. 76) "Martin's Monethe's minde," which was printed in 1589, it must be of a later date—probably about 1590. The following passage shews that the Advertisements were not then regarded as the "other order" of the Statute :—

"Craving upon my knees pardon for my boldness, I beseech your most excellent Majesty to hear me a little. . . . . The laws expect a further Reformation of the Church. . . . . It is (1 Eliz., c. 2) enacted, that all ornaments of the Church and Ministers thereof (such as are surplice, copes, &c.) shall be retained and be in use as was appointed by King Edward the 6, not for unchangeable continuance, but until other order were taken by your Majesty, and your Highness' Ecclesiastical Commissioners." (Pages 4, 5.)

Also " The (*First Rubric*) minister should use the ornaments appointed by King Edward, yet not he alone, but the clerk also doth wear a surplice in many churches." (Page 63.)

At p. 69 the writer refers to the "*Bishops*' Advertisements."

" The party presented to the Bishop should wear a plain alb (by the book of Ordering Ministers confirmed by Parliament). . . . . The Deacon must read the Gospel in the day of his ordination, putting on a tunicle." (Page 64.)

"All the Bishops that be present at the consecration of Bishops should wear copes and surplices, having their pastoral staves in their hands." (Page 66.)

The material discrepancies between the two cases will be best seen by the following comparative statement of facts:—

THE DECREE.	THE ADVERTISEMENTS.
1. It was, according to the 37 Hen. VIII., c. 12, to be made before March 1, 1546. (*See Note to No. 7.*)	1. The Statute, 1 Eliz., c. 2, did not specify any time within which the "other order" therein mentioned was to be made.
2. It was made and duly signed by the persons appointed in the Act.*	2. They were "agreed upon, and subscribed by" the Metropolitan and five Bishops "Commissioners in causes Ecclesiastical, with others": but "the authority of the Queen's Majesty" required by the Act is not mentioned; on the contrary, the words which, in the original draft submitted to Cecil (*conf.* pp. 60 & 71), asserted the Queen's sanction, were omitted.
3. Its wording recognized and recited the Act under which it was made.	3. They do not profess to have been made under the authority of 1 Eliz., c. 2, but only "by virtue of the Queen's Letters" of Jan. 25, 1564-5, which Letters moreover do not refer to the Act: whereas in an earlier and a later case of making "other order" under the Statute (See pp. 22 and 86) its provision was expressly recited.
4. It was delivered at once to the custody of a proper officer—the Bishop of London (Bonner)—and was in a Register Book of the Diocese, 1539-59, preserved in St. Paul's Cathedral at the date of the Suit, 1830.	4. They were not sent to the Bishop of London for distribution to his Comprovincial Bishops until a year after they were prepared: the delay arose from the Archbishop's inability to obtain the Queen's formal sanction to them, and they were ultimately issued without it.

* *Lord Eldon.*—" These men (very many of them eminent men) did certainly make such a Decree, and the question in the cause is, whether that Act of Parliament has made it necessary that in all future times, at the distance of three centuries or five centuries, you shall be able to prove by demonstration that there was an enrolment of that Decree. Upon looking at the whole of the Act I am very far from saying that I think the enrolment was not made necessary by the Act of Parliament. I think it probable, after all that has passed, that the enrolment was made necessary; and then comes the question whether, because at this day, within a very few years I think of three centuries, that enrolment cannot be found, you are to say that the Act is good for nothing; or whether, on the other hand, you are not justified, in point of Law, in presuming that there was an enrolment, although it is not producible at this day." (*Report,* p. 173.)

5. It "had been constantly printed by the King's printers along with the existing Statutes of this Realm, and as forming part of the said Act of Hen. VIII., and as having been duly made in pursuance of the said Act." (*Report*, p. 446.)

6. It "had been uniformly received and acted upon in the Courts of Justice in this Kingdom, and considered by the King's Judges in all times since the making thereof as a valid and existing Decree, and as having been duly made and enrolled, and as having the force and effect of an Act of Parliament; and that many decrees and orders [no fewer, it is said, than 24] of the King's Court of Justice had been made and founded on [? it], pursuant to the said Act of Parliament and Decree." (*Ibid.*, 446.)*

7. It was not required, by the Statute, to be "enrolled" at any fixed time, and therefore might have been enrolled at any subsequent date.†

5. They were never printed as having any Statutable Authority or as made in pursuance of the Elizabethan Act of Uniformity.

6. They do not appear to have ever been the subject of any Judicial decision until the Dean of the Arches in 1870 pronounced that they were not made in conformity with the 1 Eliz., c. 2: there seems no evidence that they were ever acted upon by the Ecclesiastical Authorities as being the "other order" provided for in that Statute; on the contrary, in Visitation Articles and other Documents, they were almost uniformly mentioned in terms which implied that they were of inferior authority to Royal Injunctions: and the few recorded opinions during the three centuries since they were issued are mostly adverse to the allegation that they were made in pursuance of the Act of Uniformity of 1559.

7. The "other order" of the Elizabethan Act of Uniformity was one which, whenever made, required the *concurrent* action of the Queen and the other persons

---

* *Lord Eldon.*—"With respect to the evidence of enrolment in this case, I observe, first, that from the time when this Act of Parliament passed to the present time, which is now nearly 300 years, cases have occurred again and again, in every one of which the Judgment has been founded upon the idea that an enrolment must be presumed; and when the question arises whether an impropriator is within the Act, am I to presume, when Judges of that day, one after another, have decided that an impropriator was entitled, that there was no enrolment, if, according to the true construction of the Act, enrolment was necessary." (*Report*, p. 475.)

† *Lord Wynford.*—"It was argued, that you cannot presume in this case because it must be enrolled on a given day, and you have only to search at that time, and if you find it was not enrolled, then it is conclusive that it never was registered; but undoubtedly that argument proceeds upon a mistake. The decree of the noble and learned persons to give effect to the Statute was to be made before the 1st of March, but there is no time fixed for it being enrolled;

named in the Statute; and therefore it was essential that this simultaneous proceeding should in some way be indicated by the "Order" itself.

It is, plain, then, from this comparison that the DECREE only failed (if indeed it did fail) to comply with the provision of the Statute in not being proved to be enrolled in the proper Court of Record: whereas the whole history of the ADVERTISEMENTS shews that from the first they lacked that Royal Assent which was essential to their being a valid instrument under the Statute which the Judicial Committee considers them to have satisfied.

Would any Counsel, in a contested Suit, have ventured to cite the Case of Macdougall *v.* Purrier for the purpose to which it is applied, in an undefended Cause, by the Judges of the Court of Final Appeal in Causes Ecclesiastical?

XXIV. The Court next thus introduces a fresh point in the Argument :—

> "Their Lordships are now called on to determine the force of the Rubric of 1662, and its effect upon other regulations, such as the Canons of 1603-4. They do not disguise from themselves that the task is difficult."

Their Lordships here remark for the second time upon the *difficulty* of construing this Rubric: this being their view it seems a somewhat harsh proceeding to condemn Mr. Purchas in all the costs of a Suit which he did not institute; which was professedly promoted only to ascertain the Law, nominally by an individual, but notoriously at the expense of the Church Association; where no personal interest was at stake; and where the current of interpretation and even the Judgment of the same Court were mainly in favour of the impugned prac-

---

there is no point of time we can fix upon and say, that not having been found there, you are to presume it is not enrolled. That being the case, you must look for this proof at the Rolls for nearly three hundred years before you can say with safety it is not enrolled. What a dangerous litigation this would lead to. In a case of this sort you must take it for granted it was enrolled, though at this day it is impossible to prove the fact." (*Report*, p. 482.)

"dayes and holy dayes, and in administring of the Sacraments, "doth vse and weare the Surples, yea or no?" (See p. 41); they omit these words which immediately succeed—" or doe suffer any " other to saye the common prayer, or minister either of the Sacra- "ments in your Church, not wearing the same?" (2nd *Ritual Report*, p. 422): the natural inference surely from these latter words (one would have thought also from the former) is that Sandys was guarding against *omission* not *addition*—that, like all others who made a similar inquiry, he was bent upon suppressing the practice, which some had introduced, of saying the Service after the Genevan fashion, in a Cloak, or Gown, or in their ordinary Garments.

The Court has not " quoted " any question of Aylmer's as to the *use* of the Surplice, nor do his Articles contain any inquiry corresponding to that which they quote from Sandys: Aylmer does indeed (like Sandys, No. 2, p. 422) ask " 2. Whether you "haue in your parish Churches and Chappels all things necessary " and requisite for common prayer and administration of the Sacra- "mentes, specially . . . . a decent large Surplesse with sleues. ". . . . (*Ib.*, p. 418): Sandys, however, is rather more precise, adding the words " for your Minister to weare," saying further "and all other things necessary for the premisses ": Alymer also ends his question nearly in the same words, viz. " and all other thinges necessarye in and to the premisses." What were these " other things necessary "? was the Hood *e.g.* one of them? if so, it could only be because it was considered, in the Prayer Book of 1549, " seemly " for preaching; the Advertisements do not *mention* it for Parish Churches, and in fact it was forbidden there just as much as the Cope, on the theory of the Judicial Committee that silence is prohibition. Was there any known Rule which could decide the question? It seems there was, for Aylmer himself asks " 23 . . . . whether they "[the Clergy] read the Queenes Maiesties Iniunctions every "quarter of a yeare once or no " (*Ib.*, p. 419): Sandys refers to them (*Ib.*, p. 422, Nos. 8 and 9) though he does not ask whether they are " read ": if they were to be thus read or regarded they could not be like an old Almanack—only a very partial guide to the current period—and in truth Alymer also asks " 56. Whether the Queenes Maiesties iniunctions be duely "and preciselye obserued both on the part of the Clergie and the "laity according to the articles therein conteyned," (*Ib.*, p. 421) : if the Injunctions were the full authority, then they did not contain a single word which *limited* the Rubric of 1559; if they were to be read with their " Interpretations" of 1561, then they at least required the Cope as well as the Surplice in all Parochial Churches. So that, from any point of view, no one can be bound to "think" with the Judicial Committee that Sandys and Alymer held that the Surplice was " the only Vestment of " the Parochial Clergy."

It is very strange, however, that their Lordships should not have referred to the Visitation Articles of Parker in 1569 and to the Injunctions of Cox in 1570—4, both of whom had previously signed the Advertisements issued in 1566, whereas the names of Aylmer and Sandys do not occur : Parker asks (See p. 107) whether the Clergy "weare a surples prescribed by the "Quene's Majestie's Injunctions and the boke of Common "Prayer": yet he could not have meant to exclude the Cope which was expressly mentioned in the Interpretations of the Injunctions as being the " one apparell" *required* to be used " in "the ministration of the Lorde's Supper " out of these Vestments of the Second year which the Prayer Book of 1559 retained. The same remark applies even more forcibly to Cox who orders " that euery Parson, Vicar, and Curate shall vse in "the tyme of the celebration of diuine seruice, to weare a sur-"plesse, prescribed by the Queenes maiesties Iniunctions and the "booke of Common prayer, and shall kepe and obserue all other "rightes and orders prescribed in the same booke of Common "prayer and Iniunctions, as well about the celebration of the "sacramentes, as also in their comely and priestlyke apparell, to be "worne accordyng to the precept set forth in the booke called "Aduertisementes." (2nd *Rit. Report*, p. 406.) This demand for the Surplice was fortified by referring to the Book of Common Prayer as well as to the Injunctions for its authority : but Cox does not here mention for *what part* " of Divine Service" it was to be used, and the Book of 1549 prescribed the Albe for Celebration of Holy Communion : though in his Injunctions " For the

"Churchwardens and Inquirers" (See p. 107) he asks whether the Clergy " do not weare at the celebration of the diuine ser-" uice and sacramentes a comely surplesse " : if, however, as is likely, he did not mean to enjoin more of the Rubrical prescription than was positively ordered by the Injunctions with their Interpretations, it is nevertheless certain that Surplice and Cope were the Vestments required for the Eucharistic Service.

The supposition of the Court, in this next passage, is partly anticipated by the remarks at p. 104 and also at pp. 118-23 touching Cosin's inquiry which their Lordships especially select for comment :—

> "They think that the Articles of Visitation (cited Ritual Commission, Report 2), issued at and after the passing of the Act of Uniformity, which ask after the 'fair surplice for the minister to wear at all times of his ministration,' without any suggestion of any other vestment, could scarcely have been put forth by Bishops desirous of a more elaborate Ritual and aware that the vestments were now of statutable obligation."

The Articles which seem here to be referred to are the following :—

1662. Cosin (Bp. of Durham) I.—" 6. Have you a large and decent Surplice (one or more) for the Minister to wear at all times of his public Ministration in the Church, and another for the Clerk, if he hath heretofore been accustomed to wear it, when he assisteth the Minister ? Are not either of their Surplices now grown old and torn ? and what are they at this time worth ? or if new have been lately bought, how much did they cost by the yard ?" (2nd *Rit. Report*, p. 601.)

1662. Hacket (Bp. of Lichfield)—" V. . . . . Have you also a decent Surplice (one or more) for your Parson, Vicar, Curate, or Lecturer to wear in the time of all public Ministrations ?" (*Ibid*, p. 609.),

1662. Morley (Bp. of Winchester)—" V. Have you a comely large Surplice for the Minister to wear at all times of his Publick Ministration in the Church provided, and to be duely washed at the Charge of the Parish ?" (*Ibid*, p. 615.)

1664. Henchman (Bp. of London) —" VII. Have you a fair Surplice for the Minister to wear at all times of his publick Ministration, provided at the charge of the Parish ?" (*Ibid*, p. 632.)

1679. Barlow (Bp. of Lincoln)—" VII. Have you a fair Surplice for the Minister to wear at all times of his publick Ministration, provided at the charge of the Parish ?" (*Ibid*, p. 645.)

1679. Gunning (Bp. of Ely)—"8. Have you a large and decent Surplice, one, or more, for the Minister to wear at all times of his publick Ministration?" . . . . (*Ibid*, p. 651.)

1686. Sancroft (Bp. of Lincoln) I.—"5. Have you a comely large Surplice for the Minister to wear at all times of his publick Ministration in the Church, provided and washed at the charge of your Parish? . . . .' (*Ibid*, p. 653.)

1710-20. Booth (Archn. of Durham) Tit. I.—" *Section* 6. Have you a large and decent Surplice (one or more) for your Minister to wear at all Times of his public Ministration in the Church . . . .?" (*Ibid*, p. 683.)

These *eight* are all the instances out of the *twenty-eight* Sets of Visitation Articles to which the Judicial Committee refer as having been "issued at and after" the Act of 1662, which inquire for the Surplice in terms *nearly like the words* cited by the Court; not one, however, corresponds *exactly* with those words: the inquiry might naturally enough have been made in the exact language of the Rubrick; and that all the eight questions mean the same thing as that Rubric, will not, I suppose, be doubted. I have shown, however, at p. 120 -23, that Cosin's Inquiry, upon which the Court so much relies, was framed and used *before* the Rubric of 1662 was authorized; and as I have also shown (See p. 108) that Cosin used substantially the same words *thirty-five years* before, it follows surely that he must have meant the same thing at both times: it is, therefore, at least a reasonable inference that the other six Bishops and Archdeacon Booth used the words in the same sense as Bishop Cosin. But that, in 1627, Cosin did not consider "the Vestments" had ceased to be "of Statutable obligation," in consequence of the Canons of 1603 seems certain from his *First Series* of "*Notes* "*on the Common Prayer*" written probably between 1619 and 1638; for, commenting on the Rubric of 1603, he says :—

"*As were in use.*] And then were in use, not a surplice and hood, as we now use, but a plain white alb, with a vestment or cope over it; and therefore, according to this Rubric, are we still bound to wear albs and vestments, as have been so long time worn in the Church of God, howsoever it is neglected. For the disuse of these Ornaments, we may thank them that came from Geneva, and in the beginning of Queen Elizabeth's reign, being set in places of government, suffered every negligent Priest to do what him listed, so he would but profess a difference and opposition in all things (though never so lawful otherwise) against the Church of Rome, and the Ceremonies therein used. If any man shall answer, that now the 58th Canon hath appointed it otherwise, and that these things are alterable by the direction of the Church wherein we live; I answer, that such matters are to be altered by the same authority wherewith they were established, and that if that authority be the Convocation of the Clergy, as I think it is (only that), that the 14th Canon commands us to observe all the Ceremonies prescribed in this book. I would fain know how we should observe both Canons. (But the Act of Parliament, I see, refers to the Canon, and until such time as other order shall be taken.)" (*Works, Ang. Cath. Lib.* V., p. 42.)

It has been thought, however, that these last words in parenthesis, which the Editor of the Oxford Edition says " were " added at a later time," removed Cosin's earlier difficulty :* if the *date* of this addition could be discovered it might be easier to ascertain whether it was Cosin's ultimate opinion: that it was not written after 1662 may be taken for granted, because the Statute of that year does not contain the proviso for taking "other " order" which Cosin mentions as being in "the Act of Parlia- " ment :" therefore he must have added it when the Prayer Book of 1604 was in use, for the Rubric then referred to the Elizabethan Act of 1559. Cosin's words, however, cannot be taken literally, because they would involve the anachronism that the *earlier* Statute " refers " to the *later* Canon; they must be read as though he had written—" But the Act of Parliament, I see, " *applies* to the Canon, and until such time as other order shall be " taken." Unless, however, it can be proved that he wrote this, *after* his SECOND SERIES of Notes, which he is believed to have prepared after 1638 and 1656, no reliance must be placed upon it, for in this later Series, referring to the Proviso, he says, " Which other order, so qualified as is here appointed to be, was " never made " (*Ib.*, p. 233),—language this which shows plainly that he had no idea of the *Advertisements* having been that " other " order," whatever he really held about the Canon of 1604. On the other hand, if his remark about the Canon was written *before* his Second Series of Notes, then it is no less plain that he did not consider the Canon to have been a compliance with the 25th Section of the Elizabethan Act.

* See *The Guardian* of February 14th and 28th, 1866, Letters from Rev. W. Milton and Mr. H. R. Droop.

That the Rubric had not been altered, either by the Advertisements or by the Canons, appears to be beyond question when it is recollected that the Lords' Committee in 1641 advised "that " the Rubric, with regard to Vestments, should be altered." (*Cardwell Conf.*, p. 241.) And that Cosin and the other Bishops in 1661 did not consider it to have been altered, seems certain from the fact that, when the Nonconformists at the Savoy Conference desired to have it "wholly left out," on the ground that it "seemeth " to bring back the Cope, Albe, &c., and other Vestments forbidden "by " the Prayer Book of 1552 (*Ibid,* p. 314), no suggestion even was made by the Bishops that the request was needless *because the Rubric had been altered;* they merely said, " For the reasons " given in our answer to the 18th general, whither you refer us, we " think it fit that the Rubric continue as it is " (*Ibid*, p. 351); and that the Presbyterians did not misunderstand the Bishops, or suppose them to mean that the " answer to the 18th general " implied that the Surplice only was then required by the Rubric, is clear from their " Rejoinder," in which they say, " We have given you "reason enough against the imposition of the usual Ceremonies; "and would you draw forth those absolute ones to increase the "burthen?" ("*The Grand Debate between the most Reverend the Bishops, and the Presbyterian Divines, appointed by His Sacred Majesty, as Commissioners for the Review and Alteration of the Book of Common Prayer, &c. Being an Exact Account of their whole Proceedings. The most perfect copy. London, Printed 1661.*" p. 118.) If the Bishops had felt that the Rubric had no power to "draw " them "forth," nothing was easier than for them to say so and thus reassure the complainants.

The Judicial Committee think that the Visitation Articles, at and after 1662, upon which I have now been commenting, "could "scarcely have been put forth by Bishops desirous of a more "elaborate Ritual, and aware that the Vestments were now of "statutable obligation " : that they were not " desirous " of it there is no proof, and therefore others are perfectly free to " think " differently from their Lordships: that the Bishops and other Ordinaries did not *require* it, is certain from the subsequent history; and that, among other reasons for not attempting to *enforce* the Rubric—apparently not even the Canon as to Copes in Cathedrals—it may readily be believed that they were influenced by the appeal of the Non-Conforming Clergy not to "draw "forth those absolute" prescriptions of Rubric and Canon "to "increase the burthen" of the Surplice which they were so unwilling to bear.

If, however, an *exclusive* character is to be fixed upon these *eight* cases, referred to by their Lordships, in *seven* of which the words "at all times of his [public] ministration" occur; an *inclusive* character may as reasonably be claimed for the following *three* cases in which, not only do these words not occur, but inquiries are made which, literally taken, are certainly capable of covering the Cope if not the Albe and Chasuble:—

1662. Henchman (Bishop of Salisbury) II.—"2. Have you in your said Church or Chappell, a convenient seat for your Minister to read Divine Service in, together with a comely Pulpit set up in a convenient place, with a decent cloth or cushion for the same, a comely, large, and fine Surplice, a fair Communion cup, a Flagon of silver or pewter, with all other things and ornaments necessary for the celebration of Divine Service, and administration of the Sacraments . . . ?" (2nd *Rit. Report*, p. 610.)

1662. Layfield (Archdeacon of Essex).—"4. Whether haue you a convenient seat for the Minister to read service in, together with a comly Pulpit set up in a convenient place, with a decent cloth or Cushion for the same; a comely large Surples, a faire Communion Cup of Silver, and a cover agreeable for the same, with all other things and ornaments necessary for the celebration of Divine Service, and administration of the Sacraments . . . ." (*Ibid*, p. 622.)

1662. Quarles (Archdeacon of Northampton).—"IV. Whether ye have a comely Pulpit well placed within your Church, a decent Table for the Holy Communion, with a fair linnen cloath to lay upon the same, and some Carpet of Silk, Stuff, or fine Wollen cloath, for the clean keeping thereof; a fair comely Communion-cup, and cover of silver for the same, and a decent large Surplice with sleeves . . . ? V. . . . And have ye all other necessary things appointed to be had by lawful Authority?" (*Ibid*, p. 630.)

Now if these Articles had not mentioned the usual Ornaments, including Chalice and its Cover (commonly used for a Paten), Flagon, Altar Cloth, and Linen Cloth, it would naturally be thought that these were intended by "the other things and "Ornaments:" yet, although I do not therefore contend that the Inquiries were *designed* to refer to some other Vestment than the

Surplice which they named, it is as fair to hold that they *require something more* as to hold that the other Articles *forbid anything more* than that garment.

The Judicial Committee thus concludes its expression of disagreement with the Dean of the Arches as to the interpretation to be put on the Advertisements and Visitation Articles :—

> "They think that in prescribing the surplice only, the Advertisements meant what they said, the surplice only: and that strong steps were taken to insure that only the surplice should be used."

But when a Court, and especially a Court of Final Appeal, expresses its thoughts, it ought at least to take particular care that its statements should be consistent with Facts and Documents: if their Lordships had thought and had expressed their thought that the Advertisements prescribed *only the Surplice* for Parish Churches, no one could have differed from them: but to think that they prescribed "*the Surplice only*" implies, to say the least, an inattention to language which is certainly not to be excused by the assertion that "the Advertisements meant what they said, "the surplice only:" whereas the word "only" is not to be found in any one of these Orders relating to the Ornaments of the Minister. Nor, again, had their Lordships, I submit, any warrant from history for thinking that "strong steps were taken to insure that "*only* the Surplice should be used;" though there is abundant proof that such a course was adopted to secure that *that Vesture should be worn* by those who were indifferent or careless, as to its use; or who were unwilling or refused to comply with this lowest demand of the Ecclesiastical Law. If a *negative* and *prohibitory* meaning may be put upon the Advertisement which *prescribes* a SURPLICE in Parish Churches (See p. 127); then, in all consistency, the Advertisement which orders that in Cathedral Churches "the principal Minister" and others "shall use a COPE" (See p. 126) must be held to forbid his wearing a Surplice under it.

XXV. The Judgment proceeds thus:—

> "Their Lordships remark further that the doctrine of a minimum of ritual represented by the surplice, with

a maximum represented by a return to the mediæval vestments is inconsistent with the fact that the Rubric is a positive order, under a penal Statute, accepted by each clergyman in a remarkably strong expression of 'assent and consent' and capable of being enforced with severe penalties. It is not to be assumed without proof that such a statute was framed so as to leave a choice between contrary interpretations, in a question that had ever been regarded as momentous, and had stirred, as the learned Judge remarks, some of the strongest passions of man. Historically all the communications between Archbishop Parker and the Queen and her Government indicate a strong desire for uniformity, and the Articles of Visitation after 1662 were all framed with the like object. If the minister is ordered to wear a surplice at all times of his ministration, he cannot wear an alb and tunicle when assisting at the Holy Communion; if he is to celebrate the Holy Communion in a chasuble, he cannot celebrate in a surplice."

Now upon these propositions it may be observed, *First*, that if this "doctrine" be "inconsistent" with the positive and penal character of the Rubric, the inconsistency was long anterior to the Prayer Book of 1662; for in 1563 Archbishop Parker asked only for "a minimum," viz., the Surplice (See p. 43), when it is perfectly certain that the Rubric ordered a "maximum," viz., the other Vestments; and when even the "Interpretations" of the Injunctions (issued only two years before, *i.e.* 1561, and which no one has alleged to be the "other order" of the 25th Sect. of the Elizabethan Act) made the Cope obligatory in *all* Churches. *Next*, if neither the Advertisements nor the Canons of 1604 were the "other order" (as I think has been proved) this supposed "in-"consistent" rule existed at all events until 1662. *Thirdly*, the inconsistency exists in reference to another Rubric—that which by necessary implication requires *weekly* Celebration in "Cathedral "and Collegiate Churches, and Colleges," because it orders the Clergy attached to them to "receive the Communion with the "Priest every Sunday at least, except they have a reasonable "cause to the contrary;" whereas the 24th Canon renders a *weekly* Celebration needless by declaring that "such limitation" of

z

Administration " as is specified in the Book of Common Prayer " may be regulated by only *requiring* those Clergy to " receive the " Communion four times yearly at the least." Yet, whether from this or from whatever cause, certain it is that in most of our Cathedrals *monthly* Celebrations had, unhappily, come to be the rule, and is still so in some of them.

Again, the " penal " character of the Statute, referred to by the Court, is of itself a sufficient reason for the non-enforcement of *any* Rubric which it was not *essential* to insist upon ; more especially when, as in the case of the Ornaments Rubric, it had become obsolete, was obnoxious to others besides the Non-conformists, and would involve charges which were certain to be resisted by Parishes many of which reluctantly furnished a Surplice, or even kept it clean.

Further, the " unfeigned assent and consent " of the Clergy " to all and everything contained and prescribed in and by the " Book " of Common Prayer, (even had it been any new requirement, though it certainly was not*) could neither strengthen the

---

* A Declaration which was *substantially* the same had been required of the Clergy from 1559 to 1662, as the following quotations prove :—

1559. "*A declaration of certain principal articles of religion set out by the order of both archbishops metropolitans, and the rest of the bishops for the uniformity of doctrine, to be taught and holden of all parsons, vicars and curates, as well in testification of their common consent in the said doctrine to the stopping of the mouths of them, that go about to slander the ministers of the Church for diversity of judgment, as necessary for the instruction of their people; to be read by the said parsons, vicars, and curates at their possession-taking, or first entry into their cures, and also after that, yearly at two several times, that is to say, the Sunday next following Easter day, and St. Michael the archangel, or on some other Sunday within one month after those feasts, immediately after the Gospel.*" (*Cardwell, D.A.,* i., p. 263.) " VII. Furthermore I do grant and confess, that the book of common prayer and administration of the holy sacraments, set forth by the authority of parliament, is agreeable to the scriptures, and that it is catholic, apostolic, and most for the advancing of God's glory, and the edifying of God's people, both for that it is in a tongue, that may be understood of the people, and also for the doctrine and form of ministration contained in the same." (*Ibid.,* p. 265.)

1561. "*Articles agreed upon at the second session in Lambeth the 12th day of April, A.D.* 1561, *by the most reverend fathers in God, Matthew, lord archbishop of Cant., Thomas, lord archbishop of York, with the assent of their brethren the bishops to the same.*—Ex. Reg. Parker." (*Ibid.,* p. 298.) " Item, That the declaration devised for unitye of doctrine may be enjoyned throughout the realm uniformly." (*Ibid.*)

1564-5. "*Protestations to be made, promised, and subscribed by them that shall hereafter bee admitted to any office, roome, or cure in any churche, or other place ecclesiasticall.*" Annexed to the Advertisements. " I shall reade the service appoynted playnly, distinctly, and audibly, that all the people may heare and understande." (*Ibid.,* p. 330.)

legal obligation of any Rubric, nor make compliance with it *morally* binding where by general consent or acquiescence the Ordinaries allowed it to remain inoperative. Moreover it cannot well be doubted that, however " capable of being enforced," and however much a Clergyman may be free to adopt the Vestments in virtue of his "assent and consent," the long and continuous non-enforcement of them would have protected from " severe penal-"ties" any Clergyman who might chance to have been prosecuted for not observing the Rubric; this, in fact, on May 23rd, 1857, was the opinion of a member of the present Court, Lord Chelmsford, who, in conjunction with Dr. Deane, thus advised upon a case submitted to them :—

"Upon the question of Dress we are of opinion that the present Prayer Book, taken in conjunction with the First Prayer Book of Edward VI., sanctions the use of the Vestments worn by Mr. Lowder in the Ministration of the Holy Communion; and that he may, in executing the Holy Ministry, lawfully put on a white alb plain, with a vestment, and that such dress is ' according to the form prescribed in the Book of Common Prayer made and published by authority of Parliament.'

"I do also faithfully promise . . . . . to observe, kepe, and mentayne suche order and uniformity in all external policye, rites, and ceremonies of the church as by the lawes, good usages and orders are already well provided and established." (*Ibid.*, p. 331.)

1584. "*Articles touching preachers, and other orders for the church.* Reg. I. Whitgift, fol. 97a." (*Ibid.*, p. 466.) Art. VI. requires subscription "before the ordinary of the diocese" to the following Article (with two others) :—"2. That the book of common prayer, and of ordering bushops, prestes, and deacons, conteyneth nothing in it contrary to the word of God, and that the same may lawfully be used, and that he himself will use the forme of the said book prescribed in public prayer, and administration of the sacraments, and none other." (*Ibid.*, p. 468.)

1604. *Canon* 36. "*Subscription required of such as are to be made Ministers,*" includes the following Article (with two others) :—"II. That the Book of Common Prayer, and of ordering of bishops, priests, and deacons, containeth in it nothing contrary to the Word of God, and that it may lawfully so be used ; and that he himself will use the form in the said book prescribed in public prayer, and administration of the sacraments, and none other." The person consenting to these three Articles thus attests them :—" I N. N. do willingly and *ex animo* subscribe to three articles above mentioned, and to all things that are contained in them."

Can it be maintained that there is any *practical* difference between the above Declarations and the following one of 1662 ? I think not.

1662. *Stat.* 13 & 14 *Charles* 2nd, *cap.* 4, *sect.* iv. " I, *A. B.,* do here declare my unfeigned assent and consent to all and every thing contained and prescribed in and by the book, intituled, The Book of Common Prayer and Administration of the Sacraments, and other Rites and Ceremonies of the Church, according to the use of the Church of England: together with the Psalter or Psalms of David, pointed as they are to be sung or said in Churches; and the Form or Manner of making, ordaining, and consecrating of Bishops, Priests, and Deacons."

"But this dress has been so long allowed to go out of use, that we cannot advise Mr. Lowder that the wearing such dress is now 'legally obligatory,' in the sense that a Priest of the Church of England not wearing such dress is liable to punishment or censure as for an offence." (1st *Rit. Report*, p. 157.)

The Judicial Committee say "It is not to be assumed without "proof that such a Statute was framed so as to leave a choice "between contrary interpretations, in a question that had ever "been regarded as momentous;" the idea here conveyed is—that a new Rule being set forth it would be clear and precise : whereas the *primâ facie* view is that the old Rule was retained as being plain and definite ; the instructions in Charles II.'s Warrant for the Savoy Conference certainly favour this latter impression, for the Commissioners are directed :—

"To take into" their "serious and grave considerations, the several directions, rules and forms of prayer, and things in the said Book of Common Prayer contained, and to advise and consult upon and about the same, and the several objections and exceptions which shall now be raised against the same. And if occasion be, to make such reasonable and necessary alterations, corrections and amendments therein, as . . . . shall be agreed upon to be needful or expedient for the giving satisfaction unto tender consciences, and the restoring and continuance of peace and unity, in the Churches under our protection and government; but avoiding, as much as may be, all unnecessary alterations of the forms and Liturgy wherewith the people are already acquainted, and have so long received in the Church of England." (*Cardwell, Conf.*, p. 300.)

Moreover, the following considerations are very important to be noticed .—

(1) There were no "*contrary* interpretations" of the Rubric and Statute up to the time of the Savoy Conference.

(2) The Presbyterians at that Conference interpreted it as including the Cope and other Vestments; and the Bishops did not deny that this was its meaning, although the Surplice was at that time the only one of them required, except the Cope in Cathedrals.

(3) The Bishops,[*] as the Court says (See p. 99), "determined "that the Rubric 'should continue as it is.'"

---

[*] Richard Baxter, in his account of the Proceedings of the Savoy Conference, in 1661, says :—"And here, because they would abate us nothing at all considerable, but made things far harder and heavier than before, I will annex the Concessions of Archbishop Ussher, Archbishop Williams, Bishop Morton, Bishop Holdsworth, and many others in a Committee at Westminster (before mentioned), 1641." Then, in a List of these Concessions, under the Title of "Considerations

(4) Six years afterwards the Puritans, including BAXTER (who was one of their leaders at the Savoy Conference), regarded it as unchanged, for "among the most necessary alterations of the "Liturgy" (1668) they proposed that "The Rubric for the old "Ornaments which were in use in the Second Year of Edw. VI. "[be] put out." *

(5) Fifteen years later THOMAS DE LAUNE, in "A Plea for the "Non-conformists," 1683, for which he was fined and imprisoned, regarded the Rubric as *unaltered;* for he complains of it in common with other points in the Prayer Book which unquestionably had not been altered in deference to the demands of the Presbyterians; he writes thus:—

"How faulty the liturgy appeared in many of these things, to many learned episcopal divines, is manifest by that paper, which was drawn up A.D. 1641, touching innovations, in the doctrine and discipline of the church of England, together with considerations upon the Common Prayer; and subscribed by arch-bishop Usher, Dr. Williams, bishop of Lincoln, Dr. Prideaux, afterwards bishop of Worcester, Dr. Browning, afterwards bishop of Exeter, Dr. Hacket, afterwards bishop of Litchfield and Coventry, Dr. Ward, Dr. Featly, &c., and presented to the parliament; wherein they give thirty-five exceptions against several things in the liturgy: and amongst others, against the corrupt translation of the Epistles, Gospels, and Psalms; against the Apocrypha enjoined to be read in the lessons; against singing of service; against adding *Gloria Patri* to the Psalms; against the hymns taken out of the mass-book, *Benedicite omnia opera*, &c.; against priests vestments, enjoined as were used, 2 Edw. 6th; against the sign of the cross in baptism, which was heretofore its concomitant afore they went always together; against prohibiting times of marriage, &c." (Pp. 65-6; *Cambridge*, 1789.)

(6) The Royal Commissioners in 1689 proposed to substitute for the present Rubric the following:—

"Whereas ye Surplice is appointed to be used by all Ministers in performing Divine Offices, it is hereby declared, That it is continued onely as being an Antient & Decent Habit. But yet if any Minister shall come & declare to his Bishop that he cannot satisfye his Conscience in ye Use of ye Surplice in Divine Service, In That case y^e

of the Book of Common Prayer," he mentions the following :—"3. Whether the Rubrick should not be mended, where all vestments in time of Divine Service are now commanded, which were used, 2 Edw. VI." (*Sylvester's Life and Times of Baxter*, 1696; pt. ii., pp. 369 and 371.)

* "Reliquiæ Baxterianæ, or Mr. Richard Baxter's Narrative of the most memorable Events of his life and times, faithfully published from his own original Manuscript by Matthew Sylvester." (*Part* iii., *p.* 39, *fol.* 1696.) Baxter died Dec. 8, 1691.

Bishop shall dispense with his not using it, and if he shall see cause for it, He shall appoint a Curate to Officiate in a Surplice."

"Mē: This Rubric was suggested, but not agreed to, but left to further Consideration."

On the margin of the omitted Rubric this is written—"Mem: A *Canon* to specify ye Vestments."*

The fair inference from this proposal to omit the Rubric and to provide "A Canon to specify the Vestments" is that the Canons of 1603-4 were not then held to *fully* " specify " the Vestments or to *control* the Rubric which, though it did not " specify " what was to be used, *referred* to some things which undoubtedly the Commissioners could not have wished to enforce, seeing that they were not disinclined to "dispense" with the Surplice in certain cases.

(7) Not one of the Commentators on the Rubric of 1662, from 1708 to 1869, above quoted (See pp. 111—19), nor any other, so far as I am aware, appears to have considered that it left " a " choice between contrary interpretations;" the larger *prescription* of it was not denied, although the Surplice alone was regarded as of obligation.

These considerations would seem to throw *upon the Court* the duty of furnishing "proof" that its new construction of the Statute is according to the minds of those who " framed " it ; or rather by it *continued* the Rubric which had existed since 1559, although it had only been in part enforced. Supposing, however, that their Lordships' construction did not, as it does, conflict with all the known evidence, it could not, as it did not (though the Court appears to hold the contrary), dispose of " a question "that had ever been regarded as momentous;" for the imposition of the *Surplice* alone " had stirred . . . . some of the strongest "passions of men" quite as much at least as the other Vestments to which the Judicial Committee allude when citing this remark from the Dean of the Arches.

No doubt their Lordships are correct in saying that " a strong " desire for Uniformity" characterised ",all the communications "between Archbishop Parker and the Queen and her government," and also "the Articles of Visitation after 1662"; though they might with equal truth have included the Visitation Articles *before* 1662 : but the obvious remark is that it was a Uniformity *of the very*

* " Copy of the Alterations in the Book of Common Prayer, prepared by the Royal Commissioners for the Revision of the Liturgy in 1689." (*Parliamentary Paper*, 2 June, 1854.)

lowest type, and one dictated by the necessity of securing some degree of general compliance with the Ecclesiastical Laws during a long period of marked indifference and positive opposition to their smallest requirements. Modern Visitation Articles have had to encounter the same difficulties, though not always to the same extent; they too have been "framed" upon the "minimum" of compulsory Laws; and it is notorious that generally admitted improvements in the Ritual and Ornaments of the Church are due far less to them than to the greater piety, increased zeal, improved taste, and larger liberality which have gradually manifested themselves among Laity and Clergy during the last half century, and especially in the latter portion of it.

Possibly it was not without a smile that their Lordships sought to fortify their argument against a "minimum" and "maxi-"mum" use by suggesting, what they deem the barrier of a Ritual impossibility, that:—"If the minister is ordered to wear a Surplice "at all times of his ministration, he cannot wear an alb and tunicle "when assisting at the Holy Communion": that "he *cannot*" I must take leave to deny; though it might not be quite *convenient* to have an Albe under a Surplice—the sleeves of the latter being confined within the body of the Tunicle. To say that "if he is "to celebrate the Holy Communion in a Chasuble, he cannot cele-"brate in a Surplice," is a mistake unless "cannot" means *may not*, and might lead people to think that their Lordships had never seen a Chasuble; for nothing could be easier; and indeed the sleeves of the Surplice might perhaps be thought more graceful than those of the Albe. That *three* Vestments *can* be worn together by a Bishop, and therefore are not *impossible* to a Priest when Celebrating or to a Deacon when assisting at the Holy Communion, is plain from the following direction in the First Prayer Book of K. Edward VI.:—

"And whensoever the Bishop shall celebrate the Holy Communion in the Church, or execute any other public ministration, he shall have upon him, beside his Rochette, a Surplice or Albe, and a Cope or Vestment; and also his Pastoral Staff in his hand, or else borne or holden by his Chaplain."

It has not been suggested by their Lordships that a Surplice and Cope "cannot" be worn together: perhaps they did not intend to present a bar to their combined use in *Parish* Churches, in view of having to decide later "that the Cope is to be worn in "ministering the Holy Communion on high feast-days in Cathe-"drals and Collegiate Churches."

If the Court, while condemning the other Eucharistic Vestments, had held that the language of the 58th Canon was not *prohibitory* of the Cope in Parish Churches,* the "Ritualists" might perhaps have been content to limit themselves to the use of a Vestment which even some of their strongest opponents have since either expressed their willingness to wear, or have actually adopted on the Great Festivals.

There is, however, a further and very important question arising out of a remark in that passage of the Judgment upon which I have been commenting. Their Lordships speak of "the fact that the Rubric is a positive order, under a penal "Statute," (See p. 169); this, no doubt, has been the accepted view: but is it a "fact"? For myself I own that I never doubted it until, soon after the Judgment was delivered, I read the passage quoted at p. 52 from a Tract printed in 1605, and referred to by the Judicial Committee touching the Authority of the Advertisements (See p. 50). The writer argues, as I have noticed at p. 51, that no *penalty* attached to the non-use of the *Ornaments* prescribed by the Rubric and Statute of 1559, because the Penal Clauses of the Statute *precede* the Proviso as to the Ornaments; and certainly a consideration of the Act seems to sustain his contention, though Lawyers may be able to furnish satisfactory reasons for a different conclusion.

But it will probably be said that, assuming the truth of this argument employed by the Author of "*Considerations against the* "*Deprivation of a Minister 'for the not use of a Surplice in Divine* "*Service,*'" his conclusion is inapplicable since the Act of 1662, and therefore is immaterial to us; because, while this latter Statute does not contain the Proviso of the Act of 1559, it enforces the use of the Prayer Book of 1662 which does

* The following account shows that this Canon was not deemed *prohibitory* in 1640:—" The like [persecution by the House of Commons] happened also unto Heywood, Vicar of St. Giles's-in-the-Fields; Squire, of St. Leonard's, in Shoreditch; and Finch, of Christ-Church. The articles against which four and some others more, being for the most part of the same nature and effect, as, namely, railing in the Communion-table, adoration toward it, calling up the parishioners to the rail to receive the Sacrament, reading the second service at the table so placed, preaching in surplices and hoods, *administering the Sacrament in Copes*, beautifying and adorning churches with painted glass, and others of the like condition; which either were to be held for crimes *in the clergy generally*, or else accounted none in them." (*Cyprianus Anglicus*, p. 471. Quoted in *Hierurgia Anglicana*, p. 165.)

contain the Ornaments' Rubric, and moreover the Act keeps in force the previous Statutes of Uniformity, which were then "in "*force*," *with all their penalties* for the very purpose of "establish-"ing and confirming the said book."

To meet this objection it is necessary to compare carefully the corresponding Clauses of the four Acts which bear upon the subject: they will be best seen by being placed, as is here done, in parallel columns.

N.B. The figures in square brackets shew the Nos. of the Sections in "The Statutes Revised," 1870.

2 & 3 Edw. VI, c. 1, 1548.	5 & 6 Edw. VI, c. 1, 1552.	1 Elizabeth, c. 2, 1558-9.	13 & 14 Car. II. c. 4, 1662.
Sect. 1 [1] Provided a new order of Service called "The Book of the Common Prayer and Administration of the Sacraments, and other Rites and Ceremonies of the Church, after the use of the Church of England."	Sect. 5 [4], recites that "because there hath arisen in the use and exercise of the" Book of 1549 "divers doubts for the fashion and manner of the ministration of the same," therefore the said Book has been "godly perused, explained, and made fully perfect," and "annexed" to this Statute, together with the Ordinal also provided.	Sect. 2 [1] Restored "the said Book [of 1552], with the order of service, and of the administration of sacraments, rites, and ceremonies, with the alterations and additions therein added and appointed by this Statute."	Sect. 1 [1]. Recites that the Convocations of Canterbury and York had "made some alterations . . . . and some additional Prayers" in the Book of 1559 which the King "fully approved and allowed," and "recommended" to Parliament as the Book to be used in future.
Required "all and singular ministers in any cathedral or parish church, or other place within this realm of England, Wales, Calice, and the Marches of the same, or other the King's dominions," to use it "from and after the Feast of Pentecost next coming."	Which by Sect. 6 was to come into use on the next Feast of all Saints.	Sect. 3 [2]. Required "all and singular Ministers in any cathedral or parish church, or other place within this realm of England, Wales, and the Marches of the same, or other the Queen's dominions" to use it "from and after the Feast of the Nativity of St. John Baptist next coming."	Sect. 2 [1]. Requires "all and singular ministers in any cathedral, collegiate, or parish church or chapel, or other place of public worship within this realm of England, dominion of Wales, and town of Berwick-upon-Tweed" to use the same: and Section 32 "Provided also that the Book of Common Prayer, and Administration of the Sacraments, and other Rites and Ceremonies of this Church of England, together with the form and manner of ordaining and consecrating Bishops, Priests, and
Sec. 1 [2] Enacts "that if any manner of parson, vicar, or other whatsoever minister . . . shall after the said feast of Pentecost next coming refuse to use the said common		Sec. 4 [2]. Enacts that "if any manner of parson, vicar, or other whatsoever minister . . . from and after the Feast of the Nativity of St. John Baptist next coming, refuse	

2 & 3 EDW. VI, c. 1, 1548.	5 & 6 EDW. VI, c. 1, 1552.	1 ELIZABETH, c. 2, 1558-9.	13 & 14 CAR. II, c. 4, 1662.
prayers, or to minister the Sacraments . . . ..in such order and form as they be mentioned and set forth in the said book; or shall use, wilfully and obstinately standing in the same, any other rite, ceremony, order, form, or manner of mass, openly or privily, or mattens, evensong, administration of the Sacraments, or other open prayer than is mentioned and set forth in the said book; (open prayer in and throughout this Act, is meant that prayer which is for other to come unto or hear, either in common churches or private chapels or oratories, commonly called the Service of the Church;) or shall preach, declare, or speak anything in the derogation or depraving of the said book, or anything therein contained, or of any part thereof; and shall be thereof lawfully convicted according to the laws of this realm, by verdict of twelve men, or by his own confession, or by the notorious evidence of the fact shall," if beneficed *For his 1st offence,* forfeit to the Crown one year's profits of *one* of his benefices; and suffer six months' imprisonment without bail or mainprize. *For his 2d offence,* suffer imprisonment		to use the said common prayers, or to minister the sacraments . . . . in such order and form as they be mentioned and set forth in the said book; or shall wilfully or obstinately, standing in the same, use any other rite, ceremony, order, form or manner of celebrating of the Lord's Supper, openly, or privily, or mattens, evensong, administration of the Sacraments, or other open prayers, than is mentioned and set forth in the said book; (open prayer in and throughout this act, is meant that prayer which is for others to come unto or hear, either in common churches, or private chapels or oratories, commonly called the service of the church;) or shall preach, declare or speak anything in the derogation or depraving of the said book, or anything therein contained, or of any part thereof, and shall be thereof lawfully convicted, according to the laws of this realm, by verdict of twelve men, or by his own confession, or by the notorious evidence of the fact, shall" if beneficed *For his 1st offence,* forfeit to the Crown one year's profits of ALL his benefices; and suffer six months' imprisonment without bail or mainprize. *For his 2d offence,* Section 5 [2],	Deacons, heretofore in use, and respectively established by Act of Parliament in the first and eighth years of Queen Elizabeth, shall be still used and observed in the Church of England, until the Feast of St. Bartholomew, which shall be in the year of our Lord God one thousand six hundred sixty and two." Sect. 3 to 6 [2 & 3] Require, for " Uniformity," every Beneficed person to read the Morning and Evening Prayers and to make a Declaration, in a prescribed form, " before the congregation " of " his unfeigned assent and consent to the use of all things in the said Book contained and prescribed." The same same to be done within a given time upon pain of deprivation *ipso facto*. S. 17 [13]. Enacts " that no form or order of common prayers, administration of sacraments, rites, or ceremonies, shall be openly used in any church, chapel, or other public place of or in any college or hall in either of the Universities, the Colleges of Westminster, Winchester, or Eton, or any of them, other than what is prescribed and appointed to be used in and by the said book."

2 & 3 Edw. VI, c. 1, 1548.	5 & 6 Edw. VI, c. 1, 1552.	1 Elizabeth, c. 2, 1558-9.	13 & 14 Car. II, c. 4, 1662.
for one year; and be deprived *ipso facto* of all his spiritual promotions. *For his 3d offence*, suffer imprisonment during his life. If unbeneficed, shall—*For the 1st offence*, suffer imprisonment during SIX MONTHS, without bail, or mainprize. *For the 2d offence*, suffer imprisonment during his life. Sec. 2 [3]. Makes it penal to deprave the Book "in any interludes, plays, songs, rhimes, or by other open words"; or to "compel or cause, or otherwise procure or maintain any parson, vicar, or other minister," to say "any common and open prayer, or to minister any Sacrament, otherwise or in any other manner or form than is mentioned in the said book"; or to "unlawfully interrupt or let any parson," &c., in using the said Book: the penalty being— *For the 1st offence*, a forfeit to the Crown of TEN POUNDS. *For the 2d offence*, a forfeit to the Crown of TWENTY POUNDS. *For the 3d offence*, a forfeit to the Crown of "all his goods and chattels," and the suffering		suffer imprisonment for one year; and be deprived *ipso facto* of all his spiritual promotions. *For his 3d offence*, Sect. 6 [2], be DEPRIVED, *ipso facto*, OF ALL HIS SPIRITUAL PROMOTIONS, and also be imprisoned for life. If unbeneficed, Sect. 7 [2]—*For the 1st offence*, suffer imprisonment for ONE YEAR, without bail or mainprize. *For the 2d offence*, Sect. 8 [2], suffer imprisonment during his life. Sect. 9 [3]. Makes it penal to deprave the Book "in any interludes, plays, songs, rhymes, or by other open words"; or "by open threatenings, compel or cause, or otherwise procure or maintain any parson, vicar, or other minister" to say "any common or open prayer, or to minister any sacrament otherwise, or in any other manner and form, than is mentioned in the said book"; or to "unlawfully interrupt or let any parson," &c., in using the said Book, the penalty being— *For the 1st offence*, a forfeit to the Crown of a HUNDRED MARKS. *For the 2d offence*, Sect. 10 [3], a forfeit to the Crown of FOUR HUNDRED MARKS. *For the 3d offence*, Sect. 11 [3], a forfeit to the Crown of "all his goods and chattels"; and the	

2 & 3 Edw. VI, c. 1. 1548.	5 & 6 Edw. VI, c. 1. 1552.	1 Elizabeth, c. 2, 1559.	13 & 14 Car. II. c. 4, 1662.
imprisonment for life. If the convicted person fail to pay the penalty within six weeks he is, instead of the fine, *For the 1st offence,* to "suffer imprisonment by the space of THREE months, without bail or mainprize." *For the 2d offence,* to "suffer imprisonment during SIX months, without bail or mainprize."	Sect. 1 to 4 [1 to 3] Require every person to come to Church upon Sundays and Holy Days upon pain of Ecclesiastical Censure, which the Ordinaries are empowered to inflict. Sect. 6 [5] Makes it penal to be present at any other Common Prayer or Sacraments or "making of ministers," the penalty being— *For the 1st offence,* "imprisonment for six months, without bail or mainprize." *For the 2d offence,* "imprisonment for one whole year." *For the 3d offence,* "imprisonment during his or their lives." N.B. In the Chronological Index to the Revised Statutes (vol. i., lxxviii.) it is stated that this 6th Sect. is repealed by 9 & 10 Vict., c. 59, s. 1; and, accordingly, it is omitted from this new Edition of the Statutes.	suffering imprisonment for life. If the convicted person failed to pay the Penalty within six weeks, he is, instead of the fine, *For the 1st offence,* Sect. 12 [3], to "suffer imprisonment by the space of SIX months, without bail or mainprize." *For the 2d offence,* Sect. 13 [3], to "suffer imprisonment during TWELVE months, without bail or mainprize."	Sec. 14 to 16 Require every person to come to Church upon Sundays and Holy Days, under censure of the Church, which the Ordinaries and others are empowered to inflict. "And also upon pain" of forfeiting "twelve pence" for every absence except for a reasonable cause.
Sect. 3 [4]. Gives power to "the justices of Oyer and		Sect. 17 [5] Gives power to "all and every justices of	

2 & 3 EDW. VI, c. 1, 1548.	5 & 6 EDW. VI, c. 1, 1552.	1 ELIZABETH, c. 2, 1558-9.	13 & 14 CAR. II., c. 4, 1662.
Determiner, or Justices of assize" to hear and determine these offences.		Oyer and Determiner, or justices of assize" to hear and determine these offences.	
Sect. 4 [5]. Allows the Bishop of the Diocese to join with the justices.		Sect. 18 [6]. Allows the Bishop of the Diocese to join with the Justices.	
Sect. 8 [8]. Orders at whose charge and when the Books shall be provided.		Sect. 19 Orders when the Books shall be provided.	
Sect. 9 [9]. Is a limitation of prosecutions.		Sec. 20 [8]. Is a limitation of prosecutions.	
S. 10 [10]. Enacts that Peers shall be tried by Peers.		S. 21 [9]. Enacts that Peers shall be tried by Peers.	
Sect. 11 [11]. Empowered the Mayor and other chief officers of corporate Towns, "to the which Justices of Assize do not commonly repair," to hear and determine these offences.		Sect. 22 [10]. Empowers the Mayor and other chief officers of corporate Towns, "to the which Justices of Assize do not commonly repair" to hear and determine these offences.	
Sect. 12 [12]. Made these offences also inquirable and punishable by the *Ecclesiastical* Jurisdiction.		Sect. 23 [11]. Made these offences also inquirable and punishable by the *Ecclesiastical* Jurisdiction.	
Sect. 13 [13]. Provided that a person should only be *once* punished for the said first offence, notwithstanding the two Jurisdictions.		Sect. 24 [12]. Provided that a person should only be *once* punished, for the same offence notwithstanding the two Jurisdictions.	
Sect. 5 & 6 [6]. Declare by whom and in what places the Prayers might be used in another language.			Sect. 18 [14]. Declares where the Service may be used in Latin.
Sect. 7 [7]. "Provided also, that it shall be lawful for all men, as well in churches, chapels, oratories, or other places, to use openly any psalm or prayer taken out of the Bible, at any due time, not letting or omitting thereby the service or any part thereof mentioned in the said Book."			

2 & 3 EDW. VI, c. 1, 1548.	5 & 6 EDW. VI., c. 1, 1552.	1 ELIZABETH, c. 2. 1558-9.	13 & 14 CAR. II., c. 4, 1662.
	Sect. 5 [4] Ordered the "former act to stand in full force and strength, to all intents, and constructions, and to be applied, practised, and put in use to and for the Establishing of 'The Book of Common Prayer,' now explained, and hereunto annexed, and also the said form of making of archbishops, bishops, priests, and deacons hereunto annexed, as it was for the former book."	Sect. 25 [13.] Enacted that the Ornaments of the 2nd year of Edw. 6, should "be retained and be in use" until the "other order" provided should be made. Sect. 26 [13]. Provided for the ordaining of "further ceremonies or rites" in case of "any contempt or irreverence ... by the misusing of the orders appointed in this Book. Sect. 27 [14]. Enacted "that all laws, statutes, and ordinances, wherein or whereby any other service, administration of sacraments, or common prayer, is limited, established, or set forth to be used within this realm, or any other the Queen's dominions or countries, shall from henceforth be utterly void and of none effect."	S. 24 [20]. Enacts "that the several good laws and statutes of this realm, which have been formerly made, and are now in force, for the uniformity of prayer and administration of the sacraments, within this Realm of England and places aforesaid, shall stand in full force and strength, to all intents and purposes whatsoever, for the establishing and confirming of the said book, intituled 'The Book of Common Prayer,' &c., "and shall be applied, practised, and put in ure for the punishing of all offences contrary to the said laws, with relation to the Book aforesaid, and no other."

In the foregoing Analysis, it is assumed that these four Statutes are all "in force, ... for the establishing and confirming" of the Prayer Book of 1662, for they have been usually so regarded, and they are retained in the "The Revised Statutes" of 1870: yet it seems very doubtful whether the two Acts of Edward the Sixth which were repealed by Queen Mary were ever revived. It is, indeed, commonly held that the Act of 1552 was revived by the 1st Eliz. cap. 2, §§ 1 & 2; and that as the Act of 1548 was kept in force by the Act of 1552 "for the establishing of" the Prayer Book of 1552, so it was also revived by the Elizabethan Act of Uniformity. But did the Act of 1559 really revive either of these Acts? I think not; for the following reasons:—

(1.) The Statute of Elizabeth refers to the *Book* of 1552 as having "remained" at the death of King Edward 6th in virtue of the Act of 1552, "the which Act," it says, "was repealed and "taken away by Act of Parliament in the first year of" Queen Mary. The 2nd Section then enacts "that the said statute of "repeal, and everything therein contained, only concerning the "said book, and the service, administration of the sacraments, "rites, and ceremonies, contained or appointed in or by the said "book, shall be void and of none effect, from and after the feast "of the Nativity of St. John Baptist next coming"; and then it authorizes "the said book" of 1552 "with the alterations and "additions" made in it and mentioned in the 3rd Section; "any-"thing in the aforesaid statute of repeal to the contrary notwith-"standing." Therefore it would appear that *only the* BOOK of 1552 was revived, and not the Act of 1552.

(2.) All the Clauses of the Act of 1548, penal and other, which were necessarily kept in force by the Act of 1552 to maintain the book of 1552, and also such Clauses of the Act of 1552 as it was needful to preserve, were incorporated almost *verbatim* with the Statute of 1559, and therefore the Acts of 1548 and 1552 were *wholly unnecessary* for enforcing the revived and altered BOOK of 1552.

(3.) Most of the Penalties contained in the Act of 1559 were materially different from those in the Acts of 1548 and 1552, being made severer: thus, the forfeit in 1548 of a year's profit from *one* of the Clerk's Benefices, was increased in 1559 to the like forfeit from *all* his Benefices; *deprivation of all spiritual promotions* is added to imprisonment for life after a *third* offence; *six months'* imprisonment is increased to *one year*; fines of £10 and £20 are augmented respectively to 100 Marks and 400 Marks; *three* and *six* months imprisonment became in 1559 *six* and *twelve* months; absence from Church, which in 1552 was punishable by *Ecclesiastical censure*, also incurred a *fine* in 1559. So that if the Acts of 1548 and 1552 had really been revived by the Act of 1559 there would have been the anomaly of contemporary Statutes compelling the use of the Prayer Book by *differing* Penalties, and these much heavier in the later Statute.

(4.) The last Section of the Act of 1559 made " utterly void" and " of none effect" from that time " all laws, statutes, and " ordinances, wherein or whereby any other service, administra- " tion of sacraments or common prayer, is limited, established, or " set forth to be used within this realm, or any other the Queen's " dominions or countries." There was sufficient difference between the Books of 1552 and 1559 to make them not the *same* Service; the latter consisted of "one alteration or addition of certain lessons to be used on every Sunday in the year, and the form of the Litany " altered and corrected, and two sentences only added in the " delivery of the sacrament to the communicants": besides this, the Ornaments Rubric was wholly unlike in the two Books. The Book of 1549 varied very considerably from both these in the Services, though agreeing with that of 1559 as to the Ornaments to be used in them. So that, as it appears to me, the language of Sect. 27 of 1 Eliz. c. 2, is not satisfied if it be held to refer only to the " other Service " revived by Queen Mary. The Judicial Committee, in Martin *v.* Mackonochie, when dealing with the question of Lighted Candles as " a ceremony or cere- "monial act," held that their use " would be prohibited by Queen " Elizabeth's Act of Uniformity, Sec. 4, which is now applicable to "the present Prayer Book," and that " any prior authority for the "practice, from usage or otherwise, would be avoided by Sect. 27 " of the same Statute. Their Lordships' argument may, I think, be fairly cited to prove that King Edward's two Acts of Uniformity were not "in force" when the Act of 1662 passed, and consequently are not in force now, although the Court's definition of the word "ceremonies," as used in the Prayer Book, may well be seriously questioned.

(5.) Probably, however, it will be objected—that as this view leaves "in force" only the Elizabethan Act of Uniformity, at the time of making the Act of 1662, the words of the latter would not be true; for they plainly speak of more than one Statute when they say—

"The several good laws and statutes of this realm, which have been formerly made, and are now in force, for the uniformity of prayer and administration of the Sacraments, within this realm of England and places aforesaid, shall stand in full force and strength, to all intents and purposes whatsoever, for the establishing and confirming of the said Book" of 1662.

But the terms of Sect. 24 of the 13 and 14 Car. 2, c. 4, were, at that time, applicable to the following Statutes:—

1 Edw. 6, c. 1, A.D. 1547. "An Act against such as shall unreverently speak against the Sacrament of the Altar, and of the receiving thereof under both kinds." Repealed by 1 Mary, sess. 2, c. 2. Revived by 1 Eliz., 1, s. 14.

2 & 3 Edw. VI., c. 19, A.D. 1548. "An Act touching Abstinence from Flesh in Lent, and at other usual Times."

5 & 6 Edw. VI., c. 3, A.D. 1552. "An Act for the keeping of Holy-Days and Fasting-Days."

5 & 6 Edw. VI., c. 4, A.D. 1552. "Against Quarrelling and Fighting in Churches and Church-yards."

1 Mary, Sess. 2, c. 3, A.D. 1553, "An Act against offenders of Preachers, and other Ministers in the Church."

5 Eliz., c. 28, A.D. 1562. "An Act for the Translating of the Bible and the Divine Service into the Welsh Tongue."

8 Eliz., c. 1, A.D. 1565. "An Act declaring the Making and Consecrating of the Archbishops and Bishops of this Realm to be good, lawful, and perfect."

13 Eliz., c. 12, A.D. 1570. "An Act for the Ministers of the Church to be of sound Religion."

3 Jac. I., c. 1, A.D. 1605. "An Act for a Public Thanksgiving to Almighty God every year on the Fifth day of November."

12 Car. II., c. 14, A.D. 1660. "An Act for a perpetual anniversary Thanksgiving on the Nine-and-twentieth Day of May."

These ten Acts could all, more or less, be applied to "the "establishing and confirming of the" Book of Common Prayer of 1662, although they are not *expressly* "for the uniformity "of Prayer and administration of the Sacraments"; at all events, being *Acts of Parliament*, they are *primâ facie* more likely to be "the several good Law and Statutes of this realm," referred to in this 24th Section, than are the Canons of 1604, which nevertheless this Judgment holds to be kept "in full force and "strength" by the same Section.

Assuming, then, for the sake of argument, that the two Edwardine Acts of Uniformity have been shown not to be now in force, it follows that the Penalties for breaches of the last Act of Uniformity must be sought in the Act of 1559; and if the latter Act does not, as it would seem that it does not, apply those Penalties to the Ornaments' Clause, then it would appear that they could not have been applied to the Ornaments' Rubric of 1559 which that Clause authorized, nor yet to the same Rubric of 1662.

Supposing, however, that the two Edwardine Acts are now in force, they must be construed, I submit, with the later Act of 1559; consequently the terms "rite, ceremony, order, form, or "manner of mass, openly or privily, or mattens, evensong, "administration of the Sacraments, or other open prayer," in the Act of 1548 must be held to mean precisely the same as the terms "rite, ceremony, order, form, or manner of celebrating of, "the Lord's Supper, openly or privily, or mattens, evensong "administration of the Sacraments, or other open prayers," in the Act of 1559; especially as the Clauses which contain them and the Penalties affecting them are imported bodily into the Act of 1559. Now if these terms, occurring in the Act of 1559, all *precede* the Ornaments' Clause, and are not in any way made to refer to it; surely it cannot successfully be maintained that to use the Ornaments authorized by that Clause, in addition to those *expressly prescribed* in the Rubrics of the Services, is to "use "any other rite, ceremony, order, form, or manner" than the Book provides; and consequently none of the *Penalties* for "wilfully and obstinately standing in the same" forbidden use, can be inflicted upon any Minister for either using or not using the *Ornaments* referred to in the Ornaments' Rubric.

But when a non-legal person presumes to suggest a construction of a Statute, especially if it be at variance with the received interpretation, he ought candidly to state any objections which have been made to his contention. I must therefore mention the difficulties raised by a legal friend to the interpretation here proposed: it is said, then, that:—

(*a*) "The 1 Eliz., c. 2, repeals the Statute of Mary, in so far as that Statute repealed anything concerning the Second Prayer-book: that must include the Act enforcing the Second Prayer-book, without which the Second Book had no Parliamentary existence."

The question, however, suggests itself—Was it necessary for the purposes of this Statute, that the Book should have a Parliamentary existence? The Act of Elizabeth was to give it Parliamentary life and, as it seems to me, there was no need to resuscitate the *Act* of 1552 in order to revive the *Book* of 1552. The Statute of Mary "and everything therein contained, "only concerning the said Book" which it prohibited was to "be void and of none effect;" and "the said Book" was to "stand and be . . . in full force and effect, according to the "tenor and effect of this Statute" of Elizabeth. If the Act of 1559 revived the Acts of 1548 and 1552, the obstacles, which I have already noticed, again present themselves; and it must be asked—What need was there to insert the substance of those Acts in the Act of Elizabeth? Again, if the effect of the Act of 1559 was to make the two former Acts concurrent and contemporaneous, which penalties were to be inflicted upon an offender—the later and heavier, or the earlier and lighter?

Another difficulty pointed out to me is that:—

(*b*) "The whole repealing Act of Mary was afterwards swept away by the 1 Jac. 1, c. 25, § 8, and therefore then, at any rate, if not before, the whole of the Act enforcing the Second Prayer-book came anew into existence."

Upon this I venture to remark that the Act of James seems to me itself to suggest an objection to this, the usual, view of the subject. The first part of Clause viii. does certainly appear to be of the most sweeping character; it says:—

"And be it further enacted by the Authoritie of this present Parliament, That an Acte made in the first yere of the raigne of Queen Marie, intituled an Acte for the repeal of certain Statutes made in the tyme of Kinge Edward the Sixte, shall stande repealed and voide." (*Stat. of the Realm, Vol.* 4, *pt.* 2, *p.* 1052.)

Yet the words which *immediately* follow would appear to *limit* the repealing effect to the two Statutes which the Clause mentions, for it goes on to say:—

"And that an Acte .... to take away all positive Lawes made against the Marriage of Priests; And an Acte .... made for declaration of a Statute made for the Marriage of Priests, and for the Legitimation of their Children [*i.e.* 2 & 3 Edw. 6, c. 21; and 5 & 6 Edw. 6, c. 12,] shall stande revived and be in force for ever; ·The saide. Act of Repeale notwithstandinge: And the Children of Ecclesiasticall persons in the saide Acte mentioned, shalbe and continue legitimate and inheritable to all intents and purposes in such sorte as Children of Lay persons doe enjoy and may inherit; Any Canon or Constitution to the contrarie notwithstandinge." (*Ibid.*)

Moreover, if the Elizabethan Act of Uniformity revived the two Edwardine Acts of Uniformity this Statute of K. James was a work of supererogation, not only as regards them, but also with reference to the 1 Edw. 6, c. 1, touching "the Sacrament of the Altar" which had been clearly revived by the 1 Eliz., c. 1, s. 14. On the other hand, if they had not been resuscitated, the question arises— Would not their revival in 1604 repeal the Act of 1559 so far as the latter was, as it was, at variance with them? And further, besides the Penalties, might not this difficulty have arisen—that the Act and Book of 1552 would have superseded the Elizabethan Act and Rubric as to the Ornaments?

There is a further difficulty, as it seems to me, involved in the supposed effect of this repealing Clause in King James's Act. One of the Statutes repealed by the Act of Queen Mary was the 1 Edw. VI., c. 2: "An Act for the Election of Bishops." Now if the Marian was *wholly* repealed by the Jacobean Statute, it would appear to follow that this Act of Edward was revived with all the rest; and as by this Act "all Bishoprics were made "donative again" (*Burn, E. L.*, i., 201) the Statute 25 Hen. VIII., c. 20, for the *Election* of Bishops, which was revived by the 1 Eliz., c. 1, s. 7, would have been in effect repealed 46 years later, and thus the Crown could have appointed the English Bishops by Letters Patent.

Bishop Gibson (*Codex*, 113, 114) mentions that this difficulty "was moved and urged, at a grand Committee of Lords and "Commons (12 *Co.*, 7)"; and adds:—

"But upon consideration had of this matter by command of the King, it was answered and resolved by *Popham* (Chief Justice), *Coke* (Attorney), the Chief Baron, and other Justices, then attendant on Parliament, that although the said Act 1 Mar. be repealed, yet the Act 1 Edw. VI. is not now in force, but remains repealed; and that principally for this cause, that the foregoing Act, 25 Hen. VIII., c. 20, which directs the making of bishops by election (though repealed by 1 & 2 P. & M., c. 8), was revived expressly and by name in Eliz., c. 1, s. 7, and by consequence did revive and re-establish the ancient method of election and confirmation. From hence it follows, (says my Lord Coke,) that the Act. of Eliz. reviving the 25 Hen. VIII. hath repealed the Act of 1 Edw. VI." (See also *Stephens, Eccl. Stat.*, i., 347.)

Nor does this case exhaust the difficulty; for the Marian Statute repealed the 3 & 4 Edw. VI., c. 12, "An Acte for the "orderinge of Ecclesiasticall Ministers." The Ordinal framed under this Act contained Rubrics directing " the Chalice, or cup, with "the Bread " to be given into the hand of him who was being Ordained a *Priest;* and " the Pastoral Staff " into the hand of one being Consecrated a *Bishop:* these directions were omitted in the Ordinal of 1552 which was expressly restored by the Elizabethan Act of Uniformity: but they would seem to have been revived in 1604 if the Act of that year repealed the *whole* of the repealing Statute of 1 Mary, St. 2, c. 2.

There were two other Statutes which this Act of Queen Mary repealed, viz., the 3 & 4 Edw. VI., c. 10, "An Act for the "Abolishing and putting away of divers Books and Images"; and the 5 & 6 Edw. VI., c. 3, " An Act for the keeping Holy- "Days and Fasting-Days." The Books of Statutes give these two Acts as being still in force; and Dr. Stephens has the following Note upon the later Act:—

"*Holy-days and Fasting-days:*—' In the 1st of Queen Elizabeth, a Bill to revive the act of parliament made anno 5 Edw. VI., for keeping of holy-days and fasting-days, was brought into Parliament, but passed not; so that the repeal of Queen Mary remained upon this Act till Stat. 1 Jac. I., c. 25, by which her repeal was repealed; and it is a rule, that by repealing of a repeal, the first act is revived.' 2 Inst. 686." (*Eccl. Stat.*, i., 346.)

But it seems worth considering whether the *principle* involved in the reason, just above mentioned, for the decision of the Judges—that the 1 Edw. VI., c. 2, was *not revived* by the Statute of James, viz. that the 25 Hen. VIII., c. 20, had been previously " revived expressly and by name in 1 Eliz., c. 1, s. 7 "—does not also, so far as regards the Kalendar, apply to this case. The Kalendar, as altered in 1561 for the Elizabethan Prayer Book, contained the entire List of Holy Days and Fast Days named in the repealed Act of Edward, so that the Act was not requisite for enforcing the observance of the Days; but, further, the Elizabethan Kalendar contained also the Feast of the Conversion of St. Paul and the Feast of St. Barnabas: these were not mentioned in the Act, and, consequently, they would seem not to have been *obligatory*, like the other days named in the Kalendar, if the Act of Edward had been revived: the following Article in the Advertisements of 1564-5 appears to recognize this difference between the two:—

"Item, That there be none other holidayes observed besides the Sundayes, but onelye suche as be set out for holidayes, as in the Statute, 'anno quinto et sexto Edwardi sexti,' and in the new calendar authorysed by the Queenes majesty." (*Card.*, *D.A.*, i., 327.)

This difficulty of conflicting with another Statute does not indeed apply to the 3 & 4 Edw. VI., c. 10, for "putting away "divers Books and images"; but it was not "revived, expressly "and by name," though included in the repealing Statute of Mary; and it may be doubted whether, if revived, it would have been operative, owing to the dates mentioned in it: moreover, there does not seem to have been any reason for reviving in 1604 an Act whose object was to prevent the concealment of certain Books and Images ordered to be removed from the Churches in 1549. If it be conjectured that it was revived with reference to "Popish Recusants," it should be considered that the discovery of the Gunpowder Plot was subsequent to it; and, further, that the Act 3 James I., c. 5, which was made expressly against them, distinctly prohibited, in Sections 25 and 26, "popish books and "relicts of popery" and ordered them to be searched for and defaced or destroyed.

It would seem, then, that although the 1 Jac. I., c. 25, removed the *repealing* power of the 1 Mary, St. 2, c. 2, there was no *express reviver*, in this or in any other Statute, of any of the Nine Acts, repealed by the Marian Statute, except the 1 Edw. VI., c. 1, as to the Sacrament of the Altar, revived by 1 Eliz., c. 1. § 14, and the two Statutes relative to Priests' Marriages, revived by the Act of James,—viz., 2 & 3 Edw. VI., c. 21, and 5 & 6 Edw.

VI., c. 12. If to this circumstance be added the considerations already mentioned—that the remaining Six Statutes were either (*a*) not needed or (*b*) would in part have contradicted other Statutes—there does seem a reasonable probability that they did not recover that force of which they were deprived by the Marian Statute.

Having thus noticed the objections made to the view which I have ventured to suggest, I leave where and as it is the whole statement, in case it should be thought worth while on any future occasion to have the subject fully discussed with a view to settling the questions now and heretofore raised.*

* It seems worth while, however, to notice a remark in a Letter from Abp. Parker to Sir W. Cecil dated March 12, 1565-6 (already quoted in part at p. 62), because it appears to shew that the Penalties of the Elizabethan Act of Uniformity were not then held to apply to the Ornaments' Clause of the Statute. The Archbishop was anxious to secure the Queen's sanction to the Advertisements because, as he says, " by Statute we be inhibited to set out any Constitutions without License obtained of the Prince": he complains that "once this last year certain of us consulted and agreed upon some particularities in Apparell" which he "sent" to Cecil " to be presented " to the Queen, but found "they could not be allowed then"; these, he adds, " I now send again, humbly praying that if not all yet so many as be thought good, may be returned with some authority, at the least way for particular Apparell : or else we shall not be able to do so much at the Queen's Majesty expecteth for, of us to be done." (*Parker Correspondence*, p. 263.) As a further reason for pressing his request he mentions " that some lawyers be in opinion that it is hard to proceed to deprivation, having no more warrant but the Queen's Majesty's only word of mouth." (*Ibid.*, p. 264.)

Now "deprivation" is one of the Penalties of the Elizabethan Act of Uniformity (*Sect.* 4) for a second and third offence against that Statute; if, therefore, this Penalty or any other of the Penalties applied to non-compliance with the Ornaments' Clause, what need was there for the Archbishop to ask for power thus to punish offenders? The Penalties of the Statute were in fact *heavier* than he sought to impose under the Advertisements; for in a *Postscript* of this same Letter (See p. 62) he draws Cecil's attention to the fact that "in our book of Articles . . . we made the pain sequestration, and not deprivation." (*Ibid.*) If it be thought that the Archbishop wished to have a greater Penalty for the *first* offence than the Statute provided, the answer is that the "book of Articles" which he mentions proves the contrary; for it is there proposed to "suspend the offenders *ab executione officii*: or if the contumacie of anye offender increase, then to aggravate the peine with sequestration of the fruites of his lyving." (*Strype, Life of Parker*, App. No. xxviii., Vol. iii., p. 92, Oxford, 1821.) It is important also to recollect that the entire Article (See p. 63), containing this proposed Penalty was withdrawn from the Advertisements when they were ultimately issued.

Moreover, it should be borne in mind that the Ornaments' Clause of the Elizabethan Statute contemplated the case of some "other Order" being taken with regard to the Ornaments; and if Sandy's "gloss" upon Parker's report to him touching the "Proviso" for Ornaments (See pp. 17 and 18) be correct, viz.,—" that we shall not be forced to use them, but that others in the mean time shall not convey them away, but that they may remain for the Queen "— the probability is all the greater, that it was not *intended* to attach a penalty to the Ornaments' Clause and that therefore it was purposely placed at the end of

XXVI. The Judgment goes on to say that :—

"In order to decide the question before the Committee, it seems desirable first to examine the effect of the Church legislation of 1603-4. The 14th Canon orders the use of the Prayer Book without omission or innovation, and the 80th Canon directs that copies of the Prayer Book are to be provided, in its lately revised form, and, by implication, the Ornaments-Rubric is thus made binding on the clergy. Canon 24th directs the use of the cope in Cathedral and Collegiate Churches upon principal feast days, 'according to the Advertisements for this end [*for* for this end *read* published], anno 7 Elizabeth.' Canon 58th says that 'every Minister saying the public prayers, or ministering the Sacraments or other rites of the Church, shall wear a decent and comely surplice with sleeves, to be provided at the charge of the parish.'"

Their Lordships do not here repeat *in terms* the strange error already noticed (See XV. p. 83) and subsequently twice repeated (See pp. 193 and 204), but the passage conveys the same misleading notion, especially when read, as it must be, with the context and with that error; that notion is, that "by implication the Orna- "ments-Rubric" became "binding on the Clergy" in virtue of the 14th and 80th Canons; whereas, as I have already shown (at pp. 85 to 89), the Book was in force, under the Elizabethan Act of Uniformity, before the Canons themselves were made.

Moreover, although the 80th Canon ordered the Book to be provided by "the Churchwardens or Quest men .... at the "charge of the Parish," the Canon alone could not have *compelled* the Parishioners, not being *legally* binding on them ; the King's Proclamation of March 5, 1603-4, had already directed the "Archbishops and Bishops" to "take order, that every parish "do procure to themselves" the Book "explained" under the

the Act and after the Penal Clauses which certainly do not *in terms* refer to that Clause. If, however, it should be said that—this view, though correct, is *immaterial* because the Ecclesiastical Commission had then large *punitive* powers—it seems a sufficient answer to say, that (while this does not dispose of the question as to the application of the Penal Clauses of. the Elizabethan Act) these powers ceased with the extinction of the Commission itself (by the 1 Car. i., cap. 11, A.D. 1640), twenty-two years before the Act of Uniformity of 1662.

Provisions of Sections 25 & 26 of the Elizabethan Act of Uniformity (See pp. 86 and 87); and thus legally substituted it for the Book of 1559 which Section 19 of the same Statute had ordered to be procured "at the costs and charges of the "Parishioners of every Parish and Cathedral Church."

However, on the Court's own theory, the Ornaments-Rubric was "binding" in 1603-4, notwithstanding the Advertisements; although it is extremely improbable that the words "Orders, "Rites, and Ceremonies prescribed in the Book of Common "Prayer," refer at all to that Rubric.* But construing the 14th and 80th Canons, which their Lordships allege as imposing the Rubric, with the 24th and 58th Canons which order two of its Ornaments, the Judicial Committee conclude that:—

> "There can be no doubt that the intention here was not to set up a contradictory rule, by prescribing vestments in the Prayer Book and a surplice in the Canons which give authority to the Prayer Book."

The fallacy of this assertion, apart from its erroneous statement already noticed—that the Canons "give Authority to the Prayer "Book" of 1604—lies in the allegation that the rule was "contra-"dictory." If indeed the 24th and 58th Canons had said that *no* Vestment should be used but what they named, they would have been plainly "contradictory"† of the fuller command of the Rubric; but when the *greater* of *two* Rules includes the *less*, and only the less is insisted upon by the Authority which administers both, it seems a misapplication of terms to call them "contradictory,"

* For a full discussion of this point see A Letter "Of Ceremonies, Lights, and Custom." By the REV. WILLIAM COOKE, Honorary Canon of Chester. James Parker & Co. 1868.

† It has been thought (See p. 165) that COSIN was perplexed by a seeming "contradictory rule" (as the Judicial Committee term it) in the Statute and Canon (*Notes, 1st Series*): but I do not understand him to be imagining a discrepancy between them. COSIN asserts the full force of the Ornaments Rubric of 1559: but he supposes an objector to allege "that now the 58th Canon hath ordered it otherwise": he answers "that the 14th Canon commands us to observe all the Ceremonies prescribed in this Book"; and then he says, "I would fain know how we should observe both Canons." His difficulty (if indeed it was *his*) was to reconcile the two Canons—not the Statute and Canon; yet he seems to have thought that the *larger* prescription of Canon 14 should govern the *smaller* requirement of Canon 58. If, then, he considered that Canon 14 of 1604 agreed with the Statute of 1559, it follows that, when importing the words of the Act into the Rubric, as he professed to do in 1661 (See p. 92), he did not design to limit the Vestments by the *lower requirement* of Canons 24 and 58.

especially as the Canons were and are *Statutably* binding on the Clergy,* owing to their having received the King's Ratification.

To countenance this fallacy the Court uses an argument which itself involves two misstatements; they say :—

> "It could not be intended, in recognizing the legal force of the Advertisements, to bring back the things which the Advertisements had taken away, nor could it be expected that either the Minister or people should provide vestments in lieu of those which had been destroyed, and accordingly no direction is given with regard to them."

Yet no recognition of any "legal force" as attaching to the Advertisements is contained in the 24th Canon, which only says that they were "published Ann. 7 Elizabethæ:"† and it has been demonstrated, I think, at pp. 35 to 41, that the Vestments now in question were not "taken away" by the Advertisements. That being "taken away" (whether legally or illegally), their replacement should not be demanded at a time when it was difficult to get the Surplice and the simplest necessaries provided, is not in the least surprising; and it is a reason quite sufficient to warrant their Lordships' statement that "no direction is given "with regard to them," although it cannot sustain the Court's inferential conclusion—that silence about them is a direction against them.

XXVII. The Court expresses its opinion of "the effect of the "Church Legislation of 1603-4" in these words :—

> "The provisions of the Canons and Prayer Book must be read together, as far as possible, and the Canons upon the vesture of the Ministers must be held to be an exposition of and limitation of the Rubric of Ornaments."

---

* See the Judgment of Lord Hardwicke, *Middleton* v. *Croft*, cited Stephens's Eccl. Stat., I., p. 660.

† The Lords' Committee, in 1641, declared that "the Injunctions and Advertisements of Queen Elizabeth" were "not in force, but by way of commentary and imposition." (*Cardwell, Conf. p.* 272.) This must mean, I presume, that the Documents were consecutive and authorized current expositions of the *required compliance* with the Ornaments Rubric; in other words—that they set forth a *minimum* obligation of the Rubric.

There can be no difficulty in accepting the first part of this statement, for, no doubt, the construction of the Canons and Prayer Book should be harmonious; and they would be so if a *negative* meaning were not affixed to the Canons, as has been here done by the Court. Nor need the latter part of the statement be objected to if the words "exposition" and "limitation" only mean—that the Canons set forth what cannot be dispensed with. Their Lordships, however, use them in a *positive* and *exclusive* sense: they hold that—"the Vesture of the Ministers" which the Canons prescribe *must be worn* and that that *alone may be worn*. Now, passing over the consideration that this is not the principle on which the Judicial Committee has hitherto professed to construe Ecclesiastical Documents, it only needs to test the Rubric by this theory of the controlling power of the Canons in order to see the weakness of the argument.

The Rubrical "Ornaments" of "the Ministers" in the Public Services are, according to the Court, those *prescribed by name* in the Prayer Book of 1549: the difference between them and those *prescribed* in the Canons is as follows:—

Prayer Book of 1549.	Bishops. Canons of 1603-4.
In every public ministration. The Bishop "shall have upon him, besides his Rochette, a Surplice or Albe, and a Cope or Vestment." (*Certain Notes*) *i.e.*, as it would appear to mean:— 1. Rochette with Albe and Vestment, for the Holy Communion. 2. Rochette with Surplice and Cope, for other Offices . . "and also his Pastoral Staff in his hand, or else borne or holden by his Chaplain."	*In Cathedral and Collegiate Churches.* For Holy Communion—Cope. For other Offices—nothing named. No Pastoral Staff prescribed.
In Parish Churches—nothing is prescribed by the Canon for the Bishop's use at any Office.	
Cathedral and Collegiate Clergy.	
For Holy Communion—Albe with Vestment or Cope for the Celebrant: Albes with Tunicles for all Assistants.	For Holy Communion—Cope, for the Principal Minister, *i.e.*, the Celebrant (xxiv). "Gospeller and Epistler agreeably, according to the Advertisements."

For Ante-Communion Service.

ALBE or SURPLICE, with COPE.　　Surplice "sufficient," with Hood for the Superior Members, being graduates. (xxv)

For other offices.

SURPLICE, with HOOD for the Superior Members, being graduates.　　Surplice "sufficient," with Hood for the Superior Members, being graduates. (xxv)

PAROCHIAL CLERGY.

For Holy Communion.

ALBE with VESTMENT or COPE for the Celebrant: ALBES with TUNICLES for Assistants.　　SURPLICE with HOOD for graduates, or TIPPET for non-graduates. (lviii)

For Ante-Communion Service.

ALBE or SURPLICE, with COPE.　　SURPLICE with HOOD for graduates, or TIPPET for non-graduates. (*Ib.*)

For Other Offices.

SURPLICE.　　SURPLICE with HOOD for graduates, or TIPPET for non-graduates. (*Ib.*)

*** Neither in the Prayer Book of 1549 nor in the Canons of 1603-4 is any Dress *prescribed* for Preaching: the former only says it is "seemly" for "graduates" then to use HOODS; the latter that "Deans, Masters, and Heads of Collegiate Churches, Canons and Prebendaries, being Graduates, shall" then wear HOODS with their SURPLICES.

From this comparison it will be seen that if (as the Judicial Committee rule) the Canons "must be held to be an exposition "of and limitation of the Rubric of Ornaments"—and, too, in an *exclusive* sense—no more than *four* Vestments are *legally* usable in the Public Service by Bishop, Priest, and Deacon; viz., COPE, SURPLICE, HOOD, and TIPPET.

The consequence of their Lordships' literal and exclusive construction of the Canon, however unintended, is really, though absurdly, this:—

(1) A Bishop may not Celebrate in a Cathedral or Collegiate Church with any Ecclesiastical Vestment whatever except a *Cope*—he must not wear his *Rochet*, nor yet "the rest of the "Episcopal habit" referred to in the Office for the Consecration of Bishops, whether that is the *Black Chimere with Sleeves* or whatever else it may be.

At other times and Services in these Churches and at all times and Services in other Churches he must not wear any Ecclesiastical Vestment, for the Canons are silent about his Dress.

(2) Cathedral and Collegiate Clergy, whether Celebrating or assisting as Gospeller and Epistler, must wear the *Cope*, but not a *Surplice* under it.

At other times of Service "it shall be *sufficient*" for the Superior Cathedral and Collegiate Clergy (who are mentioned in Canon xxv) to wear Surplices and also Hoods if Graduates; but they *may* wear Copes: if it be objected—that the Hoods prevent this, it is an obvious answer—that the objection does not apply to the non-graduate Clergy, for in this Canon they are not ordered to wear Tippets.

(3) No Bishop, Priest, or Deacon may wear in any public ministration a *Scarf* or *Stole* or *Gown* or *Bands*.

(4) In Parish Churches, Graduate Clergy *must* and non-graduate Clergy *may* exceed the Rubric, the former by wearing the *Hood* and the latter the *Tippet* upon the Surplice.

No doubt their Lordships would, reasonably enough, plead CUSTOM for the continued *use* of what their LAW thus *abolishes*: but, then, as the Judicial Committee (in Martin *v.* Mackonochie) would not allow *contemporaneous custom* to qualify their alleged exclusive strictness of the Rubric of 1549 in the matter of Altar Lights, the same Court cannot consistently claim *contemporaneous custom* to qualify its alleged exclusive strictness of the Canons of 1603-4.

If it were not for other statements in this Judgment it might be thought that the earlier part of this next paragraph did not regard the Rubric as *excluding* every Ornament which it does not prescribe *nominatim* (according to the ruling in Martin *v.* Mackonochie); but as *allowing* what was "used under" the Prayer Book of 1549 (according to the language in Liddell *v.* Westerton); for their Lordships say:—

> "Such ornaments are to be used as were in use in the Second year of Edward VI, limited as to the vestments by the special provisions of the Canons themselves; and the contemporaneous exposition

of universal practice show that this was regarded as the meaning of the Canons. There does not appear to have been any return to the vestments in any quarter whatever."

The passage, however, only strengthens the unavoidable inference that in the mind of the Court the only way of reading together the Rubric and Canons " as far as possible " is to subordinate the former to the latter, thus making the Canons absolute: but the absence of " any return to the Vestments " no more proves that their *prohibition* by the Canons " was regarded as the "meaning " of those Rules, than did the non-restoration of the Weekly Celebrations (required in Parish Churches by the First Prayer Book) prove that Canon xxi. was understood to *prohibit* them because it only ordered Celebrations " so often, and at "such times as every Parishioner may Communicate, at the least "thrice in the year." The proposal to alter the Rubric, made by the Lords' Committee in 1641 (See p. 166); the Order of the House of Commons, in 1643 and 1644, to destroy Vestments, &c. (See p. 91) and the desire that the Rubric should be "wholly "left out," expressed by the Ministers at the Savoy Conference in 1661 (See p. 96), all alike negative the theory of the Court as to the then received "meaning of the Canons."*

XXVIII. The Judgment proceeds thus:—

"The Act of 1662 sanctioned a Prayer Book with a different Rubric, but it referred back to the Second of Edward VI, and in some sense or other revived the Rubric of King Edward's First Book; the question is in what sense and in what degree. There seem to be three opinions on this point.
"One, that the Act of 1662 repealed all legislation on the subject of the ornaments of the Minister; the second, that the Act and the Canons set up two distinct standards of ritual on this subject; and the

---

* It would seem to be open to argument whether even the Rubric of 1552 really *prohibited* the use of the Vestments prescribed in the Book of 1549: its words are "And here is to be noted, that the Minister at the time of the Communion, and at all other times in his Ministration, shall use neither Albe, Vestment, nor Cope: but, being Archbishop, or Bishop, he shall have and wear a Rochet: and being a Priest or Deacon, he shall have and wear a Surplice only." May it not have been that, in yielding to the objections of the

third, that the Act of 1662 is to be read with the Canons of 1602 [*read* 1603-4] still in force, and harmonized with them."

Upon these passages it is only necessary to remark—*First*, that to call the Rubric of 1662 "a *different* Rubric" is to assume what has not been proved: and *next*, that it is not correct to say that "the Act of 1662" in "some sense or other *revived* the Rubric of King Edward's first Book"; for no evidence has been produced which proves that it had been repealed: in fact their Lordships had just before said (See p. 192) that, according to their own theory of the effect of the Canons of 1603-4, the Ornaments Rubric was "made "binding on the Clergy." The Act of 1662 *continued* that Rubric—whether *materially* or only *verbally* changed is a point to be further considered—always recollecting, however, that in 1857 the Judicial Committee decided that the different forms of the Rubric and Statute "all obviously meant the "same thing."

XXIX. The "three opinions" as to the "sense" in which the Rubric of 1549 was "revived" are next considered: the Court says :—

> "I. The first is that expressed by Dr. Lushington, in the case of Westerton *v.* Liddell, that in reviving the Rubric of 1549 the Act of 1662 excluded and repealed all provisions whatever of Act of Parliament or Canon which had been made after 1549 and

Foreign party to wear the Vestments, it was not intended to compel those to disuse them who wished to retain them? It is certain that the Commissioners who were then appointed to deal with the Church Goods throughout the country, had distinct Authority to leave in the Churches, besides the Ornaments named in their Commissions, "also such other Ornaments as by their discretion shall seem requisite for the Divine Service in every such place for the time." The Inventories of the period plainly shew that in hundreds of Parishes they did leave many and various ancient Ornaments of the Church and of the Ministers "for the Administration of the Communion," or "for the Divine Service," or "for the administration within the same Church": these and similar expressions abound in those Records. (See 1st *Report of Ritual Commission*, App. 149—151). If the words of the Rubric "shall use," "shall have and wear" may be read "shall [be required to] use," shall [be required to] have and wear," the action of the Commissioners derives additional force from the Rubric.

prior to 1662. This view was adopted by Sir John Dodson in the same case, when it reached the Arches Court. The consequence of this must be that every celebration of the Holy Communion in a surplice only, from 1662 to the present day, would be a violation of the Statute. The Canons of 1603-4 being repealed as to this matter, together with the Advertisements on which the Canons built, there would be no legal warrant for using the surplice and omitting to use the vestments at the Holy Communion. Yet there is no doubt of the practice. For 180 years the vestment was never worn. And thus there would be the unusual occurrence of a Statute repealing former legislation and fortified with heavy penalties, which was systematically broken not only by one and all of those who had declared their unfeigned assent and consent to all and everything contained in the Book of Common Prayer, but by the framers of the Rubric themselves immediately after the confirmation of it by Act of Parliament. Nor is there during that time one single instance of calling to account or censuring any one for his particular share in a universal violation of the law. It appears plain to their Lordships from these facts that the idea of the repealing power of this Rubric is a modern one."

In this passage several points call for remark: FIRSTLY, as to Dr. Lushington's view that the Rubric of 1662 repealed the Canons of 1603-4; for I pass over Sir John Dodson, who can scarcely be considered to have "adopted" it, since he only said, "It seemed to be admitted on all sides .... that the "Rubric .... was to be deemed the *primary* law," a word which certainly implies some *secondary* Rule: whether Dr. Lushington was right or wrong in his opinion, the Judicial Committee itself (in Martin *v.* Mackonochie) construed the Act of Uniformity in a way which, if applied to the Canons, must have abolished them. Their Lordships, dealing with "cere-"monies" in reference to the question of Altar Lights, held that "all are abolished which are not expressly retained" in the Book of Common Prayer; and therefore they ruled that the Injunction of 1547,—

"so far as it could be taken to authorise the use of Lights as a ceremony or ceremonial act, was abrogated or repealed by the Act 1 Eliz., cap. 2, particularly by section 27 . . . . and by the present Prayer Book and Act of Uniformity, and that the use of Lighted Candles, viewed as a ceremony or ceremonial act, can derive no warrant from that Injunction." (4th Report *Rit. Com.*, p. 236.)

Now apply this argument to the *Surplice:* it is not once mentioned in the Prayer Book of 1662 in any Office whatever: in the Prayer Book of 1549 an *Albe* is prescribed for the Celebration of the Holy Communion: therefore to Celebrate in a Surplice according to the Canon is, to use their Lordships' language, an act by which "the integrity of the ceremony is " broken, and it ceases to be the same ceremony": consequently (substituting *Surplice* for *Lights*) "the use of [the Surplice in " Celebrating the Holy Communion] viewed as a ceremony or "ceremonial act, can derive no warrant from that [Canon]." That such use is "a ceremony or ceremonial act," on the theory laid down in Martin *v.* Mackonochie, is certain ; for the Court held that an "inert" *Ornament* became altered in character by "active use . . . as a part of the administration of a Sacrament," so that "the act must be justified, if at all, as part of a cere- "monial law."

Further, the Court having been referred, as an authority for the Lights, to one of the Ecclesiastical Constitutions always supposed to be legally binding by the 35 Hen. viii., c. 16, decided that—

"As to these constitutions it is sufficient to say, that in their Lord- "ships' opinion, they must be taken, if of force at the time of passing "of any of the Acts of Uniformity, to have been repealed by those "Acts." (*Ibid*, p. 236.)

Substitute " Canons of 1603-4 " for " Constitutions " and those Canons are thus declared to have been "repealed."

SECONDLY, the Judicial Committee, in Hebbert *v.* Purchas, (whether recollecting or forgetting their own previous ruling is not very material) seem alarmed at " the consequence " of the alleged repeal of the Canons exhibited in, as they assume, the *illegal* use of the Surplice for 180 years, and the concurrent systematic breach of "a Statute repealing former legislation "and fortified with heavy penalties." If the argument already advanced (See pp. 176-91) has proved that no such "heavy "penalties" are attached to the Statute, there is no cause for their Lordships' consternation. Yet even if the case were as the Court contends, it need be no matter of surprise that "the "framers" and imposers of the Ornaments Rubric in 1662 did not attempt a fuller enforcement of it than had long been customary, though it had acquired new vitality by its re-enactment. On the contrary, they would have proved themselves most impolitic Ecclesiastical Rulers if, despite great opposition and long disuse combined, they had endeavoured to restore the use of the Eucharistic Vestments at a time when, in a very large proportion of places, it required a struggle to maintain or revive the employment of a Surplice only.

THIRDLY, the Court seems to shrink from the bare contemplation of the notion that for 180 years after the passing of the Statute there must have been "a universal violation of the law" by the "Celebration of the Holy Communion in a Surplice" and remarks that "during that time" there is not "one single "instance of calling to account or censuring any one for his "particular share" in this common illegality. But the Court appears to have entirely forgotten the strictly analagous case of Episcopal Ministrations for which special Ornaments are prescribed in the following Rubric of the Prayer Book of 1549, already referred to (See p. 195):—

" And whensoever the Bishop shall celebrate the Holy Communion in the Church, or execute any other public Ministration, he shall have upon him, beside his Rochette, a Surplice or Albe, and a Cope or Vestment; and also his Pastoral Staff in his hand, or else borne or holden by his Chaplain."

Now it has never been pretended, I believe, that *this* Rubric was ever qualified or limited by the Advertisements or Canons; and therefore, whatever be the true relation of the Canons to the Ornaments Rubric of 1662, they cannot affect the bearing of that Rubric upon the Rubric of 1549. Consequently, (to apply their Lordships' argument to this case) "there would be "no legal warrant for [the Bishop] using [his usual Episcopal "Dress only] and omitting to use the [other Ornaments] at the

"Holy Communion [or 'any other public Ministration']." Yet "[there is no more] doubt of the practice" of the Bishops "from "1662 to the present day," any more than there is of the other Clergy during the same period; except that within the last few years a small minority of Bishops have become "innovators" by using the Pastoral Staff, and a small minority of Priests and Deacons have gained the same title by using the Eucharistic Vestments—all alike believing that they acted *legally* in so doing.

If, then, the last Act of Uniformity has been thus "syste-"matically broken" by all the Bishops without any reproach, it can be no wonder that they allowed their Clergy to act similarly with regard to the Edwardian Ornaments referred to in the Ornaments Rubric. Yet the Judicial Committee knew enough of the condition of the Church of England in 1662 and of its subsequent decadence, to prevent them from affecting astonishment at "the unusual occurrence of a Statute" being disregarded "not only by one and all of those who had declared their un-"feigned assent and consent to all and everything contained in "the Book of Common Prayer"—a point, however, which I have already disposed of (See p. 170)—" but by the framers of the "Rubric themselves immediately after the confirmation of it "by an Act of Parliament." That other Rubrics, imposed or re-imposed at the same time have been alike disregarded during the same period is only too notorious.

FOURTHLY, the Court regards the points just discussed, as "facts," a term which I venture to think is hardly accurate; and considers it "plain" from them "that the idea of the "repealing power of this Rubric is a modern one": it is certain however that for the last 160 years the Rubric has been accepted as the *greater* authority, by a succession of Commentators (See pp. 111—19); and even granting that its "repealing power" is only a "modern" theory, the arguments which seem to make this "plain" to their Lordships have just been shown, I think, to be by no means conclusive.

Their Lordships are not content, however, with holding that the Rubric did not *repeal* the Canons of 1604; they further say:—

> "But the 24th Clause of the Act of Uniformity shows that it was not the intention of the passers of the Act to repeal past laws. It provides that 'the several good Laws and Statutes of this realm which [have formerly been made and *sic*] are now in force, for the uniformity of prayer and the [*dele* the] administration of the Sacraments . . . shall stand in full force and strength, to all intents and purposes what[so *sic*]ever, for the establishing and confirming [of *sic*] the said Book.' The laws were to remain; but they were to bear on the new Book of Common Prayer, and not upon any former one. Now, the Prayer Book up to that time in use—the Book which was the subject of the Hampton Court Conference—rested upon the Canons of 1603-4; and it is hard to suppose that the most obvious 'laws' of all, those in force up to that moment, were excluded from the saving power of this 24th Clause. Their Lordships think that the Canons relating to the vestments of the Ministers were not repealed by the Act of Uniformity, and that the Canons had the same force after the passing of that Act which they had before."

What are "the several good Laws and Statutes" here referred to, I have already endeavoured to shew at pp. 185 ff. Also at pp. 84 to 88 and 192-3 the statement is, I think, fully disproved which the Court for the third time (See pp. 84 and 193) here makes, viz. that the Prayer Book of 1604 "rested upon the "Canons of 1603-4." Upon these two points, therefore, it is unnecessary to say more in this place.

But the Court goes on to speak of the Canons of 1604 (*i.e.*, I suppose, those Canons which relate to the Prayer Book) as being "the most obvious 'laws' of all those in force up to that "moment." Yet it is necessary to ask in the first place—whether, in the Statute, the word "Laws" is not used in the *restricted* sense of *Acts of Parliament ?* The following instances would seem to answer the question in the affirmative :—

(1) 1548. 2 & 3 EDW. 6, c. 2, s. 2.—"Be it therefore enacted . . . . that all and every LAW and LAWS positive, CANONS, CONSTITUTIONS, and ORDINANCES . . . . which do prohibit or forbid marriage to any ecclesiastical or spiritual person . . . . shall be utterly void. . . ."

(2) 1552. 5 & 6 EDW. 6, c. 1, s. 5.—". . . . the said former ACT [2 & 3 Edw. 6, c. 1] to stand in full force and strength . . . . for the establishing of 'the Book of Common Prayer.' . . . ."

(3) 1552. 5 & 6 EDW. 6, c. 12, s. 1.—". . . . in the second year of the reign of the King's Majesty that now is, it was ordained . . . . that all and every LAW and LAWS positive, CANONS, CONSTITUTIONS, and ORDINANCES . . . . which . . . . forbid marriage to any ecclesiastical or spiritual person . . . . should be utterly void. . . ."

(4) 1558. 1 ELIZ. c. 1, s. 1.—". . . . in time of . . . . King Henry the Eighth, divers good LAWS and STATUTES were made and established . . . . for the utter extinguishment and putting away of all usurped and foreign powers. . . ."

(5) IBID, s. 3.—"And that also for the reviving of divers of the said good LAWS and STATUTES . . . . it may also please your highness, that one ACT and STATUTE made in the 23rd year" of Hen. 8th " shall be revived."

(6) IBID, s. 13.—"And that . . . . all other LAWS and STATUTES . . . . not in this present act specially mentioned . . . . shall stand . . . . repealed."

(7) IBID s. 35.—". . . . no manner of ORDER, ACT, or DETERMINATION for any matter of religion, or cause ecclesiastical. . . . shall be . . . . adjudged . . . . any error, heresy, schism, or schismatical opinion; any ORDER, DECREE, SENTENCE, CONSTITUTION, or LAW . . . . to the contrary notwithstanding."

(8) IBID. s. 42.—Provided for a possible Appeal within the Realm, in a given time, in the case of *Chetwood* which had gone to the Pope before the passing of the Act, enacting that it should be valid " any LAW, CUSTOM, USAGE, CANON, CONSTITUTION, or any other matter or cause to the contrary notwithstanding."

(9) 1559. 1 ELIZ. c. 2, s. 16.—". . . . any other LAW, STATUTE, PRIVILEGE, LIBERTY, or PROVISION heretofore made . . . ."

(10) IBID, s. 27.—" And be it further enacted . . . . that all LAWS, STATUTES, and ORDINANCES, wherein or whereby any other service . . . . is . . . . set forth . . . . shall from henceforth be utterly void . . ."

(11) 1559. INJUNCTIONS OF Q. ELIZ.—"1. . . . That all . . . . ecclesiastical persons shall faithfully keep . . . . all and singular LAWS and STATUTES made for restoring to the Crown the ancient jurisdiction over the state ecclesiastical, and abolishing of all foreign power repugnant to the same." (*Cardwell, D. A.,* I., 212.)

In these instances it must be observed that there is a marked distinction in the terms used: in Nos. 2, 4, 5, 6, and 11 where *only* an Act of Parliament could be involved, there the words are " Act " and " Statute " or " LAWS and STATUTES "; whereas in Nos. 1, 3, 7, 8, 9, and 10, where *other* laws might or did touch the case, there the language is more comprehensive, and *additional* terms are employed, viz., ORDINANCE, PRIVILEGE, LIBERTY, PROVISION, ORDER, DETERMINATION, DECREE, SENTENCE, CONSTITUTION, CUSTOM, USAGE, CANON. The inference from this comparison seems obvious and inevitable—viz. that nothing was referred to under the expression "the several good laws and statutes of this "realm," used in the Act of 1662, except *Statutes of the Realm* at that time in force: had it been intended to include the Canons of 1604 they would, surely, have been either expressly mentioned or designated by some term adequate to include them; for it is most unlikely that the precedent of former Acts should have been overlooked or disregarded in an enactment which required precision of language.

It may very well have been, as " their Lordships think that " the Canons relating to the vestments of the Ministers were " not repealed by the Act of Uniformity;" for, *being positive orders* with *no negative words* and being Statutably binding upon the Clergy, they necessarily contributed to "the establish-" ing and confirming" of the Prayer Book of 1662; and so no enactment was necessary to maintain them for that purpose: it may consequently be admitted that, to use their Lordships' language, " the Canons had the same force after the passing of " that Act which they had before; " for, of course, a *Canon* which *commands* a Cope or a Surplice must maintain a *Rubric* which *includes* them. But if the Canons were included by the word "Laws" they must thus have acquired a *Parliamentary* Authority which therefore was not "the same force" as they had before, but a greater power and one which the Parliament only a year before had been most careful to exclude; for the 13th Charles II., c. 12., (which maintained the Ecclesiastical coercive Jurisdiction of which "some doubt" had " been made" since the passing of the 16 Car. I., c. 11.,) expressly provided in Sect. 5 that the Act was not to "be construed" so as to abridge " or diminish the King's majesty's supremacy in Ecclesiastical " matters and affairs, nor to confirm the canons made in the " year one thousand six hundred and forty, nor any of them, "*nor any other ecclesiastical laws or canons not formerly con-* "*firmed, allowed, or enacted by parliament, or by the established* "*laws of the land,* as they stood in the year of our Lord one "thousand six hundred thirty-nine."

If, however, the Canons did not acquire any new force by their supposed recognition in the Statute: it follows that, unless they previously *prohibited* either the Vestments or anything else which they did not prescribe, they cannot have the power of excluding them now. Their Lordships though erroneously assuming (See p. 84) that the Prayer Book of 1604 depended for its sanction upon the Canons of 1604, say that "whilst thus implicitly sanctioning the Ornaments-Rubric, "the Canons also provide specially for the vesture of the "Minister:" but they do not resort to the absurdity of *saying* that the Canons *forbid* things ordered by the very Rubric which those Canons sanction.

Further if, as the Court says, "the Canons had the same force "after the passing of" the Act of 1662 "which they had "before," and if, as their Lordships imply, that "force" was superior to the Ornaments-Rubric of 1604, then the 59th Canon distinctly annuls a Rubric the meaning of which no one questions; for the Rubric orders Catechizing "after the Second "Lesson at Evening Prayer," whereas the Canon directs it to be "before Evening Prayer." There was no difficulty under the Book of 1604, for it and the Canon gave the same rule: but if the Court be right as to the present force of the Canons, it must be asked—at which of the two times can the Clergy *legally* Catechize in the Church?

In support of its view the Court says that:—

> "The contemporary exposition on this point is very strong. Bishop Henchman, of Salisbury, in 1662, in enquiring whether his Churches are provided with the Prayer Book 'newly established,' enquires for the 'comely, large, and fine surplice,' and for no other vestment. The same enquiry for the 'comely large surplice, for the minister to wear at all times of his ministration,' is found in a great number of Visitation Articles, republished by the Ritual Commission (Report 2, Appendix, p. 606, 614 and following), extending from 1662 to the end of the century. Bishop Fuller, of Lincoln, A.D.

1671, Bishop Gunning, of Ely, A.D. 1679, and Bishop Trimnell, of Norwich, A.D. 1716, refer to the 58th Canon as unrepealed, in the margin of their Visitation Articles upon the surplice. Their Lordships are of opinion that the Canon was not repealed, and that the Ecclesiastical authorities had no suspicion that it had been."

The remarks made at pp. 163-67 upon the inquiry for the Surplice, in these Visitation Articles, make it needless further to discuss the subject here: though I must observe that as Henchman (like the other Ordinaries) did not inquire for a Black Stole or Scarf, those Ornaments must be *illegal* now according to the Court's reasoning. But it is requisite to notice their Lordships' observation that three of the Bishops "refer to the 58th Canon as unrepealed, in the margin of their "Visitation Articles upon the Surplice." The Court might have cited a stronger proof from the Articles of Archdeacon Booth, 1710-20, who asks:—

"*Section* 8. Whether doth he [your Minister] in his Parish Church or Chapel, read the Book of Canons and Constitutions agreed on at the Synod holden at London, Anno. 1603, upon some Sundays or Holy-Days in the Afternoon, before Divine Service, dividing the same in such Sort, as that the one half may be read on one day, and the other on another day?" And as his authority for the requirement, he refers to the "*Ratification of the Canons at the End of them*." (2nd *Rit. Report*, p. 682.)*

But if the *Marginal References* to which their Lordships refer, and these definite inquiries which they have not noticed, prove that the Canons of 1604 were "not repealed" by the Act of 1662, then, in all consistency, any other references or questions in the same Articles which point to other Laws or Ordinances are alike entitled to be considered as proofs of their being also operative. Now Archdeacon Booth's "Articles "of Enquiry: according to the Rubricks of the Book of

---

* The Canons of 1604 are also recognised in the following Visitation Articles printed in the same Report: those marked thus † show that the Canons were to be publicly read in Church.

1662. Henchman, Bp., II., 2, 610.	1679. Barlow, Bp., I., 4, 645.
1662. Morley, Bp., I., 4, 615.	†1679. Gunning, Bp., 27, 649 : 6, 651.
†1662. Layfield, Archn., 1, 621 : 1, 622.	1686. Sancroft, Abp., I., 4, 653.
†1670. Hammond, Archn., II., 3, 637.	1703. Peculiars of Cant., I., 4, 662.
†1671. Fuller, Bp., III., 6, 639.	1728. Stanley, Archn., I., 4, 680.

"Common Prayer and other Ecclesiastical Laws now in "force" contain the following, among other, Inquiries and References:—

"*Section* 1. Is your Minister conformable in his Life and Doctrine to the holy Rule and great Example of our Lord Jesus Christ? Or doth he give any just Scandal or Offence, by haunting Taverns, Inns or Alehouses, or other Suspected Places? Or doth he in any other respect walk unworthy of his Vocation and Ministry?

"1. *Sober Conversation required in Ministers,* Can. 75.

"2. *Constit.* Rich. Wethershed *Archiepi. Cant. Lynd.* K. Edward VI. *his Injunct.* Sparrow *p.* 4. 2 *Eliz. Injunct.* Sparrow 69.

"*Can. Apost.* 54. *Concil. Carthag.* 3 *um. Can.* 27. *Concil. Rhemense.* 2 *um.* 813. *Can.* 26. *De vita & honestate Clericorum, Lyndwood Lib.* 3. *Tit.* 1." (2nd *Rit. Report*, p. 681.)

"*Section* 4. . . . . Doth he give notice of the Yearly *Perambulation* in *Rogation-week*, for preserving the Bounds of the Parish, and for desiring God's blessing upon the Fruits of the Earth? And doth he at certain convenient places sing or say, the two Psalms, beginning, *Benedic, anima mea* (*i.e.* 103, 104) with the Litany and Suffrages thereunto, with one Homily of Thanksgiving to God, already devised and divided into four Parts.

. . . .

"3. *Q. Eliz.* Injunct. 1559, 1564. Concil. Aurelianense 1, *mum. Anno* 511, Can. 24." (*Ibid.* p. 682.)

"*Section* 11. Whether hath he married any Persons in the Time wherein Marriage is by Law restrained, without a lawful License, *viz.* from the Saturday next before *Advent Sunday* until the 14th of *January*, and from the *Sunday* next before *Septuagesima Sunday*, until the *Monday* next after *Low Sunday*; and from the *Sunday* next before the Rogation week until Trinity *Sunday*? . . .

"1. *Extr. de Feriis Cap. Capellanus Lynd.* L. 3. *Tit.* 16. p. 185. L. 4. *Tit.* 2. p. 274." (*Ibid.* p. 682.)

"*Section* 3. Have you a decent Font set up at the lower Part of your Church for the administration of the Sacrament of Baptism?

"*Can.* 81. *Lynd.* 3. *Tit.* 24. *Lib.* 3. *Tit.* 27." (*Ibid.* p. 683.)

"*Section* 5. Have you a decent *Communion Table*, for the Administration of the Sacrament of the Lord's Supper? Are there two fair and large Coverings for it, one of Silk, Stuff, or fine Cloth; another of fine Linen; with a Plate or Paten, and a Cup or Chalice of Silver, and two fair Flagons of Pewter or purer Metal belonging to it?

"1. *Can.* 82. 2. *Can.* 82. *Rubrick before the Communion. Articles for Doctrine and Preaching*, 7th *Eliz. Constit. de Archidiac. Lynd. Constit. Provinc. Concil. Oxon. Steph. Cant. Archiepi. Lynd.*

"3. *Constit. Provinc. Concil. Oxon. Steph. Cant. Archiepi. Lynd. Constit.* Rich. Wethershed. *Cant. Archiep. Lynd. Concil. Triburiense. Anno* 895. *Canon* 18."

"*Section* 6. Have you a large and decent Surplice (one or more) for your Minister to wear at all Times of his public Ministration in the

Church, with an Hood or Tippet to wear over it? Have you a Terrier of the Glebe-Lands, and other Possessions belonging to your Church? Have you a Book of Parchment, wherein to Register the Christenings, Marriages and Burials of your Parish? Another Book, wherein to Record the Licenses of all strange Ministers, that are admitted at any Time to preach in your Church or Chapel? And a third Book, wherein to write down the Accounts of the Church-Wardens; and to keep an Inventory of all Things provided and belonging to your Church? Have you a strong *Chest*, with Locks and Keys, wherein to keep all those Books, and other Books, and other Furniture for Divine Services, in safe Custody? And lastly, have you a *Box*, wherein to put and keep Alms for the Poor, and a *Bier*, with a Black Herse-Cloth, for the Burial of the Dead?

"1. *Can.* 58.   2. *Lynd. de Officio. Archidiac.*   3. *Can.* 58.   4. *Can.* 87.   5. *Can.* 70.   *K.* Edward's *Injunction.*   6. *Can.* 52.   7. *Can.* 84.   8. *K.* Edward's *Injunctions.*   Q. Eliz. *Injunctions*, 1559.   9. *Lynd. Lib.* 3. *Tit.* 27." (*Ib.* p. 683.)

Now an Archdeacon's Visitation Articles have quite as much Authority as those of a Bishop, they are in fact the intermediate glances of the "*Oculus Episcopi*"; and here we find Archdeacon Booth citing as "Ecclesiastical Laws now in force" Constitutions, Canons, and Injunctions which according to the Judicial Committee (Martin *v.* Mackonochie, see p. 199) had been wholly repealed by the Elizabethan and Caroline Acts of Uniformity. It may, indeed, be urged that in some of the Inquiries the Archdeacon only asks for things retained by the Canons of 1604 out of those required by former Laws, and therefore he did not inaccurately call them "Laws now in "force": but the reasoning will not apply to other questions which he asks—viz. (Sect. 4) as to the Service for Rogation Days* ordered by the Elizabethan Injunctions but not mentioned in the Canons of 1604 or the Prayer Book of 1662;

---

* The following Visitation Articles (2nd Rit. Report) also recognise for use on Rogation Days the Office prescribed in the Elizabethan Injunctions; thus showing that the Injunctions were not supposed to have been abrogated by the Canons of 1604: those marked (I) mention the Injunctions; and those marked (L) have the words "appointed by Law."

1604. Chaderton, Bp., 31, 449.   (I)
1607. Babington, Bp., 22, 454.
1612. King, Bp., 23, 464.   (L)
1616. Abbot, Abp., 11, 471.   (L)
1619. Overall, Bp., IV. 16, 483.   (L)
1622. Laud, Bp., 13, 489.   (L)
1625. Andrewes, Bp., 36, 495.

1635. Williams, Bp., 12, 552.   (L)
1636. Wren, Bp., 6, 565.
1636. Pearson, Archn., V. 5, 570.   (L)
1638. Duppa, Bp., 18, 577.
1638. Montague, Bp., 15, 582.
1640. Juxon, Bp., 3, 591.   (I. L)
1640. Bostock, Archn., 13, 597.   (L)

(Sect. 11) as to the seasons in which he considers "Marriage* is by Law restrained, without a lawful License;" and (Sect. 6) as to "a Bier with a Black Herse Cloth, for the Burial of the "Dead"†—matters which certainly are not recognised in these same latest Laws.

Probably, their Lordships might say that Archdeacon Booth's question (Sect. 6) "Have you a large and decent "Surplice (one or more) for your Minister to wear at all Times "of his public ministration in the Church?" supports their contention that "The contemporary exposition on this point "[of the non-repeal of the Canons] is very strong"; and that he, too, "enquires . . . . for no other vestment:" all this may be conceded and yet be no proof that he could not *legally* have asked for more than the 58th Canon expressly prescribes. And that he did not consider himself *limited* by the requirements of the Canons is plain from the fact that (Sect. 5) he asks for "*two* "fair Flagons of Pewter or purer Metal"; whereas Canon 20, in ordering the Wine to be provided, only says "which wine

1628. Davenant, Bp., 15, 501. (L)
1630. Curle, Bp., 24, 513. (L)
1632. Bancroft, Bp., 14, 529.
1633. Curle, Bp., 24, 534. (L)
1633. Lindsell, Bp., 31, 540. (L)
1635. Laud, Abp., 12, 548. (L)

1662. Cosin, Bp., III. 9, 601.§
1662. Pory, Archn., 3, 627. (I. L)§
1662. Henchman, Bp., III. 18, 612. (L)
1662. Layfield, Archn., 19, 622. (L)
1679. Gunning, Bp., 16, 648. (l)

* The following Visitation Articles (2nd Rit. Report) also recognise a Law restraining Marriage without Dispensation at Seasons when it was anciently prohibited.

1612. King, Bp., 20, 464.
1619. Andrewes, Bp., 12, 476.
1625. Andrewes, Bp., 11, 495.
1628. Davenant, Bp., III. 3, 500.
1628. Neile, Bp., 14, 505.
1630. Curle, Bp., 21, 513.
1630-32. White, Archn., 6, 517.
1630. Williams, Bp., 18, 519.
1632. Bancroft, Bp., 12, 529.
1633. Curle, Bp., 21, 534.
1634. Goodman, Bp., 18, 544.
1635. Laud, Abp., 4, 548.
1635. Williams, Bp., 4, 552; 27, 553.
1636. Kingsley, Archn., 21, 567.

1636. Pearson, Archn., V. 3, 570; VI. 6, 571.
1637. Peculiars of Canterbury 11, 573.
1638. Montagu, Bp., 13, 17, 583.
1638. Thornburgh, Archn., 39, 586.
1640. Bostock, Archn., V. 9, 597; VI. 6, 598.
1640. White, Archn., II. 4; III. 5, 600.
1662. Pory, Archn., 22, 627.§
1662. Henchman, Bp., III. 3, 611.
1664. Henchman, Bp., II. 8, 632.
1679. Barlow, Bp., II., 8, 645.
1679. Gunning, Bp., 21, 649.

§ Cosin's Articles (See p. 121) and Pory's were prepared while the Book of 1604 was in use: Pory (20 p. 67) asks whether the Catechizing is for "half an hour" before Evensong, as ordered in that Book.

† See similar enquiries, p. 213.

"we require to be brought to the Communion-table in *a* clean
"and sweet standing pot or stoop of pewter, if not of purer
"metal."

It is worth noticing here that Bishop Cosin asked the same
question in 1662. "Are there .... a Cup or Chalice of
"Silver; and two fair flagons of pewter or purer mettal
"belonging to it?" (2nd Rit. *Report* I. 4. 601) The specific
mention of "two" suggests the *probability* that one of them
was intended to contain *Water* for the mixed Chalice especially
as Cosin had himself said "Our Church forbids it not, for aught
"I know, and they that think fit may use it, as some most
"eminent* among us do at this day" (*Notes* 1st Series, p. 154.
A. C. L.) It cannot well be contended that the "two" were
designed to provide an adequate quantity of Wine in Churches
where the number of Communicants was very large; for this was
not likely to have been the case in the majority of Parishes,
especially in Country places; yet if this were the design the
inquiry was more likely to have been made in an *optional* form—
"one or more"—or in some equivalent term—as was frequently
done: though even this form of Inquiry is quite consistent
with the supposition that a second Flagon might be provided
where the permitted practice of the Mixed Chalice was
followed. The following instances of the *optional* form of
inquiry occur in the Visitation Articles printed in the 2nd
Ritual Report:—

1628. Neile, Bp., 6, 503—"or two."
1633. Eland, Archn., 6, 509; Note ††—"or two."
1662. Earle, Bp., I., 3, 604—"flagons."
1662. Hacket, Bp., 3, 608—"one or more."
1662. Morley, Bp., I., 3, 615—"one or more."
1662. Reynolds, Bp., 3, 619—"flagons."
1664. Henchman, Bishop, 2, 632—"flagons."
1670. Hammond, Archn., I., 6, 637—"flagons."
1671. Fuller, Bp., II., 2, 638—"flagons."
1674. Pearson, Bishop, I., 2, 642—"flagons."
1679. Barlow, Bp., I., 2, 645—"flagons."
1692. Ironside, Bp., 2, 658—"one or more."
1701. Strafford, Bp., I., 2, 660—"one or more."
1716. Trimnell, Bp., I., 3, 677—"one or more."
1728. Stanley, Archn., I., 3, 680—"one or more."

* The Editor of Cosin's Notes here refers to p. 105 where Cosin gives the
following Note of Bp. Andrewes—"Postea panes e canistro in patinam ponit.
Dein vinum e dolio, adinstar sanguinis dirumpens in calicem, haurit. Tum
aquam e tricanali seypho immiscet." He also refers to "the description of
Bp. Andrewes's Chapel, in the Appendix to his *Life* prefixed to his Minor
English Works." In the "Hierurgia Anglicana" p. 8, there is also a Plan
and Description of the Chapel

Moreover other Ordinaries inquired for Ornaments or Utensils which certainly are neither prescribed nor necessarily implied either in the Canons of 1604 or in the Prayer Book; this is shown by the following instances from Visitation Articles printed in the same Report:—

1620. Vail to be used at Churching—Harsnet, Bp., II., 11, 485.

1632. Surplice to be worn in the perambulation in Rogation Week—Bancroft, Bp., 14, 529.

Bier (B) and Herse-Cloth (H) for Funerals.

1620. Harsnet, Bp., VI., 5, 487. (B.)	1664. Henchman,Bp.,I.,8,632. (B.&H.)
1631. Kent, Archn., 38, 527. (B.)	1670. Hammond, An.,I.,8, 637. (B.&H.)
1662. Cosin, Bp., I., 7, 601. (B. & H.)	1674. Pearson, Bp., I., 8, 642. (B. & H.)
1662. Earle, Bp., I., 8, 604. (B. & H.)	1679. Barlow, Bp., I., 8, 645. (B. & H.)
1662. Reynolds, Bp., 7, 619. (B. & H.)	1716. Trimnell,Bp.,I., 6,677. (B. &H.)

Chancel Screen to be provided.

1640. Juxon, Bp., 3, 589. "As is required by the Law." He refers to "Rubric before Morning Prayer. Orders of Queen Elizabeth. An. 1561. Ib. Order 3."

1662. Cosin, Bp., I., 4, 601. 1662. Pory, Archn., 3, 625. "As is required by the Law."* He refers to the same Authorities as Bp. Juxon.

⁎ The Articles of Cosin and Pory are certainly (Earle's are probably) *prior* to the Book of 1662.

There is one other illustration—viz. THE MANUAL ACTS—which requires separate and special notice as being a *Ceremony*, and also as entirely disproving the theory enunciated by the Judicial Committee in Martin *v.* Mackonochie and adopted by their Lordships in the present case—viz. that OMISSION IS PROHIBITION. Dr. Stephens when arguing before this Court for the Appellant, in Sheppard *v.* Bennett (*See* The Guardian, Nov. 29, 1871, p. 1409) contended that the Manuals Acts, prescribed for the Consecration of the Eucharist in the Prayer Book of 1549, were illegal from 1552 to 1662 because they were omitted in the Books of 1552, 1559, and 1604; and in reply to the objection of the Court, that "there must *ex-necessitate* "here be some manual acts," he said, "My contention is that "there were none; and your Lordships have already ruled that "omission is prohibition . . . . in point of fact the Clergy did "not [take the Paten or the Chalice in their hands, and]

---

* It is desirable to record here Pory's interpretation of the Rubric as to Chancels: he asks in this same Article—"Do the Chancels remain as they have done in times past, that is to say, in the convenient situation of the Seates, and in the ascent or steps unto the place appointed anciently for the standing of the Holy Table?"

if they "had done it they would have been liable to punish-"ment."

Now the 9th of the Canons of 1640 (which it must be remembered have precisely the same Authority as the Canons of 1604) is intituled "One book of articles of inquiry to be "used at all parochial visitations." (*Cardwell, Synodalia*, I. 407), and it recites that "this synod hath now caused a "summary or collection of visitatory articles (out of the "rubrics of the service book, and the canons and warrantable "rules of the Church) to be made and for future direction to "be deposited in the records of the Archbishop of Canterbury"; these alone, subject to such variation as the Metropolitan might allow, were to be used under the pain of suspension.

A copy of these Articles, as used by Juxon, Bishop of London, in 1640, is printed in the 2nd Report, of the Ritual Commission p. 588 ; this Note being prefixed :—

"[The following MS. note is written on the title of one of the Bodleian copies :—
"'This Book of Articles was compiled by the Bps. and Clergy in Convocation, Ano. 1640, first published for the visitation of the Bp. of London, and by him fitted in some points for the use of that Diocess. Heylyn, Cypr. &c. p. 441. 'Tis injoyned by the 5 [?9] Canon as an uniforme booke of Articles to be used in every diocess of each Province.']"

At p. 590 there is the following inquiry: " 14 . . . . Doth " the Minister take the same [Bread] into his hands to blesse "and consecrate it to that holy use [of the Lord's Supper] as "oft as he administereth the Communion ? Doth he so like-" wise with the wine provided?"

Thus, then, we find Convocation in 1640 treating, as still binding upon the Clergy, the very same two Manual Acts which were prescribed in the First Prayer Book of Edward VI., though they were not restored until twenty-two years afterwards in the Book of 1662.

Precisely the same question is asked by Archdeacon Pory in his Visitation Articles of 1662 (*Ib.* 14. 626): these Articles being prior to the Book of 1662 coming into use, as is shown by a comparison of his questions No. 13,* p. 625; 20,† p. 627; and 8, p. 630.

From all this it follows that, though there may be sufficient reasons for accepting their Lordships' "opinion that the Canon "was not repealed, and that the Ecclesiastical authorities had "no suspicion that it had been," the argument of the Court involves a principle which sustains previous Ecclesiastical Laws and Ordinances alleged by the Judicial Committee, in Martin *v.* Mackonochie, to have been repealed by Statutes which it is not pretended contain any *explicit* reference to them. If the Inquiries of Visitation Articles and even a reference in their "margin" are to be regarded as a "very strong" "contemporary "exposition" of the Law on one point, they must, in all consistency, be allowed the like force on other points to which they similarly refer; and it is clear, from the instances which have now been produced, "that the Ecclesiastical Authorities" upon whom the Court relies "had no suspicion" that by omission or implication, those Laws had been repealed which, until of late, Ecclesiastical Courts and Ecclesiastical Lawyers were wont to rely upon in defence of Ornaments and Practices now declared to be illegal.

XXX. The Court proceeds to discuss the second sense in which the Rubric of 1549 is, by others, held to be "revived"; their Lordships say :—

> "II. The next opinion is, that the Canons and the Act of Uniformity, being irreconcileable, set up distinct standards of Ritual, the one of a more elaborate and the other of a severer type, the one a maximum and the other a minimum, the one represented by the Rubric and the other by the 58th Canon. To

---

* "Have . . . you A Book of Prayers for the 5th of *November*, and for the 30th of *January*, and the 29th of *May* ?" Cosin has the same inquiry (I. 5. p. 601). These forms were ordered to be printed "at ye end of" the Book of 1662. (4th *Rit. Report*, p. 40).

† "Doth your Minister . . . . on every Sunday and Holy-day before Evening Prayer for space of half an hour and more instruct the youth and ignorant persons of the Parish, according to the Catechism set forth in the Common Prayer Book?" He cites in the Margin "Can. 59" which agreed with the Rubric in the Catechism.

this view the learned Judge in the Court below appears to incline. Their Lordships, notwithstanding this authority, are obliged to come to the conclusion that this view is at variance with all the facts of the case. They have already observed that the chasuble, alb, and tunicle were swept away with severe exactness in the time of Queen Elizabeth, and that there was no trace of any attempt to revive them."

It seems to me that their Lordships in part misrepresent the "opinion" which they here combat: the notion of "the "Canons" of 1604 and the Statute of 1662 "*being irreconcile-* "*able*" is surely their own, certainly it did not emanate from the Dean of the Arches; any how, whosesoever it may be, the remarks already made at p. 193 are sufficient, I think, to refute it. Nor is it accurate to say that "the learned Judge in the "Court below appears to incline" to the theory that the two Rules "set up *distinct* standards of Ritual": his Lordship's idea is rather that of a *higher* and *lower* standard; for he says "the gloss which all Ecclesiastical History, contemporaneous "and subsequent, would give to the Advertisements [and "therefore, I may add, to the Canons also] is, that they "provided that the Ornaments of the Minister should not fall "below a certain point; not that it should not exceed that point." The lower Standard exhibited two *Vestures*—the Cope and the Surplice—and was raised during a period when a continuous effort was made to abolish every distinctive garment which the Clergy of the Church of England had been accustomed to use in the Services: the higher Standard was emblazoned with other Ornaments besides these, and could be lifted up whenever the Episcopal Officers thought it likely to rally any to a somewhat more advanced Ritual.

The Court alleges that the theory of a "maximum" and a "minimum" Standard "is at variance" with the "facts"— "that the chasuble, alb, and tunicle were swept away with "severe exactness in the time of Queen Elizabeth, and that "there was no trace of any attempt to revive them." The remarks already made at pp. 39 and 45 to 48 as to the destruction of Church Ornaments at that period, render it needless to consider here the accuracy or sufficiency of their Lordships' assertion: but, admitting it to be an adequate representation of the case, the most it could show would be that the temper of the period was very adverse to replacing what had been destroyed and consequently to the necessary expenditure which must have been incurred: it wholly fails to prove that the Law precluded their restoration if the circumstances of the time had favoured it. That this is a reasonable view of the case, may be inferred from the fact that the "severe exactness" then shewn in sweeping out the Ecclesiastical Repertories of Ornament, exhibited little or no regard for Furniture and Utensils which by no ordinary construction can be placed in the category of things excluded by any hitherto supposed limitation of the Elizabethan Ornaments Rubric.

In support of their "conclusion" that "a maximum" and "a minimum" of Ornament could not have been contemplated, the Court makes the following remarks:—

> "The Act of Uniformity reflects, by the strictness of its provisions, the temper of the framers. The fate of a 'proviso as to the dispensation with deprivation, for not using the cross and surplice,' which was sent down from the House of Lords to the House of Commons illustrates this. The Commons rejected the proviso (Commons' Journals, VIII, 413), and in the subsequent conference between the two Houses, the Manager, Serjeant Charlton, gave, amongst other reasons for rejecting the proviso, 'that it would unavoidably establish schism, . . . that he thought it better to impose no ceremonies than to dispense with any; and he thought it very incongruous at the same time when you are settling uniformity to establish schism' (Lords' Journals, vol. xi., p. 449 *a*). And the House of Lords agreed that this proviso should be struck out (Lords' Journals, vol. xi., pp. 450 *a*, 450 *b*.")

But it seems to me that the two cases are wholly dissimilar in character. The one proposed a proviso designed to protect those who sought to get rid of a Ceremony viz., the Cross in Baptism, and of the one Vestment—and that the simplest, viz., the Surplice—the use of the two being alike required by both

Statute and Canon from every Minister: the other claims a liberty to advance beyond that precise requirement in which Canon and Statute coincide, and would proceed in the direction to which the Statute points; so that, in fact, (apart from the Cross in Baptism) it was a question of *no* Vestment against *one* Vestment or *more* than one. No wonder, then, that Sergeant Charlton thought that to sanction modern Presbyterian practices in a Church which claimed to inherit the Customs of Catholic Antiquity would "unavoidably establish schism." Moreover, his objection to "dispense" any one from the barest "cere-"monies" which Church and State were about to "impose" absolutely upon all, was natural and reasonable; but this was a wholly different thing from not requiring *more* of what was actually *prescribed* than the people had long been *accustomed* to.

The maxim that "*silence gives consent*" may well show that in this case there was no intention to "impose" all that the Rubric included; for thus apparently it was that the "Bishops" answered the "Ministers" in 1661; the latter had taken "Exception" to the Ornaments Rubric in these words:—

"For as much as the Rubrick seemeth to bring back the Cope, Albe, and other Vestments forbidden in the Common Prayer Book, 5, 6, of *Edw. VI.*, and for the* reasons alledged against Ceremonies under our 18. general Exception, we desire it may be wholly left out." ("*The Grand Debate between The most Reverend the Bishops, and the Presbyterian Divines,*" &c., "*the most perfect* Copy. London, Printed 1661." p. 12.)

To which the Bishops replied:—

"Sect. 2. Rub. For the reasons given in our Answer to the 18th General, whither you refer us, we think it fit that the Rubrick continue as it is." (*Ibid* p. 118; *Cardwell, Conf.*, p. 351; Documents &c., p. 162.)

And the Rejoinder of the Ministers was:—

"We have given you reason enough against the imposition of the usual Ceremonies; and would you draw forth those absolute ones to increase the burden?" (*Grand Debate*, p. 118; *Documents* &c., p. 305.)

---

* Conf. *Cardwell, Conf.*, 2nd Ed. 1841, p. 314; "so our"; also "*Documents relating to the settlement of the Church of England by the Act of Uniformity of 1662.* London, 1862, where the same reading is given."

So far as it appears, no response was made by the Bishops to this last expression of the Ministers' fears: but this *acquiescence by silence*, while it shows that the Bishops did not dream of urging, much less of *enforcing* all the Rubrical requirements, is perfectly consistent with the reasonable supposition that they were not unwilling to see an advance in the direction of its complete provisions.

The grounds of the Commons' objection to "the Proviso as "to the Dispensation for not using the Cross and Surplice," will, however, be the better understood by reading the whole of their "Reasons" as given by Sergeant Charlton the Manager of the Conference between the two Houses; they are these:—

"1. It is a Proviso without Precedent.
"2. That it would establish Schism.
"3. That it would not gratify such for whom it was intended.

"To the First, he said, It was very apparent in England, that it was without Precedent; and, as he thought, in the World also, for they never heard that ever any National Church did the like.

"It was one Thing, he said, to allow a differing Religion in a Nation, an other Thing, to allow men to receive Profits for that Church unto which Men would not conform.

"Secondly, Though there was Dissenters in the Particulars of the Proviso in the Time of Queen Eliz. and King James; yet in those days those Opinions stayed there, and went no further.

"To the Second Head, that it would unavoidably establish Schism, All Persons of different Inclinations would apply to such as should have the Liberty, and that necessarily [would] make Parties, especially in great cities. He did observe these two Ceremonies of the Cross and Surplice were long in Use in the Church; and he found a High Commendation of the use of the Cross in Baptism in the Book sent to the Commons from the Lords, wherein it is so clearly explained, as there can be no Suspicion of Popery in it. It was used, he said, to quicken the Memory, as to the Benefits of Baptism; and if that were omitted, much of the Service belonging to Baptism must be omitted also, many Passages depending upon the Use of that Ceremony.

"The Gentleman added, That he thought it better to impose no Ceremonies, than to dispense with any, and he thought it very incongruous, at the same Time when you are settling Uniformity, to establish Schism.

"To the Third Head, It would not satisfy those for whom it was intended; for such chiefly reject it upon these Grounds, that Things indifferent ought not to be enjoined; which Opinion, he said, took away all the Weight of human Authority, which consists in commanding Things otherwise indifferent, so as, when this shall be yielded, you give them nothing, they opposing for the Imposition sake.

"He added, These were Reasons as to the Nature of the Thing; and as to the Reasons given by their Lordships to the Commons, he answered as followeth:

"The King's Engagement at Breda as to tender Consciences; unto which he said, That His Majesty could not understand the Misleaders of the People, but the Misled. It would be very strange to call a schismatical Conscience a tender Conscience. He said A tender Conscience denoted an Impression from without, received from another, and that upon which another strikes.

"Secondly, Suppose these had been meant, yet he said there could be no Inference of any Breach of Promise in His Majesty, because that Declaration had these Two Limitations,

"First, A Reference to Parliament.

"Secondly, Such liberties to be granted only as consisted with the Peace of the Kingdom." (*Lords' Journals*, Vol. II., p. 449. Mercurii 7° die Maii.)

Now I submit that these Reasons, taken together, put a considerably different complexion upon "the fate" of this Proviso, from that presented by the fragmentary sentence which the Judicial Committee selected to sustain their contention.

The House of Commons, warned by experience of the Practices and demands which culminated in the banishment of the Prayer Book and the substitution of the Directory, was wholly adverse to such a legalized liberty as could only tend to denude the Church of England of the barest accessories of Divine Service, and to reduce it in that respect to the level of the Genevan platform. Their "Reasons" involve the following Considerations, which certainly were strong arguments against the Proviso:—

1. That it would encourage Non-conformity within the Church.
2. That it would, in the case of the Cross in Baptism, affect the *language* of the Baptismal Office.
3. That it *legalized* disregard of what was considered *necessary* for the due order of Service.
4. That it would not satisfy the Non-conformists who objected to things indifferent being enjoined.

But not one of these Considerations, or of the other Reasons, has the slightest application to those who, while readily conforming to the use of the Ceremonial Act and the Vesture from which it was proposed to dispense *others*, might at a future time, and under favourable circumstances, desire to restore some of those Ornaments which the Rubric unquestionably had recognized. This, I think, is an answer to the main argument of the Court in the following passage :—

> "It cannot be supposed that an Act which applied the the principle of uniformity so strictly in one direction was intended on the other to open the door to a return to practices that were suspected as Romish, and this without serious remonstrance in either House from the minority. The purpose of the Act is clear. It was to establish an uniformity upon all parties alike. That is its language, and that is the interpretation it bore with those in authority who had to expound it in visitation articles and the like."

The "uniformity" aimed at was the very lowest which could well be prescribed unless the *conforming* Clergy were not to be comprehended in the National Church; and therefore to apply this "principle" thus "strictly in one direction" was not inconsistent with permitting the boundary line to be passed in a direction where, certainly, it would not lead to Puritan territory. To speak of such a permission as indicating an intention "to open the door to a return to practices that were "suspected as Romish," is an ignoring of the fact—that to make the Sign of the Cross in Baptism, and to wear a Surplice,* was as abhorrently "Romish" to those who desired the Dispensation as were the Albe and the Chasuble which the Rubric in terms ordered.

---

* That this stigma of "Romish" as applied to the Surplice has survived the Rebellion, is a fact too well known to require proof: the Riots at Exeter in 1843 were a disgraceful witness to it, and the following Letter from THE ROCK, 1872, is a recent illustration of it :—

"Sir,—Can you spare me a line for the very important and interesting question that rightly excites great interest at this time; gown *v* surplice? Some of the reasons against the surplice seem to be :—1. It is a vestment borrowed from idolatrous Popish priests, and therefore unsuited to Protestants. 2. It was borrowed by Papists from the idolatrous heathen Priests, and so unsuited for Christian Ministers to imitate. (See *Hislop. Two Babylons*, &c.) 3. It is the favorite dress and badge of Puseyites, Ritualists, Sacerdotalists, Sacramentarians, and all who are endeavouring to Romanize our pure Church. 4. It is no distinctively Clerical dress, because it is worn by choristers,

If this view be correct, as I believe it is, the absence of "serious remonstrance in either House from the minority" need not be surprising; and, even had it been made, the Commons† were in no mood then to make a precautionary Law against Ritual development. No doubt the Act was designed "to establish an Uniformity upon all parties alike:" but the opening language of the Statute shews that the object uppermost in the minds of the Legislators was (1) to constrain those who did "wilfully and schismatically abstain and refuse to "come to their parish churches, and other places where common "prayer, administration of the Sacraments, and preaching of "the word of God is used;" and (2) to remedy "the great "and scandalous neglect of Ministers in using the said order" set forth in the Book of 1559. It was the *Substance*, not the *Accidents*, of Divine Service which they were then most intent upon restoring; and they only so far regarded the latter as to insist that they should not fall below the requirements of the Canons of 1604: the refusal to dispense with the Cross in Baptism and with the Surplice is evidence of this, and also

organists, choir-boys, students, &c. 5. It is a dress invented for and suited to a sacrificing Priest when ministering at an altar, but not to a Pastor. 6. It is inconvenient in form and size. 7. It is a dress symbolical of Anti-Protestantism. Some of the reasons in favour of the gown seem to be:—1. It was specially introduced by the Reformers. 2. It was used by the noble Genevan Reformers. 3. It was the favourite dress of the Puritans and other zealous but maligned preachers and ministers. 4. It is the only ministerial dress used by our Nonconforming Protestant ministerial brethren. 5. If it's [*sic*] a university gown, it has a distinctive meaning of qualification, and cannot be worn by anyone. 7. It is preferred by the laity generally to the gown [*sic?* surplice]. 8. It is far more convenient than a surplice. 9. If at all symbolical, it is of Protestantism. If this proves too much, and that the gown only should be used, we may well ask, Why not? For one minister in the Church, I should be very glad to use only the black gown, and believe it would commend itself to the laity generally, if indeed, not universally. We should thus be a step nearer to union in our essentials [*sic?* accidentals] (as we are already in essentials almost) with all true Protestant Christians, and one outward step further from conformity with Romanism, Heathenism, Idolatry, and Ritualism. DEO JUVANTE." (*The Rock* Feb. 16, 1872.)

† I am indebted as before to Mr. Ornsby (see p. 122) for the following Extract from a Letter of R. Neile to Stapylton:—

"Deare Mr. Stapylton....... For our journey [apparently with Bp. Cosin to the North] I long for as much as you, but when it will yet be I know not. There is every day alarums of the Queene's landing, but nowe [we] gett word shee is hourely expected, and then the Parliament will adjourne for a fortnight, as most people say, and sitt againe: but others that they will adjourne till winter upon the Queene's arrivall. The great divell that scareth them is the

implies that the fuller prescription of the Rubric was not meant to be enforced though the demand for its alteration was *in terms* refused and was not, as I venture to maintain, conceded *in fact* by that slightly altered wording of the Rubric upon which the Court in part relied for the construction which it laid down. The "interpretation" given to the Rubric "in "visitation articles and the like" seems to me entirely consistent with this requirement of the lower prescription of the Canon and with a practical dispensation from the higher prescription of the Rubric; though, as I have shown at pp. 211—13, the Bishops and others inquired for Ornaments and Furniture which were not warranted either by the Canons of 1604 or by the Rubric of 1662 even if the latter be limited by the Rubric of 1549.

XXXI. Their Lordships then discuss the third sense in which, according to some, the Rubric of 1549 was "revived" by the Act of 1662. They say :—

> "III. The third opinion remains, that the provisions of the Rubric of Edward the Sixth are continued, so far as they are not contrariant to other provisions still in force. And here it is to be observed again that the Rubric was altered, after refusal to listen to the Puritan objections, to a form different from that of any former Rubric, by introducing the word 'retained.' Both in the statute of Elizabeth and in the Rubric in question the word 'retain' seems to mean that things should remain as they were at the time of the enactment. Chasuble, alb, and tunicle had disappeared for more than sixty years; and it

Act of Uniformity, which is now in the House of Commons who have throwne out both the provisoes which in one of yours you so rightly guessed. The Pu : [ritan] Lords are much troubled at it, but the Commons are resolute, and will passe noe Bills of concernment (as for money or the like) till the Bill of Uniformity [is] passed. . . . . .

"Yo^r much loving and
"affectionate friend,
" Apr. ye 29th, 1662.   "R. Neile.
" Dr. Sand: [croft] saith the Presbyterian Ministers in Suffolke begine now to say that the Lords' house is the house of the Lord, and soe they pray for itt."

Since this was in type the Surtees Society has published (1872) Vol. ii. of the *Cosin Correspondence*; the Letter will be found in the Introduction p. xviii.

has been argued fairly that this word would not have force to bring back anything that had disappeared more than a generation ago. To retain means, in common parlance, to continue something now in existence. It is reasonable to presume that the alteration was not made without some purpose; and it appears to their Lordships that the words of the Rubric strictly construed, would not suffice to revive ornaments which had been lawfully set aside, although they were in use in the second year of Edward VI."

Now there are but two ways in which the Rubric of 1549 could be "contrariant to other provisions still in force": either it was legally limited, and so far repealed, by the Injunctions of 1559, or by the Advertisements of 1564, or by the Canons of 1604; or it was barred by the Rubric of 1662. I have already, at considerable length, endeavoured to prove that nothing which was done between the passing of the Elizabethan and the Caroline Acts of Uniformity had any *prohibitory* effect upon the Rubric of 1549 : it is needless, therefore, to dwell further on this point. But the Court, recurring here again to the *alteration* of the Rubric, as they allege, in 1662, says that it was changed "to a form different from that of any former "Rubric, by introducing the word 'retained.'" It is perfectly true that this word did not occur in the *Rubric* of 1559 or 1604; but as it was in the *Act* and as both Rubrics referred to the Act, the meaning * of the Rubric from 1559 to 1662 could be none other than that of the Act.

---

* The argument of the Court as to the force of the word "retained" substantially agrees with the "Further Reasons for the Opinion given, May 1866, by Sir Roundell Palmer, Sir H. M. Cairns, Mr. Mellish, and Mr. Barrow," dated 17th June 1867, and printed at pp. 139—40 of the 1st Report of the Ritual Commission. One Paper of Reasons is signed R. P., the other F. B. The latter gentleman, Mr. Barrow, says that his own "observations" had been "submitted to and approved of by" Sir R. Palmer (now Lord Selborne) and that Lord Selborne's reasons had been "submitted to Mr. Mellish [now Lord Justice Mellish]," who had given him "authority to express his entire concurrence with them." As Sir H. M. Cairns had then become Lord Chancellor, Mr. Barrow remarks that "for obvious reasons no communication could be made to" his Lordship.

In these Papers (I) the idea is repudiated "that the Vestments, &c., of the first Prayer Book of Edward VI. had become abrogated by mere desuetude," or that it "in any way operated as a repeal of the Law."

The Court, however, proceeds to construe the word "retain" in the Statute and in the Rubric, and remarks that it "seems "to mean that things should remain as they were at the time " of the Enactment." If this were so it must follow that in

(II.) It is contended "that they had been made actually ILLEGAL" by "the Advertisements of 1565-6" which "were issued by the Royal Authority and had the force of law under the Statute; and that, if this had not been the case, the Canons of 1604, to which both the King and the Metropolitan were parties, would be sufficient for the same purpose" (R.P); and it is added "that the Law enacted by the latter still remains in force, being untouched by the Rubric of 1662." (F.B.) I venture to think that enough has been said in the preceding pages to disprove, or at least to make it in the highest degree improbable, that the Advertisements were an exercise of the power given in 1 Eliz. cap. 2. sect. 25, as the "Reasons" allege to have been the case. That the Canons of 1604 were not an exercise of this power seems abundantly clear from two considerations—(First) That an act done in a Convocation summoned by the King's Writ, which act was afterwards ratified by the King; could not be the proceeding contemplated in the Elizabethan Statute, for the latter is expressly defined to be an act of the "Queen's Majesty" (probably not of Her successors) done with the advice of either of two Authorities, viz., *The Ecclesiastical Commissioners* or *The Metropolitan*, neither of whom could be regarded as the counterpart of Convocation, whether of the Province of Canterbury alone, or of the two Provinces concurring in the Proceedings taken. (Secondly), That the King's Ratification of the Canons of 1604 is distinctly declared to be "according to the Form of a certain Statute or Act of Parliament made in that behalf, in the 25th year of the Reign of King Henry the Eighth, and by Our said Prerogative Royal [*i.e.*, to Sanction the making of Canons] and Supreme Authority in Causes Ecclesiastical, to ratifie by Our Letters Patents under under Our Great Seal of England to confirm the same."

The following passage (for which I am indebted to the Rev. J. Fuller Russell) shews that, three years after the Enactment of the Canons of 1604, the writer understood the Ornaments Rubric to be still in force and so to *legally* require the Eucharistic Vestments :—"A Brownist will suspect a Pharisaicall spirit in them [" *our opposites* "] laying burthens upon others, which they will not touch themselues with their least finger : who charge good men with authoritie in things indifferent, wherin they keepe not the law themselues. This is to be seene in their apparel against the statute ; in their eating flesh on fishe dayes against the lawe ; in their neglect of more profitable Canons ; yea, by their omission of the like ceremonies, as the *Alba*, the *Cappa*, the *Casula*, the *Baculus Pastoralis*, all which are enjoined by law, as well as the Crosse and Surplice, because named in *K. Edw.* communion booke, to which our Law (Eliz. I. c. 2. rubric in init leiturg.) and Rubric sendeth us." ("*A scholastical Discourse against symbolizing with Antichrist in ceremonies especially in the signe of the Crosse.*" [By Robert Parker] part I. pp. 150-51. Fol. 1607. The Book is in the Lambeth Library. 11. D. 3.

And again—". . . why doeth not a Crozier staff appeare in the handes of a Bishopp, as well as the crosse in Baptisme, sith the lawe requireth the one as well as the other ? Is it because there is a meaning not to use that gentle direction which the upper ende betokeneth, but that rigour which the lower ende doeth signifie, according to the auncient verse, *curva trahit quos recta regit pars ultima pungit.* (*Ib.* part II. p. 109.)

(III.) The "Reasons" of Lord Selborne state that :—"IV. It is clear, that the Act of Uniformity of Charles II. did not repeal, but left in force, the Act of *Eliz. cap.* 2, with everything which had been done under the authority

1559 much more was legalized than the Rubric of 1549 prescribed as to *the Ornaments of the Ministers* (to say nothing of *the Ornaments of the Church*), for Q. Mary had restored all that was in use in "the last year of Henry 8th," and therefore the

of that Statute, except so far as the particular enactments of the Act of Car. 2, were at variance therewith." If, as I venture to contend, *nothing* "had been done under the authority of that Statute" by issuing the Advertisements and Canons: then the primary Elizabethan Law, as to Vestments, remains under the Act of 1662.

His Lordship thinks the use "of the very language of Sect. 25 of the Act 1 Eliz. cap. 2" to be "quite intelligible" if the Advertisements and Canons are held to be under that Section : is the language not equally intelligible if they are not so regarded?

"V. The words of the so-called 'Rubric' of 1662 . . . . do not seem to me to be intended, nor to be apt in themselves to *restore* anything which at that date was not 'retained' and 'in use' in the Church of England"; or to revive "an old state of things, long before prohibited by law." But, where is the *prohibition?* If there was none, then the Rubric of 1662 simply keeps in *legal* existence what the Elizabethan Act and Rubric authorized.

"VI. It is to be noted that this so-called *Rubric* appears, on the face of it, to relate only to *The Order for Morning and Evening Prayer daily to be said and used throughout the year*, not expressly mentioning the Communion Office, nor any other special Office." The main reason assigned for this opinion is, "the change" of "at the time of the Communion, and at all other times in his ministration," as in the Books of 1559 to 1604, into "at all times of their ministration," in the Book of 1662. Yet, surely, only the necessities of a theory could urge that the latter term was not as extensive as the former: "at all times," of a person's actions, obviously must mean quite as much as, at *one* time, "and at all other times." Moreover, the fact that the "Ornaments of the Church, and of the Ministers" at the period referred to, were Ornaments used in the Communion Office and in other Offices, necessarily excludes the notion that the direction as to Ornaments relates only to those required for Morning and Evening Prayer.

(IV.) Mr. Barrow, in his "Reasons," refers especially to the Savoy Conference, feeling "how strongly the history of what occurred at" it "tends to confirm the opinions which" he and the other Counsel "formed" : though, as he says, "not in the idea that every fact to which I allude could be necessarily available for arguing the case in a Court of law."

1. He contends "that the utmost" the Nonconformists "could say was, "that the Rubric *seemed* to bring back the Vestments. They could not with truth say, that it had brought them back, or that it required them to be used : for it is all subject to the limitation 'according to the Act of Parliament set at the beginning of the book' . . . . which required the use of the Vestments, only until the other order should be taken under the 25th Section." He considers that this and the Bishops' Answer shew (1) That both parties were alone contending about the *Surplice*, (2) That "the very form of" the Ministers' "objection shows that no *real* grievance was felt in respect of the use of the alb, cope, &c."

But (1) the Bishops' "Answer to the 18th general" objection, here referred to, by no means implies that they were "alone" contending for the Surplice: they were dealing with the "demand" for "the abolishing the laws which impose any ceremonies, *especially* three, the surplice, the sign of the cross, and kneeling." To yield the *Surplice* was, as they well knew, to abandon every superior Vestment as well : therefore to contend for more than

Clergy were bound to employ in Divine Service *all* the Ornaments which were actually in the Churches on the accession of Q. Elizabeth. But the Legislature did not mean the practice of that period to be the Rule, and therefore "the

the Surplice would have been a worse than useless argument. (2) Bearing in mind the *animus* which had been shown towards other Vestments before the Great Rebellion (See *e.g.* pp. 90-91 and 228-9) it is a very gratuitous assumption that the Rubric was not a "*real grievance*" as to the Cope when it was also the authority for the Surplice. There is, however, proof that they did mean to complain of both; for the Bishops, having said in their Answer that "we must not perform public Services undecently or disorderly for the ease of tender consciences." (*Cardwell, Conf.* p, 347), the Ministers rejoined "we are as confident that Surplices and Copes are undecent, and kneeling at the Lord's Table disorderly, as you are of the contrary." *The Grand Debate, &c., London,* 1661, p. 97, and *Documents relating to the Act of Uniformity, London,* 1862, p. 275.) This latter Volume states, p. 204, that this rejoinder of the Ministers, or "reply was drawn up by Baxter—Reliquiæ, Baxterianæ, p. 334." Compare this with Baxter's complaint in 1668 (See p. 173) as shewing that before and after the Act of 1662 he took the same view of the Rubric. It is, moreover, important to observe—that even if the Advertisements of 1566 and the Canons of 1604 were, either or both, the "other Order" of the Elizabethan Act of Uniformity, it is clear that Baxter and the other objectors did not consider COPES to be *unlawful* and SURPLICES to be *lawful*—they regarded both as having the like Authority.

2. Mr. Barrow argues that "the Church party "desiring" to avoid even the appearance of the smallest concession" substituted the words of the Elizabethan Act for the words of the Rubric; and so, on the one hand, if "taunted," could deny that they had "made any concession"; "on the other hand (if charged with bigotry), could allege that they had relaxed the Rubric by introducing the word "retained," which could only apply to such Vestments "as the Rubric finds in existence." This seems to me to imply a want of courage and candour on the part of the Bishops which the history of their conduct does not warrant; and certainly their opponents did not regard their concessions as designed to be of any importance, for, in their *Rejoinder* to the Bishops' *Answer* they describe them as "for the most part verbal and literal, rather than real and substantial," and they say "you indulge not the omission of any one ceremony." (*Grand Debate,* p. 30—31 or *Documents, &c.,* p. 201—2.) If Mr. Barrow should be inclined to adopt the language of the Judicial Committee "that the Rubric was altered, after refusal to listen to the Puritan objections, to a form different from that of any former Rubric, by introducing the word 'retained'" (See p. 221); there is the great fact to be faced—that Baxter and others six years afterwards did not consider that it had been altered. (See p. 173.)

3. Mr. Barrow asks "is it for one moment to be believed that the framers of the present Rubric really and deliberately intended to restore the use of Vestments, the bare phantoms of which would have set the country in a flame from one end to the other; and that they made the alteration with that intention?" I am not aware that any one has alleged such a purpose. All that they did was to preserve the existing Law, touching the Ornaments of both *Church* and *Minister* by combining the language of the Act and the Rubric; omitting, however, the reference to the then abolished Ecclesiastical Commission, and withdrawing the Power given in the Act to the Crown and the Metropolitan to make alterations—leaving these, if required, to the more Constitutional action of Convocation, Parliament, and the Crown combined Yet it is reasonable to believe that a hope was entertained that the Rubric

"second year" of Edward 6th was mentioned as the standard to be referred to. In this case, then, the argument of the Court proves a great deal too much.

On the other hand, if "retained" means "that things should "remain as they were at the time of the Enactment" in 1662, because, as the Court says "to retain means, in common "parlance, to continue something now in existence," it is obviously necessary to ask—What did exist at that time? Their Lordship's remark—that "Chasuble, alb, and tunicle "had disappeared for more than sixty years"—is not without some parallel in the case of other Ornaments; the History of the period shews (See Notes pp. 90 & 91) that "Copes and "Surplices" had also "disappeared" for twenty years. Nor were these the only "monuments of superstition and "idolatry" which were consigned to destruction in the same period; Altars;* Fonts;† Altar Coverings, Cloths, and Cushions; Organs; Hangings;‡ Candlesticks; Basons; ¶

remaining substantially unchanged, might in time lead to the restoration of some of those Accessories of Divine Service, which had been cast out in that general destruction of Ecclesiastical Ornaments and Furniture which preceded the overthrow of the Government in Church and State.

4. "What then," asks Mr. Barrow, "is the difference between the faulty Rubric and the sound? Compare them, and it will be found that the only absolutely new idea introduced is that conveyed by the word 'retain.'" But there was no "new idea," unless the fact be ignored that the word was in the Act to which the old Rubric *expressly referred* and with which it had to be read. This being so, whatever Ornaments were *legally* "retained" by the Act and Rubric of 1559 must have been also *legally* "retained" by the Rubric of 1662, unless it can be proved that the qualifying "other order" of 1559 is recognized in the Statute of 1662 as having been carried out, and as therefore necessarily limiting the general words of the present Rubric.

* The House of Commons, Jan. 23, 1640-1, "Ordered, That Commissioners be sent into all Counties for the defacing, demolishing, and quite taking away of all Images, Altars, or Tables turned Altar-wise, Crucifixes, superstitious Pictures, Monuments and Reliques of Idolatry, out of all Churches, or Chappels." (*Rushworth, Hist. Coll., Vol. I,* pt. 3, p. 95.)

† See P. 91.

‡ In *Stow's London*, Vol. II, bk. 4, c. 4, p. 83, (quoted in *Lawful Church Ornaments* p. 353) there is a detailed account of Ornaments given in 1631 to St. Giles in the Fields; and then it is added ". . . . all the forenamed Ornaments of the Church (being counted superstitious and Popish) were demolished and sold (under pretence of relieving the poor out of the money received for them) by the *Reformers* (as they were called) in the Civil War Time."

¶ Sep. 8, 1641, the House of Commons ordered "That all Tapers, Candlesticks and Basons be removed from the Communion Table." (*Rush. H. C.*, part 3, Vol. I, p. 387 : *Collier, E. H.*, II., 9, 806.)

Crosses; § Altar Plate; ‖ all shared the same fate. Perhaps it will be said that the Surplice, at all events, had to some extent at least come into use again before the Act of 1662 passed, encouraged probably by the refusal of Charles 2nd to comply with the request of the Presbyterian Ministers (in their interview with him at Breda in 1660) "that the use of the Surplice "might be discontinued by his Chaplains, because the sight "of it would give great offence and scandal to the people," (*Clarendon's Rebellion*, bk. xvi., Oxford, 1843, p. 909.) But it would be absurd to suppose that a Statute, enjoining the use of certain things described by a well-known definition, left it to the accident of any of those being "in existence" at the time to decide whether they were included under its provisions: a Law of such a character would have needed a Schedule stating what Ornaments were actually "in existence" in 1662 after the general destruction which had been effected during the Rebellion.

The word "retained" must, therefore, have referred to a *legal* "existence" and a *legal* "use" which was known and

§ "By virtue of an ordinance which had passed in 1643, all crosses, crucifixes, representations of saints and angels, copes, surplices, hangings, candlesticks, basins, organs, &c., were carried out of the cathedral and other churches." (*Milner's Hist. of Winchester*, Vol. I., pp. 411-12. 4to. 1809. Quoted *Hierurgia Anglicana*, p. 31.)

‖ "The rebels, under the conduct of Sir William Waller, entering the city of Chichester on Innocent's Day 1642, the next day their first business was to plunder the Cathedral Church; the Marshal, therefore, and some other officers, having entered the Church, went into the vestry; there they seize upon the vestments and ornaments of the Church, together with the consecrated plate serving for the altar and administration of the Lord's Supper: they left not so much as a cushion for the pulpit, nor a chalice for the Blessed Sacrament." (*Mercurius Rusticus*, p. 223, 12° 1646. Quoted *Hierurgia Anglicana*, p. 23.) See *Ibid.* as to Winchester and Exeter; p. 161 as to Peterborough, p. 163 as to Norwich and York.

Some illustrations of the manner in which the Iconoclastic Decrees of Parliament were carried out, are furnished by "The Journal of William Dowsing, of Stratford, Parliamentary Visitor, appointed under a warrant from the Earl of Manchester, for demolishing the Superstitious Pictures and Ornaments of Churches, &c., within the County of Suffolk, in the years 1643—44.

"Woodbridge: printed by and for R. Loder, sold by J. Nichols, London. 1786." ["Reprinted for John W. Parker, West Strand, London, 1844." 12°)

The Book mentions 152 places in which the Visitor did his work, and did it most thoroughly as it would seem: besides other things, the following are stated to have been demolished in the instances numbered:—Crucifix 13, Picture of Christ 8, Picture of Christ on the Cross 3, Picture of Christ on the Cross outside the Steeple 1, Cross on the Church 46, Crosses in Church 3, Cross in Chancel 5,

could be at once pointed out,* not to an *actual* "existence" and an *actual* "use" which it would have been impossible to define after the "much disorder and undecency in the exercise "of God's worship" to which the King referred as having grown up in those "late ill times," (*Ibid.* p. 909). There was such a *legal* existence and use recognized in the Act and Rubric with which the Revisers of 1661 had to deal; and there is no evidence, so far as I know, to suggest that they wished, instead of this, to give a *legal existence* to what could not even be called *the use* of their own time.

It may be said, perhaps, in reply—that Ornaments, both of the Church and the Ministers, having a *legal existence* were to be found in the Canons of 1604; but this is not the contention of the Judicial Committee in using the word "existence"; and, moreover, thus to refer to those Canons is to assume what has all along been disputed viz., that the Canons had legally excluded the larger range of Ornaments which the Rubric contemplated.

The Court says "It is reasonable to presume that the "alteration [in the Rubric] was not made without some "purpose;" no doubt this is true, but *a* (probably *the*) purpose seems very obvious, viz. *simplicity*—for by inserting in the Rubric, as Cosin had proposed, (*See* p. 92), "Y^e words of y^e "Act itself," it would be needless longer to encumber the Rubric with a reference to the Statute in the then existing

---

Cross (apparently) in Church 6, Cross on font 3, Cross in the glass 4, "my flesh is meat indeed, and my blood is drink indeed" 1, "Jesus's written in capital letters on the roof" 6, "holy water fount" 9, "a pot for holy water" 1, cover of the font 2, organs 1, organ cases 1, levelling steps 49, levelling steps in Chancel 12, the Rails 2.

The following notices also occur :—" 129 Elmsett, Aug. the 22d. . . . We rent apieces there the Hood and Surplice."—"139 Holton . . . Aug. the 29th. . . . I*H*S the Jesuit's Badge, in the Chancel Window; . . . ." There is a second instance of this.

* This is true whether "second year" be legally referable to *the Book* of 1549, or to *the year* 1547; for, if the former, Ornaments were specified in it; if the latter, it was expressly declared in the Council's Letter of May 13, 1548, to the Licensed Preachers, where it is said that "What is abolished, taken away, reformed and commanded it is easy to see by the Acts of Parliament, the injunctions, and homilies : . . . ." (*Cardwell Doc. Ann.* I. p. 65.)

words, "according to the Acte of Parliament set in the be-
"ginning of this booke": indeed, it was necessary to omit the
reference, for, otherwise, the following words of the Elizabethan
Act would have remained in force,—"until other order shall be
"therein taken by the authority of the Queen's Majesty, with
"the advice of her Commissioners appointed and authorized
"under the great Seal of England, for causes Ecclesiastical, or
"of the Metropolitan of this Realm,"—but this power was not
intended to be continued, nor, indeed, could it have been
exercised so far as the Ecclesiastical Commission was concerned,
for (See p. 192) that Commission had been abolished.

"It appears to their Lordships that the words of the Rubric
"strictly construed, would not suffice to revive Ornaments which
"had been lawfully set aside, although they were in use in the
"second year of Edward VI." But this assumes as true, what
I think has been already disproved, viz.—that they were
"lawfully set aside," *i.e.*, in the sense of being *prohibited;* for,
no doubt, they were "set aside" by the Advertisements and
the Canons (so far as they, respectively, had authority) in the
sense of not being *required*. Further, in speaking of "the
"Rubric" being "strictly construed," their Lordships clearly
seem to refer to their own interpretation of the word "re-
"tained"; but if that interpretation cannot stand, as I think
has been shown to be the case (See pp. 224-30), then their
construction of the Rubric fails, and the Ornaments which
"were in use in the Second Year of Edward VI" are legally
usable now.

In the event, however, of their Lordships' construction of
the Rubric failing, they put forward again a theory which they
had already advanced in somewhat different language (See p.
192); the Court says:—

> "But whether this be so or not, their Lordships are of
> opinion that as the Canons of 1603-4, which in one
> part seemed to revive the vestments, and in another,
> to order the surplice for all ministrations, ought to
> be construed together, so the Act of Uniformity is
> to be construed with the two canons on this subject,
> which it did not repeal, and that the result is that

the cope is to be worn in ministering the Holy Communion on high feast days in Cathedrals, and Collegiate Churches, and the Surplice in all other ministrations."

The chief point to be here noticed is the supposed opposition between some of the Canons, whereas their Lordships reasonably contend that they "ought to be construed together": to do this they, somewhat strangely, subordinate (what they admit seem to be) the higher requirements of Canon 14 to the lower prescription of Canons 24 and 58. But does Canon 14 relate at all to the Ornaments? I think not; for the reasons following:—

i. The *Title* of the Canon—" The Prescript Form of Divine "Service to be used on Sundays and Holy-days"—shews that it relates to the *Office* provided for use. Canon 16 bears a similar Title—" Colleges to use the prescript Form of Divine "Service."

ii. Wherever the Canons treat of Ornaments of the Church or of the Ministers, the Titles expressly indicate the subject, and do not employ any such language as is used in the Titles of Canons 14 and 16.

iii. If the terms "Orders, Rites, and Ceremonies" in Canon 14; and the terms "Order, Form, and Ceremonies" in Canon 16, referred to the Vestures of the Ministers "prescribed in "the Book of Common Prayer," it was useless also to give directions about Vestures in other Canons.

iv. The terms *Orders, Form, Rites, Ceremony*, had their counterpart in the Elizabethan Prayer Book, and in the Book of 1604, which was in use when the Canons were made; and thus it is plain to what the Canons referred when they required conformity to the Prayer Book directions touching the following matters:—

"ORDERS"—*Institutam*, Can. 14.   "ORDER"—*Ordinem*, Can. 16.

1. "The *Order* how the Psalter is appointed to be read."
2. "The *Order* how the rest of Holy Scripture (beside the Psalter) is appointed to be read."
3. "The *Order* where Morning and Evening Prayer shall be used and said."

4. "An *Order* for Morning Prayer daily throughout the year."
5. "An *Order* for Evening Prayer throughout the year."
6. "Thus endeth the *Order* of Morning and Evening Prayer through [throughout–1604] the whole year."
7. "The *Order* for the Administration of the Lord's Supper or Holy Communion."
8. "The *Order* of Confirmation." (1604)
9. "The *Order* for the Visitation of the Sick."
10. "The *Order* for the Burial of the Dead."

"Form"—*formam*, Can. 16.
1. "The *Form* of Solemnization of Matrimony."
2. "The *Form* and Manner of Making and Consecrating Bishops, Priests, and Deacons."

"Rites"—*ritus*, Can. 14.
1. "And note, that every Parishioner shall communicate at the least three times in the year, of which Easter to be one, and shall also receive the Sacraments and other *Rites*, according to the order in this Book appointed."

Here the term "*Rites*" plainly means some Means of Grace analogous to a Sacrament: such would be *Absolution* and *Confirmation*. Also it would include the Receiving into the Congregation those who had been privately baptized. The term *Order* also occurs here.

2. In the Communion Office the Minister is to deliver the Sacrament "to the people in their hands *kneeling*": Canon 23 describes "kneeling" as being "according to the Order [*ritum*] of the Communion Book."

"Ceremonies"—*ceremonias*, Can. 14 and 16.
1. "Then the Priest shall make a Cross upon the Child's forehead, saying '*We receive*,'" &c.

Canon 30 mentions "the Sign of the Cross in Baptism" as one "amongst some other very ancient Ceremonies [*ceremonias*]" which have been retained in this Church."

v. The illustrations just given shew plainly enough that the requirements of Canon 14 can be fully complied with, apart from any supposed reference to *Vestures*; for in the Offices of the Prayer Book there are "prescribed," as the Canon says, many and various "Orders, Rites, and Ceremonies" to be used, "as well in reading the Holy Scriptures and saying of "Prayers, as in Administration of the Sacraments."

vi. Further, the direction for "Ministers" to "observe" the "Orders, Rites, and Ceremonies," which are thus "pre-"scribed," followed as it is by the words "without either "diminishing in regard of preaching, or in any other respect," makes it evident that the purpose of the Canon was to prevent any curtailment or omission of the Offices of the Church and to secure a full and proper discharge of their public Functions by the Clergy.

vii. Once more, another expression in the Canon furnishes additional evidence of its object: "all Ministers" are prohibited from "adding anything in the matter or form "[*materiæ sive formæ*]" of the prescribed Offices: these being technical terms which refer to the SUBSTANCE and ARRANGEMENT—not to the mere ACCESSORIES—of Divine Service, are in themselves sufficient proof that it was not the purpose of *this* Canon to deal with the Ornaments to be worn by the Minister when employed in these Public Offices of the Church. Canon 56 confirms this view, for it orders "Preachers and Lecturers" to administer Baptism and the Lord's Supper "in such manner "and form, and with the observation of all such Rites and "Ceremonies as are prescribed by the Book of Common Prayer "in that behalf."

If, then, I have rightly interpreted this 14th Canon, there is no difficulty whatever in construing it with Canons 24 and 58, which do treat of the Ornaments of the Ministers: there can be no contradiction between them, because the former relates to the *structure* and *arrangement* of the Prayer Book Offices, the the two latter refer to the *Dress* to be worn in ministering these Offices. It is not necessary to discuss again their Lordships' mode of construing* together "the Act of Uniformity," and "the two Canons on this subject," or to point out "that the "result is" not necessarily the *exclusive* one at which they arrive: a reference to what has been already stated at length (See pp. 125-31) will, I think, prove their Lordships' conclusion to be at least *deficient*, viz., "that the Cope is to be worn in minis- "tering the Holy Communion on high feast days in Cathedrals

---

* See p. 204.—The Court held that the Canons of 1604 were among the "good laws" kept in force by the last Act of Uniformity; but against this theory is to be set the facts that (*a*) on Ap. 8, 1662 the House of Commons "Ordered, That such Persons as shall be employed to manage the Conference with the Lords, do intimate the desire of this House, That it be recommended to the Convocation, to take Order for reverent and uniform Gestures and Demeanours to be enjoined at the time of Divine Service and Preaching." (*Journals Vol.* 8, p. 415): that (*b*) on May 9th the Lords informed the Commons that they had agreed to their Amendments in the Bill of Uniformity (*Ib.* p. 424): and that (*c*) on May 10th & 12th Canon 18 was "approved and confirmed" in both Houses of Convocation as satisfying the Order which the House of Commons had desired Convocation to take. (*Gibson, Syn. Ang.* 231 *Ed.* 1854; *Kennet's Register*, 684; *and Lathbury's Hist. of Conv.* 295 & 296.)

"and Collegiate Churches, and the Surplice in all other "ministrations."

The Customs at the Chapel Royal, St. James's Palace, subsequent to these Canons of 1604, prove that their Lordships' view of the legal effect of the Canons was not taken by some of the Ecclesiastical Authorities at that period, at least as regards that Chapel: consequently, unless it can be shewn that the Ministrations there were exempt from the general Ecclesiastical Law, the Records of the Chapel Royal prove that the Cope was considered a Lawful Ornament of the Minister in Baptism, Churching, and Confirmation; for the following notices of its use on all these occasions occur in the *"Cheque-Book"* * of that Chapel:—

BAPTISM.

"'1605, May 5. At Greenwhich. The order and manner of the Service performed in and by the Chappell at the Christninge of Marye the daughter of the Mightie Kinge, James, &c. the fyfte of Maye, Anno 1605.

'At the tyme when the Royall Infant should be brought to the Chappell, the gentlemen of that place (after many companies goinge before) went out of the Chappell two and two in their surplesses unto the nurcerie doore, there following them the Deane of the Chappell, next after came the Arch Bishop of Canterbury, both in rich Copes of Needleworke. . . . When the Royall Infant was thus brought unto the lower Chappell doore, there did the Archbishop and the Deane of the Chappell receave the Babe and came next before it into the higher Chappell . . . . When all were placed, then begane an Antheme . . . . the which Antheme being endid the child was brought from the Traverce to the Font, whome the Arch Bishop baptized with great reverence (beinge still in his rich cope), who was assistid in the administracōn of the Sacrament by the Deane of the Chappell (he allso beinge in his cope) . . . . Then begun an offertorye to be played, in which tyme the noble baptized Infant was brought to the Holye Table and there it offered, by the person of the Lord Treasurer. Then the God Father and God Mothers did severallye offer allso, being fett [fetched] from their seates by the Lord Chamberlaine, the Deane of the Chappell receavinge the offeringes at the Communion Table in his cope. Then followed a full Anthem (Singe joyfullye) in the singinge whereof the Gossip's great giftes weare brought out of the vestrie (by certain Knightes) and placed uppon the Communion Table, at thend of which Antheme the Collect for the Kinge was read, and therewith the service ended . . . [f. 32*b*]'" *p.* 167.

* "The old Cheque-Book, or Book of Remembrance, of the Chapel Royal, from 1561 to 1744. Edited, from the original MS. preserved among the Muniments of the Chapel Royal, St. James's Palace, by Edward F. Rimbault, LL.D., Printed for the Camden Society, 1872."

CHURCHING.

"'1605, The Order of the Queen's Highnes Churchinge, which
May 19. was in the Chappell, uppon Whitsondaye 1605.

'.... When the Kinge and Queene weare so seated, then ended the offertory, and a full Anthem (beginninge Blessed art thou that fearest God) was songe, at the end whereof the Bishop of Canterbury, beinge assisted by Mr. Deane of the Chappell (and both in rich copes) did read the ordinary service of Churchinge of women, appointed by the booke, her highnes kneelinge the while in her Travase. The churchinge beinge ended, the Queene rose up and cam forth and offered at the Holye Table, as the Kinges Majestie had formerly done, Mr. Deane receavinge both their offeringes in his Cope, and the Organs playinge at each tyme . . . . [f. 33].'" *p.* 169.

CONFIRMATION.

"'1607, The Order of the Prince's Confirmacōn in the Chappell,
Apl 3. the third of Aprill 1607, beinge then Good Fridaye.

'.... in the time of singinge of the first Anthem before the Sermon began, wher, at the lower step in the Quier there, a carpett and cushions beinge prepared, he there kneelinge was confirmed in his faithe in Christ, by the Reverend Father the Archbishop of Canterbury (the Deane of the Chappell assistinge him, and bothe in rich copes) . . . . [f. 78*b*].'" *p.* 171.

"'1610-11 The Order of the Ladie Elizabeth her Grace's Con-
Mar. 22. firmacōn in the Chappell the 22th of Marche, beinge Good Frydaye.

'.... in the tyme of singinge of the first Anthem, before the Sermon began, wher at the lower Step in the Quier there, a carpett and cushions beinge prepared, she there kneelinge was confirmed in her fayth in Christe by the Reverend Father the Bishopp of Bathe and Wells, Deane of his Maj. Chappell, the Subdeane therof assistinge him, and both in riche copes . . . [f. 79].'" *p.* 172.

"'1613, Prince Charell's Confirmacōn in the Chappell the 5th of
Ap. 5. Aprill 1613, beinge the Mondaie in Easter Week.

'.... in the singinge of the first Anthem, wher at the lower step in the Queere there, a carpet and cusshions beinge prepared, he there kneelinge was confirmed in his faithe in Christe by the Reverend Father in God the Bishopp of Bathe and Welles, Deane of his Majesties Chappell (assistinge him, and bothe in riche coapes.) . . . [f. 79].'" ' *p.* 172.

To support their conclusion from Canons 14, 24, and 58 (as expressed in the words quoted at p. 232) a resort is again made to *contemporaneous exposition* in the words following:—

"Their Lordships attach great weight to the abundant evidence which now exists that from the days of Elizabeth to about 1840, the practice is uniformly in accordance with this view; and is irreconcileable with either of the other views. Through the researches that have been referred to in these remarks a clear and abundant *expositio contemporanea* has been supplied which compensates for the scantiness of some other materials for a judgment."

There might have been some force in this appeal to custom if the Ecclesiastical History of the period had shown (1) That changes (whether in the Rule or in the Practice) touching the Ornaments of the Church and of the Ministers, were deliberately made by Authority in conformity with a common desire to abolish the Legal Standard; (2.) That there had been a general and continuous practice "from the days of Elizabeth to about " 1840," to use and to use exclusively, (*a*) the Cope, "in minis- " tering the Holy Communion on high feast days in Cathedrals " and Collegiate Churches," only—as the Court seems to have misread the Canon, (*b*) "the Surplice in all other ministra- "tions" of that Sacrament in those Churches, (*c*) the Surplice in all ministrations, whether of the Eucharistic or of any other Office in Parish Churches.*

But the History of the period in question is certainly not in accordance with either of these propositions, as may be gathered, I think, from the Documentary evidence already given in these pages; and I venture to maintain that "the "practice" to which their Lordships refer, so far from being " uniformly in accordance with this view" which they exhibit, and being "irreconcileable with either of the other views" which they examine, is in fact quite consistent with the "maximum" and " minimum" view of the Dean of the Arches, (See p. 216), which, however, the Judicial Committtee held to be "at variance with all the facts of the case."†

---

* Their Lordships' language is not wholly unambiguous, but, having regard to their argument in the context, the above must be considered as their meaning in saying—"The result is that the Cope is to be worn in ministering the Holy Communion on high feast days in Cathedrals and Collegiate Churches, and the Surplice in all other ministrations."

† The Court, erroneously assuming (See p. 25) that the Advertisements "appeared" in "1564," concluded that they made the Vestments illegal, and further that, as a consequence, "the operation of the Advertisements had been rapid and complete" in causing their general destruction. It has been proved, I think, that, whatever were the causes of this destruction, the Advertisements cannot be charged with it. It has been shewn, further (See p. 64) that the Advertisements were not issued until May 21, 1566, and that the latest of the Lincolnshire Inventories in Mr. Peacock's Book (See p. 38) is dated May 26, 1556, five days only after the Advertisements were issued in London, and

There is, moreover, some further evidence bearing upon the three points (*a*), (*b*), and (*c*) which I have above mentioned, and which it may be useful to furnish here.

The 24th Canon of 1604 (upon which the Court erroneously based its decision that the Cope is only to be worn "on high "feast days" in Cathedrals and Collegiate Churches at the Celebration of the Holy Communion) refers, as I have already noticed (See p. 126), to the Advertisements in illustration of its that consequently the Court was wholly mistaken in supposing that these Inventories proved the effect of the Advertisements. Yet, on the other hand, there is some evidence which furnishes a reasonable presumption that the use of the Ornaments of the 2nd year of Edward 6th, authorized by the Elizabethan Act of Uniformity, was not imagined to have been prohibited by the later Advertisements.

I. Among the Municipal Records of BODMIN, in the County of Cornwall, there exists a Document of which the following extract was furnished to me in 1868 by Sir John Maclean, F.S.A., (who has since printed it in his "Parochial and Family History of the Deanery of Trigg Minor in the County of Cornwall," 1870, Part II., p. 341) :—

"ASSIGNMENT OF CHURCH GOODS, PRESERVED AMONG THE CORPORATION RECORDS AT BODMIN.

(*Extracted*, Sept. 7th, 1868.)

'Thys Indentuer made at Bodmyn the Sunday next after the ffeast of Seynt Mygell the archangell ynn the eyght yere of the Raygne of our Soueraygne Lady Elyzabeth by the grace of god of Englond Ffrancie and Irelond quene defender of the ffayth &c Betwyne Nycholas Cory mayor of the towne of bodmyn of thone pty, and Richard Water and Thomas Cole taunr Wardens of the Churche of St. Petherick yn bodmyn aforesayd of thother pty Wyttnesseth that the said Rychard Water and Thomas Cole Wardens and ther successors Wardens hath taken and receved into ther handes & kepyng of the sayd Nycholas Cory mayor & of all the hole pyshe [parish] aforesayd to be used and occupied to the honer of God yn the same churche from the day & yere aforesayd fourthward all suche goods & ornaments as folowth and hath taken uppon them for them & ther successors to yeld a true rekynyng of all the same goods & ornaments & delyvry thereof to make wthut deley to the sayd Nycholas Cory & his successors for the tyme beyng mayor & to all the hole pyshe of bodmyn aforesayd this tyme xii monethes that ys to wete fyrst—ffive bells wth one wch servyth for ye clock to be rung dayly at ffower of the clock yn the mornyng & at eyght yn the evynyng a warning bell for printyses & others. Item one Vestment of grene satyn of bryddes, Item one hole sute of blew velut decon subdecon and pistholere, a pere of vestments of whyte damaske, one cope of red satyn of bryddes, Item a vestment of blue velut, one whyte cope of satyn, Item one whyte vestment of satyn & more toe copes used on good fryday and a obe [albe] of sylck, Item one crosse ban^r of grene sylck, Item one frunt of yelo [& gr]ene satyn of bryddes, toe cortens [curtains] wherof one of sylck a nother frunt of Arres, a nother frunt of sey & a curtens of the same. Item [a cu]sshyn of velut for the commuyon tabell & a cusshyng of sylcke for Mr Mayor ys chere [his chair] & a cloth of cheker w[o]rk [for Mr] Mayor ys chere a shype of tyn [i.e. for Incense] viij pere of surpeles wth one new for Mr. Vycar iiij rachetes [rochets], a bybell & [paraphase] of Erasmus ij pere of candelstyckes a bason of laten a lamp before the hye auter one corperul of red velut and a nother of green ....a corpus cloth one dex cloth, toe stoles for sett at the comuio tabell a herse cloth of velut & a nother of black bocoron [Item a] sencer of

"ENDORSED
'betwene N Cory
Mayor Ric Wat^r
and T Cole tann^r
Wardens Inv'nt^t
ornament Ecclie"

directions: those Advertisements unquestionably do not make any such limitation; subsequently, in 1567, Archbishop Parker (who was the main Author of the Advertisements) issued "*Articles to be enquired of in the metropolitical visitation of* " . . . . *al and singular cathedral and collegiate Churches* "*within his province of Canterbury ;*" the 3rd of these (already quoted at p. 67,) asks " Whether your divine service be used, and " your sacraments ministred in manner and forme prescribed by " the Quenes majesties injunctions, and none other way ?" (*Cardwell, Doc. Ann* I. 339).

Again, in a Letter from the Privy Council, Nov. 7, 1573, which refers to the Queen's Proclamation of Oct. 20, the Bishops are urged " to the keeping of the order allowed by the said Parlia- " ment [in the Book of Common Prayer], and by her Majesty's Injunctions "; no reference being made to the Advertisements. (*Strype*, Bk. iv. ch. 36, p. 454.)

Further, Archbishop Grindal (who as Bishop of London, signed

latten......toe lent clothes for the commyo tabell ij polys [poles] one of brasse & a nother of yron ij newe vant clothes [and a nold, *cancelled*] a sacryng bell a cruat iij Jesus cotes ij red wosterd & one of red bocrom iij tormenttowers cotes of satyn of bryddes of yolo & blue......ij cappes of sylck toe develes cotes wherof one ys newe [toe sandyers cotes of whyte, *cancelled*] a croune of black a nother for ....a......ell a crosse & a nold crosse......one comonyn cup of sylvr and one other gylt wth hery cock used at weddyngs.. ....andy......& toe clottes of led In [witten]es herof the ptes to the psent Indentuer intrchayngabelly have putte [ther hands &] seles ye day & yere above w[ritten]'

"[Then follow other items, written in paler ink and scarcely legible. The lower part of the paper is decayed and torn.]"

Now, whether the Advertisements were published in the 7th or in the 8th year of Elizabeth, this Assignment is full four Months subsequent to the later date; and therefore, upon the Court's own showing, the Mayor of Bodmin and the Churchwardens of St. Petherick ought to have known that the Advertisements had so far repealed the Elizabethan Act of Uniformity as to render unlawful all the Vestures mentioned in this Document except the Surplices. Yet here we find the Civil Magistrate and the Ecclesiastical Officers uniting in preserving these same Vestures and other Church goods "*to be used and occupied to the honour of God in the same* [*parish*] *Church* [*of St. Petherick*] *from the day and year aforesaid forthward.*" There is not the least indication of misgiving on their part that the use of such "Ornaments of the Church and of the Ministers thereof," authorized by the Statute of 1559, subjected them to heavy pains and penalties : on the contrary, assuming with the Court that they could not have been ignorant of the Advertisements, it is plain that they did not regard the "*minimum*" requirement of these later Orders as excluding their use of the "*maximum*" prescribed by the earlier Law. It cannot be reasonably contended —that probably some or most of these things were not really meant to be used, for the Assignment applies to all and makes no distinction between *e.g.* the Vestments for the Service and the Cushion for the Mayor's Chair.

II. WILLS of the period serve also to shew the impression which the Testators had of the existing state of the Law : a few years ago a gentleman examined many of them in Doctors Commons and published some extracts in *The Church*

the Advertisements) in his Visitation Articles for "*all and sin-*
"*gular Cathedral and Collegiate Churches within his province of*
"*Canterbury,*" 1576, makes the same enquiry as Parker: he asks
"VI. Item, Whether your divine service be used, and the Sacra-
"ments ministred in manner and forme prescribed in the Quenes
"majesties injunctions, and none otherwaies; . . ." (*Ibid.* I. 419.)

The Judicial Committee (Martin *v.* Mackonochie, 1868) held that the words, "form or manner," in the Elizabethan Act of Uniformity, prohibited the use of Lighted Candles as "a Cere-"monial Act" in the Celebration of the Lord's Supper: if that be the true construction of the words "form or manner" (though I venture respectfully to question it) then those words, as used by Parker and Grindal, included any Ceremonial pre-scribed in Queen Elizabeth's Injunctions for the Ministration of the Eucharist and consequently the Vesture of the Clergy at that time; for the two Prelates expressly refer to the "Injunc-"tions" which, moreover, were published in 1559 contempo-raneously with the Act of Uniformity which had just passed.

Review: circumstances prevented him from continuing his researches and he died about four years since, but he informed me that many more similar Bequests could be produced. I quote the following:—

Humphrey Colles, Esq., of Beerton, Somerset, was a Justice of the Peace for that County: in 1569 he, with some 800 other Magistrates, signed the Declaration of adhesion to the Act of Uniformity, in which the Signatories said, "Neither shall any of us that hath subscribed do, or say, or suffer anything to be done or said, by our procurement or allowance, in contempt, lack, or reproof of any part of Religion established by the aforesaid Act;" and a service to which he was appointed in 1570 appears to have placed him in somewhat intimate connexion with Cecil and other Members of the Privy Council, so that he was likely to know the state of the Law touching the Goods and Ornaments of the Church. His Will is dated June 10, 8th Elizabeth, 1566, and was proved in London before Abp. Parker in 1571: it has three Codicils dated respectively 16 Oct. 12 Elizabeth, 24 Nov. & 17 Dec. 13 Elizabeth; these Codicils make no alteration or revocation of the following Bequest.

"Furthermore, I will to the Churchwardens of the Parish Church of Corff, in the County of Somerset, to the use of the same Church, and maintainance of Divine Service there, the Cope of velvet embroidered that my wife lent to the parishioners there, and all Vestments and other furniture of mine whatsover the Churchwardens have, meet for the maintainance of Divine Service there."

"Also I give and bequeath to the said Churchwardens, for the use and maintainance of the Ornaments, and reparations of the said Parish Church of Corff, 20s."

One of his Executors was Wm. Rowsewill the then Solicitor General, and another Sir Hugh Paulet, Kt., who signed with him the Declaration above mentioned.

It appears to me that these two Documents strengthen the proof already given (See pp. 28—30, 54, 73 & 165) that at and after the date of the promul-gation of the Advertisements, they were not regarded as repealing the provisions of the Elizabethan Act and Rubric in reference to the Ornaments of the Church and the Clergy.

Now those Injunctions make no reference whatever to the *Eucharistic Vestments*: they do prescribe (No. 30) the *ordinary Dress* of the Clergy; they order (No. 23) the removal from the Churches of certain "monuments of feigned miracles, pil-"grimages, idolatry, and superstition"; they prescribe (No. 24) a Pulpit and (No. 25) an Alms Chest to be provided in the Church; they give directions as to the character and position of the Altar-Table; they prescribe the kind of Wafer-bread to be used; and (No. 47) they require "the Inventories of Vest-"ments, Copes, and other Ornaments, Plate, Books," &c, "appertaining to the Church," to be delivered to the Queen's Visitors. The very fact that these Injunctions do not vary or limit (much less forbid) the use of the Eucharistic Vestments (though they do regulate other things used in Divine Service) shows that the Rubric of 1559 was then the *general* Law as to the Ornaments of the Church and of the Ministers.

Two years later, however, apparently about March 1561,* there appeared under the authority of the Archbishops and Bishops, certain "Interpretations and further Considerations" of the Queen's Injunctions in which, among other things, the *full* requirements of the Rubric as to the Eucharistic Vestments were dispensed with; for "Concerning the Book of Service," it was directed "That there be used only but one apparel, as the "Cope in the ministration of the Lord's Supper, and the Surplice "in all other ministrations." (*Cardwell*, Doc. Ann. I. 238). But this Dispensation made no difference between Cathedral and Parish Churches, both were to observe the *same* rule,† though it

---

* Strype, writing under the date of 1561, says:—"Other things also were drawn up by the diligent Archbishop [Parker] in his own name, and in the name of the rest of the Bishops: which were *Interpretations and Considerations* of certain of the Queen's Injunctions, for the better instructions of the Clergy: which are too long to be here set down; but may be found among the Archbishop's own MSS. preserved in the Bene't College library, in the volume entitled *Synodalia*, and in the Annals of the Reformation." (*Life and Acts of Parker*, I. bk. 2. p. 183. 8°., or fol. 92.)

In the "Annals," to which Strype here refers, he says:—"Another thing also was now drawn up in writing by the Archbishop and Bishops, for the further regulation of the inferior clergy. This paper consisted of *interpretations and further considerations* of certain of the Queen's *injunctions*, for the better direction of the Clergy, and for keeping good order in the Church. It was framed, as it seems to me, by the pen of Cox, Bishop of Ely, and revised by the Archbishop, and was as followeth." (Vol. I. chap. xvii. p. 318. 88., or fol. 213). See also Cardwell (Doc. Ann. I. 236) who also gives the Paper.

† Compare Abp. Sheldon's Letter, 1670, quoted p. 24. Note.

was a relaxation of the fuller requirements of the Rubric. Five years after, indeed, 1566, the Advertisements still further relaxed the Rule in favour of *Parish* Churches by not requiring more than the Surplice:* nevertheless Parker, Abp. of Canterbury, in his Visitation Articles for Parishes, 1569,† mentions "the lawes "of this realme," the "Injunctions" and "the Advertisements" as rules to be observed in the Ministration of the Public Offices of the Church in " Paryshe churches," though, very noticeably, he speaks of the Injunctions as the *Queen's*, while for the Advertisements he only claims " publike authority." Grindal (Abp. of York) in 1571, recognises the Injunctions‡ as binding : and Whitgift (Abp. of Canterbury) in his Visitation of the Diocese of Sarum, 1588, asks "the Churchwardens and sworne men" whether "her majesties lawes and injunctions" are obeyed. ǁ

Looking then at this *Documentary* "evidence," it seems to me to prove that, however "uniformly" lax may have been " the practice " as to the Vestments worn "from the days of " Elizabeth to about 1840," it was a practice quite as much at

* "Item, That every minister sayinge any publique prayers, or ministringe of the sacramentes or other rites of the Churche, shall weare a comely surples with sleeves, to be provided at the charges of the parishe ; . . . ." (*Cardwell, Doc. Ann.* I. 326.)

† " Inprimis, Whether Divine Service be sayde or songe by youre minister or ministers in your severall churches duely and reverently, as it is set forth by the lawes of this realme, without any kind of variation. And whether the holy sacramentes be likewise ministred reverently in such manner, as by the lawes of this realme, and by the Quene's majesties injunctions and by thadvertisements set forthe by publike authority is appointed and prescribed."

"III. Item. Whether youre prestes, curates, or ministers do use in the time of the celebration of divine service to weare a surples, prescribed by the quene's majesties injunctions, and the boke of common prayer." (*Cardwell, Doc. Ann.* I. 355-56.)

‡ " The queen's injunctions to be read in time of divine service, in churches and chapels, once every quarter; . . . ." (*Ibid.* 370, and 2nd Ritual Report, p. 412.)

ǁ " II. Item, ... Whether doth he [your minister] use in his ministration the ornaments appointed by the lawes now in force ?"

"III. Item, Whether you have in your church all things necessary for the common prayer, and due administration of the sacramentes, according to her majesties lawes and injunctions ?" (*Ibid.* II. 33.)

In his Visitation Articles for the Diocese of Chichester, 1585, Whitgift asks " V. Whether doth your minister in public prayer time wear a surplesse, and go abroad apparelled, as by her majesties injunctions and advertisements prescribed . . . ? (*Ibid.* II. 25). It may be as well to anticipate a remark which might be made upon this question, viz. that the " injunctions and advertisements" are both called " her majesties" and that thus Whitgift accords the *Queen's authority* for the advertisements : but (as I have pointed out at p. 59) he had, only the year before, drawn a clear distinction between them in describing them as " the Book of Advertisements, and Her Majesty's Injunctions."

variance with the requirements of the Laws and Regulations referred to by Parker, Grindal, and Whitgift, as were other notorious departures from the plainest directions of the Book of Common Prayer, not only during the same period, but even up to the present time.

XXXII. Their Lordships, however, proceed to support their view of the bearing of the "practice," which they notice, upon the Rubric which they had to explain; they say:—

> "It is quite true that neither contrary practice nor disuse can repeal the positive enactment of a statute, but contemporaneous and continuous usage is of the greatest efficacy in law for determining the true construction of obscurely framed documents. In the case of the Bristol Charities (2 Jac, and Walker, 321) Lord Eldon observes, 'length of time (though it must be admitted that the charity is not barred by it) is a very material consideration when the question is, what is the effect and true construction of the instrument? Is it according to the practice and enjoyment which has obtained for more than two centuries, or has that practice and enjoyment been a breach of trust?'"

This passage starts with the assumption that the Ornaments Rubric is an "obscurely framed" document: such, however, was not the opinion of the same Court in 1857, in the case of Liddell *v.* Westerton ; then the Judicial Committee thought it *plain*, holding that the Rubric and Statute of 1559, the Rubric of 1604, and the Rubric of 1662 "all obviously mean the same thing, "that the same dresses and the same utensils, or articles, which "were used under the first Prayer Book of Edward the Sixth, may "still be used." (*Moore*, p. 159). Nor do the various Commentators from 1708 to 1845, whom I have cited at pp. 111 to 119, appear to take a contrary view. The notion of the Rubric being in itself *obscure*, or, as some have also said, *ambiguous*, seems to be a very modern one; though, no doubt, various opinions have been held as to the limiting effect upon it of Canon or Custom.

With regard, however, to the opinion of Lord Eldon, which the Judicial Committee cited to support its construction of the Rubric, the question arises—whether there is any true analogy between the Purchas Case and the Bristol Charities, and consequently, whether Lord Eldon's dictum is really applicable to the point for which the Court cited it, or would have been so applied by the learned Judge who is thus relied upon? In order to consider this question properly, it is necessary to ascertain what was the issue raised in the case upon which Lord Eldon adjudicated.

It appears, then, from the Report (*Jacob and Walker*, Vol. II.) that, in 1820, an Information and Bill was filed in Chancery—

"to obtain a Decree, declaring that the increased Rents of certain Estates, out of which, in the year 1566, annual sums of a given amount were covenanted to be paid by the Corporation of Bristol, to certain Charities in rotation, ought to be applied for the benefit of those Charities. To this Information and Bill, the Mayor, Burgesses, and Commonalty of Bristol, and their Chamberlain, put in a general Demurrer, which was overruled by his Honour, the Vice-Chancellor." (p. 294.)

"The Defendants having appealed from the Order overruling the Demurrer, the relators moved before the Lord Chancellor for the appointment of a receiver." (*Ib.*)

"In the course of the arguments in support of this motion, his Lordship expressed considerable doubt, whether, after an enjoyment of more than two Centuries, under a practical construction of this deed, the Court, pending an appeal from a contrary judicial construction, would change the possession, and remove persons who had so long enjoyed it, and particularly when more than twenty bodies, seeing that construction acted upon, *de anno in annum*, and interested in changing it, had never interfered." (*Ib.*)

The Report goes on to state (p. 321) that "His Lordship then read the report of the case [Atty.-General *v.* Mayor and Corporation of Coventry] from *Vernon*, and on coming to that part of the Judgment in which it is stated that a Charity is not barred by length of time, proceeded as follows. The statute of limitations undoubtedly does not apply; but length of time," &c.

Then follows the passage quoted by the Judicial Committee (See p. 243); upon which their Lordships remark :—

> "We may ask in like manner what is the true construction of the Act of 1662 and of the Rubric which it sanctioned? Is it according to the practice of two centuries, or was the practice a continual breach of the law, commanded and enforced by the Bishops, including the very Bishops who aided in framing the Act?"

But that "the practice of two Centuries" would not have been sufficient to deter Lord Eldon from disregarding it, if the Document he was construing had clearly shown that that "practice and enjoyment" had been "a breach of trust," is plain from his Lordship's own words which immediately follow the passage cited by the Judicial Committee; for he says, "If "it has we must not scruple to disturb it . . . ."

The fact is, however, that Lord Eldon did not decide the question before him upon the ground of "the practice of two "Centuries," but (unlike the Court in the Purchas Case) "upon "the construction of the deed alone," as the Report says (p. 297): his Lordship's words are:—

"Upon the best judgment I can form, and laying out of view everything but the question, whether this deed appropriates the surplus rents to these charities, I am of opinion, that they cannot, under the effect of this instrument merely, call for a distribution of the surplus. My judgment may be set right elsewhere, or the case may be reheard; but that is my opinion upon the effect of this deed, and the consequence is, that by putting some special words into the order, it does appear to me, this demurrer ought to be allowed." (p. 332.)

Supposing, however, that Lord Eldon, instead of thus deciding the Case before him, had determined it upon "the "practice of two centuries," I venture nevertheless to contend that no two issues could well be more at variance than those raised in this and in the Purchas Case.

In the Bristol Charity Case it was sought to compel a Corporation to pay out of increased Rents a larger sum to twenty-three Charities than it had been accustomed to pay for 250 years under a Covenant which, as it seems, it was not denied had been complied with according to the value of the Property when the Charity was founded. The Corporation held that the Donor of the Charity did not contemplate an increased payment, and Lord Eldon decided that the Deed of Gift did not appropriate to the twenty-three Charities the Surplus Rents. The endeavour was to enforce payment of a supposed liability: in other words, to require obedience to an alleged Law.

In the Purchas Case, on the contrary, the object was to prevent the Defendant from complying with what he believed to be a Law (made in 1559, seven years before the Bristol Charity was given, and re-enacted in 1662) which, however, had since that time been very generally, if not almost entirely, neglected until a recent period. Moreover, his doing so did not entail a pecuniary charge upon an unwilling Congregation or Parish; but, on the contrary, only the use of Ornaments in Divine Service, which were the Voluntary Gifts of both Pastor and People.

Lord Eldon decided in favour of the Bristol Corporation, upon the construction of the Deed alone, and without recourse to a *contemporaneous exposition* arising from Practice: the Judicial Committee decided against Mr. Purchas, chiefly by resorting to the *contemporaneous exposition* of Practice for the construction of the Ornaments Rubric, in the elucidation of which they heeded less its literal, grammatical, and historical meaning.

Had the case before their Lordships been one in which it was endeavoured to compel the use of the Eucharistic Vestments by an unwilling Minister and in an unwilling Congregation, it would have been only natural and reasonable for the Court to hold that long and recognised disuse justified it in not condemning a Defendant as having violated a Statute : this indeed would only have been in accordance with an Opinion (already quoted at p. 171) given by a Member of the Court, who, as Attorney-General, said with Dr. Deane, on May 23, 1857 :—

"Upon the question of Dress we are of opinion that the present Prayer Book, taken in conjunction with the First Prayer Book of Edward VI., sanctions the use of the Vestments worn by Mr. Lowder in the ministration of the Holy Communion ; and that he may, in executing the holy ministry, lawfully put on a white Alb plain, with a Vestment, and that such Dress is 'according to the form prescribed in the Book of Common Prayer, made and published by authority of Parliament.'

"But this dress has been so long allowed to go out of use, that we cannot advise Mr. Lowder that the wearing such Dress is now 'legally obligatory,' in the sense that a Priest of the Church of England not wearing such Dress is liable to punishment or censure as for an offence." (1st *Report of the Royal Commission on Ritual*, p. 157).

Two months before this Opinion was given, the Judicial Committee, in Liddell *v.* Westerton, had enunciated the Interpretation of the Ornaments Rubric already quoted at pp. 5 and 243 ; and it would have been surprising if the Attorney-General of that day had not followed their construction of that Rubric: fourteen years after, the learned gentleman was a Member of the same Court, when it not only declared the Eucharistic Vestments to be unlawful, but moreover both *censured* and *punished*, "as for an offence," Mr. Purchas who had worn what Mr. Lowder had been advised by Sir Frederick Thesiger he might "lawfully put on," though it was not "legally obliga-

"tory." How far individual Members of the Court are committed by its Report to Her Majesty, is concealed by the practice which prevails in the Judicial Committee of not stating who concur in, or who dissent from, their Report.

When thus condemning Mr. Purchas, the Judicial Committee applied the language of Lord Eldon to test "the true "Construction of the Act of 1662 and of the Rubric which it "sanctioned." They thereupon asked, First, "Is it according to "the practice of two centuries?" Now it can hardly be doubted that "the practice of two Centuries" since the Revision (so far as known evidence exists) has not much, if at all, agreed with that construction of the Ornaments Rubric which maintains that what are therein termed, the Ornaments "of the Ministers," include those Vestments which are prescribed by name in the Prayer Book of 1549; or with that other construction which regards the term "second year" as meaning the second regnal year of Edward VI. But does it therefore follow, as the Court would seem to imply, that the true construction of the Rubric "may" be inferred from the "practice" of the period mentioned? There are other Rubrics of which it cannot possibly or reasonably be suggested, I think, that they are "obscurely "framed" (as their Lordships seem to say is the case with the Ornaments Rubric); yet, probably, the evidence of compliance with their requirements, is as deficient as the evidence touching compliance with the Ornaments Rubric; take the following Rubrics as being more or less strictly, in point:—

THE OFFICE OF THE HOLY COMMUNION.

1. "So many as intend to be partakers of the holy Communion shall signify their names to the Curate, at least some time the day before.
2. "And when there is a Communion, the Priest shall then [*i.e.*, after the presentation of the Alms*] place upon the Table so much Bread and Wine as he shall think sufficient."
3. "And note that every Parishioner shall communicate at the least three times in the year, of which Easter to be one. And yearly at Easter every Parishioner shall reckon with the Parson, Vicar, or Curate, or his or their Deputy or Deputies; and pay to them or him

---

* "The Rubric directs that at a certain point in the course of the Communion Service (for this is, no doubt, the true meaning of the Rubric) the Minister shall place the bread and wine on the Communion Table, but where they are to be placed previously is nowhere stated. In practice they are usually placed on the Communion Table before the commencement of the service, but this certainly is not according to the order prescribed." (*Liddell v. Westerton*, Moore, p. 187.)

all Ecclesiastical Duties, accustomably due, then and at that time to be paid."

The Office of Infant Baptism.

4. "And the Priest coming to the Font (which is then* to be filled with pure Water) and standing there, shall say, HATH THIS CHILD," &c.

5. "And then naming it after them (if they shall certify him that the Child may well endure it) he shall dip it in the Water discreetly and warily, saying, N., I BAPTIZE THEE," &c.

"But if they certify that the Child is weak, it shall suffice to pour Water upon it, saying the foresaid words, N.," &c.

The Form of Solemnization of Matrimony.

6. "At the day and time appointed for solemnization of Matrimony, the persons to be married shall come into the body of the Church with their friends and neighbours: and there standing together, the Man on the right hand, and the Woman on the left, the Priest shall say, DEARLY BELOVED," &c.

"Then the Minister or Clerks, going to the Lord's Table, shall say or sing this Psalm following, BLESSED ARE ALL THEY," &c.

Having regard, then, to these Rubrics, the appeal "to the "practice of two centuries" to determine the true meaning of the Ornaments Rubric (while in itself not analagous to the case in which the Judicial Committee propose to follow Lord Eldon's dictum) can only be accepted as a legitimate test upon condition that the true meaning of these other Rubrics is to be determined in the same manner.

Their Lordships, however, ask an alternative question, viz:— "was the practice a continual breach of the law, commanded "and enforced by the Bishops, including the very Bishops who "aided in framing the Act?" To this I venture respectfully the reply—that, in strictness, the practice was a breach of the *Rubric,* as it had been for a Century before; but that, so far from its being "commanded and enforced by the Bishops," the one thing, apparently, which they were, for the most part, intent upon doing was, to get the Law observed so far as they found it possible to obtain compliance; and that even in this endeavour, which had been made from a few years after Queen Elizabeth's accession, they were continually foiled; for Injunctions, Advertisements, and Canons were all alike resisted by those whose declared or obvious purpose was to avoid compliance with any Ecclesiastical requirements in the Church of England at variance with that Continental Regime which they mainly

---

* See previous Note as to the meaning of the word "then."

desired to follow, because it was the most opposed to the Law and Custom of those Churches which were in communion with the See of Rome.

To include in the hypothetical charge of Episcopal command and enforcement of "a continual breach of the Law," those "very Bishops who aided in framing the Act" of 1662, seems to me wholly visionary and unpractical: they had the very difficult task of preventing the old Legal Standard of Church and Ministerial Ornaments from being destroyed altogether, or else so lowered that it would have been quite undistinguishable from that maintained by the followers of the Continental Reformation, and which was alien to the belief and feelings of the Caroline Bishops and Divines. But although the re-enactment of the Ornaments Clause of the Act of 1559 and the Ornaments Rubric of 1559, by combining them in the Ornaments Rubric of 1662 (which the Judicial Committee in 1857 held to "obviously mean the same thing") revived the abstract legal authority of the Ornaments; no one surely would have thought of accusing the Caroline Bishops of countenancing a "breach of the Law," because the circumstances of the times rendered it practically impossible for them to have "commanded "and enforced" more of the Rubrical prescription than custom, on the one hand, had long regarded as a compliance with the Law; while, on the other hand, innovation had been and still was striving to establish a rule of non-compliance with even the lesser requirements of the Canons of 1604 which the Bishops endeavoured, though often in vain, to uphold as a standard which could not be dispensed with, unless indeed there was to be an end of all decency and reverence in the Public Offices of the Church of England. It needs no great acquaintance with English Church History to know that from the Caroline period until "about 1840" (the date fixed by the Judicial Committee as marking the departure from that habit which they regard as the Rubrical equivalent) there was little, if any opportunity for the Prelates who succeeded the Caroline Bishops to overcome that "continual breach of the law" which, on the Court's hypothesis, they also indeed must have "commanded and enforced" if the true meaning of the Ornaments Rubric be that which their Lordships decline to admit.

The Court having thus disposed of the various general arguments and authorities which it cited as to the meaning of the Ornaments Rubric, goes on to observe with reference to the Judgment of the Arches Court, from which they had been appealed to, that:—

> "The learned Judge relies on two former judgments of this Committee, as having almost determined the question of vestments; one of them in the case of Liddell *v.* Westerton, and the other in the case of Martin *v.* Mackonochie."

Upon this the Court observes that:—

> "In Liddell *v.* Westerton, the question which their Lordships had to decide was whether the Rubric which excluded all use of crosses in the service affected crosses not used in the service, but employed for decoration of the building only, and they determined that these were unaffected by the Rubric."

But a reference to that judgment will show, I think, that this is an incomplete view of "the question which their Lordships "had to decide" in 1857; for, in dealing with the subject of Crosses, their Lordships referred to the "difference between the "reasons assigned for their decisions" by Dr. Lushington in the Consistory Court and by Sir John Dodson in the Arches Court, though both Judges had ordered the *Altar Crosses* at St. Paul's and St. Barnabas and the *Chancel Screen Cross* in the latter church "all to be removed, as illegal Ornaments." (*Moore's Report*, p. 155). Their Lordships proceeded to mention the authorities upon which the two Judges relatively held the question of the lawfulness of Crosses to depend, and then said (the Italics are mine):—

> "It will be necessary to examine both these grounds of decision with the attention and respect which are due to the eminent persons who have adopted them; *and first, as to the effect of the Rubric.*
>
> "In dealing with this question it is necessary to remember that there were many crosses, some with, some without, the image of the Saviour, which were in use in the Roman Catholic ritual; altar crosses, processional crosses, funeral crosses, and others, as well as painted or

carved representations of the cross not used in the services, but set up as architectural decorations of Churches; *and the question is, whether the Rubric applies to the latter class.* (*Ibid.*)

The Court went on to state that:—

"Dr. Lushington was of opinion, that by the true construction of these words [*i. e.*, the Ornaments Rubric], reference must be had to the Act of the second and third, Edward the Sixth, and the Prayer Book which it established, for the purpose of determining what Ornaments were thereby sanctioned, but he was perplexed by the difficulty that al hough there were words in that Prayer Book describing the Ornaments of the Ministers, there were none which applied to ornaments of the Church, in his understanding of this expression." (*Ibid.* p. 156.)

And they add :—

"Their Lordships, after much consideration, are satisfied that the construction of this Rubric which they suggested at the hearing of the case is its true meaning, and that the word 'ornaments' applies, and in this Rubric is confined to those articles, the use of which in the Services and Ministrations of the Church is prescribed by the Prayer Book of Edward the Sixth." (*Ibid.*)

Their next step was to define and illustrate the meaning of "the term 'ornaments' in Ecclesiastical law;" then to point out the changes which took place as to the use of these Ornaments during the reigns of Edward VI., and Mary; afterwards to state the provisions of the Act and Rubric of Elizabeth; and finally to speak as follows of the succeeding Rubrics:—

"The Rubric to the Prayer Book of January 1st, 1604, adopts the language of the Rubric of Elizabeth. The Rubric to the present Prayer Book adopts the language of the Statute of Elizabeth, but they all obviously mean the same thing, that the same dresses and the same utensils, or articles, which were used under the First Prayer Book of Edward the Sixth may still be used." (*Ibid.* 159.)

But it was not until their Lordships had thus declared distinctly the meaning of the Rubric, that they added these words:—

"None of them, therefore, can have any reference to articles not used in the Services, but set up in Churches as ornaments in the sense of decorations." (*Ib.*)

And it is some distance further on in their Judgment that the following passage occurs:—

"Their Lordships, therefore, are of opinion that, although the Rubric excluded all use of crosses in the Services, the general question of crosses not used in the Services, but employed only as decorations of Churches, is entirely unaffected by the Rubric." (*Ib.* p. 161.)

It seems to me that this history of what occurred in the case of Liddell *v.* Westerton furnishes a larger view of what the Judicial Committee had to, and did, perform, than could be gathered from the very brief account of it given in the six lines of the Purchas Judgment upon which I am commenting. Those lines must, I think, convey to the reader whose information is limited to them, the notion that the Court in 1859 had only "the [one] question" before it, viz., to decide whether the Ornaments Rubric applied to "crosses not used in the service;" whereas they had also to decide two previous questions (1) what the Rubric really meant, and (2) whether in its true construction, it "excluded all use of crosses in the Service."

The Judicial Committee in the following passage, glances at the decision given by the Court, in Liddell *v.* Westerton, as to the meaning of the Ornaments Rubric :—

> "They decided that the Rubric in question referred to the Act passed in 2 and 3 Edward VI., adopting the first Prayer Book, and not to any canons or injunctions having the authority of Parliament, but adopted at an earlier period. Their Lordships feel quite free to adopt both the positive and the negative conclusions thus arrived at. In construing the expressions made use of in that judgment, it should be borne in mind that this question of the vestments was not before the Court."

To the public mind, however, the language of their Lordships would probably convey very little idea of the meaning which the Court in 1857 distinctly attached to that Rubric in the language already quoted at p. 251. Their Lordships, referring to this decision, say that they "feel quite free to adopt both the "positive and negative conclusions thus arrived at" in Liddell *v.* Westerton, viz., that the Rubric of 1662 "referred to the Act "passed in 2 and 3 Edward VI., adopting the first Prayer Book, "and not to any canons or injunctions having the authority of

"Parliament, but adopted at an earlier period." Nevertheless, the question arises, whether the Court in 1857 did not, by its interpretation of the Rubric, equally exclude all Rubrics, Injunctions, Advertisements, Canons and the like, between 1549 and 1662 (more especially if they had not any Authority of Parliament) which altered those Ornaments of the Book of 1549 to which they decided that the Rubric of 1662 refers? Considering the conclusion at which that Court arrived, as to the meaning of the Ornaments Rubric, it can hardly be doubted that this question must be answered in the affirmative; and it may well be believed that their Lordships really concurred in the opinion of Dr. Lushington as expressed in the following words:—

"I am well aware of the irresistible argument, that the last Statute of Uniformity, by referring to the First Book of Common Prayer of Edward the Sixth, excluded, not only the Second Book of Common Prayer, but everything else effected in the interval between 1549 and 1662, whether by Act of Parliament or by Canon, which could or might have altered what existed in 1549; and, consequently, I am equally aware that nothing done from 1549 to 1662, however lawful during that period, has in itself force or binding authority after the Statute of 1662 came into operation." (*Moore*, p. 31.)

The Judicial Committee of 1871 consider, however, that "in "construing the expressions made use of in that Judgment" of the same Court, which was given 14 years before, "it should be "borne in mind that this question of the Vestments was not before "the Court." No doubt this is quite true so far—that they had not to adjudicate, as in the Purchas Case, upon a charge of wearing unlawful Vestments; and therefore, it would seem that nothing could have been easier for their Lordships than to avoid, with the ordinary caution of Courts, any intimation of opinion upon a point not then distinctly in issue. Yet it is, surely, plain enough from the language used on that occasion, that the eye of the Court clearly saw that its interpretation of the Rubric must involve the question of the lawfulness of "Ornaments of the Church and of the Ministers thereof," other than those which it had to pronounce upon, and therefore deemed it right not to conceal its opinion of the full force of the Rubric which it was compelled to expound in order to decide upon the points submitted to its Judgment. That a leading member of that Court was fully aware of the lawfulness of the Vestments being covered by the Court's interpretation of the Rubric, was within my own knowledge at that time : though his Lordship's opinion of the *policy* of Clergy then acting upon that interpretation was quite another matter.

The Judicial Committee in Hebbert *v.* Purchas remark that :—

> "In Martin *v.* Mackonochie the Committee stated anew the substance of the judgment in Liddell *v.* Westerton upon this point, but did not propose to take up any new ground."

But, notwithstanding this, their Lordships, in condemning Mr. Purchas, did in fact place themselves in a very different position; for they expressed an opinion, (seemingly quite the opposite of that enunciated or implied in Liddell *v.* Westerton) that the Rubric of 1662 is governed by the Elizabethan Advertisements and Jacobean Canons issued, as they were, before it; and must be construed in the limited sense of those Ecclesiastical Instruments.

Having thus interpreted the Rubric adversely to the commonly received theory of its meaning, and to what certainly appeared to be the mind of the Judicial Committee in Liddell *v.* Westerton and in Martin *v.* Mackonochie, it was no surprise to learn that :—

> "Their Lordships will advise Her Majesty that the Defendant Mr. Purchas has offended against the Laws Ecclesiastical in wearing the chasuble, alb and tunicle; and that a monition shall issue against the Defendant accordingly."

The two following passages of their Lordship's Judgment do not call for any remark in these Notes.

The Biretta.

> "With respect to the cap, called a biretta, which the Defendant is said to have carried in his hand, but not to have worn in church, their Lordships would not be justified, upon the evidence before them, in pronouncing that the Defendant did an unlawful act."

HOLY OR CONSECRATED WATER.

"As to the holy or consecrated water in the church the evidence does not go to the full extent of the charge. There is no proof whatever that the water placed in the church was consecrated at all, nor that it was put there by the Defendant with the purpose of its being used as the congregation seem to have used it. This is a penal proceeding, and each charge must be strictly proved as alleged. Upon this point, too, the appeal must be disallowed."

THE MIXED CHALICE.

XXXIII. The next subject considered by the Court is that of the Mixed Chalice: the Report to Her Majesty introduces it thus:—

"Their Lordships now proceed to the 16th Article, which charges that, on a certain day, the Defendant 'administered wine mixed with water instead of wine to the communicants at the Lord's Supper.' The learned Judge in the Court below has decided that it is illegal to mix water with the wine at the time of the service of Holy Communion; but he decides that water may be mixed with the wine 'provided that the mingling be not made at the time of the celebration.' For this view the learned Judge quotes, amongst other authorities, Bishop Andrewes, but it has escaped him that the practice of Bishop Andrewes was that which he condemns; in his Consecration Service, the Bishop directs as follows:—*Episcopus de novo in calicem ex poculo quod in sacrâ mensâ stabat, effundit, admistâque aquâ, recitat clare verba illa consecratoria.* (Sparrow's Articles, &c.) The learned Judge considers that the act of mixing has some symbolical meaning, but he holds that it was 'wholly unconnected with any papal superstition, or any doctrine which the Church of England has rejected.' (Appendix p. 88.) Nor does it appear that the controversy between the Romish and Reformed churches turned so much upon the symbolism of the mixed cup, as upon the necessity of its use."

It may be as well to notice that in this passage, the Court seems under the impression that the Dean of the Arches cited Bishop Andrewes as an authority for using the Mixed Chalice if the Mixture be not made at the time of the Service. But, on consideration, this does not seem to be the meaning of the learned Judge: he had been quoting his former judgment (Martin *v.* Mackonochie) where, while holding "the ceremony or manual "act of mixing the Water with the Wine during the celebration "of the Eucharist" to be "illegal," he "added," as he says, the following remark, "I do not say that it is illegal to "administer to the communicants wine in which a little water "had been previously mixed." (4*th Report of the Ritual Commission*, p. 247.) In his later judgment (*Elphinston v. Purchas*), which the Judicial Committee were reviewing, the Dean of the Arches gave his reason for this opinion, he says:—

"At that time I had in my mind, among other authorities, that of Bp. Andrewes, who appears to have used the mixed chalice in the Chapel Royal all the time he was Dean of it, and who, in the form that he drew up for the Consecration of a Church, expressly directed it to be used (Wheatley, Common Prayer, p. 281); and that of Bp. Cosin, who, speaking of the practice under the Elizabethan Prayer Books, says, 'Our Church forbids it not, for aught I know, and they that think fit may use it, as some most eminent among us do at this day.' (Notes on the Book of Common Prayer, 1st Series, p. 154, Works, vol. v.)" (4th *Rit. Report, p.* 247.)

Of this passage the Judicial Committee remark—"It has "escaped him [the Judge] that the practice of Bp. Andrewes "was that which he condemns," and they quote, in proof of it, the Office referred to as having been provided by Bp. Andrewes for the Consecration of a Church. But the Dean's reference to it is quite consistent with a knowledge of the Bishop's practice; and the fact that his Lordship cites Cosin's opinion, at the same time and for the same purpose, though there seems no evidence of what his *practice* was, leads, I think, to the conclusion—that the Judge's object was to show, that *the Mixture* was deemed *legal* by Authorities such as Andrewes and Cosin, prior to the Revised Book of 1662, though it had not been *prescribed* in the Rubric since the Prayer Book of 1549.

The remarks of Cosin, which include his reference to the practice of "some most eminent" in his own time, among them

Bishop Andrewes himself [*] may advantageously be re-produced here: he is commenting upon words of the Catechism, "Bread and "wine which the Lord hath commanded," &c., and he says:—

"Now for wine, which is the other part, the matter is somewhat more difficult. For cheapness, of old some would have milk, &c., which was condemned by ancient councils, and some only water, which Epiphanius saith was the heresy of the Ebionites, that began in Africa about St. Cyprian's time; Ep. iii. lib. ii.[n] is written wholly against them; and St. Chrys., *Hom.* liii. *in S. Matth.*[o], refels the heresy from Christ's own institution, *Christus non bibebat aquam, sed vinum.* This were enough to free our Church from any heinous offence, though it uses not commonly to mix water with wine, as the Church of Rome doth. And yet, we must confess the custom is very ancient, consonant to the figures of the Old Testament, which St. Cyprian, Ep. iii. lib. ii., reckons up, and of the New, where water and blood issued out of Christ's side; and agreeable (as there is great probability) to Christ's own practice, when He did first institute this holy Sacrament; for it is not so likely, that He used wine alone in His sacred supper, both because it was the custom of the Jews, *diluere vinum*, as Prov. ix., *Bibite vinum quod miscui vobis*, and because all the evangelists use the name of *calix, quod nomen* (saith Maldonate[p]) *significat vinum conjunctum cum aqua, juxta ritum.* The ancient liturgies are all for *vinum cum aqua mixtum.* So Justin Martyr, *Apol* 2[q]; Iren., lib. iv. cap 57[r]; and lib. v. *initio*[s]; Cypr., *Ep.* iii. lib. ii.[t]; Ambr., lib. v. *de*

[*] "*Dein vinum e dolio, adinstar sanguinis dirumpens in calicem, haurit. Tum aquam e tricanali scypho immiscet.*" (Cosin's Notes, p. 105.)

NOTES BY THE EDITOR OF COSIN.

[n] [S. Cypr., Ep. 63. ad Cœcilium, (ed. Erasm., lib. ii. Ep. 3.) Op. pp. 148—157.]

[o] [καὶ τίνος ἕνεκεν οὐχ ὕδωρ ἔπιεν ἀναστάς, ἀλλ' οἶνον; ἄλλην αἵρεσιν πονηρὰν πρόρριζον ἀνασπῶν, ἐπειδὴ γάρ τινες εἰσὶν ἐν τοῖς μυστηρίοις ὕδατι κεχρημένοι, δεικνὺς ὅτι ἡνίκα τὰ μυστήρια παρέδωκεν οἶνον παρέδωκε. καὶ ἡνίκα ἀναστὰς χωρὶς μυστηρίων ψιλὴν τράπεζαν παρετίθετο οἴνῳ ἐκέχρητο.—S. Chrysost., Hom. in Matt. 26. Hom. 82, (al. 83.) Op. tom. vii. p. 784, B.]

[p] [See Maldonatus, as above.]

[q] [ἔπειτα προσφέρεται τῷ προεστῶτι τῶν ἀδελφῶν ἄρτος, καὶ ποτήριον ὕδατος καὶ κράματος.—S. Justin, Mart., Apol. 1. (al. Apol. 2.) § 65. Op. p. 82, D.]

[r] [Quomodo autem juste Dominus, si alterius patris existit, hujus conditionis quæ est secundum nos accipiens panem, suum corpus esse confitebatur, et temperamentum calicis suam sanguinem confirmavit.—S. Irenæus cont. Hæres., lib. iv. cap. 33. (al. cap. 57.) Op. p. 170-2.]

[s] [ὅποτε οὖν καὶ τὸ κεκραμένον ποτήριον, καὶ ὁ γεγονὼς ἄρτος ἐπιδέχεται τὸν λόγον τοῦ Θεοῦ, καὶ γίγνεται ἡ εὐχαριστία σῶμα Χριστοῦ.—Id. ibid., lib. v. cap. 2. Op. p. 294.]

[t] [Vinum mixtum declarat, id est calicem Domini aqua et vino mixtum prophetica voce prænunciat.—S. Cypr., Ep. 63. ad Cœcilium, (alit. lib. ii. Ep. 3.) Op. p. 150.

Sic autem in sanctificando calice Domini, offerri aqua sola non potest,

Sacram., cap. i.ᵘ; Gennad., *de Eccl. dogm.*, cap. 75ˣ; *Patres Concil, Trullani*ʸ, and many others, *Vide notas in Gennadium*ᶻ. Our Church forbids it not, for aught I know, and they that think fit may use it, as some most eminent among us do at this day*ᵃ*; yet for the approbation of our most common practice, which is to consecrate wine alone without water, we have all this on our side; the Greeks did it, Niceph. Callist; lib. xviii. cap. 53ᵇ; Innocent III., *de myst. Miss.*, lib. iv. cap. 32.ᶜ; Durand., lib. iv. *d.* 12. *q.* 5ᵈ; Lomb., lib. iv. *d.* 11ᵉ; Bonav.,

quomodo nec vinum solum potest; nam si vinum tantum quis offerat Sanguis Christi incipit esse sine nobis: si vero aqua sit sola, plebs incipit esse sine Christo: quando autem utrumque miscetur, et adunatione confusa sibi invicem copulatur, tunc sacramentum spiritale et coeleste perficitur. Sic vero calix Domini non est aqua sola, aut vinum solum, nisi utrumque sibi misceatur.—Ibid., p. 154.]

u [Diximus ergo quod in altari constituatur calix et panis. In calicem quid mittitur? Vinum. Et quid aliud? Aqua.—S. Ambros. de Sacr,, lib. v. cap. 1. § 2. Op. tom. ii. col. 373, C.]

ˣ [In eucharistia non debet pura aqua offerri, ut quidam sobrietatis falluntur imagine, sed vinum cum aqua mixtum; quia et vinum fuit in redemptionis nostrae mysterio, cum dixit: non bibam amodo de hoc genimine vitis: et aqua mixtum, non quod post coenam dabatur, sed quod de latere ejus lancea perfosso aqua cum sanguine egressa, vinum de vera ejus carnis vite cum aqua expressum ostenditur.—Gennadii Massiliensis de Eccles. Dogmatibus, c. 75: ed. G. Elmenhorstius. Hamburg, 1614. Maldonatus cites this as Augustine's, to whom this tract was (wrongly) attributed. See S. Aug. Op. tom. viii. Append. col. 75, sqq.]

ʸ [ἐπειδὴ εἰς γνῶσιν ἡμετέραν ἦλθεν, ὡς ἐν τῇ Ἀρμενίων χώρᾳ οἶνον μόνον ἐν τῇ ἱερᾷ τραπέζῃ προσάγουσιν, ὕδωρ αὐτῷ μὴ μιγνύντες .... εἴ τις οὖν ἐπίσκοπος ἢ πρεσβύτερος μὴ κατὰ τὴν παραδοθεῖσαν ὑπὸ τῶν ἀποστόλων τάξιν ποιεῖ, καὶ ὕδωρ οἴνῳ μιγνὺς, οὕτω τὴν ἄχραντον προσάγει θυσίαν, καθαιρείσθω.—Conc. Quinisext. seu Trullani, cap. xxxii. Concilia, tom. vii. col. 1361, B, 1363, A.]

ᶻ [The notes referred to are those of Elmenhorstius, Hamburg, 1614, p. 174, where many passages illustrating this point are brought together.]

ᵃ [See the note of Bp. Andrewes above, p. 105; and the account of the furniture of his chapel, Minor English Works, Angl. Cath. ed.] The "note" of Bp. Andrewes is given at p. 257 *supra*.

ᵇ [οἱ δὲ αὐτοὶ καὶ ἄζυμον οὐκ ἄρτον ἐν ταῖς ἱεραῖς ἁγιστείαις προσφέρουσι, καὶ οἶνον ἀκέραστον ὕδατι, μίαν διὰ τοῦτο φύσιν ἐν τῷ Χριστῷ καταγγέλλοντες, καὶ οὐχ ὡς ἡμεῖς κιρνῶσι τὴν ἕνωσιν δύο φυσίων.—Nicephor. Callist., Hist. Eccles., lib. xviii. cap. 53. Op. tom. ii. p. 883, C.]

ᶜ [Quæritur an irritum sit quod geritur si forte praetermittitur aqua. Alii concedunt, quod si quisquam non intendens haeresim introducere, oblivione vel ignorantia praetermiserit aquam, ille quidem vehementer est corripiendus et graviter, non tamen sit irritum sacramentum. Quod ergo praedictum est, hoc est, verum vinum solum offerri non posse, determinari debet; quia recipit exceptionem, hoc modo, non potest nisi fiat simpliciter vel ignoranter; vel non potest, id est, non debet.—Innoc. III. de sacro altaris Mysterio, lib. iv. c. 32. fol. 197.]

ᵈ [Appositio vini non est de necessitate sacramenti, unde de vino sine aqua potest confici, peccaret tamen qui scienter non apponeret aquam. Dicitur etiam quod Græci aquam non apponunt, et tamen vere conficiunt.—Durandi de S. Portiano sup. Sententias, lib. iv. dist. 11. Quaest. 5. § 7. The statement about the Greeks is not true. The Nestorians only omitted the water.]

ᵉ [Si quis tamen, &c., (as in Innocent, who cites Lombard's words.)—P. Lombard., Sentent., lib. iv. dist. xii. § 8.]

Ibid.[f]; *neque est de necessitate Sacramenti,* saith Aquinas, p. 3. *q.* 74. ar. 7[g]; Paschasius *de Sacram. Euch.*, cap. 11[h]; Bernard., Ep. 69[i]; Rab. Maurus, *de Euch.*, cap. 11[k], *et alii.*" (*Notes,* 1st *Series;* Works vol. v. pp. 152-5.)

The Court thus proceeds with its argument:

"Their Lordships find here two questions for their consideration. Since it has been decided by this Committee that additional ceremonies or innovations are excluded by implication by the Service for Holy Communion; or, in other words, that the service for Holy Communion is not only a guide but a sufficient guide in its celebration; and since the learned Judge has decided that the act of mingling wine with water in the Service, with a view to its administration, is one of the additional ceremonies so excluded, the first question is whether the doing the act before the service, and in the vestry or elsewhere, could so alter the symbolical character of the act that the cup might be brought in and consecrated and administered to the people, without constituting an innovation or additional ceremonial act, beyond what is ordered in the service."

"If this question be decided in the affirmative, the second question would be whether upon a fair con-

[f] [Aqua non est de integritate Sacramenti Eucharistiæ, sed est quid annexum materiæ, et de congruitate.—S. Bonaventuræ Expos. in Sentent., lib. iv. dist. xi. pars ii. art. 1. quæsti 3. conclusio, p. 347. Op. tom. v. Romæ, 1596.]

[g] [Utrum permixtio aquæ sit de necessitate hujus sacramenti; which is decided in the negative.—S. Thom. Aquin., Summa Theol., part iii. quæst. 74. art. 7.]

[h] [Ut quid aqua cum vino misceatur dum in cœna Domini factum non legitur, is the title of the chapter referred to, and expresses its substance. Paschasius does not go into the question of the validity of consecrating wine only; but says, Plane aqua in Sanguine quare misceatur, dum in natali calicis factum fuisse a Christo non legitur.—Paschasius Radbertus de Corpore et Sanguine Domini, c. xi. Bibl. Patr. Max., tom. xiv. col. 740, A.]

[i] [The title of the Epistle is, Ad Guidonem, qui incuria ministrantium in consecratione calicis erraverat ob defectum vini. Guido had said the words of consecration without the wine being in the chalice. S. Bernard incidentally speaks of the water to be mixed with the wine, but does not discuss this particular question. Epist. lxix. Op. tom. i. pp. 70, 71.]

[k] [See Rabanus Maurus de Institutione Clericorum, lib. i. c. 31; de Eucharistia, Op. tom. vi. p. 12, E. He also gives the reasons for mixing water with the wine, but does not treat the question of the validity of consecration with it.]

struction of the directions of the Rubrics, this previous mingling could take place without violation of the Rubrics."

The statement in these passages as to what "this Committee" decided on a former occasion (in Martin *v.* Mackonochie apparently) does not seem to be quite borne out upon reference to that Judgment; the statements therein which touch this subject are the following:—

1. The adoption of the following dictum in Liddell *v.* Westerton that "In the performance of the Services, rites, and ceremonies, ordered by the Prayer Book, the directions contained in it must be strictly observed; no omission and no addition can be permitted." (4th *Rit. Report*, p. 234.)

2. The allegation that "The various stages of the [Communion] Service are, as has already been shewn, fenced and guarded by directions of the most exact kind as to standing and kneeling, the former attitude being prescribed even for prayers, during which a direction to kneel might have been expected." (*Ib.* p. 234.)

3. The Court's own dictum that "the lighting of the candles and the consuming them by burning throughout, and with reference to a Service, in which they are to act as symbols and illustrations, is itself either a ceremony, or else a ceremonial act forming part of a ceremony, and making the whole ceremony a different one from what it would have been had the lights been omitted." (*Ib.* p. 235.)

4. The remark that the ".... ceremonial mixing [of water] with the Sacramental wine .... must be justified, if at all, as part of a ceremonial law." (*Ib.* p. 236.)

5. The assertion that ".... in the Preface [of the Prayer Book] ..... it is assumed that all [Ceremonies] are abolished which are not expressly retained." (*Ib.*)

6. The assumption ".... nor can a separate and independent ornament previously in use be said to be consistent with a Rubric, which is silent as to it, and which, by necessary implication, abolishes what it does not retain." (*Ib.* p. 237.)

Now, even if it could be admitted that these passages accurately define the meaning of "Ceremonies" as used in the Prayer Book, or correctly represent the intended effect of Rubrical changes therein, they are not, I think, exactly represented by the gloss in Hebbert *v.* Purchas—" that the Service " for Holy Communion is not only a guide but a sufficient guide " in its celebration." Cosin, as is shown by his " Particulars to " be considered, explained, and corrected, in the " Book of Com-

"mon Prayer," did not so regard the Book;[*] and he endeavoured to supply its defects: but although in the last Revision many of his suggestions were adopted, difficulties still remain. If it were not so, some well known questions as to difference of practice could hardly have arisen, *e. g.*, when the Elements for the Sacrament should be placed on the Altar; whether the Celebrant should stand (following the ancient practice) or kneel when receiving the Sacrament; whether he should use any or what words in communicating himself. Moreover, the Recommendations of the Ritual Commission, and the consequent proposals of Convocation, abundantly shew that those who, by experience or investigation, had acquired some knowledge of the subject, were convinced that the existing Rubrics do not in all cases guide, or guide sufficiently those who have to officiate in the Services of the Church.

XXXIV. Their Lordships next put their difficulty in the form of the two following questions:—

> "The first question is, whether this is an additional ceremony, not provided in the Rubric? The second question is, whether it is contrary to the express directions of the Rubric?"

And then they thus discuss the first question:—

> "On the former question their Lordships observe that, whether the water mingled with the wine be used because Christ himself is believed to have used it, or in order to symbolize the water from the rock given to the thirsty Israelites, or the blood and water from the side of the Lord, or the union of Christ with His people (the water being a type of the people), or the union of two natures in the one Lord, it can scarcely be said that the reception of the mingled chalice had no share in this symbolism, but only the act of mingling. Their Lordships are unable to arrive at the conclusion that, if the

---

[*] Yet Cosin considered that the Prayer-Book was not meant to be a *complete* Manual of directions, for he says—"And it is to be noted, that the Book does not everywhere enjoin and prescribe every little order, what should be said or done, but take it for granted that people are acquainted with such common, and things always used already. Let the Puritans then here give over their endless cavils, and let ancient custom prevail, the thing which our Church chiefly intended in the review of this Service." (*Notes, 1st Series; Works* v. p. 65.)

> mingling and administering in the service water and wine is an additional ceremony, and so unlawful, it becomes lawful by removing from the service the act of mingling but keeping the mingled cup itself and administering it. But neither Eastern nor Western Church, so far as the Committee is aware, has any custom of mixing the water with wine apart from and before the service."

Here their Lordships, by way of reply to their own first question, appear to hold that the Mixture is in itself illegal, whether made in or out of the Service, and on this ground,—that whatever may be the symbolism of the Mixed Chalice, "the reception of it can scarcely be said" to have "had no "share in this symbolism, but only the act of mingling." Now it is easy to understand that, upon the mere symbolical doctrine of the Eucharist, the oral *reception* of the Species symbolizes *e. g.*, the mental or moral reception of Christ; but it is difficult to realize that either the symbolisms mentioned by the Court or any other symbolisms suggested by the Mixed Chalice, continue to be exhibited by the oral participation of a symbolical mixture. The language of their Lordships' ruling is, indeed, somewhat obscure, but probably they mean to imply that, whatever may be the abstract truth of the various symbolical interpretations of The Mixed Chalice, no one of them being referred to in any Rubric or Prayer of the Prayer Book Communion Office, it is not permissible to import any such symbolism into the Office by introducing a Ceremony meant to suggest it. Perhaps, too, they thought that the Congregation might come to know that the Mixture was made privately, and thus the Symbolism would be as truly suggested by giving The Mixed Chalice to the Communicants, though it would not be so conspicuously effected as by mingling it publicly before the People.

Yet a ruling which thus prohibits The Mixed Chalice, virtually condemns a very common practice which it is most unlikely the Court would think of interfering with, though there are those now who, like the Lord's Committee in 1641, hold "the "Minister's turning his back to the West, and his face to the "East, when he pronounceth the Creed, or reads Prayers" to be "Innovations in Discipline." (*Cardwell, Hist. Conf. p.* 272.)

These Ceremonial Actions are not ordered in any Rubric, neither is their Symbolism* recognised in any part of the Prayer Book ; and therefore they come under the theory (untenable though it is) laid down by the Judicial Committee in Martin *v.* Mackonochie and affirmed by the same Court in the Judgment here under consideration—" that additional ceremonies "or innovations are excluded by implication by the service for Holy "Communion," (See p. 259), and *à fortiori* in all other Offices of the Book of Common Prayer. The only pretence, therefore, upon which Turning to the East in the Creed and the Prayers could be allowed and The Mixed Chalice proscribed, is—that the latter practice has been exceptional, while the former has been a not uncommon Custom.

It may be as well, however, to remark here that such *continuity* of Symbolism as the Court appears to contemplate, does not seem to have been designed when our old English Eucharistic Office, in prescribing the Mixed Chalice, recognised a Symbolism. Thus, in the Sarum Missal,† between the reading of the Epistle and Gospel, a Rubric directs :—

---

* "Turning at the same time [viz. when saying the Creed] towards the East, as many do, is an ancient custom ; as indeed, in most religions men have directed their worship some particular way. And this practice being intended only to honour Christ, ' the Sun of Righteousness,' who hath risen upon us, to enlighten us with that doctrine of salvation, to which we thus declare our adherence; it ought not to be condemned as superstitious : and yet, being neither obligatory in itself nor commanded by authority, the omission of it ought not to be censured, as irreverence or disobedience. *Abp. Secker.*

" Most Churches are so contrived that the greater part of the Congregation faces the East. The Jews in their dispersion throughout the world, when they prayed, turned their faces towards the mercy seat and cherubim, where the ark stood. (See 2 Chron. vi. 36—38.) Daniel was found praying toward Jerusalem, Dan. vi. 10, because of the situation of the temple. And this has always been esteemed a very becoming way of expressing our belief in God, namely, by turning to the East, that quarter of the heavens, where He is supposed to have His peculiar residence of glory.—*Collis.* The Christians from the beginning built their Churches, and worshipped towards the East, because they expected our Saviour, who is called the Day-Spring from on high, to come from thence. In that part also the holy table or altar is placed, where God affords His most gracious and mysterious presence.—*Clutterbuck.* See note from Dr. Bisse before the Nicene Creed." (*Mant on the Book of Common Prayer*, 4th Ed. 1830, p. 32.)

† In the " Rationale " of the Offices of the Church, prepared shortly before 1541, when a new Edition was issued of the " Portiforium secundum usum Sarum," &c., it is said, " At which time [*i.e.*, the Offertory] the Minister, laying the Bread upon the Altar, makes the Chalice, mixing the Water with the Wine : signifying, thereby, how that Blood and Water ran out of Christ's side in His Passion ; and admonishing us of the inseparable coupling and joining of Christ and His Church." (*Collier, E. H.*, v. p. 113.)

"... let the Sub-deacon take the bread and wine and water with the Chalice, and prepare them for the Service of the Eucharist; the blessing of the water being first asked of the Priest thus, the Priest in the mean time sitting: Bless. *The Priest answers:* The Lord. By Him be it blessed out of Whose side came forth blood and water. In the Name of the Father, and of the Son, and of the Holy Ghost." (*The Sarum Missal, in English* p. 296: The Church Press Co: 1868.)*

But, after this, the symbolism is not noticed throughout the Office: † indeed, not one of the passages where it might seem likely to occur makes the slightest allusion to it but, on the contrary, language is used which would naturally be held even to *exclude* the symbolism. They are these following:—

"*Here, making the sign of the Cross, let him [the Priest] place the said third particle of the Host in the Sacrament of the Blood, saying:*
Let this most ✠ holy union of the Body and Blood of our Lord Jesus Christ be to me and all who receive It health of mind and body, and a saving preparation for worthily attaining unto eternal life. Through." (*Sarum Missal, in English*, p. 317.)

"*Before the Peace is given, let the Priest say:*
"O Lord, Holy Father, Almighty, Everlasting God, grant me so worthily to receive this most holy Body and Blood of Thy Son our Lord Jesus Christ that I may thereby receive forgiveness of all my sins," &c. (*Ibid.*)

"*After the giving of the Peace, let the Priest say these Prayers privately, before communicating, holding the Host in both hands:*
"O Lord Jesu Christ, ... deliver me, I beseech Thee, by this Thy most holy Body and Blood, from all mine iniquities and from every evil," &c. (*Ibid.* p. 318.)

"Let not the Sacrament of Thy Body and Blood, O Lord Jesu Christ, ... be to me for judgment," &c. (*Ib.*)

"... *Then to the Blood let him say, with great devotion:*
"Hail for evermore, Heavenly Drink, ... The Body and Blood of our Lord Jesus Christ be unto me a perpetual healing," &c. (*Ibid.* p. 319.)

"*Here let him receive the Blood; which taken, let the Priest incline, and say with devotion the prayer following:*

---

* See also "*Missale ad usum insignis et præclare Ecclesiæ Sarum,*" col. p. 587; Burntisland Ed. 1861.

† This remark applies to the present Roman Office, where, in the Ordinary of the Mass, after the Offertory, occur the following Rubric and Prayer, "*The Priest pours Wine and Water into the Chalice, blessing the Water before it is mixed, saying:* O God + who, in creating human nature, didst wonderfully dignify it; and hast still more wonderfully renewed it; grant that, by the mystery of this Water and Wine, we may be made partakers of His Divinity, Who vouchsafed to become partaker of our humanity, Jesus Christ, Thy Son, our Lord; Who liveth and reigneth with Thee in the Unity of, &c." (*The Roman Missal for the use of the Laity.* Imp. Card. Wiseman, Dec. 15, 1851. London: Burns.) See also *Missale Romanum*, Mechliniæ, 1850.

"I give thanks unto Thee, O Lord, Holy Father, Almighty, Everlasting God, Who hast refreshed me with the most sacred Body and Blood of Thy Son our Lord Jesu Christ," &c. (*Ib.*)

The Prayer Book of 1549 prescribes the Mixture in the following words of the Rubric which succeeds the Offertory Sentences:—

". . . . . and putting the Wine into the Chalice, or else in some fair or convenient cup prepared for that use, (if the Chalice will not serve,) putting thereto a little pure and clean Water, and setting both the Bread and Wine upon the Altar . . . ."

Here, as in the rest of the Prayer of Consecration—the only other part of the Office where the species is named—the *Mixture* is called "Wine": but the Office throughout is silent as to the Symbolism.

However, their Lordships "are unable to arrive at the con-"clusion that, if the mingling and administering in the service "water and wine is an additional ceremony, and so unlawful, it "becomes lawful by removing from the service the act of "mingling but keeping the mingled cup itself and administering "it." If the Court understood the Dean of the Arches as saying that "the mingling and administering in the service" what had been there mixed, were both "unlawful," then it would be difficult to hold that the "administering" what had been mixed before the Service would be "lawful:" but that was not the position taken by his Lordship: he, while deciding (whether rightly or wrongly is not here the question) in Martin *v.* Mackonochie, "that the mixing may not take place during the "service, because such mixing would be a ceremony designedly "omitted in and therefore prohibited by the Rubrics of the "present Prayer Book" (*2nd Report of Rit. Com^n. p.* 388), would "not say that it is illegal to administer to the communi-"cants wine in which a little water has been previously mixed," and consequently he did not condemn Mr. Mackonochie for the *latter* act, but only for the *former*, though he was charged with *both* as being *alike* offences against the Ecclesiastical Law. In Mr. Purchas's case, Sir R. Phillimore quoted his former decision and distinctly affirmed it: in doing so he cited Sir William Palmer, (*Orig. Litur.* ii. 76) as saying that "the Rubric which "enjoins the priest to place bread and wine on the table, does not "prohibit him from mingling water with that wine," and then remarked, " In this opinion, provided that the mingling be not "made at the time of the celebration so as to constitute a new "rite or ceremony, I agree." (4*th Rit. Report, p.* 247.)

Now in Liddell *v.* Westerton and in Martin *v.* Mackonochie the Judicial Committee in the plainest words limited their remarks upon and definition of lawful or unlawful Ceremonies, to Acts *done in the Service,* whether in excess or defect of "the "directions contained in " the " Prayer Book " (*Moore, p.* 187) ; but, in Hebbert *v.* Purchas, their Lordships go out of the Book, and, looking into the Church "before the service, and in the "Vestry or elsewhere," pronounce—that then or there to mingle the Chalice, afterwards to be used in the Service, constitutes "an innovation or additional ceremonial act, beyond what is "ordered in the Service," and is therefore unlawful. Yet there is no order in the Communion Office as to the preparation of the Bread, therefore, to apply the reasoning of the Court, the usual practice of cutting up the Bread into small pieces, "before the Service, and in the vestry or elsewhere " is an unlawful Ceremonial Act, because it is only ordered to be broken during the Prayer of Consecration.

Passing from Rubrics their Lordships refer to the practice of the Church, remarking—"But neither Eastern nor Western "Church, so far as the Committee is aware, has any custom "of mixing the water with wine apart from and before the Ser- "vice." Now, though there may not be such a custom, or it may be difficult to find it, at the present time in the Western* Church, owing to the way in which local uses have been superseded by the enforcement of uniformity in respect of the

---

* Mr. Scudamore (*Notitia Eucharistica,* p. 396) says that "At Auxerre the old Rubric ordered the Priest to 'minister bread on the Paten, and Wine and Water in the Chalice,' before vesting if he pleased, but at least to do this before the Gospel. At Châlons-sur-Marne he was ordered to do it before vesting, without the liberty of choice permitted at Auxerre." And there is said to be evidence of a similar custom elsewhere in France and also in Germany, Italy, and Spain, before the National uses were superseded in the beginning of the 18th century.

The Editor of *The Sarum Missal in English,* describing the English Use as to Low Mass from the 11th to the 16th century, mentions that the Celebrant "prepares the Chalice" &c. in the Sacristy, and observes—that " When Low Masses first began, the Priest was in the habit of putting the Wine and Water here before Mass." (p. xliv.)

Roman Liturgy; yet it is certain that the custom is general in the Eastern Church, *the Office of the Prothesis* expressly prescribing it. It can hardly be supposed that, at least, the *Episcopal* Members of the Committee, were not aware of this provision of the Greek Liturgies; and so it may be that, in their remark upon this point, the Committee regarded the Rite of Prothesis as the commencement of the *public* Office, whereas it is the *private* preparation for that Office and is made in the Chapel of the Prothesis, which adjoins the Bema or Sanctuary, and, in a great degree, corresponds to the Sacristy or Vestry of an English Church. In the course of that Office the following directions occur :—

" *The Deacon then poureth into the holy Cup Wine and Water together, first saying to the Priest,* Master [Sir—*Neale*], bless the Holy Union. *And the Priest blesseth them, saying:* Blessed be the union of Thy saints always, now and ever, and to the age of ages. Amen. (*Service of the Divine and Sacred Liturgy of our Holy Father John Chrysostom,* p. 94. Masters, 1866. See also *Translations of the Primitive Liturgies,* p. 182. Neale & Littledale, Hayes 1869.)

Towards the end of the Office the Deacon says to the Priest "It is time to perform unto the Lord. Give the blessing, holy " Master [Sir—*Neale*]," (*Service* &c. p. 105 ; *Neale*, p. 192) and at the end of the Office it is directed " *Then shall the Veil* " *before the holy Doors be withdrawn, and the Deacon beginneth* " *the holy Liturgy*" (*Ib.* p. 106.)

Mr. Scudamore, in his very learned Work *Notitia Eucharistica,* (p. 395, 2nd Ed. Rivington, 1876) thus remarks upon this subject :—

"In the Greek Church the Cup is mixed by the Deacon before the Liturgy at the table of Prothesis or Credence, and generally in a side Chapel [*Goar*, p. 61.] The practice appears to be the same throughout the East. The Ordo Communis of the Syrians [*Renaud*, tom. ii. pp. 4, 12] gives a direction for the admixture by the Priest and a form of words to be said at the time. The Ethiopic [*Ibid.* tom. i. p. 502] has a prayer to be said (with others used 'before the Liturgy begins,') 'when the water is mixed with the wine.' In the Coptic [*Ibid.* tom. i. p. 3] rite the *previous* mixture is indicated by a prayer of Prothesis, in which the Priest dedicates to their sacred use 'this Bread and this Cup, which' (to give the very words employed by him) 'We have placed upon this Thy Sacerdotal Table.' This prayer is said at the Great

Entrance, which among the Copts takes place before the Lessons are read. [*Ibid.* p. 186]. The Nestorians of Malabar prepare the bread and the wine on the Altar before the Lessons. [*Le Brun. Diss.* xi. Art. xii. tom. 6, pp. 481, 486]. The Chaldeans prepare them before; but set them on the Altar after. [*Ibid.* p. 491 *Renaud*, tome ii. p. 586.]"

So much, then, with regard to the existing "Eastern" custom of which the Court speaks.

XXXV. But their Lordships go on to remark thus:—

> "As to the second question, the addition of water is prescribed in the Prayer Book of 1549; it has disappeared from all the later books, and this omission must have been designed."

Now, in all likelihood, the omission was "designed;" but if their Lordships meant to imply (as it would seem they did) that this designed omission was intended to be a *prohibition* of the mixture—whether in or out of the Service—such a conclusion may well be doubted. For, if we take the Book of 1552 and compare the Communion Office with that of 1549, there are omissions which "must have been designed" quite as much as "the addition of water," but which it cannot seriously be pretended were therefore to be abolitions. I pass over now the notable instance of the omitted Directions for the Manual Acts[*] in the Prayer of Consecration, as they have been already referred to (See p. 213–14), merely remarking that (in Sheppard *v.* Bennett) the Court said "there must *ex necessitate* here be some "Manual Acts," and proceed to notice only the following instances: it will be seen that the bracketed words do not appear in the later Books:—

---

[*] Cosin, remarking upon their omission in the Book of 1552 (as in his own time) in deference he thinks to Bucer (though this seems doubtful) says. "And yet the use could not for all that be left off, it being a general custom among us to do so still." (*Notes 3rd. Series.* Vol. v. p. 478). Also in his "Particulars to be considered, explained, and corrected in the Book of Common Prayer," he says—" 57. Again, at the words there, 'He took bread and He brake it, and He took the cup,' no direction is given to the priest, (as in King Edward's Service-Book there was, and as in most places it is still in use,) to 'take the bread and cup into his hands,' nor to 'break the bread before the people'; which is a needful circumstance belonging to this sacrament; and therefore, for his better warrant therein, such a direction ought here to be set in the margin of the book." (*Ib.* p. 516.)

1549.	1552, 1559, 1604, 1662.
"*The Collects ended, the Priest, [or he that is appointed,] shall read the Epistle [in a place assigned for the purpose], saying,* The Epistle," &c.	"*Immediately after the Collects,* the Priest shall read the Epistle, beginning thus,†* The Epistle,"&c.
"*Immediately after the Epistle ended, the Priest [or one appointed to read the Gospel,] shall say,* The Holy Gospel," &c.	"*And the Epistle ended, he shall say the Gospel, beginning thus:* ‡ The Gospel written," &c.
["*The Clerks and people shall answer,* Glory be to Thee, O Lord."]	Omitted.
["*Then shall the Minister take so much Bread and Wine, as shall suffice for the persons appointed to receive the holy Communion, laying the bread upon the corporas, or else in the paten, or in some other comely thing, prepared for that purpose; and putting the wine into the Chalice, or else in some fair or convenient cup, prepared for that use, (if the Chalice will not serve) putting thereto a little pure and clean water, and setting both the bread and wine upon the Altar:*" &c.]	Wholly omitted in 1552, 1559, and 1604. In 1662 the following Rubric was inserted—"*And when there is a Communion, the Priest shall then place upon the Table so much Bread and Wine, as he shall think sufficient.*"
"*And the Minister delivering the Sacrament of the Blood, [and giving every one to drink once and no more], shall say,* The Blood," &c.	"*And the Minister that delivereth the Cup¶ shall say,* The Blood," &c.

Looking, then, at these omitted Rubrics or portions of Rubrics, can it be seriously contended that for 300 years it has been, and still is, *illegal* (1) For the Epistle to be read "in a "place assigned;" (2) For a Deacon to read the Epistle; (3) For a Deacon or for any other Priest than the Celebrant, to read the Gospel; (4) to say "Glory be to Thee, O Lord" before the

---

* 1662—"*Collect.*"   † 1662—"*the Epistle, saying.*"   ‡ 1662—"*Then shall be read the Gospel (the people all standing up) saying.*"   ¶ 1662—"*To anyone.*"

Gospel; and (5) from 1552 to 1662, to put the Bread and Wine upon the Altar immediately after the Offertory, * or indeed at any period of the Service, seeing that no direction whatever is given about it; or further (6) will it be alleged to have been lawful since 1552 and to be lawful still, to give the Chalice *more than* " once " to every Communicant? Yet it is not so many years ago that Bishops and others held it to be wrong for a Clergyman to cross from the North to the South side of the Altar to read the Epistle; and for " Glory be to " Thee, O Lord " to be said or sung before the Gospel.

Why these various omissions were made—and *designedly* made, as I see no reason for doubting—is another question: in the absence of other Documentary evidence some slight clue seems furnished by the language of the Act which authorized the Book of 1552: it is there declared (5 & 6 Edw. vi. c. 1. § 5.):—

"And because there hath arisen in the use and exercise of the aforesaid common service [*i.e.*, the Prayer Book of 1549] in the Church heretofore set forth, divers doubts for the fashion and manner of the ministration of the same, rather by the curiosity of the minister and mistakers, than of any other worthy cause; therefore, as well for the more plain and manifest explanation hereof, as for the more perfection of the said order of common service, in some places where it is necessary to make the same prayers and fashion of service more earnest and fit to stir Christian people to the true honouring of Almighty God; the King's most excellent Majesty, with the assent of the lords and commons, in this present parliament assembled, and by the authority of the same, hath caused the aforesaid order of common service, entitled

---

* The following Visitation Articles show that, in the opinion of their Authors, it was a duty to put the Oblation on the Altar in the course of the Office, notwithstanding the omission of the Rubric of 1549 :—

Harsnet, Bp. of Norwich, 1620—" Item, whether haue the Church-wardens at euery Communion prouided sufficient Bread and Wine for the Communicants, and set the same vpon the Communion Table, in the presence of the Minister before he beginne the administration of the said Sacrament?" (2nd *Rit. Report*, p. 487, Tit. 9, 4.)

Laud, Bp. of St. David's, 1622—" Have you . . . . a faire Communion cup . . . . a flagon . . . . to put the Wine in, whereby it may be set vpon the Communion Table, at the time of the blessing and consecrating thereof . . ." (*Ib.* p. 488. 2. See the same question in his Articles for Norwich, as Abp. of Canterbury in 1635-p. 547. 3.)

Williams, Bp. of Lincoln, 1635—"Item, whether have you . . . . a fair Communion Cup . . . . a flagon . . . . to put the Wine in, whereby it may be set upon the Communion Table, at the time of the blessing thereof. . . . ." (*Ib.* p. 531. 3.)

'the Book of Common Prayer,' to be faithfully and godly perused, explained, and made fully perfect, and by the aforesaid authority hath annexed and joined it, so explained and perfected, to this present statute: . . . . . . (*Stephens, Eccl. Stat. I.* p. 332.)

COLLIER, writing of the Revision in 1551-2 and commenting upon this passage of the Act of 1552, thus remarks:—

"By this Statute, the First Common Prayer-book authorized by a Parliament, in the second and third year of this reign, is called 'a very godly order, agreeable to the Word of God, and the Primitive Church, very comfortable to all good people desiring to live in Christian conversation, and most profitable to the estate of this realm.'

"This is a very honourable testimony. The first book is said to be formed upon the doctrine of the Scriptures, and the practice of the best Antiquity. And that it is very serviceable for the promoting of piety, and public advantage. This commendation is given without abatement. There is no stroke of censure, no charge of superstition, no blemish either with respect to doctrine, or ceremonies, thrown upon it. Thus Bucer's* and Calvin's animadversions are in effect declared frivolous and of no weight. The men, it is likely, meant well: but then they ventured beyond their talent, and their judgment failed them.

"But if the book was in this good condition, why was it brought under a review? Why are some parts expunged? Some added, and some transposed? The Statute accounts for this. There were 'divers doubts risen for the fashion and manner of the ministration of the same.' Then, it seems, there was no exception touching any part of the matter. But were these doubts well-founded? No; the Act says they proceeded 'rather by the curiosity of the Minister and mistakers, than of any other worthy cause.' From hence we may infer, that the explanations, as they are called, in the Second Book, were not made without compliance with the weakness of some people: not without condescension to those who had more scruples than understanding, more heat than light in them. When this Bill for discharging the first Book, and appointing the Second, was read in the House of Lords, the Earl of Derby, the Bishops of Carlisle and Norwich, the Lords Stourton and Windsor, protested against it. (*Journal Procer. Biblioth. Cotton. Tiberius*, D. 1.)

"From the full approbation given by the Statute to the first Book, one may reasonably infer, that the following Clause, which mentions the 'explaining, perfecting, and making the same prayers and service more earnest and fit to stir Christian people to the honouring of

---

* It is important to bear in mind that, although Bucer's opinion was asked about the Book of 1549, the changes to be made in the Book, appear to have been determined upon before his "Censures" reached Abp. Cranmer in January 1551-2: Bucer died on Feb. 28. The Act of Uniformity was passed on April 6th. Information on this point will be found in Hardwick's *Reformation*, p. 223; Proctor, *on the Common Prayer*, p. 34; and my *Historical Considerations on the Declaration on Kneeling*, pp. 89 & 402.

Almighty God'; from hence, I say, we may reasonably infer, that this clause was added rather to recommend the, Second, than to fasten any blemish or abatement on the First Book.

"The Ordinal for making Archbishops, Bishops, Priests, and Deacons, was annexed to the Bill, and passed with it. The Statute was not to inure till the Feast of All Saints following, which was almost three quarters of a year. This is another argument of the inoffensiveness of the First Common Prayer-book, and that the Parliament believed the people would not receive any harm from the use of it." (*Eccl. Hist.* V. 454-5.)

The *principle* upon which this Revision was conducted generally, seems to have been, in part, *simplicity* : Peter Martyr, writing from Oxford to Bucer at Cambridge, early in Feb. 1551-2, says:—

"Concerning the Reformation of the Rituals, I cannot write anything else as to what will be [done], except that the Bishops have agreed among themselves on many emendations and corrections in the published Book. Indeed, I have seen the alterations on which they have decided, noted in their places; but, as I am ignorant of English, and could not understand them, so I am unable to give you any certain information about them. However, I do not think they have gone so far, as to determine on adopting the whole of your and my suggestions. To our [Archbishop], indeed, I said, more than once, that, having undertaken this correction of the Rituals, they ought to look well to it, that the restoration they make should be so simple, chaste, and pure, that there may be no further need for emendation: for, if frequent changes should take place in these matters, it might at length easily come to pass that they would fall into general contempt. And I am persuaded that, if the business had been committed to his individual hand, purity of ceremonies would without difficulty have been attained by him : but he has colleagues who offer resolute opposition. Cheke* is the only person there, who openly and earnestly favours simplicity." (*Gorham's Reformation Gleanings*, 1857, p. 232.)

Further, as the Foreign party urged that *the directions of Scripture* rather *than the practice of Antiquity* should be the model for reforming the Public Offices of Religion, so it would appear that this was not without its influence in the Revision of 1552; for Cox, writing to Bullinger, from Windsor on Oct. 5th, though hardly in a tone of satisfaction, says:—

". . . . We have now for the second time altered the administration of the public prayers and even of the sacraments themselves, and have

---

* viz., Sir John Cheke who was Tutor to Edward VIth and a Privy Councillor.

framed them according to the rule of God's Word: but the severe institutions of Christian discipline we most utterly abominate. We would be sons, and heirs also, but we tremble at the rod . . . ." (*Original Letters relative to the Reformation.* Parker Society, P^t. I. p. 123.)

Yet it would be an error to suppose that those, or at least all of them, who maintained this view were therefore opposed to every rule and practice, whether ancient or modern, because it was not ordered in Scripture: on the contrary, some used language of a very different kind: thus, for instance, Bucer, who is commonly claimed as pressing upon Cranmer the mere Scriptural model, writing to Hooper, in Nov. 1550, in reference to his " letter and papers on the Vestments," says thus :—

"It is evident that our Lord Jesus Christ, as regards the ministry, and the word, and the Sacraments, has prescribed to us, in His own words, only the substance; and has left His Church at liberty to order everything else which appertains to the decent and useful administration of His mysteries. Hence we celebrate the Sacred Supper, neither in the evening,* nor in a private house, nor recumbent, nor among men only . . . . . the celebration of the Lord's Supper so rarely,— and the partaking of it by so few,—I judge to be in themselves Papistical: for they are in direct opposition to the Word of God. But those other matters,—the place,—the time,—the posture of body, in the celebration or participation of the Sacred Supper,—the admitting women to communion,—the method of conducting prayers and hymns to God,—the Vestment,† and other things appertaining to outward

---

* See also *Ib.* p. 206. And Peter Martyr, in writing on Nov. 4, 1550, to Hooper on the same subject of Vestments, says (*Ib.* p. 195). "At this day we so administer the Eucharist in the morning time, that after dinner we will not have the communion in the sacred assembly. But who will say, that this, which we all do with the like will and consent, is tyrannical? To myself truly, as I have now often mentioned, it would be more agreeable, that we should only do what Christ did and delivered to His Apostles."

† There is much in this Letter and in another of his (*Ib.* p. 214) to Abp. Cranmer, Dec. 8, 1550, in reply to two questions from the Archbishop about the Vestments, also in the Letter of Peter Martyr quoted in the preceding Note, which is well worth the notice of those who condemn the Eucharistic Vestments: I quote only the following passages:—

P. Martyr to *Hooper*, Nov. 4, 1550.—" Doubtless we must take care, that we afflict not the Church of Christ with the undue bondage of being able to adopt nothing which is of the Pope." (*Ib.* p. 192.) "It appears, therefore, that there were some distinctions of Vestments in the Church, earlier than the Papal tyranny. But admit that these things were invented by the Pope, I do not persuade myself, that the wickedness of the Papacy is so great, that it renders whatever it touches altogether defiled and polluted, so as not possibly to be given to virtuous and godly men for a holy use," (*Ib.* p. 193.)

Bucer to *Hooper* Nov. 1550.—" However, to affirm that these Vestments abused by Antichrist, have become so contaminated, that they can be suffered

decorum, have been left by the Lord with full power to His Church of determining and ordering on these matters what each Church may judge to be most conducive to sustain and increase among their people reverence for all the sacred things of the Lord." (*Gorham's Reformation Gleanings,* pp. 204-5.)

Moreover Cranmer himself gives contemporary testimony that he had no intention of ignoring the customs of the Church in yielding, so far as he did, to the pressure of the Protestant party in favour of what they deemed a more Scriptural Liturgy; for in his Letter to the Privy Council, October 7, 1552,[*] in reference to their wish that he would consult " the bushop of " London and some other learned men as Mr. Peter Martyr or " suche like," whether the order to kneel at receiving the Holy Communion " bee fitt to remayn as a commaundement or to bee " left out of the boke" of 1552, then being printed, he says :—

"I knowe yor L. wisdome to bee suche, that I trust ye will not bee moved w^t thes gloriouse and unquiet spirites wch can like nothing in no Church, even though she knows her Christ and prizes her liberty in all things, is a proposition which I scruple to adopt; for I find no warrant in Scripture for such a condemnation of any good creature of God," (*Ib.* p. 203.) " Now if such true Christians . . . . were to decide that anything should be done in order to commend the sacred ministry to plain men and to children— [for instance] that ministers should use some particular vestment when discharging their office, aye, even a vestment which the Papists had abused,—why ought I not to leave Christians of this sort to [follow] their own judgment? In truth I see no passage of Scripture which teaches me [that I *ought not*]. But that *I ought*, is clearly taught, beyond a doubt, in Romans xiv., in 1 Corinthians viii. and ix., and in many other places; wherever, indeed, we are instructed in our liberty and good use of the creatures, which administer food or serve any other purpose." (*Ib.* p. 204.)

Bucer to *Cranmer*, Dec. 8, 1550.—" [They should consider] also, that ministers must be clothed in *some* Vestments; and that [it is most befitting] it should be in such as may not merely cover and cherish their bodies, but may have some good signification and suggestion. Since it has now seemed good to the King's Majesty, and to the Chief Council of the Kingdom, that the use of these Vestments should still be retained, they ought to change the abuse of the Papists for a pious use of these good creatures of God, to the glory of God and the honour of the King's Majesty; and to declare distinctly that to the holy and pure all things are holy and pure, and are verily sanctified by the Word of God and by prayer; that neither demons nor men can so contaminate any creature of God, as that the pious cannot use it piously and to the glory of God, even by the use of signification not merely by the enjoyment of natural effects," (*Ib* p. 217.)

[*] This Letter is printed in full, from the MS. in The State Paper Office, at pp. 77 and 78 of my " Some Historical Declarations relating to the Declaration on Kneeling, appended to the Communion Office of the English Book of Common Prayer."—London, Masters & Co., 1863. It is there shown (pp. 92 ff) that John Knox was the probable leader of those " gloriouse and unquiet spirites " (as Cranmer calls them) who complained of the Rubric on Kneeling.

but that is after their own fansye and cease not to make troble and disquietnes when thinges bee most quiet and in good ordre. If suche men should bee hearde although the boke were made everye yere anewe, yet should it not lacke faultes in their opinion. But (saie thei) it is not commaunded in the scripture to kneele, and whatsoever is not commaunded in the scriptura is against the scripture and utterly unlaufull and ungodlie. But this saing is the chief foundation of therro' of thanabaptists and of divers other sectes. This sainge is a subvertion of all ordre aswell in religion as in common pollicye. If this sainge bee true, take awaie the hole boke of service. For what should men travell to set an ordre in the forme of service, if no ordre can be sett, but that is alreadye prescribed by the scripture . . . . . . But it is not expreslye conteigned in the scripture (saie thei) that Christ ministred the sacrament to his apostles kneelinge. Nor thei find it not expresly in scriptur that he ministered it staundinge or sittinge; but if wee will followe the plaine wourdes of scripture, wee shall rather receave it lyinge downe on the grounde, as the custome of the wourlde at that tyme almost every where, and as the Tartars and Turkes use yet at this daie to eate their meate lying upon the grounde."

These quotations tend, I think, to show that the Revision for the Book of 1552 was intended to be based, more or less, upon (a) Simplicity, or (b) Scripturalness, or (c) Custom; and so some indication is furnished as to the meaning of the statement in the Statute of 1552—that the Book of Common Prayer had been "explained, and made fully perfect;" and that there had been a consideration of what was required "in some places where it "is necessary to make the same prayers and fashion of service "more earnest and fit to stir Christian people to the true "honouring of Almighty God." Whether the changes made produced the desired effect, may well be doubted by those who have given attention to the subsequent History of the Church of England. One object, however, of those who were responsible for this Second Prayer Book seems to have been—to keep within her Communion those whose tendencies were towards the Foreign Reformation and who disliked being fettered by Rubrical requirements which they deemed at variance with the Protestant freedom they sought in the English Church: but to this, the Ecclesiastical and even the Civil Authorities felt there must be a limit: therefore, as it seems to me, they resolved that toleration must be bounded by compliance with what was *prescribed* in the Book of 1552 and that more could not be conceded in relaxation of the fuller Rubrical requirements of the Book of 1549: hence the language of the Act which, in sanctioning the Book, said that it was "made fully perfect;" in other words—that this Revision was final, as yielding all that could fairly be asked or allowed; and requiring all that was now ordered.

But it appears to me unreasonable to suppose that, in thus charitably consulting the wishes and difficulties—even the prejudices—of the Foreign Reforming School, the Rulers in Church and State were not equally mindful of the desires and habits of Clergy and Laity who had no inclination to *exchange* the English for the Genevan Ritual and Ceremonial, however willing they might be to abandon Rules and Practices which the Bishops generally held to be not Primitive and Catholic. It is wholly improbable that they were *expected to*, and altogether unlikely that they *did*, when the Book of 1552 appeared, cease from everything which they had been accustomed to under the Sarum Offices and under the Book of 1549 when they found it was not prescribed in the Revised Book of Service. It would be an utter delusion, surely, to suppose that the *mere absence* of Rubrics such *e.g.* as those mentioned at p. 269, was an *order* to them to *abstain* from the acts which those Rubrics embodied: while, even with regard to what seemed like *prohibitory* language in the Vestment Rubric, they could hardly do other than qualify it by the "discretion" reposed in the Commissioners who had to deal with the goods of the Churches, and who (as mentioned at p. 198 Note) actually *exercised* that "discretion," to a very great extent, by not depriving Parishes of the Eucharistic Vestments and other Ornaments which the *terms* of the Rubric alone appeared to forbid. The conclusion to which I am led by the circumstances attending the publication of the Prayer Book of 1552 is, that its omissions were, on the one hand, designed to provide liberty in certain things to the Protestant party; but, on the other hand, were not meant to reduce the Catholic party to a standard of Ceremonial which they were indisposed to accept, and which they could only have complied with by doing violence to habits, officially or naturally life long, with which prudent Ecclesiastical Governors would be slow to interfere.

Perhaps, however, it will be said—that it is immaterial to enquire for the cause of the omissions in the Second Prayer Book, because the language of the Statute which authorized the Book refers to the Book of 1549 as "appointed" by the Act of 1549 "for the uniformity of service and adminis-" tration of the sacraments throughout the realm," and applies the provisions of that Act to the Book of 1552. But to advance this as an argument against the use of the Mixed Chalice under the Book of 1552, which omitted the order of 1549 prescribing the mixture, would prove much more than the person employing it would be likely to admit; for it would be necessary to hold that "throughout the realm" the required "uniformity" would have been broken for 100 years, viz., from 1552 to 1662, in every Church where a Paten or Corporas Cloth was used for the Sacramental Bread, because those Articles were omitted in the Rubrics during that period though prescribed in the Book of 1549.

XXXVI. In continuation of their argument their Lordships observe that :—

> "The Rubric of 1662, following that of 1604, says ' The bread and wine for the Communion shall be provided by the Curate and [the] Churchwardens at the charges of the parish.' So far wine, not mixed with water, must be intended."

This, no doubt, is true enough : no one would imagine, I suppose, either that a charge was made upon the "Parish" for the "little pure and clean water" which the Rubric of 1549 ordered to be added to the Wine which was to be Consecrated, or that the "Parish" was to be charged for Wine and Water instead of Wine. But the Rubric of 1604 (which was also the Rubric of 1559 and 1552) is no proof whatever that the use of Water was intended to cease; for the Book of 1549, which prescribed the Water, also directed that the Bread and Wine should be paid for by the Parishioners; the Rubric runs thus :—

> "*And forsomuch as the Pastors and Curates within this Realm shall continually find at their costs and charges in their Cures, sufficient Bread and Wine for the Holy Communion, (as oft as their Parishioners shall be disposed for their spiritual comfort to receive the same,) it is therefore*

ordered, that in recompense of such costs and charges the Parishioners of every Parish shall offer every Sunday, at the time of the Offertory, the just valour and price of the holy loaf, (with all such money, and other things as were wont to be offered with the same,) to the use of their Pastors and Curates, and that in such order and course as they were wont to find and pay the said holy loaf."

If any one should think that this Rubric only requires the Parishioners to provide the *Bread*, but makes no order upon them as to the *Wine*, it is enough to reply—that, while the " other things " may include the Wine, or " such money " may include the cost of it; the words of the Rubric of 1552 clearly shew that the previous custom was for the Parishioners to provide both; for, the Rubric quoted by the Court, (viz., that " the " Bread and Wine for the Communion shall be provided by the " Curate and the Churchwardens at the charges of the Parish ") is immediately followed (in 1552, 1559, and 1604) by this plain notification :—

" and the Parish shall be discharged of such sums of money, or other duties, which hitherto they have paid for the same, by order of their houses every Sunday."

It is very likely that the origin of this part of the Rubric of 1552 and the consequent omission of the above Rubric of 1549 may be traced to a growing difficulty of obtaining compliance with the latter, as seems to be indicated in the following passage of an Order in Council, dated Decr. 25, 1549, and addressed to the Abp. of Canterbury :—

"And furthermore whereas it is comme to oure knowledge that dyvers frowarde and obstinate persons do refuse to pay towards the fyndinge of bredde and wyne for the holy communion, according to the ordre prescribed by the shide boke, by reasone whereof the holie communion ys manny tymes omitted upon the Sonday; these are to will and commaunde you to convent such obstinate persons before you and themc to admonyshe and commaunde to kepe th' order prescribed in the saide boke; and if any shall refuse so to do, to ponyshe them by suspension, excommunication or other censures of the Church." (*Cardwell, Doc. Ann.* I. p. 87.)

Still, however this may be, it is reasonable to believe that Andrewes and Cosin, ministering as they did under the Prayer Book of 1604 (to which the Judicial Committee here refer) were as likely to know the meaning of this Rubric as their Lordships or any one else 250 years afterwards; and it is certain (See pp. 256-7), from the *practice* of Andrewes and the *language* of Cosin, that *they* did not consider it illegal to use The Mixed Chalice.

XXXVII. The Court, however, have more to urge, from the Rubrics, against the Mixture: they go on to say:—

> "The priest is directed in the Rubric before the Prayer for the Church Militant to place on the table 'so much bread and wine as he shall think sufficient.' Of so much of this wine as may remain unconsecrated it is said that 'the Curate shall have it to his own use.' These directions make it appear that the wine has not been mingled with water but remains the same throughout. If the wine had been mingled with water before being placed upon the table, then the portion of it that might revert to the Curate would have undergone this symbolical mixing; which cannot surely have been intended."

Now it is somewhat misleading thus to quote the latter Rubric; for to persons only cursorily acquainted with the Rubrics (and they are far from few, even among educated people) it might, naturally enough, be thought that it is the unconsecrated *Wine* only which "the Curate" is to have "to his own use:" whereas the Rubric says "Bread and Wine." The omission of their Lordships to mention the *Bread* is, moreover, not unimportant, as might be thought; for the *Bread*, as well as the *Wine*, has been *symbolically* used in making the *Oblation* of the Sacramental Elements in the Church Militant Prayer; and there seems no more ground for saying that it "cannot surely have been intended" to let "the "Curate" have "to his own use" the unconsecrated Wine which "would have undergone this symbolical mixing," than for saying the same of the unconsecrated Bread and Wine which have been *offered*. The conclusion—that "these directions," cited by the Court, "make it appear that the wine has not been mingled "with water"—is one which certainly is far from self evident; and what has just been mentioned seems to me to render it all the more difficult of acceptance.

Indeed, except for a most lax and very unrubrical custom which has superseded the practice contemplated by the two Rubrics, the question raised by the Court could, probably, scarcely have arisen: I mean the Custom, once very general and still not uncommon (notwithstanding the ruling of this same Court in *Liddell* v. *Westerton* touching the Credence Table) of putting the Bread and Wine upon the Altar before the Service begins, and (especially where the whole Congregation remained until the end of the Church Militant Prayer) thus making an Oblation of all the Elements brought for the Sacrament: as a, not uncommon, consequence, either much remains unconsecrated or much more is Consecrated than is required for the Communicants: whereas if the Bread and Wine were not put upon the Altar until the Offertory, and the Celebrant then only placed there "so much" as he deemed "sufficient," no more would be Offered or Consecrated than could be conveniently consumed by the Communicants during or after the Celebration. The provision, both of Rubric and Canon, for a second Consecration, plainly shews that it was supposed, somewhat *less*, not much *more*, than was requisite might perhaps be Consecrated.

It may be that if what has now been advanced had been urged in an Argument for the Defence, the Court would not have terminated its Judgment upon the Mixed Chalice in the language following:—

> "Their Lordships gladly leave these niceties of examination, to observe that they doubt whether this part of the article is of much importance. As the learned Judge has decided that the act of mingling the water with the wine in the service is illegal, the private mingling of the wine is not likely to find favour with any. Whilst the former practice has prevailed both in the East and the West, and is of great antiquity, the latter practice has not prevailed at all; and it would be a manifest deviation from the Rubric of the Prayer Book of Edward VI. as well as from the exceptional practice and directions of Bishop Andrewes. Upon this 16th Article, however, whether it be more or less important, their Lordships allow the Appeal, and will advise that a monition should issue against the Defendant."

WAFER-BREAD.

XXXVIII. The Court next deals with the subject of Wafer-bread, which Mr. Purchas was alleged to have illegally substituted for ordinary Bread when celebrating the Lord's Supper; their Lordships thus introduce the discussion :—

> "The 20th Article charges the Defendant with using on divers occasions 'wafer bread, being bread made in the special shape and fashion of circular wafers, instead of bread such as is usual to be eaten,' and with administering the same to the communicants."

It is worth noting here that Mr. Purchas was not charged with not using *Bread :* nor do their Lordships anywhere say or even imply that the "Wafer-bread" used was not *Bread*, though the contrary has been and is said respecting Wafers such as Mr. Purchas is known to have employed. Further, it was not alleged by the Complainant that any Law prescribed "the special shape" of the bread to be administered to the Communicants; and it may well be asked why Bread in the form "of circular wafers" should be objectionable, and not Bread in the form of cubes or thin squares as is commonly used. It might be answered, perhaps, that the latter is more like the Greek practice and the former more like the Roman practice: whether this was in the mind of the Prosecution, and whether the Prosecutors and those who hold with them would tolerate Eastern but not Western use, does not appear. In the absence of other charges it may be thought that there was really nothing for this Court, or for the Court below, to entertain as to the Bread.

However, the Judicial Committee in dealing with the charge, such as it was, proceed to notice the Rubrics of the several Prayer Books, in the following passages :—

> "The Rubric of the Prayer Book now in force, runs thus :—'And to take away all occasion of dissension and superstition which any person hath or might have concerning the bread and wine, it shall suffice that the bread be such as is usual to be eaten, but the best and purest wheat bread that conveniently

may be gotten.' This is the same with the Rubric of 1552, 1559, and 1604, with two exceptions. The present Rubric omits after 'eaten' the words 'at the table with other meats,' and it introduces words which have been prominent in the argument in this case; instead of 'to take away the superstition,' it reads 'to take away all occasion of dissension and superstition.'"*

"In the first book of Edward VI. the direction is different: 'For avoiding [of *sic*] all matter[s *sic*] and occasion of dissension, it is meet that the bread prepared for the Communion be made, through all this realm, after one sort or [*for* or *read* and] fashion, that is to say, unleavened and round, as it was afore, but without all manner of print, and something more larger and thicker than it was, so that it may be aptly divided into [*for* into *read* in] divers pieces, and every one shall be divided in two pieces at the least, or more by the discretion of the minister, and so distributed."

XXXIX. But they raise a question and announce a conclusion in these words :—

"One of the Elizabethan injunctions is at variance with the Elizabethan Rubric, continued from the 2nd book of King Edward, and provides as follows :—' Where also it was in the time of King Edward VI. used to have the sacramental bread of common fine bread, it is ordered for the more reverence to be given to the [*for* the *read* these] holy mysteries, being the Sacraments of the body and blood of our Saviour Jesus Christ, that this [*for* this *read* the] same sacramental bread be made and formed plain, without any figure thereupon, of the same fineness and fashion, [*dele*,] round [*insert*,] though somewhat bigger in compass and thickness, as the usual bread and wafer [*insert* ,] heretofore named singing-cakes, which served for the use of the private masses [*for* masses *read* mass].' (Cardwell.) The learned Judge calls this injunction a *contemporanea expositio*

---

* "It is as well to notice here two other slight variations viz.—"concerning" *for* "in" and "usual," which is a restoration of the word employed in 1552 and 1559, instead of "usually" as given in 1604.

of the Rubric, but it is in fact a superseding of the Rubric, nor can it be regarded as at all reconcileable with it."

Yet a fuller consideration of the case will, I think, shew that their Lordships' conclusion is erroneous, and that the Dean of the Arches took a correct view of the Injunction: to say the least, it is highly improbable that the Prayer Book and the Injunctions should be "at variance," issuing, as they both did, at the same date (1559) and with concurring Authority. The Rubric runs thus :—

"And to take away the superstition, which any person hath, or might have in the bread and wine, it shall suffice that the bread be such as is usual to be eaten at the table, with other meats, but the best and purest wheat bread, that conveniently may be gotten."

This Rubric, "continued," (as the Court says) "from the 2nd Book of King Edward," was a relaxation of the stricter Rubric of 1549 which deemed it "meet that the bread prepared "for the Communion be made through all this realm, after one "sort and fashion: that is to say, unleavened, and round ...." This order was not an *exclusive* one, though it was a clear recognition of the *fitness* ("meet") of continuing to use the bread "as it was afore, but without all manner of print, and "something more larger and thicker than it was, ..."

It should be borne in mind that when this Rubric was introduced, another, already noticed (See p. 277), was also inserted to compensate the Parochial Clergy for the cost of the Saracmental Elements, by providing that the Parishioners should continue to pay "the just valour and price of the holy loaf" which had been used for the "Blessed Bread"* given at the

---

* It is thus described in the "*Rationale*," intitled "*Ceremonies to be used in the Church of England*," "*together with an explanation of the meaning and significancy of them*," prepared by Authority about 1540,—"*Holy Water* and *holy Bread* be two godly ceremonies, and to be continued in the Church. The one to put us in remembrance of our baptism, and of the bloud of Christ sprinkled for our redemption upon the cros. And the other, to put us in remembrance, that al Christen men be one mystical body of Christ: as the bread is made of many grains, and yet but one loaf. And to put us in remembrance also of the receiving of the H. Sacrament and body of Christ in right charity. Which in the beginning of Christs Church, men did more often receive than they use now a dayes to do." (*Strype, Eccl. Mem.* App. Vol. I. pt. ii. p, 433, Oxf. Ed.: or 295 fol.)

Mass—a Ceremony not continued in the Eucharistic Office of 1549.* It is likely that some people (especially of the poorer sort) continued to pay in kind; and if this "holy loaf" had been occasionally used previously for *Sacramental* Bread (as seems to have been the case), it is very probable that it continued to be used sometimes or in some places, as well as or instead of the particular kind of Bread prescribed in the Rubric of 1549 as "meet" to be "prepared for the Communion."

The Rubric of 1552 in saying, "it shall suffice that the bread " be such as is usual to be eaten at the table, with other meats," implied that it might be of *leavened* "sort" and of *loaf* "fashion": but the Rubric excluded all *inferior* "table" bread, by directing that it must be "the best and purest wheat " bread, that conveniently may be gotten." The Rubric did not discountenance, much less forbid, the use of the "un- "leavened and round" bread.

Moreover, the following new Rubric (already referred to at p. 278) had also been introduced in 1552, and was continued in 1559:—

"The Bread and Wine for the Communion shall be provided by the Curate and the Churchwardens, at the charges of the Parish; and the Parish shall be discharged of such sums of money, or other duties, which hitherto they have paid for the same, by order of their houses every Sunday." . . . .

The fact that the *duty* of providing the Sacramental Elements was thus no longer left to "the Pastors and Curates" alone— to be recompensed or not according as the Parishioners' offerings might serve—but was to be shared by "the Churchwardens," and that "the parish" was to be "at the charges" for it, would naturally make the Clergy less likely to use inferior materials for the Sacrament than else they might have been tempted to employ.

The Elizabethan Prayer Book retained unaltered the Rubric of 1552: but the contemporaneous Injunction plainly implies

---

* As shown by the complaint of the Devonshire Rebels in 1549, one of whose Demands was, "We will have holy bread and holy water, every Sunday, palms and ashes at the times accustomed; images to be set up again in every church; and all other ancient old ceremonies used heretofore by our mother holy Church." (*Cranmer's Remains.* Parker Society, p. 176.)

that some laxity or irreverence had either developed itself or was thought likely to arise under that Rubric; possibly from the very circumstance just noticed—of the Churchwardens being concerned in making the provision; for some of them might be inclined then, as in our time, to save expense to the Parishioners; all the more so in cases where the Parish Priest himself was careless or was a favourer of the extreme Reforming party. Accordingly, as Abp. Parker stated some years afterwards in a Letter presently to be noticed (See p. 294), the Queen, "for the more reverence to be given to" the Eucharist, used the power given Her in Her Act of Uniformity (Sect. 26) and issued the direction of the Injunction touching the Bread. The Judicial Committee assert that this Injunction "is in fact a superseding of the Rubric": but an examination of it would seem to prove that the object was to make the Rubric more effective; for the Injunction recognises the Rubric by saying that "it was in the time of King Edward "the Sixth used to have the sacramental bread of common fine "bread" *i.e.*, leavened Bread of a superior quality: this kind of Bread the Injunction did not abolish, but merely required, for the reason assigned, that it should be the better distinguished from other "common" Bread, by making it of a particular shape and size—which indeed the Rubric had not excluded—and which, moreover, would be in, these respects, similar to the Bread prescribed in the Rubric of 1549.

Their Lordships further declare that this Injunction of 1559 cannot "be regarded as at all reconcileable with" the Rubric of 1559: it seems to me that what has just been said really disposes of this assertion: another reply, however, is to be found in the "Interpretations" of the Injunctions which the Bishops published two years later: under the Title "Concerning the "Book of Service," it is said "that there be no other manner "and form of ministering the sacraments, but as the service "book doth precisely describe, with the declaration of the "Injunctions; as for example, the common * bread." (*Cardwell*,

---

* The word "common" seemed to me to be an error, and I find it is "communion" in the Petyt MS. from which Strype quotes: the transcriber probably did not observe the contraction in the original: Strype also refers to "MSS.

Doc. Ann. I. p. 238 or *Strype, Ann. Ch.* xvii. p. 214. or 8o. Vol. I, pt. 1 p. 320.) Here, then, is an authorised comment on the Injunction which shews that, so far from its being *irreconcileable* with the Rubric, they both provide for using the same material, viz., "the common fine bread" which the Injunction says was "used" in K. Edward's time, and which is described in the Rubric as "the best and purest wheat bread, "that conveniently may be gotten." The Injunction, however, orders this "same sacramental bread" to be made in a particular form. This "Interpretation" is followed by another viz., "That the Communion bread be thicker and broader than "it is now commonly used." (*Ibid.*) This appears to be a direction with reference to the Sacramental Wafer-Bread generally: whether that of the Injunction or the thinner Wafer which, probably, having been more or less resumed in Mary's reign, may still have partially remained in use at the date of the "Interpretations."

If, however, their Lordships' view of the Injunction be correct, then, on this ground, their decision against Wafer-bread is directly opposed to the principle on which they condemned the Eucharistic Vestments. In the latter case they held that the Advertisements were an exercise of the power given to the Queen, under Sect. 25 of the Elizabethan Act of Uniformity, to take "other order" touching the "ornaments "of the Church and of the Ministers thereof"; and that, consequently, certain of the Vestments prescribed in the Elizabethan Prayer Book had become illegal: in the former case they held that the Injunction (which Abp. Parker says was an exercise of the 26th Sect. of the same Act) by ordering Wafer-bread, *superseded* the Rubric; nevertheless they decided that Wafer-bread is illegal also.

C.C. Vol. intit Synodal:" but the Librarian of Corpus Christi College, Cambridge, who has been good enough to examine the MS., informs me that he has not been able to trace the Document. Cardwell quotes it from Strype. If, however, "common" were the true reading it would even more plainly show that the Court erred in holding that the Rubric and Injunction are not "at all reconcileable ;" for, while the Rubric mentions "usual" bread, provided it was "the best and purest wheat bread" to be had; the Injunction, referring to this "*common* fine bread," wished it to be made in a particular shape.

XL. The Court, having (erroneously, as I think has been shewn), disputed the opinion of the Dean of the Arches—that the Injunction is "a *contemporanea expositio* of the Rubric"—goes on to say :—

> "Upon these facts the learned Judge decides as follows: 'It appears, therefore, that while the first Rubric prescribed a uniformity of size and material, the later and the present Rubric are contented with the order that the purest wheaten flour shall suffice, and the bread may be leavened according to the use of the Eastern or unleavened according to the use of the Western Church.'"

Upon this decision the Court remarks that :—

> "Their Lordships do not find any mention of flour, and apart from this slight inadvertence, their Lordships are unable to accept this view of the passages that have been quoted. The first Book of Edward has in view uniformity of practice, and not the choice of two practices; the bread is to be made 'through all this realm after the same sort and fashion.'"

It is somewhat unfortunate that the writer of the Judgment, being so critical upon the use of the word "flour," should have himself fallen into the errors of quotation just now and before noticed: though indeed the Dean of the Arches was, apparently, not quoting the Rubric, but expressing in other words its meaning *viz.*, that the material for the Bread *i.e.* flour, must be of a particular kind. Ps. 81. 17 (P. Bk. ver.) mentions "finest wheat flour." (See also Ps. 147. 14.) But this by the way. Their Lordships, however, are not strictly accurate in assuming here that by the Book of 1549 an absolute uniformity was required : their words "the Bread is to be "made" cannot be considered as the exact equivalent of the Rubric "it is meet that the Bread .... be made": no doubt the Rubric had "in view uniformity of practice," but more than this cannot, I think, be strictly claimed for it; and I have already pointed out (See p. 284.) that it is not unlikely the "*holy loaf*" (originally offered for the "blessed "bread," and under the Rubric of 1549 probably still offered *in kind* instead of *in money* to defray the cost of the Sacramental Elements), was then sometimes consecrated for the Communion of the people.

Nor, so far as I am aware, is there the slightest proof that the Court is at all warranted in the conclusion stated in the following passage :—

> "The 2nd Book of Edward VI. is not so positive in form, for the words 'it shall suffice' are used; but it produced uniformity and not diversity, for the Injunction of 1559 says, 'it was in the time of King Edward the Sixth, used to have the Sacramental bread of common fine bread.'

The Book of 1552 could not, at the very outside, have been employed legally for more than one year and 20 days; for it was to come into use on Nov. 1, 1552, and, by the Marian Statute, after Dec. 20, 1553 the old Offices as used "in the last year of "Henry Eighth" were to be restored; it is most unlikely, to say the least, that in so short a time there should have been "uni-"formity" in the use of a Sacramental Bread touching which, as their Lordships say, the direction "is not so positive in form" as that relating to the Bread which for three years had been authorised by the Book of 1549, and which differed little from that which had been previously used under the Missal. The Clergy who used the Book of 1552 must have been, for the greater part, those who all their Official life had been accustomed to this Bread: it needs only to imagine ourselves in their position in order to understand that, by the mere force of habit, they would continue to use the same Bread unless there was a "positive" order for them to substitute a different kind of Bread. If the Court, viewing the Rubric of 1552 in the light of present custom, sees that it "is not so positive in form" as the Rubric of 1549 because "the words 'it shall suffice' are "used," is it in the least probable that the Clergy of 1552-3 would perceive in it any *direction* to abandon the use of the Sacramental Bread then commonly provided, and to resort to a different kind of Bread? Moreover, though there were some differences of opinion at that time about the Bread to be used, there is no evidence (so far as I know) of any great or general dissatisfaction with Wafer Bread *; or any eagerness on the part of the Clergy at large to lay aside the First Prayer Book and to adopt the Second. Some, no doubt, were urgent for change and lost no time in effecting it when the opportunity offered: but, beyond this, there seems no reason for supposing that, in this respect, the " uniformity " or "diversity" which previously existed was much altered under the Prayer Book of 1552.

It is necessary, however, to notice the reason assigned by the Court for concluding that the Rubric of 1552 " produced " uniformity and not diversity ": their Lordships find a witness to this in the words of the Elizabethan Injunction, that "it was "in the time of King Edward used to have the Sacramental " bread of common fine bread." But the word " used " would seem to be employed here in a *legal* not in an *historical* sense; and to refer to *the direction of the Rubric* rather than to any *general adoption* of ordinary Bread whether "such as is usual to "be eaten at the table with other meats " or " the best and "purest wheat bread, that conveniently may be gotten." The word "used" was a technical Rubrical term *e.g.* " The Morn- "ing and Evening Prayer shall be *used* "—" the Litany to be "*used* on Sundays," &c.—" The Collects, Epistles, and Gospels "to be *used* at the Celebration," &c.—" The Ministration of " Baptism, to be *used* in the Church "; and therefore the word was likely to be employed in an Injunction which pointed to a Rubrical direction.

Yet, even if it be admitted that the word "used" was employed by the Injunction in an *historical* sense, as shewing what occurred " in the time of King Edward the Sixth," it by no means follows that the Injunction intended to express an *unvarying* practice: to state that a certain thing was "used" during a given period, need not, often does not, mean that it

---

* Cosin, stating Bucer's objections to the Book of 1549, only mentions his desire (*Censura* p. 459) "That liberty might be given to use leavened and common bread, as well as wafers and unleavened." (*Notes, 3rd Series, Works* v. p. 475). And Collier remarks of him that " In his third chapter, speaking of the Holy Eucharist, he has nothing to except against the figure of the consecrated bread, and concludes it indifferent whether it is round or otherwise . . . ." (*Eccl. Hist.* v. 389. ed. 8o. 1852.)

was *uniformly* used. It is remarkable that in one of the *Interpretations of the Injunctions*, (already quoted at p. 286) which orders that "the Communion Bread be thicker and "broader," it is described as that "now *commonly* used," thus indicating the *extent* of the use; but whether the word "used" be here employed in a *legal* or in an *historical* sense, the contrast between the "used to have" of the Injunction and the "now "commonly used" of the Interpretation, deprives the Judicial Committee of the testimony which they assume to be furnished by the Injunction to a supposed uniformity of practice caused by the Rubric of the 2nd Prayer Book.

Having thus assumed (erroneously, as I believe) a "general "use" of Loaf Bread, either the "usual" or a better sort, to have prevailed under the Rubric of 1552, the Court says :—

> "This general use the Injunction proposes to change; but again the order is universal and binds the very minutest details; the bread is to be plain without any figure, fashioned round but somewhat bigger in compass and thickness than the cakes used in private masses: there is no trace of an intention to leave men free to follow the fashion of the Eastern or of the Western Church."

But, if what has just been advanced is correct, it cannot be rightly alleged that "the Injunction proposes to change" the "general use" under the Book of 1552; for (so far as there is any distinct evidence upon the subject) the *actual* "use" is not likely to have been much at variance with the ordering of the Injunction. Supposing, however, it was as greatly at variance as their Lordships contend, the argument overlooks the fact—that the Injunction had not to operate upon what existed in 1552-3, but upon what existed in 1559 when the five years of Mary's reign would have restored the general use of Wafer-bread, even if it had come to an end with the last year of Edward. The Court's reasoning blots out or bridges over all that occurred between Dec. 20, 1553, when Mary restored the Missal, and June 24, 1559 on which day the Prayer Book of 1552 was revived, though somewhat altered and improved in the Elizabethan version of 1559. Moreover it ignores the fact that during the seven months between Elizabeth's Accession (Nov. 17, 1558) and the Prayer Book of 1559 coming into use, the Missal Office was continued; for, to stop Innovations, a Proclamation of Dec. 27th, 1558, forbad "to use any "other manner of public prayer, rite, or ceremony in the "Church, but that which is already used, and by law "received, or the Common letany used at this present in her "majestys own chappel, and the Lord's prayer, and the Crede in "English; untill consultation may be had by parliament, by her "majesty and her three * estates of this realme, for the better "conciliation and accord of such causes, as at this present are "moved in matters and ceremonies of religion." (*Cardwell, Doc. Ann.* I. 209.)

The Rubric of 1559 was the result of *this* "consultation" so far as concerned the Sacramental Bread: it was not a *new* Rubric, but one existing in the then restored Book of 1552. This revived *Rubric* did not *forbid* the Bread then, and for the five years before, in use at the Mass; but it *sanctioned* another kind to avoid a contingent objection. Nor did the contemporary *Injunction* in terms affect the existing use, except in so far as the words "plain, without any figure thereupon" may have been designed to apply to all Sacramental Bread : otherwise, its purpose seems limited to *regulating* the form and size of the "common fine bread" which it mentions. It sounds somewhat exaggerated to speak of this regulation as one that "binds the "very minutest details." It may readily be admitted of the Injunction that, as their Lordships say, "there is no trace of an "intention to leave men free to follow the fashion of the Eastern "or of the Western Church;" for the professed object of the Injunction was only to secure "the more reverence" in following a recognised *English* "fashion": in seeking to effect this object, the Queen's advisers were fully impressed with the importance of conciliating, what may be termed, the Catholic and the Protestant parties then in the Church of England; consequently

---

* Can "*three* estates" mean anything but the Lords, the Commons, and the Convocation ? The Solicitor General's speech, Oct. 23, 1641, on the Impeachment of the 13 Bishops, seems to show that they did not sit in the House of Lords as "a third estate and degree." (*Rushworth.* pt. 3. v. 1. 396.)

they avoided a too rigid and exclusive rule in this matter of the Sacramental Bread (as indeed in other Ecclesiastical Regulations), by giving, in the combined directions of the Rubric and the Injunction, a liberty which, as it seems to me, consulted the wishes and covered the reasonable demands of both parties.

XLI. Reviewing their references to and remarks upon the Rubrics and the Injunction, the Court sums them up thus:—

> "So there are three distinct orders, first, for wafer bread, unleavened as before, but larger and without print; then for common bread usual at the table; then for a new kind of bread thicker than the wafer and without symbolical figures; and the first and last are in their form universal and absolute; and the second also had brought about a general usage and not a diversity. There was, no doubt, a great division of opinion upon this question; and this makes it all the more remarkable, that none of the three orders takes the natural course of leaving the matter free. Each seems to have aimed at uniformity but each in a different practice."

But if what I have been saying about these directions is correct, they do not involve "three distinct orders" in the sense of being *exclusive* in their language or effect, as their Lordships seem to regard them. It has been shewn, I think, (See p. 283) that not even the Rubric of 1549, much less (See p. 285) the Injunction of 1559 can be correctly described as "in "their form universal and absolute;" and that (See pp. 288–90) there is no real ground for asserting of the Rubric of 1552 that it "had brought about a general usage and not a diversity." It is to be remarked that this second order is not correctly described as one "for common bread usual at the table": it was to be "such," that is, the *sort* "usual to be eaten" there; but its *quality* was to be better—"the best and purest wheat "bread, that conveniently may be gotten." The language seems even *prohibitory* of any *inferior* bread "usual to be eaten "at the table with other meats." Their Lordships believe that "a great division of opinion" existed "upon this question;" no doubt there was a diversity of opinion, though not, apparently, to any such extent as the Court seem to suppose, at least until after the Injunction was issued; though even then the advocates of the Loaf Bread appear, from Parker's statements, (See pp. 294, 5, & 6), to have been only a small minority. But the very fact of this difference suggests, I think, that some liberty was likely to be allowed; and " the three orders " (though not taking what their Lordships call " the natural " course of leaving the matter free "—a course which in all likelihood would have aggravated the divisions) do appear to provide a degree of freedom within certain defined limits. Had these directions been either laxer or more rigid, they would not have satisfied objectors on either side: but, as issued, they were adapted to meet all reasonable requirements. The Court regards each Order as having "aimed at uniformity" though "in a " different practice": yet the Injunction of 1559 only assigns as its object " the more reverence;" the Rubric of 1552 merely seeks " to take away the superstition, which any person hath or " might have in the bread and wine*;" and the Rubric of 1549 is but desirous of " avoiding all matters and occasion of dissension." Having regard to the history of parties at these three periods, is it at all likely that the insisting upon "uniformity" would have produced any one of these wished-for results?

XLII. The Report of the Judicial Committee now enters upon a discussion as to the meaning of the Rubrical expression " it " shall suffice," with this remark :—

> "But it has been argued by some that the phrase 'it shall suffice' implies a permission; that the words may mean 'it shall be sufficient, but another usage is allowed and might even be better.'"

It is reasonable to suppose that one who was Abp. of Canterbury in 1559, when the Prayer Book of 1552 was revived (with a few alterations) would be likely to know the meaning of the words in question; and, fortunately, Abp. Parker has plainly recorded his understanding of them in the following Letter which, from its importance, it is best not to curtail:—

"ARCHBISHOP PARKER TO SIR WILLIAM CECIL," 8th January, 1570-1. Petyt MS., Inner Temple, No. 47, fol. 53, Parker's draft.

" Sir, Where upon the return of my lord of London [Bp. Sandys]

---

* How " to take away the superstition " in " the wine " is not said: possibly it was effected by the next Rubric—" *And if any of the bread or wine remain* [*i.e.* unconsecrated], *the Curate shall have it to his own use.*"

from the Court we had communication of the communion* bread, and he seeming to signify to me that your honour did not know of any rule passed by law in the Communion-Book that † it may be such bread as is usually eaten at the table with other meats,‡ &c.; I thought it good to put you in remembrance, and to move your consideration in the same. For it is a matter of much contention in the realm: where most part of protestants think it most meet to be in wafer-bread, as the injunction prescribeth; divers others, I cannot tell of what spirit, would have the loaf-bread, &c. And hereupon one time at a sessions would one Master Fogg have indicted a priest for using wafer-bread, and me indirectly for charging the wafer-bread by Injunction: where the Judges were Mr. Southcoots and Mr. Gerrard, who were greatly astonied upon the exhibiting of the book. And I being then in the country, they counselled with me, and I made reasons to have the Injunction prevail.

"First, I said, as her Highness talked with me once or twice in that point, and signified that there was one provisio in the act of the uniformity of Common Prayer, that by law is granted unto her, that if there be any contempt or irreverence used in the ceremonies or rites of the Church by the misusing of the orders appointed in the book, the Queen's Majesty may, by the advice of her commissioners, or metropolitan, ordain and publish such further ceremonies, or rites, as may be most for the reverence of Christ's holy mysteries and sacraments, and but for which law her Highness would not have agreed to divers orders of the book. And by virtue of which law she published further order in her Injunctions both for the communion-bread, and for the placing of the tables within the quire. They that like not the injunctions force much the statute in the book. I tell them that they do evil to make odious comparison betwixt statute and injunction, and yet I say and hold, that the injunction hath authority by proviso of the statute. And whereas it is said in the rule, that 'to take away the superstition which any person hath or might have in the bread and wine, it shall suffice that the bread be such as is usually to be eaten at the table with other meats, &c.'; 'it shall suffice,' I expound where either there wanteth such fine usual§ bread, or superstition be feared

---

* *Strype* prints this "common," but it is "communion" in the original. See Note p. 285.

† "but that," *Strype*. ‡ "meals," *Strype*.

§ In *Strype's life of Parker*, Bk. IV., chap. iii., p. 310, fol. or 8vo., Vol. ii., p. 35, the words are "in usual bread," (see p. 295) and so it has been suggested that the word "fine" is an error: but, by the courtesy of the Librarian at the Inner Temple, I have examined the original Letter in the Petyt MSS. and find that the reading is "fine usual bread." Canon Robertson ("*How shall we conform to the Liturgy?*" p. 167, ed. 1869) has the following Note:—"In Parker's Correspondence, edited by Mr. Bruce (p. 376), the reading is 'such fine usual bread,' and the editor informs me that this is according to the manuscript. Yet surely an error must have crept in, as the word "usual" makes nonsense. I have therefore followed Strype (Parker, 310) in reading 'such fine bread'— *i.e.*, of the kind ordered by the injunctions." But, with all respect to the

in the wafer-bread, they may have the Communion in fine usual * bread: which is rather a toleration in these two necessities, than is in plain ordering, as is in the injunction.

"This I say to shew you the ground which hath moved me and others to have it in the wafer-bread; a matter not greatly material, but only obeying the Queen's Highness, and for that the most part of her subjects disliketh the common bread for the sacrament. And therefore, as her Highness and you shall determine, I can soon alter my order, although now quietly received in my diocese, and I think would breed some variance to alter it. I hear also that in the Court you be come to the usual bread. Sir, the great disquiet babbling that the realm is in in this matter maketh me thus long to babble, and would be loth that now your saying or judgment should so be taken as ye saw a law that should prejudice the injunction.

"Sir, I thank your honour for your prudent secrecy, that you did use toward that party that laboureth to know who did write letters to the Queen to signify such innovation. He saith he is promised to know, &c. It would breed but unkindness, and therefore I left him in his suspense, as in my last long letter I would I had spared one word written which might work unkindness, but that I say your wisdom will rather make charity than break it.

"If this unhandsome weather, or my casual body, shall defer the longer my duty of coming to the Queen, I pray you ease it with some word. And thus God make you strong. This 8th of January."
(*Correspondence of Abp. Parker*, Parker Society, pp. 375-6.)

Strype, in giving this Letter, introduces it with the following remarks:—

"There was now in the Churches of the kingdom great variety used in the sacramental bread, as to the form of it. As in some (and they the most) the form of it was round, wafer-like: in some the form was otherwise, as ordinary bread: though the wafer-form of the bread to be used in the Communion had been before agreed upon, upon good deliberation, between the Archbishop and the Bishop of London; yet this order about the bread would not prevail to bring in an uniformity therein. The tidings of this variety came new to the Court and gave great offence. Of this the Secretary informed the Archbishop, and withal desired of him to certify him of what form it was agreed the

---

Canon, the word not only makes sense, but the omission of it by Strype renders Parker's argument less clear: the Archbishop was *expounding* the Rubric, not the Injunction; and he says that the "it shall suffice" applies to the lack of. "*such* fine usual bread," *i.e.*, what the Injunction refers to as the "common fine bread," viz., "fine bread" (purposely prepared, as it would seem) *leavened* and in *loaf* shape (as distinguished from *unleavened* wafers) of which "in the time of King Edward the Sixth" it was "used to have the Sacramental bread" provided. In that case they might have "fine usual bread," *i.e.*, the *leavened loaf*, "usual to be eaten at the table with other meats," only it must be "the best and purest wheat bread that conveniently may be gotten."

* "in usual bread," (*Strype's Parker*, Bk. IV., ch. iii. 310 fol. *or* 8°., II. 35).

bread should be. The Archbishop, in satisfaction to the Secretary, gave him this answer.

"'As you desire, I send you here the form of the bread used, and was so appointed by order of my late Lord of London [now elect of York]* and myself, as we took it, not disagreeable to the Injunctions. And how so many Churches have of late varied, I cannot tell; except it be the practice of the common adversary, the Devil, to make variance and dissension in the sacrament of unity. For where we be in one uniform doctrine of the same, and so cut off much matter of variance, which the Lutherans and Zwinglians do hatefully maintain; yet because we will have some matter of dissension, we will quarrel in a small circumstance of the same: neither regarding God in his word, who earnestly driveth us to charity, neither regarding the love and subjection we should bear to our Prince, who zealously would wish the devout administration of the Sacrament; nor yet consider what comfort we might receive ourselves in the said Sacrament, if dissension were not so great with us. Sir, I pray help to pacify it, whether by proclamation, or by any other way; as in wisdom of government, you see, sometimes things must be forced or remitted.'" (*Life of Parker*, Bk. IV., chap. iii., p. 309, *fol.* or 8vo., Vol. II., p. 32. The Letter is also printed in the *Parker Correspondence* p. 378.)

The date of this Letter is Feb. 6, 1570-1, a month later than the one just before quoted, and was written, apparently, in reply to a communication from the Secretary to the Archbishop: Strype introduces it before the Letter of January 8th but then goes on to remark thus:—

"And as there was this stir at this time about the form of the bread, so there was not long before as great about the kind of it, whether wafer bread, or loaf, or common bread. The Archbishop had appointed it to be wafer bread; and so he enjoined it in his Injunctions to his Clergy. And it was generally so used; though some would rather make use of the loaf bread; which did not please the Archbishop: and of the same mind seemed the Secretary to be, the particular sort of bread not being prescribed by the Rubric. And even in the Court they were come to the usual bread. The Archbishop was pretty indifferent which bread soever it were, and was ready to follow orders that should be sent to him thereabout. But he thought it might breed some disturbance, seeing the other, that is, the wafer bread, was already appointed. But this matter occasioned this Letter to the Secretary, written either this, or perhaps the last year." (*Life of Parker, Ibid.*)

Then follows the Letter of Jan. 8th., 1570—1, already printed

---

* The bracketed words are *Strype's*. *Grindal* is the Bishop referred to by Parker.

at pp. 293-5, from the *Parker Correspondence* where this date is given, and there is no ground for questioning its accuracy.

Now, considering the great value which the Judicial Committee, who decided the Purchas Case, attached to *contemporaneous exposition*, it is surprising that their Lordships did not take the least notice of this Letter though it was cited by the Dean of the Arches with the remark—" This is an authority which " must command great respect in this Court, and from which I " see no reason to dissent, more especially as it proceeds upon a " principle of construction similar to that to which I have already " adverted as having been adopted in Westerton *v* Liddell, with " respect to the covering of the Holy Table." *(4th Report of Rit. Com^n p. 248.)* In this Letter, the Archbishop not only states distinctly his own understanding of the Rubric, but says that his exposition of its meaning satisfied two " Judges" who had to try a Priest (charged like Mr. Purchas) with illegally " using Wafer-bread." To them he " made reasons to " have the Injunction prevail "; and part of his reasoning was just the reverse of that of the Judicial Committee who held that the Injunction "is in fact a superseding of the Rubric, nor can " it be regarded as at all reconcileable with it." The Archbishop, on the contrary, deemed it " evil to make odious comparison " betwixt statute [*i.e.* the Rubric which he also calls 'the statute "'in the book'] and injunction"; for, while he held "that the " injunction hath authority by proviso of the statute", *i.e.* Sect. 26 of the Act of Uniformity of 1559, the Rubric was "rather a " toleration," under " two necessities," of another kind of Sacramental Bread " than " such as " is in plain ordering " described " in the injunction." The " two necessities " in which the Archbishop held the Rubric to be tolerant of Bread " such " as is usually* to be eaten at the table with other meats," *viz.*, leavened loaf bread, are *First*, where, " there wanteth such " fine usual bread " *i.e.*, the " common fine bread" of which the Injunction says " it was in the time of " King Edward VI. " used to have the Sacramental bread," and *Secondly*, where " superstition be feared in the wafer-bread." In either circumstance they might " have the Communion in fine usual

* *Sic.* in Parker's letter (see p. 294), but "usual" in the Rubrics of 1552 and 1559.

2 Q

" bread," *i.e.*, the *leavened loaf* of " the best and purest wheat " bread, that conveniently may be gotten." This, says Archbishop Parker, " I expound " to be the meaning of "it shall " suffice ; " and, surely, His Grace was much more likely, than any Court or person 300 years after he wrote, to know the meaning of a Rubrical expression, first inserted in the Prayer-Book only 18 years before the date of his Letter and revived under his own auspices 7 years later, in the Prayer Book of 1559.

Upon this interpretation, by which he reconciled the Rubric and the Injunction, the Archbishop appears to have acted, some three years afterwards, where difficulties arose in his own Diocese touching the Bread to be used ; and also when advising Parkhurst the Bishop of Norwich under similar circumstances ; for Strype states that :—

"A great question now arose, or rather was renewed, in Norfolk, as well as in other places, what bread ought to be used in the Communion ; partly occasioned by Sergeant Flowerdew : who, in his charge the last sessions, made mention of common bread to be used by authority of the statute. This the Bishop of the diocese signified to his Metropolitan at the same time he wrote his letter last mentioned, dated Jan. 21 [1573–4], shewing him, how men were hereby in doubt what to do; especially remembering what the Queen had said to the Archbishop and other the Bishops, when they had been not long before in her presence, in exposition, as it seems, of her own Injunctions; which was in effect to continue the use of the wafer-bread. And accordingly, in obedience hereto, he did use that sort of bread in his church at Ludham. Of this therefore he desired the Archbishop's advice to be signified to him.

" All that I find answered by the Archbishop to him in this matter was, that in a letter to this Bishop, wrote in May 1574, he hath these words : ' You would needs be informed by me, whether I would warrant you either loaf-bread or wafer-bread : and yet you know the Queen's pleasure : you have her Injunctions ; and you have also the Service-book. And furthermore, because I would deal brotherly with you, I wrote in my last Letters how I used in my diocese for peace-sake and quietness. I would your Lordship and others were nearer, to hear what is said sometimes ' ; (meaning, I suppose [says Strype], by the Queen, in displeasure towards some of the Bishops.) On the other hand, the Bishop, in excuse of himself for requiring so earnestly his judgment and direction herein, shewed his Grace the great contentions and unquiet disputes that arose hence in his diocese. ' If your Grace, said he, did hear and see what contention and heart-burning is kindled in many places, and what earnest disputes are maintained abroad for the bread, either part diversely affected ; the one alleging the Book, the other her Majesty's Injunctions ; the one affirming this, the other that, to be of more force ; in such dangerous, bitter, and daily striving, your Grace would think it not impertinent for me to wish a certainty; and one way to be set down for everybody, by such as are placed in high authority.' *

"But the grave Archbishop did not think it advisable positively to determine this matter at present, but rather to leave it as it was; lest perhaps the Queen might be offended, as an infringement of her Injunctions. And therefore he again gave this gentle advice to the same Bishop, in relation to the contentions of some for wafer-bread and loaf-bread; 'That if the order he had taken' (to allow of it [says Strype] in some places and for a time) 'would not suffice them, they might fortune hereafter to wish they had been more conformable. And he furthermore told the Bishop, he trusted, that he meant not universally in his diocese to command the use of the loaf-bread, or to wink at it, but only for peace and quietness here and there to be contented that it might be used.'" (*Strype's Parker Bk.* iv. ch. xxxv. p. 453, fol. or 8vo., Vol. ii. pp. 343 & 4. These two Letters are also given in the *Parker Correspondence*, Nos. cccli. and ccclii., where the Letter of May is dated the 17th, and that of June the 14th, 1574.)

If this evidence of Archbishop Parker's opinion and practice had been fully brought before their Lordships, it would surely have been sufficient to warrant the Court's adoption of at least the opinion first referred to in the Judgment, namely, "that "the words ['it shall suffice'] may mean 'it shall be sufficient, "but another usage is allowed and might even be better.'"

XLIII. However, their Lordships proceed to consider another opinion; they say:—

"On the other hand, it has been argued, that in other places in the Liturgy 'it shall suffice' must be construed into a positive direction; that if 'it shall suffice' to pour water on a sickly child, this ought to restrain the clergyman from immersing a child known to be sickly; that even the weaker form 'it may suffice' in the Rubric as to children and infants, brought to be baptized, conveys to the minister a distinct direction as to what he is to do, and leaves no alternative course apparent; that 'it shall suffice that the Litany be once read [*for* read *put* said]' for both deacons and priests is meant to be, and is received as a positive order; and that in such cases 'it shall suffice' means 'it shall be sufficient for the completeness of a sacrament or for the observance by the minister of the Rubric.'"

Upon the validity of this argument the Court does not express its opinion: yet it is just worth while to consider

* See the Letter, June 5, 1574, in *Gorham's Reformation Gleanings*. 1857. *p.*490.

whether the argument is really tenable. In the first place, then, it may be observed generally—that it is not according to the analogy of the Rubrics, to use terms which seem to imply a discretion or liberty, when "a positive direction" or "no alter-"native course" or "a positive order" is intended; and therefore it is unlikely that the Rubrical terms quoted in this argument would have been used if they were intended to be construed as the argument alleges. It is contended that, in the instances cited, "'it shall "'suffice' means 'it shall be sufficient;'" the converse therefore must surely be admitted. Now the expression "it shall suffice" occurs in the Baptismal Office of 1549, and in that same Book the expression "it shall be sufficient" occurs at the end of the First Exhortation in the Communion Office, " Dearly beloved "in the Lord" &c.: of this, the Rubric says: " In Cathedral " Churches, or other places where there is daily Communion, *it* "*shall be sufficient* to read this exhortation above written, once " in a month:" can it be seriously supposed that the Clergy of that day would have regarded this as a prohibition to use it more frequently? Moreover this same Rubric adds, " And in "parish Churches, upon the week days *it may be left unsaid;*" yet what Parish Priest would have thought himself precluded from using it on any week day if he considered it necessary or desirable to do so? Is there any real difference of meaning between "it may be left unsaid," and " it may suffice " in the Rubric quoted by the Court's arguer from the Office for Adult Baptism?

With these general observations the above passage in the Judgment might be left: but it may be useful to consider whether the three Rubrics quoted therein are patient of the permissive character which is denied to them.

Of the *First* Rubric it is said "that if 'it shall suffice' to pour " water on a sickly child, this ought to restrain the clergyman " from immersing a child known to be sickly ": the Rubrical term, indeed, is "weak" not "sickly"; but *weakness* (and perhaps even *sickliness*) would not necessarily preclude Baptismal washing by "immersion", any more than it would forbid Bodily washing by a bath. Immersion is *ordered* if the Sponsors "shall certify" the Priest "that the child may well endure "it";

he may dispense with it "if they certify that the child is " weak "; but *immersion* is plainly contemplated as the rule : if immersion were not (as it is) the exception, it is easy to understand that it might be preferred or desired by Parents or Sponsors even when it was doubtful whether the child could "*well* endure it"; in such a case would it be contended that "it shall suffice" was so far an obligation as that it " ought to " restrain the clergyman from immersing the child "?

Of the *Second* Rubric it is said that it " conveys to the " minister a distinct direction as to what he is to do, and leaves "no alternative course apparent." Before discussing this interpretation I must just observe, that this Rubric is incorrectly described by terming it as the Judgment does, " the Rubric as "to children and infants, brought to be baptized"; unless indeed the word " Infants " was meant to be used in a Legal sense. The Rubric relates only to " persons not baptized in "their infancy" and provides that if any such "shall be brought " to be baptized before they come to years of discretion to " answer for themselves; it may suffice to use the Office for " Publick Baptism of Infants, or (in case of extreme danger) " the Office for Private Baptism "; and *Infants* are distinctly excluded from the provision of the Rubric by its concluding direction, viz. "only changing the word [Infant] for [Child *or* " Person] as occasion requireth."

There are two other instances of the use of the word "may" which can fairly be compared with its employment in this Rubric: in the "Forms of Prayer to be used at Sea" it is said that "At the Burial of their Dead at Sea. The Office in " the Common Prayer-Book *may be used*"; and in "The Order-" ing of Deacons " it is provided that if the Deacon " be found " faithful and diligent, *he may be admitted* by his Diocesan to " the Order of Priesthood, at the times appointed in the " Canon ": yet no one, I suppose, would construe " may " to mean "must" in these two places.

The case, in the Office for " The ministration of Baptism to " such as are of riper years, and able to answer for themselves," to which the words " it may suffice " refers, is that of " persons " not baptized in their infancy " who " shall be brought to be " baptized before they come to years of discretion to answer

" for themselves." Now " The Order of Confirmation " is to be used with those " baptized " persons who are " come to " years of discretion," and it (or the being "ready and desirous" for it) is the warrant for being " admitted to the Holy Com- " munion :" the Baptismal Office to which the Court refers has a Rubric, preceding the one in question, which says " It is ex- " pedient that every person, thus baptized, should be confirmed " by the Bishop so soon after his Baptism as conveniently may " be; that so he may be admitted to the Holy Communion." Comparing, then, this Rubric with the language just cited from the Confirmation Service, it would appear that the expression " years of discretion to answer for themselves " is equivalent to the age of fitness for receiving the Holy Communion. But most Clergymen, of much Parochial experience, could probably recollect instances of children "not baptized in their infancy" who were sufficiently competent to understand the Questions and Answers in the Baptismal Office, and at whose Baptism they did use, or would have felt able to use, the Office for the Baptism of Persons of Riper years; though such children might not be then quite fit for Confirmation or Communion. Indeed the cases are abundant in which, from either the ignorance or the character of those who might present themselves as Sponsors, it would be even preferable that the children should answer for themselves.

On the other hand, there is the case of either deaf and dumb, or else deaf or dumb, persons who have attained "years of dis- " cretion" but are physically unable "to answer for themselves," or are greatly hindered from doing so by reason of deafness: circumstances alone can determine which of the two Offices it may be the more convenient to use. Then, as regards Idiots, this Office for Adults would probably be generally unuseable; yet often it could even hardly be that "it may suffice to use the " Office for Public Baptism of Infants," because there may not be the remotest prospect of the Exhortation to the Sponsors being acted upon; and therefore no choice might be left but to employ the Office for Private Baptism.

Further, the fact, mentioned in " The Preface " to the Prayer Book of 1662—that it was considered that the Office for " The Ministration of Baptism to such as are of riper years," then first provided, "may be always useful for the baptizing of "natives in our plantations, and others converted to the faith," suggests various considerations which would render it necessary to exercise a *discretion* as to employing this Office or one of those two which the Rubric says that "it may suffice to use" instead.

Of the *Third* Rubric it is said " that 'it shall suffice that the " Litany be once read [*for* read *put* said]' for both deacons and " priests is meant to be, and is received as a positive order." No proof is offered that it was "*meant* to be" so received; and the assertion may fairly be questioned on the ground that the corresponding Rubric—"And it shall suffice, the Litany to be " said once"—appears in the Ordinal of 1559; and in the Communion Office of 1559 the words "It shall suffice," in the Rubric as to the Bread, also occur: Abp. Parker, as we have seen (See p. 294) did not construe *them* "as a positive order;" it is at least a reasonable supposition that he might not so have interpreted the direction as to the Litany. That in practice the Litany is only "once said" when Deacons and Priests are ordained on the same occasion, is not necessarily a proof that the Rubric is "*received* as a positive order:" under conceivable circumstances a Bishop might wish to duplicate the Litany and not consider himself prohibited by the Rubric from so doing.

Finally, the arguer is represented as saying of the three Rubrics which have just been considered—" that in such cases " 'it shall suffice' means 'it shall be sufficient for the complete- " 'ness of a sacrament or for the observance by the Minister of " 'the Rubric.'" There is no need to dispute this proposition, but it must be considered that to do *more* or *other*, than the arguer alleges in the three previous propositions, neither detracts from such " completeness " nor hinders such " observance."

XLIV. Having mentioned the anonymous argument which has now been considered, the Judgment goes on to say :—

> " Their Lordships are disposed to construe this phrase in each case according to the context. Here the expression is 'to do [*for* do *read* take] away all occasion of dissension and superstition . . . it shall suffice.' If these words left the whole matter open, and only provided that the usual bread should be sufficient where it happened to be used, it is difficult

to see how either dissension or superstition would be taken away: not dissension, for there would be a licence that had not existed since the Reformation; not superstition, for the old wafer with its 'print,' its 'figures,' which the first Book of Edward and the injunctions desired might be excluded, might now be used if this Rubric were the only restraint. Their Lordships are therefore inclined to think on this ground alone that the Rubric contains a positive direction to employ at the Holy Communion the usual bread."

The Rubric quoted by the Court has not, indeed, "left the "whole matter open;" for, as already observed (See p. 292) it limits the *quality*, though describing the *character* of the Bread which " shall suffice:" while in *form* "such as is usual " to be eaten" *i.e. leavened* and *loaf* Bread, in *quality* it must be " the best and purest Wheat Bread that conveniently may "be gotten,"—not *ordinary household* Bread if it can be avoided. Nor, as the Court correctly implies, is it " only provided that " the usual bread should be sufficient where it happened to be " used:" the aim of the Rubric lies beyond such a mere contingency. It preserved the liberty which, as I think has been shown, *had* " existed since the Reformation;" and so, as it seems to me, declared that no real " occasion " was left for " dissension."

But the Court not only fears "a licence" unknown "since " the Reformation" if the Rubric is held to be permissive of any other Bread than "the usual bread;" it further fears that "superstition" would not "be taken away" if this interpretation be allowed,"for the old wafer with its 'print,' its 'figures' ".... might now be used." Their Lordships assume, apparently that " the first Book of Edward and the Injunctions " of Elizabeth " desired" that the " print" or "figure" on the Wafer-bread " might be excluded" on the ground of "super-"stition" connected with them: but the Book of 1549 does not assign this as the ground for omitting "all manner of print;" the reason given is—" for avoiding all matters and occasion of " *dissension*"—nothing is even hinted about " superstition." Nor does the Injunction imply the view of the Court; for, though it refers to the Bread mentioned in the revised Rubric of 1552, in which the word "superstition" was substituted for "dissension," the Injunction merely prescribes the kind of Wafer-Bread specified in the Rubric of 1549; it is silent as to the "superstition" which the Rubric of 1552 desired to guard against by its provision touching "the bread," and is bent upon securing "more reverence" than, as it implies, was obtained under that Rubric. The Rubric of 1552 in seeking "to take away the superstition which any person hath or might "have in the bread and wine" had not to do away with Wafer-bread stamped with "print"* or "figure"—that had been done three years before—the "superstition" which it deprecated is not likely therefore to have referred to anything save questions as to the *form* of the Bread and whether it was to be *leavened* or *unleavened* :† indeed the very terms of the Rubric, allowing "such as is usual to be eaten at the table, with other meats," seem plainly to imply that the "superstition" chiefly concerned an exclusive claim for *unleavened* Bread. Whitgift's reply to Cartwright (1574) serves to prove this (for the Rubric of 1559 was in the same words); and at the same time shews, that a species of Wafer-bread was then used.

In his *"Admonition to the Parliament,"* T.C. (believed to be Thomas Cartwright) had said :—

"Then they ministered with (Acts ii. 46) common and (Acts xx. 7) usual bread; now with wafer-cakes brought in by pope Alexander, being, in form, fashion, and substance, like their God of the Altar." (*Whitgift's Works*, III., p. 82. Parker Society.)

Whitgift, having stated that "learned interpreters, and "especially M. Calvin, deny this place to be meant of the "ministration of the supper," further remarks :—

"Alexander lived *anno* 111, and was a good and godly bishop: it is

---

* Myles Hogarde (*The Displaying of Protestants*, Lond. 1556) says, "in anywyse the prynte of the name of Jesus left out." (*p.* 81.)

† Wheatley (whom the Court quotes in reference to the Position of the Celebrant) says :—" § 5. The fifth Rubric is designed to take away all those scruples which over-conscientious people used to make about the Bread and Wine. As to the Bread, some made it essential to the Sacrament to have *leavened*, others *unleavened*; each side, in that, as well as in other matters of as small moment, superstitiously making an indifferent thing a matter of conscience." (*Rational Illustration of the Book of Common Prayer*, p. 298, ed. 1794.)

reported in some writers that he appointed unleavened bread to be used in the eucharist, because that Christ himself used the same according to the law written Exod. xii., Deut. xvi. But that he brought in wafer-cakes, or appointed any certain form of bread, you cannot prove; neither doth any credible author write it." (*Ib.* p. 84.)

"The truth is, that it skills not what kind of bread is used, leavened or unleavened, so it be bread; although it were to be wished, for the avoiding of superstition, that common and usual bread were used, and also that the form were altered, and the quantity increased. But these things are not *de substantia sacramenti*, and therefore not sufficient to prove that the supper is not sincerely ministered.

"M. Bucer likewise, in his Censure upon the book of common prayers, is of the same judgment: his words be these: 'The third chapter is of the substance, form, and breaking of bread, which all do well enough agree with the institution of Christ, whom it is manifest to have used unleavened Bread, and easy to be broken; for he brake it, and gave to his disciples pieces of the bread broken. Touching the form and figure, whether it were round or square, there is nothing declared of the evangelists. And because this bread is used only for a sign, and not for corporal nourishment, I see not what can be reprehended in this description of the bread which is in this book;. except some would peradventure have it thicker, that it may the more fully represent the form of true bread." (*Works*, Parker Society, III. 84.)

T. C. in his Reply, referred to the Rubric as directing the kind of bread to be used in order "to avoid superstition," and said:—

"... it is certainly known by experience, that in divers places the ignorant people, that have been misled in popery, have knocked and kneeled unto it, and held up their hands whilst the minister hath given it, not only those which have received it, but those which have been in the church and looked on. I speak of that which I know and have seen with my eyes." (*Ib.* p. 85.)

Whitgift, in his "Defence," answers:—

"The danger that you speak of is in the form and figure of the bread, not in the other qualities, nor in the substance; and therefore not pertaining to anything that I have spoken. For the question is of leavened or unleavened bread, not of roundness or squareness, &c. Although the form and figure also is indifferent, and in the power of the Church to appoint; wherefore there may no schism or division in the church be made for it." (*Ib.*)

Once more, T. C. had argued:—

"Besides that, we be called by the example of our Saviour Christ to use in the supper usual and common bread; for what time our

Saviour Christ celebrated his supper there was no other bread to be gotten but unleavened bread, there being a strait charge given by the law, that there should be then no leavened bread; and it is not to be doubted but that, if there had been then when he celebrated his supper, as at other times, nothing but leavened bread, he would not have caused unleavened bread to have been made for that purpose of celebrating his supper." (*Ib.* p. 86.)

To this Whitgift urges in his " Defence " :—

"It was not usual bread, but properly appointed for the celebrating of the passover, and then to be used, and not otherwise usually and commonly; for their usual and common bread was leavened; wherefore this maketh against you; and if you will have the commandments that appertain to the eating of the passover perpetual, and to be referred to the celebrating of the Lord's supper, as, by that precept 2 Chron. xxxv., before alleged, it seemeth you would, then must we make it a matter of necessity to have unleavened bread: but, as that is untrue, so is this also; for the kind of bread is indifferent, although (as M. Bucer saith) it cometh nearer to the institution of Christ to use unleavened bread, because he did celebrate his supper with it, if there were not other circumstances and reasons to move the church sometimes to use the contrary." (*Ib.*)

The Rubric of 1662 combines the object of the Rubric of 1549, viz., "the avoiding of all matters and occasion of dis-"sension," and the object of the Rubrics of 1552, 1559, and 1604, viz., "to take away the superstition," as to the Sacramental Bread: unless, then, " superstition " is a lesser evil than " dissension," or is not a cause of it, Whitgift's words may be reasonably urged as proving that Wafer-bread is, to say the very least, not *excluded* by the language of the present Rubric: that the use of Wafer-bread was retained in the Chapel Royal, St. James's, nineteen years after Whitgift wrote, is plain from the following account of Queen Elizabeth's Communion on Easter day, April 15, 1593, recorded in the "Cheque-Book" from which extracts have already been given at pp. 235-36. I have put in *Italics* the words which describe the Bread then used.

Aprill 15 "The Princelye comminge of her Majestie to the Holy
Estreday Communion at Estre [Easter].
1593. The moste sacred Queene Elizabethe upon Estre day, after the Holy Gospell was redd in the Chaple at St. James, came downe into her Majestes Travess: beffore her highness came the gentle-

men pencioners, then the Barons, the Bushopps, London and Landaffe, the Erls, and the ho: Councell in their colors of State, the Harolds at Arms, the Lord Keeper bearinge the Great Seal himselfe, and the Erle of Herefford bearinge the sword beffore her Majestie. Then her Majesties Royal person came moste chearfully, havinge as noble supporters the Right Honorable the Erle of Essex, Master of her Majestes Horse, on the right hande, and the Right Hon. the Lord Admyral on the lefte hand, the Lord Chambrelen to her Majestie (also nexte beffore her Majeste) attendante al the while. Dr. Bull was at the organ playinge the Offertorye. Her Majestie entred her travess moste devoutly, there knyelinge: after some prayers she came princely beffore the Table, and there humbly knielinge did offer the golden obeysant, the Bushop the hon. Father of Worcester holdinge the golden bason, the Subdean and the Epistler in riche coaps assistante to the sayd Bushop: which done her Majestie retorned to her princely travess sumptuously sett forthe, untyl the present action of the Holy Communion, contynually exercysed in ernest prayer, and then the blessed Sacrament first receyved of the sayd Bushop and administred to the Subdean, the gospeller for that day, and to the Epistler, her sacred person presented her selfe beffore the Lord's Table, Royally attended as beffore, where was sett a stately stoole and qwssians [cushions] for her Majestie, and so humbly knielinge with most singuler devocion and holye reverence dyd most comfortablye receyve the most blessed Sacramente of Christes bodye and blood, in the kinds of bread and wyne, *according to the laws established by her Majestie and Godly laws in Parliament. The bread beinge waffer bread of some thicker substance,* which her Majestie in most reverend manner toke of the Lord Bushop in her naked right hand, her setisfyed hert fixinge her semblant eyes most entirely uppon the woorthye words Sacramental pronounced by the Bushop, &c. that with soche an holye aspecte as it did mightelye adde comfforts to the godlye beholders (wherof this writer was one very neare): and likewise her Majestie receaved the cuppe, havinge a moste princely lynned clothe layd on her cushion pillowe and borne at the four ends by the noble Erle of Herefford, the Erle of Essex, the Erle of Worcester, and the Erle of Oxford: the side of the sayd clothe her Majestie toke up in her hande, and therewith toke the ffoote of the golden and nowe sacred cuppe, and with like holy reverend attention as beffore to the sacramentaon words, did drinke of the same most devoutly (all this while knielinge on her knies) to the confirmation of her faythe and absolute comfforte in her purged conscience by the holy spirit of God in the exercise of this holye Communion, of her participation of and in the merits and deathe of Christe Jesus our Lorde, and the perfecte communion and spiritual ffoode of the very bodye and bloode of Christe our Lord Saviour: and so retoringe to her sayd Travess their devoutly stayed the end of prayers, which done her Majestie Royally ascended the way and stayrs into her presence, whom the Lord bless for ever and ever. Amen.

Ant. Anderson, Subdean.   [f. 14b.]" p. 150.

It is at least fair matter of opinion whether the use of Sacramental Breads impressed with some Sacred Symbol—the practice of the Greek no less than of the Latin Communion—has any "superstition"* attached to it which requires "restraint:" yet, supposing it to be so, their Lordships, in arguing that "if "the Rubric were the only restraint" upon practice "it is

---

* Bp. Cosin, Notes 1st Series (*Works*, p. 130) has the following :—
"*And, to take away superstition, it shall suffice that the bread be as usual.*] Survey, Exc. 26, p. 79."
The Title of the Book to which Cosin refers is the following, and the passage which he mentions connects the "superstition" as to Wafer Bread with a Doctrinal view of either Transubstantiation or Consubstantiation : the passage also proves the use of "Wafer-cakes" at that time " at Westminster."

"A Survey of the Booke of Common Prayer, by way *of* 197 *Queres grounded upon* 58 *places*, ministring iust matter of question, with a view of *London* Ministers exceptions. All humbly propounded, *That* They may be syncerely answered : *Or els* Offences Religiously remoued.
1 Cor. 4. 19. 20. I will come to you shortly if the Lord will, and will know, not the wordes of them that are puffed vp, but the power. For the Kingdome of God is not in word, but in power.
Anno Dni 1606."

Rub. a com. sect. 5.	"26. And to take away the superstition which any person hath, or might haue in the Bread and Wine, it shall suffice, that the Bread be such as is vsuall at the Table with other meates.
Quær. 71.	Quære. *Whither any person haue not, or may haue superstition in kneeling in the very acte of receiving, as well as in a wafer cake.*
Induc. 1.	Seeing it is not knowne that supirstitious persons had, or haue superstition in the wafer cake, as it is a wafer cake, more then in wine, as it is wine, but only as they were consecrated, and transubstantiated, or consubstantiated ; whereas *kneeling* it selfe, is the principall part of their superstition.
2.	Seeing Christ ministred the Communion in vnleauened bread, whereas *kneeling* in the very acte of receiving came from Antichrist with transubstantiation, vid. Q 60. and

" difficult to see how either dissension or superstition would be
" taken away," seem to have overlooked the bearing of two
other Rubrics upon the Rubric in question: one of these directs
that " The Bread and Wine for the Communion shall be pro-
" vided by the Curate and Churchwardens, at the charges of the
" Parish," the other empowers the " Ordinary" to decide upon
the disposal of " the money given at the Offertory " if " the
" Minister and Churchwardens" should " disagree" about it.
So that if there were " occasion of dissension or superstition "
touching the Sacramental Bread provided " at the charges of
" the Parish," whether through the Offertory or otherwise,
some " restraint " could be exercised ; and this consideration,
apart from the evidence which has been adduced as to the
meaning of " it shall suffice," is a reason for respectfully
differing from their Lordships who are " inclined to think on
" this ground alone that the Rubric contains a positive direction
" to employ at the Holy Communion the usual bread."

3.	Seeing there is no inquisition either after ministring in Wafer cakes or not kneeling in th' action of prayer as there is after not kneeling in the very acte of receiving, vid. Q. 57.
Quær. 72.	Quære. *Whither it may not be supposed that the State doth not directly command kneeling in the very acte of receiving.*
Induc. 1.	Seeing it not only leaveth out that section which immediately goeth before this in 5. E. where it is said, *that it is ordained in the booke of common prayer, that communicants kneeling, should receyve,* as is said, Quæres 56 and 79. But also, to prevent superstition that may be in any person, it prescribeth vsual bread
k Rub. a. com. se. 4.	(k) whereas in 2. E. round vnleavened cakes be prescribed for the communio. The premises considred.
Quæe. 73.	Quaere. *Whither it be not as great an offence to minister the communion in wafer cakes, which they do at Westminster, as to minister to people, that do not kneele in the act of receyuing, Except either superstition agree better with collegiat then parish Churches, or the Prelates intend to advaunce superstition in all places by piece-meale."* (*pp.* 79-81.)

XLV. The Judicial Committee next advance another objection to Wafer-Bread, drawn from what occurred at the Revision of 1661; they say:—

> "It is at least worthy of notice that when Cosin and others at the last revision desired to insert the words making the wafer also lawful, these words were rejected."

But to put the case thus is somewhat misleading; for the inference would be very natural—that "the Wafer" was not considered "lawful" either by those who proposed or by those who rejected the words referred to: this, however, is not borne out by the evidence on the subject. Cosin's own opinion is plainly given in the following passage:—

"*And to take away superstition, it shall suffice that the bread be such as is usual to be eaten*]. It is not here commanded that no unleavened or wafer bread be used, but it is said only 'that the other bread shall suffice.' So that though there was no necessity, yet there was a liberty still reserved of using wafer-bread, which was continued in divers churches of the kingdom, and Westminster for one, till the 17th of King Charles. [*Editor's Note—i.e.* till 1643].

"The first use of the common bread was begun by Farel and Viret at Geneva, 1538, which so offended the people there, and their neighbours at Lausanne and Berne, (who had called a synod about it) that both Farel and Viret, and Calvin and all, were banished for it from the town, where afterwards the wafer-bread being restored, Calvin thought fit to continue it, and so it is at this day. *Vid. Vitam Calvini per Bezam, ad. an.* 1538, *et. Ep. Calv.*[k]" (*Notes*, 3rd *Series Works* V. Ang. Cath. Lib. p. 481.)

So again, in his "Particulars to be considered, explained, and "corrected, in the Book of Common Prayer,"[a] he says:—

Editor's Note. "[k] [The statement in Beza's Life is that common bread was in use at Geneva, but not at Berne, and that in the year 1538, the Bernese calling a Synod at Lausanne, ordered the use of wafers at Geneva; that Calvin and his friends were, on refusing to celebrate, expelled from Geneva by the civil magistrates; that afterwards they agreed to use wafers, and returned.—See Joannis Calvini Vita, a Th. Beza, ad. ann. 1538, prefixed to the firstvolume of his works, Amsterd. 1671.]"

Editor's Note. "[a] [These observations, contained in several leaves, are bound up at the end of the interleaved Book of Common Prayer of 1619, in which the first series of notes is written, but the handwriting is of a later hand than the notes themselves. They were printed by Nichols at the end of the additional notes, p. 67, with the following notice:—'Whether or no these following obser-

" 64. In the next rubric it is said, that at the Communion 'it shall suffice, that the bread be such as is usual to be eaten, so it be the best and purest that may be gotten.' It is questioned here, whether by virtue of this order any Church is restrained from their custom of using wafers at the sacrament, as in Westminster, and many other places, they have been always wont to do. To avoid dispute and contention herein, an order would be annexed for that purpose." *Editor's Note.* "[Cosin suggested this, and the bishops allowed it, but it was not passed.]" (*Ibid.* p. 518.)

Cosin's proposed alteration of the Rubric was in these words:—

" . . . . . . it shall suffice that the Bread shall be such as is usuall, yet the best and purest wheat bread that conveniently may be gotten, though wafer Bread, pure and without any figure, shall not be forbidden, especially in such Churches where it hath bin accustomed. The Wine also shalbe of the best and purest that may be had." (*Cosin Correspondence*, Vol. II. p. 62.)

Bp. Wren, who was one of the Committee of the Upper House of Convocation appointed in 1661 to revise the Prayer Book, makes the following remark:—

"Ibidem . . . . in the Bread and Wine, it shall suffice that the Bread, *where it is not of fine Wafer, pure, and without any figure or print*, be such as is usual to be eaten &c.

"This would be put thus, because in some places, (at Westminster, if I remember aright, and elsewhere) plain Wafers have ever been used." (*Fragmentary Illustrations of the Book of Common Prayer, from Manuscript Sources.* Edited by William Jacobson, D.D., Bishop of Chester, *London*, Murray, 1874, p. 84.)

Bishop Wren was one of the Bishops to whom the SCOTCH vations were drawn up by Dr. Cosins before the restoration of King Charles, or afterwards upon the last review of the C. P., I cannot say; but this is plain that those reviewers had very great regard to these remarks, they having altered most things according as was therein desired. And it is probable, that they were laid before the board, Bishop Cosin being one of the principal commissioners.'

"The handwriting, however, is of a much earlier period of Cosin's life, and the observation No. 30, shews that they were made in the reign of Charles I., as does their tone throughout. It appears, however, from additions in a later hand, that Cosin retained and improved this paper, and it is by no means improbable that he made use of it in 1661. Most of the alterations set down here as required were suggested by Cosin in his proposed changes of the Prayer-Book, (See the end of the Preface to this volume,) and almost all were adopted. The observations refer to the Prayer-Books as commonly printed with many typographical errors in the reign of Charles I. The marginal notes indicating the alterations made in 1662 are Dr. Nichols', here reprinted.]" *Ibid.* p. 502.

LITURGY of 1637 had been submitted before its publication;[*] that Office Book, which certainly was not designed to be materially at variance with the English Prayer Book, recognized distinctly the use of Wafer Bread in the parenthetical words of the following Rubric:—

"And to take away the superstition which any person hath or might have in the bread and wine, (though it be lawful to have wafer bread) it shall suffice that the Bread be such as is usual: yet the best and purest wheat bread that conveniently may be gotten."

These passages shew that their Authors did not consider the Wafer-bread to be *unlawful*, but that "to avoid dispute and "contention herein," as Cosin said, they wished to remove the doubt which had been raised as to the *restraining* power of the Rubric; and at the same time to *secure* the liberty of choice which they understood that Rubric to afford. The Court says that the "words" which they proposed for this purpose "were "rejected;" but this is no proof that their interpretation of the Rubric was accounted wrong or that their object was opposed. It is said, indeed, of Cosin's suggested alteration that "the

---

[*] Mr. Keeling, in the Preface (p. v.) to his "Liturgiæ Britannicæ," London, 1851, has the following Note upon this Book—"This Liturgy was framed by the Scottish Bishops; and submitted, by the King's command, to the review of Laud, Archbishop of Canterbury, Juxon, Bishop of London, and Wren, Bishop of Norwich.—*Collier's Eccl. Hist. vol.* 8, p. 113, 8vo. Ed.

"Upon the application of the Bishops of Scotland for a Liturgy for that Church, it was the opinion of Abp. Laud (to use his own words) that, 'if his Majesty would have a Liturgy settled there, it were best to take the English Liturgy without any variation, that so the same Service-book might be established in all his Majesty's Dominions . . . . His Majesty inclined to my opinion, to have the English Service without any alteration to be established there; and in this conclusion I held that business for two, if not three, years at least. Afterwards, the Scottish Bishops still pressing his Majesty that a Liturgy framed by themselves, and in some few things different from ours, would relish better with their countrymen, they at last prevailed with his Majesty to have it so, and carried it against me, notwithstanding all I could say or do to the contrary. Then his Majesty commanded me to give the Bishops of Scotland my best assistance in this way and work. I delayed as much as I could with my obedience; and when nothing would serve but it must go on, I confess I was then very serious, and gave them the best help I could. But wheresoever I had any doubt, I did not only acquaint his Majesty with it, but writ down most of the amendments or alterations in his Majesty's presence. And I do verily believe there is no one thing in that Book, which may not stand with the conscience of a right-good Protestant. Sure I am his Majesty approved them all; and I have his warrant under his Royal Hand for all that I did about that Book.'—*Hist. of the Troubles and Trial of Abp. Laud. Wrote by himself during his imprisonment in the Tower,* pp. 168, 169."

"Bishops allowed it, but it was not passed;" this *allowance* is a witness for Cosin's view of the Rubric: its having been "not "passed" (or, as the Court says, its having been "rejected") need not imply an opposite view in the minds of those who did not assent to the proposal: their dissent probably arose from the feeling that the alteration might provoke complaints and that therefore it was best to leave the Rubric as it was, seeing that it gave a discretionary use and that in the King's Warrant for the Savoy Conference there was a direction for "avoiding, "as much as may be, all unnecessary alterations of the forms and "liturgy wherewith the people are already acquainted, and have "so long received in the Church of England." (*Cardwell Hist. Conf.* p. 300.) The experience of the Ritual Commission may fairly be referred to in confirmation of the probability of this view: several times it happened that after long discussions upon a Rubric, which it was thought might be made plainer or which was deemed to need alteration, the various suggestions were either negatived or withdrawn on the ground that, between the advantages of change and the risks of leaving ancient Rubrics as they were, it was the safer course to make no alterations.

XLVI. The Court next turns to another source of information in order to ascertain the meaning of the Rubric; the Judgment says:—

> "But their Lordships attach greater weight to the exposition of this rubric furnished by the history of the question. From a large collection of Visitation Articles, from the time of Charles II it is clear that the best and purest wheat bread was to be provided for the Holy Communion, and no other kind of bread. They believe that from that time till about 1840 the practice of using the usual wheat bread was universal."

The Visitation Articles here referred to are, I presume, those published in the 2nd Report of the Ritual Commission, from which quotations are previously made in the Judgment: as the Inquiries are dispersed through 80 pages, and none of them are specified by the Court, it will be convenient to collect them here; they are as follows:—

1662. Cosin (Bp. of Durham), VII. 6.—"Do you against the time of every holy Communion appointed in your Church or Chappel, provide a sufficient quantity of fine white bread, and of good Wine, according to the advice and direction given you by your Minister for the number of Communicants?" (2 *Rit. Report*, p. 603.)

1662. [Earle?] (Bp. of Worcester), VII. 5.—"Do you provide fine White-Bread and good Wine against every Communion, according to the number of Communicants?" (*Ib.* 606.)

1662. Morley (Bp. of Winchester), VII. 6.—"Do you against every Communion appointed in your Church or Chappel, provide a sufficient quantity of fine white Bread, and of good Wine, according to the number of Communicants?" (*Ib.* 619.)

1662. Pory (Archn. of Middlesex), 14.—"Is the Bread provided for the Holy Sacrament of the Lord's Supper, of the best and purest white-bread that may conveniently be gotten . . . . ?" (*Ib.* 626.)

 3.—"Do you against the time of every Communion, at the charge of the Parish provide a sufficient quantity of fine white bread, and of good and wholesome wine, for the number of the Communicants? . . . ." (*Ib.* 630.)

₊ These Articles of Cosin, Earle, Morley, and Pory, are *before* the Book of 1662.

1662. Hacket (Bp. of Lichfield), VIII.—". . . And have they [the Churchwardens] provided such fine white Bread, and good Wine, as was fit for the Sacrament, according to advice taken with the Minister?" (*Ib.* 610.)

1662. Ironside (Bp. of Bristol), I.—". . . And doth the Churchwardens provide a sufficient quantity of Bread and Wine for the same [Sacrament]?" (*Ib.* p. 614.)

1662. Layfield (Archn. of Essex), 2.—"Whether the Churchwardens doe provide against every Communion with the advice of the Minister, a sufficient quantity of fine white Bread, and of good and wholesome Wine for the number of the Communicants that shall receive? . . . ." (*Ib.* 623.)

1670. Hammond (Archn. of Huntingdon), IV. 2.—"Do they [the Churchwardens] against every Communion appointed in your Church or Chappel provide a sufficient quantity of fine white Bread, and of good Wine, according to the number of Communicants?" (*Ib.* 638.)

1671. Fuller (Bp. of Lincoln), VIII. 6.—"Can. 20. Do they [the Churchwardens] against every Communion provide a sufficient quantity of fine White-Bread, and of good Wine, according to the number of Communicants?" (*Ib.* 642.)

1679. Gunning (Bp. of Ely), 3.—"Rubrick. Can. 20. 3. Do you the Churchwardens against every Communion provide a sufficient quantity of fine white Bread, and good and wholesome Wine according to the number of the Communicants? . . ." (*Ib.* 650.)

1683. Fielding (Archn. of Dorset), 2.—". . . And do the Churchwardens provide a sufficient quantity of Bread and Wine for the same [Sacrament], as by the 20, 21, 22 Canons is required?" (*Ib.* 652.)

1686. Sancroft (Abp. of Canterbury) for Lincoln, as Metropolitan, VIII. 6.—"Do they [the Churchwardens] against every Communion appointed in your Church or Chapel, provide a sufficient quantity of fine white Bread, and of good Wine, according to the number of Communicants, at the Parish-charge?" (*Ib.* 656.)

1692. Ironside (Bp. of Hereford), 2.—"Rubr. Can. 20. Do they [the Churchwardens] against every Communion provide Bread and Wine at the Parish charges, ..." (*Ib.* 659.)

1701. Strafford (Bp. of Chester), VII. 3.—"7th Rubric after the Communion and Can. 20. Do they [the Churchwardens] provide against every Communion appointed in your Church or Chapel a sufficient quantity of fine white Bread, and good Wine, at the Charges of the Parish?" (*Ib.* 661.)

1710. Fleetwood (Bp. of St. Asaph), III. 3.—"Is fine White-Bread, and wholesome Wine provided against every Communion, according to the number of the Communicants, by the Curate and Churchwardens at the Charges of the Parish?" (*Ib.* 672.) The Bishop forbids the continuance of a Custom "in some places in this Diocese . . . that the Minister should be put to provide Bread and Wine for all the Communicants at Easter."

1716. Trimnell (Bp. of Norwich), VII. 3.—"Rubrick after Communion. Do they [the Churchwardens] provide against every Communion appointed in your Church or Chapel, a sufficient quantity of fine White Bread, and good Wine, according to the number of the Communicants, at the Charge of the Parish?" (*Ib.* 679.)

1728. Stanley (Archn. of London), VII. 3.—". . . . Do they [the Churchwardens] take care against every Communion-Day to provide a sufficient quantity of fine white Bread, and wholesome Wine for the Communicants, as in the Rubric to that Service is directed and required . . .?" (*Ib.* 681.)

Now it is certain that Abp. Sancroft and Bp. Cosin held Wafer-Bread to be lawful; yet the Inquiry in their Articles is for "fine white bread"—the very words which are used in *twelve* out of the *sixteen* other Visitation Articles. It cannot, surely, be said of Cosin and Sancroft that their Articles make "it clear" that "no other kind of Bread," except "the "best and purest Wheat-Bread" was to be provided for "the "Holy Communion;" and it can hardly be reasonably doubted that they would, if asked, have repudiated such an interpretation of their language. Unless, therefore, there is other evidence to show that the Authors of the rest of the Visitation Articles designed to exclude Wafer-Bread, I venture to contend that such an intention cannot be proved from their questions: they contain no expression or indication of a *negative* character; and the term "fine white Bread" shews that a *special* kind of Bread was meant to be provided; moreover, there is nothing whatever to shew that this Bread was to be limited in *size* or *shape* to ordinary Loaf-Bread; on the contrary, the absence of the Rubrical term "usual" may have had the object and the effect of procuring this "fine white Bread" in a more convenient *form* than ordinary Bread. Their Lordships "believe" that for 180 years " till about 1840 the practice of using the usual "wheat bread was universal:" it seems to me that for the first 68 years of this period, namely down to the date (1728) of the latest Visitation Articles to which they refer, the natural inference from those Articles would be that "the usual wheat "bread" was not employed, at least if the *practice* was conformable to the *demand* of the Articles. It may, often, not have been so; and no doubt the custom of the greater part of this Nineteenth Century would go very far to prove the general use of ordinary Wheaten Bread for the Sacrament: but to claim that use as the legitimate interpreter of a Rubrical expression to which Ecclesiastical Authorities, contemporaneous with its first introduction in 1552, have given the opposite meaning, seems to me a false Canon of Exposition.

Moreover, in the Collection of Visitation Articles published by the Ritual Commission, there are also 24 instances, ranging from 1605 to 1638, in which the same expression—"fine white "bread"—occurs: among the Authors of these Articles are Andrewes, Laud, and Wren whose opinions are known to have been in favour of the Lawfulness of Wafer-bread (See Wren's, p. 312); it will hardly be pretended that in their questions they meant it to be understood that "no other kind of bread" than "the best and purest wheat bread" might be "provided"; and, therefore, it is highly improbable that the Archbishops, Bishops, and Archdeacons "who issued the other Articles" designed to take an opposite course. This conclusion is strengthened by the fact that in one instance only, among the Articles published by the Ritual Commission, are there any words prohibitory, apparently, of Wafer-bread : though, indeed, the language is equally adverse to ordinary Bread; Overton, Bp. of Lichfield, 1584, gives the following direction :—

"7. Item that the ordinance of the Booke of Common Praier bee from henceforth obserued in this, that the Bread deliuered to the Communicants, be such as is vsual to be eaten at the Table with other meats, yet of the purest and finest Wheat : and no other bread to be vsed by the Minister, nor to be prouided for by the Churchwardens and Parishners then such finest common bread." (2nd *Rit. Report* p. 430.)

There are eight other instances in this Collection of Visitation Articles where the question as to the Communion Bread varies from the term "fine white bread; " they are these :—

1563. Parker (Abp. of Canterbury), 5.—"Item, whether they [your Prestes, Curates, or Ministers] do vse to minister the communion in wafer bread, according vnto the Queenes Maiesties Injunctions, or in common bread." (*Ib.* 403.) *

1571. Grindal (Abp. of York), 4.—". . . And the Churchwardens also shal from time to time, at the charges of the Parish, provide bread and wine for the communion . . ." (*Ib.* 413.)

1575. Parker (Abp. of Canterbury), 17.—". . . Whether they [your Parsons and Vicars] . . . minister the holy Communion in wafer bread or common bread. . ." (*Ib.* 416.)

1608. Jagon (Archn. of Norfolk), 7.—". . . if the churchwardens prouide not sufficient bread and wine for the communion. . . ." (*Ib.* 457.)

1620. Harsnet (Bp. of Norwich), 9. 4.—"Item, whether haue the Church-wardens at euery Communion prouided sufficient Bread and Wine for the Communicants, . . ." (*Ib.* 487.)

1624. Kent (Archn. of Surrey), 4.—"Doe the Church-wardens (with the aduice of the Minister) prouide bread and wine for the communicants, . . . ? " (*Ib.* 493.)

1638. Duppa (Bp. of Chichester), 6.—"Is the bread and wine of the best sort . . . ? " *Ib.* 5, 7.)

1638. Mountagu (Bp. of Norwich), 7. 11—"Is the bread and wine of the best sort, fine, clean, sweet, not musty, or unsauoury . . . ? " (*Ib.* 584.)

* The Return to Secretary CECIL, Feb. 14, 1564–5, in Answer to Parker's Inquiries as to the Varieties in the Public Services, shews that this difference of use continued; it says :—" Some with unleavened bread, and some with leavened." Strype remarks, "He might have added, some with common manchet bread." (*Strype's Parker*, fol. 152, *or*, 8°. Vol. II. 302.) "MANCHET. A small loaf of fine bread." (*Imperial Dictionary*, 1851.)

And in the Return from Canterbury Cathedral, 1564, it is stated that—" For the ministering of the Communion we use bread appointed by the Queen's Highness Injunctions." (*Ib.* fol. 183, *or*, 8°. Vol. I. 365.)

Two of these Inquiries, Abp. Parker's, undoubtedly recognize the lawfulness of Wafer-bread : a third, Grindal's, furnishes no description of the Bread, but cannot justly be thought to exclude Wafer-bread, seeing that, when Bp. of London, it "was "so appointed by" his and Parker's "order," as they "took it, "not disagreeable to the Injunctions." (See p. 296): of the other five it may certainly be said—that they do not afford the slightest reason for supposing their Authors to have held that Wafer-bread was then illegal, or even that they objected to the use of it on any other ground.

XLVII. From the Visitation Articles their Lordships turn to the Canons of 1604, remarking that:—

> "The words of the 20th Canon, to which the Visitation Articles refer, point the same way. The churchwardens are bound to supply 'wheaten bread,' and this alone is mentioned. If wafer bread is equally permitted, or the special cakes of Edward VI.'s first Book and of the injunctions, it is hard to see why the parish is to supply wheaten bread, in cases where wafers are to be supplied by the minister or from some other source. And if wafers were to be in use, a general injunction to all churchwardens to supply wheaten bread, would be quite inapplicable to all churches where there would be another usage.'"

Probably most persons reading this passage would consider that the words "wheaten bread" are a quotation from the Canon, whereas they are a slight variation of the words "Wheat "Bread" used in the Rubric: the words of the Canon are "fine "white bread;" and this term, no doubt, is either referred to or mentioned in most of the Visitation Articles, whether after the date of the Canon or after the date of the present Prayer Book. I think it has already been proved that the description of the Bread given in the Canon cannot be correctly construed as opposed to, much less excluding, the use of wafer bread. Their Lordships seem to assume that "wafer bread" or the "un- "leavened and round" "bread" of the First Prayer Book, or "the common fine bread . . . formed plain" and "round," according to the Injunction, are, none of them, equivalent to the "fine white bread" of the Canon, or "the best and purest wheat "bread" of the Rubric; whereas the *quality* of all three was meant to be, and most probably was, very much more in accordance with the directions both of Rubric and Canon, than is "the usual wheat bread" which the Court "inclined to think" is "a positive direction" of "the Rubric," and did also "believe" to have been "universal" in practice" from 1660 "till about 1840." If then, "Wafer bread" is, as it is, "fine "white" "wheaten bread," though *unleavened*, it fulfils the requirements of both the Rubric and the Canon; and, therefore, it is but an imaginary difficulty advanced by the Court, when it finds it "hard to see why the parish is to supply wheaten "bread, in cases where wafers are to be supplied by the minister "or from some other source:" neither Rubric nor Canon suggests any such conflict of duties. The Rubric orders that "the "Bread and Wine for the Communion shall be provided by "the Curate and the Churchwardens, at the Charges of the "Parish"—a direction which clearly points to concurrent action between the Minister and these Parochial Officers: the Canon has the same object, it says—"The Churchwardens of "every Parish, against the time of every Communion, shall at "the charge of the Parish, with the advice and direction of the "Minister, provide a sufficient quantity of fine white Bread, "and of good and wholesom Wine for the number of Commu- "nicants that shall from time to time receive there: ..." The Court considers that this "general injunction . . . would be "quite inapplicable to all churches where there should be "another usage" namely of "Wafers:" but this view, again, overlooks the *joint action* directed in the Rubric and more particularly defined in the Canon, where the "advice" of the Minister seems to refer to the *description* of Bread to be provided; and his "direction," to the "quantity" needed, of which indeed he is assumed to be the judge, as being supposed to know how many persons are likely to communicate. That the Canon does not contemplate the use of what the Court calls "the usual "wheat bread," is a reasonable inference not only from its direction that the Bread is to be "fine white," but also from the order to "provide" it "against the time of every Commu- nion"—an order very needless if time was not required for preparing it; because, ordinarily at least, Bread "such as is "usual to be eaten" could readily be obtained.*

Their Lordships hold rightly, as it seems to me, that the Canon and the Rubric mean the same thing: but they, wrongly, as I venture to think, allege that both exclude Wafer-Bread and therefore its provision by the Churchwardens: they hold, moreover, that the present Rubric is substantially the same as the Rubrics of 1552, 1559, and 1604 (See p. 282): the following extracts which were sent to me two years ago from the Parish Registers of Eltham, Kent, are instances (by no means uncommon probably) of the provision of Wafer-bread "at the "Charges of the Parish."

1579. Item paid unto John Bonner for Wafers for the Communion vj$d$.
Item paid for a boxe to put in ye Communion bread iiij$d$.
1580. For wafer bread for the Communion ij$d$.

These Extracts are the more pertinent because they not only shew that "Wafers" were considered to be "*Bread*," but they give the three names by which this description of the Sacramental Bread was commonly known, viz. (1) Wafers (2) Communion Bread (3) Wafer-bread. It may, possibly, be objected that this provision of Wafer-bread was made when the Injunction was in force and that the Court held it to be "a super-"seding of the Rubric;" but, as already pointed out (See p. 297) Abp. Parker, who was responsible for both, did not so regard the matter and in fact considered the Wafer-bread of the Injunction to be the Rule, rather than the Exception, of the Rubric.

---

* The following occurrence sustains the inference above stated. "There happened also in the town of Tadlow a very ill accident on Christmas day, 1638, by reason of not having the Communion-table railed in, that it might be kept from profanations. For in Sermon time a dog came to the Table, and took the loaf of Bread prepared for the Holy Sacrament, in his mouth, and ran away with it. Some of the parishioners took the same from the dog, and set it again upon the Table. After Sermon, the Minister could not think fit to consecrate this bread: and other fit for the Sacrament was not to be had in that town; and the day so far spent, that they could not send for it to another town: so there was no Communion. And this was presented by four sworn men of the town aforesaid." (*Laud's Works*, V. pt. ii. p. 367. Oxford, 1853.)

This appears to be the occurrence mentioned by Bp. Wren who describes the Bread as *white*, saying, "they could have no Communion that day, there being not another Loaf of white-Bread in the Town, except that which the Dog had defiled." (*Parentalia*, p. 76). Tadlow was in the Diocese of Ely.

That the Privy Council at this period held Wafer-Bread to be lawful is clear from the following Documents which are given in Peck's "Desiderata Curiosa." London, 1732.

JULY 26, 1580. No. XVII. p. 15.

"*The Lords and others of the Council to* William Chaderton, *Lord Bp. of Chester, thanking him for his great Pains and Care in the Execution of his Trust as one of the Queen's High Commissioners in* Lancashire; *and exhorting him always to consult his brother Commissioner* Henry Stanley *Earl of* Darby. *And whereas the People in those Parts had a great Dispute about the Bread for the Holy Sacrament (whether it should be common Bread, or of the Wafer Sort?) that either should be severally allowed as every Parish liked best, till the Parliament take further Order. With a word or two about Fairs and Mercats on the Lord's day.*" "July 26. 1580. 22 Eliz. M.S. Chaderton, fol. 32. b."

After exhorting him "to see those Countryes under your Charge speedilie purged of that dangerous Infection of Poperie" they say :—

"3. And where [as] your Lordshippe desireth to be resolved, from us, touchinge two speciall Points worthy of Reformation; thone, for the Lords Supper, with Wafers, or with common Bread? and the other, touchinge Faires and Marketts kept upon the Saboth Daies (the Remedie of both which we thinke meete to referre unto the next session of Parliament, where the necessarie Reformation of them is onlie to be had) in the mean Time, for the Appeasinge of such Division and Bitterness as doth and maie aryse of the Use of both these Kinds of Bread, we thinke yt meete,

"4. That in such Parishes as doe use the common Bread, and in others that embrase the Wafer, they be severallie continued as they are at this present. Untill which Time alsoe your Lordshippe is to be carefull, accordinge to youre good Discretion, to perswade and procure a Quietnes amongst such as shall strive for the publique Maintaininge ether of thone or thother: whereof we hope youre Lordshippe will take Care, as appertaineth.

"5. We bid your Lordshipp right hartie farewell. From the Court at Ottlands, the XXVI of *Julye*, 1580.

"*Youre Lordshippe's verey lovinge Frends,*

T. Bromley,	Canc.	F. Bedford.	Chr. Hatton.
W. Burgheley.		Ro. Lecester.	Fra. Walsingham.
E. Lincolne.		James Croft.	John Wilson.
T. Sussex.			

"To our verie good Lord, the Lord Bishop of *Chester*."

The Council here, while advising that the use of both kinds of Bread should be allowed, distinctly states that the "necessarie Reformation" of the existing Divisions on the matter "is onlie to be had" in "Parliament;" and their Lordships say the same "touching Faires Markets kept upon the Saboth

"Daies"—shewing plainly that, in their view, both the one and the other were alike authorized by the Law of the Land. That Law—viz. the Rubric of 1559 relating to the Bread—has not since been substantially changed, though its wording was slightly altered in Convocation and authorized by " Parliament" in 1662 : consequently, if the Privy Council rightly held, in 1580, that Wafer-Bread was then lawful; the Judicial Committee of the Privy Council wrongly held, in 1871, that Wafer-Bread is now unlawful. Their Lordships afterwards wrote :—

AUGUST 21, 1580. No. xx. p. 18.

"Wm. *Lord* Burghley and *Sir* Francis Walsingham *to* Wm. Chaderton *Lord Bp. of* Chester . . . . . *wishing him to indulge the Sticklers for Wafer Bread in that Particular, they being as yet Children in* Christ, and therefore rather *to be fed with Milk than strong Meat.*

"Concerninge the last Pointe of youre Letter, contained in a Postscript, wherebie appereth that some are troubled aboute the Substance of the Communion Bread: yt were good to teach them, that are weake in conscience, in esteeming of the Wafer Bread; not to make Difference. But yf there Weakness continue, yt were not amisse, in our Opinions, charitabley to tollerate them, as Children, with Milk. Which we refer to youre Lordshipps better Consideration.

". . . From the Court at Otlands, the XXI. of Aug. 1580."

Here, again, the Privy Council evidently felt that they had no authority to forbid the Wafer-Bread : but they treated the use of it as a " weakness " on the part of those who contended for it : it would be interesting to know what their Royal Mistress may have thought of their Lordship's decision, if she knew of it, to "tolerate" the advocates of Wafer-Bread " as " Children, with Milk," seeing that she herself was Communicated with it in 1593, nearly thirteen years later, and in her old age. (See p. 308.)

The Court thus concludes its examination of the Charge against Mr. Purchas of using " wafer bread, being bread made "in the special shape and fashion of circular wafers, instead of " bread such as is usual to be eaten " :—

" Upon the whole their Lordships think that the law of the Church has directed the use of pure wheat bread, and they must so advise Her Majesty."

Yet, unless " pure wheat bread " is "bread such as is usual to "be eaten"—a proposition which may well be doubted—the Court advised the Queen "that the law of the Church" is something different from what the Prosecution alleged it to be: though, in doing so, their Lordships used words which are not to be found in the Rubric or the Canon : the Rubric says "the "best and purest Wheat Bread that conveniently may be gotten" and the Canon says "fine white Bread": whether " pure "wheat bread" is the equivalent of either term, is certainly open to question: that it combines both terms, can hardly be affirmed : but, even assuming that their Lordships' expression defines with sufficient accuracy what "the Church has directed" it is not disrespectful to the Court to hold that (Wafers being *pure wheat bread**) the " shape" of the " bread " complained of could not really be an infraction of "the law" which prescribes, as the Court says "the use of pure wheat bread."

It was not necessary for the Promoter of this Suit to allege that the use of Wafer-bread is a Popish Custom, as well as an infraction of the Law of the Church of England ; but, that he would have been ready so to declare, is not in the least an uncharitable assumption: had he done so the Court might not have deemed it wholly beyond its province to express its opinion in the following words of " The judicious Hooker :"

"In the meanwhile sorry we are that any good and godly mind should be grieved with that which is done. But to remedy their grief lieth not so much in us as in themselves. They do not wish to be made glad with the hurt of the Church: and to remove all out of the Church whereat they shew themselves to be sorrowful, would be, as we are persuaded, hurtful if not pernicious thereunto. Till they be able to persuade the contrary, they must and will I doubt not find out some other good means to cheer up themselves. Amongst which means the example of Geneva may serve for one. Have not they the old popish custom of using god-fathers and godmothers in Baptism? the old popish custom of administering the blessed sacrament of the holy Eucharist with wafer-cakes? These things the godly there can digest. Wherefore should not the godly here learn to do the like both in these and in the rest of the like nature?" (*Book* iv. ch. x. 1. Vol. I. Keble's ed. p. 449.)

* It has been contended that the Wafer is not Bread: but Bp. Wren did not so think, for, in a proposed Rubric, he says :—" Ibidem. *What remaineth of the Bread of any Loaf or Wafer that was broken for the use of the Communion, or of the Wine that was poured out, or had the Benediction, the Curate shall, after the Service is ended, take some of the Communicants to him, there to eat and drink the same. But all the rest in both kinds, the Curate shall have to his own use.*" (*Fragmentary Illustrations*, p. 84.)

THE POSITION OF THE CELEBRANT.

XLVIII. The last point which the Judicial Committee had to Report upon to the Crown is—The Position of the Celebrant at the Altar: the Court states the Case in the words following:—

> "It remains to consider part of the 17th Article of charge, which sets out that the Respondent during the whole of the prayer of consecration at the Holy Communion 'stood at the middle of that side of the holy table which if the said holy table stood at the east end of the said church or chapel (the said table in St. James's Chapel, in fact, standing at the west end thereof), would be the west side of such table, in such wise that you then stood between the people and the said holy Table, with your back to the people, so that the people could not see you break the bread or take the cup into your hand.' The learned Judge deals with this charge very briefly, believing it to have been settled by this Committee in the Judgment in Martin *v.* Mackonochie. He says, 'I must observe that the Rubric does not require that the people should see the breaking of the bread, or the taking of the cup into the priest's hands; and, if it did so prescribe, the evidence in this case would establish that all the congregation could see him take the cup into his hand, and some of them at least could see him break the bread.' The Rubric on this point is this: 'When the priest, standing before the table, hath so ordered the bread and wine [*insert,*] that he may with the more readiness and decency break the bread before the people, and take the cup into his hands, he shall say the Prayer of Consecration, as followeth.'"

Having thus introduced the subject, the Court proceeds to comment upon the meaning of the Rubric which they had just quoted, saying:—

> "Their Lordships are of opinion that these words mean that the priest is so to stand that the people present may see him break the bread and take the cup into his hands; although the learned Judge is right if he means to say that the mere words do not speak of seeing."

The Court only puts forward this interpretation of the Rubric as a matter of "opinion;" there can be nothing disrespectful, therefore, in presuming to question it: I am not aware of any *authoritative statement* which would uphold or prove the view here taken by their Lordships: in default of this, the only satisfactory mode, as it seems to me, of arriving at the probable meaning of the Rubric, is, to consider its History. Now this new Rubric of 1662 would appear to have been derived from three sources—Bp. Cosin, Bp. Wren, and the Scotch Prayer Book of 1636: Cosin and Wren were both on the Committee of the Upper House of Convocation, appointed Nov. 21, 1661, for revising the Prayer Book; and Wren had been employed to review the Scotch Prayer Book when it was prepared in 1636: a comparison of the Rubric of 1662 with the three Documents, set out in the following parallel arrangement, seems to prove that it was the outcome of them all.

PRAYER BOOK, 1662. *4th Rit. Report* p. 19, copied from *MS. Book in House of Lords.*	BP. COSIN. P. Bk. 1619 as altered by him (in Durham Cath. Library.) Cosin Corresp. II. p. 57.	BP. WREN "*Fragmentary Illustrations*"— (Bp. of Chester. 1874. p. 81.)	SCOTCH PRAYER BOOK, 1636.
"When the Priest, standing before the Table, hath so ordered the Bread and Wine, that	"When the Priest, standing before the Table, hath so ordered the Bread and Wine that	" Then the Priest standing before the Table shall so order and set the Bread and Wine that, while he is pronouncing the following Collect,	" Then the Presbyter standing up,
he may with the more readiness and decency	he may with the more readiness and decency	he may readily	
break the Bread before the people, and take the Cup into his hands;	break the Bread before the people and take the Cup into his hands,	take the Bread and break it, and also take the Cup, to pour Wine into it (if he pour it not before), and	
he shall say the Prayer of Consecration as followeth."	he shall say as followeth."	then he shall say,	shall say the Prayer of Consecration, as followeth, but

then during the time of Consecration, he shall stand at such a part of the holy Table, where he may with the more ease and decency use both his hands."
" ALMIGHTY GOD, OUR HEAVENLY FATHER, WHO OF THY TENDER MERCY," &c.

It will be observed, at once, that Cosin's proposed form entirely corresponds with the new Rubric except that he does not supply the words—" the Prayer of Consecration," these appear to have been copied from the Scotch Book of 1636: his words " the " more readiness and decency " are also, except " readiness," in that same Book : this word " readiness " (agreeing with Wren's word "readily ") seems to have been substituted for the word "ease" which occurs in the Book of 1636; Cosin had used it in his Note upon the direction "*standing up*" (2nd Series, written in a Prayer Book of 1638) where he says " Which is a posture " of reverence, and here ordered for the priest to use, that he " may with the more readiness perform his office in consecrating " the elements." (*Works.* Vol. v. p. 332.)

Another expression in this new Rubric of 1662 needs to be accounted for—the substitution of the words "standing before " the Table" for the words " standing up " which are found in the Scotch Book of 1636 and in the English Books of 1604, 1559, and 1552: did this intend to introduce a *change* of Position or was it only meant as an explanation of the latter term ?

As regards the Scotch Book, it would seem that " standing "up" could be taken in the restricted sense of "standing "before " *i.e.*, in front; for the Rubric of that Book said that " during the time of Consecration " the Celebrant " shall stand " at such a part of the holy Table, where he may with the " more ease and decency use both his hands ; " and if, up to this time, he had been " standing at the North . . . End " of " the holy Table," as the Rubric allowed (it said " side or " end "), he would be likely to find the *front* of it the more convenient place when the Altar stood " at the uppermost part of " the Chancel" and close against the Wall behind it. One of the Charges against Abp. Laud referred to this Rubric: he replied as follows :—

" Yea, but (35) they find fault with the reason given in the rubric. For they say :—

"*He must have the use of both his hands, not for anything that he hath to do about the bread and the wine; (for that may' be done at the north end of the table, and be better seen of the people;) but (as we are told by the Rationalists⁸) that he may, by stretching out ͭ his arms, represent the extension of Christ on the cross ͧ.*

"But the reason given in the Rubric doth not satisfy them; for they say plainly, 'they have no use of both their hands for anything that is to be done about the bread and the wine. Surely these men consecrate their elements in a very loose & mean way, if they can say truly, 'that they have not use of both their hands' in this work. Or, that whatsoever is done, 'may as well be done at the north end of the table;' which, in most places is too narrow, and wants room, to lay the Service-book open before him that officiates and to place the bread and wine within his reach. So that in that place 'tis hard for the presbyter to avoid the unseemly disordering of something or other that is before him, perhaps the very elements themselves; which may give scandal to them which come to communicate: especially since, in the margin of the Prayer of Consecration, he is ordered to lay his hand upon the bread and wine which he consecrates.¹ As for 'his being better seen of the people,' that varies according to the nature of the place, and the position of the table; so that in some places he may be better seen, and in some not. Though I am not of opinion, that it is any end of the administration of the Sacrament 'to have the priest better seen of the people.'

"Thus much against the reason given in the rubric. Next, they produce other reasons of this position of his at the holy table. And first, they say, 'tis not for the more convenient use of both his hands in the celebration of that work; but it is, (say they,) 'that he may, by stretching out his arms, represent the extension of Christ on the cross.' Why, but I say not this; nor is there any such thing ordered or required in the Book; nor doth any English divine practise this that I know. Why then is this charged upon me? Nor is it sufficient for them to say, 'they are taught thus by the Rationalists'; unless I did affirm, or practise, as those Rationalists do. Here's a great deal of charity wanting." (*Works.* Vol. iii. p. 346. Oxford, 1853.)

The case of the English Book is somewhat different: the Rubric at the time of the Revision was also "standing up:" the *posture* was the same as in the Scotch Book, but no choice of position was *mentioned* in it or in the earlier Books: it was merely "standing up" in 1552 and 1559 as well as in 1604 and in the later Editions of this last Book: the alterations made at the Revision in 1661 were written in the Edition of 1636,

"ʳ 'Must,' Rush.   ˢ [Admirers of Durand's Rationale].
  ᵗ Forth,' Rushw. and Pryn.
"ᵘ [See Durandi Rationale, lib. iv. cap xliii. § 3, p. 176.]
"¹ [' or other that is . . . . consecrates' on opposite page.]"

where the Rubric containing the words "standing up" is erased, and the present Rubric substituted. This interesting and important Volume was *Photozincographed* for the Ritual Commission in 1871.

There is, however, in these three Books another Rubric which is retained in the Book of 1662: it occurs at the beginning of the Office and directs the Priest to be "*standing at "the North-side of the Table:*" this is an order for both *posture* and *position*: moreover, throughout the Office, there is no direction to alter the *position*, though changes of *posture* are prescribed, viz. twice "*kneeling*," twice "*standing up*" (for "*standing up*" at the Collect after the Commandments is not a *change* of posture), and once "*turning himself to the people*" at the Absolution—a direction which shews that at the Confession the Priest was turning from them, whatever may have been his *position* towards them at the other parts of the Service. If the words "*the North-side of the Table*" meant the Northern part of its Front (a point which will have to be considered later in reference to the question of the Court "what is meant by '"the north side of the Table?"'") there can be no doubt that the Celebrant's normal *position* was, *Rubrically*, turning from them and looking Eastward. Whether his *position* at the commencement of the Office—"*standing at the North-side of the "Table*"—was not to be changed during the Office, will have to be discussed in connection with the meaning of " North side:" that a change was not *excluded*, I cannot myself doubt, having regard to the existing Rule and Practice when the Rubric was first introduced in 1552.

In the Book of 1549 there is a corresponding Rubric at the commencement of the Office, after the Introit: it *defines* only *one place* for the Celebrant throughout the whole Service, unless he had to read the Epistle or Gospel; although it does not *forbid* his taking another place at Collects, in continuance of the Rule he had been accustomed to under the Sarum Book: its words are "*standing at God's board;*" and there can be no question (as I shall show hereafter) what " at" meant, it was— in the middle of the Altar's front and turned away from the people: in other words—the Eastward position with back to the people.

Before the Revision of 1661 certain " Exceptions against the "Book of Common Prayer" of 1604 were tendered to the Bishops by the Puritan party: one of these was to the Rubric before the Absolution in the Communion Office—

"*Then shall the Priest or the Bishop (being present) stand up, and turning himself to the people, say thus.*"

The Exception to this was—

" The Minister turning himself to the people is most convenient throughout the whole ministration." (*Cardwell Conf.* p. 320: *or* the *Grand Debate*, 1661, p. 16, where " Ministers" (*i.e.* Minister's) is the word used.)

To this Exception the Bishops answered—

" § 6. Minister's turning. The Minister's turning to the people is not most convenient throughout the whole ministration. When he speaks to them, as in Lessons, Absolution, and Benedictions, it is convenient that he turn to them. When he speaks for them to God, it is fit that they should all turn another way, as the ancient church ever did: the reasons of which you may see Aug. lib. 2. de Ser. Dom. in monte." (*Cardwell*, 353: *Grand Debate*, 125.) *

The Ministers made the following " Reply" (not given by Cardwell) to this Answer of the Bishops:—

" It is not yet understood by us, why the Ministers, or people, (for which you mean by [they all] we know not) should turn another way in prayer: we think, the people should hear the prayers of the Minister; if not, Latine prayers may serve; and then you need not except against extemporate prayers, because the people cannot own them; for how can most of them own what they hear not, whatever it

---

* Bp. Wren's hand seems traceable in this Answer: as appears by his Answer to the Lords upon his Impeachment by the Commons in 1641: the 4th Article of Charge was this—"IV. The more to advance blind Superstition, he in the same year, caus'd all the Pews in the Churches to be so alter'd, that all the People might kneel with their Faces Eastward towards the Communion-Table, so set Altar-wise." (*Parentalia*, p. 13). His Answer was:—
" To the fourth Article, this Defendant answereth, and denieth" the charge in certain respects (*Ib.* p. 77): yet, in defence, he says (p. 78) " It was also the constant Observation of the Primitive Church in the Time of Prayer, to kneel towards the East [*Ad Orientem convertimus*, says *Gregory Nyssen, Lib. de Orat.* and *St. Augustin, Lib. ii. de Serm. Dom. Cap.* 19. *Ad Orientem adoramus*, says *Athanasius, Quæst. Neces.* 14. *Spectamus Orientem cum precamur*, says *St. Basil, Lib di Spir, Cap.* 27. *Epiphanius, Lib. i. Tom. i. Cap.* 19.] And that it was so accustomed here in *England*, after the Reformation, appears by the ancient Forms of their Seats in many Churches, and by Mr. *Cartwright's*

be? As for *August*. reason for looking towards the East, when we pray, (*Ut admoneatur animus ad naturam excellentiorem se convertere, id est, ad Dominum; cum ipsum corpus ejus, quod est terrenum, ad corpus excellentius, id est, ad corpus celeste convertitur*): We suppose you will not expect that we should be much moved by it; if we should, Why should we not worship towards any of the creatures visible, when we can pretend such Reasons for it, as minding us of superiour things? and why should we not look Southward when the sun is in the South?

"And we fear the worshipping towards the Sun, as representing or minding us of Christ's heavenly body, is too like to the prohibited worshipping before an Image, and too like that worshipping before the Host of Heaven, in which the old Idolatry consisted, or at least which was the introduction of it; of which our Protestant Writers treat at large against the Papists, on the point of Image-Worship; See also *Vossius de Idolatriâ, lib. 2. cap. 23, &c.*" *(The Grand Debate,* p. 125; or *Documents relating to the Settlement of the Church of England by the Act of Uniformity of* 1662, *p.* 313. London. 1862. p. 313.)

This Exception, Answer, and Rejoinder shew that the Rubric of 1604 (and the same must be true of 1559 and 1552) was regarded alike by the Bishops and by the Ministers, as recognizing the Eastward Position of the Celebrant in the Eucharistic Office: if they believed otherwise, nothing would have been easier than for both parties to declare that the Rubric was opposed to the Practice which the Ministers deprecated: whereas the Answer of the Bishops and their appeal to St. Augustine in support of it, indicate that they did not regard the "standing at" of the Rubric of 1604 as opposed to the "standing at" of the Rubric of 1549, so far, at least, as the Eastward Position was concerned. It would seem indeed that

Complaint, that the Minister at Prayer was in the Chancel with his Back to the People: And by the Rubrick before *Te Deum*, appointing the Minister, when he reads the Lessons, to stand and turn himself so as he may best be heard."

"This Defendant therefore could have no other Intention in that Enquiry but this, that the East being the highest End of the Church, and the holy Table standing there, by kneeling all that way, People would give no Offence or Disturbance to one another, and would also the better hear and see, what the Minister said and did in his Administration.

"And to the same Purpose, that in the time of the holy Communion, Mens Thoughts might be less disturbed with other Objects, and the Minister himself, and his Administration be less liable to Disturbance; and the Place itself be freer for that holy Service, and for Access of the Communicants, he enquired whether any Seats were above the Table, or up even with it, as holding it a thing, in his own Judgment, under Correction, for divers Causes very unfitting."

Bp. Cosin regarded the *Position* indicated by the Rubric of 1549 as truer to Antiquity than that of the Rubric of 1604; for his Note upon the latter is this:—

"*At the north side.*] *Antiquitus vero ad medium Divini altaris adstitit.* Dionys., *Eccl. Hier.*, cap. 3," (*Notes 2nd Series.* Written in a Prayer Book of 1638. Works. Vol. v. p. 308.

In "The King's Warrant for the Conference at the Savoy" the persons therein appointed were directed "to advise upon " and review the said Book of Common Prayer, comparing the " same with the most ancient liturgies which have been used in "the Church, in the primitive and purest times." (*Cardwell. Conf.* p. 300): considering, then, the Bishops' Defence of the Rubric impugned by the Ministers, it is not surprising that they appear to have acted upon this Instruction from the Crown, in reference to so important a part of the Communion Service as the Prayer of Consecration, by making the Rubric which preceded it *clearly* consistent with those "Liturgies:" this they did in altering "standing up" into "standing before "the Table:" though, indeed, it must not be assumed (as will be seen hereafter) that "standing up" did not mean "standing "before."

But the "Opinion" of the Court "that the priest is so " to stand that the people present may see him break the bread " and take the cup into his hands" seems mainly founded upon the words "before the people," which are another portion of the new Rubric of 1662: therefore, in considering this opinion, it is further necessary to investigate the origin of these words. So far as anything to the contrary appears, they were taken from what is known as Cosin's Durham Book, which is " a Book of Common Prayer of the year 1619, corrected and " altered throughout in Bp. Cosin's hand, with further cor- "rections of Cosin's suggested alterations, made in Sancroft's "handwriting" (*Preface to Cosin's Notes,* Vol. v. p. xxi:) this Book,* or Sancroft's copy of it in the Bodleian Library,

---

* A comparison of the proposals in this Durham Book with the alterations made in 1662 is given in the COSIN CORRESPONDENCE, published by THE SURTEES SOCIETY, 1872. This Rubric is already given at p. 326.

is believed to have been used at the Revision in 1661, as so many of its suggestions were then adopted. Whence Cosin derived the words "before the people" is another question: a clue to the enquiry is to be found, I think, in one of his "Particulars to be considered, explained, and corrected, in "the Book of Common Prayer," which, though already quoted (See p. 268), it will be convenient to repeat here, it runs thus:—

"57. Again, at the words there, 'He took bread and He brake it, and He took the cup,' no direction is given to the Priest, (as in King Edward's Service-book there was, and as in most places it is still in use,) to 'take the bread and cup into his hands,' nor to 'break the bread before the people;' which is a needful circumstance belonging to this Sacrament; and therefore, for his better warrant therein, such a direction ought here to be set in the margin of the book." (*Works*, Vol. v. p. 516.)

Here Cosin gives the words "break the bread before the "people"—the very words of the later Rubric of 1662— apparently as a *quotation* from the Prayer Book of 1549, to which he was referring: but they do not occur there, though the Manual Acts, "to take the bread and cup into his hands," are there in separate marginal directions. In fact there is no order to *break* the Bread at all in the Act of Consecration, a circumstance which, so far, corresponds with the Rubric in the Sarum Missal which, at the word "brake," says only, "Hic "tangat hostiam."† In the MISSAL, the fraction was not made until the Consecration was ended and had been followed by the Lord's Prayer and some Collects. But even this is not pre-

† So also in the Bangor and York Missals: the Hereford was "Signat Hostiam;" and the Roman is "Signat Super Hostiam" (*Maskell*, p. 41. Ed. 1844.) In "The Sarum Missal in English" a fuller Rubric is given—"Here let him touch the Host, but not so as to break it, as some do; for although the order of the words seems to imply that Christ brake before consecrating, tradition teaches the contrary." (p. 310.) The Burntisland Reprint (1861) gives the shorter Rubric—"Hic tangat hostiam" and also this longer one: "Hic non debet tangi hostia, modo fractionis sicut aliqui fatui tangunt et male faciunt. Videtur tamen ex ordine verborum quod prius debet frangi quam consecrari cum dicat, *benedixit, fregit*: per hæc verba videtur quod prius est fractio quam consecratio. Sed Ecclesia prius consecrat quam frangit: sic aliter facit Ecclesia quam Christus fecit; et sic Ecclesia videtur errare et per consequens delinquit. Solutio. Dicendum est, quod Ecclesia non delinquit; quia Christus post consecrationem et benedictionem fregit; licet ordo verborum aliter sonat. Et dicat sacerdos inclinando.—M. 54. [*i.e.* Missal 1554.]" (Col. 616.)

scribed in the Book of 1549. Yet it seems clear that Cosin considered that "to 'break the bread before the people,'" was *warranted* either by that Book or by some other Authority, or by Custom; quite as much as the other *prescribed* Manual Acts: it may be that he had regard to that part of the Rubric at the end of the Office, which, after directing the Bread to be made "so that it may be aptly divided in divers "pieces;" goes on to direct that "every one [of the Breads] "shall be divided in two pieces at the least, or more, by the "discretion of the Minister, and so distributed." This division of the Bread was, obviously, to be made in the course of the Service itself; for the division is mentioned in connexion with the direction that it is to be "so distributed;" upon which these words follow—"And men must not think less to be received in "part than in the whole, but in each of them the whole Body of "our Saviour Jesu Christ."

But Cosin's reference to the Book, touching the Manual Acts, shews that he is not likely to have meant that the Priest must be in such a position towards the people as that, in the manner implied by the Court, they "may see him break the bread "and take the Cup into his hands;" for that Book shows in the plainest manner that the Priest was not to be turned towards the people, but the contrary; immediately after the words of Consecration is the Rubric following—"These words before "rehearsed are to be said, turning still to the Altar, without "any elevation or shewing the Sacrament to the people." This direction equally applies if the *Practice* under that Book was to *break* the Bread in the Act of Consecration: in which case, even if Cosin's quoted words "break the bread before the "people" had been a Marginal Note or a Rubric, they could only have meant *in the presence* of the people.

Cosin considered, however, that this fraction of the Bread and the other two Manual Acts, which he mentioned as being in the Book of 1549, were "a needful circumstance belonging "to this Sacrament" and that as they were not ordered in the Book then in use, "such a direction ought to be" given for the "better warrant" of the Priest: he inserted such directions in his Durham Book: the Ministers in their *Exceptions* had said

"We conceive that the manner of consecrating of the Elements is "not here explicite and distinct enough: and the Ministers "breaking of the bread is not so much as mentioned." (*Grand Debate*, p. 17, or *Cardwell Conf.* p. 321:) the Bishops made no *Answer*, thus shewing that they agreed with the Exception; and so Cosin's proposal was adopted at the Revision of 1661. None of these persons however seem to have raised any question or expressed any wish about the people *seeing* these Acts—indeed the *Exception* touching the Minister's turning from the People only referred to his being *heard*. There seems, therefore, no real ground for the opinion which the Court expressed as to the meaning of this Rubric. It is not out of place, moreover, to observe that even if " the Priest is so to stand that the people "present may see him break the bread and take the cup into "his hands," the Judicial Committee itself has (if its language is final) made it extremely difficult to most of a Congregation—impossible to some—to witness the action which it is assumed they are intended clearly to observe; because, in an Application to their Lordships " for an order to enforce compliance with a " Monition issued in the case of Martin *v.* Mackonochie the Court said, on Dec. 4, 1869:—

"It is most desirable, and their Lordships are all of opinion, that it should be distinctly understood that they give no sanction whatever to a notion that any elevation whatever of the Elements, as distinguished from the mere act of removing them from the Table, and taking them into the hand of the Minister, is sanctioned by Law. It is not necessary for their Lordships to say more (but most undoubtedly less we cannot say) than that we feel nothing has taken place in the course of this cause, that can possibly justify a conclusion, that any elevation whatever, as distinguished from the raising from the Table, is proper or sanctioned. All that their Lordships can say on the present occasion is, that the point has never yet been in these proceedings raised, ... nothing, therefore, which we are now determining can be pleaded hereafter as a justification for any mode of elevation, which is to be distinguished from the mere act of removing the Elements from the Table, and taking them into the hands of the Minister." (*Brooke, Six Privy Council Judgments*, p. 140.)

Having expressed its opinion on the meaning of the Rubric the Court continues thus:—

" Their Lordships think that the evidence of the witness

Verrall, which there is no reason to doubt, proves that 'generally the congregation could not see' the breaking of the bread, because the Respondent had his back turned to them. As regards the cup, the witness said that they could see him take the cup into his hand, but being asked further, he says, 'I could tell he was taking the cup into his hand.' This is consistently explained by supposing that the witness and others could see a certain motion of the Respondent which from their knowledge of the service and from the subsequent elevation they were sure was the taking of the cup into his hands. It would probably be impossible in any position so to act that all the congregation could see or that all should be unable to see; but we take it as proved that the greater part of the congregation could not see the breaking of the bread or the act of taking the cup into the hands."

As this passage does not affect the Argument and, perhaps, could have no bearing on any other case, it might be passed over: but, in reference to their Lordships' remark that "It would probably be impossible in any position so to act that all the congregation could see or that all should be unable to see," I may observe that, from my own knowledge of this Building, it would be difficult to find a Church or Chapel in which the majority of the Congregation could see the Actions of the Celebrant at the *North end* of the Altar as *plainly* as the Congregation generally could observe what was done by the Celebrant at St. James's Chapel standing in front of the Altar with his back towards the people. The Chapel was a plain oblong room, with nothing to obstruct the sight of the Altar from, I think, any part of the building; it had three Galleries, and the floor was mostly covered by somewhat high pews: but the Altar was raised on a Platform not much lower than the tops of the Pews, so that the Celebrant occupied a very conspicuous position and could be well seen and heard.

The Report next makes this remark:—

"The facts being established, their Lordships proceed to consider the question itself. In default of argument on the Respondent's side, they have been somewhat aided by a large mass of controversial literature, which shows how much interest this question excites, and which has probably left few of the facts unnoticed."

And then it sets out the following particulars as to the Position of the Altar and of the Priest:—

" The Rubric upon the position of the table directs that it shall 'stand in the body of the church [*insert*,] or in the chancel, where morning and evening prayer are appointed to be said.' This is the same as the Rubric of 1552, 1559, and 1604, excepting the verbal alteration of *are* for *be*. It goes on, 'And the Priest standing at the north side of the table, shall say the Lord's Prayer with the * Collect following.' The table is a moveable table. By the injunctions of Queen Elizabeth (Cardwell, Doc. Annals 1, p. 210) it is ordered 'that the holy table in every church be decently made and set in the place where the Altar stood, and there commonly covered as thereto belongeth, and as shall be appointed by the visitors, and so to stand, saving when the Communion of the Sacrament is to be distributed; at which time the same shall be so placed in good sort within the chancel, as whereby the minister may be more conveniently heard of the communicants in his prayer and ministrations [*dele* s], and the communicants also more conveniently and in more number communicate with the said minister. And after the Communion is [*dele* is] done, from time to time, the same holy table to be placed where it stood before."

XLIX. Upon this Rubric and Injunction their Lordships comment thus:—

" If this custom still prevailed of bringing the table from the east and placing it in the chancel, the two Rubrics would present no difficulty. The priest standing on [*read* at] the north side as directed by the one, would also be standing before the table so as to break the bread before the people, and take the cup into his hand as required by the other."

---

* " this " in 1604, 1559, and 1552.

Now in this passage two points seem to be assumed with regard to the Injunction :—

1. That it required the Holy Table to be *always* moved, at a Communion, from "the place where the altar stood."

2. That, when so removed, it was to stand with its ends East and West.

But the Injunction does not, as I read it, say or mean this: it was issued, as the earlier part shews,[*] to prevent the "riotous " or disordered manner" which, it seems, had been " used " in taking down the Altars ; and also to secure some " uniformity " in the " tables " substituted for them.

1. As regards their *Place*, the Injunction refers to " the "form of the law therefore provided," and says that its directions were designed " for the better imitation of the law in that "behalf:" that "law" was the Rubric of 1552, revived in 1559, which said that :—

" The Table . . . . shall stand in the body of the Church, or in the Chancel, where Morning Prayer and Evening Prayer be appointed to be said . . . ."

The *place* of the Lord's Table here prescribed, depended upon the action taken under the following " Order " as to " where Morning and Evening Prayer shall be used and " said : "—

" The Morning and Evening Prayer shall be used in[†] the accustomed place of the church, chapel, or chancel, except it shall be otherwise determined by the ordinary of the place, and the chancels shall remain as they have done in times past."

---

[*] "*For tables in the Church.* Whereas her majesty understandeth, that in many and sundry parts of the realm the altars of the churches be removed, and tables placed for the administration of the holy sacrament, according to the form of the law therefore provided ; and in some other places, the altars be not yet removed, upon opinion conceived of some other order therein to be taken by her majesty's visitors ; in the other whereof, saving for an uniformity, there seemeth no matter of great moment, so that the sacrament be duly and reverently ministered; yet for observation of one uniformity through the whole realm, and for the better imitation of the law in that behalf, it is ordered, that no altar be taken down, but by oversight of the curate of the church, and the churchwardens, or one of them at the least, wherein no riotous or disordered manner to be used. And that the holy table in every church be decently made. And" &c. (*Cardwell, Doc. Ann.* I. 234) as in the rest of the Injunction quoted by the Court. (See p. 337).

[†] In 1552 the words were " such place of the church, chapel, or chancel, and the minister shall so turn him, as the people may best hear. And if there be any controversy therein, the matter shall be referred to the Ordinary, and he or his deputy shall appoint the place, and the chancels," &c.

So that if the Ordinary, in any case, directed the Morning and Evening Prayer to be said, either "in the body of the Church" or "in the Chancel," whichever was not "the accustomed "place," the "Table" was to "stand" in either of these places according as the one or the other was ruled by the Ordinary to be used for Matins and Evensong. The Injunction would also seem to have read the Rubric as to the *place* of "The "Table" in connexion with the Order in Council* of Nov. 24,

---

* Ridley, Bp. of London, issued in 1550 certain Injunctions for his diocese one of which was the following:—

"*Item.* Whereas in divers places some use the Lord's board after the form of a table, and some of an altar, whereby dissension is perceived to arise among the unlearned; therefore wishing a godly unity to be observed in all our diocese, and for that the form of a table may more move and turn the simple from the old superstitious opinions of the popish mass, and to the right use of the Lord's supper, we exhort the curates, church-wardens, and questmen here present, to erect and set up the Lord's board after the form of an honest table, decently covered, in such place of the quire or chancel, as shall be thought most meet by their discretion and agreement, so that the ministers, with the communicants, may have their place separated from the rest of the people; and to take down and abolish all other by-altars or tables." (*Ridley's Works*, Parker Society, p. 319.)

But, as the Judicial Committee (Liddell *v.* Westerton) observed, this Injunction "probably had no binding force" in Ridley's Diocese (*Moore's Report*, p. 182): consequently, as it seems, the Order in Council, above noted, was issued: it is styled "The King's Letter to Nicholas Ridley, Bishop of London, &c.," and states that, in order to persuade the people who were opposed to the change, "we send unto you herewith certain considerations gathered and collected, that make for the purpose:" (*Ridley's Works*, p. 507). These "Considerations" were, as it appears, the Six "Reasons" prepared by Bp. Ridley to shew "why the Lord's Board should rather be after the form of a table, than of an altar:" Dr. Townsend, in his Edition of Foxe's Acts and Monuments (Appendix to Vol. vi. p. 743) says:—

"The Order in Council from the King to Ridley is in the [Ridley] Register dated 'the xxiii day of November' . . . . The 'Reasons' are thus introduced in the Register immediately after the Order in Council:—'Roman. I. I am not ashamed of the gospel, because it is the power of God unto salvation, to every one that believeth. Londini A°. dm. M.D.L." and he further remarks—" There is no doubt that these 'Reasons' were drawn up by Ridley, and it is as clear that they are identical with the 'Considerations' referred to in the Order of Council. That they are Ridley's appears from the preamble to them, which expressly says so; and the marginal title [Considerationes superius mentionatae in proxime prescriptis literis, p. 5] in the Register (omitted by Foxe, but given in this Edition) equally identifies them with the 'Considerations' mentioned in the King's letter. Moreover it appears from the Council Book, quoted in Strype's life of Cranmer (book ii. ch. 20) and Collier's History, that Day, Bishop of Chichester, was before the Council November 30th, for not complying with the King's letter of November 23rd; and next day stated to them that he saw no force in the Six Reasons which were set forth by the Bishop of London, to persuade the taking down of altars and erection of tables. It is pretty plain, then, that he and every other Bishop, had received the Order in Council and the

1550 which, to aid Bp. Ridley in overcoming the "contention " and strife about the standing or taking away" of the Altars, directed "instead thereof a table to be set up in some con- " venient part of the chancel, within every such Church or " Chapel, to serve for the ministration of the blessed Commu- " nion." (*Cardwell, Doc. Ann.* I. 101, or *Ridley's Works*, Parker Society, p. 506); for both this Order and the Injunction, nine years later, limit the place of the Table to " the Chancel."

The Injunction, while thus keeping the Table at all times *within* the Chancel, further ordered it to be "set in the place " where the altar stood :" but it allowed it to be removed to *another part* of the Chancel "when the Communion of the " Sacrament is to be distributed :" the Injunction does not say that it *must always* be so *removed :* it says—

"At which time the same shall be so placed in good sort within the

---

'Reasons' together." The "Reasons" will be found in *Ridley's Works*, Parker Society, pp. 321–3, and are as follows :—

("Certain reasons why the reverend father, Nicholas, bishop of London, amongst other his injunctions given in his late visitation, did exhort those churches in his diocese, where the altars, as then, did remain, to conform themselves to those other churches which had taken them down, and had set up, instead of the multitude of their altars, one decent table in every church. And that herein he did not only not anything contrary unto the Book of Common Prayer, or to the King's majesty's pro- ceedings, but that he was, induced to do the same, partly moved by his office and duty, wherewith he is charged in the same book, and partly for the advancement and sincere setting forward of God's holy Word, and the King's majesty's most godly proceedings).

" *First Reason.*

"The form of a table shall more move the simple from the superstitious opinions of the popish mass, unto the right use of the Lord's Supper. For the use of an altar is to make sacrifice upon it; the use of a table is to serve for men to eat upon. Now, when we come unto the Lord's board, what do we come for ? to sacrifice Christ again, and to crucify him again, or to feed upon him that was once only crucified, and offered up for us? If we come to feed upon him, spiritually to eat his body, and spiritually to drink his blood (which is the true use of the Lord's Supper), then no man can deny but the form of a table is more meet for the Lord's board, than the form of an altar.

" *Second Reason.*

"Whereas it is said, ' The Book of Common Prayer maketh mention of an altar ; wherefore it is not lawful to abolish that which the book alloweth :'" to this it is thus answered : The Book of Common Prayer calleth the thing whereupon the Lord's Supper is ministered indifferently a table, an altar, or the Lord's board ; without prescription of any form thereof, either of a table or of an altar : so that whether the Lord's board have the form of an altar, or of a table, the Book of Common Prayer calleth it both an altar and a table. For as it calleth it an altar, whereupon the Lord's Supper is ministered, a table, and the Lord's board, so it calleth the table, where the holy communion is distributed with lauds and thanks- giving unto the Lord, an altar, for that there is offered the same sacrifice of praise

"chancel as whereby the minister may be more conveniently heard of "the communicants in his prayer and ministrations, and the communi- "cants also more conveniently and in more number communicate with "the said minister."

"So placed" means, as it seems to me, *so situated:* if the Chancel was large enough to accommodate the Communicants, who in the short Exhortation were invited to "draw near," * probably "the place where the Altar stood" would be the most convenient place for the purposes mentioned in the Injunction; as, indeed, Archn. Kent says in his Visitation Articles 1631–9 and thanksgiving. And thus it appeareth, that here is nothing either said or meant contrary to the Book of Common Prayer.

"*Third Reason.*

"The popish opinion of mass was, that it might not be celebrated but upon an altar, or at the lesst upon a superaltar; to supply the fault of the altar, which must have had its prints and characters; or else it was thought that the thing was not lawfully done. But this superstitious opinion is more holden in the minds of the simple and ignorant by the form of an alter, than of a table; wherefore it is more meet, for the abolishment of this superstitious opinion, to have the Lord's board after the form of a table, than of an altar.

"*Fourth Reason.*

"The form of an altar was ordained for the sacrifices of the law, and therefore the altar in Greek is called θυσιαστήριον, *quasi sacrificii locus.* But now both the law and the sacrifices thereof do cease: wherefore the form of the altar used in the altar ought to cease withal.

"*Fifth Reason.*

"Christ did institute the Sacrament of his body and blood at his last supper at a table, and not at an altar; as it appeareth manifestly by the three Evangelists. And St. Paul calleth the coming to the holy communion, the coming unto the Lord's Supper. And also it is not read that any of the apostles or the primitive church did ever use any altar in ministration of the holy communion.

"Wherefore, seeing the form of a table is more agreeable to Christ's institution, and with the usage of the apostles and of the primitive church, than the form of an altar, therefore the form of a table is rather to be used, than the form of an altar, in the administration of the holy communion.

"*Sixth and last Reason.*

"It is said in the preface of the Book of Common Prayer, that if any doubt do arise in the use and practising of the same book, to appease all such diversity, the matter shall be referred unto the bishop of the diocese, who by his discretion shall take order for the quieting and appeasing of the same, so that the same order be not contrary unto any thing contained in that book."

* Bp. Mountagu, in his Visitation Articles for Norwich, 1638, makes the following inquiry—"7. Before the Communicants ascend up into the Chancell out of their seats in the Church, that Exhortation is to be said, which in the Communion-Book beginneth, *We be come together at this time, &c.* And then this Exhortation, *Dearly beloved, we are come together, &c.* When after this exhortation, the Communicants are come up into the Chancell, before they dispose themselves to kneel in their severall places, (which are orderly and decently to be appointed for them) this is to be said, *You that do truly and earnestly repent you of your sinnes, &c.* Is this order of the Communion-Book observed? if not, let it be amended hereafter." (2nd *Report Rit. Com.* p. 583.)

(See p. 345): if, on the contrary, the Chancell was not so adapted, then, the Communicants having to remain in the Body of the Church, the Table would have to be *removed* in order to be "so placed" as to comply with the object of the Injunction; and the bringing it down to the West end of the Chancel would, practically, be causing it to "stand in the body of the Church," according to the alternative given in the Rubric.

That this mode of placing the Holy Table at the West End of the Chancel is not mere surmise, is shewn by the following Injunction of Middleton, Bp. of St. David's, 1583:—

"6. Item, when there is a Communion to be ministered, that the Communion Table bee placed at the lower ende of the Chancell, as nere vnto the people as maie bee conuenient, and when the Ministration is doen, remoue it to the vpper end of the saied Chauncell." (2*nd. Rit. Report*, p. 426.)

So much, then, with regard to the seeming opinion of the Court—that the Table was always to be removed from the old Site of the Altar when there was to be a Celebration of the Holy Communion. The further view of the Court has also to be examined, namely:—

2. That at the time of the Communion, the Table, by the Elizabethan Injunction, was to stand with its ends East and West.

There is one important piece of contemporary Evidence which, at first sight, may seem to favour this view: Strype mentions it as occurring in "the Certificate made to the Archbishop's "Commissary" by "the Vice-Dean" and "Prebendaries" of Canterbury Cathedral, owing to the general Inquiry by the Bishops, in consequence of the Queen's complaint of "sundry "varieties and novelties" in the Service of the Church, made in her Letter to Abp. Parker, January 25, 1564-5. (See pp. 26 & 56.) This return states that:—

"The holy Communion is ministered ordinarily the first Sunday of every month through the year. At what time the table is set *east* and *west*. The Priest which ministereth, the Pystoler and Gospeler, at that time wear copes. And none are suffered then to tarry within that chancel but the communicants." (*Life of Parker, Bk.* II. ch. xxvi.) p. 183, *fol.* Vol. I. p. 365, 8°.

Here two facts are plainly stated (1) that the Table was in the Chancel (2) that its ends were East and West. But this is no proof that its *position*, East and West, was conformable to the Injunction; for the same Certificate states that, out of Communion time the position of the Table was *North* and *South*, and that the Minister stood on the *East* side of it to say daily the Common Prayer—a position which unquestionably he was not authorized to take. By "Common Prayer" seems to be meant that portion of the Communion Office which was used when there was "no Communion." If the *Morning Prayer* was meant, it only proves all the more how irregular the Practices were in that Cathedral. These are the words of the Certificate :—

"The Common Prayer daily through the year, though there be no Communion, is sung at the communion-table, standing *north* and *south*, where the high altar did stand. The Minister, when there is no Communion, useth a surplice only, standing on the east side of the table with his face toward the people. (*Ib*.)

Further, Strype speaking of "the confused varieties that "divers Ministers in these days used in the Service of God," says :—

"I find a paper among the Secretary's [Cecil's] MSS. specifying these varieties, dated Febr. 14. 1564 [5], which was the month before the articles for uniformity, afterward mentioned [*i.e.* the Advertisements] were devised by the Archbishop and the other Bishops." (*Ib*. fol. 183. 8v. I. 301.)

The second of these "varieties" is the following :—

"The Table standeth in the body of the church in some places; in others it standeth in the chancel. In some places the table standeth altarwise, distant from the wall [? a] yard. In some others in the middle of the chancel, north and south. In some places the table is joined; in others it standeth upon tressels. In some the table hath a carpet; in others it hath none." (*Ib*.)

This passage mentions four different *places* of the Table : but as to its *position* it only describes it as "altarwise" and "north "and south."

The Advertisements " of 1565-6 may, reasonably, be thought

to have discouraged (in consequence of these varieties) the liberty given by the Injunctions of 1559 to remove the Table for Celebrations; for the Advertisements direct:—

"Item. That they shal decentlie cover with carpet, silke, or other decente coveringe, and with a fayre lynnen clothe (at the time of the ministration) the communyon table, and to sett the Tenne Commaundmentes upon the easte wall over the said table." (*Cardwell, Doc. Ann.* I 326.)

Their Lordships, in the previous part of their Judgment, have quoted or referred to, in support of their Arguments, the Visitation Articles and Injunctions published by the Ritual Commission; and later, on the subject of the Celebrant's position, they have done the same: it is desirable, therefore, to examine these Documents in order to ascertain whether they afford any and what countenance to the opinion of the Court touching the intended *position* of the Holy Table under the Injunction, at the time of Communion.

1563. Parker (Abp. of Canterbury), 8.—"Item, whether the communion table be decentlye couered and set in conuenient place, according to the Queenes Maiesties Iniunctions." (2 *Rit. Report*, p. 403.)

1583. Middleton (Bp. of St. David's), 6.—(See p. 342.)

The following are under the Canon of 1604 which, however, employs nearly verbatim the language of the Injunction, though it has "Church or Chancel" (as in the Rubric) and not "Chancel" only.

1607. Babington (Bp. of Worcester), 3.—". . . And whether is the same table then [*i.e.*, "at the Communion time"] placed in such conuenient sort within the Chancell or Church as that the Minister may be best heard in his prayer and administration, and that the greater number may communicate?" (*Ib.* p. 454.)

1612. King (Bp. of London), 3.— same as Babington. (*Ib.* p. 465.)

1616. Abbot (Abp. of Canterbury), 1,—same, but "greatest" instead of "greater." (*Ib.* p. 470.)

1619. Overall (Bp. of Norwich), III. 1.—". . . And whether is the same Table placed conueniently as it ought." (*Ib.* p. 481.)

1622. Laud (Bp. of St. David's), 1.—". · · And whether is the same Table placed in conuenient sort within the Chancell?" (*Ib.* p. 488.)

1630. Curle (Bp. of Bath and Wells), 3.—same as Babington. (*Ib.* p. 514.)

1630. White (Archdn. of Norfolk). 6.—" conveniently placed." (*Ib.* p. 516.)

1631-9. Kent Archdn. of Sudbury). 37.—". . . and whether is the same table then [*i.e.*, "at the Communion time"] placed in such convenient sort, as that the Minister may be best heard in his prayer and administration, and that the greater number may communicate. To that end, doth it ordinarily stand up at the East end of the Chancell, where the altar in former times stood ; the ends thereof being placed north and south? (*Ib.* p. 527.)

1632. White (Archdn. of Norfolk), 5.—"conueniently placed." (*Ib.* p. 532.)

1633. Curle (Bp. of Winchester), 3.—Same as Babington. (*Ib.* p. 533.)

1633. Lindsell (Bp. of Peterborough), 2—" placed conveniently, as it ought to be?" (*Ib.* p. 538.)

1635. Laud (Abp. of Canterbury—for Norwich), 1.—". . . And whether is the same table placed in such conuenient sort within the Chancell or Church [as hath beene appointed by the Ordinary. *Added in* 1638], as that the Minister may bee best heard in his Prayer and Administration : and that the greatest number may communicate." (*Ib.* p. 547.)

1635. Williams (Bp. of Lincoln), 1.—". . . And whether is the same Table placed in such convenient sort within the Chancell or Church, as that the Minister may be best heard in his prayer and administration, and that the greatest number may communicate ? [And whether it is so used out of time of divine service, as is not agreeable to the holy use of it ; as by sitting on it, throwing hats on it, writing on it, or is it abused to other profaner uses?]." In 1641 the words bracketed are omitted and the following substituted—" Doth your said Communion table stand in the ancient place where it ought to doe, or where it hath done for the greatest part of these sixty years last past, or hath it been removed to the East end, and placed Altar-wise, and by whom, and whose authority hath it been so placed." (*Ib.* p. 551.)

1636. Wren (Bp. of Norwich), Chap. 3. 2.—"And is the same Table placed conueniently, so as the Minister may best be heard in his administration, and the greatest number may reuerently communicate ? To that end doth it ordinarily stand vp at the East end of the Chancell, where the Altar in former times stood, the ends thereof being placed North and South ?" (*Ib.* p. 557.)

" 3. That the Communion table in everie Church doe alwayes stand vnder theast wall of the Chancell, the ends thereof north and south, vnless the Ordinarie give particular directions otherwise." (*Ib.* p. 564.)

1636. Kingsley (Archn. of Canterbury), 6.—" Whether haue you a decent Communion Table placed as it ought to be, so as may be most conuenient for the due celebration of the holy Communion, and of that part of Divine Service then appointed to be said : . . . (*Ib.* p. 566.)

1636. Pearson (Archn. of Suffolk), I. 1.—". . . and whether is the same Table placed conveniently as it ought . . ." (*Ib.* p. 569.)

1637. Peculiars of Canterbury, 2.—"Whether is the Communion Table placed in such sort within the Chancell or Church, as that the greatest number of Parishioners may most conueniently receiue?" (*Ib.* p. 592.)

1638. Duppa (Bp. of Chichester), 6.—"Is your Communion Table, or Altar, strong, faire, and decent? is it set according to the practice of the ancient Church, vpon an ascent at the East end of the Chancell, with the ends of it North and South? . . ." (*Ib.* p. 576.)

1638. Mountagu (Bp. of Norwich), Tit. 3. 12.—"Is the Communion-table fixedly set, in such convenient sort and place within the Chancell, as hath been appointed by Authority, according to the practice of the ancient Church, that is, at the East-end of the Chancell, close unto the wall, upon an ascent or higher ground, that the officiating Priest may be best seen and heard of the Communicants, in that Sacred action?" (*Ib.* p. 580.)

"13. Whether is the Communion-table removed down at any time, either for, or without Communion, into the lower part of the Chancell, or body of the Church? by whom, at whose instance, direction or command is it done?" (*Ib.*)

1640. Juxon (Bp. of London), 6.—Have you in the Chancell of your Church or Chappell a decent and convenient Table for the celebration of the Holy Communion? Is it so set as is directed in the Queenes Injunctions, and appointed by the Canon * made in the Synod held at *London, Anno* 1640." (*Ib.* p. 589.)

---

* The following is the Canon of 1640—"That the standing of the Communion-Table side-way under the East window of every Church or Chappel, is in its own nature indifferent, neither commanded nor condemned by the Word of God, either expressly, or by immediate deduction, and therefore that no Religion is to be placed therein, or scruple to be made thereon. And albeit at the time of Reforming this Church from that gross superstition of Popery, it was carefully provided that all means should be used to root out of the minds of the people, both the inclination thereunto, and memory thereof; especially of the Idolatry committed in the Mass, for which cause all Popish Altars were demolished; yet notwithstanding it was then ordered by the Injunctions and Advertisements † of Queen *Elizabeth* of blessed memory, that the holy Tables should stand in the place where the Altars stood, and accordingly have been continued in the Royal Chappels of three famous and pious

† This must refer to the following "Item" of the Advertisements—"*That they shall decentlie cover with carpet, silke, or other decente coveringe, and with a fayre linen clothe (at the time of the Ministration) the communyon table, and to sett the Tenne Commandmentes upon the Easte walle over the said table.*"—(Cardwell, Doc. Ann. I. 326.)

1640. Bostock (Achn. of Suffolk), III. 2.—" . . . is the same Table placed conveniently, so as the Minister may best be heard in his administration, and the greatest number may reverently communicate? to that end, doth it ordinarily stand up at the East end of the Chancell, . . . ?" (*Ib.* p. 596.)

1662. Cosin (Bp. of Durham). *Before the Prayer Book of* 1662.— " Tit. I. 4. Is there a partition between your Church and your Chancel, a comely fair Table there, placed at the upper part of it, for the administration of the Sacrament of the Lord's Supper?"—(*Ib.* p. 601.)

1662. Pory (Archn. of Middlesex). *Before the Prayer Book of* 1662.—" 6. Have you in the Chancel of your Church or Chappel a decent and convenient table for the celebration of the Holy Communion? Is it so set as is directed in the Queene's Injunctions, and appointed by the Canon made in the Synod held at *London, Anno* 1640. . . . ?" (*Ib.* p. 625.)

Now of these 25 Inquiries, 16 make no mention of the *Position* of the Lord's Table; viz., Parker, Middleton, Babington, King, Abbot, Overall, Laud (2), Curle (2), White (2) Lindsell, Kingsley, Pearson, Peculiars of Canterbury: 3 say that its Ends are to be pointed North and South; viz. Kent Wren, Duppa,: 2 direct it to be in the place of Altar; viz. Juxon, Pory: 1 mentions the East end of the Chancel; viz. Bostock: 1 names the Upper part of the Chancell: viz. Cosin: 1 says the East End of the Chancel, close unto the Wall; viz. Mountagu: and 1, viz. Williams, though not saying anything about *Position* in 1635, apparently deprecates, in 1641, *i.e.* after and contrary to the Canons of 1640, its being "removed " to the East end, and placed Altar-wise."

The silence of Bp. Middleton (See p. 342) in 1583 calls for some further attention; for he says that:—

"Because I understande, there is vsed in moste partes of my Dioces, an infinite number of Popishe Ceremonies and other thynges, contrarie to the Lawes of God, and the Quenes maiesties moste godlie Princes, and in most Cathedral, and some Parochial Churches, which doth sufficiently acquit the manner of placing the said Tables from any allegality, or just suspition of Popish superstition or innovation. And therefore we judge it fit and convenient, that all Churches and Chappels do conform themselves in this particular to the example of the Cathedral or Mother Churches, saving always the general liberty left to the Bishop by Law, during the time of Administration of the holy Communion. And we declare that this scituation of the holy Table, doth not imply that it is, or ought to be esteemed a true and proper Altar, whereon Christ is again really sacrificed; but it is, and may he called an Altar by us, in that sence in which the Primitive Church called it an Altar, and in no other."

proceedynges: I thought good, for the auoiding of the same to sett doune the Injunctions following." (2nd. *Rit. Report*, p. 426.)

One of these was for " the auoiding" of "horrible Idolatries" touching the Eucharist: so he—

"decreed that no Persone, Vicare, or Curate, whatsoeuer, hereafter shall handle, lifte vp, or shewe vnto the people, the bread and wine, but shall let it lie still vpon the Table, untill the distribution thereof . . ." (*Ib.*)

Another for the like purpose, was :—

" 4. Item, that there bee no recourse by the Minister, to the Communion Table, to saie any parte of seruice there, sauyng onely when there is a Communion to bee ministered : for it doeth retaine a memorie of the Idolatrous Masse : For the auoiding whereof, all the seruice shal be said by the Minister, in his owne seate or Pulpit, with his face turned downe towardes the people: . . ." (*Ib.*)

Nevertheless, in describing precisely the *place* of the Lord's Table " when there is a Communion," he says nothing whatever to imply either that its ends were to point *East* and *West*, or that the Celebrant was to turn his face towards the people.

Excepting, then, Bp. Williams (whose language on another occasion, as quoted by the Court, will have to be considered later) it seems to me that this analysis of Episcopal and Archidiaconal Inquiries does not warrant the view apparently taken by the Court as to the *placing* and the *position* of the Holy Table required by the Elizabethan Injunction.

But the Court also appears to have regarded the *practice* of the period as being conformable to its construction of the wording of this Injunction; for they say " If this custom still " prevailed of bringing the table from the East and placing it " in the chancel, the two Rubrics would present no difficulty." I venture, however, to think it very doubtful whether " this " custom," to which their Lordships refer, ever " prevailed " to the extent supposed.

The following passages are taken from the Publications of four * Writers, who, (so far as I am aware) have collected all that is known on this point : the first two are altogether opposed

---

* Dean Howson—" Before the Table." 1875. Macmillan—does not produce any evidence on this point.

to the Eastward Position of the Celebrant; the last two strongly advocate that Position as being authorized, by the Rubric of 1662, for the Prayer of Consecration; but they do not consider the North *End* Position to be contrary to the word "North "side," though they would prefer not to use that Position; the Works are these :—

1. Rev. C. J. Elliott—"The North side of the Table." 1866. Parker & Co.
2. H. R. Droop, Esq.—"The North side of the Table." 1866. Hatchard & Co.
3. Revd. H. B. Walton—"The Rubrical Determination of the Celebrant's Position." 1866. Rivingtons, 2nd Ed. 1870, Masters & Co.
4. Revd. W. E. Scudamore—"The North side of the Table ; what it was." 1870. Rivingtons.
5. Revd. W. E. Scudamore— "Notitia Eucharistica." 1876. 2nd. Ed. Rivingtons.

** The Letters before and after the square brackets indicate how much of any passage is quoted by each writer.

1. *Elliott*, p. 35: 5. *Scudamore*, p. 163.—Laud's speech, 1636, at the censure of Bastwick and others. Works, VI. pt. 1. p. 59. Oxford. Ed. ᴱ["For in the King's Royal Chapels, and divers Cathedrals, the Holy Table hath, ever since the Reformation, stood at the upper end of the quire, with the large or full side towards the people. And though it stood in *most* parish churches the other way, yet whether there be not more reason,]ᴱ the *Parish Churches* should be made *conformable* to the *Cathedrall* and *Mother Churches*, than the *Cathedrals* to them, I leave to any reasonable man to judge." (p. 53.)

It may fairly be doubted whether Abp. Laud intended his words to apply so far back as 1550, when the Altars were first taken down: it is most likely that he referred to what occurred in Elizabeth's reign, after Mary had restored the Altars: his language, therefore, is not necessarily descriptive of the state of things in K. Edward's reign. Yet if it were so, Laud's comment shews that he considered the Law to have been complied with in those Parish Churches which followed the example of the Cathedrals.

1. *Elliott*, p. 116: 3. *Walton*, p. 57: 5. *Scudamore*, p. 189. Thomas Dorman [1564], in his book called *A Proof* (p. 110).

ᵂ "'This day your [Communion] table placed in the midst of the the quire; next day removed into the body of the church; at the third time placed in the chancel again after the manner of an altar, but yet removeable as there is any communion to be had. ᴱ[Then, your Minister's face one while to be turned towards the South, another while towards the North],ᵃ that the weathercock on the top of the steeple hath been noted not to have turned so often in the space of one quarter of a year, as your Minister hath been caused beneath in the bottom of the Church in less than one month]: ʷ as though you could not sufficiently declare how restless an evil heresy is; except you must make your communion table to run about the church, the minister first after it and then round about it, to express the same." (See also *Strype Ann. I.* 163 fol. or 8vo. I. pt. 1. p. 242.)

But Strype quotes Dorman, who wrote in 1564, not as evidence of what occurred in *K. Edward's* reign, but of what happened early in *Q. Elizabeth's* time, for, referring to the Injunctions, Strype says:—

"This order for the table and the bread was occasioned from the variety used in both, for some time, until these Injunctions came forth. For indeed in the beginning of the Queen's reign the protestants were much divided in their opinion and practice about them; which was the cause of some disturbance. And the papists made their advantage of it; laying to the charge of the protestants their mutability and inconstancy. Thus did Thomas Dorman, in his book called *A Proof.* 'This day your table is placed'" &c. (*Ann.* I. 163 fol.—8vo. I. pt. 1. p. 242.)

Whatever, then, may be the value of Dorman's statement as regards the *place* or *position* of the Table in 1559, prior to the Injunctions of that year; or between that date and when Dorman wrote; it has no bearing upon the *place* or *position* of it in the Reign of Edward VIth.

1 Elliott, p. 20—Miles Huggard [1556] quoted by Heylin. "For in K. Edward's first Liturgie, An. 1549. the Minister was appointed, as before is said, to stand *in medio Altaris* with his back towards the people. After, when as the King had commanded to take downe the *Altars*, and to set up *Tables*, then followed first a difference about the situation of those *Tables;* some being *placed* like *Altars*, and some like *tables*, according as we have it in the Acts and Monuments, *part* 2. pag. 700. Hereupon followed that confusion which *Miles Huggard* speakes of, amongst the Ministers themselves: *some standing northward, some southward, and some westward.* For remedy whereof, it was appointed in the Second Liturgie, that hee, the Minister, should have some certaine point, whereupon to fixe: your selfe [*i.e.* Williams] affirming (pag. 48) that *this contention was determined by the* Rubric, *still in force, for the* North-side *of the Table.*" (Heylin, "*Antidotum Lincolniense*," 1637. p. 57.)

This passage is no proof that, either by design or in fact, the Tables set up in Edward's reign were to any great extent, much less generally, placed with their ends East and West: all

it states upon this point is that "some" were "*placed* like
"*Altars*, and some like *Tables*." The other point of the passage
is, that Heylin cites Williams as agreeing with him—that the
dispute was settled by the "North-side" Rubric of 1552. But it
will be seen further on (See p. 358 ff) that this Rubric can
reasonably be accounted for on an entirely different ground.

1. *Elliott*, p. 101: 2. *Droop*, p. 3: 3. *Walton*, pp. 3 & 66: 5. *Scudamore*, p. 189.—Miles Huggard, "Displaying of Protestants" [1556] quoted by Heylin.

"But where you [*i.e.*, Bp. Williams] knock it on the head, with saying that the placing of the Table end-long, with one end towards the East great window, was the last situation of that Table in K. *Edward's* time; and call (pag. 47, 48) *Miles Huggard* for a witnesse: most sure *Miles Huggard* tels you no such matter (displaying of *Protestants*. An. 1556. p. 81.) For thus saith *Miles*: [D & W] [' *How long* were they learning to set their *Table*, to minister the said Communion upon?' [First they placed it *aloft*, where the *High Altar* stood. Then must it bee set from the wall that one might go betweene: [the Ministers being in contention on whether part to turne their faces, either towards the West, the North, or South] . Some would stand West-ward, some North-ward, some South-ward.'] D. E. W. How say you now. Doth *Miles* say anything of *placing the Table end-long*. *No point*. He saith it was removed from the wall where at first it stood, that one might goe betweene the said wall and it; and so I hope it might standing *North* and *South*: but that it was placed end-long, not one word saith Miles." (Heylin, "*Antidotum Lincolniense*," 1637. p. 51.)

All that this statement proves is—that Heylin and Williams did not agree as to the meaning of Miles Huggard's language ; and, therefore, it is open to choose between the two interpretations, and to hold, with Heylin, that "Miles" does not "say "anything of placing the Table end long:" though his words may fairly be quoted to show that some Ministers stood *behind* or at *either end* of the Table placed Altarwise; not, however, proving that none stood in front and looking East—a Position which he was not likely to blame.

3. *Walton*. p. 57—John Rastell, in his counter-challenge to Jewel (1564), asks where it is ever read in Catholic Antiquity, 'that the Communion Table (if any then were) was removeable up and down, hither and thither, and brought at any time into the lower parts of the Church, there to execute the Lord's Supper?' (*Confutation*, f. 162.)"

Nothing more can be even inferred from these words—than that the liberty given by the Elizabethan Injunction of moving the Lord's Table at the times of Communion, was exercised between 1559 and 1564 when Rastell wrote; and that he regarded the practice as being unsanctioned "in Catholic "Antiquity." But this does not touch the question—where or how the Lord's Table was placed when substituted, in K. Edward's reign, for the Altar.

4. *Scudamore.* p. 16.—"At the last examination of Ridley, 1555, White, the Bishop of Lincoln, is reported to have said, 'when your Table was constituted, you could never be content in placing the same now East, now North, now one way, now another, until it pleased God of His goodness to place it clean out of the Church.' (*Ridley's Works*, p. 281. Camb. 1841)." [or Parker Society, 1843. p. 281.]

But, even assuming that there was no exaggeration in White's language, it by no means follows that such variety was meant to be allowed when the Altars were removed: indeed Ridley's language may fairly be taken to imply the contrary: he had said:—

"As for the taking down of the Altars, it was done upon just considerations,* for that they seemed to come too nigh to the Jews' usage: neither was the Supper of the Lord at any time better ministered, [or] more duly received, than in those latter days when all things were brought to the rites and usage of the primitive church." (*Works.* Parker Society. p. 281.)

To which it was replied by:—

"*Lincoln:*—'A goodly receiving, I promise you, to set an oyster table † instead of an Altar, and to come from puddings at Westminster, to receive: and yet, when your table," &c. (*Ibid.*), as in Mr. Scudamore's quotation above.

Ridley rejoined thus:—

"Your Lordship's unreverend terms do not elevate the thing. Perhaps some men came more devoutly from puddings, than other men now do from other things." (*Ibid.*)

---

* See also (*ante* p. 341) his "Reasons why the Lord's Board should rather be after the form of a Table than of an Altar." *Fourth Reason.*

† Mr. Scudamore (p. 17) referring to this and to a complaint of Becon's, says—"It was called by them an 'oyster-board' or 'table,' apparently because it stood free on either side, and lengthways up and down the Church, as we see oyster-tables in the season stand it our streets." This comparison will hardly hold, I think: the term seems to have arisen from some of the Tables being merely Boards placed on "Tressels," as mentioned in the Return p. 343: hence, probably, the order in a proposed Canon of 1571 that it should be "a fayre joyned table."

In saying, as Ridley did, that "things were brought to the "rites and usage of the primitive church," he could not have meant to defend the placing *any way* of the Lord's Table.

That the removal of it had not been unfrequent, there is no reason to doubt; but that the instances were so numerous as to warrant the term "custom," or that they can be said to have "prevailed," remains to be proved. To have effected such a change in the Place and Position which the Altar occupied when the Prayer Book of 1549 came into use, or when Queen Mary's reign had restored it to the Place whence it had been removed in the later years of King Edward's life, would have required a combination of circumstances which, I believe, will be sought in vain. There must have been (1) a plain command, (2) a common abandonment of long habits, (3) a general prevalence of the opinions held by the Genevan party in England. But the first did not exist; the second is most improbable; the third is opposed to fact. What may conveniently be called the *Puritan* Leaven (though so to term it is, in part, an anachronism) which was working during the Century before 1662, by no means leavened the whole lump of English Priests or Laymen; and consequently the Innovations, upon the customary status of the Altars in 1549, were not likely to have been so extensive as the Court seems to have supposed.

Unless, therefore, the contrary of this can be proved, and *prevailing custom*, during the period referred to by the Court, is satisfactorily shewn to have been such as their Lordships assume that it was, it may reasonably be doubted whether "the "Priest" was "generally standing on the north side" of the Table, *i.e.* as I understand to be here meant—l ookingSouth, with the Table before him, having its sides parallel with the side Walls of the Chancel, and consequently its Ends pointing East and West, or whatever may have been the Orientation of the Church.

Now it will be allowed, probably, that if the *Position* of the Priest came into question near the time at which the Royal Injunction was issued, the occurrence may be better trusted, as an exposition of that Order than later practice or statements of an indefinite or merely negative character. One such occurrence is related by Strype as having happened in 1564-5; he states that:—

"The Archbishop had placed one Richard Kechyn in some benefice near Bocking in Essex, which seemed to be one of his Peculiars: and upon his admission had charged him to follow the orders and rules appointed and established by law, and to make no variation, whatsoever others should or might do or persuade him to the contrary. But now this year in his ministerial course, he met with many rubs and checks by one, a neighbouring preacher, (or English Doctor, as they loved to call themselves,) who came into his pulpit, being a licensed preacher, and there openly condemned him, the incumbent, for certain things. We must know that Kechyn had in Rogation-week gone the perambulation with his parishioners; and according to the old custom and the Queen's injunctions, had said certain offices in certain places of the parish. . . . . . He also constantly wore the surplice in his ministration, and in reading the divine service turned his face to the East.

"The Dean of Bocking, (who, I think, was Mr. Cole,) having some jurisdiction over Kechyn and some other ministers thereabouts, had charged him and the rest not to turn their faces to the high altar in service-saying, which was a new charge and not given before. But this Dean in his visitation usually gave new articles every year. And lastly, offence was taken against him that he used the surplice.

"Upon this occasion, the said Minister thought convenient to acquaint Peerson, the Archbishop's Almoner and Chaplain, with these things, to impart them to the Archbishop, that he might have his counsel and direction. He told the Almoner in a letter to him what his practice was, that though he turned his face upward, as he had done hitherto, yet his Church was small,* and his voice might be heard. That the Litany he said in the body of the church; and when he said the service he kept the chancel, and turned his face to the east; and that he was not zealous in setting forth predestination. And for these matters they were much offended with him. He beseeched the Almoner therefore to let him understand his Grace's mind. . . . . . . Further, that he would gladly learn what articles his Grace caused to be inquired of in his visitation; because the Dean their Visitor had every year a new scroll of articles. And this, of charging all not to turn their faces to the high altar was one; which be called a *new charge*." (*Life of Parker*, Bk II. ch. xix. p. 153 *fol.* or 8vo. Vol. I. pp. 303-5.)

Whether anything further happened or what (if any) reply the Archbishop made, Strype does not mention: but it may fairly be presumed what he would have said in reference to the

---

* "A remark which was, of course, equally applicable to hundreds of other Churches throughout the Kingdom, in Town as well as in Country; the proofs of which are abundant now, for mostly the Churches of that period remain in their former size and general structure."

inquiry about his Visitation Articles; for in those for the Diocese of Canterbury, 1560-1, he had asked :—

"2. *Item*, Whether you have in your parish churches . . . a comely and decent table for the holy Communion, set in place prescribed by the Queene's Majesties Injunctions : . . ." (*Ib.* Bk. I. App. XI. *fol.*, or 8vo. Vol. III. p. 28.)

In 1563 his question was similar (See p. 344); and that his ruling upon the point was not changed when Kechyn asked his question, may be inferred from the Advertisements which were occasioned by the disorders of the time. Moreover, as the use of the Surplice was one of the complaints against Kechyn and as it is certain that Abp. Parker would have upheld him in that, it is not probable that the complaint against his Eastward Position could, any more than the Surplice, have been regarded by the Archbishop as a breach of the Law.

These Inquiries shew, that the Abp. endeavoured to keep the Holy Table as much as possible where the Altars used to stand; and the "Interpretations of the Injunctions," issued by him and the other Bishops in 1561, support this view; for they prescribe, more precisely than the Injunctions, the circumstances under which the Table may be moved from the Chancel; they order :—

"That the table be removed out of the Choir into the body of the Church, before the Chancel door; where either the choir seemeth to be too little, or at great feasts of receivings. And at the end of the Communion to be set up again, according to the Injunctions." (*Cardwell, Doc. Ann.* I. 238.)

It is plain, indeed, that at this period the *Altarwise* position of the Lord's Table (implied in this very passage) was obnoxious to many of the Clergy who, as Strype says, " seem to have been " exiles " and " much biassed . . . towards those platforms " which were received in the Reformed Churches where they had " a little before sojourned." (*Ann.* I. pt. 1. 502, 8vo.) For, in the Convocation of 1562, it was proposed, but not carried :—

"That the table from henceforth stand no more altarwise, but stand in such place as is appointed by the Book of Common Prayer." (*Ib.* I. pt. 1, 475, or *Cardwell, Syn.* II. 498.)

The like opposition was shewn to the *Eastward Position* of

the Minister in the Service; for in the same Synod it was proposed (among other things) but lost by 59 to 58 :—

"That in all Parish Churches, the Minister in Common Prayer turn his face towards the people; and there distinctly read the Divine Service appointed, where all the people assembled may hear and be edified." (*Strype, Ann.* I., pt. 1, 502.)

Another contemporary illustration of the received meaning of the Law, occurs in a letter from Kings College, Cambridge, Dec. 17, 1565, which states:—

"That he [the Provost] had used one Mr. Wolwerd very roughly (he was afterwards fellow of Eton) because he would not officiate with his face towards the East, and his back sometimes towards ye Altar according to ye manner of ye Mass, for his refusal of w^h he had been expelled, was it not for an injunction from the queen and that, one of the Conducts then so celebrated. (*Le Keux's Memorials of Cambridge.* II. 24, ed. 1841.)

The Provost indeed, after the fashion of the time, was accused of favouring the Papists; although he had been commended by the Queen when she was at Cambridge in the previous year.

The following observation of the Court cannot indeed be questioned:—

"No direction was given for a change of position in the Prayer of Consecration in the second book of King Edward VI, but only a change of posture in the words 'standing up.'

But, as has been already shewn (See p. 269), the silence of the Book on other points cannot with any reason be accounted a prohibition, and therefore in this case the absence of a "direction" does not warrant the conclusion that "a change of "position" was not meant to be allowed. It can only fairly be inferred from the paucity of Rubrical directions in the Book of 1552, that a greater liberty was conceded to those who objected to the more stringent directions of the Book of 1549; though, at the same time, those who did not so object were not to be compelled to abandon customs not actually forbidden in the later Book.* The remark of the Court seems somewhat in place

---

* The remarkable case of *Robert Johnson,* in 1573, shews that a Practice could even be *required,* though not prescribed in a Rubric. Johnson was charged before the High Commission Court with omitting "to repeat the words of Institution" when more Wine was needed than had been Consecrated at

here, for if the opinion just before expressed (as to the Position of the Table and the Priest) were warranted, any " change of "position" would have been both difficult and useless, the Table standing East and West, as the Court appears to assume that it was.

This next sentence continues, seemingly, to take it as historically correct that a contrary custom had been *general* as to the place of the Table, in saying :—

> "But before the time of the Revision of 1662, the custom of placing the table along the east wall was becoming general, and it may fairly be said that the revisers must have had this in view."

No doubt "the custom" of which the Court here speaks applies to those Tables which had been removed from their Altarwise place; and this greater uniformity of practice would not be absent from the minds of the Revisers in 1661: but that it led them to make " a change of position in the Prayer of " Consecration " (as the Court seems to imply by the connexion of this with the preceding sentence) is a theory not supported, I think, by the History of the Revision or by a comparison of the Rubrics of 1604 and 1662: the latter are more explicit than the former; but that the two are at variance, is at least a very doubtful, if not an erroneous, view; and will appear to be so, I think, in considering the points mentioned by the Court in this next passage of its judgment :—

> "The following questions appear to require an answer, in order to dispose of this part of the case; what is

first: one part of his Defence was—"that in the Book of Common Prayer there is no such order appointed, unto which in this case I do refer myself." *The Dean of Westminster* said, " . . . . when you did send for more bread and wine you should have again rehearsed the order of Institution." *Johnson:* "The Book appointed no such order." *Bp. of London:* "Yes, Sir, the Book sayeth you shall have there sufficient Bread and Wine, and then the Prayer of Institution must be recited; for as much as you had not sufficient, therefore you should have repeated the Institution." *Johnson:* "There is no such caveat nor proviso appointed in the Book." *Bp. of London:* "But that is the meaning of the Book." *Johnson:* "Men may make what meaning they list, but I refer myself to the Book, whether it be so appointed or no." (*Part of a Register,* cir. 1590, p. 116). The needful *order* was afterwards given in the xxist. Canon of 1604.

meant by 'the north side of the table?' What change, if any, is ordered by the Rubric before the Prayer of Consecration? And what is the meaning of 'before the people' in that Rubric?"

L. The Court now proceeds to discuss the questions in order; remarking thus:—

"As to the first question, their Lordships are of opinion that 'north side of the table' means that side which looks towards the north.

To ascertain whether their Lordships have correctly answered their own question—"what is meant by 'the north side of the 'table?'" it is necessary to consider when and under what circumstances the term was first employed in the English Prayer Book. Now, as is commonly known, it originally appeared in the Second Prayer Book of K. Edward VIth., 1552; and it has been assumed by writers of varying and even opposite opinions on Doctrine and Ritual—that it was designed to fix the Position of the Celebrant at a period when the Altars being abolished in the Church of England and Tables were substituted for them (a) they were in a different *place* from that which the Altars had occupied; or (b) the Tables, standing in the Place of the Altars, were set with their Ends *East* and *West;* or (c) the *Place* of the Tables was not where the Altars stood, and their *Position* was also the reverse of the Altars. This opinion as to the *situation* and *orientation* of the Lord's Table thus substituted, has in part been discussed already and will have to be further noticed hereafter. The point now to be considered is whether there is any other mode of accounting for the term in question: it seems to me that there is. At the request of a friend, in 1859, who was cognisant of a Proposal, by some of the Bishops, that an Episcopal Manifesto should be issued in reference to the Position of the Celebrant, I stated this opinion in writing; and since then I have had occasion to mention it. It may be wholly erroneous, nevertheless I venture to reproduce it now in a more distinct and public form than it has before occupied, hoping that it may, perchance, aid some little in "the resolution" of the "doubts "concerning the manner how to understand" the Rubrics of the present Prayer Book which relate to the Position of the Celebrant at the Altar.

It appears, then, to me, that sufficient attention has not been paid to the fact that the ORDER of the Communion Office in the Book of 1552 was *materially changed* from that which was provided in the Book of 1549; and that this *transposition* of leading portions of the Office necessitated a corresponding alteration of the Rubrics. This will be best seen by placing in parallel columns those Rubrics of the two Books which control the Position of the Celebrant; and at the same time the language of the Rubrics may be better understood by also giving the corresponding Rubrics of the Sarum Missal and the Latin translation of the Rubrics of 1549, made by Alesius for the benefit of Bucer and other foreign Divines. This is done in the following arrangement:—

I.	II.	III.	IV.
SARUM MISSAL.*	PRAYER BOOK, 1549	ALESIUS'S TRANSLATION. P.B.1549.†	PRAYER BOOK, 1552
"Ad Missam dicendam, dum sacerdos induit se sacris vestibus, dicat Hymnum sequentem. "Hymnus. "VENI, CREATOR SPIRITUS, &c. (*Col.* 577).	"Upon the day, and at the time appointed for the ministration of the holy Communion, the Priest that shall execute the holy ministry, shall put upon him the vesture appointed for that ministration, that is to say, a white Albe plain, with a Vestment or Cope. And where there be many Priests, or Deacons, there so many shall be ready to help the Priest in the ministration, as shall be requisite; and shall have upon them likewise the vestures appointed for their ministry, that is to say, Albes with Tunacles. Then shall the Clerks sing in English, for the Office or Introit, (as they call it,) a Psalm appointed for that day."	"Die destinato ad celebrationem Cœnae Domini, Sacerdos indutus Alba Casula, vel Cappa, astabit altari, & in locis, ubi sunt plures sacerdotes & Diaconi tot ex his iuuabunt Pastorem, quot opus habuerit, induti vestibus destinatis ad corum ministerium, hoc est, Albis & Tunicis. His paratis, Clerici incipiant cantare officium Misse lingua Anglica, vel Introitum, ut vocāt, hoc est, Psalmum assignatum ad hunc diem."	"And here is to be noted, that the Minister at the time of the Communion, and at all other times in his ministration, shall use neither Alb, Vestment, nor Cope: but being Archbishop, or Bishop, he shall have and wear a rochet: and being a Priest or Deacon, he shall have and wear a surplice only."

* " Missale ad usum insignis et præclaræ Ecclesiæ SARUM. Pars prima; Temporale.—BURNTISLAND: e prelo de PITSLIGO. Londini: Veneunt apud C. J. STEWART. 1861."

† The Title is—"Ordinatio Ecclesiæ sev Ministerii Ecclesiastici, in florentissimo Regno Angliæ, conscripta sermone patrio, & in Latinam linguam bona fide conuersa, & ad consolationem Ecclesiarum Christi, ubicunque locorum ac gentium, his tristissimis temporibus, EDITA AB ALEXANDRO ALESIO SCOTO SACRAE THEOLOGIAE DOCTORE, Lipsiæ in officina vvolfgangi GVNTERI. Anno. M.D.LI."

I.	II.	III.	IV.
"His finitis, et Officio Missae inchoato, cum post Officium GLORIA PATRI incipitur, accedat Sacerdos cum suis ministris ad gradum altaris, et dicat ipse confessionem, diacono assistente a dextris et subdiacono a sinistris. Hoc modo incipiendo, "ET NE NOS INDUCAS IN TENTATIONEM, SED LIBERA NOS A MALO," [said before going to the Altar.] "DEUS, CUI OMNE COR PATET," &c. (Ib. 577).	"The Priest, standing humbly afore the midst of the Altar, shall say the Lord's Prayer, with this Collect. "ALMIGHTY GOD, UNTO WHOM," &c.	"Sacerdos stans ante altare orabit precationem Dominicam, cum hac Collecta. "OMNIPOTENS DEUS," &c.	
"Deinde sequatur Antiphona, INTROIBO AD ALTARE DEI, Ps. JUDICA ME, DEUS, ET DISCERNE. Totus Psalmus dicitur cum GLORIA PATRI. Deinde dicitur Antiphona, "INTROIBO AD ALTARE DEI, "KYRIE ELEYSON, &c. (Ib. 579).	"Then shall he say a Psalm appointed for the Introit: which Psalm ended, the Priest shall say, or else the Clerks shall sing, "iii. LORD HAVE MERCY UPON US," &c.	"Tunc recitabit Psalmum destinatum ad Introitum Missæ huius diei quo finito Sacerdos dicet, aut Clerici canent: "KYRIE ELEISON," &c.	
"Quo facto, sacerdos et sui ministri in sedibus paratis se recipiant et exspectent usque ad GLORIA IN EXCELSIS, quod incipiatur semper in medio Altaris quandocunque dicitur. (Ib. 583). ". . . vertat se sacerdos ad populum, . . . dicat. . "DOMINUS VOBISCUM." "Oremus."	"Then the Priest, standing at God's board, shall begin, "GLORY BE TO GOD ON HIGH." "Then the Priest shall turn him to the people, and say, "THE LORD BE WITH YOU." "The Priest. "Let us pray."	"Sacerdos stans ad medium altaris canet, "GLORIA IN EXCELSIS DEO." "Tunc Sacerdos conversus ad populum dicet: "DOMINUS VOBISCUM." "SACERDOS. "Oremus.	"The Table having at the Communion time a fair white linen cloth upon it, shall stand in the body of the Church, or in the Chancel, where Morning Prayer and Evening Prayer be appointed to be said. And the Priest standing at the north side of the Table, shall say the Lord's prayer, with this Collect following. "ALMIGHTY GOD, UNTO WHOM," &c. "Then shall the Priest rehearse distinctly all the Ten Commandments: and the people kneeling, shall after every Commandment ask God's mercy for their transgression of the same, . . ."

I.	II.	III.	IV.
"Deinde dicitur oratio, sic determinando: "PER OMNIA SÆCULA SÆCULORUM."	"Then shall follow the Collect of the day, with one of these two Collects following, for the King." "ALMIGHTY GOD," &c.	"Tunc sequetur Collecta de die, cum una ex his quae subscriptæ sunt. "OMNIPOTENS DEUS," &c.	"Then shall follow the Collect of the day, with one of these two Collects following for the King: the Priest standing up and saying. "Let us pray." "ALMIGHTY GOD," &c.
"... Subdiaconus per medium chori ad legendum epistolam in pulpitum accedat." (Maskell Ancient Liturgy &c. Ed. 1844, p. 16).	"The Collects ended, the Priest, or he that is appointed, shall read the Epistle in a place assigned for that purpose, saying, "The Epistle," &c "The Minister then shall read the Epistle. Immediately after the Epistle ended, the Priest, or one appointed to read the Gospel, shall say,	"His finitis, Sacerdos aut subdiaconus legat Epistolam loco ad hoc deputato, & sic incipiat. "Epistola," &c. "Post Epistolam Sacerdos, aut Diaconus continuò legat Euangelium, & sic incipiat:	"Immediately after the Collects, the Priest shall read the Epistle, beginning thus. "The Epistle," &c. "And the Epistle ended, he shall say the Gospel beginning thus,
"In fine alleluia, vel sequentiæ, vel tractus Diaconus antequam accedat ad evangelium pronuntiandum thurificet medium altaris tantum. Deinde accipiat textum, silicet librum Evangeliorum, ... ad pulpitum accedat ... (Ib. 18.)			
"Evangelium secundum," &c.	"The Holy Gospel" &c. "The Clerks and people shall answer, "GLORY BE TO THEE, O LORD." "The Priest or Deacon then shall read the Gospel. After the Gospel ended, the Priest shall begin, "I BELIEVE IN ONE GOD." "The Clerks shall sing the rest: "THE FATHER," &c "After the Creed ended, shall follow the Sermon or Homily, or some portion of one of the Homilies, as they shall be hereafter divided: wherein if the peo-	"Sanctum Euangelium" &c. "Clerici & populus respondebunt: "GLORIA TIBI DOMINE." "Post Euangelium sequetur Symbolum. "CREDO IN UNUM DEO." "Post Symbolum sequetur sermo ad populum, uel Homilia, aut pars aliqua Homiliæ, quas, Deo uolente, postea diuidemus. Quod si in sermone uel Hom-	"The Gospel written" &c. "And the Epistle and Gospel being ended, shall be said the Creed. "I BELIEVE IN ONE GOD," &c. "After the Creed, if there be no sermon, shall follow one of the homilies already set forth, or hereafter to be set forth by common authority."
"Finito evangelio, incipiat sacerdos in medio altaris: "CREDO IN UNUM DEUM." (Ib. 20.)			

I.	II.	III.	IV.
	ple be not exhorted to the worthy receiving of the Holy Sacrament of the Body and Blood of our Saviour Christ, then shall the Curate give this exhortation to those that be minded to receive the same. "DEARLY BELOVED IN THE LORD, YE THAT MIND," &c.	ilia non fuerit exhortatio ad populum, de digna præparatione, & perceptione Sacramenti Corporis & Sanguinis Domini: Sacerdos utetur hac forma exhortationis ad communicantes. "DILECTO IN DOMINO, QUI CONSTITUISTIS COMMUNICARE," &c.	
	"In Cathedral Churches, or other places where there is daily Communion, it shall be sufficient to read this exhortation above written once in a month. And in Parish Churches, upon the week days, it may be left unsaid.	"In Cathedralibus Ecclesiis, & in aliis locis, ubi est quotidiana Communio, satis erit si legatur prædicta exhortatio semel in Mense, & in Parrochialibus Ecclesiis in aliis diebus, præter Dominicam diem, per totam Septimanam potest omitti.	
	"And if upon the Sunday or Holy-day the people be negligent to come to the Communion, then shall the Priest earnestly exhort his Parishioners to dispose themselves to the receiving of the holy Communion more diligently, saying these or like words unto them, "DEAR FRIENDS, AND YOU ESPECIALLY," &c.	"Si autem populus sit negligens, & diebus Dominicis, & aliis Festis diebus, non accedat ad Communionem, tunc Pastor serio exhortetur suos Parrochianos, ut sese præparent ad perceptionem Sacramenti, adhibita maiore diligentia, & utetur hac, uel simili forma exhortationis: "DILECTI IN DOMINO, & UOS NOMINATIM," &c.	
"Deinde dicitur Offertorium." (*Col.* 593.)	"Then shall follow for the Offertory one or mo of these sentences of holy Scripture, to be sung whiles the people do offer; or else one of them to be said by the Minister immediately afore the offering, "LET YOUR LIGHT," &c.	"Tunc sequetur Offertorium, unum ex his quæ subscripta sunt, quod canitur interim, dum populus offert munera ad altare, "SIC LUCEAT," &c.	"After such sermon, homily, or exhortation, the Curate shall declare unto the people whether there be any holy days or fasting days the week following: and earnestly exhort them to remember the poor, saying one or more of these Sentences following, as he thinketh most convenient by his discretion. "LET YOUR LIGHT," &c.

I.	II.	III.	IV.
	"Where there be Clerks, they shall sing one or many of the sentences above written, according to the length and shortness of the time that the people be offering. "In the mean time, whiles the Clerks do sing the Offertory, so many as are disposed shall offer to the poor men's box everyone according to his habilitie and charitable mind. And at the offering days appointed, every man and woman shall pay to the Curate the due and accustomed offerings. "Then so many as shall be partakers of the Holy Communion shall tarry still in the Quire, or in some convenient place nigh the Quire, the men on the one side, and the women on the other side. All other (that mind not to receive the said Holy Communion) shall depart out of the Quire, except the Ministers and Clerks."	"Harum & similium sententiarum ex Thobia, Prouerbiis, uel Psalmis, una aut plures canantur, ut tempus oblationis, & numerus offerentium postulabit. "Tempore quo canitur offertorium, quilibet qui communionem cupit percipere, imponet aliquid æris in erario pauperum. "Die autem oblationum, quilibet per soluet Pastori debitam pensionem. "Tunc communicaturi poruenient in Chorum, uel locum uicinum, uiri à dextris, mulieres à sinistris separatim, & disiuncti genuflectant, reliqui chorum egrediuntur, præter Clericos & ministros."	
"Post offertorium vero porrigat diaconus sacerdoti calicem cum patena et sacrificio, et osculetur manum ejus utraque vice. Ipse vero accipiens ab eo calicem, diligenter ponat in loco suo debito super medium altare. . . . (Ib.) ". . . ponatque panem super corporalia decenter ante calicem vinum et aquam continentem; et osculetur patenam et reponat eam a dextris sacrificii super altare sub	"Then shall the Minister take so much Bread and Wine as shall suffice for the persons appointed to receive the Holy Communion, laying the Bread upon the Corporas, or else in the Paten, or in some other comely thing prepared for that purpose: and putting the Wine into the Chalice, or else in some fair or convenient cup prepared for that use, (if the Chalice will not serve,) putting	"Tunc Sacerdos tot hostias calici aut corporali imponet, quot sufficient communicantibus, &c. tantum vini, cui admiscebitur parum aquæ puræ, quantum opus est, in calice, vel in pateris infundet, & collocabit in altari,	

I.	II.	III.	IV.
"corporalibus parum cooperiendo." (*Ib.*)	thereto a little pure and clean Water, and setting both the Bread and Wine upon the Altar. Then the Priest shall say, "THE LORD BE WITH YOU."	Sacerdos, "DOMINUS VOBISCUM."	
"Sequuntur Præfationes." (*Ib.*596).	"Here shall follow the proper Preface, according to the time, (if there be any specially appointed,) or else immediately shall follow,	"Tunc sequetur propria præfatio Festi.	
"Sequitur. "ET IDEO CUM ANGELIS," &c.	"THEREFORE WITH ANGELS," &c.		
			"Then shall the Churchwardens, or some other by them appointed, gather the devotion of the people, and put the same into the poor men's box: And upon the offering days appointed, every man and woman shall pay to the Curate the due and accustomed offerings:
	"When the Clerks have done singing [the Sanctus], then shall the Priest or Deacon turn him to the people, and say, "Let us pray for the whole state," &c. "Then the Priest, turning him to the Altar, shall say or sing, plainly and distinctly, this prayer following:	"Tunc Sacerdos, uel Diaconus, conuersus ad plebem dicet: "Oremus pro statu univesalis Ecclesiæ, & mox hanc Orationem clara uoce, & distincti, canet, aut leget:	after which done the Priest shall say, "Let us pray for the whole state of Christ's Church militant here in earth."
	"ALMIGHTY AND EVERLIVING GOD, WHICH," &c. [Marginal Notes.] "Here the Priest must take the Bread into his hands."	"OMNIPOTENS ÆTERNE DEUS, QUI," &c. [The Manual Acts are not mentioned in the margin or elsewhere.]	"ALMIGHTY AND EVERLIVING GOD, WHICH," &c. [No Manual Acts mentioned.]
"Hic tangat hostiam."* (*Ib.* 616.) "Hic elevet sacerdos parumper calicem, ..." (Col. 617.)	"Here the Priest shall take the Cup into his hands." "These words before rehearsed are to be said, turning still to the Altar, without any elevation or shewing the Sacrament to the people."	"Haec dicantur sine eleuatione aut ostensione Sacramenti."	

* A fuller Rubric says—"Hic non debet tangi hostia, modo fractionis, sicut aliqui fatui tangunt et male faciunt," &c. Col. 616, and See p. 333.

I.	II.	III.	IV.
			"Then shall follow this exhortation at certain times when the Curate shall see the people negligent to come to the Holy Communion, "WE BE COME TOGETHER," &c. "And sometime shall be said this also, at the discretion of the Curate. "DEARLY BELOVED, FORASMUCH, &c. "Then shall the Priest say this exhortation. "DEARLY BELOVED IN THE LORD, YE THAT MIND," &c.
"Hic elevet sacerdos manus, dicens,	"Let us pray. "As our Saviour Christ hath commanded and taught us, we are bold to say:	"Oremus. "Præceptis salutaribus moniti, & divina institutione formati, audemus dicere:	
"PATER NOSTER" &c. "Chorus dicat. "SED LIBERA NOS A MALO. Amen. ". . . dicens,	"OUR FATHER, &c." "The Answer. "BUT DELIVER US FROM EVIL. Amen. "Then shall the Priest say,	PATER NOSTER, &c. "Chorus respondeat: "SED LIBERA NOS A MALO. "Sacerdos.	
"PAX DOMINI + SIT SEM + PER VO + BISCUM. "Chorus respondeat. "Et cum Spiritu tuo. ". . . . accedant diaconus et subdiaconus ad sacerdotem . . . et dicant privatim, "AGNUS DEI QUI TOLLIS," &c.	"THE PEACE OF THE LORD BE ALWAY WITH YOU. "The Clerks. "AND WITH THY SPIRIT. "The Priest.	"PAX DOMINI SIT SEMPER VOBISCUM. "Chorus. "ET CUM SPIRITU TUO. "Sacerdos.	
	"CHRIST OUR PASCHAL LAMB," &c	"CHRISTUS NOSTER AGNUS," &c.	
	"Here the Priest shall turn him toward those that come to the holy Communion, and shall say, "YOU THAT DO TRULY," &c.	"Hic Sacerdos conversus ad confitentes, dicet: "VOS, QUOS SERIO," &c.	"Then shall the Priest say to them that come to receive the holy Communion. "YOU THAT DO TRULY," &c.

II.

"Then shall this general Confession be made, in the name of all those that are minded to receive the holy Communion, either by one of them, or else by one of the Ministers, or by the Priest himself, all kneeling humbly upon their knees.

"ALMIGHTY GOD, FATHER OF," &c.

"Then shall the Priest stand up, and turning himself to the people, say thus:

"ALMIGHTY GOD, OUR HEAVENLY FATHER," &c.

"Then shall the Priest also say,

"Hear what comfortable words," &c.

"Then shall the Priest, turning him to God's board, kneel down, and say in the name of all them that shall receive the Communion, this prayer following:

"WE DO NOT PRESUME," &c.

III.

"Tunc fiet generalis confessio nomine eorum, qui volunt communicare, uel per eorum aliquem, uel per unum ex Ministris altaris, uel per ipsum Sacerdotem, omnibus interim flectentibus genua.

"OMNIPOTENS DEUS PATER," &c.

"Tunc eriget se Sacerdos, & conversus ad populum, sic loquetur.

"DOMINUS NOSTER JESUS CHRISTUS," &c.

"Sic stans conversus ad populum dicet:
"Audite," &c.

"Tunc genuflectet Sacerdos, & nomine eorum, qui volunt communicare, sic orabit, genibus flexis:

"NON AUDEMUS," &c.

IV.

"Then shall this general Confession be made, in the name of all those that are minded to receive the holy Communion, either by one of them, or else by one of the ministers, or by the Priest himself, all kneeling humbly upon their knees.

"ALMIGHTY GOD, FATHER OF," &c.

"Then shall the Priest or the Bishop (being present) stand up, and turning himself to the people, say thus.

"ALMIGHTY GOD, OUR HEAVENLY FATHER," &c.

"Then shall the Priest also say.

"Hear what comfortable words," &c.
"After the which, the Priest shall proceed, saying.
"LIFT UP YOUR HEARTS," &c.

"Here shall follow the proper Preface, according to the time, if there be any specially appointed: or else immediately shall follow: Therefore with Angels, &c."
"After which preface, shall follow immediately.
"THEREFORE WITH ANGELS," &c.

"Then shall the Priest, kneeling down at God's board, say in the name of all them that shall receive the Communion, this prayer following.

"WE DO NOT PRESUME," &c.

I.	II.	III.	IV.
			"Then the Priest standing up shall say, as followeth. "ALMIGHTY GOD, OUR HEAVENLY FATHER," &c.
	"Then shall the Priest first receive the Communion in both kinds himself, and next deliver it to other Ministers, if any be there present, (that they may be ready to help the chief Minister,) and after to the people. "And when he delivereth the Sacrament of the Body of Christ, he shall say to every one these words:	"Tunc surget Sacerdos, populo adhuc genuflectente, & communicabit ipse primo sub utraque specie: & deinde ministri, ut possint eum iuvare in communicando populo, et cum exhibet Sacramentum corporis, utatur hac forma orationis.	"Then shall the Minister first receive the Communion in both kinds himself, and next deliver it to other ministers, if any be there present (that they may help the chief minister), and after to the people in their hands kneeling. And when he delivereth the bread, he shall say.
	"THE BODY OF OUR LORD," &c.	"CORPUS DOMINI," &c.	"TAKE AND EAT THIS," &c.
	"And the Minister delivering the Sacrament of the Blood, and giving every one to drink once, and no more, shall say,	"Et cum porrigit Sacramentum sanguinis sic orabit:	"And the minister that delivereth the cup, shall say.
	"THE BLOOD OF OUR LORD," &c.	"SANGUINIS DOMINI," &c.	"DRINK THIS" &c.
	"If there be a Deacon or other Priest, then shall he follow with the Chalice; and as the Priest ministereth the Sacrament of the Body, so shall he (for more expedition) minister the Sacrament of the Blood, in form before written."	"Sic affuerit Diaconus, aut alter Sacerdos, is priorem qui porrigit corpus Domini, sequatur cum calice, quem continuò exhibeat."	
	"In the Communion time the Clerks shall sing. "ii. O LAMB OF GOD," &c.	"Tempore communionis cantet Chorus. "2. AGNUS DEI," &c.	
	"Beginning so soon as the Priest doth receive the holy Communion: and when the Communion is ended, then shall the Clerks sing the post-Communion."		

I.	II.	III.	IV.
	"Sentences of holy Scripture to be said or sung, every day one, after the holy Communion, called the post-Communion.	"Post communionem canatur:	
	"If any man," &c.	"Si quis uult post me uenire," &c.	
	"Then the Priest shall give thanks to God, in the name of all them that have communicated, turning him first to the people, and saying,	"Tunc Sacerdos conuersus ad populum orabit:	
	"The Lord be with you."	"Dominus vobiscum."	
	"The Answer, "And with thy spirit."	Chorus. "Et cum Spiritu tuo.	
	The Priest. "Let us pray."	Sacerdos. "Oremus,	"Then shall the Priest say the Lord's Prayer, the people repeating after him every petition.
			"After shall be said as followeth, "O Lord and heavenly Father," &c.
			Or this,
	"Almighty and everliving God, we most heartily thank thee, for that thou hast vouchsafed" &c.	"Diuinis refecti mysteriis & spiritualibus faciati Sacramenti, corpore & sanguine" &c.	"Almighty and everliving God, we most heartily thank thee, for that thou hast vouchsafed" &c.
			"Then shall be said or sung, "Glory be to God on high," &c.
	"Then the Priest, turning him to the people, shall let them depart with this blessing:	"Tunc Sacerdos conuersus ad populum, orabit.	"Then the Priest or the Bishop, if he be present, shall let them depart with this blessing,
	"The peace of God," &c.	"Et pax Dei," &c.	"The Peace of God," &c.
	"Then the people shall answer, Amen.	"Cui populus respondebit, Amen.	
	"Where there are no Clerks, there the Priest shall say all things appointed here for them to sing."	"Vbi non sunt cantores, dicantur omnia, non canantur."	
	"When the holy Communion is celebrate on the workday, or in private houses, then may be	"In diebus per septimanam, & cum celebratur communio in priuatis aedibus possunt	[Nothing corresponding here or in the Office for the Communion of the Sick.]

I.	II.	III.	IV.
—	omitted the Gloria in Excelsis, the Creed, the Homily, and the Exhortation, beginning, "DEARLY BELOVED," &c.	omitti : Gloria in Excelsis Deo, Credo, Homilia, Exhortatio, & sic incipiatur : "DILECTI IN DOMINO," &c.	
	"Collects to be said after the Offertory, when there is no Communion, every such day one. "ASSIST US MERCIFULLY," &c.	"Sequuntur Collectæ dicendæ post Offertorium, quando non adsunt communicantes. "ADESTO SUPPLICATIONIBUS NOSTRIS," &c.	"Collects to be said after the Offertory, when there is no Communion, every such day one," &c. "ASSIST US MERCIFULLY," &c.
	"Upon Wednesdays and Fridays the English Litany shall be said or sung in all places, after such form as is appointed by the King's majesty's Injunctions; or as is or shall be otherwise appointed by his Highness. And though there be none to communicate with the Priest, yet these days (after the Litany ended) the Priest shall put upon him a plain Albe or Surplice, with a Cope, and say all things at the Altar, (appointed to be said at the celebration of the Lord's Supper,) until after the Offertory : And then shall add one or two of the Collects afore written, as occasion shall serve, by his discretion. And then, turning him to the people, shall let them depart with the accustomed Blessing. "And the same order shall be used all other days, whensoever the people be customably assembled to pray in the Church, and none disposed to communicate with the Priest."	"Diebus Mercurii, & Veneris, Letania Anglica canatur, uel dicatur omnibus locis, sicut à Serenissimo Rege est præscriptum. Cum autem non adsunt communicantes, tamen diebus dictis, post Letanium Sacerdos indutus Alba, aut linea, cum Cappa, recitabit ea, quæ in cœna Domini recitari solent, usque dum perueniat ad Offertorium. Tunc enim post unam aut alteram Collectam, demittet populum, cum benedictione consueta. "Nusquam celebratur cœna Domini, uel Missa, (ut uocatur) sine communicantibus."	"Upon the holy days, if there be no Communion, shall be said all that is appointed at the Communion, until the end of the Homily, concluding with the general prayer, for the whole state of Christ's church militant here in earth : and one or more of these Collects before rehearsed, as occasion shall serve. "And there shall be no celebration of the Lord's Supper, except there be a good number to communicate with the Priest, according to his discretion."

Now it will be seen, by comparing Columns I. and II. (p. 360) that the *First* POSTURE and POSITION occupied by the Priest (Celebrant) under the Prayer Book of 1549 were the same which he had been accustomed to under the Sarum Missal; and which, moreover, he had been ordered, only a year before, still to occupy while that Office remained in use; for "The "Order of Communion," 1548, which was designed as a temporary Supplement to the Canon of the Mass, contains the Rubric following:—

"The time of the Communion shall be immediately after that the Priest himself hath received the Sacrament, without the varying of any other rite or ceremony in the Mass, (until other order shall be provided.) . . ."

This *First* POSTURE and POSITION are—" standing humbly "afore the midst of the Altar," or, as Alesius translates it, "stans ante altare," *i.e.*, as the Missal Rubric shews, at the *Step* of the Altar ("ad gradum Altaris"): here he was to say the Lord's Prayer and the Collect "Almighty God, unto whom all hearts "be open," &c: this was his Preparation for commencing the Office; and was the counterpart, in this place, of the Sarum Office, except that the Collect was said earlier in the Sarum Preparatio.

After the Introit, &c., the *Second* POSTURE and POSITION of the Priest are—" standing at God's board," which Alesius translates " stans ad medium altaris: " here the Priest was to begin the Office with "Glory be to God on high," &c. which, says the Sarum Rubric, "incipiatur semper in medio altaris "quandocuncque dicitur." That the Priest was looking Eastward *i.e.* having his back to the people, is plain from the next Rubric, "Then the Priest shall turn him to the people, and "say, The Lord be with you:" this being, in fact, the "vertat "se Sacerdos ad populum" of Sarum, and the "Sacerdos conver- "sus ad populum" of Alesius.

Thus far, then, it is perfectly clear what were the POSTURE and POSITION of the Celebrant at the commencement of the Office while the Book of 1549 remained in use.

But in 1552 it was decided to supersede the Book of 1549,

and the new Communion Office, *in its structural arrangement*, differed considerably from the previous one: into the reason of this change it is unnecessary here to inquire. But it must be noticed—that the *first* POSITION occupied by the Priest is neither his *first* nor his *second* Position under the Book of 1549 (See Column IV. p. 360: he takes a wholly new POSITION, though not POSTURE, for the commencement of the Office, viz., "stand-"ing at the North side of the Table:" there he says the Lord's Prayer and Collect, whether still as his Preparation or as the beginning of the Office itself, it is immaterial to consider for the purpose of the present inquiry. Yet the question arises—Why this change of POSITION? On what principle, if any, did he not place himself at first before the *middle* of the Table, whether at the Step or at the Table itself, as he had hitherto done according to the Book of 1549?

As regards the Priest not first standing at the *Step* of the Lord's Table, the omission of the former direction would be fully accounted for by the omission of all the *Introits* in the Book of 1552: though it is very likely that the mere force of habit caused them still to be used, as they were not *forbidden* in the new Office and could be said in the old place, before the Lord's Prayer and Collect, without in the least conflicting with the new Rubric which merely ordered the Lord's Prayer and Collect to be said later, and in a different place, than before. Where, indeed, the Altar Steps had been removed (if such was the case): or where, in consequence of the King's Letter to Ridley, Nov. 24. 1550 (See p. 340) the "Table" may have been "set up in some convenient part of the chancel" other than the place where the Altar stood, there the absence of the former Rubric would concur with these altered conditions.

But these considerations do not account for the Priest not going to the *Middle* of the Table itself to begin the Office, though this had been his position "at God's board" when he commenced the Office in the Book of 1549. Yet there must have been some ground for this alteration; and as it seems to me, the explanation is to be found in the fact that the new Office did not begin with the "Gloria in Excelsis." In the absence of any known Historical Record about it, the reasonable way of accounting for what was done, is to place ourselves as much as may be in the position of the Revisers of 1552: they were reconstructing an Office (that of 1549) which only three years before they had constructed, so far as it went, mainly upon the lines of the Sarum Ordinary and Canon of the Mass; and it is utterly unlikely that the "greate menny "bushops and other of the best learned within this realme" who, as Cranmer said (in his Letter already partly quoted at p. 274), with himself and Ridley were "appointed" for "the "making of the boke" of 1552, disregarded, when doing so, the Rules of that old Office with which, up to four years before, they had been thoroughly familiar; and could not but be reminded of it in using the Book of 1549.

Therefore, when these Revisers determined (among other things) to transpose the order of the Book of 1549 and to remove the "Gloria in Excelsis" from *the very beginning* to *nearly the end* of the Office, they must, surely, have considered where the Celebrant was to be placed under this altered state of things. In doing so, they would of course recollect the following Sarum Rubric:—

"*Sciendum est autem quod quicquid a sacerdote dicitur ante Epistolam, in dextro cornu altaris expleatur; præter inceptionem Gloria in excelsis. Similiter fiat post perceptionem sacramenti. Cætera omnia in medio Altaris expleantur, nisi forte diaconus defuerit. Tunc enim in sinistro cornu Altaris legatur Evangelium.*" (Ed. Burntisland. 1861. Col. 589; or Maskell, *Ancient Liturgy* &c. 1844, p. 12.)

With this before them, nothing could be more natural than for them to say—We cannot direct the Priest, when he goes to the Lord's Table, to stand at the *middle* of it for the "Gloria in "Excelsis" does not now begin the Office: therefore he must be placed elsewhere. By the analogy of the Sarum Rubric he should have been sent to the *dexter horn*, *i.e.*, to the right-hand corner, or South of the middle of the Altar-table: whereas the Rubric of 1552 puts him "at the North side of the Table;" this, by the same analogy, would be the *sinister horn*, *i.e.*, the left hand corner, or North of the middle of the Altar-table. But why was he sent *North* and not *South*? It would seem that the reason is to be gathered from what occured two years before. It was natural that the Clergy in using the Book of 1549, especially those of them who did not greatly favour it, should continue their old customs where the Rubrics of the new Book were not inconsistent with them; and that this did happen is shewn, for example, by Hooper's Letter to Bullinger, Dec. 27, 1549, in which he complains of the similarity in using the new and the old Offices; saying, for instance, "where they had the "principal, or high *Mass*, they now have, as they call it, the high "*Communion* . . . . . God knows to what perils and anxieties "we are exposed by men of this kind . . ." (*Original Letters*, Parker Society, p. 71). This circumstance may have led Bp. Ridley, in 1550, to issue his Injunctions for the Diocese of London, the Second of which directs "That no minister do "counterfeit the popish mass;" and then, among the ways of counterfeiting it, this is mentioned—"shifting the book from "one place to another." (*Works*, Parker Society, p. 319.)

This shows plainly that the old Custom of moving the Missal from one part of the Altar to another, was followed when the Book of 1549 came into use, though the latter contained no such Rule as that upon which the Sarum practice was founded.

In the year 1551 Bp. Hooper, in his "Visitation Booke" for the Diocese of Gloucester, gave a like direction to that of Ridley—"Item, that none of you do counterfeit the Popish "mass in . . . shifting the book from one place unto another." (*Later Writings*, Parker Society, p. 118)

This same Prohibition of—"shifting of the book from one "place to another"—occurs also in a Document called "Articles "to be followed and observed according to the King's Majesty's "Injunctions and Proceedings" (*Cardwell, Doc. Ann.* I. 74): they have no Date, but are supposed to be Royal Injunctions of 1549 (though both Date and Authority are doubtful):* however, the existence of these three Documents may well imply that the Injunction was also issued by some other Prelates,† and if so it

---

* See my "Reasonable Limits of Lawful Ritualism." In "The Church and the World," 1866. p. 455.

† After the Book of 1552 had been restored by Q. Elizabeth, Parkhurst, Bp. of Norwich, gave the following Injunction in 1561—"4. Item that they neither suffer the Lordes Table to be hanged and decked like an aulter, neyther vse any gestures of the popish masse in the time of the ministracion of the communion, as shifting of the boke, washing, breathing, crossing or such like." (2nd *Rit. Report*, p. 401): thus showing that practices which had been resumed in Q. Mary's reign, clung to the Clergy under the Book of 1559.

would be all the more likely to lead to some mode of giving a general effect to it when the Book of 1552 was prepared. The "North side" Position would accomplish this better than the South side: for, even supposing that this direction was intended to keep the Celebrant in this one place throughout the whole Service, there would be no more change of the Book than if he had been sent to the *South* side; and, further, his normal Position would be on that side of the Church where it had been customary for the Gospel to be read, especially when the Celebrant, being unassisted, had to read it himself. Moreover, whether the Priest was to Consecrate the Sacrament in his normal Position or, as is more likely, in the middle* of the Lord's Table, it is obvious that he could do so much more conveniently than if the Book were placed on his right hand *i.e.* the South side. And, once more, he could turn to the people, when required, more naturally from the Northern than from the Southern part of the Table, if he was, as I here assume, standing with his back to the people.

That the Bishops, in 1552, intended to send the Celebrant to an END (whether *North* or *South*) of the Lord's Table, standing Altar-wise, seems to me to be a notion so wholly improbable, that it ought to be at once rejected unless there is some reliable evidence in its favour. The Position would be so entirely foreign to all their Ritual knowledge and experience, that they were not in the least likely to propose it—most probably not even to think of it: Bp. Hooper was, perhaps, more likely than any of them to propose such a departure from the Rule and Practice of the Church, whether in England or elsewhere; yet, though he does (in his Visitation Book, 1551-2) direct "that the "minister in the use of the communion and prayers thereof turn "his face towards the people" (*Later Writings*, Parker Society. p. 118), the Order implies a Position looking *Westward*, whether the Celebrant was *behind* or *before* the Table—the latter, however, being a most unlikely place for him to take, in order

---

* Even FULKE, replying in 1597 to RASTEL one of the "Arch-patriarchs of the Popishe Synagogue," as he was called, says—"... as though we did not vse ordinarily ... to take the bread and breake it, and with the cup set it before vs, and not to let it stand at the ende of the Table, as he belyeth vs, as though we were ashamed to follow Christ." (*D. Hoskins, D. Sanders, and M. Rastel ... overthrown*" ... &c. "Anno 1579.")

to "face" the people. Moreover, this direction of Bp. Hooper's is, remarkably enough, an addition to Bishop Ridley's Injunction of 1550, though the rest of Hooper's Article is mainly a repetition* of Ridley's Injunction.

Further, it is most important to notice—that in the minute description † of ways in which "the Popish Mass" was *counterfeited*, (as stated by Ridley, Hooper, and the alleged Royal "Articles" already quoted p. 373) the Position of the Celebrant in front of the Altar, looking East, is not even hinted at as being any such "counterfeit;" though it was a far more *prominent* feature of the Mass than any one of the counterfeits mentioned in those Documents.

It has, however, been contended (by the writers ‡ already

---

* The following is Ridley's Injunction. Hooper's variations are put in brackets:—"Whereas in divers places some use the Lord's board after the form of a table, and some of an altar, whereby dissention is perceived to arise among the unlearned; therefore wishing a godly unity to be observed in all our diocese, and for that the form of a table may more move and turn the simple from the old svperstitious opinions of the Popish mass, and to the right use of the Lord's Supper, we exhort the Curates, church-wardens, and questmen here present [*Hooper*, we exhort you] to erect and set up the Lord's board after the form of an honest table, decently covered, in such place of the choir or chancel [*Hooper*, in such place] as shall be thought most meet by their discretion and agreement [*Hooper*, thought most meet], so that the ministers, with the [*Hooper*, and] communicants, may have their place separated from the rest of the people; [*Hooper*, Communicants may be seen, heard, and understood of all the people there being present]; and to [*Hooper*—and that ye do] take down and abolish all other by altars or tables. [*Hooper*, Further, that the Minister in the use of the communion and prayers thereof turn his face towards the people." [*Works of Ridley* p. 319; *Later Writings of Bp. Hooper*, p. 118. Parker Society.]

† *Ridley.* "That no minister do counterfeit the popish mass, in kissing the Lord's board; washing his hands or fingers after the gospel, or the receipt of the holy communion; shifting the book from one place to another; laying down and licking the chalice after the communion; blessing his eyes with the sudarie thereof, or paten, or crossing his head with the same, holding his fore-fingers and thumbs joined together toward the temples of his head, after the receiving of the sacrament; breathing on the bread, or chalice; saying the Agnus before the communion; shewing the Sacrament openly before the distribution, or making any elevation thereof; ringing of the sacrying bell, or setting any light upon the Lord's board. And finally that the Minister, in the time of the holy communion, do use only the ceremonies and gestures appointed by the Book of Common Prayer, and none other, so that there do not appear in them any counterfeiting of the Popish mass." (*Works.* p. 319. Parker Society: or *Cardwell Doc. Ann.* Vol. I. p. 93.) *Hooper* and the supposed *Royal Articles* are almost identical in language with *Ridley;* but *Hooper* does not give the direction, "And finally that the Minister," &c.

‡ Mr. *Elliott*, p. 20. ". . . . the Rubric of 1552, following upon the general demolition of altars, and substitution of tables, ordered that 'the *table* should stand *in the body of the Church*, or *in the Chancel*, where Morning and Evening

mentioned, at p. 349, as being either *for* or *against* the Eastward Position) that the term "North side" was employed in the Book of 1552 to suit the altered position of the Lord's Table which, it is said, had at that time ceased to stand with its ends North and South, and was placed lengthwise in the Chancel or Church with its Ends East and West: that, consequently, the Celebrant was to stand on the long side of the Table, with his

Prayer be appointed to be said,' and the same Rubric directs that the Priest should stand, no longer, as in 1549, '*afore the midst of the Altar*,' but 'at the North side of the Table.'"

p. 22.—"Altars having been abolished in 1550, and tables of no prescribed form ordered to be set up 'in some convenient part of the Chancel,' in every Church, and the position of those tables being commonly no longer N. and S., but E. and W., the words 'North side,' even if applicable to the *northern portion* of the *West side* of the *Altar*, standing N. and S., (of which, however, there seems to be no proof adduced from English sources,) would have been utterly unintelligible in their application to any *one particular part* of the *North side* of the Table, standing E. and W.: . . ."

p. 25.—"It seems almost superfluous, after what has been already advanced, to state my own conviction that 'North side,' in the original Rubric of 1552, (if meant to denote any particular side of the Table, and not merely to determine the position of the Priest at the *North* of it,) had reference to its broad side, when placed E. and W., and not to its short side, or end, when placed N. and S."

Mr. Droop, p. 6.—". . . . the Rubric of 1552 was speaking not of an altar at the East end of the chancel, but of a table to be placed rather in the body of the church than in the chancel. In November 1550, King Edward and his Council had issued orders to every bishop (Cardwell, Doc. Ann. Vol. i., p. 89) to cause 'that with all diligence all the altars be taken down, and instead of them a table to be set up in some convenient part of the chancel, to serve for the ministration of the blessed Communion.'"

p. 9.—". . . . there is nothing to show that the Prayer-book of 1552 intended the bearings of the table to remain the same as those of the altars in use before 1550."

Mr. Walton, p. 3.—"The Rubric of 1549, directing the Priest to stand 'humbly afore the midst of the Altar,' points to the time when the ancient consecrated Altars remained 'as in times past' erected against the east wall of Chancels; it belongs to that period referred to in our Prayer Book as 'the second year of the reign of King Edward the Sixth.' But with the Rubric of 1552 a wholly different state of things had come in. The sinister influences of Foreign Reformers had told upon the Ritual of the English Church; not only had the ancient Altars been violently pulled down from the east end of the Churches, but the Tables substituted for them, in order to contrast as much as possible with the form and appearance of an Altar, were now placed lengthwise down the Chancel, or in the body of the Church, *i.e.*, the Nave, the two ends of the Table being set east and west."

Mr. Scudamore ("The North side," &c.) p. 9.—"Our next step is to show that when the Table was thus placed, ready for the celebration, 'in the body of the church, or in the chancel,' it was *always* set east and west, or, as the phrase ran, *tablewise*. In doing this we shall be led to see that it was also *generally* set in the same way when in its ordinary place."

p. 10.—"In most churches the Tables would from necessity alone have been set east and west when moved into the nave or low down in the chancel.

back to the North and his face looking South. But it appears clearly to me that the passages, which have been produced to prove this alleged general Position of the Altar-Tables when the Prayer Book of 1552 was published, are not to the purpose (See pp. 349–52) and do not in the least conflict with the theory which I have ventured to propound as fully accounting for the term "North side."*

There would not have been room between the seats to admit of their being set lengthways across the church."†

* * * * * * * * *

p. 11.—"It is evident, then, that men had what they imagined to be a good reason for the tablewise position of the Altar. But as the reason for this position was the same as that for moving it at all, we cannot suppose that the Revisers would secure one of these changes by a written law, and not the other. The Revisers of 1552, doubtless, supposed that they had done both . . . . . . That the Rubric was meant to be thus understood, we might infer from the two facts: (1) that only so could the altar-like appearance, so offensive to the then prevailing party, be quite done away; and (2) that the Tables were every where so set, i.e., with one *side* properly so-called, towards the north, from the first publication of the Rubric."

* * * * * * * * *

p. 16.—"At the last examination of Ridley, 1555, White, the Bishop of Lincoln, is reported to have said, 'When your Table was constituted, you could never be content in placing the same now east, now north, now one way, now another, until it pleased God of His goodness to place it clean out of the church.' (Ridley's Works, p. 281, Camb. 1841.) Thomas Dorman somewhat later, 'This day your Table is placed in the midst of the quire; the next day removed into the body of the Church; at the third time placed in the chancel again *after the manner of an altar*, but yet removable as there is a Communion to be had.' (Proof, p. 110; in Strype's Annals of Q. Eliz. Vol. i. c. 12, p. 163.) It was called by them an 'oyster-board' or 'table,'‡ apparently because it stood free on either side, and lengthways up and down the church, as we see oyster-tables in the season stand in our streets."

p. 17.—"This, then, is the state of things to which our Rubric applies. The Table was to stand east and west, and the minister to stand against that long edge of it which was then turned towards the north."

p. 26.—"'Looking one day west, and another day east; one that way, and another this way.' (Weston, in Foxe, Acts and Mon. Vol. iii., p. 70.)"

† But this is to assume that in 1552, when the Rubric was made, the Chancels and Naves of Churches were crowded with fixed Pews or Seats, such as we were accustomed to see 40 or 50 years ago. There seems, however, no evidence (1) That at that time the Seats would have been a hindrance to placing the Table Altarwise; (2) That, then, the Tables were generally moved, except in large Churches.

‡ "Bishop White at Ridley's Examination: 'A goodly receiving! . . . to set an oyster-table instead of an altar.'—Ridley's Works, p. 281. 'The sacrificing sorcerers,' says Becon, in Mary's reign, in language as reprehensible as that which he condemns, 'shame not, both in their private talk, and in their open sermons, spitefully to call the Lord's Table an oyster-board.'—The Supplication, Prayers, and other Pieces. p. 229, Camb. 1844."

* COSIN, though appearing to hold that "North Side," in the Book of 1638 (which contains his 3rd Series of Notes) meant *North end*, does not seem to have considered that the Tables in K. Edward's Reign were placed with their

On the other hand, this theory derives, I think, strong inferential support from some proceedings of Bp. Ridley at this period, 1550-52. STOW (who as a contemporary[*] and a resident in the City of London was likely to be well informed) makes the following statements in his " Chronicles : "

"The 12 of April [1550], D. Nich. Ridley late bishop of Rochester, was enstalled bishop of London at Paules." (*Chronicles*, p. 549).

"The 11 of June being S. Barnabies day was kept-holyday all London ouer, and the same day at night the high aulter in Paules Church was pulled downe, and a table set where the aulter stood, with a vayle drawen beneath the steps, and on the Sunday next, a Communion was sung at the same table, and shortly after all the aultars in London were taken downe, and tables placed in their roomths." (*Ib.* p. 551).

FOXE (another contemporary[†]), writing of Ridley's Visitation in 1550 and of his directions about the Altars, says :—

"And so appointed he the form of a right table to be used in his diocese, and in the Church of Paul brake down the wall[‡] standing then by the high altar's, side." (*Acts and Mon.* VI. p. 7, Townsend's Ed. 1846. And *Works of Ridley*, Parker Society, p. 324.)[||]

Ends *East* and *West ;* for, commenting on the Rubric ". . . *the priest standing at the north side of the table shall say the* Lord's Prayer, &c.," he says :—

"There was much ado about the posture of the table and the priests standing at it in King Edward's time ; for in the second year the altar stood still in the usual place, and the priest was appointed to stand before the midst of the altar with his face towards it, and this was confirmed by act of parliament. Notwithstanding which act, there were so many exceptions taken, and opposition made against that order, (some standing at the west side of the altar, with their faces turned towards the people, others at the east, others at the south, and others at the north,) that at last they agreed to set forth this rule in the fifth of King Edward, instead of the former set forth in the second year, where the tenor and sequence of the service was ordered after this manner; . . ." (*Notes*, 3rd Series, p. 458.) Then COSIN gives the arrangement of the Office in the Book of 1549 ; but he does not notice the transposition of the Services in 1552 ; and it does not seem to have occurred to him that this might have led, as I have suggested, to the "North side" Rubric.

[*] Stow was born in the Parish of St. Michael, Cornhill, in 1525, and was buried April 8, 1605 in St. Andrew's, Undershaft.
[†] Born 1517, died 1587.
[‡] It would be interesting to know whether this "wall" had any connexion with the Altar as thus described by DUGDALE—"The High Altar. This, as appeareth by the indented covenants betwixte Raphe de Baldock, Bishop of London, and one Richard Pickerell, a citizen, had a beautiful tablet made and fitted to set thereon in an. 1309 (3 Ed. II.), variously adorned with many precious stones, and enammelled work ; as also with divers images of metal : which tablet stood betwixt two columns, within a frame of wood to cover it, richly set out with curious pictures, the charge whereof amounted to two hundred marks." (*History of St. Paul's Cathedral*, ed. Sir Henry Ellis, 1818.— p. 11.)
[||] Some time after this was printed I noticed the following passage in

From these statements the following are legitimate conclusions:—

1. That the new Table in St. Paul's was placed Altarwise; for (a) it was " set where the aulter stood ; " (b) the " steps " remained, and (c) the " wall " behind the Altar being taken down, a Curtain was substituted, apparently to hide the back of the Steps.

2. That the "side" of the Altar then meant its longer portion; for there seems no conceivable reason for supposing that the " wall " which was taken down was at either *end* of the Altar.

3. That Ridley must have officiated in front of the Table, looking East, for the " Communion " which " was sung at the " same Table " could only have been the Office of 1549.

4. That the Tables which were substituted for the other Altars in London which "shortly after" this "were taken " downe," were, generally at least, placed in the same Place and Position as that at St. Paul's, and that the Clergy officiated in the Positions which they had occupied at the Altars.

Passing now to 1552, we have the following account in Stow :—

"The first of Nouember, being the feast of All Saints, the new seruice booke, called Of common prayer, begun in Paules church, and

Wheatley :—" Another dispute arising, viz. Whether the Table placed in the room of the Altar ought to stand *Altar-wise*, *i.e.* in the same place and situation as the Altar formerly stood ? This was the occasion that in some Churches the Tables were placed in the middle of the chancels, in others at the East part thereof next the wall; some again placing it Endwise, and others placing it at length.⁶⁶ Bishop Ridley endeavoured to compromise this matter, and therefore in St. Paul's Cathedral, suffered the Table to stand in the place of the old Altar.; but beating down the wainscot partition behind, laid all the choir open to the East, leaving the Table then to stand in the middle of the chancel,⁶⁷ which indeed was more agreeable to the primitive custom.⁶⁸ Under this diversity of usage, things went on till the death of King Edward; when Queen Mary coming to the throne, Altars were again restored wherever they had been demolished : but her reign proving short, and Queen Elizabeth succeeding her, the people (just got free again from the tyranny of Popery), through a mistaken zeal fell in a tumultuous manner to the pulling down of Altars : though indeed this happened for the generality only in private churches, they not being meddled with in any of the Queen's Palaces, and in but very few of the Cathedrals." He then goes on to mention Q. Elizabeth's Injunctions, (p. 245-6. Ed. 1794).

" 66 Huggard's Display of Protestants, p. 81, printed Anno 1556, as cited in Heylin's Antidot, Lincoln, page 50."

" 67 Acts and Monuments, Part II. p. 700."

" 68 See Bingham's Antiquities, l. 8. c. 6. ? 11."

the like thorow the whole citie. The bishop of London, doctor Ridley, executing the seruice in Paules church in the forenoone, in his rochet onely, without cope or vestment, preached in the quire, and at afternoone he preached at Paules crosse, the lord mayor, aldermen, and crafts, in their best liveries being present, which sermon, tending to the setting forth the said late made booke of common prayer, continued till almost five of the clock at night, so that the mayor, aldermen, and companies entered not into Paules church as had bene accustomed, but departed home by torchlight. By this booke of common prayer, all copes and vestments were forbidden thorow England, and prebends of Paules left off their hoods, and the bishops left theyr crosses, &c. as by an act of parliament more at large is set out." (*Chron.* 1590, p. 557; and Strype's Summary, *Cranmer*, Bk. II. ch. 33. pp. 289–90.)

"After the feast of All Saints, the upper quire in Saint Paules church in London, where the high altar stoode, was broken downe, and all the quire therabout: and the table of the communion was set in the lower quire, where the priests sing." (*Ibid.*)

From this account we learn that the "Table" which, in June 1550, had been "set where the aulter stood" remained there when Bp. Ridley himself began the use of the Second Prayer Book on All Saints Day 1552, though it was afterwards " set " in the lower quire:" but Stow does not even imply any change of its Altarwise *Position*—a silence from which it is most reasonable to conclude that it still retained the old *position* though it was *placed* nearer to the people: the circumstantial character of Stow's account warrants the belief that he would have mentioned so marked an alteration had it been made.

Further, the precision with which Stow notes the alteration in the Bp. of London's Dress—saying that he was "in his "rochet onely without cope or vestment," justifies the belief that there was nothing unusual in the *place* or *position* occupied by the Bishop when "executing the Service:" it seems to me wholly improbable that, if Ridley had gone to the North *End* of the Table, the careful Chronicler would have left unnoticed so remarkable a departure from the ancient Custom.

Whatever, then, may be thought of Ridley's proceedings, in substituting new moveable Tables for the old structural Altars, there seems no evidence that he had any intention of introducing or allowing such an innovation as that of setting the Lord's Table with its ends East and West; or of Celebrating the Holy Communion at one End of that Table set in the Position or

Place of the old Altar, or elsewhere in the Chancel, with its Ends North and South. Where, as in this case, positive proof is wanting of the alleged-change, it is all the more needful to put ourselves into the position of the Bishops and Clergy of that period and judge of what they probably did by considering what we should probably have done in their circumstances. No more misleading method could be adopted than that which is so commonly followed—of looking at their proceedings in the middle of the 16th Century from our own stand point in this 19th Century. It is wholly unreasonable to suppose that Clergy who had been Officiating for Three Years with an Office Book, which in its main features corresponded with another Office Book which they had used all their Ministerial lives, should have divested themselves, all at once, of old habits in discharging their Public functions; and it is the less likely when, as in this case of the Position of the Celebrant, there was no order of a *prohibitory* kind, such as the same Book of 1552 gave with reference to the Vestments: there was, indeed, a new directory Rubric prescribing a different place for the *commencement* of the Office; yet even that place the Clergy had been accustomed to for another part of the old Office. The mere absence of the directory Rubrics, as to the Position of the Celebrant at other parts of the Service, would no more lead him to abandon his habit, than did the omission of the Manual Acts in this same Book lead to their general disuse by the Priests of that day, unless indeed they were those who deemed that those Acts ought not to have been retained in the Book of 1549.

LI. Their Lordships, in order to maintain their own "opinion that 'north side of the table' means that side which "looks towards the north," make the following remarks :—

> "They have considered some ingenious arguments intended to prove that 'north side' means that part of the west side that is nearest to the north. One of these is that the middle of the altar before the Reformation was occupied by a stone or slab, called *mensa consecratoria* and *sigillum altaris*, that the part of the altar north of this was called north side, and that to the south of it was called the south side. Without inquiring whether English altars were

generally so constructed, which is to say the least doubtful, their Lordships observe that in the directions for the substitution of a moveable table for the altar and for its decent covering, and its position at various times, there is no hint that this is to revive this peculiarity of the altar which it replaced; and they do not believe that the table was so arranged or divided."

In this passage there seems to be a reference to Archdeacon Freeman's "Rites and Ritual"—a portion perhaps of that "large "mass of controversial literature" by which the Court "have "been somewhat aided:" the Archdeacon says:—

". . . . the slab or surface of the Altar, or Holy Table—there is a wonderful *equableness* in the use of the two terms by antiquity*—was always conceived of as divided into *three* portions of about equal size. The central one, called the *media pars*, was exclusively used for actual celebration, and often had a slab of stone † let into it, called *mensa consecratoria*. The other portions were called the *latus sinistrum* and *dextrum*, or *Septentrionale et Australe*.‡ These would be in English the 'midst of the Altar,' the 'left or north side,' and the 'right or south side:' the term 'side' being used with reference to the 'middle portion.' The most solemn parts of the rite, then, were performed '*at* the middle' of the Table; the subordinate parts '*at* the northern or southern portions. In all cases '*at*' certainly meant with the face turned *eastwards*," (p. 71, 4th. Ed. 1866).

Now if there were no other evidence to shew that this or any similar description of old "English altars," which the Court appears here to dispute, is maintainable, one of Bp. Ridley's

* "The Fathers generally prefer 'Altar,' the Liturgies, 'Holy Table.'"

† "Syriac Liturgy of St. James, 'pars *altaris* in quâ tabula defixa est;' 'pars media mensæ vitæ.'"

‡ "Syriac Liturgy of St. James, Renaudot; the 'Ancient English and Communion Offices' (Maskell), where 'cornu' is used. The Roman 'Ritus celebrandi Missam,' 4. 4; 'Thurificat *aliud latus* altaris.'"

Mr. Elliott ("*The North side of the Table*:" p. 111) commenting upon the language of Archdeacon Freeman (and also of Dr. Littledale: "*The North side of the Altar*," &c.) admits that "the two authorities to which the Archdeacon and Dr. Littledale alike appeal in support of their entirely divergent theories," establish "beyond doubt the threefold position of the Priest at the Altar, and *so far*, in a *general* way, the threefold division of the Altar ⁱ itself;" nevertheless, he denies that they give support to the "division of the slab into a central portion and two *sides* of 'about equal size.'"

"ⁱ As *e.g.* in the following Rubric 'Sacerdos inclinat se et osculatur altare primum in medio, tum ad duo latera dextrum et sinistrum.'—Renaudot ii., 586."

"Reasons" for abolishing the old Altars in 1550, furnishes at least a probable proof that the description is not incorrect: for his "*Third Reason*" is that:—

"The popish opinion of mass was, that it might not be celebrated but upon an altar, or at the least upon a super-altar, to supply the fault of the altar, which must have had its prints and characters; or else it was thought that the thing was not lawfully done." (*Works*, Parker Society, p. 322.)

Here the Bishop speaks of two Articles of Church Furniture, well known to have been used in England at that time, viz. (1) Consecrated Altars, (2) Consecrated Slabs, called "super-altars," which were placed on or let into the Altar slab when not Consecrated—sometimes used upon it when it had been Consecrated. So that the "stone or slab," which their Lordships seem to question, is distinctly recognised by Ridley. Moreover, the the "prints and characters," which Ridley mentions as being deemed essential, were common features of English Altars or Super Altars—five Crosses, at least, being, I think it may be said, always found upon them as indicating their Consecration.*

If, as some hold, the substitution of Tables for Altars was designed also to get rid of "the Popish" practice of Celebrating with the Priest's back to the people, it seems an unaccountable thing that Ridley in his "Reasons" (which had, too, the Royal sanction) does not any where give even a hint of such a purpose : there is not a word which could lead to a surmise that the old Position of the Priest was to be abandoned in order to "more move the simple from the superstitious opinions of the "popish mass, unto the right use of the Lord's Supper," (*First Reason*. See p. 340). It seems incredible that so prominent a feature in the Mass, as the Position of the Priest, should have been left unnoticed on such an occasion, if it had been deemed a practice needful to be abolished.

* Dr. Rock (*Church of our Fathers*, Vol. I. pp. 243-63) furnishes much information on this subject. A simple Super-Altar, being merely a piece of Slate in a wooden frame, 7½ Inches long by 5½ Inches broad, and having the five Crosses, was found (with some Books) in pulling down the Chancel of St. Mary the Virgin, Addington, Bucks, in 1857; the Articles appear to have been concealed there by the then Rector, Richard Andrewes, between 1576 and 1587 when he died.

The language of the Court, in the passage now under consideration, implies also a doubt of the contention—that, "the "part of the altar north of this [stone or slab] was called north "side, and that to the south of it was called the south side." It is true that in the English Missals "*cornu*," not "*latus*," is the term: but then the words "dexter" and "sinister" occur without "cornu,"* though identified with the *Northern* and *Southern* portions of the Altar; and, whether the term "side" was or was not generally known to be the Foreign usage, it is at least probable that it was more likely to be "the Vulgar "tongue" than "horn", when the Altar was spoken of.

Their Lordships are more positive in their opinion that "the "directions for the substitution of a moveable table for the "altar" give "no hint that this is to revive the peculiarity of "the altar which it replaced:" no doubt this is so: but, on the other hand, there is no "hint" that the Clergy were not to occupy at the New Tables the *Positions* at that very time prescribed for them in the Prayer Book of 1549, which was the one Office Book they had still to use: not to have done so, would have been a breach of the Act of Uniformity, rendering them liable to penalties, unless some Dispensation had been given; but, so far as I am aware, no indication of any such relaxation has ever been produced.

It has indeed, been alleged (See p. 375ff) that, owing to the various *Positions* taken by the Clergy in consequence of the removal of the Altars, the Rubric, "The Priest standing at the "North side of the Table," was inserted to fix his *Place* at the New Tables. I have already stated what seems to be the true reason of its introduction (See pp. 370-75). But, among other arguments (which have been employed to prove that "North "side" was designed to mean, either that *End* or that *Side* of the Lord's Table which stood *North* and standing at which the

---

* *e.g.*—SARUM and BANGOR: "accedat sacerdos cum suis ministris ad gradum altaris, et dicat ipse confessionem diacono assistente a dextris, et subdiacono a sinistris . . ." (*Maskell*, Ed. 1844, p. 6. SARUM: *Burntisland*, Ed. 599.)

SARUM, BANGOR, HEREFORD—". . . et osculetur patenam et reponat eam a dextris super altare sub corporalibus parum cooperiendo." (*Maskell*, p. 24. SARUM, *Burntisland*, col. 593.)

SARUM, BANGOR, YORK—". . . osculetur altare a dextris sacrificii . . ." (*Maskell*, p. 44. SARUM, *Burntisland*, col. 618.)

Priest would look *South*,) it is said that "North-side" was not an expression likely to be employed: the objection may be conveniently put as thus stated by Mr. Droop :—

"(2) If it could be shown that in 1552 the phrase 'north side' was in common use in England in the non-natural sense now contended for, the argument [he had been opposing] might deserve some attention; but the language of foreign missals must have been altogether unknown to the large majority of English Clergy at the End of Edward the Sixth's reign. The English missals, I believe, never use any other phrase except *cornu*; and if the Revisers of 1552 had taken the language of this Rubric from any previous Liturgy, they would have said either 'corner,' 'horn,' or 'end,' not 'side.' But it is exceedingly improbable that they should have assumed any knowledge of any missals or other former service-books, either English or foreign, as an Act passed in 1550—the 3rd and 4th Edw. VI. cap. 10—had provided for these service-books being all burnt, or otherwise defaced and destroyed." (*The North side of the Table,* p. 4.)

I have already (See p. 382) suggested a reason for the phrase "North side" being probably used in England before and in 1550, if so, it was not likely to have been disused two years later. It is quite immaterial whether "the lan- "guage of foreign missals" was or was not known "to the "large majority of English clergy" in 1551 and 1552: they were not the Revisers of the Book of 1549. But Cranmer and other Bishops were not likely to be wholly ignorant of some of the foreign Missals. As to its being "improbable" for them to assume "any knowledge of any missals or other "former service-books," owing to the Act for abolishing such Books; it implies great faith in the operation of the Act to suppose that Cranmer e.g. (who certainly was not one of "such perverse persons as do impugn the....book of Common "Prayer") might not retain an English or Foreign Missal in his Library at Lambeth; or that the King's Council must burn any copy they had at Westminster. Supposing, however, that every copy had been destroyed, in what peril were the Revisers if they did import partially or wholly some Missal Rubric into the Book of 1552? They did retain Rubrics which were in the Book of 1549 and which had been drawn from these condemned Books: their minds, moreover, were fully charged with the Rubrics of the Sarum Missal which, only four years before, they were constantly using; and so, in this respect, it was of no consequence if they had no access to the old Books.

To have translated "cornu" by "corner" (as Mr. Droop assumes might have been one choice of the Revisers if they had resorted to the old Office Books) would probably have been perplexing to Clergy who had not read it quite in that sense: "horn," surely would the rather have kept alive that notion of a sacrificial Altar which it was deemed necessary to get rid of, because it was then popularly associated with a carnal doctrine of Transubstantiation at that time commonly held: "end" is a term which, as it seems to me, would have been wholly foreign to the minds of the Revisers of that day; the Judicial Committee "do not believe that the table was so arranged or divided" as had been contended: it is not too confident to "believe" (as strongly as their Lordships do in reference to the Table) that "end" was not thought of as *any position* for the Priest to take when Celebrating the Holy Eucharist.

But, without resorting to any old Service-Book the word "side" was well known in 1552 and was at hand to find in a Book of the fullest Authority at that time, viz. the First Prayer Book of K. Edward VI. There, in the Communion Office, the following Rubric was to be found after the Offertory Sentences (See p. 363, Col. II.):—

"Then so many as shall be partakers of the holy Communion, shall tarry still in the quire, or in some convenient place nigh the quire, the men on the one side, and the women on the other side. All other (that mind not to receive the said holy Communion) shall depart out of the quire, except the Ministers and Clerks."

Here the whole Quire is divided into two SIDES which, of course, relatively to the End Wall of the Chancel (even if it chanced not to be East), would be called, respectively, the *North* "side" and the *South* "side." The Rubric precludes any suggestion—that only a single row of people remained close to the Wall on either "side" and that they were looking North or South, according to the "side" which they occupied. It is plain that all who could find room in the Quire remained there; and it will hardly be disputed, I think, that they faced in the same (Eastward) direction as the Priest. Thus, then, being (the Women) on the *North Side* and (the Men) on the *South Side* of the Chancel, they were in fact on the *North Side* and the *South Side* of the Altar and of the Celebrant who, at that period of the Service, undoubtedly was " standing at God's " board" *i.e.* in the *middle* of its *West* Front, with his back to the people.

Under these circumstances and having to find another place for the Priest who, owing to the transposition of the Service in the new Book of 1552, would not have to begin the Office at the Middle of the Lord's Table (See p. 360. Col. iv.), nothing was more likely than for the Revisers to adopt from the Book of 1549 the word " side " (which everybody would understand) when needing to describe in a Rubric the new Place intended to be assigned to the Celebrant at the commencement of the Communion Service.

There is a passage, in Bp. Wren's Answer to the *Second* Article* of his Impeachment, which (though not referring to the Revision of 1552 but to that 2nd Book as revived in 1559) shews his belief that " North side " was a common phrase used in reference to the Altars and applied later to the Tables which were substituted for them in Elizabeth's reign; his Answer begins thus :—

"To the second Article he answereth and denieth that he did in the Year 1636, order that the Communion Table should be set at the East-end of the Chancel altarwise, and not to be removed from thence.

"And he saith, that he was ever so far from having any Thought or Intention of resembling the popish Manner of Altars, that he believeth that he never did by any Words of his own, so much as name the Word *Altar*, in any of his Articles or Directions; much less did he ever term the Table an Altar.

"And whereas he mentioned† the North-end of the Communion Table, he humbly conceiveth, that (even by that) he did the more distinguish it from an Altar: For that the Altars being very nearly equilateral, or four square, the North-end, or South-end of an Altar, hath never yet been heard of. Only in 1 *Eliz.* when the use of Altars was but as yesterday out of their Eyes, and the Name of Altars but newly out of their Mouths, Custom of Speech led them to call the North end, or North part of the Table, the North-side thereof, as they

---

* " II. . In the same year he order'd that the Communion-Table, appointed by the Rubrick, to be placed in the Body of the Church, should be set at the East End of the Chancel." (*Parentalia*, p. 13.)

† The reference here seems to be to his Visitation Article (1636) where he asks (See p. 345) " . . . doth it ordinarily stand up at the East End of the Chancell, where the Altar in former times stood, the Ends thereof being placed North and South ?"

had used to call it the North-side of the Altar. And he the rather believeth this to be so, because that in 2 Eliz. when they best understood their own Meaning, the Queen causing the Liturgy to be translated into *Latin*, the Rubrick before the Communion Service reads it *Ad septentrionalem mensæ partem stans*, and not *ad septentrionale latus*, so that North-part, North-side, and North-end were all one." (*Parentalia,* p. 75.)

This passage appears, at first sight, to be opposed to the view for which I am contending, and therefore it might seem unfair to pass it over; though, indeed, Wren was referring to the beginning of Q. Elizabeth's Reign, whereas the point in question is—what "North Side" meant when first used in the Prayer Book of 1552, in K. Edward the VIth Reign ? One remark of Wren's, however, seems to be at variance with fact, at either period; he speaks of " the Altars being very nearly equilateral " or four square ; " but of this we are, perhaps, better able to judge 300 years after, than he was at a distance of 80 years. The destruction of old Office Books and the Penalties to which those who kept them were liable, would probably deprive him of the information we are able to gather from contemporary pictorial illustrations in numerous volumes which somehow were preserved and are now accessible in Public Libraries and Private Collections. At an early period Altars were indeed commonly of the form which Wren mentions : but the oblong shape apparently prevailed in mediæval times and at the period of the Reformation.

Moreover, all that is said about the Tables substituted for the Altars shews that they were usually of an oblong form: even the opprobrious term " oyster board " given to them by some of the Roman party serves to prove this : the Commissioners who had to deal with the Church Ornaments in 1552 were directed to leave in the Churches " the honest and comely furniture of " coverynges upon the Communion Table : " the Injunction of Elizabeth directed "that the holy Table in every Church be " decently made, and set in the place where the Altar stood, " and there commonly covered, as thereto belongeth : " Ridley's Reasons, for Tables instead of Altars, do not imply that the difference which he desired to make turned upon OBLONG *versus* SQUARE ; but upon fixity, consecration marks, and the other grounds which he gives (See pp. 340–41.) It may, therefore, be fairly assumed that, in respect of mere shape, there was no material difference between the Old Altars and the New Tables.

It is likely enough that "Custom of speech," as Wren says, led people to apply to the New Tables the description, which they had been accustomed to use as regards the Altars; yet, while their doing so would be quite consistent with that origin of the term "North Side" which I have already suggested (See pp. 379–81): it would not necessarily follow that it was intended in 1559 to send the Celebrant to the North End of the Table.

Wren's reference to the Rubric of the Elizabethan Latin Prayer Book, supports, I think, the view—that "side" may properly be understood of the whole portion of the Altar right and left of the Celebrant though he also includes the *End*, strictly so called. For if, as he says," the "North-end, " or South-end of an Altar, hath never yet been heard of;" and "*latus*" (the word which he implies did describe that part of the Altar) not being used to translate "side," the inference surely is—that "partem," which was used, was not employed in the exclusive sense of "side" *i.e.* "end;" though, as describing the *whole northern* portion* of the Table, it would include the End: "so that," as Wren says, "North-"part, North-side, and North-end were all one." It should be borne in mind, too, that "partem" was an old Rubrical word,†

* Mr. Elliott ("The North side of the Table," p. 37) arguing against Dr. Littledale's conclusions from Bp. Andrewes's Form of Service for the Consecration of a Church, A.D. 1620, draws a distinction between "the *North*" and "the *North part* of the Holy Table;" for he says—". . . whilst the position of the Bishop at the North side or End of the Table during the whole of that portion of the Communion Office which is read by himself, though not directly affirmed, may be inferred from the fact that that position is expressly assigned to him during the Post Communion Service, in the words 'ad sacræ mensæ *Septentrionem* (*i.e.* at the North of the Holy Table); whilst the position of the Chaplain who officiates at the beginning of the Service is described in the words 'ad *Septentrionulem partem* sacræ mensæ' (*i.e.* at the North part of the Holy Table)." The *Italics* are Mr. Elliott's.

† *e.g.* In the *Sarum Missal* "Sacerdos thurificet medium Altaris, et utrumque cornu Altaris, primo in dextera, secundo in sinistra parte, et interim in medio." (*Burntisland Ed.* col. 581).

Hereford Missal.—"Ad dicendam vel cantandam præfationem erigat se sacerdos honeste et ponat manus super altare ex utraque parte calicis et dicat hoc modo: PER omnia sæcula sæculorum" &c. (*Maskell* p. 33, Ed. 1844). *Sarum* and *Bangor* Missals.—"Hic osculetur sacerdos corporalia in dextera parte . . " (*Ib.* p. 54.)

used in this sense, and therefore the Translator would be likely to use it; and would be most unlikely to choose a new word for " end," especially if he knew that " side " of the Altar=" end " of the Table was not intended to be described.

Besides, the Bishop while thus defending his use of the word "Ends" in the Inquiry, of his Visitation Articles, as to the Place and Position of the Table, does not ask anything as to the Position of the Minister thereat; nor does he even imply in any way that it would be wrong for the Celebrant to interpret "North Side" by standing at the Northern part of the Table's front, and looking East, the Table being "placed North and "South," as he considered it should be, " where the Altar in " former times stood."

LII. The Court next remarks as follows :—

> "Another argument is drawn from the Jewish Ritual. On offering sacrifices before the Lord, the altar was to be sprinkled with the blood, and a red line was drawn across the altar to mark the height at which it should be sprinkled; and it is argued that the line being only in front, the Priest must have stood in front in order to see it and be guided by it. But on the other hand the line probably went all round the altar, and the sprinkling was applied to all the sides. And even if the fact was rightly stated, it would be impossible to allow an argument so remote and shadowy to supersede the plain sense of a direction so clear in itself. When the Table was placed in the body of the Church or chancel, the Priest or Minister was to stand on the north side of it, looking south."

This paragraph of their Lordships' Report appears to be based upon a comment by Mr. Elliott (" *The North side of the Table* " pp. 4 & 5) upon a statement made by Dr. Littledale (" *The North side of the Altar, a Liturgical Essay* "). It may be thought that it was scarcely necessary to consider this question in reference to an Expression in a Rubric consequent upon certain Ritual changes in 1552; and therefore unimportant to pursue it here: as, however, the Court has drawn attention to the point, it seems as well to know what may be said in reference to their Lordships' remarks: Dr. Littledale's comments upon them will be found in the following statement with which he has been good enough to furnish me:—

"As regards the Jewish rite of sacrifice, the fact is simply that the mere slaughtering of the victim, to prepare it for oblation, was performed at the north of the altar; but the officiating priest made the actual presentation of it at the east side, facing west, and looking towards the veil which hid the Holy of holies and the Mercy-seat from view. This latter attitude was the technical and recognized interpretation of the phrase 'before 'the Lord.' See Lightfoot, *Temple Service*, and Edersheim, *The Temple, its Ministry and Service*."

"Now, the analogue for this is found exactly in the Eastern Liturgies, which borrow largely from Jewish ritual. The Bread and Wine for the Eucharist are prepared in the Chapel of Prothesis, always the northern of the three apses which usually terminate an Oriental Church, and there is a symbolical slaying or cutting up of the altar-loaf, technically called the Holy Lamb, performed there previous to the Liturgy. But the actual presentation of the Bread and Wine on the altar is invariably at the west side, facing east. The Chapel of Prothesis thus answers exactly to the Western Credence-table, but does not serve any more than it does to fix the attitude of the Celebrant at the actual time of the Liturgy.

"I may just add that the Court has misunderstood the nature of the argument I drew from Jewish usage. No idea that a Levitical rubric could interpret an English one was present to my mind. I should as soon have imagined that a Canon of 1604 could repeal a statute of 1661, or a set of Visitation Articles issued in 1627 serve as a gloss on a rubric which did not exist till thirty-four years later. My object was to shew that the whole course of precedent, Jewish and Christian alike, anterior to 1552, is non-cognizant of a north-end position; and that it was unknown to and unpractised by even the Continental Protestants of that date (as indeed of the present day also), so that no reason nor probability for its adoption existed."

Whatever may be the pertinency of these remarks, the Court,

perhaps, would have deemed them to be as "remote and shadowy" as the "argument" which they (not unreasonably) would not "allow . . . to supersede the plain sense of a direction so clear "in itself" as the Rubric under discussion. Whether the interpretation given to it in the following words is its "clear" meaning, is the very point in dispute: I humbly think that what has been advanced in the preceding pages makes it, at least, extremely doubtful whether their Lordships had any real warrant either from the History of the period or from the contemporaneous usage of the Rubric's terminology, to assert that "when the Table was placed in the body of the "Church or Chancel, the Priest or Minister was to stand on the "north side of it, looking south." In this sentence the Table is, apparently, regarded as placed with its Sides parallel to the North and South Walls of the Church and its Ends pointing East and West.

LIII. But their Lordships go on to remark upon the Position of the Celebrant under an altered situation of the Table; they say :—

> "When it became the custom to place the table altarwise against the east wall, the Rubric remained the same. And there are many authorities to show that the position of the Minister was still upon the north side or end, facing south. It is only necessary to cite a few. Archdeacon Pory (1662), in his Visitation Articles, says, 'The Minister standing, as he is appointed, at the north side or end of the table when he celebrates [*for* he celebrates *read* he prepares to celebrate—2nd *Rit. Report*, p. 629] the Holy Communion.'"

Here, however, the Court uses the word "side" in a different sense from that in which they employed it in the preceding sentence; there it was dealt with as meaning the *longer* portion of the Table, here it is applied to the *shorter* portion—the "end," as their Lordships' call it: the terms they use seem to be drawn from Archdeacon Pory's Visitation Article which they quote; no reference is given, but if, as may be presumed, it was taken from the 2nd Ritual Report, it will be seen above that the reading given by the Court has an error which might mislead to the belief that Pory considered " the north side or " end " to be the Minister's place *during* the Celebration, whereas Pory's words only apply it to the *preparing* to Celebrate. The object of the Inquiry will be best understood by giving the entire Article ; it is this:—

"9. The Minister standing as he is appointed at the North side, or end of the Table, when he prepares to celebrate the holy Communion, and calling on those who do intend to communicate, to draw near and take that holy Sacrament to their comfort, as it is in the words of the Common prayer book, have you any in your Parish that keep their seats, and sit still in their places not drawing near as is commanded by the Church, but looking that the Minister should forsake the place of his station, by the Church appointed, to bring it to them?" (2nd *Rit. Report*, 9. p. 629.)

It is important to mention here that Pory's Articles, though dated 1662, are prior to the Book of that date; for he frames Article 20, (p. 627) touching Catechising, upon the Rubric of 1604, asking whether it is " before Evening Prayer: " whereas the Book of 1662 appoints it "after the Second Lesson."

Archn. Pory's Inquiry (which really relates to *the Place of the Communicants* rather than to *the Position of the Minister*) was also made in 1640 by *Juxon*, when Bp. of London (2nd *Rit. Report*, 9. p. 592): in fact the two Sets of Articles correspond, except so far as they were necessarily varied by the differences in the Office of the Bishop and the Archdeacon: they both followed the Visitation Articles compiled by the Convocation of 1640, already mentioned (See p. 214). This particular Inquiry does not occur, however, in any of the other 64 Sets of Visitation Articles after 1640 nor in any of the 63 Sets before 1640, as given in the 2nd Report of the Ritual Commission. In truth, from whatever cause, these Visitation Articles, ordered by the Canon of 1640 for general use, seem to have been but little followed.

The word "end," as employed in them, was not used in any English Prayer Book before 1640, nor does it occur in the Book of 1662: the Convocation of 1640 appears to have borrowed the expression " North side or end " from the Scotch Book of 1637; and, if so, its meaning would seem to depend upon the force of the words in that Book—whether *i.e.* they were designed to afford a liberty in Scotland, or whether "end" was a mere expletive of "side." There were other examples of *alternative* use in that Book, as well as in the English Prayer Book of that period, for instance :—" Then shall be said or "sung" the Venite; the Athanasian Creed "shall be sung or "said:" the Banns of Marriage were to be asked "three "several Sundays or Holy Days." And, in the Prayer Book of 1662, there are the following expressions in which certainly the words used are not *synonymes* though the word "or" intervenes :—" The Evens or Vigils before" the Days named; yet a Vigil is not an Eve when a Sunday comes between the Vigil and the Festival on the following Monday. "Days of fasting or Absti-"nence;" but Abstinence is not Fasting. If the Authors of the Scotch Rubric intended to place the Celebrant at the *End* of the Holy Table, it is certainly strange that they did not say so, instead of using two words "side" and "end." It is quite probable that the contention, shortly before, in the case of the Vicar of Grantham (which the Court next notices) induced Laud and Wren, (especially in the difficulties Laud felt as to providing a Liturgy for Scotland) to allow an *alternative* position for the Celebrant. Yet, even if it were certain that "end" was meant to be the synonyme of "side" in the Scotch Book and in the Visitation Articles of 1640, this would not prove that "side" meant "end" in the Prayer Book of 1552. There is no difficulty in understanding that, in the strife and confusion as to the Place of the Lord's Table and the Position of the Celebrant, subsequent to the revival in 1559 of the Book of 1552, practices grew up which sheltered themselves under the Rubrics relating to the Chancel, the Holy Table, and the Place of the Officiant. But it by no means follows that such Practices were, or were considered by the Prelates generally to be, the true exposition of Rubrics; though they did not deem it necessary or prudent to insist upon an abandonment of Custom, or to demand an absolute Uniformity.

LIV. The Court next calls another Witness, observing that :—

"In the dispute between the Vicar of Grantham and his

parishioners (1627), Bishop Williams plainly shows that whichever way the table was to stand, which was the matter in dispute, the position of the Minister was on the north. 'If you mean by altar-wise that the table shall stand along close by the wall, so that you be forced to officiate at one end thereof (as you may have observed in great men's Chapels), I do not believe that ever the Communion Tables were otherwise than by casualty so placed in country churches.' He also says, 'I conceive the alteration was made in the Rubric to show which way the celebrant was to face.' (Heylin, 'Coale from the Altar,' and Williams, ' Holy Table.') "

Before considering this passage it may be convenient to state the circumstances of this Case and the Publications to which it gave rise.

1. It appears, then, that the Vicar of Grantham, in Lincolnshire, had been "removing of the *Communion Table* from the " *upper part* of the *Quire* (where it was *comely placed*, and had " stood time out of minde) to the *Altar-place*, as he called it." (*Holy Table, Name and Thing*—p. 6.) Whether, before its removal, it stood in this Position or was placed with its Ends East and West is not stated or implied.

2. In consequence of a complaint from some of the Townspeople, "about June or July 1627 " (*Holy Table*, &c. p. 7) the Bishop of Lincoln (Williams) sent a "Letter" " to the Vicar of " Gr.: against the placing of the Communion Table at the " East End of the Chancell." The Bishop begins his Letter thus :—

"When I spoke with you last, I told you that the standing of the Communion Table, was unto me a thing so indifferent, that unlesse offence and umbrages were taken by the Towne against it, I should never move it, or remove it. That which I did not then suspect, is come to passe. The Alderman whom I have known this 17 or 18 yeares, to bee a discreet and modest man, and farre from any humour of innovation, together with the better sorte of the Towne, have complained against it : And I have (without taking notice of your Act, or touching in one syllable upon your reputation) appointed the *Church Wardens* (whom it principally doth concerne under the *Diocesan*) to settle it for this time, as you may see by this Copy inclosed.

" Now for your owne satisfaction, and my poor advise for the future, I have written unto you somewhat more at large, then I use to express myself in this kinde."

3. The Bishop's Letter led to the following Publication, where it is printed at pp. 67-78 :—

"A Coale from the Altar. Or an Answer to a Letter not long since written to the Vicar of Gr. against the placing of the Communion Table at the East end of the Chancell; and now of late dispersed abroad to the disturbance of the Church. First sent by a Judicious and learned Divine, for the satisfaction of his private Friend; and by him commended to the Presse, for the benefit of others. The third Impression. Heb. xiii. 10. *We haue an* ALTAR, *whereof they haue no right to eate, which serue the Tabernacle.* LONDON, Printed for Robert Milbornd, at the signe of the Vnicorn, neere Floet-bridge, 1637."

The Author (PETER HEYLIN, as is believed) assigns his reason for thus Writing to his "Friend," in the following opening words of his Letter:—

"Sir, I have read your Letter and cannot but extreamely wonder, that you should be so easilie over-weighed as I see you are. You say that you were willing once, of youre owne accord, to have removed your Communion Table unto the East end of your *Chancell*, according as it is in his Majesties *Chappell*, and generally in all *Collegiate* and *Cathedrall* Churches: and that you had intended so to doe, had you not mett with a Discourse written in way of Letter, to the *Vicar* of GR. (and as you have taken it upon common report) by a Reverend Prelate of this Church; whose Arguments have so prevailed with you, that you are almost taken off from that resolution, though it be now exacted of you by your *Ordinarie*."

4. Heylin's "Coal from the Altar" was replied to in the following Publication:—

"The Holy Table, Name and Thing, more Anciently, properly, and literally used under the New Testament, then that of an Altar: Written long ago by a Minister in Lincolnshire, in answer to D. COAL, a judicious Divine of Q. MARIES dayes. *Illa Sacramenti donatrix Mensa.*—Aurel. Prudent. in Peristeph. Hymno 11. Printed for the Diocese of *Lincoln*, 1637."

Bp. Williams, in his Approbation of it, signed "Jo. Lincoln. "*Deane of Westminster*" and dated "the last day of *November*," treats it as "written by some Minister of this Diocesse," and says it is "most Orthodox in *Doctrine*, and consonant in "Discipline, to the Church of England:" so that (if not written by himself, as has been believed) it had his entire sanction and may be considered to express his own mind.

5. To "The Holy Table, Name and Thing," a Rejoinder was

published by *Peter Heylin* in 1637 and Dedicated to K. Charles 1st, its Title is as follows :—

"Antidotum Lincolniense. Or an Answer to a Book entituled, The Holy Table, Name, and Thing, &c. Said to be written long agoe by a Minister in *Lincolnshire*, and Printed for the Diocese of *Lincoln*, A°. 1637. Written and inscribed to the grave, learned, and religious Clergie of the Diocese of *Lincoln*. The Second Edition, revised and enlarged, by PET. HEYLIN Chapleine in Ordinary to his M^{atie}. 1 Cor. xiv. 40. *Let all things be done decently and in order.* London, Printed for JOHN CLARK, and to be sold at his shop under *St. Peter's* Church in Cornhill, 1637."

6. There was a further Publication on the subject, by another Author, it is called :—

"Altare Christianum : or the dead *Vicar's* Plea. Wherein the Vicar of Gr. being dead, yet speaketh, and pleadeth out of Antiquity, against him that hath broken downe his Altar. Presented, and humbly submitted to the consideration of his Superiours, the Governours of our Church. By JOHN POCKLINGTON, DR. D. . . . . The Second Edition, Corrected by the Author, and enlarged, to give answer in sundry particulars to a Lincolnshire Minister, his *Holy Table*. London, Printed by Richard Badger, 1637."

The Judicial Committee, quoting the First of these Publications—viz.—The Bishop's Letter to the Vicar of Grantham—says that "Bishop Williams plainly shows that whichever way "the table was to stand, which was the matter in dispute, the "position of the Minister was on the north." If their Lordships only mean that the Bishop's reference to what "you may "have observed in great men's chapels," shews that "to officiate "at one end" of the Table was then a custom in such places, the conclusion may be admitted, though it proves nothing as to the practice in Cathedrals, or in Collegiate or Parish Churches where the Tables stood Altarwise. The Bishop assumes, indeed, that "the Communion Tables were" only "by casualty so placed "in country churches : " but, as Heylin, remarks, upon this and a previous passage which he quotes (*Coal from the Altar*, p. 18) this is "rather matter of opinion and hearesay, than of "proof, reason, or authoritie: For it stands onely on *I thinke*, "and *I conceive*, and *I have heard*, and *I believe not :* which no "man can interpret to be *Demonstrations.*" Recollecting, moreover, that the reason assigned for the removing of the Tables, when in use, was—that the Minister might be better seen and heard—it is unlikely that they were removed at all in the smaller Churches where no difficulty would arise on this point; and, as I have already shown (See pp. 342-48), to whatever extent this practice prevailed, neither the Order in Council in 1550 nor the Elizabethan Injunctions of 1559, appear to contemplate the placing of the Tables with their ends East and West, much less do they give any direction for so placing them. Heylin very decidedly expresses his view of the Injunctions in the following passage :—

"The Queenes *Injunctions* were set out for the reiglement and direction of all the Churches in this Kingdome, and it is said in them, that *the holy Table in every Church shall be decently made*, (in case the *Altars* were removed, which they left at liberty) *and set in the place where the* Altar *stood, and there commonly covered, as thereto belongeth*. If in the place where the *Altar* stood, then certainly it must stand along close by the wall, because the Altars alwaies stood so : and that as well in Countrey Churches, as in great mens Chappells, all being equally regarded in the same *Injunctions*, as in the Preface to the same doth at full appeare. Whereas in case the Table were to stand 'with one end towards the East great Window,' as is after said ; it could not possibly stand in the place where the *Altar* did, as the *Injunctions* have appointed; the *Altar* taking up much roome to the North and South, which the *Table* placed end long doth not take up; and contrary, the *Table* taking up much roome to the East and West, which the *Altar* did not." (*Coal from the Altar*, p. 19.)

On the other hand, if the Court regards Bp. Williams's language as shewing that the *North End* of the Table was a proper Position for the Celebrant when Officiating, it is plain from another passage that the Bishop entirely condemned it; for he says :—

"2. This Table must not stand *Altarwise*, and you at the North end thereof, but *Tablewise*, as you must officiate at the *Northside* of the same." (*Letter in Coal from the Altar*, p. 77.)*

* A contemporary illustration of the meaning of the term "Northside" occurs. in 1630, in the "Articles, or Instructions for Articles, to be exhibited by His Majestie's Heigh Commissioners, against Mr. John Cosin, Mr. Francis Burgoine, Mr. Marmaduke Blaxton, Doctor Hunt, Doctor Lindsell, Mr. William James, all learned clerks of the Cathedrall Church of Durham." (*Cosin Correspondence*, Surtees Society, Vol. I. 1869). The following are the passages : the *Italics* are mine :—
"This Altar stands upon 6 stone pillers curiously polished, and fastened to the ground, having upon every black pillar 3 cherubim-faces as white as snow, and it is placed at the end of the quire, along by the wall, with *neither side toward the North*, al which is contrary to the Booke of Common-prayer, and Injunctions, which command

Their Lordships further cite Bishop Williams as saying—"'I conceive the alteration was made in the Rubric to show which way the celebrant was to face:'" they only give a general reference to "Heylin, 'Coal from the Altar,' and Williams "'Holy Table,'" no pages being mentioned: I have carefully examined the two Books but have not succeeded in finding the words: it may be that the Writer of the Judgment found it thus quoted elsewhere ; yet, if so, it does not seem to really represent the two following passages which are the only ones I can discover as bearing upon it.

In "Holy Table, Name and Thing" the Author (thought to be Bp. Williams) quoting *Miles Huggard* ("How long were "they learning," &c. See p. 351) says, "And this contention was "determined (by the Rubric still in force) for the North-side of "the Table."

This sentence is quoted by Heylin ("*Antidotum Lincolniense*," p. 58) and at p. 127 he thus comments upon it:—

"But *this diversity* [of the holy Table, p. 48] say you, *was settled by the Rubrick, confirmed by Law*. What universally? There is no question but you meane it; or to what purpose do you say so? Yet in another place you tell us, that notwithstanding the said *Rubrick*, the *Tables* stood like *Altars* in *Cathedrall* Churches; in some of them at least, which had no priviledge, I am sure, more than others had. For thus say you (pag. 183), *In some of the* Cathedrals, *where the* stepes *were not transposed in* tertio *of the* Queene, *and the wall on the back-side* it to be a portable table, and to stand, when the Communion is administred, in the middest of the church or chancell, where morning and evening prayers are appointed to be sayd; which evening praier is never said where the table standeth now: and that the Minister should stand at the *north syde* of the Table, which cannot be done when *neither syde* of the Table standeth *northward*." (p. 169.)

"And allthough the Communion Booke" &c. "appointing it to be placed at the Administration of the Holy Communion, both in Cathedrall and Parish-Churches, in the body of the Church or Chancell, where morning and evening prayers are appointed to be said, and so to stand that the Minister may stand at the *north side of* the Table, . . . you will needs sett it at the east end of the church, ... Again, you have lately so set it, that the Minister can not possibly stand on the *north side* of the Table, ther being neyther side standing northward, ..." (pp. 178–9.)

Again, in Mr. Peter Smart's Sermon in Durham Cathedral, Sunday July 27, 1628, he says:—

"Neither must the table be placed along from north to south, as the altar is set, but from east to west, as the custom is of all reformed churches, otherwise the minister cannot stand at the *north side*, there being *neither side toward the north*. And I trow there are but two *sides* of a long table, and two *ends*: make it square, and then it will have four *sides* and no *end*, or four *ends* and no *side* at which any minister can stand to celebrate. I confess it is not material which way a man turn his face, when he ministers and prayeth, if it be left as a thing indifferent, without superstition." (*The Acts of the High Commission Court within the Diocese of Durham*. Surtees Society 1858, p. 216.)

of the Altar *untaken downe,* the Table *might stand all along, as the* Altar *did.* If it did stand in some, it might stand in all; and if in the *Cathedralls,* then also in *Parochiall* Churches; unlesse you show us by what means they procured that *might,* which could not bee attained unto by any others."

LV. Referring again to the first Publication in the Grantham controversy, their Lordships remark that:—

> " Heylin says, quoting the Latin Prayer Book of 1560, 'I presume that no man of reason can deny but that the northern end or side, call it which you will, is *pars septentrionalis,* the northern part.' ('Coale from the Altar.')"

This sentence is contained in the following passage, and its bearing will be best seen by considering it with the context:—

" 4. Nor doth it helpe the cause undertaken by the *Epistoler,* that 'the Minister appoynted to reade the Communion, is directed to reade the Commandements, not at the ende, but at the North-side of the Table:' there being no difference in this case betweene the *North-end,* and the *North-side,* which come both to one. For in all quadrilaterall, and quadrangular figures, whether they be a perfect Square, which *Geometricians* call *Quadratum,* or a long square (as commonly our Communion Tables are) which they call *Oblongum:* it's plaine that if wee speake according to the rules of Art, (as certainly they did which composed that *Rubricke*) every part of it is a side; however Custome hath prevailed to call the narrow sides by the name of ends. When therefore hee that ministreth at the *Altar,* stands at the *North-end* of the same, as wee use to call it; hee stands no question at the *North-side* thereof, as in proprietie of speech wee ought to call it; and so implies not, as it is supposed by the *Epistoler;* that the end, or narrower part thereof, *is to bee placed towards the East great Window.* And this Interpretation of the *Rubricke,* I the rather stand to, because that in the *Common Prayer* Book done into *Latine* by command, and authorized by the great Seale of Queene *Elizabeth,* Anno. 2do, of her reign, it is thus translated: *Ad cujus mensæ septentrionalem partem, Minister stans, orabit orationem Dominicam,* viz. That the Minister standing at the *North part* of the Table, shall say the Lord's Prayer. And I presume no man of reason can deny, but that the Northern end or side, call it which you will, is *pars septentrionalis,* the Northerne part; though I expect e'ere long, in spight of Dictionaries and the Grammar, to heare the contrary from this trim *Epistoler.* So that the Rubrick is fulfilled, as well by standing at the *Northerne end,* the *Table* being placed where the *Altar* stood; as standing at the *Northerne side,* in case it stood with 'one end towards the East great Window,' as the *Epistoler* would faine have it." (*A Coale from the Altar,* pp. 23 and 24.)

To this Argument the Author of "Holy Table, Name and "Thing," thus replies at pp. 56 & 57:—

> "I do presume, gentle *Doctour, that no man of reason can deny but that every* End *is a* Part: but I hope a man may stoutly deny that every *Part* is an *End,* and yet with the help of a warm Night-cap keep his Reason safe enough. Every *side* of a man is a *part:* but he that will say that every *part* of a man is a side, hath neither head nor brains of his own, nor hath he ever studied *Vesalius* his Anatomy. . . . . So in this particular, when you officiate at the *end* of the *Table,* you may officiate at a *part* (and well enough, for ought the *writer* of the *Letter* saith to the contrary) but you cannot officiate at that part of the *Table,* to the which by the *Rubrick,* confirmed by *Act of Parliament,* you are literally directed and appointed."

The remarks already made (See p. 388) upon Bp. Wren's quotation of this same Rubrick from the Elizabethan Latin Prayer Book, apply equally to Heylin's citation of it; and there is nothing in this passage to show that he, any more than Wren, would have denied that the Northern part of the Front of a Table standing Altarwise came within the definition "septen-"trionalem partem:" to hold this opinion in no way hinders agreement with his contention "that the Rubrick is fulfilled, as "well by" the Celebrant "standing at the *Northerne* end," as he says, of the Table placed Altarwise, as by "standing at the "*Northerne side*" of the Table placed with Ends East and West according to Bishop Williams's ruling. The real question, however, is whether the Rubric *originally* contemplated the Celebrant standing in the Position allotted to him by either *Heylin* or *Williams*. If there is any force in the argument by which I have endeavoured to account for the expression "North "Side" (See pp. 370ff), it is hardly likely that they "which "composed that *Rubricke*" did "speake according to the rules "of [Geometricians] Art," as Heylin assumes; but much more probable that they designed to use the language of old Ritualists. Yet be this as it may, Heylin and Williams seem to have been alike influenced, in their interpretation of the Rubric, by the *opposite* Practices which then existed; they, respectively, accepted this *contemporaneous exposition;* instead of resorting to the uniform custom just prior to the time when the Rubric was made—a course which, perhaps, might have led both to somewhat different conclusions from those which they enunciated.

LVI. The Court proceeds to support its view, further, in these words :—

> "When Bishop Wren was impeached in the House of Lords, A.D. 1636, [*read* 1641] for consecrating the elements on the west side of the table, he, answered that he stood on the north side at all the rest of the service except at the Prayer of Consecration. 'He humbly conceiveth it is a plain demonstration that he came to the west side only for the more conveniency of executing his office, and no way at all in any superstition, much less in any imitation of the Romish priests, for they place themselves there at all the service before and at all after, with no less strictness than at the time of consecrating the bread and wine.'"

Now, of course, this passage shews what Bp. Wren did on the occasion referred to; and, so far, is an authority "to show," as their Lordships say, that when the Table regained the Altarwise position, " the position of the Minister was still upon the "north side or end, facing south." (See p. 392). It must, however, be borne in mind that, in contending for this Position, the Court's aim was to prove "that the priest is so to stand that the "people present may see him break the bread and take the cup "into his hands." (See p. 325). But Wren's position in Consecrating is foreign to this theory: moreover the complaint against him was not that they could not "see" what he did—quite the reverse ; the Charge was this :—

"XVIII. He in the same year 1636, in a Church at *Ipswich*, used idolatrous actions in administering the Lord's-Supper, consecrating the Bread and Wine with his Face towards the East, and his Back towards the People, elevating them so high, that they might be seen above his Shoulders, and bowing low either to or before them, when set down on the Table." (*Parentalia*, p. 14.)

The Bishop's Defence, as to the first part of this Charge, is in these words :—

" To the eighteenth Article this Defendant answereth and denieth that in *Anno*. 1636, he did in his own Person use any superstitious or idolatrous Actions and Gestures in the Administration of the Lord's Supper.

"But he saith, that he doth ever use, and observe the Form of preparing or consecrating the Bread and Wine for the holy Sacrament which the Church of *England* hath appointed, and no other, *viz.* He doth it standing at the Lord's Table, with the Bread and Wine placed openly before him: and that as well by holy Prayer and supplication according to the Manner of the Eastern Church; as also by rehearsing of our Saviour *Christs'* Institution, according to the Manner of the Western Church, both which the Church of England, to avoid all Question, hath with great Wisdom conjoined in the Collect next before the Delivery of the Sacrament.

"And he acknowledgeth, that for the better taking of the Bread, and for the easier reaching both of the Flaggon and the Cup for the Wine, because they stood upon the Table farther from the end thereof, then he, being but low of Stature, could reach over his Book unto them, and yet still proceed on in reading of the Words without Stop or Interruption, and without Danger of spilling the Bread and Wine, he did in Tower Church in *Ipswich, anno.* 1636, turn unto the West-side of the Table, but it was only while he rehearsed the forementioned Collect, in which he was to take the Bread and Wine, and at no other time.

"And he humbly conceiveth, that altho' the Rubrick says, that the Minister shall stand at the North-side of the Table, yet it is not so to be meant, as that upon no Occasion, during all the Communion-time, he shall step from it: For it is usual to go before the Table to read the Epistle and Gospel, and necessary to go from the Table to the Pulpit to preach, and with the Bason to receive the Offerings, if any be; and with the Bread and Wine to distribute to the Communicants. Inasmuch therefore as he did stand at the North-side, all the while before he came to that Collect, wherein he was to take the Bread and Wine into his Hands, and as soon as that was done, thither he returned again; he humbly conceiveth, it is a plain Demonstration that he came to the West-side, only for more Conveniency of executing his Office, and no way at all in any Superstition, much less in any Imitation of the *Romish* Priests; for, they place themselves there, at all the service before, and at all after, with no less Strictness, than at the Time of their consecrating the Bread and Wine." (Ibid. pp. 103 & 4.)

It will be seen that Bp. Wren distinctly defends his mode of Consecration as being what "the Church of England hath "appointed;" and his admission that he did "turn to the "West-side of the Table" to Consecrate, is, in fact, his interpretation of the Rubric before the Prayer of Consecration— "Then the Priest standing up, shall say as followeth;" (See Col. iv. p. 367) for he says that "he doth it standing at the Lord's "Table, with the Bread and Wine placed openly before him."

This traditional meaning of " at " is plainly to be traced to the corresponding Rubric in the Book of 1549 (See Cols. II. & III. p. 360) where "standing at God's board" is the direction; and this is translated by Alesius "stans ad medium altaris." He further says that though the Rubrical direction is to "stand at the "North-side of the Table, yet it is not so to be meant, as that upon "no Occasion, during the Communion-time, he shall step from "it;" and in giving instances of this necessary liberty, it can hardly be thought that he excluded the very Eastward Position which he was defending himself for occupying. The Bishop's Defence has, indeed, been alleged to afford no support to the Eastward Position of the Celebrant being Rubrical, because he pleaded that "he being but low of Stature, could not reach "over his book unto" the Elements which, evidently, were at the middle of the Altar: yet his plea, as in part quoted by the Court, "that he came to the West-side, only for the more con- "veniency of executing his Office," was one for which he could quote the Rubric of the Scotch Office which he had assisted in framing: the Bishop wished to consecrate "with the more ease "and decency" which that Office assigned as the reason for authorizing the Minister "during the time of Consecration" to stand at a part of the holy Table where he could best "use both "his hands."

In all this, however, as well as in the rest of Wren's Defence to this 18th Article of Charge, he does not even hint at any excuse for the breaking of the Bread not being *seen* by the people (though, indeed, as already remarked, there was no Charge on this score): so far from this, his denial of the Charge as to "Elevating" the Bread and Wine, distinctly shews that his mode of Consecrating was one which may well be described in the deprecatory language of the Court, as to Mr. Purchas— " we take it as proved that the greater part of the Congregation "could not see the breaking of the bread or the act of taking "the cup into the hands." (See p. 336.) This is what the Bishop says :—

"But he denieth, that ever he did use any elevating of the Bread and Wine, much less that he made any Elevation so high, as that the Bread and Wine might be seen over his Shoulders; whereof abundant Testimony will be had of many (*omni exceptione majores*) who were then present, and well observed all Passages and Gestures, *viz.* Mr. *Larry,* Mr. *Keene,* Mr. *Norwich,* Mr. *Novell,* Mr. *Mapletoft,* and others. He therefore saith, that only in repeating the Words of Institution, he took the Silver Plate, wherein the Bread was, into his Hand, to break the Bread, and to say, *Take, Eat,* &c. But then he never lifted his Hand from the Table, whereon it rested: and no otherwise did he with the Cup also. . . . ." (*Ibid.* p. 104.)

LVII. In further support of its opinion that "the north side or end, "facing south" was meant to be the Celebrant's true position, throughout the Office, the Court remarks that:—

> " Nicholls (Commentary on Common Prayer, published 1710), Bennett (Annotations on Book of Common Prayer, 1708), Wheatley (Rational illustrations of Common Prayer, 1710), confirm the view that when the table was placed east and west, [? north and south] the Minister's position was still on the north."

It is inconvenient that the statements here alluded to are neither quoted nor more particularly indicated: perhaps the Writer of the Judgment had in mind the three passages quoted, in the same order and from the same Editions, by Mr. Elliott in his "North side of the Table" (pp. 90–92)—a Pamphlet already mentioned (See p. 390) as apparently cited by the Court. It may be useful, therefore, to re-produce here Mr. Elliott's quotations; adding such comments as they seem to require.

(I) NICHOLLS. I quote from the Edition of 1712 which does not differ from the Edition of 1710 cited by Mr. Elliott who, however, does not give the passages here put in square brackets: the *Italics* are in the original.

" *Standing before the Table.*] 'Tis quæried by some, Whether the Priest is to say the Consecration-Prayer standing before the Table, by this Rubrick; or, Whether after having prepared the Elements so standing, he is to return to the usual plan of saying the Communion-Service with us, *viz.* to the North-side of the Table? I answer, That according to the Rules of Grammar, the Participle *standing,* must refer to the Verb *ordered,* and not to *say*: so that the Priest must *order* standing before &c. and not *say* standing."

But the very fact—that Nichols was replying to another view of the Rubric—shews that his was not the only interpretation then, and therefore it need not be accepted now as necessarily the true one: however, this question will have to be discussed with reference to a later passage in the Judgment, and so it is unnecessary to say more upon it now. To support his interpretation he next observes :—

"But this will be yet clearer, if we consider, *first*, What the former Rubricks were, before the making of this; and *secondly*, The reason which is given in this Rubrick.

["1. To consider what the former Rubricks were before the making of this.

"*Way of standing at the Altar before the Reformation.* In the *Missale Romanum*, from whence a considerable part of the Communion-Service is taken, the Priest is obliged, almost during the whole Service, to turn his face towards the Altar, standing in the midst thereof. At his first entrance within the Rails he is obliged by the Popish Rubrick, *facere debitam reverentiam*, with his Face towards it, and so to continue till he comes to *the Dominus vobiscum*, &c. which Versicles are to be said by the Priest, *Versus in Populum*, and no more. Afterwards when the Prefaces are read, he is to lay both hands upon the Altar, with his Back to the People, *Præfatio incipitur ambabus manibus positis hinc inde super altare.*"]

["And when the Commemorations are made, he is *extendere manus & elevare ad cælum oculos, & statim demittens profundi* inclinatus ante altare, which still implies the same posture, *viz.* his face towards the Altar.

"When he says the Benediction Prayer, he is to *tenere manus expansas super oblata*, which must be with his Face towards the Altar.

"And in this Posture he is to *tenere ambabus manibus hostiam inter indices & pollices*, when he pronounces the Consecration words; and so likewise to adore it after Consecration. And in this posture he was to lift it up above his Forehead to be seen by the people.]

"So that from hence it is plain, that the greatest part of the Romish Service was performed with the Priest's face turned to the Altar."

This conclusion is true enough of the Office which was in use before the Book of 1549, though that Office was not "the "*Missale Romanum*," as Nicholls says, but the old English Office, especially that of Sarum; and therefore the Rubrics he quotes are only pertinent so far as they are to be found in words or in substance in those Offices. He goes on, however, to say :—

"Now our Reformers conceived a dislike of this Practice, upon several Accounts; for if the People had understood the Language of the Mass, they could not have heard the Voice of the Priest in this Posture, being directed quite from them."

Whether Nicholls had any sufficient warrant for this assertion may, at least, be reasonably doubted if tested by what has been already said upon the point in the preceding passages. Yet, whatever may be thought of this, Nicholls in fact goes far to disprove his own assertion in the following references to the P. Book of 1549 which prescribe the very "Practice" of the Priest being turned from the People which he says "our Reformers "conceived a dislike of." He goes on to remark:—

["*Way of standing enjoined afterwards.*] 2. Now let us consider what they Substituted instead of this Posture of Celebrating the Communion, in the first Book of *Edw.* VI.
"At the beginning of the Communion-Service, *Almighty God to whom all hearts are open,* &c. is to be said by the *Priest humbly standing before the middle of the Altar,* without any Posture mentioned either to the Altar or towards the People."]

["The general Confession was to be repeated with the Minister's Face towards the Table, because the Rubrick before the Absolution which immediately follows, says, *Then shall the Minister stand up, and turning himself towards the People.* When he is to say the Prayer next to the Consecration, *We do not presume,* &c. he is *turning himself to God's Board* to *kneel* down."]

["And how the Consecration-Prayer was recited, is evident from the Rubrick which follows after it: *These words before rehearsed* (viz. the Consecration-Prayer) *are to be said, turning still to the Altar, without any elevation, or shewing the Sacrament to the people.*

"So that upon the whole, besides composing many new Prayers, and the expunging several others out of the *Missale,* and the laying aside many Ceremonies therein, these things in particular were exploded: 1. Reverence towards the Altar, there being no Rubrick for it in King *Edward's* first Book. 2. Elevation of the Sacrament. 3. Ostension."]

But the "Reverence" did not depend upon a "Rubrick:" that which Nicholl quotes (See Col. I. & II. p. 364) was not in the Sarum Office: yet the Book of 1549 fully covered the Practice in the following Note.—"As touching kneeling, crossing, holding "up of hands, knocking upon the breast, and other gestures, they "may be used or left, as every man's devotion serveth, without "blame." Nicholls thus continues his comment:

"After this Book was established, the first thing moved for, to be altered therein, was to have Altars changed into Tables. [Bishop *Hooper* first motion'd this in a Sermon at Court, saying, that *as long as Altars remained, ignorant People, and Priests, would dream of Sacrifice.*] Thus an Order of Council was issued out for changing Altars into

Tables, *Anno. Edw.* VI. 4, 1550. And after that, 1551, there was a Review of the Common-Prayer; in which the Rubricks were altered, and the Priest, instead of performing the Communion-Service *standing before the middle of the Altar*, was enjoined to perform it *standing on the North-side of the Table.* [The present Rubric was likewise set down in the same words we have it, in the last Review of the Common-Prayer."]

["*Reasons for standing on the North side of the Table.*] II. But in the next place, I think this Matter will be out of all doubt, if we consider the Reason given in this Rubrick, why the Priest should stand, at this particular time, before the Altar or Table. The Papists had their particular Reasons, why they stood before the Altar, during the time of Consecration; which was not to let the People be Eyewitnesses of their Operation in working their pretended Miracle: For they would be apt to have lesser esteem thereof, whilst they looked on and saw what was done: and therefore they thought it the best way to skreen it from the People's Eyes, by the intervention of the Priest's body. But our Church enjoins the direct contrary, and that for a direct contrary Reason. He is to stand before the Table indeed, just so long as he is *ordering the Bread and Wine*; but after that, he is to go to some place where he may break the Bread *before the People*, which must be the North-side of the Table, there being, in our present Rubrick, no other place mention'd for performing any part of this Sacrament. But to say the Consecration-Prayer (in the recital of which the Bread is broken) standing before the Table, is not to break the Bread *before the People*; for then the People cannot have a View thereof, which our wise Reformers, upon very good Reasons, ordered they should."

The statements in these two paragraphs, bearing upon the point now under discussion, have been partly noticed already and will have to be remarked upon further: so it is unnecessary to comment upon them in this place.

The following passage is not noticed by Mr. Elliott, but it is as well to give it here.

["*Posture in saying the Consecration Prayer.*] But then again it may be Quæried, Whether the Priest must say the Consecration-Prayer standing or kneeling. I answer, our Church has determined neither. The Scotch Liturgy indeed says, *The Priest standing up shall say the Prayer of Consecration*: and the Old Common-Prayer Book, *The Priest standing up shall say;* but our present Common-Prayer-Book obliges the Priest only to stand whilst he is ordering the Bread and Wine, but not to stand whilst he is saying the Prayer. Now, since this is a Prayer, and not a bare Repetition of the words of the Institution, in the Popish way, the Posture of kneeling is the most proper. If it be said, that since the Church does not oblige the Minister to kneel, it supposes him to stand.

I answer, That is no Consequence; for there is not one Rubrick which obliges the Minister to kneel in all the Post-Communion-Service, and yet I do not know any one that has contended for the Posture of standing in performance of that part of the Service. However, they are not to be condemned that say the Prayer standing, the Rubrick leaving them at liberty, and they having the ancient Rubrick of Queen *Elizabeth's* Book to Countenance them therein. But whenever the Goverment pleases to call for another Review, this Matter would do well to be clearly settled, to avoid all Disputes, and that Ministers may be obliged to an exact Uniformity."]

Upon this it is sufficient to remark here that Cosin, whose NOTES Nicholls himself published in his Commentary says (Additional Notes, p. 45):—"*Standing up.*] Which is a posture of "reverence, and here ordered for the Priest to use, that he may "with the more readiness perform his office in consecrating the "Elements," (*Works* v. p. 322.) And as "readiness" is one reason assigned in the Rubric of 1662 which is clearly traceable to Cosin (See p. 326) it will hardly be believed that he meant to sanction *kneeling* by the Celebrant when Consecrating.

(II). THOMAS BENNETT. Ed. 1708. He argued thus "if it "[the Table] stand in the Chancel, I think, it ought in any "wise to stand close to the East-wall;" and, to a supposed objector, he replied "that the word *Body* has no relation to "the word Chancel": then he says, in the passage quoted by Mr. Elliott (except the part in brackets) as follows:—

"Now let us consider the Rubric before the Commandments. It says 'then shall the Priest (who stands at the North side or end of the Table) turning to the people, rehearse distinctly all the ten Commandments. [The Rubric also before the Absolution informs us, that the Absolution is to be said by the Minister *standing up and turning himself to the People.* But if the Table be in the middle of the Chancel, and the People consequently round about the Minister; how shall the Minister turn to the People at the reading of the Commandments, more than he did before?] If the Table be close to the East Wall, the Minister stands on the North side and looks Southward; and then, turning to the Westward, he looks full towards all the people. —p. 155, 2nd Edition. 1709.* [But if the Table be in the middle of the Chancel, he cannot so turn to them. See also Dr. Heylin, *Antidot.* p. 58."]

(III). CHARLES WHEATLEY. Ed. 1794. Oxford, Clarendon Press (p. 247). He was objecting to the Table being in the middle of the Church, and, quoting the two Rubrics as to the Minister turning to the People at the Commandments and at the Absolution, he says :—

"From whence I argue, that if the Table be *in the middle of the Church*, and the People consequently round about the Minister, the Minister cannot turn himself to the People any more at one time than another. Whereas [if the Table be close to the East wall, the Minister stands on the North side, and looks Southward, and consequently, by looking Westward, *turns himself to the People.*"]

The passage in Brackets is that quoted by Mr. Elliott from p. 107, Ed. 1710; and he continues it in the following Sentence which, however, does not appear in the Edition which I am quoting, and which is stated in the Preface as "being printed "from one of those which had received the Author's last "corrections :"—

"Wherever it stands, the Priest is obliged to stand at *the North side of it*, which seems to be enjoined *for no other end*, but to avoid the practice of the Romish Church, where the Priest stands *before the Table with his face towards the East.*" *

Mr. Elliott then cites the following passage from the Edition of 1720 which agrees with the Edition of 1794 and immediately follow the words "*turns himself to the people*" in the passage above quoted :—

"Wherever it be placed, the Priest is obliged to *stand at the North side (or end thereof*, as the Scotch Liturgy expresses it; which also orders, that it *shall stand at the uppermost part of the Chancel or Church*), the design of which is, that the Priest may be better seen and heard : which, as our Altars are now placed, he cannot be but at the North or South side. And therefore the north side, being the right-hand or upper side of the Altar, is certainly the most proper for

---

* Yet Mr. Lathbury (History of the Book of Common Prayer, 1868, p. 394), speaking of Practices after the Book of 1662, says,—"We are told by a writer of the period, who evidently describes the practice of many of the clergy, that the minister in reading the lessons turned towards the people, 'whereas in prayer he looks another way, towards the more eminent part of the church, where use to be placed the symbols of God's more especial presence, with whom the minister in prayer hath chiefly to do. For the same reason, we suppose, that the Christians in former times used to pray with their faces eastward.' (Elborrow's Reasonableness of the Christian Sacrifice, 47, 48.)"

Long before the Revision of 1661 Bp. Wren, in his Orders of 1636, had directed:—"20. That the Minister's reading desk do not stand with the back towards the Chancel, nor too remote or far from it." (*Cardwell Doc. Ann.* II 257, or 2nd *Rit. Report*, p. 565.)

the *officiating* Priest, that so the *assisting* Minister (if there be one) may not be obliged to stand above him. And Bishop Beveridge* has shewn that wherever, in the ancient Liturgies, the Minister is directed to stand *before* the Altar, the North side of it is always meant."

These, then, are probably the passages to which the Court alluded as helping to "confirm the view that when the table "was placed east and west," or rather, *north and south*, as the context of the Judgment (See pp. 400, 402, & 405) seems to shew that the Court meant, the Minister's Position was "still on the "north." Now, no doubt, the Writers are reliable witnesses of Practice in their time; though, indeed, the very existence of their Arguments seems to shew that there was some variation in the Practice. But the real question is—what did "North side" originally mean in 1552? The conventional meanings which, more or less widely, it subsequently acquired (whether they were the *cause* or the *effect* of the different Positions of the Lord's Table) must not be allowed to displace the meaning

---

* Wheatley refers to " *Bev.* Pandect. vol. ii. page 76, § 15. See also Renaudotius's Liturgies, tom. ii. page 24." But Bp. Beveridge affords no support to Wheatley's view: Beveridge quotes from the Liturgy of St. Chrysostom a direction beginning "ὁ ἱερεὺς καὶ ὁ διάκονος" &c., and gives the following translation, "*Sacerdos & Diaconus ante sanctam mensam tres adorationes faciunt : Tum vero Sacerdos acceptum sanctum Evangelium tradit Diacono, atque ita per portam Septentrionalis partis egressi, ad consuetum locum veniunt.*" Upon this he remarks:—"E quibus simul perspicuum redditur, in dictâ Septentrionali parte portam etiam fuisse ex bemate, ubi sancti mensa ducentem. Quandoquidem autem Bema perpetuo ad Orientalem Ecclesiæ partem extructum est, & Episcopus in eo sedet respiciens Occidentem, hic Septentrionem ad dextram, & austrum ad sinistram semper habeat necem est; . . . ."

Mr. Elliott adds, p. 92, "Any remaining doubt as to the meaning of *North side* in this extract [from Wheatley] *should such exist*, will be removed by reference to the Frontispiece affixed to the folio edition of 1720." This Frontispiece represents the Celebrant as standing at the North *end* of the Altar placed, as customarily, lengthwise against the East wall of the Chancel. If, however, any material weight is to be attached to Pictorial evidence, there are two other Pictures about the same date which clearly witness against the North *end* Position for the Celebrant.

One of these forms the Frontispiece to "The Divine Banquet of Sacramental Devotions," 1700, which has the "*Imprimatur*, Isham, R. P. D. Henric, [Compton] *Episc.* Lond. *a Sacris.*" The Picture plainly shows the Celebrant kneeling at the *Northern part* of the West side of the Altar placed close against the East Wall of the Chancel. This Picture has been re-produced at p. 373 of Mr. J. D. Chambers's valuable publication, " Divine Worship in England in the 13th & 14th Centuries contrasted with and adapted to that in the 19th." (*Pickering*, 1877.)

The other Picture is the Frontispiece to "A form of Prayers, used by his late Majesty K. William III. when he received the Holy Sacrament, and on other occasions," 1704. Here the Celebrant, a Bishop, is standing at the Northern part of the West side of the Altar, turning half round to the King who is kneeling at the Altar Rails.

which the Revisers of 1552 intended it to bear, if that meaning can be discovered. Wheatly, most certainly, was not justified in referring to the words " North side or end thereof," in the Scotch Book of 1637, as the true exposition of " North side " in the Revised book of 1662. It does not appear to have occurred to these Writers (or indeed to others) that the term " North side" originated in the way I have ventured to maintain (See p. 359 ff.) Nor do they seem to have been aware that, at the Revision of 1661, the word " side " was altered to the word " part," but that finally the word " side " was retained. Probably they had no knowledge of the Black Letter Prayer Book of 1636 in which the Revisers of 1661 inserted their MS. alterations ; or of the MS. copy of the Revised Book which was attached as the Schedule to the Act of Uniformity of 1662. These Books, at one time missing and supposed by some to be lost, were produced before the Ritual Commissioners on August 8, 1867. It may be useful to reproduce here, as nearly as mere Printing will permit, the Rubric with its alterations as found in the two Books.

The following is the Rubric of the Book of 1636 copied from the Photozincographed Fac-simile of the Book which was made by the Government at the instance of the Ritual Commission. The *Italics* shew the alterations :—

"The table at the communion time having a fair white linnen cloth upon it, shall stand in the ~~body of the church, or in the chancell, where~~ *✗ body of the Church, or in the chancell, where* morning ~~prayer~~, *and evening prayer are appointed to be said.* ~~morning prayer, and evening prayer be appointed to be said.~~ And the priest standing ~~at~~ *at* the north ~~side~~ *side* ~~part~~ of the table, shall say the Lords prayer, with ~~this~~ *the* collect following, yᵉ people kneeling."

In the left hand margin of the page this alteration occurs :—

~~✗ most conuenient place in the upper end of yᵉ Chancel (or of yᵉ body of yᵉ Church where there is no Chancel.)~~

The Rubric in the MS. Book is thus altered, the changes are printed as a foot Note in the Rubrics collated from that Book at p. 17, of the Fourth Report of the Ritual Commission: —

"¶ *The Table at the Communion time hauing a fair white Linen cloth upon it, shall stand in the* [an erased word, probably *most*, is indistinct] *of the Church, or where Morning and body* ~~convenient place~~ *in the* ~~upper end of the~~ *Chancel,* ~~(or of the body of~~ *Evening Prayer are appointed to be said.* ~~the Church where there is no Chancel).~~ *And the Priest standing at the north* ~~part~~ side *of the Table shall say the Lords Prayer with the Collect following, the people kneeling.*"

The alterations in this Rubric speak for themselves, and they shew that two changes were made and afterwards abandoned: *First*, a proposed liberty to put the Table in the "*most con-venient place* in the upper end of the Chancel (or of the body of the Church where there is no Chancel)" was cancelled and the old wording of the Rubric kept which (read, as it must be, with the Rubric as to the place of Morning and Evening Prayer) limited the situation of the Table "except it shall be otherwise determined by the Ordinary of the Place." *Secondly*, whereas it was proposed to place the Priest at the "North *part* of the Table"—a term which clearly would have allowed him the choice of the *Northern part of the Front* or the *North end*—the Revisers restored the word "side." It is noticeable that in doing this they did not follow the precedent of the Scotch Book—"North side or end thereof"—and therefore it may be fairly concluded that, whether "end" was an *alternative* or an *expletive* of "side," they saw objections to its use; and it is reasonable to suppose that their vindication of Praying Eastward, in reply to the contrary Proposal of the Ministers at the Savoy Conference (See p. 330) influenced their decision. Moreover, in all likelihood, they deemed it safest to alter as little as possible; and probably it may be said of this Rubric, as Sancroft wrote in Cosin's Durham Prayer Book in reference to a re-arrangement proposed by Cosin in part of the Office—" My Lords the bishops at Ely House ordered all in the old method." (*Preface to Cosin's Notes*, p. xxii. and *Introduction to the Cosin Correspondence*, Vol. II., p. xiii.)

The Court thus concludes its Inquiry into the meaning of the term " North side " :—

> "Their Lordships entertain no doubt whatever that when the table was set at the east end the direction to stand at the north side was understood to apply to the north end, and that this was the practice of the church."

It may readily be admitted that, at the period to which the Court refers, there was such an understanding and practice and that it was by no means uncommon; it may even have been pretty general: nor can it be denied that the tradition prevails to a considerable extent even now, and is the rule in perhaps the majority of English Churches. But a general understanding and practice is no necessary proof that the *intention* of a Rubric is observed: the History of the Church of England at various periods and at the present time furnishes proofs that Custom and Rubrics have not always coincided. The question therefore must be repeated—" What did the Rubric originally " mean"? I venture to think that, in what has been already said in the preceding pages on this subject, some ground has been furnished which might lead their Lordships to reconsider the Reasons which left them free from "doubt" on a matter which, at all events, cannot claim to be so clear that a different interpretation may not be held and acted upon without being condemned as plainly contrary to the Ecclesiastical Law.

LVIII. Another point, which the Judicial Committee proposed to investigate, is next brought forward in the following passage:—

> "It will be convenient to consider next what is the meaning of the words 'before the people,' in the Rubric, before the Consecration Prayer. Nicholls (*Op. cit.*) observes—'To say the Consecration Prayer (in the recital of which the bread is broken) standing before the table, is not to break the bread before the people; for then the people cannot have a view thereof, which our wise Reformers, upon very good reasoning, ordered that they should.'"

But this statement, which the Court appears to accept, assumes the very point in dispute, viz. that it was intended the people should "have a view" of the breaking of the Bread: Nicholls does not attempt to shew that the words of the Rubric even imply this; nor does he offer any proof whatever that "our "wise Reformers," whoever he may have meant, "ordered "that" the people "should" see the actual fraction. It has been shewn, I think, in the preceding pages, that no such direction was issued by those who were responsible for the various Revisions of the Book since 1549; and it is quite certain, from the Rubrics of the First Prayer Book, that what Nicholls asserts could not have been designed by those "Reformers" who compiled that Book. The Court itself admits (See p. 325) "that "the mere words" of the present Rubric "do not speak of "seeing"; and the fact that this Rubric has the words "before "the people," and not the words "in the sight of the people" which were used in the draft Liturgy presented at the Savoy Conference, is reasonable evidence that the Bishops did not favour the proposal and that it did not commend itself to the Revisers in 1661. The Ministers in their *Exceptions* at the Conference did not, indeed, seem to imply that "seeing" was an end which they desired (See p. 335): but, later, in the Liturgy which accompanied their "Petition for Peace" the following Rubrics occur:—

"*Then let the Minister take the Bread, and break it in the sight of the People, saying:*
"The Body of Christ was broken for us, and offered once for all to sanctifie us; Behold the sacrificed Lamb of God, that taketh away the sins of the World."
"*In like manner let him take the Cup, and pour out the Wine in the sight of the Congregation, saying;*
"Wee were redeemed with the precious Blood of Christ, as of a Lamb without blemish, and without spot." ("A Petition for Peace: with the Reformation of the Liturgy. As it was presented to the Right Reverend Bishops, by the Divines Appointed by His Majesties *Commission* to treat with them about the alteration of it. London, Printed, *Anno Dom.* MDCLXI," pp. 53 and 54. (The *Liturgy* is also printed in the "*Reliquiæ Liturgicæ*," Edited by the Revd. Peter Hall. Vol. 4. 1847.)

Their Lordships, for the more confirmation of their opinion as to the true position of the Celebrant in the act of Consecration, remark:—

> "That stress was laid on this witness of the people of the act of breaking, appears by other passages; for example, Udall says—'We press the action of

breaking the bread against the Papist. To what end, if not that the beholders might thereby be led unto the breaking of the Body of Christ.' (Communion Comeliness, 1641.)"

This short extract from Udall occurs in the following passage from Udall's Tract given by Mr. Elliott (" The North Side of "the *Table*," p. 70, Note] :—

"That the action of breaking the bread was still observed, even when not prescribed by the Rubric, and importance attached to it in connection with the Romish controversy, will appear from the following extract from 'Communion Comeliness,' by Ephraim Udall, Rector of St. Austin's :—' We press the action of breaking the bread against the Papist. To what end, if not that the beholders might thereby be led unto the breaking of the body of Christ . . . . which all shall see if there be a competent number *at the Table*, and few shall see if they sit in pews so high as the pews in London,' pp. 3—4, 1641."

It may be that the Writer of the Judgment had this passage before him, as it is highly probable that Mr. Elliott's Pamphlet was part of the " controversial literature " brought under the Court's notice : Udall's Tract being a somewhat rare book may not, perhaps, have been seen by their Lordships. Yet Udall's remark about the " pews," which Mr. Elliott quotes (not cited however in the Judgment), seems to suggest that it was not the question of the MINISTER's *Position* which prompted his remark about " the action of breaking the bread," but rather the *Place* of the PEOPLE " in pews so high as the pews in London." A perusal of the Original Tract fully supports this view ; and therefore it is desirable to quote some other passages in order to shew its general drift. Two remarks are, however, in place here : *First*, that (if nothing may be done without a Rubric) Udall had no Rubrical warrant to support his requirement; for no Manual Acts existed in the Prayer Book then in use: *Secondly*, that his opinion and practice in 1641 (even if it meant what the Court understood it to mean) is not necessarily a guide to the meaning of a Rubric not made until 20 years afterwards. The following is the Title of Udall's Publication:—

"τὸ πρέπον εὐχαριστικὸν
i.e.

" Communion comlinesse. Wherein is discovered the conveniency of the peoples drawing neere to the Table in the sight thereof when they receive the Lord's Supper. With the great unfitnesse of receiving it in

Pewes in *London,* for the Novelty of high and close Pewes. The former way of receiving tending to edification by the Sacrament, the latter to the destruction thereof.

By *Ephraim Vdall,* Rector of St. *Austin's, London.*

Colos. 2. 5. *For though I be absent from you in the Flesh, yet am I present with you in Spirit, joying and beholding your order and stedfastnesse of your Faith in Christ Jesus.*

1 Cor. 14. 26. Let all things be done to edifying. 40. Let all things be done decently and in order.

LONDON Printed, and are to be sold by *T. Bates* in the *Old Baily,* 1641."

UDALL commences his Tract (of 24 pages) by an " Epistle to " the Reader " in which he says :—

" It is ingeniously confessed, that the setting up of the Table of late like an Altar brought into many Churches, fixing it to the wall, and railing it about on the three other parts of it, whatever the intention thereof was, was not so convenient for the Communion as if it had stood in the middle of the Chancell, and the Raile beene square about it. For in the Altar way one side of the Table was wholy lost, so that the bringing of the greatest number of Communicants at one time to the Table was neither effected, neither doe I think it was intended which should be our greatest care and ayme. And peradventure one part of the intention was to see that all the Communicants did kneele at the Communion according to the Act of Parliament in that case provided. But I professe another intention in that which I desire, viz. to bring the greatest number together into the Chancell in sight of the Table, both in their Pewes and in any other additionall way that may be invented, not to bee sure they kneele for though kneeling hath ever beene my practise, and the gesture I have perswaded others too as the gesture established by Law, in which perswasion I have prevailed with divers somewhat opposite, yet if the State shall thinke fit to alter that gesture my desire remains notwithstanding as of a thing most fit for Communicating be the gesture whatsoever it shall be. And therefore, considering that the Lord's Supper is a Communion, having also divers essentiall actions about it which are signes running into our sences, and ordained to raise the heart inwardly, by that which is seene outwardly to apprehension of the thing that is signified in the signe, and because the words of Benediction by Prayer and Thanksgiving are appointed for the instruction and edification of the people in separating the elements of Bread and Wine unto that holy and Sacramentall use, and to raise them up to thankefulnesse to God, and Prayer for spirituall benefit in that heavenly banquet, which things cannot be effected but by coming up to the Table in sight and hearing of the Minister, considering also how farre we are degenerated from a due manner of receiving (in LONDON especially) by a late new kind of building the Pewes so much higher and closer then heretofore, for that all the externall actions of the Minister, doe lose their use and vertue to the greatest part of the people, together with all the prayers and benedictions, by which the elements are consecrate, sanctified and set apart from their common, to that holy use of the Supper of the Lord, to be a spirituall and Sacramentall refection to the soule which benefit these new, high, and close Pewes doe evacuate and destroy."

This passage clearly shows that Udall's complaint was—that the Pews practically shut out the Congregation generally from joining in the Office with the Celebrant: it was not one action only—the breaking of the Bread—that was hidden from them, but "all the externall actions of the Minister:" the way in which the Minister stood could make no difference in this respect: the high Pews were the offence. Moreover he complains that this—

". . . building of their high Pewes, being indeed 'a new thing' was 'forcing' the Ministers 'to make some provision in the Chancell for the Communion, which they by their high Pewes have made the body of the Church unfit for.'"

This evil, which was opposed, he says, to "my practise since "I have been a Minister for about 30 years past (when innova- "tions were not thought of), except that aboute two yeares "space when" he "came first to London," he "found the "manner of receiving the Communion in" his "judgment "marvellously intoward, and inconvenient to the Minister, and "unprofitable for the people and unworthy and incompetent to "the nature of the Sacrament." In trying to remedy this he brought upon him the "reproach" of "Popish or formall" whereas before he had been "branded" as "Puritanicall;" and he was threatened with "the Parliament" by "some one or "two," though what he had done had the "approbation of the "most wise, ancient, and Religious persons" in his Parish. The plan he adopted, he thus describes:—

"I . . . set up a square Raile in the Chancell at the Communion times onely, and that within the Pewes which were made to fold downe for that use, and went square about the Chancell,* excepting the East

* At p. 1, *Udall* refers to "*Black-Friers*, in *London*" as an example of his plan "onely with this difference, That whereas that Church hath the inner Pewes immoveable, because it useth not the ground for Buriall, which is used in that way in other Churches: the inner Pewes may be made so, as they may be removed, when the ground is to be used for Buriall; as now is practised in many Churches, where all the Pewes in the Church are so ordered, That any of them, and all of them successively are taken up, and the ground used."

end where the Pew was removed before I came, by this means I received a double row of Communicants one within the other neere the Table in a very small Chancell to the number of 40, or 50, at one time in the Pewes and at the Raile, and when they had received, another company after them, and so till all had received and administered with much ease, quick dispatch, and benefit to those that knew how to use a Sacrament and the Sacramentall actions thereabout, by discerning the things Sacramentall in their signes . . . ."

It was to "satisfy" objectors, to explain his proceedings to others who were well disposed towards him, and to induce others to adopt his plan, that he wrote his Tract, assigning the "Reasons" for his proceedings: of these I quote the following portions:—

"First, it is most agreeable to Christ's own manner of Celebration, in the first Institution; . . . . who sate downe with the twelve . . . it may be possible that Christ might stand up when hee blessed the elements of Bread and Wine, . . . his disciples that did communicate were with him in common at the same Table, within sight and hearing of his words and actions . . . not in severall Roomes, or severall corners were they all present with him in the Celebration," (p. 3.)

The next Reason is the one from which the Court quotes: I give it entire in order that the force of the words cited may be best seen by the context:—

"2. It is most sutable with his intention in the Sacrament; which is an outward Signe of an inward and spirituall Thing, to be received of the heart by Faith. Now Christ intended to use the Senses, and by them to affect and worke upon the heart: which is done most effectually, in all, when all draw neere to see and behold the sacramentall Elements, Rites and Actions about them at the Table. Wee presse the action of breaking the Bread against the Papist. To what end, if not that the beholders might thereby be led unto the breaking of the body of Christ; and in like manner, by the powring out of the Wine, unto the shedding and effusion of the Blood of Christ? Which all shall see, if there be a competent number at the Table; and few shall see, if they sit in Pewes, so high, as the Pewes in *London* be. Thus all, by Seeing, and hearing; as well as by taking, and eating, and drinking, and smelling, shall be elevated to the spirituall Actions of Faith, and comfortable apprehension of That, that these externall Actions doe represent unto them," (pp. 3 & 4.)

In his Third Reason UDALL depicts more fully the irreverences and abuses of the period, which he endeavoured to correct:—

"3. It is most agreeable to the nature of the Sacrament; which is not onely a Communion of the Faithfull with Christ, but of the

Faithfull also one with another. (1 *Cor.* 10–17). *For wee, that are many, are one Bread, and one Body :* but in high and scattered Pewes, where we are seperated so, that we can neither see, nor heare one the other, this Communion seems to be rent and divided, into so many single Societies of twoes and throes, as there be Pewfulls in the Church, more like so many private Masses and Houselings, than one Communion: for, in the private Masse, the Priest receiveth alone, and peradventure, at one time there may be three private Masses, in three severall places of the same Church, and yet all of them make not one Communion, but are justly taxed by our Divines; though the people stand, and looke on, but receive not: and so, in my apprehension, is it worthy to be taxed, though they doe receive, if they receive it scattered here and there, and are shut up close, that they neither see nor heare, untill the Minister come to the Pewes where they sit; in, which, sometimes, there are divers Pewes, and they farre distant one from the other; in which there are but one, or but two Communicants, in this corner; and one or two in the other corner, and others up in the Gallery, and so will have the Minister to hunte up and downe to search them out, and administer unto them scattered here and there in severall Pewes, remote one from the other. And I thinke shortly the Sacrament of the Lord's Supper will get up into the Steeple among the Bells with us, as the Sacrament of Baptism hath done heretofore among the Papists . . . . ." (pp. 4 & 5.)

In his *Fifth* Reason UDALL supports his proposal by the remark :—

"It hath beene the ancient practice of the Church of *England*, continued since the Reformation, in many churches. And what other construction can bee made of those words of the service as [? at] the Communion, *viz.* Draw neere, and receive ? . . . (p. 6.)

"7. It is a needlesse wearinesse put upon the Ministers, to go up and downe the Church, reaching and stretching, rending and tearing themselves in long Pewes, to hold forth the Elements, over foure or five persons; the Ministers being sometimes aged, sometimes sickly, or afflicted with one painfull infirmity or other; by which meanes they are not alwaies men of activity and fitnesse to such imployments: which many people have lesse regard unto, than to their Horse; to which the righteous man is mercifull. *Prov.* xii. 10. (p. 9.)

"8. It is also an occasion, often in this way of administering, of shedding and spilling the Bread and Wine upon the ground, or on the peoples heads; which, by reason of this reaching and stretching cannot be avoyded." (p. 9.)

"11. It cannot but be supposed far more seemely, to administer in this desired way, than for a Minister to stride and straddle, over the Laps of Maids and Women : a most indecent thing; which in long Pews cannot be avoided." (p. 10.)

"12. It is a fit thing the Minister should discerne and know the persons he administereth unto . . . but hee cannot discerne whom he receives unto the Communion, when they sit stragling, and closed up in high Pewes, not to be taken notice of by the Minister . . . ." (p. 10.)

His 13th Reason, which advocates " a Raile, or Wainscot . . . " upon the Communion daye to keepe off the people from the " Table " exhibits the great irreverences of the time; for he says :—

"2. And to leave the Table open, in such crowds of people as wee have, in many small Churches within the Walles, would expose the Furniture upon it to be pulled to the ground, and the Wine to be spilled, by jogging the Table, unlesse something be set about it, at the time, to defend it from the injuries of the people: among whom, some are very incivill; and, in a crowde, none of them able to that decent and inoffensive carriage, they be willing unto. And, in some places, the Boyes doe write on the Communion Table, the Table being prepared for the Communion, and remove the vessels of Wine that be on the Table prepared for the Communion to make roome for their writing, fouling and spotting the linnen and table at the same time with inke, and in some places upon the communion dayes, the table-cloath and carpet are throwne over the bread, and communion vessels of Wine which are wholly covered therewith, that they may use the Table at the same time to write on, which table used in that manner, stands all the Sermon-time more like a Corpse brought to the Church on a Beare to be buried then a Table prepared for the feasting of the guests of CHRIST the Lord of heaven and earth; a misusage that none of us would endure towards a table prepared in our owne houses for the entertainment of our meanest friends . . ." (pp. 11 & 12.)

"3. It is very inconvenient, in the eyes of any cleanly person, that regards what hee receives into his body, that a crowd of people should stand close to the Table, leaning upon it, and breathing on the Bread, which the Congregation is, by and by, to eate; and breathing in the Cups, out of which they are to drinke." (p. 13.)

"4. And more then this, it is possible, that by one person, that thus standeth neere unto, and breatheth on the Bread, especially, the same person being infected with the Plague, or having a Plague-sore on him (w[hich] is no rare thing, in our Churches of *London*) that a whole Congregation of communicants may be poisoned: as *Henry* an Emperouere, was poysoned in the Bread; and *Victor* a Pope, was poysoned in the Cup : to say nothing of other loathsome diseased people. In which respect, something about the Table, at the Communion times, to keepe people a distance from the Table, is a thing very convenient and desirable." (p. 13.)

Answering a supposed Objection—that his plan was an "*Innovation*," which he denies, for the reasons he assigns, he further says :—

". . . . if the people be not brought to the Table, within sight and hearing, to what end are the sacramentall actions, of breaking the Bread, of taking the Bread, of taking it by the Minister into his hands, of pouring out the wine? To what end doth he sanctifie the elements, by blessing, in their owne language more, then if there were no sacramentall actions at all, or then if the prayers, readings, thanksgivings and all were in Latine, or neither in Latine, nor in English, nor at all used, or whispered and muttered secretly, as the Popish Priestes doe some part of their Masse, that no body doth heare them? . . . . . If then, the reading of the second Service, as they called it, at the Communion Table, the people being in the Body of the Church, and therefore unable to heare, was deservedly condemned, as an unfit usage; why should we judge otherwise, of the people's abiding in their Pewes, at the Communion time? (Wherein there is, not onely use of the hearing, but of the seeing and beholding also; which, unlesse they be used, the Minister and they, are as dumbe and deafe and blind one to another) why, I say, this usage, in Communion time, should not be condemned, as unfit and unprofitable also, seemes to me an absurd thing, and void of sence and reason." (pp. 21–23.)

I have quoted thus fully from Udall's Tract because, as it seems to me, no one reading the four lines cited by the Court (See p. 415) could have any true conception of the nature and object of the Publication: yet, read with its context only, and still more when considered in the light of the whole Tract, the passage used in the Judgment would, I think, appear to most people to be far from applicable in the Case before their Lordships.

That Case really was—that Mr. Purchas, standing in Front of the Altar with his back to the People who had a full view of the whole Chancel, hindered them from seeing him " break the "Bread" or " take the Cup into his hands."

Udall's Case was :—(1) That owing to the height and closeness of the Pews in the Body of the Church, " the externall "actions of the Minister . . . . together with all the prayers "and benedictions, by which the elements are consecrate," were lost to " the greatest part of the People " (See p. 417 and Reason 2, p. 419.)

(2.) That therefore it was necessary " to make some provision " in the Chancell for the Communion." (See p. 418.)

(3.) That the Doctrine of the " Communion of the Faithfull " . . . one with another" was " rent and divided " by the people being " in high and scattered Pewes." (See p. 419.)

(4.) That to carry the Sacrament "up and downe the Church" into "the Pewes" and even "in the Gallery," was "a needlesse "wearinesse put upon the Ministers," an occasion of accidents with the Sacrament, indecent, and a hindrance to the Minister's knowing who he was going to Communicate. (See p. 420.)

(5.) That "to leave the Table open, in such crowds of people" as they had "in many small Churches within the Walles" led to gross irreverence and other evils.

Could any two Cases well be more opposed; or is it fairly conceivable that Udall would have written "Communion come-"linesse" in reference to St. James's Chapel, Brighton, or to any Church seated and arranged as we are now accustomed to see, even where the Celebrant does occupy the Eastward Position?

Udall, apparently, could not effect his object by altering the Pews in the Body of the Church; and, moreover, he seems to have thought it objectionable and unsafe to leave the Holy Table unprotected either in the Nave or in the Chancel. Further his object was "to bring the greatest number together into the "Chancell in sight of the Table, both in their Pewes, and in "any other additional way that may be invented" (See p. 417), because "the apprehension of the thing that is signified in the "signe" and the "edification of the people in separating the "elements of bread and wine" by "words of Benediction by "Prayer and Thanksgiving" are "things" which, he said, "cannot be effected but by coming up to the Table in sight and "hearing of the Minister." (*Ib.*)

To accomplish his object, Udall, "at the Communion times "onely", so placed the Lord's Table relatively to "a square "raile" which he "set up in the Chancell" and to "the "Pewes" there, that he "received a double row of Communi-"cants ... in a very small chancell to the number of, 40 or "50, at one time in the Pewes and at the Raile, and when they "had received, another company after them, and so till all had "received ..." (See p. 419.) Now, unless Udall Consecrated for each "company" (a proceeding hardly to be surmised) it is plain that only the *first* "40 or 50" could have seen the actions and heard the words of Consecration in the manner Udall desired:

the rest, remaining in their Pews, could not have been more cognizant of them than they were before: Udall did his best, as it seems, but (except as to all coming into the Chancel to *Communicate*) he could only have done all he wished by cutting down his high Pews and altering any that were square, so that all the People could look towards the East and both see and hear, though not quite so well perhaps as those in the Chancel, all that Udall desired they should listen to and behold. Yet, even in this arrangement which Udall did make in the Chancel (unless indeed he Consecrated looking Westward—a Position not even implied) there must have been some of the People behind him who, consequently, could not see the Celebrant's Actions much (if at all) better than some of those before whom any Priest stands when occupying the Eastward Position at the Altar. So that, if, in the words quoted by the Court, Udall had meant to say that everyone present must see the *actual fraction* of the Bread, he would have been condemning his own arrangements for the Celebration. What he so strongly deprecated, was the hindrance offered by high Pews to any observation of the general Actions of the Celebrant; and this he held to be a bar " to the spirituall actions of Faith " in those who came to the Holy Sacrament.

Their Lordships, having cited Nicholls, and referred to Udall, now quote another Commentator as to the meaning of " before " the Table," observing that :—

> " Wheatley (*Op. cit.*) says—' Whilst the priest is ordering the bread and wine he is to stand before the table; but when he says the Prayer he is to stand so that he may with more readiness and decency break the bread before the people, which must be on the north side. For if he stood before the table, his body would hinder the people from seeing, so that he must not stand there, and, consequently, he must stand on the north side, there being, in our present Rubric, no other place for the performance of any part of this office.' "

As, however, Wheatly professes in his Title Page to give " the Substance " of what Nicholls (and some other Commentators) had stated, what has been said (See p.405) applies equally to Wheatly's dictum that the Celebrant "must not stand" so that "his body would hinder the people from seeing:" he bases this conclusion upon Nicholls's Grammatical construction of the Rubric (See p. 405) which he evidently quotes, viz.—"according " to the rules of grammar, the participle *standing* must refer to "the verb *ordered*, and not to the word *say*." So that, in fact, here Wheatly is but a repetition of Nicholls. As to Wheatly's assertion—that the Priest " must stand on the north side, there " being, in our present Rubric, no other place for the perform- " ance of any part of this office "—I hope it has been satisfactorily shewn (See p. 356) that the silence of the Rubric. *e.g*, as to the place of reading the Epistle, does not warrant the conclusion, that it may not be read where in a former Rubric it was ordered to be read: the same argument seems to me applicable to what Wheatly here urges. It is certain that Bp. Wren did not regard the " North side " Rubric as prohibitory of any " other place " for " any part " of the Office; for he expressed the contrary belief in the First of his " Particular " Orders," &c. for the Diocese of Norwich, 1636, where he directs that—" the Communion Service, called the Second " Service, be audibly and distinctly read at the communion " table unto the end of the Nicene Creed before the sermon or " homily; yet so as in very large churches the minister may "come nearer to read the Epistle and Gospel. . . ." (*Cardwell, Doc. Ann.* II., p. 251, or 2nd *Report, Rit. Com.* p. 564.)

Having thus appealed to the statements of these two Authors, (who, however, can hardly be regarded as independent witnesses) the Court resolves its own question in the following sentence :—

> "Their Lordships consider that the Defendant, in standing with his back to the people, disobeyed the Rubric in preventing the people from seeing the breaking of the bread."

But, it must be again remarked, their Lordships have themselves admitted (See p. 325) "that the mere words" of the Rubric "do not speak of seeing:" the Court, as it seems to me, had to construe those "mere words" according to their literal signification, and not to read them in the light of an *existing practice*, though even of long continuance, unless it could be plainly shown that the framers of the Rubric had in some way made it apparent that they intended such a Practice. So far, however, from it being the case—that the Custom of Consecrating at the North End of the Holy Table derives any sanction from them—what is known of their minds is foreign to it, and authorizes the very Position which the Court condemned Mr. Purchas for adopting.

Before the Revision of 1661 the Rubric was as bare as it could well be—"*Then the Priest standing up, shall say as "followeth:"* yet even under it Cosin* and Wren (See p. 402)—(two of the Revisers) Consecrated in·Front of the Altar with their backs to the people; and the sort of apologetic defence which they deemed it needful to make against their Puritan persecutors did not in the least imply that they regarded that Position as *unlawful*, though they could not appeal to any words of the then Rubric actually *prescribing* it. Moreover, they, like Laud when he was attacked with reference to the Eastward Position in connexion with the Scotch Book† of 1637,

---

* The Proceedings in Parliament against Cosin (March 16, 1640-41) charged him with "bowing and officiating towards the East; with his back to the people, and several other postures which he used before the Altar." (*The Acts of the High Commission Court within the Diocese of Durham*, p. 216, Surtees Society, 1858.

In his Answer, he—"denieth that he did ever officiate with face purposely towards the East.[b] But he constantly stood at the north side or end of the table to read and perform all parts of the communion service there; saving that the bread and wine being usually placed in the middle of the table, which is about seven foot in length, he might haply do as others did there before him, (though he remembreth not to have so done these twelve years) and step to the former part thereof, to consecrate and bless those elements, which otherwise he could not conveniently reach; in the mean while many of the communicants kneeling as they used to do, very near to the table within the rails, on either hand of defendant, whose back was not then towards more of the people, than it would have been, if he had for that small space of time stood still at the north side of the table; whereunto he always returned immediately after distribution was made by him unto the communicants at their several forms." (*Ibid.* pp. 217-18.)

† Mr. Elliott ("The North side of the Table," p. 38) quotes the following Charge against Abp. Laud in reference to this Book—"It seems to be no great matter that, without warrant of the Book of England, the Presbyter going from the North End of the Table shall stand during the time of Consecration at such a part of the Table where he may, with the more ease and decency, use both his hands. Yet being tried, it importeth much, that he must stand with his hinder parts to the people, &c."

"[b] 'He used to officiate at the west side thereof, turning his back to the people.'—Art. 2, in Rushw."

assigned substantially the Reason given in that Book and afterwards, with a slight variation and addition, furnished in the Rubric of 1662 (See pp. 326 & 328): that Reason touched the *convenience* of the Priest, rather than the *observation* of the People: it was then, it is now, that the Celebrant might perform the Manual Acts of the Consecration (which had been inserted in the Scotch Book and were restored in the English Book 25 years later) "with the more readiness and decency."

These Acts were to be done "before the people"—*coram populo*—the objectors to the Book, at the Savoy Conference, had desired that the Consecration should be made more "ex-"plicite and distinct" and especially that the "breaking of the "bread" should be ordered (See p. 335): compliance with this wish naturally involved a provision which should guard against what LAUD regarded as "the unseemly disordering of "something or other that is before" the Priest "perhaps the "very elements themselves." Those who have witnessed or practised the Consecration at the *North End* of and *before the Table* can readily judge which is the more convenient to the Celebrant or seemly to the Congregation; and, apart from prejudices, would probably most of them admit that the *North End* has not the advantage over the *West Side* of the Altar. It is certain, as has been shewn, that some of the leading Revisionists took this view; there is nothing, so far as I am aware, to show that the rest were opposed to it: coupling this consideration with the previous declaration of the Bishops at the Savoy Conference touching the Minister's turning Eastward (See p. 330), it is not unreasonable to presume that the words "before the Table" (in the Rubric of 1662) were preferred to the words "such a part

Upon this Mr. Elliott remarks "The Archbishop's answer to the charge is remarkable on two grounds; (1) his implied admission that the English Prayer Book did not authorize the departure of the Priest from the North End of the Table ; . . . ." The words of the Answer upon which Mr. Elliott relies, are these :—"And yet here again they are offended that this is done without warrant of the Book of England. How comes this Book of England to be so much in their esteem, that nothing must be done without warrant from it?"

But, as I read the Abp's Answer, it does not at all favour the conclusion which Mr. Elliott draws from it: what Laud said was merely a remark upon the inconsistency of his Accusers, in referring, when it suited their purpose, to a Book for which he knew they had no "esteem." The fact that Laud did leave the North End and Consecrate in front of the Altar, shews that he did not consider the Rubric to forbid the change.

" of the holy Table " (in the Scotch Book), as securing a Position for the Priest when Consecrating, which, while clearly the more prominent one, would facilitate his actions " before the " people : " although, as LAUD said, " I am not of opinion, that " it is any end of the administration of the Sacrament ' to have " ' the priest better seen of the people.' "

LIX. The Court, taking its own interpretation of *North side* as being beyond dispute, next deals with another term in the Rubric, in the following passage :—

> "The north side being the proper place for the minister throughout the Communion office, and also whilst he is saying the Prayer of Consecration, the question remains, whether the words 'standing before the table' direct any temporary change of position in the minister before saying the Prayer of Consecration ? This is not the most important, but it is the most difficult question. One opinion is that of Wheatley, quoted above, that the Rubric sends the priest to the west side of the table to order the elements, and recalls him for the Prayer itself. This, however, would be needless if the elements were so placed on the table as that the priest could, 'with readiness and decency,' order them from the north side, as is often done."

The last sentence in this paragraph admits the unsuitableness of the North End for *ordering* the Elements placed in the Middle of the Altar; and, consequently, it implies the same with regard to their *Consecration*—a view which agrees with what was said by Cosin, Laud, and Wren. The Court does not *approvingly* suggest their being placed at "the north side [end], as is often "done" to overcome the difficulty : indeed, considering its reliance on the *contemporaneous exposition* of PRACTICE, it would be strange to find an abandonment of it recommended by the Judicial Committee. The Custom of the Church of England in this respect may most fairly be called *continuous* and *universal:* still more is it to be noticed that it is in harmony with the rest of the Catholic Church East and West : a circumstance which differences it entirely from the *contemporaneous exposition* of 300 years upon which their Lordships condemned the Eucharistic

Vestments *continuously* and *universally* employed in the rest of the Catholic Church. The sight which a "Communion Sunday" everywhere presented in England, long before the so-called Ritual Movement, of the "White Napkin" covering up, usually, the Eucharist Elements as well as the Altar Vessels, placed in the centre of the Altar before Morning Service began, what was it but the Catholic Tradition of the Church of England unreformed as well as reformed? And to what did this Tradition point as regards the true Position of the Celebrant when Consecrating? Could it be properly regarded as any other than the *Eastward* Position?

LX. Their Lordships go on to remark :—

> "It would also be needless in any case where the Communion Table was placed in the body of the church or in the chancel with its ends east and west. And though this position is not likely now to be adopted, the question is whether that was the law at the time this Rubric was drawn. Now the Rubric prescribes that the Table shall stand 'in the body of the church or in the chancel where morning and evening Prayers [*dele* s] are appointed to be said;' and there are two cases, which occurred in 1633, those of Crayford (Cardwell Doc. Annals, ii, 226) and St. Gregory's London (Ibid, ii, 237) which show that the Table, though placed at the east end, might be moved for convenience' sake and under competent authority."

The only object for here referring to a Position of the Table which their Lordships say "is not likely to be adopted now" is the "question" here asked. That question has, I think, been fully answered in the negative in the foregoing pages. As, however, importance is attached to Wheatly's opinion in the previous passage of the Judgment, it is well to mention here that he does not favour their Lordships apparent view, as is shown in the passage already quoted from him at p. 410.

As, however, Bp. Wren was one of the Revisers in 1661 his opinion of "the law at the time this Rubric was drawn" is of more importance than Wheatly's. In Answer to the Charge "that he did in the year 1636, order that the Communion Table

" should be set at the East-end of the Chancel, altarwise, and
" not to be removed from thence," he thus defends himself:—

"He further saith, that it was necessary the Rubrick should appoint the Table at the Time of the Communion, to stand in the Body of the Church or the Chancel, where Morning and Evening Prayer were appointed to be said; for otherwise in sundry Places where they had no Chancel, they should not have had any Table, or any Communion or Divine Service.

"But where Chancels were, it was by Law, as he humbly conceiveth, appointed, that the Table should stand up at the East-end of the Chancel. The Words of the Queen's Injunctions (set forth, 2 *Eliz.* 1559) being, that the Holy Table in every Church shall be set in the Place where the Altar stood: and that, if for more Convenience, at the Time of the Distribution of the Communion, it were set in any other Place of the Chancel, yet after the Communion done, from time to time it should be placed where it stood before. Now these Injunctions are allowed and confirmed by the Queen's Advertisements, *Cap.* 1, *Art.* 3. And those Advertisements are authorized by Law, 1 *Eliz. Cap.* 2. *Sect. penult.**

"He also saith, that his directing to have the Communion Table placed at the East-end of the Chancel was done by him, as well for an Uniformity to all cathedral and collegiate Churches, which he conceived did receive the Usage which had been therein from the Beginning of the Reformation, and to all the King's Chapels, and to very many Parish Churches, wherein it had never been otherwise: as also for a double Convenience, especially of the smaller Churches and Parishes, that, inasmuch as by the metropolitical Injunction, they were to make Rails for the Communion Tables, therefore to set the said Tables thus, did tend both to less Charge and less Incumbrance; for if the said Tables should have been placed any where else in the Chancel, they would have taken up both more Room, and more Cost in the Railing." (*Parentalia*, p. 75).

"He further addeth that an Act of State made at the Council Board by the King himself, with the Advice of the Metropolitan, and the rest of the Privy Council (who were all Commissioners for Causes Ecclesiastical) about the placing the Table in that wise at St. *Gregory's* Church in *London, Anno* 1633, was a Rule to lead this Defendant (as being the Ordinary) to give Directions for the same. Especially considering, that the fore-mentioned Advertisements 7 *Eliz.* do directly

---

* Bp. Wren appears here to treat the Advertisements as having been duly published under the Statute which he quotes: he may, very likely, have so concluded from the expression in Canon xxiv. of 1603-4, "the Advertisements published Ann. 7 Elizabethæ:" moreover he wrote after the passing of the Canon of 1640, the viith. of which speaks of "the Injunctions and Advertisements of Queen *Elizabeth* of blessed memory." But, as has been already shewn (See pp. 59, 142, & 194), the terms employed in these two Canons do not prove that Q. Elizabeth "authorized" the Advertisements as the Statute required; we know now the History of them, as Wren could not have known it; and that History is entirely adverse to the belief that they had the Queen's formal sanction.

imply, that the Table should stand there, even at the time of the Communion. [*Item*, they shall decently cover the Table with a Carpet, and with a fair Linnen Cloth at the time of the Ministration, and shall set the Ten Commandments upon the East-wall over the said Table, *Cap.* 2. Art. 7]* for if over it at the time of the Ministration, then was it at the Time to stand under the said East-wall.

" Nevertheless, he humbly supposeth, that as well by his Articles enquiring only, whether the Table did ordinarily stand up at the East-end, as also by his directions, that the Table should always stand there, unless the Ordinary gave Direction otherwise, he did thereby intimate, that the Communion Table might and should be upon any due Occasion, for more convenient hearing or communicating, be removed not only at the Communion Time, but at other Times when there was no Communion; and to this end he expressed himself afterwards, for some Churches in the said Diocese, as at St. *Edmund's-bury*, Lavenham, and other Places, where it was certified, that the End of the Chancels was too far distant from the People in the Church. And at *Yarmouth* (from the Beginning) he had given Order for the more Convenience of the People, that although there was a Rail by the Vicar-general's appointment, placed towards the East-end of the said Chancel, yet the Communion Table should always stand without and beneath the said Rail, in the Body of the said Church." (*Ibid.* p. 76).

LXI. The Court has fallen into an error about the Crayford case, for there is nothing in Abp. Abbot's Letter of July 8, 1633, even implying their Lordships' conclusion from it : His Grace says :—

" . . . we have ordered and decreed, and by these presents do order and decree as followeth : ' videlicet ' : that the parishioners and inhabitants of the said parish of Crayford, and others intending hereafter to receive the holy communion there, shall repair unto the two ascents, or foot paces in the chancel before the communion table, and there mats being laid upon the said two ascents, or foot paces, to kneel upon, and mats being also laid on either side above the said steps to kneel upon, (if by reason of the number of communicants it seems requisite, the two ascents or foot paces being first filled,) they shall in decent and reverend manner humbly kneeling upon their knees on the said two ascents or foot paces, receive the holy communion and sacrament of the body and blood of our Lord and Saviour Jesus Christ; and after the first company hath received the same, they to return to their seats and places in the said church; and to give way for a second company to receive in like manner; and the second, after they have received in like manner, to return and give way for a third company, and the third to the fourth, and so successively, until all the communicants there have received the holy communion in manner and form aforesaid. . . ." (*Cardwell, Doc. Ann.* II. pp. 227–8.)

* The brackets are in the original.

LXII. Neither does the case of St. Gregory's favour the Court's view of "the law at the time this Rubric [of 1662] was drawn." Bp. Wren's conclusion from the Case has just been given (See p. 430): the following is the Case itself:—

"*An order of Council for placing the communion table in St. Gregory's Church.*—Rushw. Col. Vol. ii. fol. 207.

"At Whitehall November 3, 1633.

"This day was debated before his majesty, sitting in council, the question and difference, which grew about the removing the communion table in St. Gregory's church, near the cathedral church of St. Paul, from the middle of the chancel to the upper end, and there placed altarwise, in such manner as it standeth in the said cathedral, and mother church, as also in all other cathedrals and in his majesty's own chapel, and as is consonant to the practice of approved antiquity; which removing and placing of it in that sort was done by order of the dean and chapter of St. Paul's, who are ordinaries thereof, as was avowed before his majesty by Dr. King, and Dr. Montford, two of the prebends there; yet some few of the parishioners, being but five in number, did complain of this act, by appeal to the court of arches, pretending that the book of Common Prayer and the 82d canon do give permission to place the communion table where it may stand with most fitness and convenience. Now his majesty having heard particular relation made by the council of both parties of all the carriage and proceedings in this cause, was pleased to declare his dislike of all innovation, and receding from ancient constitutions, grounded upon just and warrantable reasons, especially in matters concerning ecclesiastical order and government; knowing how easily men are drawn to affect novelties, and how soon weak judgments in such cases may be overtaken and abused. And he was also pleased to observe, that if those few parishioners might have had their wills, the difference thereby from the aforesaid cathedral mother church, by which all other churches depending thereon ought to be guided, would be the more notorious, and give more subject of discourse and disputes, that might be spared, by reason of the nearness of St. Gregory's, standing close to the wall thereof. And likewise for so much as concerns the liberty of the said Common Prayer Book or canon, for placing the communion table in any church or chapel with most conveniency; that liberty is not so to be understood, as if it were ever left to the discretion of the parish, much less to the particular fancy of any humorous person, but to the judgment of the ordinary, to whose place and function it doth properly belong to give direction in that point, both for the thing itself, and the time when, and how long, as he may find cause. Upon which consideration his majesty declared himself, that he well approved and confirmed the act of the said ordinary, and so gave commandment, that if those few parishioners before mentioned do proceed in their said appeal, then the dean of the arches, who was then attending at the hearing of the cause, should confirm the said order of the aforesaid dean and chapter." (*Cardwell Doc. Ann.* II. pp. 237-9.)

LXIII. Nor, as it seems to me, do their Lordships strengthen their position by saying:—

"This, too, is the view of Bishop Wren in 1636 (Ibid. ii, 252) 'That the Communion Table in every church do always stand close under the east wall of the chancel, the ends thereof north and south, unless the ordinary give particular directions [*dele* s] otherwise.'"

For although, no doubt, Bp. Wren held that under special circumstances the Table might be moved with the Ordinary's permission, it is clear, from his language already quoted (See p. 430) that he was adverse to its removal*; and, further, after "otherwise," the above order runs on thus :—

"And that the rail be made before it according to the archbishop's late injunctions, reaching cross from the north wall to the south wall, near one yard in height, so thick with pillars, that dogs may not get in."

The object of "the Rail" (which Laud seems to have ordered with a view to prevent such a case as that which was mentioned at p. 321 as having occurred at Tadlow) was to protect the Altar *during* the Celebration rather than when it was not in use ; and, surely, it can scarcely be doubted that fixed Rails were not intended to *facilitate* its being put in a different Place or in another Position either in or out of Communion-time. It cannot be pretended that the Prayer Book of 1662 *enlarged* the liberty allowed previously ; and therefore no purpose appears to be answered in the suggestion of the Court that :—

"Should the Table be placed with its ends east and west, it would be absurd to enforce a rule that the

---

* WHEATLY, quoting the Elizabethan Injunction, says—" Now it is plain from this injunction, as well as from the eighty-second Canon of the Church (which is almost verbatim the same), that there is no obligation arising from this rubric [viz. 'The Table, at the Communion-time havinge, &c.] to move the Table at the time of the Communion, unless the people cannot otherwise conveniently hear and communicate. The injunction declares, that the *holy Table is to be set in the same place where the Altar stood*, which every one knows was at the East end of the chancel. And when both the injunction and canon speak of its being moved at the time of the Communion, it supposes that the minister could not otherwise be heard : the interposition of a belfrey between the chancel and body of the church (as I have already observed, page 100 &c.) hindering the minister in some churches from being heard by the people, if he continued in the chancel. So that we are not under any obligation to move the Table, unless necessity requires." (p. 246.)

priest should go to the west end to order the elements, seeing the north side would be in every way more convenient."

Moreover, this passage seems to assume that if the Table were moved, under the exceptional circumstances to which Bp. Wren refers, it must stand " with its ends east and west ; " whereas there is not the slightest indication, in these three Cases to which their Lordships refer, that it was meant to be so placed ; on the contrary, the language of the King in Council, of Abp. Abbot, and of Bp. Wren, plainly shews that in their judgment the Table ought to be placed Altarwise at the East end of the Chancel ; and therefore it is in the highest degree improbable that they could have intended or would have sanctioned a contrary *Position* for it in the exceptional cases where it was lawful for the Ordinary to place it in another part of " the " Chancel " or even " in the body of the Church." Why their Lordships speak of the " west end " of the Table, set lengthwise, as a place " to order the elements," rather than the *East* End, I am at a loss to understand.

LXIV. The Court sums up its previous remarks and references in a passage which sets forth three Conclusions : the FIRST is in these words :—

> " Upon these facts their Lordships incline to think that the Rubric was purposely framed so as not to direct or insist on a change of position in the minister, which might be needless; though it does direct a change of posture from kneeling to standing."

Yet, surely, whatever the Rubric may have been designed to order it was something to be done *always:* there is nothing optional or discretionary in its terms, as in the Rubric touching the place of the Table : it is a positive direction to do a specified thing, and therefore is not an act " which might be needless." The Priest is quite as distinctly told to be in a defined Place and Posture, as he is told to " break the bread," to " take the Cup," and to " say the Prayer." The language is quite as express as are the words of the Rubric in 1552, 1559, 1604—" Then the " Priest standing up, shall say as followeth." Whether the Rubric of 1662 meant "to direct or insist on a *change* of Position "in the minister" would depend upon his Position when saying the previous Prayer "We do not presume," etc. There can be no doubt that, under the Book of 1549 (See Col. ii., p. 366) the Priest said this Prayer at the middle portion of the Altar; and their Lordships in the passage last noticed (in common with all who hold that the Table may or must stand with its Ends East and West) regard this middle place as the only place for the Celebrant, standing on the North side and looking South. If, as can hardly be doubted, the Revisers of 1661 contemplated that same (Eastward) Position for the *Prayers* in this Office which the Bishops defended at the Savoy Conference, the Priest would already be " before the table " and so would not have to "change" his Position in order to comply with the new Rubric: if, as is unlikely, they assumed that he would begin the Office at the North End of an Altarwise Table, then he would have to change in order to be "standing before the Table."

LXV. The Court's SECOND Conclusion is thus stated:—

> " The words are intended to set the minister free for the moment from the general direction to stand at the north side, for the special purpose of ordering the elements ; but whether for this purpose he would have to change the side or not is not determined, as it would depend on the position of the Table in the church or chancel, and on the position in which the elements were placed on the Table at first."

Here it is admitted that the Rubric was designed to free the Minister from the " North side " Position (whatever may be the true meaning of that term) " for the special purpose of order- "ing the Elements;" but for this purpose only, as their Lordships think. Here again, however, their Lordships argue that this " change of position " is not " determined " to be of obligation " as it would depend on the position of the Table in "the church or chancel." In commenting upon their First Conclusion this plea has been already considered; and, if I have rightly contended elsewhere (See p. 342 ff) that the framers of the present Rubric did not contemplate the Table being placed with its Ends East and West, their Lordships' plea is deprived of any remaining force.

Another plea is, however, advanced for the supposed indeterminate direction as to the Minister changing his Position for the purpose of ordering the Elements viz. "the Position in "which the elements were placed on the Table at first." Enough has been said, I think, to show (See p. 428) that no other place than the *middle* of the Table has any sort of warrant to be recognized as the proper " position in which the elements " are " at first" to be " placed on the Table." Their Lordships themselves only say (See p. 428) that they are " often " placed at the "north side " *i.e.* end. I assume that by the words " at "first" the Court did not mean to imply, contrary to its language in Liddell *v.* Westerton (See p. 247), that the Elements may be placed on the Altar before the Service begins. The Rubrical time for the Priest to " place " them " upon the " Table " is, plainly, immediately before the Church Militant Prayer. If their Lordships mean that then they should be placed at the North End of the Table, with a view to their Consecration, it seems enough to say—that if the Authors of the Rubric had any such intention, they would surely have directed them to be "ordered" *at this period* for Consecration, and not have uselessly deferred the *arranging* of them until the time for the Consecration arrived. There seems, then, no ground whatever for supposing, as the Court does, that it is consistent with the Rubric to place the Elements " at first" at the North End of the Table and then, at the Prayer of Consecration, for the Priest to *order* them from the North End where, as is alleged, he can only legally stand to Consecrate them.

The most important feature, however, in this Second Conclusion of the Court is the contention, already adverted to, that " standing before the Table " refers only to the *ordering of the Elements for Consecration,* and not at all to the Priest's place when saying the Prayer of Consecration. The following tabular arrangement shows the Rubric in its three Authoritative forms, viz.—I. As settled by the Revisers: II. As sanctioned by Convocation and Parliament and attached to the Act of Uniformity, 1662 : III. As examined and sealed in proof of its being correctly printed from the MS. copy (II) of (I) the Revised Book.

I.	II.	III.
Black Letter Prayer Book, 1636,* used for the Revision of 1661. MS. Rubric.	MS. Prayer Book, Schedule to the Act of Uniformity 1662. (House of Lords Library)*	Prayer Book of 1662, re-printed from the Sealed copy in the Tower of London (Pickering, 1844)
"When yᵉ Priest, standing before yᵉ Table, hath so ordered yᵉ Bread, & Wine, that he may, wᵗʰ yᵉ more readines, & decency, break yᵉ Bread before yᵉ People, & take yᵉ Cup into his hands, he shall say yᵉ Prayer of Consecration, as followeth."	"When the Priest, standing before the Table, hath so ordered the bread and wine, that he may with the more readiness and decency break the Bread before the people, and take the Cup into his hands; he shall say the Prayer of Consecration as followeth."	"When the Priest, standing before the Table, hath so ordered the Bread and Wine, that he may with the more readiness and decency break the Bread before the people, and take the Cup into his hands, he shall say the Prayer of Consecration as followeth."

There is a slight variation in the punctuation of these three forms, but it is unimportant and does not affect the relation of the words in question to the rest of the Rubric: " standing "before the Table" is in form parenthetical, the words being enclosed by Commas; so that the whole prescribed action of the Celebrant, touching the *ordering* and *consecration* of the Elements, is completely independent of the Position and Posture intended by the words whose application to the rest of the Rubric is disputed.

There are two other Rubrics in the Communion Office, where a similar independent parenthetical direction occurs, which will serve to test the applicability, to the rest of the Rubric, of the words "standing before the Table." They are the Rubric immediately preceding the Lord's Prayer, and the Rubric before the Ten Commandments.

"The Table, *at the Communion time having a fair white linen cloth upon it*, shall stand in the Body of the Church, or in the Chancel, where Morning and Evening Prayer are appointed to be said. And the Priest standing at the North-side of the Table shall say the Lord's Prayer, with the Collect following, the people kneeling."

"Then shall the Priest, *turning to the people*, rehearse distinctly all the Ten Commandments; and the people still kneeling shall, after every Commandment, ask God's mercy for their transgression thereof for the time past, and grace to keep the same for the time to come, as followeth."

The words which I have here italicized no more affect the sense of, or regulate what is prescribed in, the rest of each

Rubric in which they occur, than do the similarly placed words before the Consecration Prayer; and it may well be doubted whether a person, knowing nothing of the controversy about the words "standing before the Table," would imagine that they involved any different relation to the rest of the Rubric than do the parenthetical clauses affect the rest of the two Rubrics in which they, respectively, are found.

LXVI. The THIRD Conclusion of their Lordships is this:—

> "They think that the main object of this part of the Rubric is the ordering of the elements; and that the words 'before the Table' do not necessarily mean 'between the Table and the people,' and are not intended to limit to any side."

The first portion of this passage, being substantially a repetition of what the Court held in its Second Conclusion, need not be further remarked upon here. The other point to be considered is their Lordships' view of the meaning of the words "before the Table." Now it might be the case, if the Table were intended by the Rubric to stand apart from the East Wall of the Church, that the Celebrant could stand on the East side of it, facing the People who would be Westward of it, and so be "before the Table." Some 40 years ago a long controversy in "The Record" Newspaper ended in the Editor, I think, holding that "before the Table" meant "behind the "Table." Nor, in itself, can any reasonable objection be made to what would practically be the Basilican arrangement: yet that Position of the Celebrant is quite consistent with people being *behind* him—and this is the main objection offered to the Eastward Position. On considerations of mere policy and expediency it might be well to hold with the Court that " the "words 'before the Table' . . . are not intended to limit to "any side," and thus afford some degree of liberty, under existing circumstances, to the differing Parties in the Church of England. But this language of the Court (which, indeed, the Court did not favourably apply to Mr. Purchas) cannot fairly be considered apart from the general principle upon which the whole Judgment proceeds, viz., that "The purpose of the Act "[of Uniformity] is clear. It was to establish an uniformity "upon all parties alike." And, therefore, in whatever Place permitted by the Rubric the Table is appointed to stand, the expression "before the Table" must be (according to their Lordships' ruling) *uniformly* construed.

Assuming it, then, to have been satisfactorily shown already (See p. 342 ff) that the Lord's Table was not meant, by any Rubric from 1549 downwards, or by the Injunctions of Q. Elizabeth, or by the Advertisements, to stand with its Ends East and West, the real question to be considered is—what was intended by the words "before the Table" in reference to its Altarwise Position? Now, as is shewn in the parallel Rubrics at p. 326, both Wren and Cosin used the term before it was imported into the Rubric of 1662; and that they both occupied the Eastward Position, in front of the Holy Table, when Consecrating the Elements. This ought to be sufficient, I think, to show what, in all likelihood, was their mind when they assented to the new Rubric which contained the words; and that they did assent is plain from the fact that they signed the MS. Book annexed to the Act of Uniformity. (4th *Rit. Report*, pp. 39* and 40*.) There is, however, another proof of the meaning which Wren attached to the words, prior to the Rubric of 1662. It occurs in his "Orders and Directions given in the Diocese of Norwich" at his "Primary Visitation" in 1636: the 3rd Order, already quoted at p. 345, directs "That the communion table in every "church do always stand close under the east wall of the "chancel;" and the 15th Order proves that it was to remain there when the Holy Communion was celebrated, for it requires "That all communicants come up severally, and kneel before "the rail to receive the holy communion;" and then the 18th Order is in these words:—

"That the holy oblations in such places, where it pleaseth God at any time to put into the hearts of His people by that holy action to acknowledge His gift of all they have to them, and their tenure of all from him, and their debt of all to him, be received by the minister *standing before the table* at their coming up to make the said oblation, and then by him to be reverently presented before the Lord, and set upon the table till the service be ended." (*Cardwell, Doc. Ann.* II. 256, or 2nd *Rit. Report*, 565.)

The words "standing before the Table," which I have

italicized, read in connexion with the 3rd and 15th Orders, furnish the clearest proof that "before the table" could only mean here *in front* of the Table, "between the Table and the "people": either facing the People, when the Oblations were being received by the Minister; or having his back to the people, when presenting the Oblations upon the Holy Table. Moreover, Wren's expression helps to explain the source of the words in the Rubric of 1662 (See p. 327).

Unless, then, it can be shewn that Bp. Wren had changed his mind about the Position of the Celebrant when Consecrating, it seems most unreasonable to suppose that the words could mean in 1662* anything different from what they meant in 1636; more especially when it is recollected that the Bishops defended the Eastward Position against the Ministers at the Savoy Conference.

As the Act of Uniformity, 1662, authorizes the Office to be used in *Latin* in the Universities and some other Places, a Translation adopted there may fairly be applied in considering the meaning of the Rubrics in English. Canon Bright kindly informs me that in a Latin Communion Office, at Christ Church, Oxford, dated 1726†, the Rubric before the Consecration Prayer is in these words:—"Quum Presbyter stans ante Mensam "Domini, panem et vinum ita disposuerit, ut expeditus ac "decentius possit panem frangere coram populo, et calicem in "manus sumere, dicit orationem consecrationis, prout sequitur." He adds, that the University has in use a Latin form of Communion‡ in which the Consecration Rubric agrees exactly with the Christ Church form. It will be seen that "before the "Table" is translated "ante Mensam Domini," and "before "the people" is rendered "coram populo."

The following Rubric in the Marriage Service shews the meaning of "before the Table," and it is all the better testimony because, with the exception of substituting "Table"

---

* Dr. Brett, the Author of the Nonjuror's Prayer Book, writes to the Rev. Mr. Smith—"Therefore in ye first place, I desire that ye priest may still be directed to stand at y^e *north side* of ye table, and not at ye place wch we at this time [1717] call *before the Table*, that is, y^e *West side*, with his back to ye people." *(Letters on the Church of England*, reprinted by the Rev. Thomas Bowdler, 8o., 1850.)

† "Liber Precum Ecclesiæ Cathedralis Christi Oxon, Litania, Ordo administrandæ Cœnæ Domini, Catechismus, &c. Oxoniæ: Theatro Sheldoniano, 1726."

‡ Printed at the University Press, 1841.

for " Altar," it has remained unchanged since the Book of 1549; it is in these words :—

"The Psalm ended, and the man and the woman kneeling before the Lord's Table, the Priest standing at the Table, and turning his face towards them, shall say, LORD, HAVE MERCY," &c.

No one can dispute that the Position of the Man and Woman in this Rubric is *in front* of the Altar, looking Eastward; assuming, that is, that the Orientation of the Church is correct. Moreover, the Priest's true Position is also *in front*, " between "the Table and the people," looking Westward, although he is said to be "standing at the Table"; for there can be no question that "standing at" in the Book of 1549 meant IN THE MIDDLE OF THE FRONT—"stans ad medium altaris"—(*Alesius*, Col. iii, p. 360) and consequently must mean the same now * : in this case, too, the Practice coincides with the Rule of 1549.

LXVII. In the following passage the Court disputes the interpretation which the Dean of the Arches put upon the language used by this Court, as to this Rubric, in the Case of Martin *v.* Mackonochie: their Lordships say :—

> " The learned Judge in the Court below, in considering the charge against the Defendant that he stood with his back to the people during the Prayer of Consecration, briefly observes 'the question appears to me to have been settled by the Privy Council in the case of Martin *v.* Mackonochie.' The question before their Lordships in that case was as to the posture and not as to the position of the Minister. The words of the Judgment are: 'Their Lordships entertain no doubt on the construction of this Rubric' [before the Prayer of Consecration] 'that the Priest is intended to continue in one posture during the Prayer, and not to change from standing to kneeling, or *vice versâ;* and it appears to them equally certain that the Priest is intended to stand and not to kneel. They think that the words 'stand-

---

* Therefore "at the North side" may fairly be held to mean *before the Northern part of the Front*. The Latin Rubric in the Oxford Books (mentioned at p. 440) is " Presbyter stans ad septentrionalem partem mensæ. . . . ."

ing before the table' apply to the whole sentence; and they think this is made more apparent by the consideration that acts are to be done by the Priest before the people as the prayer proceeds (such as taking the paten and chalice into his hands, breaking the bread, and laying his hand on the various vessels) which could only be done in the attitude of standing.

"This passage refers to posture or attitude from beginning to end, and not to position with reference to the sides of the table. And it could not be construed to justify Mr. Purchas in standing with his back to the people, unless a material addition were made to it. The learned Judge reads it as if it ran, 'They think that the words standing before the table apply to the whole sentence, *and that before the table means between the table and the people on the west side.*' But these last words are mere assumption. The question of position was not before their Lordships; if it had been, no doubt the passage would have been conceived differently, and the question of position expressly settled."

All that can well be said upon this statement is—that Sir Robert Phillimore was by no means the only person of eminence who understood the Judgment to sanction the Eastward Position of the Celebrant both in Ordering the Elements and in Consecrating them. Some Bishops altered their practice in consequence of the language of the Court; and there certainly was a wide spread belief among both Clergy and Laity, that the Judgment authorized the Eastward Position. It must remain for the Court itself, whenever opportunity offers, to pronounce whether the Purchas Judgment interpreted rightly or wrongly the Judgment in Martin *v.* Mackonochie.

LXVIII. The Court, having completed its discussion of the question, thus sums up the result at which it arrived:—

"Upon the whole then, their Lordships think that the words of Archdeacon, afterwards Bishop, Cosin in A.D. 1687 express the state of the Law, 'Doth he [the minister] stand at the north side of the table, and perform all things there, but when he hath special cause to remove from it, as in reading and

> preaching upon the Gospel, or in delivering the Sacrament to the communicants, or other occasions of the like nature.' (Bishop Cosin's Correspondence. Part I., p. 106. Surtees Society.) They think that the Prayer of Consecration is to be used at the north side of the table, so that the minister looks south, whether a broader or a narrower side of the table be towards the north."

The Article here quoted (given at p. 118 of the " Correspondence," though the Document begins at p. 106) is, unfortunately for their Lordships' theory, wholly valueless to "express the "state of the Law" since the Revision of 1661, whatever may be its importance in reference to the Rubric before that date; for Cosin's Inquiry was made 35 years before the Prayer Book of 1662 was published. The date of the Visitation Articles (as given in the Cosin Correspondence from which the Court quotes) is 1627, not 1687 as probably misprinted in the Judgment. Cosin died Jan. 15, 1671-2. To make his Visitation Article of 1627 an exposition of the Rubric of 1662, it is necessary to shew that he retained and repeated the same Inquiry after the present Rubric had become Law. But his latest known Set of Visitation Articles, though dated 1662, was prepared before the Book of 1662 had come into use (See p. 120): yet even those Articles have nothing corresponding in the least to the Article of 1627 which their Lordships quote; and, considering Cosin's share in the Rubric of 1662, it is wholly beyond belief, as it appears to me, that he would have re-issued after 1662 the Visitation Article upon which their Lordships apparently rely when "They think that the Prayer "of Consecration is to be used at the north side of the table, "so that the minister looks south, whether a broader or a "narrower side of the table be towards the north."

LXIX. With the following passages the Court terminates its examination of the Case :—

> "It is mentioned that Mr. Purchas' chapel does not stand in the usual position, and that, in fact, he occupied the east side when he stood with his back towards the people. If it had happened, as it does

> in one of the Chapels Royal, that the north side had been where the west side usually is, a question between the letter and the spirit of the Rubrics would have arisen. But the Defendant seems to us to have departed, both from the letter and the spirit of the Rubrics; and our advice to Her Majesty will be that a monition should issue to him as to this charge also."

LXX. Having thus arrived at the conclusion that no excuse was to be found for the Practice which the Court deemed wholly contrary to the Rubric, their Lordships thus end their Judgment:—

> "As all the charges have been proved against the Defendant except as to two less important particulars, we direct that he shall pay the costs in this Court and in the Court below."

This Judgment led, on March 8, 1871, to the Publication of the following Remonstrance for Signature by the Clergy:—

"*To the Archbishops and Bishops of the Church of England.*

"We the undersigned Clergy of the Church of England, hereby offer our solemn Remonstrance against the Decision of the Judicial Committee of the Privy Council in the Case of 'Hebbert *v.* Purchas.'

"Without referring to all the points involved in this Judgment, we respectfully submit the following considerations touching the Position of the Minister during the Prayer of Consecration at the Holy Communion:—

"1. That the Rubrics affecting this particular question having been diversely observed ever since they were framed, the Judicial Committee has given to these Rubrics a restrictive interpretation condemnatory of a usage which has continuously existed* in the Church of England, and has for many years widely prevailed.

"2. That this decision is opposed to the comprehensive spirit of the Reformed Church of England, and thus tends to narrow the Church to the dimensions of a sect.

"3. That this restriction will press very unfairly upon a large body of Clergy who have never attempted, by resort to law or otherwise, to abridge the liberty of those whose practice differs from their own.

"4. That the rigorous enforcement of a Decision so painful as this is to the consciences of those whom it affects might involve the

---

* For some information as to this usage, see the Speech of Canon Gregory, in the Lower House of the Convocation of Canterbury, April 14, 1875, pp. 9-13. (*Church Printing Company*, 11, Burleigh Street, Strand.)

gravest consequences to a large number of the Clergy, and lead to results most disastrous to the Established Church.

"On these grounds, although many of us are not personally affected by the Judgment, we earnestly trust that your Lordships will abstain from acting upon this Decision, and thus preserve the ancient liberty of the Church of England."

The Remonstrance ultimately received 4,761 signatures, of which only 9 had any reservation; the following is a classification:—

Bishop (coadjutor)	1	Minor Canons	26
Bishop (archdeacon)	1	Priest Vicars	2
Archdeacons	10	Vicar Choral	1
Chancellors of dioceses	3	Assistant Vicars Choral	5
Rural Deans	187	Heads of Oxford and Cambridge	4
Rectors	884		
Vicars	1,260	Heads of other Colleges	18
Incumbents	170	Members of Colleges	67
Perpetual Curates	28	Chaplains	145
Assistant Curates	1,321	School Inspectors	7
Deans	4	Schoolmasters	126
Canons	16	Secretaries to Societies	6
Honorary Canons	22	Unattached	396
Prebendaries	45		
Precentors	6	Total	4,761

N.B.—In many instances the signatories held some other appointment, *e.g.*—A *Canon* is also a *Regius* (or other) *Professor*. A *Minor Canon* is also a *Rector*. A *Rural Dean* is also a *Canon* or *Prebendary*. A *Rector* or *Vicar* is also an *Honorary Canon*.

It was sent to the Archbishops and Bishops with the following letter from the Dean of Chichester:—

"24th April, 1871.

"My Lord Archbishop (or Bishop),—In the name of more than 4,700 clergymen who have signed a Remonstrance to the Archbishops and Bishops of the Church of England in reference to the late Report of the Judicial Committee in the case of Hebbert *v.* Purchas, I have the honour to lay a copy of the same with the signatures appended before your Lordship (or Grace), and to request your fatherly attention to it.—I have the honour to be your Lordship's very obedient servant,

"The Deanery, Chichester." "W. F. Hook."

Meanwhile Mr. Purchas, having most unexpectedly had a generous offer of pecuniary assistance from a private source, endeavoured by Petition to the Queen to obtain a re-hearing of the Case; by an error the Petition was treated as coming within the ordinary Rules relating to Petitions of Appeal, and was accordingly referred at once to the Judicial Committee without being presented to Her Majesty. At the sitting of the Court on March 25 to hear the application the Solicitor-General, who appeared for Mr. Purchas, questioned the proceeding; and the Court, admitting the error, decided that it could not deal with the Petition, as the Crown had not made any communication respecting it to the Judicial Committee. Steps were immediately taken to rectify the mistake, and the Petition was duly forwarded to the Queen, together with a second Petition which Counsel had advised as a precautionary measure; these two Petitions, being referred by her Majesty to the Judicial Committee to report upon, were considered (together with one to the Judicial Committee itself) on April 26 in a very full Court, consisting of the Lord Chancellor (Hatherly), Lords Chelmsford, Westbury, and Cairns, Sir James Colville, the Lords Justices James and Mellish, the Archbishop of York and the Bishop of London. The Solicitor-General (now Lord Coleridge), Dr. Deane, and Mr. C. Bowen appeared for Mr. Purchas; Dr. A. J. Stephens and Mr. Archibald for Mr. Hebbert. The Court, after argument and a long consultation refused the application, and announced its decision in the following terms:—

"Their lordships are of opinion that as regards the first two petitions, those which were presented to her Majesty, they ought to advise her Majesty that no further proceedings should be taken thereon. Having carefully weighed the arguments offered in support of the petition addressed to this Committee, and considering the grave public mischief that might arise from any doubt being thrown on the finality of the decisions of the Committee, their lordships are of opinion that expediency requires that the prayer of the petition should not be acceded to, but should be refused with costs."

Thus the Report of the Judicial Committee, read on Feb 23, stands as the present Judgment of the Final Court of Appeal on the Points submitted to it in the Suit of Hebbert v. Purchas.

Subsequently to this Decision the REMONSTRANCE COMMITTEE issued the following Circular to the Clergy who had signed the Remonstrance:—

"*The Remonstrance* in re *Hebbert* v. *Purchas.*"
"Messrs. Parker's, 377, Strand, London, W.C.,
May 22, 1871."

"Sir,—We are requested by the REMONSTRANCE COMMITTEE to forward to you the enclosed Copy of a Case submitted to the Solicitor-

General, Mr. Manisty, and Mr. Bowen, as to the effect of the Judgment in the case of 'Hebbert v. Purchas' in reference to other officiating clergymen, as respects the practices thereby adjudicated upon, and of the Opinion of those eminent counsel; and also an extract from the arguments at the late unsuccessful application to obtain a re-hearing of that Case, which elicited an important remark of Lord Cairns upon the point.

"We are further requested to transmit a copy of a resolution passed at a recent influential meeting of Churchmen, from which it will be seen that if attempts be made to enforce against other clergymen the late decision as respects the position of the Celebrant in the Prayer of Consecration at the Holy Communion, the Committee will be prepared, so far as they may lawfully do so, to assist in obtaining a full reconsideration of the recent decision of the Privy Council, which (irrespective of the other important points involved in it) is in their belief unsustainable at law and in direct contradiction to a previous determination of the same tribunal on the matter of the priest's position.

"The following is a copy of the resolution above referred to:—

"'Counsel having advised that the late proceedings in Hebbert v. Purchas were *in personam*, and not *in rem*, the REMONSTRANCE COMMITTEE have resolved to undertake the cost of resisting any proceedings which may be instituted for enforcing the Judgment, when a fitting opportunity shall present itself, with a view to secure a full discussion of the points at present determined by that Judgment upon an *ex parte* hearing.'

"We beg to remain, yours faithfully,
"THE SECRETARIES."

"CASE.

"With this Counsel will receive a Copy of the Judgment of the Judicial Committee of the Privy Council in the case of Hebbert v. Purchas.

"It will be seen that the Judgment prohibits certain proceedings in the Public Services of the Church of England as against the Prayer Book, and Canons, and the Act of Uniformity; and that it orders Monitions to be addressed to the Defendant prohibiting him from repeating the acts so alleged to be in breach of the Laws of the Church.

"A considerable difference of opinion is entertained as to whether the decision of the Court is *in personam* or *in rem*, and whether the merits of the Judgment can be questioned, and the self-same points re-discussed in a fresh case if brought before the Court in the instance of another clergyman performing all or any of the acts recently observed by Mr. Purchas, and condemned by the Judgment in question, such as the Vestments and the position of the Celebrant at the Prayer of Consecration in the Service of Holy Communion.

"We content ourselves with presenting the bare question for the consideration of Counsel, without attempting to refer them to the great Cases on the point, as it is necessary to ascertain the Law on the point with the least avoidable delay. Counsel will therefore please consider the foregoing proposition and advise thereon in consultation."

"OPINION.

"We are of opinion that the decision in the case of Hebbert v. Purchas may be questioned; and that the same points which were involved in, and decided by it, may be re-considered in the case of any other clergyman against whom proceedings may hereafter be taken. At the same time it cannot be doubted but that the Decision is an authority which every Committee of the Privy Council will respect, though they may not consider themselves absolutely bound by it.

"Having regard to the peculiar circumstances under which the Decision in Hebbert v. Purchas was arrived at, and the nature and character, as well as importance, of the questions involved in it, we think it may reasonably be expected that the Decision will not be considered conclusive in a new case. "JOHN DUKE COLERIDGE.
"H. MANISTY.
"CHARLES BOWEN."

"Extract from shorthand writer's Notes, quoted from the letter of Messrs. Few & Co., in the *Guardian* of May 17, 1871:—

"'*The Solicitor-General.*—All I propose to do is to draw your Lordships' attention to what I venture to call the direct verbal contradiction between the utterances of the Supreme Court of Appeal, and to point out to your Lordships that the Supreme Court of Appeal has now the means of reconciling them. I do not mean to say that the Supreme Court of Appeal cannot or may not reconcile them. All I say is, that these stand apparent contradictions, and as long as those contradictions stand apparent, it is surely a ground upon which the Church at large may claim to be heard, and have a right to put in a claim that there should be some more distinct examination of how it is that these judgments of equal authority, and pronounced, as I venture to think, in one sense at least, upon exactly the same points, are to be followed by persons desirous of obeying that which has been laid down by the highest tribunal as the law.

"'*Lord Cairns.*—That question might be raised in another case.'"

THE APPEAL.

RIDSDALE v. CLIFTON AND OTHERS.
1877.

Since the failure of the Application to re-hear the Purchas Case, no opportunity has offered until now of arguing before the Judicial Committee any of the points decided *exparte* in 1871. The Judgment of Lord Penzance, Feb. 3, 1876, in the Case of CLIFTON & OTHERS v. RIDSDALE, which was the first Suit under the Public Worship Regulation Act of 1874, led to an Appeal to the Judicial Committee, and that Appeal has now been heard by that Body as altered under the Judicature Act of 1876. The Lord President of the Council (The Duke of Richmond and Gordon) took his Seat at the opening of the Court which was constituted of the Ten following Members, viz:—

The Right Honourables

1. The Lord Chancellor (Cairns)
2. The Lord Selborne (R. Palmer)
3. Sir J. Colville
4. The Lord Chief Baron (Kelly)
5. The Lord Justice James
6. Sir R. J. Phillimore
7. Sir Montagu Smith
8. Sir R. Collier
9. Sir Baliol Brett
10. Sir R. P. Amphlett

And of the Five following Assessors, viz:—

1. The Most Reverend and Rt. Hon. the Lord Archbishop of Canterbury (Dr. Tait)
2. The Bishop of Chichester (Dr. Durnford)
3. The Bishop of St. Asaph (Dr. Hughes)
4. The Bishop of Ely (Dr. Woodford)
5. The Bishop of St. David's (Dr. Jones)

COUNSEL FOR THE APPELLANT, THE REV. C. J. RIDSDALE.
Sir James F. Stephen, Q.C.   Mr. Arthur Charles (now Q.C.)
Mr. Francis H. Jeune   Dr. Walter G. F. Phillimore
PROCTOR, Mr. G. H. Brooks.

COUNSEL FOR THE RESPONDENTS, CLIFTON & OTHERS.
Dr. Archibald J. Stephens, Q.C.   Mr. Benjamin Shaw.
PROCTORS, Messrs. Moore & Currey.

The Hearing occupied Eight Days, viz.: Tuesday, January 23rd; Wednesday 24th; Thursday 25th; Friday 26th; Saturday 27th; Monday 29th; Tuesday 30th; Wednesday 31st; at the conclusion of the Arguments the Court intimated that they would take time to consider their Judgment.

APPENDIX.

Date of the "Interpretations" of the "Injunctions" of 1559. Whether 1559 or 1561.

Dr. Stephens, in his Argument for the Respondents, Monday Jan. 29th, contended that the Date of the "Interpretations" of Queen Elizabeth's "Injunctions" is 1559 (the same year as the Injunctions) and not 1561 as stated by Counsel for the Appellant: the Reasons he assigned were these:—

(1) The "Interpretations" contain the following Order:—

"That one brief form of declaration be made, setting out the principal articles of our religion; the rather, for the unity of doctrine in the whole realm: especially to be spoken by the parsons, curates, or both, at their first entry; and after, twice in the year, for avoiding all doubt and suspicion of varying from the doctrine determined in the realm." (*Cardwell*, Doc. Ann. I. 239.)

(2) This Declaration is Dated by Cardwell, "1559, Elizab. I., "Sede Cant. vacante" (*Ib.* 263); therefore the "Interpretations" must have been made in 1559.

Considerations as to this theory.

I. Cardwell relies upon Strype and Burnet for the Date he assigns to the Declaration: for he says in a Note:—

"*A declaration*] Put forth by archbishop Parker after his election, with the concurrence of other bishops, and intended to be used, until articles of faith could be drawn up and enjoined by Convocation. Strype, Ann. vol. i. P. i. pp. 325–329. Burnet, H. R. vol. ii. p. 810. . . . ." [Cardwell quotes Burnet from Nares's Ed. Oxf. 1829.]

Strype, as here referred to by Cardwell, writing under Date 1560, says:—

"Now next for the form that all ministers were to read and declare publicly upon their first coming into their benefices, being a confession of their faith and belief, contained in eleven articles: this was put in print the next year by Richd. Jugg, the queen's printer, and was entitled, *A Declaration*" &c.

Then follows the Declaration; after which Strype remarks:—

"Such was the pastoral care of archbishop Parker, by whom, I believe, this Declaration was chiefly framed, that so all that came into livings, and served in the church, might be purged of popish doctrines and superstitions, and to make the best security he could of admitting none to officiate but such as consented to the gospel, and took the profession thereof upon them." (*Ann.* I. pt. i. p. 329, 8vo. *or* Ch. xvii. 220, fol.)

The passage in Burnet (writing under Date 1559), to which Cardwell appears to refer, is this:—

"Thus were the Sees filled, the worship reformed, and the queen's injunctions sent over England. Three things remained yet to be done. The first was, to set out the doctrine of the church as it had been done in King Edward's time. The second was, to translate the Bible, and publish it with short notes. And the third was, to regulate the ecclesiastical courts. The bishops therefore set about these. And for the first, though they could not by public authority set out the articles of the church till they met in a convocation; yet they soon after prepared them. And for the present, they agreed on a short profession of their doctrine, which all incumbents were obliged to read and publish to their people. This will be found in the Collection, (Numb. 11) copied from it as it was then printed." (*Vol.* ii. p. 641. Pocock's Ed. 8vo. 1865: where the old *folio* paging is also given, viz.: Part II. Book III. 405.)

The Declaration is given by Mr. Pocock in Vol. v. p. 563. The fol. reference being Pt. II. Bk. III. 365. In a Note (p. 567) he says, "This Book is mentioned as printed by Jugge in "4to, 1561, in Dibdin's Ames, vol. iv. p. 251:"

Burnet does not anywhere notice the "Interpretations" of the "Injunctions."

II. Cardwell seems merely to have followed Burnet's general Dating at the top of the Page, without reference to the particular Dates of the occurrences he relates; for, although (p. 641) under the Date 1559, Burnet says "Thus were the sees filled" &c.; he had just before (pp. 638–9) given the particulars of the Appointments, the Dates ranging from Dec. 21, 1559 to May 4, 1561. Therefore, in speaking of the Declaration as one of the "three things" that "remained yet to be done" after "the "sees" were "filled," he surely could not have meant to say that the Declaration was made in 1559. It seems, then, to me that Cardwell must have been misled by the Date (1559) in the heading of Burnet's pages.

III. There are, however, other Statements in Strype, besides the passage referred to by Cardwell, which relate to the Dates of the " Interpretations " and of the " Declaration." Thus, before his statement about the Declaration (*Ann.* I. pt. 1, 329) to which Cardwell refers, he says (writing under Date 1560) :—

"Another thing also was now drawn up in writing by the archbishop and bishops, for the further regulation of the inferior clergy. This paper consisted of *interpretations and further considerations* of certain of the queen's *injunctions,* for the better direction of the clergy, and for keeping good order in the church." (*Ann.* I. pt. i. p. 318 *or* fol. ch. xvii. 213. The passage is quoted *ante,* p. 241 Note.)

Again, Strype, in his *Life of Parker,* writing under date 1561, says :—

"The Archbishop, as he had much to do at this time, for the reformation of the Church, and of those that were to serve in it, so he had an *Assessus* of other Bishops with him at Lambhith, for his assistance, by special commission from the Queen, as it seems, according to a late Act of Parliament. And as in their first session many wholesome things were concluded upon; so at their second session (which was April 21, 1561, at Lambhith) Articles were agreed upon by our most reverend Father, and Thomas,* the other most reverend, the Archbishop of York, with the consent of their brethren the Bishops, to the same : *viz.* First, that the articles agreed on the first sessions be ratified, confirmed, and put in execution accordingly. *Item.* That the Readers be once again reviewed, and their abilities and manners examined, &c. with divers other particulars, which I omit. But one chief order by the Archbishop and this venerable assembly appointed, now or near this time, was that which follows :

"In the Church many popishly affected Priests still kept their hold by their outward compliances; but to make the best provision that could be against such for all times hereafter, all Parsons, Vicars, and Curates, that took ecclesiastical livings or cures, were now bound to make a public declaration, by the order of the Archbishop and the rest of the Bishops; and afterwards to be read by them once every half year before their people : to testify their common consent in certain sound doctrines. That hereby Papists might be refuted, who had slandered the Protestant Ministers, as if there were no agreement and unity of faith among them. This Declaration consisted in eleven articles; the sum whereof was, 'That they professed to believe in one living and true God,' " &c. (*Life of Parker,* Vol. i. pp. 181–2 : *or* fol. Bk. ii. 91.)

"The Archbishop also about this time framed another useful writing; which was to serve for the Clergy to *practise,* as the former was for them to *declare*: and this was to serve for uniformity in their ministration, and for maintenance of concord in the Church, till a Synod should meet. This also was published by the consent of all the Bishops, to be observed in both provinces. They called them *Resolu-*

---

* Thomas Young translated from St. Davids to York, Feb. 1561.

tions and Orders, viz. "That licences for preaching that had been given by the late general visitors should be called in . . . . ; and to move the people to obedience to the Book of Common Service and the Queen's injunctions,' " &c. (*Ib.* 183.)

"Other things also were drawn up by the diligent Archbishop in his own name, and in the name of the rest of the Bishops: which were *Interpretations and Considerations* of certain of the Queen's injunctions, for the better instructions of the Clergy: which are too long to be here set down; but may be found* among the Archbishop's own MSS. preserved in the Bene't college library, in the volume entitled *Synodalia;* and in the Annals of the Reformation." [*i.e.* his own *Annals*, Vol. I., pt. i., pp. 318–24 : *or* fol. ch. xvii. 213–18]." (*Ib.* 183 ; and see *ante* p. 241 Note.)

Further, Strype (at p. 194) mentions again the sitting of the Archbishops at Lambeth, here dating it April 12th, whereas he had before called it April 21st ; one or other of the Dates is probably a misprint; he says:—

"The Archbishop of Canterbury, with Thomas, Archbishop of York, the Bishops of London and Ely, and some others of the ecclesiastical Commission, were now sitting at Lambeth, upon the regulating and ordering of the matters of the Church. And on the 12th day of April, (being their second session,) certain Articles were agreed upon by them, with the assent of their brethren Bishops to the same : namely," (See *ante* p. 45.)

Then he gives the Articles from " MSS. C.C.C.C.," three of them being the following :—

"First, That the Articles agreed on at the first sessions be ratified, confirmed, and be put in execution accordingly."

"*Item.* That the Declaration devised for unity of doctrine may be enjoined to be used throughout the realm uniformly." (See Note, p. 170.)

"*Item.* That besides the Catechism for children which are to be confirmed, another, somewhat larger, may be devised for communicants, and a third in Latin for schools."

Dr. Cardwell, (*Doc. Ann.* I. p. 298) also mentions this Document, quoting from " Strype, Parker, vol. i. p. 194," but referring for the Articles themselves to " Ex. Reg. Parker." (See *ante* p. 170, Note.)

IV. The " Interpretations" of the Injunctions (as given by both Cardwell and Strype) contain the following directions which are also mentioned in the Documents already quoted :—

---

* This Document appears to be now missing (See Note p. 285); and the same seems to be the case with the "Declaration," for Mr. Pocock (*Burnet's Hist. Ref.* v. p. 567, 1865) noticing Strype's reference to "Parker's MSS. in Benet College Library," says " They are not, however, to be found there now." Archdeacon Hardwick also, (in his *History of the Articles*, 1859) says of the MS. Declaration, that he had "searched for it in vain." (p. 120 Note.)

"*Item*, to the eighth, 'That no visitors licences to preach be continued in force.'" (*Resolutions and Orders*, See p. 453.)

"*Item*, 'That there be some long catechism devised and printed, for the erudition of simple curates: homilies to be made of those arguments which be shewed in the book of homilies . . . .'"&c. (*Articles of April* 12, 1561, See p. 453)

Margin.—"ᵃ In distinction to the short catechism in the Common Prayer Book."

"*Item*, 'That the order of the articles prescribed to ministers be inserted in this form, *ut infra*.'"

"*Item*, 'That one brief form of declaration be made,'" &c. (See *ante*, p. 450; and *Articles of April* 12, p. 453)

Strype (writing under Date 1560) says of these Directions in the "Interpretations":—

"And much was done not long after, according to this reformatory platform. For there was a larger catechism composed in Latin, and published by Alex. Nowel, dean of St. Paul's, having been first revised and approved by both houses of convocation, anno. 1562. A second book of homilies was also compiled and set forth, as we have them at this day in our homily book. And articles of faith to be subscribed to by ministers, and the form of declaration to be by them openly spoken and professed, were likewise framed.

"The articles of the principal heads of religion prescribed to ministers, as was mentioned before, now follow:

"*S. scriptura in se continet omnem doctrinem pietatis*," etc. (*Ann.* I. pʳ· i. p. 323, *or* fol. ch. xvii. 216.)

The Consideration of these passages necessarily leads, as it seems to me, to the following Conclusions:—

1. That CARDWELL did not intend to assign to the *Declaration* a Date different from that given by Burnet or Strype.

2. That BURNET's language as to the *Declaration*, read in connexion with his account of the Episcopal Appointments after Parker's Consecration, points to 1561 and not 1559 as the Date of the *Declaration*.

3. That STRYPE, in his *Annals*, mentions the preparation of the "Interpretations" under the Date 1560; and, in his Life of Parker, as made at or near April 12 [or 21] 1561.

4. That the Declaration was not printed until 1561.

5. That it is wholly unlikely "Interpretations" should have been made at the very Date of the "Injunctions;" though the carrying out of the Injunctions was likely enough to raise questions which required the "Interpretations."

6. That, therefore, 1561 is most likely to be the true Date both of the "Interpretations" and of the "Declaration."

Besides these Conclusions from the previous Considerations, a comparison of the "Interpretations" and the "Declaration" leads to these two further Conclusions:—

7. That the "*Declaration*" does not go beyond the "Injunc-"tions;" for No. vii. recognizes "the Book of Common Prayer;" No. viii. justifies the omission of certain things in Baptism; Nos. ix. and x., though referring to certain matters about the Eucharist, do not hint anything about the Vestments, not even in the latter portion of No. x. where the Declarant has " to "utterly disallow the extolling of Images" and certain other things which are called "such like superstition."

8. That, therefore, if the Date of the *Interpretations* be 1559 and not 1561, the *Declaration* serves to shew that the "First" *Interpretation,* "Concerning the Book of Service," did not CONDEMN other Vestments as *unlawful,* in only *requiring* the "Cope" and "Surplice." The words "That there be used "only but one apparel; as the cope in the ministration of the "Lord's Supper, and the Surplice in all other Ministrations," need not, probably do not, mean more than this—notwithstanding the Order of the Rubric, it is not requisite that you should have Chasuble and Albe, Cope and Surplice, the last two will suffice for all purposes: and the word "as" seems to imply— you may make your choice; very likely having regard to what was left in the Churches after the great destruction of Church goods in 1559.

Since this was written I have examined the Index to the Parker Register at Lambeth to ascertain whether any Document exists which would clear up this question of the Date of the "Declaration:" in Vol. II. p. 691, the following reference occurs:—

"The Archbishop's Letter to the Archdeacon of Canterbury concerning a Declaration of certaine principall pointes of Religion by him sett forth and commanding him to see the same by his officers published within the Diocese of Canterbury. Dated from Lambeth the 4 of August, 1561, f. 232 a."

The following is the Letter itself, copied from Abp. Parker's Register, (Lambeth Library) f. 232a :—

"Lre missiue Revdendissimi script Archino Cant.

"I comend me vnto you And whereas a declaracon of certaine principall pointes of Religion was of late sette fourthe as well by myne order as also by my lord of Yorke his grace wth the Rest of our Brethren the other Busshoppes of this Realme The copie whereof I send to you herein enclosed Thes shalbe to will and Requier you to see the same by your officers published within that my dioces of Canturbery At suche tymes and in suche order as you shall thincke most convenient so that the same maye be effectuallie executed and obserued accordinglie Willing you further to see the same redde and declared at tymes therein mentioned by all suche clarkes as it dothe concerne Assuring your self of myne assistaunce against the contempners thereof And thus fare you hartelie well ffrom Lambehith the fourth of August 1561 Copia lbrarum missiuaru Rg^{ml} Script Archino Cantuar."

It will be seen that this Letter, written on August 4, 1561, states that the Declaration "was of late sette fourthe :" this is clearly in agreement with the account and the Dates given by Strype: he speaks of the "Interpretations" under two Dates, 1560 and 1561, the technical year depending simply upon the fact of their being made before or after March 25th, 1560-61: these "Interpretations" order that a "Declaration be made," (See p. 450): the "Articles" agreed upon at Lambeth, April 12 or 21, 1561, (whichever is the true Date) order the "De-"claration devised" to "be enjoined to be used," (See p. 453): thereupon Abp. Parker, on August 4, 1561, sends the "De-"claration" to the Archdeacon of Canterbury that it may be "published within" his "dioces of Canturbery." Having regard, then, to these Dates alone, there seems no real ground for supposing that the "Interpretations" of the "Injunctions" were made in 1559; on the contrary, Abp. Parker's Letter of August 4, 1561 fully sustains the other known evidence which points to 1560-61 as the true Date of the "Interpreta-"tions."

INDEX.

ABBOT, ABP., Visitation Articles, 1611. 41
Visit. Articles, 1616 344
decision as to place of the Lord's Table, at Crayford 431
"A PARTE OF A REGISTER," 1590, Puritan Tract quoted... 73, 76, 79
"ADMONITION" The "to the Parliament, by T. C.," 1572 83
ADVERTISEMENTS, The, cited by J. Com*** as of 1564; not issued till 1566 .... 25, Note 237
caused by the Queen's Letter to Abp. Parker, Jan. 25, 1564-5 . 26
Correspondence of Parker with Cecil as to original and revised draft............ 27, 60, 61, 62, 63
were not the "other Order" of Eliz. Act of Uniformity 50-55, 69, 74, 84, 135
titles given to them, shew this... 58-9, 242
"not authorized nor published," 1564, Cecil's Memo. ...... Note 60
Copies of in B. Museum ... Note 60
penalties omitted in, before published .... 63 & Note
not mentioned in certain Documents from the Queen, Parker and others—tends to shew their inferior authority 67-69, 239
difference between the original and the amended draft, Strype 71-3
held by Ho. of Lords, in 1640-41, not to be "in force, but by way of commentary and imposition " .... Note 98, 194
acted upon and enforced by Royal Commissions, thought by J. Com*** to bring them within the Statute: grounds for doubting this 135-42

ADVERTISEMENTS, THE, their Authority, as the "other Order," not proved (as held by Dr. Stephens) by marg. note on Whitgift's Articles No. 5 145
not authorized: so said in "An abstract of certain Acts of Parliament" &c., 1583-4 Note 154
reply "by some Civilian," 1584, to this "Abstract" 155
not authorized: so said in "A Petition directed to her Majesty" &c. 155
J. Com*** speak of them as prescribing "the surplice only;" the word "only" does not occur 168
further relaxed the Rule for Vestments in *Parish* Churches ... 242
as to Lord's Table, discouraged its removal from E. end of Chancel or Church 344
Bp. Wren's reference to them, Note 430
"AGREEABLY," meaning of as to Vestments of Epistoler and Gospeller .... Note 126
ALBE, The, used at Bledlow, Bucks, 1771-83 105
ALTAR, THE HIGH, in St. Paul's Cathedral, taken down in 1550: Table put in its place 378
ALTARS, in London, taken down: Tables substituted, 1550 378
ANDREWES, Bp., Visitation Articles, 1625............ 108
ARTICLES, VISITATION, of Bps. supposed by J. Com*** to prove effect of Advertisements 41
for Visitation by Commissioners, 1559............ 47
agreed upon by Abps. and Bps. at Lambeth, April, 1561...App. 453

458

ARTICLES of Whitgift and others,
1583 144-49
remarks upon the same 149-54
copy of these Articles, in the
Inner Temple Library 153
"ASSENT AND CONSENT," Declaration of, required from 1559 to
1662 ...... Note 170-1 App. 450-6
"AUTHORITY, THE QUEEN'S MAJESTY'S," meaning of in Bp. Grindal's Letter, May 21, 1566,
to D. and C. of St. Paul's, as
to the Advertisements 64-67
AYLMER, BP., Visitation Articles,
1577............................. 41

BABINGTON, BP., Visitation Articles, 1607 .... 41, 107, 344
BANCROFT, BP., Visitation Articles,
1601........................... 107
BANCROFT, ABP., revived the use of
Copes &c., 1605 90
BARLOW, BP., Visitation Articles,
1679......................... 106, 163
BARNES, BP., Monitions and Injunctions, Oct. 1, 1577, does
not mention The Advertisements............................ 69, 140
Returns to, as Commissioner in
the North, 1577-86 ...... Note 81
BARROW, MR. F., his Reasons for
Opinion as to Ornaments Rubric, 1867 .... Note 226-8
BAXTER, RICHARD, after Savoy Conference, shews that the Ornaments Rubric remained unaltered .... Note 172, 173
BENNET, THOMAS, 1708, on the
Ornaments Rubric 111
on Position of the Celebrant ... 409
"BEORE THE PEOPLE," Nicholls
quoted as to it by J. Com^r:
not intended, as he thinks, that
the *fraction* of the Bread must
be seen 414
Udall also quoted: his statements are really a complaint
against *high Pews* 415-24
Wheatley also cited: he only
follows Nicholls................. 424
means "coram populo" 427
"BEFORE THE TABLE," meaning
assigned to it by Nicholls,
Bennett, Wheatly (cited by

J. Com^r): remarks upon their
statements.................... 405-12
Laud's defence of it 327-8, 427
Cosin, his excuse for it ... Note 426
Bp. Wren's use of the expression,
proof of its meaning 439
meaning of the words, in the
Marriage Service 441
Brett's use of the words, 1717
Note 440
"BLESSED BREAD," Symbolism of,
Note 283
A ceremony not continued in
Bk. of 1549 .... 284 & Note
BODMIN, Assignment of Vestments
&c. for use in the Church, 8th
Elizabeth 238
"BOOK OF THE DISCIPLINE of the
Church of England," prob. the
Canons of 1571 82
BOOTH, ARCHN., Visitation Articles,
1710-20 164
BOSTOCK, ARCHN., Visitation Articles, 1640 .... 110, 347
BREAD, for the Communion, P. Bk.
1549 did not require absolute
Uniformity as to it 287
Rubric of 1552 not long enough
in use to have "produced uniformity," as J. Com^r thinks 288
fraction of, direction as to, Sarum
Missal .... Note 333
BRISTOL CHARITIES, Case of, cited
by J. Com^r as to value of contemporaneous usage in construing obscure Documents—
not applicable to Ornaments
Rubric 243-8
BUCER, whether his "Censures"
much influenced the Revision
of the Book in 1552...... Note 271
not opposed to Rule and Practice
in the Church because not
ordered in Scripture; *e.g.*,
Communions *not* in the Evening, and Vestments: Letter to
Hooper, Nov. 1550 ... 273 & Note
Vestments not to be rejected
because "abused by Antichrist." Letter to Hooper,
Nov. 1550 .... Note 273
Letter to Cranmer, Dec. 8, 1550,
Note 274
did not object to Wafer-bread,

459

only wanted liberty to use leavened Bread also...... Note 289
BURN, DR. RICHARD, 1763, On the Ornaments Rubric............... 115
BURNET, BP., his notice of the "Declaration" of Clergy as to Doctrine, 1560-1 .... App. 454

CALVIN and others banished from Geneva, in 1538, for using common Bread at Communion .... 311 & Note
CANON 30, 1603-4, principle of, opposed to such destruction of Ornaments as occurred in 1559 39
24, 1603-4, Title therein given to The Advertisements......... 59
58, Cosin's remark upon it, explained 165
does not prohibit Cope in Parish Churches........................ 176
Arch. Sharp on the force of...Note 130
CANONS of 1603-4, compared with The Advertisements, as to Vestments 126-7
not the Authority for the P. Book of 1604...................... 85-9
date of their passing the two Convocations...................... 87-9
held by J. Com*s to be among the "Laws" kept in force by Act of 1662—the question considered 204-7
ask for "fine white bread": do not exclude Wafers 319
14, 24, 58, not inconsistent, as J. Com*s seem to consider: explanation of their object: meaning of Order, Form, Rites, Ceremonies 232-4
1571, not sanctioned by the Queen, quoted 82
1640, as to example of Cathedrals to Parish Churches ...... Note 24
Title therein given to the Advertisements 59
as to Position of the Lord's Table .... Note 346
CANTERBURY, PECULIARS OF, Visitation Articles for, 1637 ... 42, 346
CARDWELL, error as to Date of "Declaration," not 1559 but 1560-1 ....Abp. 450-6

CARTWRIGHT, THOS., opposed to Copes, Surplices, &c. 83
controversy with Whitgift as to Wafer Bread 305-7
CATHEDRALS, to be the Standard of Parish Churches ...... Note 24
no Copes in some in 1635, but ordered by the Visitors......... 90
Bishop, Dean, or other chief Dignitary to celebrate on principal Feast Days, Can. xxiv. 126
CECIL, SECY, Abp. Parker's Letters to, about The Advertisements 27
Returns to him, 1564-5, as to Varieties in Service 26
as to varieties of Communion bread .... Note 318
as to varieties of place of the Lord's Table 343
CELEBRANT, Position of, change as to (See Position).
"CEREMONIES OR RITES," Q. Eliz. power as to ordaining them under Act. of Unif., 1559 14
CHADERTON, BP., Visitation Articles, 1604 107
complaint to P. Council, 1580, of disputes about Wafer Bread or Common Bread 322-3
CHALICE, THE MIXED, Charge as to 255
Symbolism of ... 261, Note 263, 264
not forbidden, so held by Cosin 212, 256
used by Bp. Andrewes 256
decision of The Dean of the Arches (Sir R. Phillimore) as to 256
not mixed before Service in Eastern or Western Church—error of Jud. Committee as to this... 266-8
not inconsistent, as held by J. Com*s, with the Law that the Churchwardens are to provide the Bread and Wine... 277
not inconsistent, as said by J. Com*s, with the Curate having for his own use the remains of unconsecrated Elements 279
mixing Water with the Wine during the Service, an additional Ceremony excluded by P. Book: J. Com* 259
Symbolical character of this Act not altered by being done

	PAGE
before the Service: J. Com^{ers}: remarks upon this	262
CHANCELS, Rubric as to, Archn. Pory's Interpretation of it, 1662	Note 213
CHARGES, The, against Mr. Purchas	2
CHASUBLE &c., as obnoxious as Surplices to Cartwright and others	83
CHICHESTER CATHEDRAL, destruction of Ornaments by the Rebels in 1642	Note 229
CHURCHES, ruinous state of in the North, 1577-80	Note 81
CHURCHING VEIL, ordered, Visit. Art., 1620	213
CHURCHWARDENS to provide Bread and Wine, not opposed to use of Mixed Chalice, as alleged by J. Com^{ers}	277
COLLIER, on Articles for Visitation Commissioners and destruction of Ornaments in 1559	47
account of revival of Copes &c. in 1605	90
on revision of 1st P. Bk. in 1552	271
COMMISSION, for Visiting the Province of York, 1559, description of it Note 32; 1561	141
1570	140
COMMISSIONS, GENERAL, to Visitors, issued probably under 1 Eliz., c. 1 and 2	40
no evidence that they authorized the destruction of Ornaments	40
COMMISSIONERS, for Visiting the Parishes, 1559, York &c.	31
Returns to from Parishes in the North, 1578-80	Note 81
COMMISSIONERS, ECCLESIASTICAL, the Queen's Letter to, 1560-1, as to condition of Churches	22
did not order destruction of Vestments in 1561	45
Royal, 1689, proposed to alter Ornaments Rubric	173
COMMONS, Com^{ers} of Ho. of, 1643-4, ordered destruction of Church Ornaments	Notes 90-1, 228
House of, 1662, did not want to oppose all Ritual; Letter of Neile to Stapylton, Ap. 29, 1662	Note 232
COMMUNION, The, time at which to	

	PAGE
place Elements on the Altar— Lid. & West	Notes 247, 270, 280
COMMUNION-BREAD, "orders" as to, not correctly described by J. Com^{ers}	292
varieties of 1564-5	318
varieties of, in 1571	295
ordinary household Bread not to be used without necessity	304
Canons of 1604 are for "fine white bread"	319
carried off by dog, in Tadlow Church, 1638	Note 321
CONFERENCE of two Houses of Parliament (See Parliament).	
CONSECRATION, PRAYER OF, error as to, Liddell v. Westerton and Hebbert v. Purchas	15
"CONSIDERATIONS against the deprivation of a Minister, for the not use of a Surplice in divine service"—Puritan Tract, 1605	52
COPES (as well as Chasubles) destroyed, though ordered by the "Interpretations of the Injunctions"	39
not forbidden, by The Advertisements, in Parish Churches: Visit. Art. of Aylmer, Grindal, Sandys	42, 43, & Note
nor by Canon 58 of 1604	176
Inquiries for, in Parish Churches, York Visitation, 1571	Note 44
instances of their retention in Parish Churches, Lincolnshire Inventories	Note 77, 91, 74-6
used in the Chapel Royal for Baptism, Confirmation, Churching, 1605-13	235-6
used in St. Paul's Cathedral by Bp. of London, in 1567	76
disused at Durham Cathedral, 1759	Note 49
in Westminster Abbey, ordered by Parliament to be destroyed, 1643	Note 49
proposal to abolish them, Convocation 1562-3, rejected	78
complaint of in "The Admonition to the Parliament by T. C."	83
revived use of in 1605	90
neglect of in some Cathedrals in 1635, but ordered to be procured	90

	PAGE		PAGE
COPES, forbidden by Parliament in 1643	90	junction for Tables instead of Altars	Note 339
error of J. Com^{rs.} that Copes are only to be worn on "Principal Feast-days" in Cathedrals	128	Cox, to Bullinger, Oct. 5, 1552, on revision of the P. Bk. in 1552	272
CORPORAS (or "fair linen cloth") not asked for in many Visitation Articles—not therefore forbidden	124	Cox, BP., Injunctions of, 1570-74, Title of Advertisements	59, 107
COSIN, BP., fac-simile of his proposed form of Ornaments Rubric in 1661	92	CRANMER, ABP., did not mean to disregard the Custom of the Church when revising the P. Bk. of 1549 in 1552: his Letter to the Council, Oct. 7, 1552	274
Notes on the P. Book, as to the Ornaments	Note 93-7	Order in Council, 1549, to, about Parishioners who would not provide Bread and Wine for the Sacrament	278
Visitation Articles, 1627	108-9		
1662 (before P. Bk of 1662)	106, 163, 315, 347	CRIPPS, H. W., 1845, on the Ornaments Rubric	119
proofs of this	120-3	CROSSES, illegally destroyed in 1559-60, Jewel to P. Martyr	Note 39
his reference to Canon 58, 1603-4, explained	165, 193	CURATE, THE, to have remains of unconsecrated Bread and Wine, thought, by J. Com^{rs.}, opposed Mixed Chalice, because of the "symbolical mixing": remarks on this	279
his opinion as to the Mixed Chalice: Authorities cited by him	257-9		
did not hold the Rubrics to be always a sufficient guide	260-1 & Note	CURLE, BP., Visit. Art. 1680	345
his note on the omission of The Manual Acts in P.Bk., Note 263,333		1633	345
held wafer bread to be lawful	311	DECLARATION of "Assent and Consent," required from 1559 to 1662	Note 170-1
proposed to order it	312		
North side	Note 377	true Date of	450-6
implies Lawfulnes of Eastward Position, though excusing himself for having taken it	Note 426	issued by Abp. Parker in his Diocese, Aug 4, 1561	App. 456
author of the Rubric before Prayer of Consecration	326	DE LAUNE, THOMAS, 1683, complains of the Ornaments Rubric	173
Visitation Articles 1627 (when Archdeacon), cited by J.Com^{rs.}, not an exposition of Rubric as to position of Celebrant in P. Bk. of 1662	442	DEVONSHIRE REBELS, 1549, demanded back "Holy Bread" and other old Ceremonies	284
		DODSON, SIR JOHN, the Ornaments Rubric as affecting Crosses	250
COUNCIL, The P., Order of, Nov. 3, 1633, as to Holy Table in St. Gregory's, near St. Pauls,	Note 24, 432	DORMAN, THOS., 1564, position of Lord's Table	349
in a Letter about Uniformity, Nov. 7, 1573, does not mention The Advertisements	69	DOWSING, WILLIAM, Journal of his proceedings, as Parliamentary Visitor in 1643-44, in destroying Ornaments	Note 229
Order in, about Parishioners who refused to provide Bread and Wine for Sacrament	278	DUGDALE, his account of the High Altar at St. Paul's Cathedral, 1300	Note 378
did not regard Wafer-bread as unlawful, in 1580	322-3	DUPPA, BP., Visit. Art. 1638	318,346
Order to support Ridley's In-		EARLE, BP. [?], Visitation Articles, 1662	315

EASTWARD POSITION, in the Creed or at Prayers, an "Innovation" — so held by Lords' Com^{ee} in 1641 262
in Common Prayer, proposed in Convocation 1562 to be forbidden: not carried 356
Eastward Position in Prayers, used after 1662............ Note 410
EASTERN LITURGY, S. Chrysostom, mixture of Chalice made before the Public Office, in the Chapel of the Prothesis 267
ECCLESIASTICALL COMMISSIONERS, The, proceedings of (See Commissioners).
ELAND, ARCHN.,Visit. Articles, 1620 109
ELDON, LORD, his Decision, in Case of Bristol Charities, as to value of contemporaneous usage when interpreting obscurely framed Documents............. 243-8
ELEMENTS FOR COMMUNION, some Parishioners would not provide them, in 1549............... 273
when to be placed on the Altar Note 247, 270
ELIZABETH, Q., Her Letter to Eccl. Com^{rs}, Jan. 22, 1560-1, as to condition of Churches &c. ... 22
Her Letter to Abp. Parker, as to neglect of Rites and Ceremonies in Churches, 1564-5 ... 26, 50
Her unwillingness to Authorize The Advertisements 27
does not mention the Advertisements in her Letter to Abp. Parker, Aug. 20, 1571; Proclamation, June 11 and Oct. 20, 1573 68-69
communicated in Wafer-bread,at ChapelRoyal,St.James's,1593,307-8
ELPHINSTONE, C. J., Promoter of Suit: Hebbert, H., substituted 2
ELTHAM, KENT, Parish Accounts, 1579-80, contain Payments for Wafer Bread 321
EVENING COMMUNIONS, opposed to the custom of the Church: so contended by Bucer and P. Martyr .... Note 273

FIELDING, ARCHN., Visit. Articles, 1683 316

FLAGON or FLAGONS, inquiries for in Visit. Art. 1628-1728 212
FLEETWOOD, BP., Visitation Articles, 1710 316
FOXE, his account of taking down wall behind the Altar at St. Paul's Cath. 1550 378
FREEMAN, ARCHN., meaning of "North Side" 382
FULKE, 1579, repels charge of Consecrating at the End of the Table .... Note 374
FULLER, BP., Visit. Articles, 1671, 315

GIBSON, EDMUND, BP., 1713, on the Ornaments Rubric 114
GRIFFITHS, BP., Visit. Art., 1662 Note 121
GRINDAL, BP., Letter to D. and C. of St. Pauls, May 21, 1566, as to The Advertisements........ 64
Visit. Art. for Canterbury, 1576, do not mention the Advertisements 69
Visit. Art. for York, 1571, Injunctions binding ...... 242 & Note
ABP., Letter to Zanchius, 1571 or 1572, the Law as to Ornaments not altered 29
Visitation Articles, York, 1571 . 41, 318
GUNNING, BP., Visitation Articles, 1679 .... 106, 164, 315

HACKET, BP., Visitation Articles, 1662 .... Note 121, 163, 315
HAMMOND, ARCHN., Visitation Articles, 1670 .... 106, 315
HAMPTON COURT CONFERENCE, referred to by J. Com^{ee} 83
HARSNETT, BP., Visitation Articles, 1620 ...... 108, 213, 270, 318
HENCHMAN, BP., Visitation Articles, 1662 167
1664 163
HEYLIN, PETER, "A Coale from the Altar" 396, 397, 398
"Antidotum Lincolniense" 397, 399
HOGARDE (or HUGGARD), MYLES, 1556, describes Print omitted on Wafer-bread .... Note 305
Position of Lord's Table 350-1
HOOKER, defended Wafer-bread ... 324
HOOPER to BULLINGER, 1549, com-

plains that old customs were retained under P. Bk. 1549 ... 373
Howson, Bp., Visit. Articles, 1619   42

Injunction, Bp. Ridley's, 1550, for changing Altars into Tables Note 339
Order in Council supporting it Note 339
Six Reasons for this Order. Note 340-1
Injunctions, 1547, shew what Ornaments, &c., were abolished before P. Bk. 1549 ...13, Note 14
1559, not new but a revision of 1547 14
30, orders destruction of "monuments" of "superstition" Note 46
do not mention the Vestments: what they do prescribe 241
1559, Authority of, Parker to Cecil 14
1559, No. 30 quoted .... Note 46
as to Wafer-bread, not at variance with Rubric of 1559 283
nor "a superseding" of it, as held by J. Com^{rs}....................... 285
"For Tables in Church"... Note 338
did not require the Lord's Table to be always moved from the Altar's place, for a Celebration 338-42
nor that its Ends should be East and West .... 342 ff
Interpretations of the Injunctions, prob. date of, 1561 24, Note 241
further proof of................... 450-56
Dispense with, but do not prohibit, some of the Vestments: yet make no difference between Cathedrals & Parish Churches 241
prescribe when the Lord's Table may be removed from Chancel 355
Inventories of Church Goods, to be received by the Visitors, 1559 21
Ironside, Bp., Visit. Articles, 1662, Note 121, 315
1692, 316
"It shall suffice," meaning of it given by J. Com^{rs} (see Suffice).

Jebb, Dr. John, 1843, on the Ornaments Rubric 117

Jegon [?] Archn., Visitation Articles, 1608 .... 108, 318
Jewel, to P. Martyr, Crosses illegally destroyed, Letter Feb. 4., 1559-60 .... Note 39
Johnson, Robert, 1573. condemned by High Commission Court for not Consecrating the Elements newly brought, when not sufficient had been Consecrated .... Note 356
Judicial Committee, Names of in Liddell v. Westerton............ 15
Names of in Hebbert v. Purchas 1
Names of in Ridsdale v. Clifton & others 449
Juxon, Bp., Visitation Articles, 1640 .... 110, 346

Kalendar, of Lessons, to be revised, Q. Eliz. Letter 1560-1 23
Keeling, Mr., remarks on preparation of Scotch P. Book, 1637 .... Note 313
Kent, Archn., Visit. Articles, 1624 318
1631-9 345
King, Archn., Visitation Articles, 1599 107
King, Bp., Visitation Articles, 1612 42, 344
Kingsley, Archn., Visit. Articles, 1636 346

Lathbury, Rev. T., The Advertisments had not the Queen's Authority 69
History of the Canons of 1603-4 87-9
quotes Elborrow as to Eastward Position in Prayer, after 1662 Note 410
Latimer, Bp., character of P. Books of 1549 & 1552 15
Laud, Bp., of St. David's Visitation Articles, 1622 ...... Note 270, 344
Laud, Abp., Visitation Articles, 1635, order Copes to be procured in some Cathedrals...... 90
place of Table, 1635 90
charge against him as to Position of Celebrant, in Scotch Book, 1637, when Consecrating .... 327-8, Note 426
unwillingness to Scotch P. Book being prepared............... Note 313

PAGE	PAGE
LAUD, ABP., Position of the Holy Table in Cathedrals & Parish Churches 340	MARTYR, PETER, opposed to Evening Communions; Letter to Hooper Nov. 4, 1550 ... Note 273
"LAWS," meaning of the Word in Act of 1662, Statutes which illustrate it 205	objects to the bondage of using "nothing which is of the Pope" e.g. Vestments .... Note 273
LAYFIELD, ARCHN., Visitation Articles, 1662 .... 107, 315	MAXIMUM AND MINIMUM OF RITUAL, inconsistent with Penal character of Act of Unifor.—this opinion of J. Com[ee] discussed 169 ff.. 216-17
LESSONS, NEW, to be provided, Q. Eliz. Letter 1560-61 23	
LIDDELL v. WESTERTON, J. Com[ee] as to character of P. Bk. 1559 11 did not decide upon Vestments —the point considered 250-4	History of the use of Ornaments since the Reformation is consistent therewith 237
LINDSELL, BP., Visitation Articles, 1633 .... 109, 345	MICKLETON MSS., Letter from Neile to Stapylton, as to Visitation Articles of Bp. Cosin, 1662 122
LORDS, HOUSE OF, Committee in 1640-1, suggestion to alter the Ornaments Rubric 103, 194	MIDDLETON, BP., Visit. Articles, 1583, Place of Table at Celebration, viz., lower end of the Chancel 342, 348
Eastward Position at Prayers or the Creed an "Innovation" 262 as to force of Injunctions and Advertisements .... Note 194	MIXED CHALICE, The (see Chalice)
	MORLEY, BP., Visitation Articles, 1662 .... 163, 315
LUSHINGTON, DR., nothing done between 1549 & 1662 binding after Act of Uniformity, 1662, came into operation 253	MOUNTAGUE, BP., Visitation Articles, 1638 .... 110, 318, 346
	NEILE, BP., Visit. Articles, 1628... 109
MACDOUGALL v. PURRIER, cited by J. Com[ee], does not support their view of the Authority of The Advertisements 143-58	NICHOLLS, WILLIAM, 1710, on the Ornaments Rubric .... 111 on the Position of the Celebrant 405-9
MANT, BP., 1820, on the Ornaments Rubric .... 115-17 turning to the East at Prayers, ancient .... Note 263	"NORTH SIDE OF THE TABLE," the, origin of the term in 1552... 370 ff "manifold shiftings of the Book" forbidden: probable cause ... 373 ff
MANUAL ACTS, THE, in Consecration Prayer, in force though not mentioned in P. Bks., 1552, 1559, & 1604.................. 213-15 notice of their omission, by Cosin .... Note 268 remarks on their use, J. Com[ee] Martin v. Mackonochie ...... 335 Bp. Middleton, 1583 347-8	four writers, Mr. Elliott, Mr. Droop, Mr. Walton, and Mr. Scudamore, hold that "North side" was inserted in 1552 to meet the changed Position of the Lord's Table, then placed East & West: reasons against this view .... 375 ff & Notes J. Com[ee] on meaning of "North side" .... 381 ff
MARRIAGE, PROHIBITED TIMES OF, mentioned in Visit. Art., 1612 to 1679 .... Note 211	Mr. Droop's opinion of meaning of it: remarks thereon 385
MARTYN, PETER, to BUCER, Feb., 1551-2, "simplicity" the principle on which he thought the P. Bk. of 1549 should be revised 272	"side" probably taken from Rubric, 1549, "Then so many as shall be partakers . . . . . men on the one side," etc. ... 386
	argument from Jewish Altar— Dr. Littledale 390-91

| | PAGE | | PAGE |

"NORTH SIDE OF THE TABLE,"
Visitation Articles, *e.g.* Pory cited by the Court, to shew that *End* is the Celebrant's *North side* position: remarks upon 392-4
meaning of, shewn in the Charges against Cosin, 1630...... Note 308
alterations of the Rubric, 1661, fac-simile of 412-13
Wheatley's reference to "*Bev.* Pandect" adverse to his view, as to .... Note 411
Pictures illustrating it...... Note 411

"ORDERS, THREE," as to Communion Bread, not correctly described by J. Com**rs** 292
"ORDINANCE" OF PARLIAMENT, 1643, forbids Copes, Surplices, &c. 90
ORNAMENTS, &c., abolished before P. Book of 1549, could be known by the Injunctions,&c.— Letter of P. Council, May 13, 1548 .... Note 230
ORNAMENTS, destruction of in 1559, opinion of J. Com**rs**, in L. and W. 47-8
of 2nd year Edw. 6 to "be retained and be in use," until "further order" as to Act of Unifor**y** 1559 .... Note 56
the same now as in 2 Edw. vi., Dr. A. J. Stephens 69
destruction of in 1640-1, by order of Parliament ... Note 228
use of, forbidden by Parliament, 1643 .... 90 & Note
Cosin's Notes upon, before P. Book of 1662 .... Note 93-7
not inquired for in Visitation Articles, not therefore meant to be disused, as supposed: e.g. "a fair linen cloth" not asked for in many cases...... 123-4
not prescribed, asked for in Visit. Art., 1620-70 213
Opinion of their Lawfulness, Sir F. Thesiger (Lord Chelmsford), 1857 161
of Ministers, comparative Table of those prescribed in P. B. 1549 and Canons 1604 195-6

ORNAMENTS RUBRIC, history of, in 1549 and 1552, by J. Com**rs** 3
of 1552, things not therein ordered might be left in Churches at discretion of Commissioners .... 3 & 4
1559, Sandys' "gloss" upon it, and remarks thereon 17-19
1559, whether meant to be only temporary, conf. J. Com**rs** in Liddell *v.* Westerton and Hebbert *v.* Purchas 11
not affected in its *legal* force by Injunctions of 1559, or by Interpretations of 1561 ... 20, 125
only relaxed, as to its full observance, by Injunctions, Interpretations, and Advertisements 30-31
1559, the Law as to, not altered in 1571 or 1572. See Grindal to Zanchius 29
J. Com**rs** considered it binding in 1604............................ 103
Lords' Com**rs** in 1641 suggested that it "be mended"............ 103
comparative Table as to, and fac-simile of Cosin's alteration of 92
Bps. at Savoy Conference said it "should continue as it is" 99
Rejoinder of the Ministers to the Bps. at Savoy Conference ... 100
J. Com**rs** think they afterwards re-cast" it and so altered it: reasons against this view 99-103, 172-3
necessity for rewording it in 1662, because the Ecc· Com**rs** had been abolished 230
of 1662, Commentators on, from 1708 to 1845 .... Note 111-19
Articles not mentioned in, not therefore illegal, Lid. & West. 132
in what sense it revived the Rubric of 1549, remarks of J. Com**rs** upon the opinions of Dr. Lushington & Sir J. Dodson—considered...... 199 ff., 250-1
meaning not *obscure*, Liddell *v.* Westerton 243
meaning of the word "retained:" opinion of J. Com**rs** and Rea-

3 o

	PAGE
sons of Counsel in 1866, considered	224 & Note
true construction of, Liddell v. Westerton	251
non-compliance with it no proof that it is not in force; for other Rubrics not complied with, though admitted to be in force	247
if in force after 1662 its neglect a continued breach of the Law by Bps.; remarks upon	248-50
in Scotch P. Bk., 1637	Note 100
ORNSBY, REV. G., extracts from Mickleton and Tanner MSS. as to true date of Bp. Cosin's Visitation Articles, 1662	122
on the MS. of Cosin's Visitation Articles of 1627	Note 108
OVERALL, BP., Visitation Articles, 1619	108, 344
PALMER, SIR WILLIAM, 1832, on the Ornaments Rubric	117
on the Mixed Chalice	265
PARISH CHURCHES, to follow Rule of Cathedrals	Note 24, 241
PARKER. ABP., Letter to the Archn. of Cant^y., Aug. 4, 1561, to publish and execute the "Declaration" of Faith to be signed by Clergy	App. 456
Letters to Sec^y Cecil about the Advertisements, March 3, 1564-5, first draft for Cecil's perusal	60
March 8, 1564-5, begging the Queen's consent	27, 61
March 24, 1564-5, complains of delay	27, 61
April 7, 1565, says that it is alleged the Queen is indifferent	27, 62
March 12, 1565-6, sends them again, mentions an alteration, and asks that some, at least, may be allowed	27, 62
March 28, 1566, means to send them to Bp. of London; stays till he hears Cecil's advice, has weeded out the Doctrinal portions as they may have hindered the Queen's approbation	27

	PAGE
PARKER, ABP., April 4, 1566, dismissed some Non-conformists "with our Advertisements"	62
April 28, 1566, the Queen willed "the order to go forward," but he despairs of doing anything if the Queen will not aid him	63
Jan. 8, 1570-1, as to further "Ceremonies or Rites"	14
Visitation Articles, 1563	318, 344
to Bp. of London, Feb. 15, 1560-1, as to Queen's Letter about state of Churches, and New Lessons	23
to Bp. of London, March 28, 1566, Title of Advertisements	58, 63
Visitation Articles, 1567, 1569, Advertisements not mentioned	67
Visitation Articles, 1569, 1575, Title of Advertisements	59
inquiries for Wafer bread	318
to his Peculiars, March 28, 1566, as to the Advertisements	66
Letter to Lord Burleigh, May 9, 1573, does not mention the Advertisements	69
Letter to Sandys, Bp. of London, Nov. 24, 1573, does not mention the Advertisements	69
Letter to Lord Burleigh, Nov. 15, 1573, does not prove the Advertisements Authorized	70
Visitation Articles: 1569... 107.	242 & Note
Wafer Bread, Letter to Cecil thereon, Jan. 8, 1570-1	293-5
sends a specimen of it to Cecil, Letter, Feb. 6, 1570-1	296
Letters on the subject, 1573-4, to Parkhurst, Bp. of Norwich	298-9
wished to keep the Lord's Table, as much as possible, in the Altar's place	355
PARKHURST, BP. of Norwich, application to Abp. Parker about the use of Wafer-bread	298-9
PARLIAMENT, Conference of two Houses of, 1662: proposed to dispense with use of Cross and Surplice, rejected	217
PEACOCK, MR. EDW., Lincolnshire Inventories, 1566, J. Com^{rs} misled as to; the destruction	

of Ornaments therein recorded was before the Advertisements were issued............... 35-40, 160
Table of Ornaments destroyed, and Dates of destruction 37
they prove too much as to the purpose for which they are quoted............................. 38
instances of Copes, &c., retained in Parish Churches 74-6, Note 176
PEARSON, ARCHN., Visitation Articles, 1636, 1639 .... 110, 346
BP., Visitation Articles, 1674 ... 106
PENALTIES, none in Act of Unif., 1599, as to Ornaments, so held in Puritan Tract, 1605, "Considerations," &c. 52-4
the subject discussed ...... 177-91, Note 191
PETITION of 15,000 to Ho. of Com., 1640, complaining of increased use of Cope and Surplice...... 90
PHILLIMORE, SIR ROBERT, Judgment re Purchas, his opinion of Whitgift's Articles, 1583 ... 149
decision as to Mixed Chalice ... 256
PHILLPOTTS, BP., 1844, on the Ornaments Rubric............... 118
POCKLINGTON, JOHN D., "Altare Christianum"................... 397
"POPERY, grosse points of," viz., Black Chimere of Bps., &c. ... 80
POPISH RECUSANTS, Statutes against 24
PORY, ARCHN., Visitation Articles, 1662, before P. Book 1662 106, Note 121, 315, 347
POSITION OF THE CELEBRANT, Jud. Com⁰⁰ admits Sir R. Phillimore to be right in saying that the words of the Rubric "do not speak of seeing"............. 325
and Posture of in 1549, same as under Sarum Missal 370
changed Position to "North side," at beginning of Office in 1552, reason for this 371
Bishops, in 1552, wholly unlikely to send the Celebrant to an END of the Lord's Table 374
change of, not necessarily forbidden because not ordered in P. Bk. of 1552 356
proposed in Convocation, 1562, that "the Minister in Common Prayer turn his face towards the people": not carried 356
Richard Kechyn, 1564-5, charged with facing Eastward 354
Mr. Wolwerd, King's Coll. Camb. nearly expelled for not Celebrating Eastward 356
discussion at Savoy Conference as to .... 330-32 & Note 330
Source of the Rubric, 1662, Table shewing the 326
"standing before" substituted for "standing up"—remarks on................................... 327
"north side of the Table," retained, in 1662, from Books 1552, 1559, & 1604, compared with Rubric in 1549,—meaning of 329
Cosin's Visit. Art., 1627, referred to by J. Com⁰⁰, not an exposition of the Rubric of 1662 442
charge as to,—the people could not see him break the Bread or take the Cup into his hands 325
POTTER, BP., Visitation Articles, 1629................................. 109
PRACTICES directed in P. Bk., 1549, not necessarily prohibited because not ordered in P. Bk., 1552 269-70
why omitted probably 270-77
old, clung to Clergy under revised Office Books................ 371
PRAYER BOOK, 1549, not a *sole* Rule then for Ornaments 13
"a very godly order," &c., Act of Unif., 1552..................... 16
order of Office transposed in 1552 372
Rubrics of, compared with Alesius's translation, Sarum Missal, & P. Bk. of 1552... 359-69
1552, Latimer's opinion of it, and of Bk. 1549 15
probable principle of its preparation, viz., Simplicity, Scripturalness, Custom 270-77
its omissions meant to give liberty on both sides 276
only in use for a year 288
1559, "a compromise" between Services and Ornaments, J. Com⁰⁰ 1857...................... 11
1604, not dependent upon Canons

of 1604, as held by J. Com⁻., but upon Royal Proclamation............ 85-9, 192
1636, fac-simile of altered Rubric as to place of the Lord's Table ; from Photozincographic copy 412
1662, MS. copy of, MS. Table of Alterations in 100
fac-simile of altered Rubric as to place of the Table 413
PRIVY COUNCIL, (See Council).
PROCLAMATION, authorizing P. Bk. 1604, issued March 5, 1603-4 87
of Eliz., Nov. 17, 1558, forbad change in the Services until new Service authorized 291
PROCLAMATIONS, ROYAL, valid as Acts, 31 Hen. viii., c. 8, and 34 and 35, c. 23 12
repealed 1 Edw. vi., c. 12. s. 4 12
PURCHAS, REV. JOHN, the Charges against him 2
PURCHAS JUDGMENT, Clerical Remontrance as to, 1871 444
Application for re-hearing of ... 446
Case and Opinion of Counsel as to it 448
PURITANS, The, their opposition to the Surplice, shewn by Visitation Articles, 1563 to 1728 ... 50

QUARLES, ARCHN., Visitation Articles, 1662 (before P. Bk. 1662) .... 106, Note 121, 167

RAINE, REVD. J., misinformed as to Return from York Com⁻ 1559.............................. 33
on the Authority of the Advertisements .... Note 133
on the supposed effect of the Advertisements 138, 141
RASTALL, JOHN, 1564, Position of Lord's Table 351
"RATIONALE, The," 1541, Symbolism of Mixed Chalice ... Note 263
Symbolism of Blessed Bread Note 283
REALM, *three* Estates of, meaning of the Term 291
RECUSANTS, Popish, Statutes against 43
"RETAINED," meaning of, in Ornaments Rubric, discussed ..... 224 ff. & Note

RETURN, from York Com⁻, 1559, nature of it mistaken by J. Com⁻.............................. 32-4
REVISION OF P. BK. in 1552, probable principle of it 270-77
RIDLEY, BP., Injunction,¹ 1550, for changing Altars into Tables Note 340, 375
and Six Reasons for this... Note 340
officiated at St. Paul's with new P. Bk., 1552 379
RIDSDALE APPEAL, 1877, statement as to............................. 449
RITUAL, Minimum and Maximum of, opposed to Act of Uniformity: so held by Jud. Com⁻: this considered 168
ROBERTSON, CANON, as to use of Cope under Canons of 1604 Note 90 & 129
ROCK, DR., on Altars and Super-Altars............ Note 383
ROGATION DAYS, Service for, in the Injunctions, recognized in Visit. Art., 1604-79... Note 210-11
"ROMISH," Surplice still so called Note 221
RUBRIC, AS TO COMMUNION BREAD, Cosin's and Wren's proposed form of, to include Wafer-bread 312
before Prayer of Consecration, comparative Table of, from Black Letter Bk., MS. Book, and Sealed Book 437
RUBRICS OF P. BOOK, not always a sufficient guide 200-1
1549, omitted in 1552 not always meant to prohibit former Practices 269

SAMPSON, Letter to P. Martyr, as to the Vestments &c. in the Queen's Chapel, 1560...... Note 46
SANCROFT, BP., Visitation Articles, 1686........................... 164, 316
SANDYS, EDWIN, (Abp. of York, 1576), his opinion in 1559, as to intention of Ornaments Rubric 17
acts with Parker as to Wafer Bread, in 1571 .... 293, 296
Visitation Articles for York, 1578 .... 41, 107
SARUM MISSAL, Chalice mixed be-

469

fore Low Mass, 11th to 16th Cent. ....Note 266
Rubrics of, compared with Rubrics of 1549. Alesius's Latin translation, & Rubrics of 1552 359ff
SAVOY CONFERENCE, Ornaments Rubric, Ministers' objections to, Bps. defence of, Ministers' Rejoinder 218
Position of Celebrant 330
Consecration of the Elements desired to be more explicit ... 335
SCOTCH P. BK., 1637, a proof that the Ornaments Rubric of Eliz. had not been altered ... Note 100
SCUDAMORE, MR., instances of Mixing the Chalice before Service. Note 266
Mixture of the Chalice, before the Public Office, in the Greek Church 267
"SECOND YEAR OF THE REIGN OF K. EDW, VI." Jud. Com. held it to mean the P. Bk. of 1549: reasons for doubting this ... 4-10
SHARP, THOMAS, 1735, 1746, on the Ornaments Rubric............... 114
on meaning of Canon 58 of 1604 Note 130
SHARPE, ARCHN., Visitation Articles, 1615....................... 108
SELBORNE, LORD, his Reasons for Opinion as to Ornaments Rubric, 1867, considered Note 225-6
SHELDON, ABP., Circular Letter to Cathedrals, June 4, 1670...... Note 24 & 128
"SHIFTINGS OF THE BOOK" forbidden, by. Ridley, Hooper, supposed Royal Injunctions, Parkhurst...................... 373-4 & Note
SIDE OF ALTAR, meaning of 378
STANLEY, ARCHN., Visit. Articles, 1728............................ 316
STATUTE, 1548, Legalizing 1st. P. Bk. 16
1552, Legalizing 2nd P. Bk.: whether revived by 1 Jac. 1. c. 25, § 8 187
1558, 1 Eliz. c. 1, to restore Eccl. Jurisⁿ. of the Crown 57
1558, 1 Eliz. c. 2., Sect. xxv. Ornaments retained until "other Order" .... Note 56

STATUTE, "further Ceremonies or Rites" if needed............ Note 56
1 Jac. I. c. 25, repealing Marian Stat. 187
1604, 2 James I. c. 4, 1604, and 3 James I. c. 4. 1695, against Popish Recusants 42
1662, Sect. 24, keeping former Acts for enforcing P. Bk. 1662 185
what included under "several good Laws and Statutes of this Realm" 185
STEPHENS, DR. A. J., The "other Order" of 1 Eliz. 2., Sect. xxv. never made...... 69, Note 116
1845, 1849, on the Ornaments Rubric........................ 118
on Whitgift's Articles, 1583, as proving Authority of the Advertisements 149
his Argument in Ridsdale Appeal that 1559 is the date of the "Interpretations," answered App. 450-6
STOW, his account of taking down the Altar at St. Paul's, and elsewhere in London, 1550 ... 378
his account of Bp. Ridley officiating at St. Paul's with Book of 1552........................... 370
STRAFFORD, BP., Visit. Articles, 1701 316
STRYPE, action of Visitors as to Ornaments in 1559 21
account of Abp. Parker's Letter to Peculiars, about the Advertisements 66
his statement of difference between the original and the altered Advertisements 71-3
his description of Whitgift's Articles, 1583 150-1
his remarks upon the variety of the Sacramental Bread in 1570 295, 296
his relation of disputes in Norwich and elsewhere as to the Communion Bread, and Abp. Parker's letters thereon to Bp. Parkhurst 298
his account of the "Declaration," 1560-1, to be signed by beneficed Clergy .... App. 450 ff
"SUFFICE," meaning attached to it by J. Com^m, discussed ...... 293 ff

	PAGE
"SUFFICE," Cosin's Note on the Rubric: reference to "survey" Note	309
SUPERSTITION, "monuments of," described by Injunction xxviii. 1547 Note	14
Eliz[th] Injunction xxiii. 1559 Note	46
Visitation Articles as to	41, 47
SURPLICE, Visitation Articles as to	41, 163
Puritans reluctant to use it, Visit. Articles 1563 to 1728...	50, 106-10
complained of in "The Admonition to the Parliament by T. C" 1572	83
increased use of, in 1640, complained of to Ho. of Com.	90
ordered to be disused by Ordinance of Parliament, 1643	90
J. Com[rs] think it was to be "the only vestment of the Parochial Clergy" the Inquiries of Aylmer and Sandys, cited by the Court, do not prove this	161
Articles of Parker, 1569; and Injunctions of Cox, 1570-4 adverse to view of J. Com[rs]	162
other Visitation Articles, referred to by J. Com[rs], do not support the theory of J. Com[rs]	163-4
Advertisements do not order it "only"	168
condemned as Popish, Idolatrous &c.: Letter in "Rock," Feb. 16, 1872 Note	221
"SURVEY OF THE BOOK OF COMMON PRAYER," 1606, referred to by Cosin on Rubric as to Communion bread Note	309-10
SYMBOLISM OF MIXED CHALICE, given in the "Rationale," 1541 Note	263
Sarum Missal	264
Roman Missal Note	264

TABLE, THE LORD'S, not intended to be always moved from East End of the Chancel for Celebrations 338-42
Ends not meant to be placed East and West .... 342 ff
though, wrongly, so set in Cant. Cath. 1564-5 342
compare Return to Sec[r] Cecil 343
passages as to Position of Lord's Table, collected by 2 (Mr. Elliott and opposed to, and 2 more and Mr. favour of Eastw of Celebrant ...
called an "Oyster bo ing of this ....
" the North side of, when originally i 1552: shewn by Table of Rubrics Elizabethan Latin I pentrionalem par in the place of the ious to many of t proposal in Convo that the Table no Altarwise: not ca case of the Vicar c in reference to....
place of, Wren's def Abp. Abbot's deci Crayford Case.....
Order in Council Gregory's, near S
TANNER, MSS., Lette port to Sancroft, J
"THE COPIE OF A L Puritan Objectic Whitgift's Article
THORNBOROUGH, BP., Articles, 1603.....
TRIMNELL, BP., Visit. A

"USED," meaning of tion 1559 as to Bread ....
UDALL, "Communion c 1641 ....
UNIFORMITY, ACT OF, ness of its provisi to theory of Ma Minimum: this o Com[rs] considered
UNIFORMITY, ACT OF, 1552, reason given f of Bk., 1549........
1559,..................
1662, Sect. 24........
comparative Table Clauses ....
whether all 4 Acts discussed...........

	PAGE
VESTMENTS, what to be worn at Altar when no Celebration	16
not objected to by Bucer and P. Martyr because abused by Papists	Note 273
whether wholly forbidden by Rubric of 1552	Note 199
as prescribed in P. Bk. 1559, not altered by Injunctions, 1559	20
nor, as to their *legal* character, by " Interpretations of the Injunctions," 1561	20
used in Q. Elizabeth's Chapel, 1560	Note 46
not ordered to be destroyed by Eccl. Com^{rs.} in 1561	45
some dispensed with, but not prohibited, by Interpretations of the Injunctions, 1561	241
proposal to abolish them, in Convocation 1562-3, not pressed	78
retained for use in Bodmin, 8th Elizabeth	Note 238
Wills, later than the Advertisements of 1566, shew that they were not illegal	Note 239-40
the terms of some Visitation Articles, in 1662, adequate to include them	167
J. Com. think that 2 or 3 cannot be worn together: but Bp. ordered, in 1549, to wear three at Celebrations	175
their lawfulness, whether decided by Lid. v. West	250-4
VISITATION ARTICLES, as to " monuments of superstition," Grindal, 1571; Parker (38), 1575; Aylmer, 1577; Sandys, 1578; Bancroft, 1603; Babington, 1607; Abbot, 1611; King, 1610; Howson, 1619; Peculiars of Canterbury, 1637	41-2
as to time of putting the Oblation on the Altar	Note 270
as to Surplice, not prohibitory of Vestments: Parker, 1575; Sandys, 1578	41
1569 to 1670, prove difficulty of getting the Surplice used, do not shew that other Vestures were illegal	106-10
not mentioning the Advertisements; Parker 1567 and 1569	67

	PAGE
VISITATION ARTICLES, language of some in 1662, adequate to include Vestments	167
opinion of Jud. Com^{n.} that Marginal Notes in some of them, shew that Can. 58 is unrepealed: but others would thus prove that older Canons remain in force	20 8-13
recognizing Service ordered in the Injunctions for Rogation Days	Note 210-11
asking for Ornaments not prescribed, 1620-1710	213
enquire as to prohibited times of Marriage	Note 211
one form, ordered by Convocation, in 1640, to be provided for all the Dioceses: copy of, as used by Juxon, 2nd Rit. Report, p. 588	214
1662 to 1728 ask for "fine white bread:" are not opposed to Wafer-bread; but do not favour *ordinary* Bread	314-19
as to Place of the Lord's Table, 1563-1662, averse to the theory of its Ends being East and West	344-7
VISITORS, THE, 1559, authority and practice of, compared as to Ornaments	21
WAFER-BREAD, charge as to: not alleged that Mr. Purchas did not use *Bread*	281
not objected to by Bucer; he wished *leavened* also to be allowed	Note 289
any disuse of it in K. Edward's Reign restored by Q. Mary: the Injunction of 1559 operated upon this later use	290
not meant to be discountenanced by Rubric of 1552 and 1559	284
Injunction of 1559 intended for " reverence," under Sect. 26 of Eliz. Act of Uniformity	285
P. Bk. and Injunctions of 1559 not at variance as to	283
Interpretations of the Injunctions, 1561, support this 285 & Note Abp. Parker held it to be the Rule	293

WAFER-BREAD, Controversy as to between Cartwright and Whitgift 305-7
defended by Hooker against the Puritans 324
not denied to be lawful, by P. Council, in 1580 322-3
charges for it in Parish Account, Eltham, 1579-80 321
used in Chapel Royal, St. James, in 1593 307-8
and in other Churches till 17 Charles 1st 311
Jud. Com^{ee.} observes that a proposal in 1661 to specify Wafer-Bread was not accepted: this does not prove such Bread to be unlawful 311, 312
The Court afraid that Wafers would re-introduce the "print" and "figures" formerly given up: remarks upon this 304 & Note
no real objection to some Symbol upon the Bread: sufficient restraint in Rubric as to providing the Bread 309
J. Com^{ee.} does not say it is not Bread 281
Bp. Wren calls the Wafer "Bread" .... Note 324
not alleged that any *shape* is prescribed 281
decision of J. Com^{ee.} against it, inconsistent with the *principle* on which they condemned Vestments 28
Calvin and others banished from Geneva, in 1538, for not using it .... 311 & Note
mentioned in Scotch P. Book, 1636 313
WALCOTT, REV. M., gift of Cope for Parish Church, 1617 ...... Note 91
WHEATLY, CHARLES, 1710, 1720, on the Ornaments Rubric 112-13
as to object of Rubric about the Bread and Wine .... Note 305
remarks upon Ridley's proceedings about the Altars in 1550 Note 378-9
on the Position of the Celebrant 409-12

WHEATLY, CHARLES, reference to "Bev. Pandect," as to North side, inapplicable .... Note 411
The Lord's Table, its removal from E. End for Celebrations not the Rule but the Exception Note 433
WHITE, BP. OF LINCOLN, 1555, Position of Lord's Table 352
WHITE, ARCHN., Visitation Articles, 1630 345
1632 .... 109, 345
WHITGIFT, ABP., Visit. Art., 1584, Title given to the Advertisements 59
his Articles of 1583 144-49
Puritan Answer to 73
his Letter to the Bishops to execute the Articles of 1583 150
Defence of his Answer to the Admonition 83
Visit. Art. for Sarum, 1588 242 & Note
discussion with Cartwright as to Wafer-bread 305-7
WILLIAMS, BP., Visit. Articles, 1635 Note 270, 345
"Letter to the Vicar of Grantham," as to place and position of Table 395, 397
"Holy Table, Name & Thing" 396, 401
WITHERS, GEORGE, Letter to Bullinger, 1567, Title given to the Advertisements 58
WREN, BP., Visitation Articles, 1636 110, 345
proposed alteration of Rubric, to mention Wafer-bread 312
reviewed Scotch P. Book, 1636 313
white-bread stolen by dog from Tadlow Church, 1683: consequently no Communion Note 321
deemed Wafers to be Bread Note 324
defence of Eastward Position, in 1641 .... Note 330, 402-5
his language about *end* and *side* 387
reference to the Advertisements Note, 430

ZANCHIUS, Letter to from Grindal, *in* 1571, shews that the Elizabethan Ornaments Rubric had not been altered 29

W. J. PERRY, PRINTER, 22, CURSITOR STREET, CHANCERY LANE.

By the same Author.

REVIEW OF LENT TEACHING.—A Sermon preached in the Parish Church of St. Peter the Great, or Subdeanry, Chichester, on the Sunday next before Easter, 1849. 6d.

THREE PRESENT SPECIAL DANGERS TO CHRISTIAN SANCTIFICATION.—A Sermon preached in the Parish Church of St. Peter the Great, or Subdeanry, Chichester, on Sunday, February 24, 1850. 6d.

PRAISE, A DUTY IN THE CHURCH'S ADVERSITY.—A Sermon preached in the Temporary Church of All Saints, St. Marylebone, on the Feast of All Saints, 1851. 6d.

LAWFUL CHURCH ORNAMENTS:—Being an Historical Examination of the Judgment of the Right Hon. Stephen Lushington, D.C.L., in the case of Westerton v. Liddell, &c. And of "Aids for determining some disputed points in the Ceremonial of the Church of England," by the Rev. William Goode, M.A. With an Appendix on the Judgment of the Rt. Hon. Sir John Dodson, D.C.L., in the Appeal Liddell v. Westerton, &c., 1857. £1 1s.

THE ANGLICAN AUTHORITY FOR THE PRESENCE OF NON-COMMUNICANTS DURING HOLY COMMUNION.—Reprinted from "The Ecclesiologist" of August and October, 1858. 6d.

SOME HISTORICAL CONSIDERATIONS relating to the Declaration on Kneeling, appended to the Communion Office of the English Book of Common Prayer. A Letter addressed privately, in 1858, to the Right Rev. CHARLES H. TERROT, D.D., Bishop of Edinburgh, and then Primus. To which is added, a Postscript of further Authorities and Arguments; including an Examination of Statements in a Work and Supplement on the Eucharist, by the Very Rev. W. GOODE, D.D., Dean of Ripon, 1863. 12s.

SOME ANALOGIES BETWEEN THE HUMAN AND THE MYSTICAL BODY, APPLIED TO DIFFICULTIES AND DUTIES IN THE CHURCH.—Part I., DIFFICULTIES IN THE CHURCH. 1863. 1s. 6d.

REASONABLE LIMITS OF LAWFUL RITUALISM. An Essay in "The Church and the World." Longmans & Co. 1866.

THE PRESENT LEGISLATIVE RESULTS OF THE RITUAL COMMISSION. A Paper read at the Brighton and Hove Ruri-decanal Chapter, Oct. 3, and (in part) at the Sussex District English Church Union Meeting at S. Leonard's-on-Sea, Oct. 29, 1872. Published by request. Reprinted from "The Church Review." 3d.

Edited by the same.

MEDITATIONS FOR A WEEK ON THE LORD'S PRAYER, 1853. 6d.

DIRECTORIUM SCOTICANUM ET ANGLICANUM.—Directions for Celebrating the Holy Communion according to the Rite of the Church in Scotland and of the Church of England. By the late Rev. W. Wright, L.L.D., 1855. 3s. 6d.

A MANUAL OF DAILY PRAYERS—for persons who are much hindered by the duties of their calling. With a Preparation and Devotions for Holy Communion. *Fourteenth thousand, with additions.* 1870. 4d. A new and cheaper Edition *in preparation.*

www.ingramcontent.com/pod-product-compliance
Lightning Source LLC
Chambersburg PA
CBHW030322020526
44117CB00030B/391